Diversity
and Social Work in Canada

Diversity
and Social Work in Canada

Edited by Alean Al-Krenawi, John R. Graham, and Nazim Habibov

OXFORD
UNIVERSITY PRESS

Oxford University Press is a department of the University of Oxford.
It furthers the University's objective of excellence in research, scholarship,
and education by publishing worldwide. Oxford is a registered trade mark of
Oxford University Press in the UK and in certain other countries.

Published in Canada by
Oxford University Press
8 Sampson Mews, Suite 204,
Don Mills, Ontario M3C 0H5 Canada

www.oupcanada.com

Library and Archives Canada Cataloguing in Publication
Diversity and social work in Canada / edited by Alean Al-Krenawi, John R. Graham, and Nazim Habibov.

Includes bibliographical references and index.
ISBN 978-0-19-900706-6 (paperback)

1. Social service—Canada—Textbooks . 2. Cultural pluralism—Canada—Textbooks. I. Graham, John R. (John Russell), 1964-, author, editor II. Al-Krenawi, Alean, author, editor III. Habibov, Nazim, author, editor

HV105.D59 2016 361.30971 C2016-900327-2

Cover image: Roberto Machado Noa/Getty Images

Oxford University Press is committed to our environment.
This book is printed on Forest Stewardship Council® certified paper
and comes from responsible sources.

Printed and bound in Canada

3 4 5 — 23 22 21

Contents

Preface

This volume emerged from the 2003 work *Multicultural Social Work in Canada*, co-edited by Alean Al-Krenawi and John Graham. Several years in the making, *Multicultural Social Work in Canada* had its roots in a conversation between Al-Krenawi and Graham. Both authors had taught courses in multicultural social work and had jointly published over two dozen journal articles on multicultural and international practice, principally among Arab peoples indigenous to the Middle East. One of us (Al-Krenawi) had lived in Canada for a number of years; the other (Graham) had lived here all his life and was teaching in Calgary. Given our research interests, we were both immersed in diversity and multicultural literatures within and outside Canada. But within Canada we became increasingly convinced of the need for a single volume that gave voice to the country's pre-eminent practitioners and teachers of multicultural practice.

The present book's third editor, Nazim Habibov, had used the 2003 work for a decade while teaching. Periodically he inquired about plans for a new edition. The changing curriculum needs of this decade brought the three scholars together, and they jointly concluded that a broader book was merited, covering diversity rather than the narrower focus of multiculturalism. The idea was to come up with an edited book covering multiple dimensions that differentiate groups and people from one another. The guiding principle of the volume would be an appreciation of the vast array of differences among individuals, including ethnicity, gender, age, national origin, (dis)ability, sexual orientation, education, religion, socio-economics, political ideology, and so forth. Scholarly yet readable, our work would be designed as a teaching tool for the students who will be tomorrow's players in policy diversity. Of one mind as to the critical call for such a work, we contacted academic experts in the helping professions and, working carefully with Oxford University Press, moved the project forward.

Diversity is arguably the overarching feature of life. Certainly, personhood cannot be divorced from its diversity without extreme damage to its essence. This basic notion informs our charge as helping professionals who are tasked with teaching and practising in a manner that demonstrates awareness of and respect for the many ways in which people are people. The present work takes up that charge and aims to offer original insights from leaders in a wide variety of psychosocial fields.

This volume is emerging during our postmodern era of positive psychology, or what is called in social work a "strengths approach." The contributing authors are cognizant of the impact that a wide range of beliefs and behaviours can have on the expression of problems while using a strengths-based approach to build on the healing properties inherent to each individual system. Basic to the therapeutic toolkit of this sophisticated mental health treatment approach is not only cultural sensitivity and knowledge, but also methodologies that harness the power of diverse identities.

Diversity and Social Work in Canada has been written for introductory and intermediate students as well as for scholars and practitioners. It offers cutting-edge scholarship on diversity in social work. The principal theoretical propositions are fivefold. First, diversity is intrinsic to every situation and to every person. Historically, social work functioned with many assumptions about commonality in needs. Naturally, the concept of basic human needs has not been jettisoned by the field. Nonetheless, the notion of need is now undergoing an overhaul, with a great deal more sensitivity being paid to the nuances of *particularized* need. This leads to our second point: Needs vary across a single person's lifetime, and they may be far more fluid than previous perspectives assumed. Indeed, fluidity characterizes the third point: Multiple aspects of identity intersect within a particular person, community, or situation. More than this, to turn to a fourth point: Issues of identity have much to do with power, status, and other social capital. These, in turn, will be reflected in the treatment encounter. The fifth and final point pertains to knowledge, both local and global. The field of social work is in the midst of a discourse on the relative merits of localized versus globalized knowledge. It is the view of the editors of this volume that neither type of knowledge is mutually exclusive, and in fact, both types are critical to social work practice in diversity. The reader will find these topics as well as many more between the covers of this book, reflected through the prism of psychosocial intervention.

There is a growing consensus that diversity of human needs constitutes the most helpful—and authentic—paradigm for psychosocial treatment. However, the translation of this contemporary ideal into practice is fraught with difficulty, as the chapters in this book make clear. Notwithstanding this challenge, we hope that the current volume helps clinicians fulfill the privileged mandate that they have been given by people everywhere.

Acknowledgements

The editors would like to thank Dr Susan Graham, who provided unfailing support and provided key assistance with several parts of this book. David Sandoz, Sara Tropper, and Derek Campbell provided most helpful research assistance.

We also wish to thank the named and anonymous peer reviewers who provided positive feedback that helped to shape this volume:

- Shaheen Azmi, Ryerson University
- Barbara Baker, Georgian College
- Gus Hill, York University
- Judith White, University of Regina
- Jim R. Vanderwoerd, Redeemer University College

Dedication

This book is dedicated to Dr Monawar, Liali and Mohamad Al-Krenawi, and Alena Auchynnikava; Dr Susan Graham; and Tatyanna Melanie Morgan.

Contributors

Alean Al-Krenawi, Ph.D., is president of Achva Academic College and professor in the Spitzer Department of Social Work at Ben-Gurion University of the Negev, Israel. Dr Al-Krenawi's research interests include multicultural mental health and social work with Indigenous populations, political violence, and polygamy. Dr Al-Krenawi is an international authority in his area of research and has been invited to lecture in many academic institutions and conferences around the globe. He has conducted studies in Canada, Israel, and many countries in the Middle East.

Xue Bai is assistant professor in the Department of Applied Social Sciences at the Hong Kong Polytechnic University. She obtained her Ph.D. from the Department of Social Work and Social Administration at the University of Hong Kong. Her areas of research mainly include aging and health, social policy for older people, and social service evaluation. She has been actively involved in a number of research projects that have made a great impact on aging policy and service development for older people.

Natalie Blake-Noel is a professor in the Social Service Worker Diploma Program at Humber College and the Family and Community Social Services Degree Program at the University of Guelph-Humber. She is passionate about teaching and connecting students with the fundamentals of social work within an applicable and practical learning environment. Professor Blake-Noel has extensive years of experience as a social worker specializing in mental health, at-risk youth, immigrants, and community development. She continues to strongly advocate for the oppressed and marginalized.

Keith Brownlee is a professor of social work at Lakehead University and director of research at the Centre for Education and Research on Positive Youth Development. Professor Brownlee teaches research and clinical practice at the undergraduate and graduate levels. For many years he has worked and conducted research in northwestern Ontario and has had an interest in issues related to rural and remote communities.

Irene Carter is an associate professor at the University of Windsor and is the coordinator for the on-campus Master of Social Work programs. She also serves as faculty for the School of Social Work and the Disability Studies Program.

Diana Coholic is associate professor and current director of the School of Social Work at Laurentian University. She has published previously in the area of spiritually influenced social work practice, including arts-based mindfulness with vulnerable populations.

Gio Dolcecore completed their Master of Social Work at the University of Calgary. They work as a mental health clinician specializing in homelessness and working with diverse populations, including gender and sexual minorities.

Gary C. Dumbrill is an associate professor in McMaster University's School of Social Work. His research and teaching focus on service-users' theory, child welfare, anti-oppressive practice, anti-racism, and social inclusion and exclusion. Dumbrill places emphasis on connecting theory to direct practice and on conducting research that informs both policy and practice. His research is primarily participatory and community based, and it is often grounded in the knowledge, theory, and voice of service users, particularly through the use of photovoice, video, and other arts-based methods.

Douglas Durst is a professor of social work at the University of Regina and teaches social research and social policy at the undergraduate and graduate levels. Underlying his research is an anti-oppressive approach by giving voice to marginalized peoples, including people with disabilities, the elderly, and immigrants and refugees. During his years in the Northwest Territories, he developed a love for the north and its peoples.

Debashis Dutta is coordinator of the Human Services Foundation Program at Conestoga College in Kitchener, Ontario, and he also teaches in the School of Social Work at Renison University College in Waterloo, Ontario. His current research focuses on adaptation and acculturation of immigrants to Canada from the Bengal region of India, and the impacts on parenting and on socialization of children.

Sarah Fotheringham is a Ph.D. candidate in the Faculty of Social Work at the University of Calgary. Fotheringham has worked with the issue of violence against women, including sexual and domestic violence, and women's homelessness for a number of years in both research and direct service. Her current research interest is in women-centred social enterprise, a poverty reduction strategy for low-income women located within Canada's social economy.

Sulaimon Giwa is a Ph.D. candidate (ABD) in social work at York University, with research, policy, and direct practice experience at the community and federal level in youth health promotions, community and organizational practice in diverse communities, corrections, and policing. His applied research program and professional activities centralize critical race transformative pedagogies and theories as frameworks and analytic tools for social justice and equity. His research interests are in the areas of race and sexuality, critical social work pedagogy, anti-racism/oppression, and the criminal justice system. He has taught in the social work programs at Ryerson University and York University.

John Graham, formerly the Murray Fraser Professor at the University of Calgary, is director and professor of the School of Social Work at Florida Atlantic University. He has published on international social work, multicultural social work, and social policy.

Nazim Habibov is associate professor of social work at the University of Windsor. He has published extensively on social and health policies as well as poverty and inequality in the context of developed and developing countries.

Ross A. Klein is a professor of social work at Memorial University of Newfoundland. He has worked with culturally and ethnically diverse populations and has written extensively about the international cruise ship industry, including stratification and "rights" of passengers and crew based on skin colour, religion, cultural heritage, gender, sexual orientation, country of origin, and other reflections of diversity.

Marie Lacroix a professor at the School of Social Work, Université de Montréal. She has worked with asylum seekers in Montreal and has done extensive research on asylum seekers and social work.

Daniel W.L. Lai was a professor in the Faculty of Social Work and the Annual Killam Professor (2014–15) at the University of Calgary. He was also formerly Alberta Health Scholar between 2003 and 2009. Since mid-December 2015, he has been appointed as Chair Professor of Social Work and Gerontology in the Department of Applied Social Sciences at the Hong Kong Polytechnic University. His scholarly and research interests include anti-oppressive social work practice, social policy, gerontology, and working with immigrants and culturally diverse populations. His research publications and funded research focus mainly on immigrant and culturally diverse older adults and racialized population groups.

Catherine Montgomery is a professor of communications at the Université du Québec à Montréal where she teaches in the field of intercultural communication. She also directs the METISS research group in Montreal, which specializes in intercultural intervention in the health and social services. Her recent work focuses on intervention practices in contexts of diversity.

Carey Mulligan has a Master of Clinical Social Work from the University of Calgary. She is a full-time social worker in Ottawa, Ontario. Carey's clinical work and research is informed by an anti-oppressive, feminist and queer perspective. Carey is active in anti-violence work locally and sees social justice as central to the work she does.

Raymond Neckoway is an associate professor at Lakehead University's School of Social Work. He teaches in the undergraduate and graduate programs, and his research revolves around Indigenous interests in parenting, attachment theory, and social work in rural, remote communities.

Gordon Pon has a Master of Social Work and Ph.D. and is an associate professor in the School of Social Work at Ryerson University. His research interests include anti-racism and anti-colonialism, child welfare, and Asian-Canadian Studies.

Narda Razack is a professor in the School of Social Work, York University and has extensive experience in research, pedagogy, and administration. She is the Associate Dean, Global and Community Engagement in the Faculty of Liberal Arts and Professional Studies. Her research and publication areas include: North–South relations, globalization and international social work, critical race theory and post-colonialism.

Christine A. Walsh is a professor in the Faculty of Social Work at the University of Calgary. She is a feminist and activist and teaches research and social justice and anti-oppressive practice. Her program of action research prioritizes the needs of marginalized populations, including Aboriginal peoples, youth at risk, and populations impacted by poverty and homelessness.

David Welch is an associate professor at the École de service social, Université d'Ottawa. He has published extensively on social services for people of Franco-Ontarian background, community development, and policy concerns.

Miu Chung Yan is a professor at the University of British Columbia's School of Social Work. He teaches and studies culture, race, and ethnicity in social work practice, and settlement and integration needs and challenges of visible minority newcomers to Canada.

June Ying Yee is an associate professor in Ryerson University's School of Social Work as well as the academic coordinator of the Internationally Educated Social Work Professionals Bridging Program at Ryerson. Her professional and scholarly research interests are in the area of health, education, child welfare, and social services. She has published in a number of journals, including *Canadian Social Work Review*, *Social Work Education: The International Journal*, and *Critical Social Work*. Yee continues to actively work with various organizations involved with child welfare, local municipalities, and children's mental-health organizations to adopt organizational-change strategies that result in instrumental systemic change.

Part I

Theoretical Approaches to Social Work and Diversity

Multiculturalism and ethnocultural identity are now central to Canadian life—and to social work theory and practice. Differences within our communities, our families, and ourselves increasingly demand that we, as social workers, advocate for both ourselves and those we practise with and serve. Ours is a profession committed to social justice and human rights. Social workers in Canada will be expected to practise within, as well as spread, anti-oppressive social work principles throughout their careers.

The chapters within this section will discuss historical connections and current socio-cultural phenomenon that have acted and continue to act as social and governmental drivers of ethnoracial identity. But ethnoracial identity, we stress, intersects with age, socio-economic class, range of ability, sexual orientation, and other identities. This section will address the culture of the "Other" and the ways in which this sociological construct helps social workers appreciate other people's differences and the power relationships that flow out of these differences.

Privileged social positions influence our learning and practice as professional helpers in ways that will affect how we are able to advocate for and make positive change toward the elimination of discrimination and the enhancement of minority rights and future ethnocultural development. The following chapters will also explore the nature of privilege and social and structural dynamics in Canada and offer indications of what we, as professional social workers, can do to lessen the negative consequences of such social conditions in Canada.

Part I Contents

Introduction

Social Work and Diversity

By Alean Al-Krenawi, John R. Graham, and Nazim Habibov

Chapter Objectives

In this chapter, you will be introduced to:

- Ways to understand the notion of "difference"
- Current instances of social work challenges among various religious and socio-economic groups
- Definitions of cultural competence, identity, intersectionality, and indigenization/localization vis-à-vis social work practice
- The organization of this book

Introduction

French Canadian or Franco-Ontarian? Afro-Canadian or Black? Differently abled or (dis)abled? Can a straight person use the word "queer"? Can someone whose first language is not French consider themselves Québécois? Should a younger person refer to an older person in a more formal manner, such as by using the word *vous* in French, or Mr or Ms in English? Is it ever acceptable to refer to a married woman as "Mrs," or should women always be addressed as "Ms," regardless of marital status? Can cohabitating persons engaged in an intimate relationship describe themselves as "husband" and "wife," or should they use a gender-neutral term like "partner"? What is the most significant identifier of them all? Is it sex, gender, socio-economic class, race, language, geography, religion, sexual orientation? Is there something else that is even more significant? Or is it a combination of these facets, changing over the course of time and across situations and lived experiences? Whatever these concepts are, and however we define them, how do we understand them in ourselves and in others? How do we come to learn how others construe these same things in themselves and in the world around them?

These questions stand at the very forefront of debates now taking place across academic disciplines and societies. Even as our book headed to peer review, this is how a professor of English described her undergraduate experiences teaching at a diverse Bronx campus in New York City:

> "I have no connection to Africa," a black student explained one year, "so I don't want to be called African-American any more than whites want to be called European-American." Students from Africa and the Caribbean routinely object to being categorized with American blacks. A Jamaican student said that she had never experienced racism until, as an adult, she came to the United States . . . Since I began doing this exercise in the late '90s, the discussions have revolved around self-presentation and self-identification. I remember a mixed-race student loudly scolding her classmate for denying his blackness by calling himself Dominican instead of Afro-Dominican, as she did. "You have no racial pride," she yelled at him across the room. "You're denying a whole piece of your history by hiding it when you call yourself Dominican. You should be ashamed!" (Mifflin, 2014, p. B2).

Difference is the mark of healthy societies. We find differences within our communities as well as between ourselves and those with whom we learn and practice; differences between ourselves and the people we serve; differences in ourselves over the life course. These and other parameters strongly impact how we conceive of and carry out professional practice.

Naturally, differences show up in worldviews. Religion stands as a prime example of this, and social work research reflects that reality well. Two Canadian scholars have written thoughtfully on classroom experiences in which there are differences in viewpoints between Christian fundamentalist and secular students, and they provide strategies that can engender respectful dialogue (Todd & Coholic, 2007). Another Canadian author, David Hodge, addressing an American audience, ponders whether the social work profession oppresses Christian fundamentalists (Hodge, 2002). He and his coauthors provide evidence of bias against people of faith in some social work writings (Hodge, Baughman, & Cummings, 2006). A solo article by Hodge examined sexual orientation and its different epistemological frameworks among people of faith and others (Hodge, 2005). Scholars have responded to Hodge's work (Dessel, Bolen, & Shepardson, 2011), and the profession stands stronger for such dialogue.

Socio-economic class is another obvious marker—sometimes interfacing with geographic background. A secondary school teacher in New York City writes of her experiences as a student on a prestigious college campus in the late 1970s:

> The other students I encountered seemed foreign to me. Their parents had gone to Ivy League schools; they played tennis. I had never been east of Nebraska. My mother raised five children while she worked for the post office, and we kept a goat in our yard to reduce the amount of garbage we'd have to pay for at the county dump . . . It's often the subtler things, the signifiers, of who they

> are and where they come from, that cause the most trouble . . . Hardest was the awareness that my own experiences were not only undervalued but often mocked, used to indicate when someone was stupid of low-class. No one at Barnard ate Velveeta or had ever butchered a deer . . . (Madden, 2014, p. A21).

The above-noted narrative describes poignantly the pain experienced by the student who perceived herself as different and was considered inferior due to this difference. As is well known, misreadings of diversity abound.

Social science, however, has made significant strides over the past several decades in reducing the number of these misreadings. Older notions of feminist identity tended to look at gender in linear terms, with insufficient reference to age, socio-economic class, range of ability, sexual orientation, or other identities (Anthias, 2002a). Scholarship on aging (Calasanti & Slevin, 2006), race (Maher & Tetrault, 2001), and multiculturalism (Worell & Remer, 2002) has rendered feminist analyses far richer. The same is true of research on (dis)ability (Bickenbach, Chatterji, Badley, & Üstün, 1999).

Yet few social work texts, and none with a Canadian orientation, guide us in grappling with the changing complexities of Canadian society and the resulting comingling of diversity with social work knowledge, development, and practice. One may find Canadian volumes on structural social work (Mullally, 2007; Baines, 2007), multicultural social work (Al-Krenawi & Graham, 2003), disability and social policy (Prince, 2009), ethnicity/race and social work (Wallis & Kwok, 2008), and gender and social work (Swift, 1995). But no Canadian work has taken up the challenge of treating, in a single volume, the intersectionality of multiple forms of diversity.

To correct this problem, we have brought together thought leaders on a range of topics of contemporary issues of diversity. We have geared this book to senior undergraduate students and graduate students of social work—those who are well into the development stage of their thinking on how to manage and leverage the diversity that calls from every corner of practice. Collectively, the book has important implications and utility for direct practice and for the enhancement of skills in working in an increasingly diverse world. Distinctive theoretical angles are embedded in each chapter, highlighting four major concepts:

- cultural competence
- experiential phenomenological approaches to identity
- intersectionality
- localization or indigenization

The following pages in this introductory chapter deal with each concept in turn.

Cultural Competence

An expanded notion of **cultural diversity** includes the domains of race/ethnicity, culture, socio-economic status (SES), age, religion/spirituality, subcultural identification, language, physical ability, sexual orientation, gender, education, and any other identification that the client uses for self-reference (American Psychiatric Association [APA], 2000; APA, 2003; Malik & Velazquez, 2002). Diversity is differently expressed across context, resulting in an array of definitions (Zapata, 2009). Welfare, psychological services, education, and legislation are but a few of those settings.

The present work widens and deepens the frame of a prior volume, which encouraged social workers to understand their practice in a multicultural framework mediated by socio-economic class, gender, religion, geography, sexual orientation, and other subjective identities (Al-Krenawi & Graham, 2003). In the interim, scholars have explored social work practice that is anti-racist, anti-oppressive, and structural in orientation (Dominelli, 1997, 2002; Moreau, 1979; Mullaly, 2007). Authors from these traditions explore the interface of broader social structures and individual social problems, whether rooted in racism or oppression via other forms of identity or via the economic, political, and social structures of those who have power.

As Al-Krenawi and Graham (2003) have pointed out, "Canadian literature, like its American counterparts (Lum, 1992; Devore & Schlesinger, 1996), has emphasized a model of cultural competence that enables behaviours, knowledge, attitudes, and policies to respond appropriately to cultural and racial diversity" (Este, 1999; Herberg, 1993). As shown in Table 1.1, **cultural competence** goes well beyond efforts toward sensitivity. Whereas cultural sensitivity involves honing one's awareness of cultural issues, cultural competence entails a more change-committed focus on cultural issues (Este, 1999, p. 32).

Experiential Phenomenological Approaches to Identity

But how does one become culturally competent? One way of looking at the question is to think about where one might fall along a continuum. One's position might vary over time and in different contexts, but the two polarities are intellectual constructs the help us to better understand cultural competence. On one end of the continuum is **cultural literacy**; on the other, **experiential phenomenology** (see Table 1.2). For more on experiential phenomenology see Chapter 4 by Marie Lacroix.

Table 1.1 The Cultural Sophistication Framework

Dimension	Culturally Incompetent	Culturally Sensitive	Culturally Competent
Cognitive dimension	Oblivious	Aware	Knowledgeable
Affective dimension	Apathetic	Sympathetic	Committed to change
Skills dimension	Unskilled	Lacking some skills	Highly skilled
Overall effect	Destructive	Neutral	Constructive

Source: Este, D. (1999). Social work and cultural competency. In G. Lie & D. Este (Eds.), *Professional social service delivery in a multicultural world* (p. 32). Toronto: Canadian Scholars' Press.

Table 1.2 Two Models of Culturally Competent Multicultural Practice

Cultural Literacy Model	Experiential Phenomenological Model
Practitioner as expert	Practitioner as learner
Assumes superior knowledge	Naiveté and curiosity
Culture as homogeneous system	Plurality and multiplicity of internalized culture
Client as member of cultural group	Member as unique individual
Culture-specific techniques	Process-oriented techniques
Nearly impossible	Demands critical self-examination

Source: Excerpted from Tsang, A.K.T., & George, U. (1998). Towards an integrated framework for cross-cultural social work practice. *Canadian Social Work Review*, *15*(1), 83.

Some practitioners tend toward the cultural literacy end of the spectrum. Canadian scholars Tat Tsang and Usha George are critical of this position, which, they argue, presupposes that the knowledge of the social worker is superior to that of the client. Moreover, they contend that this approach takes for granted that social workers are adequately conversant with multiple cultures and that they are willing to use stereotypical "culture-specific" intervention techniques (Tsang & George, 1998, p. 82). Finally, these authors claim that cultural literacy encourages social categorization rather than trying to understand the unique nexus of each person's diversities and the nuances of individuality. For more on cultural literacy see Chapter 2 by June Ying Yee and Gary C. Dumbrill.

In contrast, the more experiential, phenomenological end of the continuum assumes a stance of openness, humility, and curiosity vis-à-vis the client. A worker's assumptions are suspended in this model, and worker–client interactions stress the former's lack of presumption in engaging with the client. Recent scholarship discusses this stance in relation to (1) understanding one's own culture and self and using this as a basis for understanding others, and (2) using social constructivist principles to guide intervention (Lee & Greene, 1999). The following chapters adhere to this approach, but with some additional consideration—cultural literacy is not entirely abandoned. For example, several contributors appear to hold, and we agree, that some culturally specific techniques *are* tenable provided they are carried out in experiential phenomenological ways and that the client is permitted to exercise his or her cultural knowledge/expertise. Likewise, clients may be members of a particular cultural group, but in a thoughtful, experiential-phenomenological model this should not mean—as a position of strong cultural literacy might assert—that the worker would then hold an essentializing set of perceptions.

Intersectionality

We shall provide definitions for three terms here. The first is **social location**, which implies one's place in society as delimited by race, ethnicity, gender, sexual orientation, religion, language, or anything else that might distinguish one person from the next.

Social location is best understood subjectively, in relation to how a person understands him or herself (Anthias, 2002b).

Second, we consider the notion of **positionality**, which is similar to social location but subsumes the notion of power. By positionality, we mean one's social position in relation to others—particularly in relation to the different levels of power that occur in those relationships. A good way to determine one's social location—those things that distinguish us from another—is through its intersection with positionality. For further reading on positionality, see Chapter 6 by Miu Chung Yan.

Third, **intersectionality** points to the idea that social location or positionality are not fixed concepts: They change with time and place, and these shifts can even seem contradictory (Anthias, 2008). A person may have, or be perceived to have, power and authority at one moment and comparably less the next moment—depending in part on those people with whom he or she is interacting and the nature of their ever-changing relationships. By "intersection" we mean the way in which all these aspects—ethnicity, gender, language, race, religion, sexual orientation, socio-economic class, and so on—contribute to the unique person that each of us is, as well as to the subjectivities in which we understand ourselves and in which others understand us (Al-Krenawi & Graham, 2003; Mehrotra, 2010).

Localization and Indigenization

Social work emerged in the late 19th and early 20th centuries in Western Europe and North America. In the period between World Wars I and II, the profession spread across the world, and after World War II that diffusion deepened. A voluminous corpus of social work scholarship, culminating in James Midgley's monumental 1981 work, describes this profusion of knowledge as a product of "imperialism," or "colonialism." The assumptions and values of the countries in which social work originated were poorly suited to newly developing countries (as they were then called), and the development of the profession was consequently curtailed in these settings. A movement to **indigenize**, or—our preferred term—**localize**, social work called for locally based understandings and practices of the profession, and the creation of knowledge from within the specific locale rather than the external imposition of knowledge from without it (Al-Krenawi & Graham, 2008; Bradshaw & Graham, 2007; Graham 2006).

How This Book Is Organized

Against the above background, how can the social work profession begin to address the growing diversity in Canada? The chapters in this book have been carefully selected to shed light on this urgent question. The chapters are divided into three parts. The chapters in Part 1, "Theoretical Approaches to Social Work and Diversity," aim to elucidate the relationship between diversity and social work. In this first chapter, Alean Al-Krenawi, John Graham, and Nazim Habibov provide a succinct summary of key issues related to diversity in social work. The authors introduce some problems, theories, and themes related to social work and diversity that have recently emerged in the literature. In Chapter 2, June Ying Yee and Gary C. Dumbrill look at the place of race, "Whiteness," and racism in Canadian social work. They introduce and examine the concept of "Whiteness," demonstrating how it reproduces racism, classism, and sexism in the delivery of social work services. In Chapter 3, Gordon Pon, Sulaimon Giwa, and Narda Razack build a solid foundation for anti-racism and anti-oppressive social work. They discuss diversity discourse against the background of colonization and racism in Canada and examine the strengths and limitations of anti-racism and anti-oppressive social work practice in the Canadian context.

In Part 2, "Social Work in Diverse Settings," the contributors offer a number of trenchant ideas for managing diversity in a variety of contemporary social work venues. In Chapter 4, Marie Lacroix suggests how multicultural social work might be harnessed in clinical and direct social work practice. The reader will learn how social workers can develop and maintain cultural competency in working with individuals, families, and groups. In Chapter 5, Douglas Durst provides a perspective on present-day challenges of macro practice with diverse communities. In doing so, he presents the skills, strategies, and values that form the bedrock of community development in a multicultural context.

In Part 3, "Social Work with Diverse Populations," the contributing authors detail the importance of cultural competency for social work practice with many groups, from First Nations to francophones to new Canadians. In Chapter 6, Miu Chung Yan identifies intersectionality as central to effective social work practice with diverse populations. Blending theory and case studies, he demonstrates how the intersection of multiple social categories may encourage the development of oppressive conditions against individuals or groups within these categories. In Chapter 7, Raymond Neckoway and Keith Brownlee develop an endogenous model of social work practice with Aboriginal families within both traditional and urban contexts. The chapter illustrates how to incorporate important elements of First Nations history and culture such as extended family, the medicine wheel, and Aboriginal parent voices into social work practice today. In Chapter 8, David Welch affords a view of the history and social construction of the Franco-Ontarian community. He vividly depicts the main socio-economic transformations of the community, which have dramatically altered social work practice with francophones in Ontario and Canada.

In Chapter 9, Debashis Dutta and Ross A. Klein re-examine the classic theories and social work approaches to adaptation and acculturation of new immigrant parents. Then, they examine the Immigrant Parent Enhancement framework as an innovative way to foster parental integration. In Chapter 10, Catherine Montgomery continues with the topic of immigrants by focusing on the most vulnerable categories of immigrants—refugees. She evaluates the existing intervention models for working with immigrant and refugee populations, and suggests using narrative techniques for understanding migration trajectories and integration processes. In Chapter 11,

Diana Coholic provides rationales for integrating spiritually sensitive methods into social work practice. Using a case study approach, she assesses multiple strategies for including spirituality in social work. In Chapter 12, Christine A. Walsh, Carey Mulligan, and Gio Dolcecore concentrate on sexual diversity and social work. After providing in-depth historical and theoretical overviews of the LGBTQ (lesbian, gay, bisexual, transgender, queer) movement and structural barriers for LGBTQ groups, the authors consider mechanisms of advocacy for LGBTQ individuals and communities. In Chapter 13, Sarah Fotheringham engages with the important topic of gender and its implications for social work. The author begins with an overview of theories of gender and continues with their critical assessment. Next, she evaluates the impact of gender on daily life, moving then to her main concern, the complexities that riddle the relationship between gender and social work practice.

In Chapter 14, Irene Carter brings the reader into the world of disability. A range of models of disability are presented, with an emphasis on two: the social model of disability and the independent living model. The former stresses that the onus for the restricted participation of persons with disabilities should be placed on negative social factors rather than on the disability itself, while the latter advocates situating the person with disabilities as an adequate decision maker capable of taking responsibility for his or her care requirements. In Chapter 15, Daniel Lai and Xue Bai focus on the diversity of Canada's aging population by providing a succinct description of the main theories and perspectives on aging and diversity and discussing practice approaches for working with older adults. In Chapter 16, Natalie Blake-Noel introduces an array of classroom exercises that are explicitly aimed at engaging group work in the classroom, critical thinking, and individual reflection related to practice with diverse populations. Chapter 17, the concluding chapter of the book, by Al-Krenawi, Graham, and Habibov, discusses how diversity and multiculturalism, while highly related notions, are nonetheless differentiated by significant factors. The volume ends with a consideration of the "culture of inclusion," a construct that is gaining much ground on a global scale.

Summary and Conclusion

The discipline of social work, arising as it did in the West, was exported with only partial success to different cultures across the world. Indeed, even in North America social work has been shown to be implicated in a variety of oppressive modes. Social work, however, is far from alone in its discovery and disclosure of less-than-ideal practices and assumptions. In point of fact, in every sector a kind of across-the-board reassessment of approach to difference is taking place. Long-standing assumptions regarding gender, ethnicity, race, ability, religion, sexual orientation, and every other element that defines us are currently under critical review. To this exhaustively evaluative approach there has been a fair amount of backlash. Authors Cummins and Sayers (1996), for instance, described cultural diversity as "the enemy from within." Others see multiculturalism as a "minority perspective" and an attempt to be "politically correct" (D'Andrea, Daniels, & Heck, 1991). However, multiculturalism and diversity do not necessarily threaten group unity; multiculturalism has the ability to enrich society with its variant social components (Al-Krenawi, 2014).

This volume actively embraces a positive reception of diversity. As noted above, the world in general, and the ambit of social work in particular, is made up of people bearing very different profiles. The present work assembles the contributions of multiple research avenues for constructive engagement with this world of diversity. The very diversity of the authors represented here reflects the wide array of viewpoints available for consideration. As such, the reader will note some disagreements in perspectives among the chapters. Notwithstanding this intellectual heterogeneity, a thread running throughout the work is that social work knowledge tends to spearhead a progressive orientation toward the Other. This hopeful thrust is manifesting itself across the discipline of social work, rendering social work practice increasingly compassionate and helpful.

Suggested Readings and Resources

Brydon, K. (2012). Promoting diversity or confirming hegemony? In search of new insights for social work. *International Social Work, 55*, 155–67.

Congress, E. P. (2004). Cultural and ethical issues in working with culturally diverse patients and their families: The use of the *culturagram* to promote cultural competent practice in health care settings. *Social Work in Health Care, 39*(3–4), 249–62.

Dhooper, S. S., and Moore, S. E. (2000). *Social work practice with culturally diverse people.* Lexington, KY: Sage Publications, Inc.

Graham, J. R., Shier, M. L., & Brownlee, K. (2012). Contexts of practice and their impact on social work: A comparative analysis of the context of geography and culture. *Journal of Ethnic & Cultural Diversity in Social Work, 21*(2), 111–28. doi: 10.1080/15313204.2012.673430

Graham, J. R., Swift, K., & Delaney, R. (2012). *Canadian social policy: An introduction* (4th ed.). Toronto, ON: Pearson Education Canada.

Gray, M., Coates, J., & Hetherington, T. (2007). Hearing Indigenous voices in mainstream social work. *Families in Society, 88*(1), 53–64.

Harrison, G., & Turner, R. Being a "culturally competent" social worker: Making sense of a murky concept in practice. *British Journal of Social Work, 41*(2), 333–50.

Jones, D. N., & Truell, R. (2012). The Global Agenda for Social Work and Social Development: A place to link together and be effective in a globalized world. *International Social Work, 55*, 454–72.

Law, K. Y., and Lee, K. M. (2014). Importing Western values versus indigenization: Social work practice with ethnic minorities in Hong Kong. *International Social Work.* doi:10.1177/0020872813500804

National Association of Social Workers. (n.d.). Diversity and cultural competence. Retrieved from https://www.socialworkers.org/pressroom/features/issue/diversity.asp

Trinidad, A. M. O. (2014). Critical Indigenous pedagogy of place: How centering Hawaiian epistemology and values in practice affects people on ecosystemic levels. *Journal of Ethnic & Cultural Diversity in Social Work, 23*(2), 110–28.

Weaver, H. N. Indigenous people and the social work profession: Defining culturally competent services. *Social Work, 44*(3), 217–25.

References

Al-Krenawi, A. (2014, May 22). What do we mean by diversity and multiculturalism in the Israeli society? Paper presented at the first conference on diversity and multiculturalism, Achva Academic College, Israel.

Al-Krenawi, A., & Graham, J. R. (2003). *Multicultural social work in Canada*. Toronto, ON: Oxford University Press.

Al-Krenawi, A., & Graham, J. R. (2008). *Helping professional practice with Indigenous peoples: The Bedouin-Arab case*. Lanham, MD: University Press of America.

American Psychiatric Association. (2000). *Diagnostic and statistical manual of mental disorders* (4th ed., text rev.). Washington, DC: Author.

American Psychological Association. (2003). *Guidelines on multicultural education, training, research, practice, and organizational change for psychologists*. Retrieved from http://www.apa.org/pi/oema/resources/policy/multicultural-guidelines.aspx

Anthias, F. (2002a). Beyond feminism and multiculturalism: Locating difference and the politics of location. *Women's Studies International Forum, 25*(3), 275–86.

Anthias, F. (2002b). Where do I belong? Narrating collective identity and translocational positionality. *Ethnicities, 2*(4), 491–514.

Anthias, F. (2008). Thinking through the lens of translocational positionality: An intersectionality frame for understanding identity and belonging. *Translocations: Migration and Social Change, 4*(1), 5–20.

Baines, D. (Ed.). (2007). *Doing anti-oppressive practice: Building transformative, politicized social work*. Halifax, NS: Fernwood Books.

Bickenbach, J. E., Chatterji, S., Badley, E. M., & Üstün, T. B. (1999). Models of disablement, universalism and the international classification of impairments, disabilities and handicaps. *Social Science and Medicine, 48*(9), 1173–87.

Bradshaw, C., & Graham, J. R. (2007). Localization of social work practice, education and research: A content analysis. *Social Development Issues, 29*(2), 92–111.

Calasanti, T. M., & Slevin, K. F. (Eds.). (2006). *Age matters: Realigning feminist thinking*. New York, NY: Taylor & Francis.

Cummins, J., & Sayers, D. (1996). Multicultural education and technology: Promises and pitfalls. *Multicultural Education, 3*(3), 4–10.

D'Andrea, M., Daniels, J., & Heck, R. (1991). Evaluating the impact of multicultural counseling training. *Journal of Counseling & Development, 70*, 143–50.

Dessel, A., Bolen, R., & Shepardson, C. (2011). Can religious expression and sexual orientation affirmation coexist in social work? A critique of Hodge's theoretical, theological, and conceptual frameworks. *Journal of Social Work Education, 47*, 213–34.

Devore, W., & Schlesinger, E. G. (1996). *Ethnic sensitive social work practice*. New York: Macmillan.

Dominelli, L. (1997). *Anti-racist social work*. London: Macmillan.

Dominelli, L. (2002). *Anti-oppressive social work theory and practice*. Hampshire, UK: Palgrave, Macmillan.

Este, D. (1999). Social work and cultural competency. In G. Lie & D. Este (Eds.), *Professional social service delivery in a multicultural world* (pp. 27–45). Toronto: Canadian Scholars' Press.

Graham, J. R. (2006). Spirituality and social work: A call for an international focus of research. *Arete: A Professional Journal Devoted to Excellence in Social Work, 30*(1), 63–77.

Herberg, D. C. (1993). Frameworks for cultural and racial diversity: Teaching and learning for practitioners. Toronto: Canadian Scholars' Press.

Hodge, D. (2002). Does social work oppress Evangelical Christians? A "new class" analysis of society and social work. *Social Work, 47*(4), 401–14.

Hodge, D. (2005). Epistemological frameworks, homosexuality, and religion: How people of faith understand the intersection between homosexuality and religion. *Social Work, 50*, 207–18.

Hodge, D., Baughman, L. M., & Cummings, J. A. (2006). Moving toward spiritual competency. *Journal of Social Service Research, 32*(4), 211–31.

Lee, M. Y., & Greene, G. J. (1999). A social constructivist framework for integrating cross-cultural issues in teaching clinical social work. *Journal of Social Work Education, 35*(1), 21–7.

Lum, D. (1992). *Social work practice and people of color: A process-stage approach*. Pacific Grove, CA: Brooks/Cole.

Madden, V. (2014, September 22). Why poor students struggle. *New York Times*, p. A21.

Maher, F. A., & Tetreault, M. K. T. (2001). *The feminist classroom: Dynamics of gender, race, and privilege*. Lanham, MD: Rowman & Littlefield.

Malik, S., & Velazquez, J. (2002, July/August). Cultural competence and the "new Americans." *Children's Voice, 11*(4), 24–30.

Mehrotra, G. (2010). Toward a continuum of intersectionality theorizing for feminist social work scholarship. *Affilia, 25*(4), 417–30.

Midgley, J. (1981). *Professional imperialism: Social work in the Third World*. London: Heinemann.

Mifflin, M. (2014, September 12). Race matters. *Chronicle of Higher Education*, p. B2.

Moreau, M. (1979). A structural approach to social work education. *Canadian Journal of Social Work Education, 5*(1), 78–94.

Mullally, R. (2007). *The new structural social work*. Toronto, ON: Oxford University Press.

Prince, M. (2009). *Absent citizens: Disability politics and policy in Canada*. Toronto, ON: University of Toronto Press.

Swift, K. (1995). *Manufacturing bad mothers: A critical perspective on child neglect*. Toronto, ON: University of Toronto Press.

Todd, S., & Coholic, D. (2007). Christian fundamentalism and anti-oppressive social work pedagogy. *Journal of Teaching in Social Work, 27*(3), 5–25.

Tsang, A. K. T., & George, U. (1998). Towards an integrated framework for cross-cultural social work practice. *Canadian Social Work Review, 15*(1), 73–93.

Wallis, M., & Kwok, S. M. (Eds.). (2008). *Daily struggles: The deepening racialization and feminization of poverty in Canada*. Toronto, ON: Canada Scholars' Press.

Worell, J., & Remer, P. (2002). *Feminist perspectives in therapy: Empowering diverse women*. Hoboken, NJ: John Wiley & Sons.

Zapata, R. (2009). Setting a research agenda on the interaction between cultural demands of immigrants and minority nations. In R. Zapata (Ed.), *Immigration and self-government of minority nations* (pp. 1–25). Bruxelles: PIE—Peter Lang.

Whiteout

Still Looking for Race in Canadian Social Work Practice

By June Ying Yee and Gary C. Dumbrill

Chapter Objectives

This chapter will help you develop an understanding of:

- The ways in which learning about the culture of the "Other" distracts social work practitioners from recognizing the ways in which Whiteness shapes the norms and values of Canadian society
- The origins of White power, which date back to the early days of colonialism, European enslavement of others, and capitalism
- How the White standpoint becomes the nation's standpoint and White cultural practices are constituted as Canada's social norms
- Whiteness as a marker of social location of privilege that is linked to broader socio-political processes, resulting in differential access to privilege
- How Whiteness has shaped the history of multicultural social work literature and, in turn, the way in which services are provided to ethnoracial communities
- The need for social work practice to make visible the power of Whiteness within organizational structures and practices
- Strategies for confronting Whiteness in social work practice

Introduction

Canada's population is racially diverse (Henry & Tator, 2010). According to the National Household Survey (Ministry of Industry, 2013), between 2006 and 2011, 78 per cent of the immigrants who arrived in Canada were visible minorities. The primary source countries of immigration were from Asia, including the Middle East, as well as Africa, the Caribbean, and Central and South America. Recognizing that social work caseloads include an increasing number of persons from diverse **ethnoracial** backgrounds brings to the fore the urgent need to provide culturally relevant and appropriate services. Many social service agencies struggle to find ways to deliver both equitable and accessible services that meet the cultural and linguistic needs of diverse ethnoracial populations (Dumbrill, 2009; Pashang, 2012; Yee, Wong, & Schlabitz, 2014). This struggle focuses on equipping service providers with knowledge about the cultures of various ethnoracial communities in the belief that ignorance and prejudice about cultures different from one's own can lead to cultural insensitivity and discrimination (Cournoyer, 2014; Hepworth, Rooney, & Larsen, 2013; McGoldrick, Giordiano, & Garcia-Preto, 2005). Many within the social work profession believe that if one can better understand the behaviour, culture, and perspectives of a different ethnoracial group, then cultural respect, validation, and acceptance should follow.

The Danger of Focusing on the "Other"

A danger of attempting to understand culture is that it can detract from the lived experiences of the ethnoracial **Other**—their "voice" easily becomes subsumed within the defining forces of the dominant culture, which presents itself as non-ideological, fair, and neutral. A focus on the "Other" can mitigate the responsibility, shared by everyone, to implement far-reaching actions to dismantle systemic, individual, and cultural discriminatory barriers within Canadian social service systems. While focusing on the "Other" allows social work practitioners to feel good about having knowledge of another culture, at the same time it allows them to be oblivious to the fact that they are reproducing the values and norms of the dominant culture and keeping oppressive and dominant structures intact. At worst, this approach reduces "culture" to a static concept and reduces people to celebrations of dress, customs, and behaviours. This reification of "culture" further mystifies people's social relations and allows one to make generalizations about people's behaviour without considering their material, lived experiences of racism, classism, sexism, ableism, and heterosexism.

Compared to the more privileged sectors of society, disadvantaged groups such as single mothers and ethnoracial minorities are disproportionately represented among those receiving social work intervention (Jones, 1994; Swift, 1995; Yee, Hackbusch, & Wong, 2015). Swift (1995) builds on Hutchinson's (1992) work to contend that the failure to apply a race analysis to the disproportionate number of Aboriginal and racialized children in care because of "neglect" maintains and legitimizes the societal inequalities that Aboriginal and racialized groups face and that have an impact on such differential outcomes (ibid., p. 127). Ethnoracial communities receive blame for inappropriate conduct, a label readily applied by a child welfare bureaucracy that fails to recognize the underlying causes sustained by racial and ethnic inequality. In turn, child welfare workers do not provide the types of support required by these ethnoracial communities to address the larger socio-economic factors that have a negative impact on parenting capacity. This difficulty in naming social processes that perpetuate the stigmatization and devaluing of cross-cultural communities has much to do with Western, liberal democratic societies, which produce male "white, Eurocentric, heterosexual and able-bodied" perspectives and practices through the preservation of their own unnamed power base (Pease, 2011).

If one is to understand the production and reproduction of such discriminatory practices, one needs to locate how and why such mechanisms of oppression operate. Several important questions arise from an effort to understand these mechanisms:

- Why focus on ethnoracial communities in multicultural social work practice in Canada?
- Do referential norms exist that are implicitly compared to one's understanding of ethnoracial communities? If so, what are these norms?
- Who really struggles with ethnoracial communities and why?

Until such unsettling questions are answered, the complex processes that allow the reification of the concepts of race, culture, and ethnicity cannot be unpacked.

Before we explore these questions, we need to define some key concepts. **Race** does not exist as a biological or social category, and any reference to the concept as real is false, other than when race is viewed as socially constructed as an ideological effect of hierarchical social relationships that have become racialized. **Culture** is a fluid and constantly changing aspect of behaviour that reflects the totality of practices by which groups can be identified according to their heritage. **Ethnicity** refers to a common heritage that particular groups identify themselves as belonging to—for example, British Isles, Caribbean-Black, Chinese, or Pakistani.

Multicultural social work practice that defines ethnoracial people by cultural characteristics becomes problematic when it ignores the socio-political context of race and ethnicity. Winant (2000) notes that "the category of race" has been replaced by "supposedly more objective categories like ethnicity, nationality, or class" (p. 182). Categorization by ethnoracial background may at times serve practical purposes of understanding the particular needs of specific communities, but this practice often avoids the more sensitive issues around inequality and racism. Does attempting to understand the cultural practices of ethnic groups create generalizations and stereotypes about people? Who benefits from such ethnoracial classification, and what meanings about such groups does this create? Indeed, a focus on race and ethnicity can allow social work practitioners to hide behind cultural misunderstandings to explain why ethnoracial communities do not receive the services they need. For instance, a child welfare agency may explain the overrepresentation of Aboriginal children in its care as a mismatch between modern societal expectations about parenting and Aboriginal culture, and completely miss the fact that the legacy of residential schools, the sixties scoop, systemic poverty, underfunding, a lack of community resources, and perhaps the agency's own attitudes are the more viable explanations for disproportionality. The reduction of race and ethnicity to identity and culture not only stereotypes the needs and aspirations of diverse communities and unique individual identities, but also covers up how Whiteness determines Canada's social service delivery system. Consequently, we contend that the key to working across ethnoracial difference is not by understanding the ethnoracial Other, but examining the power mechanisms that define such people as Other—that is, by examining Whiteness.

Naming Whiteness

To examine **Whiteness** is to identify how race shapes the lives of *both* White people and people of colour (Frankenberg, 1993; Gabriel, 1998; Todd, 2011). Multicultural social work practice cannot be undertaken effectively unless Whiteness is examined and the problem of White dominance is addressed. For this to occur, social work must move away from simply understanding ethnoracial communities and interrogate how White dominance shapes the experiences of the oppressed. Naming Whiteness in social work practice is the starting point of disrupting its power. Failing to name Whiteness colludes with oppression and perpetuates addressing issues of diversity at superficial levels without creating real change. Indeed, the delivery of social work services and the production of social work knowledge remain primarily a White, European enterprise (Dumbrill & Rice-Green, 2008). It makes little sense, therefore, to examine the "differences" of ethnoracial communities without first examining the group that defines these communities as different and the power that enables this group to consider itself the norm.

This chapter explores Whiteness in a process that needs to be mirrored in mainstream social work and within Canadian society as a whole. We, June Ying Yee, a woman of Chinese heritage, and Gary Dumbrill, a White man of British heritage, explore issues of race and ethnicity in the delivery of social work services not by presenting characteristics of our respective ethnoracial identities, but by considering the way in which Whiteness attempts to define and delimit them. By examining this delineation, we unmask how Whiteness invisibly assumes power, situates itself as the norm, and constructs the ethnoracial Other. Whiteness maintains its **hegemony** of social work by literally "whiting out" and obscuring its racial origins. Based on an examination of this power, we suggest an alternative framework for social work practice that frees both White and ethnoracial people—the "mainstream" and the "ethnic"—from producing and reproducing power dynamics that sustain institutional and society-wide oppression.

Identifying Whiteness as a Racial Position of Power

The influence of the White race on social work practice is hardly discussed in social work texts, reflecting a silence that exists in Canadian society as a whole. The significant role that the White race plays in everyday life, often referred to as "Whiteness" (Frankenberg, 1993; Gabriel, 1998; Twine & Gallagher, 2007; Yee, 2005), operates so invisibly that it is difficult to identify or define (Kincheloe, 1999). Despite its elusive nature, there is agreement among authors (Levine-Rasky, 2013; Schick, 2012) that Whiteness is a form of hegemony that allows White people to gain power over racialized people (Levine-Rasky, 2013).

In Case Example 2.1 the authors have been assigned to fixed positions in society; White Anglo-Canadians and, to a lesser extent, White French Canadians, represent

Case Example 2.1

The presence and impact of Whiteness can be demonstrated in examples from the lives of the authors, one from an established Canadian family and the other an immigrant from Britain. Many people ask June Ying Yee, a second-generation Canadian and a woman of Chinese descent, "Where do you come from?" Few people ask Gary Dumbrill, a White male, the same question, even though he is an immigrant. Such experiences are not unique: Many Canadians of colour report being asked where they come from, as though they do not belong in Canada (Drakes, 2000; Mahtani, 2002; Tettey & Puplampu, 2006). June's Chinese ethnicity does not belong in the Canadian fabric.

Consider the following observation—intended as a "compliment"—made to June by a White Anglo-Canadian person: "June, I don't even see you as Chinese." When June chose to use her middle name, Ying, stating she would not pay the expected price, the same White, Anglo-Canadian person responded: "Oh, you don't want to use that name. It sounds so ethnic." Such a statement indicates the price of June's acceptance: She has to adopt White, Anglo-Canadian ways and erase her Chinese-Canadian identity as much as possible to belong.

Gary, on the other hand, is rarely considered ethnic; because of his English ancestry and White race, he is automatically identified as Canadian. He is rarely questioned about where he comes from, even though he is an immigrant from London, England. When some people recognize Gary's accent as English, he is not treated as "foreign," and in fact he enjoys an elevated status coming from what many Canadians regard as "the motherland." To prove this, when Gary shops for his favourite "fish and chips" at the grocery store, he finds these in the regular rather than the "ethnic" food aisle.

Canada's "dominant culture" and identity. Those who do not conform to these norms are denied a full sense of belonging in Canada—this is an example of the power of Whiteness. As will be shown below, naming Whiteness and the ways in which it attempts to position and delineate each of us is the first step of awareness and resistance. By voicing her personal narrative, and coming from a social location that is not a part of the "White race," June reveals and challenges the power of Whiteness to define her by her race and ethnicity. Gary's narrative shows how his location within the "White race" absorbs him into a position of racial privilege. June's and Gary's personal narratives provide an entry point to understanding how Whiteness shapes social work practice. Indeed, June's and Gary's different experiences of acceptance and belonging within the Canadian fabric is mirrored in social work practice. The concept of "diversity" in social work acquires meaning only because a reference point exists from which "difference" can be measured—a reference point of Whiteness. "Diversity" refers to ethnoracial communities, while the White reference point remains invisible. (For a continued discussion on diversity and the profession of social work, see Chapter 12 by Christine A. Walsh, Carey Mulligan, and Gio Dolcecore.)

Frankenberg (1993) describes the three dimensions of Whiteness that enable it to establish White societal norms: "First, whiteness is a location of structural advantage, of race privilege. Second, it is a 'standpoint,' a place from which white people look at ourselves, at others, and at society. Third, 'whiteness' refers to a set of cultural practices that are usually unmarked and unnamed" (p. 1). Evidence demonstrating the existence of the latter two dimensions—a White standpoint and a set of unmarked cultural practices—can be found in James's (1996) research on ethnicity in Canada. When James asked White people to describe their ethnicity, the typical response revealed the invisibility of normative power: "To me, ethnicity was something that belonged to people that differed from the so-called average White Canadian—differing perhaps because of language, accent or skin colour. I believe my ignorance regarding my ethnicity is because I belong to the majority in Canada. Because the majority of Canadians are White, English-speaking descendants of Britain, I have only thought of myself as a Canadian. In essence, I didn't realize I had ethnicity because I did not differ from the stereotypical image of an average Canadian" (pp. 39–40). White people making similar statements view themselves, others, and society from their own White standpoint, usually without recognizing the cultural practices of their own "ethnicity." Indeed, other researchers (Bonnett, 2000; Henry & Tator, 2010; Roger, 2000) have similarly documented the failure of White, English-speaking Canadians to recognize their own ethnicity while seeing and defining Aboriginal, Chinese, Somali, and other visibly different people as ethnic. Such ethnocentrism seems innocuous at first, but because Whiteness is also a "location of structural advantage and race privilege," White ethnocentrism has the power to become the centre of the societal universe. The White standpoint becomes the nation's standpoint, and White cultural practices are constituted as Canada's social norms. Gabriel (1998) explains the power of Whiteness to wield delineating power in his expansion of Fiske's (1994) definition of Whiteness as "a set of discursive techniques, including: *exnomination*, that is the power not to be named; *naturalization*, through which whiteness establishes itself as the norm by defining 'others' and not itself; and *universalization*, where whiteness alone can make sense of a problem and its understanding becomes *the* understanding" (Gabriel, 1998, p. 13; emphasis in original).

The Origins of White Power

The essence of Whiteness lies in its power to establish and maintain a silent discourse that automatically equates normality with White culture—thus enabling this culture to become taken for granted as the norm. The origins of White power date back to the early days of colonialism, European enslavement of others, and **capitalism**. White Europeans imposed their cultural practices around the world through military and economic might. Today, rather than White cultural practices being sustained by military power and subjugation, Whiteness maintains itself through the power to define the subject. The transition from military to ideological domination can be discerned in Canada's history. Mercredi and Turpel (1993) recount how some 500 years ago the people of Turtle Island met visitors from other lands in "a momentous event in our collective history" (p. 16). White Europeans colonized and settled in a process of subjugating, invading, and engaging in acts of genocide to dominate Aboriginal peoples. By 1867, the British and French colonizers had formalized the establishment of a political entity called Canada in the northern part of Turtle Island. A part of the European subjugation of Aboriginal peoples was the building of a national institutional infrastructure, including various levels of government, judicial systems, and educational systems that decimated the cultural practices and infrastructure of First Nations communities (James, 1996). The institutions of colonial rule eventually became the vanguard of White dominance.

The shift from violent to predominantly ideological coercion and control demonstrates the ability of Whiteness to maintain subjugation by adapting to changing historical circumstances. Of course, violence is always ideological, too. Kincheloe (1999) explains how White rule was deeply embedded in the Enlightenment's notion of "[r]ationality with its privileged construction of a transcendental white, male, rational subject who operated at the recess of power while giving every indication that he escaped the confines of time and space" (p. 164). "Science" and "reason" were marshalled to justify White colonial domination (Kincheloe, 1999).

Some writers (Johnson, Rush, & Feagin, 2000) suggest that the "scientific" categorization of humans by race grew from the need to legitimate the European–American slave trade. In 1775, Johann Blumenbach developed one of the first typologies of race by dividing humans into five biological categories: Mongolians, Ethiopians, Americans, Malays, and Caucasians. He chose the term "Caucasian" to refer to White Europeans because he believed that Whites had originated in the Russian Caucasus Mountains, where they had been created by God in his own image (Akintunde, 1999; Blakey, 1999). Blumenbach ranked races in order of superiority; since he considered Caucasians as most God-like, other races fell beneath them, their degree of relative inferiority determined by their closeness to the White ideal (Akintunde, 1999; Cameron & Wycoff, 1998). With other races ranked as inferior to Whites, the justification of the enslavement and domination of other races by Whites was seen as the natural order of society. Thus, the concept of race enabled and justified the subjugation of other races by Whites.

Today, with the exception of neo-Nazis, White supremacists, and some others, most people recognize Blumenbach's "science" as flawed. Yet the White race still rules, Whiteness retains normative status, and White understanding continues to be "the understanding" (Gabriel, 1998, p. 13). Whiteness maintains dominance in part because Blumenbach did not simply construct the concept of race—he constructed an apparatus through which White systemic racial subjugation was justified.

Distinguishing Whiteness and White People

Recognizing Whiteness as a form of domination separates, to some degree, the concept of Whiteness from a description of White people. Separating Whiteness from White people is important: because biological descriptions of race such as "White," "Black," or "of colour" lack validity, one cannot claim that Whiteness is a racial characteristic. Although the concept of race has no **ontological** meaning, it has **epistemological** meaning as a **social location** that shapes the way the world is experienced. Race, therefore, gains meaning not as a descriptor of skin colour but as a marker of social location, with Whiteness representing a location of structural advantage. As such, the term "Whiteness" transcends race to represent the multiple sites of advantage and privilege of being White, male, middle class, heterosexual, and able bodied. Just as these locations transcend race, so does their antithesis of being a person of colour; female; working class; lesbian, gay, bisexual, or transsexual; or having a disability.

Ethnicity can also be included in the construct of Whiteness because, although ethnicity refers to cultural groupings rather than categorization by racial characteristics, socio-political processes determine which of the vast array of human characteristics are singled out as signifiers of ethnicity. As shown in June's and Gary's narratives, both Gary's Whiteness and his invisible ethnicity secured his acceptance as fittingly Canadian, while June was excluded by her race and ethnicity. Ethnicity, therefore, becomes interconnected with race in the array of social locations forming the power position of Whiteness.

In Britain, understanding race as a political construct resulted in members of a number of subjugated groups recognizing the oppression they experienced as having roots in their social location rather than their race or ethnicity. Consequently, many Southeast Asians, South Asians, people of African descent, and even some "White" Irish rallied together and adopted the label "Black" (Gabriel, 1998; Kincheloe, 1999). The use of the term "Black" by these groups was a political rather than a biological statement that emerged from a solidarity among groups with a shared consciousness about the nature of their common oppression. The inclusion of "White Irish" as members of the "Black" group reveals that not all White people have access to the full privilege and power of Whiteness. Recognizing different access among Whites to the power of Whiteness is important. To act as though individuals are defined by a single aspect of their oppression homogenizes and reduces people to that essence—it **essentializes** them. Such essentializing must be avoided because to claim that all White people have equal access to the power of Whiteness is inaccurate and oversimplifies the problem. McIntosh (1998) describes Whites as having an unearned "invisible knapsack" of privilege that they can draw from. Yet if Whiteness is characterized as an intersection of locations of privilege, all Whites clearly cannot access the same array of privileges. (For a more in-depth discussion on intersectional identities, see Chapter 1 by Alean Al-Krenawi, John R. Graham, and Nazim Habibov, and Chapter 6 by Miu Chung Yan.)

As Gabriel (1998) comments, "I am not suggesting that Whiteness works for all 'Whites' in the same way. Not all White ethnicities are dominant and not all 'Whites' are privileged" (p. 4). Clearly, a homeless White male, a White mother on welfare, and a White male CEO of a *Fortune* 500 company do not have equal access to **White privilege**. Whiteness does not divide the oppressed from the oppressors in a neat binary. In fact, division into the binary opposites of Black and White is a form of objectification that denies subjects their ability to act in different ways (Leonard, 1997). In other words, categorization into White oppressors and Black oppressed defines people by race and denies them the ability to resist that definition—a process Whiteness itself uses to maintain dominance.

The spectre of binary simplicity must not, however, allow Whiteness to elude interrogation. Without falling into the trap of essentialism, Whiteness must be named and unmarked. Naming Whiteness makes it visible and profoundly changes the way one engages in social work practice with ethnoracial Others. When social workers understand and name Whiteness, they fight oppression.

The Invisible History of Whiteness in Multicultural Social Work Literature

When one recognizes the pervasiveness of Whiteness in Canadian culture, the history of multicultural social work takes on new meaning. No longer is the history of multicultural practice about searching for ways of working with ethnoracial communities; rather, it is a history of how the discourse of Whiteness shapes, defines, and delineates knowledge about ethnoracial people. Social work, from the anchor point of the norms and values of the dominant culture, reappropriates the terms "race" and "ethnicity" by socially constructing these categories through the lens of Whiteness. Ethnoracial people are understood from the standpoint of the "rational" and "scientific" White understanding that both creates and reinforces Whiteness. Throughout this process, the world is divided into two camps—the definer and the delineated—with attention focused on ethnoracial people, not Whiteness itself. The object of activity for service providers, who work from a place of Whiteness, focuses on the problems that ethnoracial communities place on the system, rather than laying bare the invisible domination of the discourse of Whiteness.

The preservation of race privilege and predominance of the cultural practices of Whiteness create the ethnoracial Other. Although White societal norms manifest themselves in different ways over time, they have determined social work knowledge and literature. During the 1950s and 1960s, intergroup conflict between ethnoracial minorities and the dominant culture group in North America resulted in the creation of the **race relations**, bias, and assimilation models. These approaches assumed that racial tensions were caused by individual prejudice and a lack of cultural contact between members of the mainstream and ethnoracial people. Mainstream social scientists readily accepted these claims. They coincided neatly with state policy perspectives and the benevolent belief that Canada was not a racist society. From this point of view, responsibility for racial tensions was placed on ethnoracial groups by focusing on their acculturation and adaptation skills, rather than considering the source of conflict as emanating from the racism of the mainstream group. (For a further analysis of acculturation and adaptation, see Chapter 9 by Debashis Dutta and Ross Klein.)

Inherent in this thinking was an "us and them" attitude in which Whiteness plays a key role: Ways needed to be found for "them" (ethnoracial Others) to fit better with "us" (White society). This thinking rests on the assumption that the race and ethnicity of the Other must be identified and scrutinized. Once the ethnoracial Other has been marked and objectified, the dominant culture wields power over them, emphasizing the cultural characteristics of **minority groups** in order to define them, determine their needs, and place them within the hierarchical social order. Although such categorization makes little sense, this process of racialization helps to ameliorate the dominant group's perception that the ethnoracial Other encroaches into the space of Whiteness and potentially threatens Canada's White landscape.

A focus on difference and culture allows people to avoid dealing with racism. As noted by Back and Solomos (2009), "the language of culture and nation invokes a hidden racial narrative" (p. 20). Whiteness dominates the narrative of Canadian history and is an integral and defining force of national identity. Yet its very omnipresence renders it virtually invisible: It is simultaneously "everywhere but nowhere" in the consciousness of both White people and people of colour. For example, one of the striking powers of Whiteness lies in its ability to determine who belongs and who does not belong in the discourse of the nation. Most people are aware that the use of the term "Canadian" frequently refers to those who are of White European descent as opposed to people of colour (Mahtani, 2002). In everyday social work practice, to emphasize the differences of ethnicity and race not only diverts attention away from the way various social locations give differential access to power and privilege, but also removes any awareness about the power of the White professional to socially construct and define "ethnoracial communities."

In social service agencies, the dominant culture may constitute itself in the position of power and control through the privileged social location of Whiteness, and may determine and limit the type of social services, supports, and resources available to ethnoracial communities. A major obstacle that mainstream service providers have yet to overcome is their own inability to challenge the way mainstream agencies organize and structure service delivery and to change these systems so that such services fully and equally take into account the rights of the ethnoracial Other. Race evasion on the part of mainstream agencies—that is, failure to acknowledge the role that race plays in structuring service delivery—prevents them from equitably sharing power with and integrating services for ethnoracial communities. For example, many agencies provide workshops on educating mainstream service providers about the culture of ethnoracial communities. A consequence of such action is that the equal rights of the ethnoracial Other are perpetually undermined by the dominant culture. If ethnoracial Others are not satisfied with the services they receive from mainstream agencies, the reason must be because "they" are different, and ethnoracial Others should expect to receive culturally appropriate services only if and when funding becomes available.

Cross-Cultural Approach

Apart from socio-political interpretations of ethnoracial communities' interaction with the dominant culture, the development of psychological, biological, and social analyses of various cultural groups have predominated in social work literature, especially from the 1960s to the early 1980s. Tsang and George (1998) expanded Casas's (1985) review of cross-cultural understandings of ethnoracial people to identify five different models, all of which portray ethnoracial Others in negative terms: the inferiority or pathological model (Padilla, 1981), the deviant model (Rubington & Weinberg, 1971), the disorganizational model (Moynhihan, 1965), the culturally deficient model (Padilla, 1981), and the genetically deficient model (Herrnstein, 1971). The discourse of Whiteness that is evident in these texts does not simply portray ethnoracial people as explicitly inferior, it also implicitly portrays the dominant culture as superior, without making any explicit reference to the normality of Whiteness. This notion of White superiority complements the race relations, bias, and assimilation perspectives of the same period by taking for granted that the problem stems from ethnoracial people, not White people. In social work practice, the standard convention for dealing with the problem of race and ethnicity is to teach the ethnoracial Other how to maintain their ethnicity in appropriately "Canadian" ways and to assimilate as a "Canadian" by acting more White, rather than to help build the cultural identities of ethnoracial people in positive ways.

Cultural Literacy Approach

The policy of multiculturalism has not reduced problems of racial inequality, even though the intent of the policy was acceptance and tolerance of Canada's many cultures. Adopted in 1971 against the backdrop of institutional recognition of British and French cultures and official bilingualism, the federal government's policy of multiculturalism recognized Canada's mosaic of cultures, and it did help to propagate the idea that the ethnoracial Other need no longer assimilate and should instead be encouraged to maintain their cultural heritage. In the context of multiculturalism, understanding the ethnoracial Other became salient and important. Especially in social work practice, the **cultural literacy** approach of McGoldrick, Giordiano, and Garcia-Preto (2005) flourished, as mainstream workers sought expert knowledge of the client's culture to meet the instrumentalist need for a practical way of working with those from another culture. Cultural fairs and "ethnic" food lunches became popular, and it was fashionable to develop an appreciation for saris, samosas, and steel bands. The cultural literacy approach encouraged social work practitioners to engage in self-reflection about how their personal values, beliefs, or social locations filter and transform the cultural world of the service user to conform to their agency's mainstream practices. As long as practitioners remain consciously unaware of their Whiteness, its power remains deeply embedded and invisible in various social work practice approaches that deflect attention away from the self to the Other.

Although much of the social work literature on cultural literacy approaches carefully cautions readers to pay attention to the variability of people's experiences and to avoid making generalizations about people's behaviour, many social work practitioners unintentionally fall into the trap of essentializing and circumscribing people's social identities. More importantly, one cannot ignore the reality that the social identities of ethnoracial people intermesh with those of Whiteness. The reason for a focus on the ethnicity of racial minorities may not be so much the fault of the practitioner as the fallacy of the approach itself. As noted by Gilroy (1990), "at the end of the day, an absolute commitment to cultural insiderism is as bad as an absolute commitment to biological insiderism" (p. 80). In other words, culture cannot be treated as some kind of artifact that the social work practitioner takes for granted as true; rather, social workers should politically critique the appropriation of culture by the person who has the power to speak about it. Gilroy observed that "in our multi-cultural schools the sound of the steel pan may evoke Caribbean ethnicity, tradition and authenticity yet they originate in the oil drums of the Standard Oil Company rather than the mysterious knowledge of ancient African griots" (p. 80). Without a historical understanding of the role that economic and colonial oppression play in the lives of ethnoracial people, a White "understanding" of the Other remains unchallenged and is assumed uncritically in the media, school, and workplace.

Indeed, multiculturalism and cultural literacy approaches perpetuate and maintain Whiteness as the societal referential norm and authoritative voice from which the ethnoracial Other can be defined and measured. As Dyche and Zayas (1995) point out, culture is, "reified, lifted from its abstract status and the printed page and perceived as a description of real individuals; that is, clients are seen as their culture, not as themselves" (p. 391). The safety in examining ethnoracial people's identity through their cultures serves many purposes. First, for social work practitioners, understanding the cultures of ethnoracial people provides a cookie-cutter approach to social work practice and maintains the illusion that we treat everybody the same. Second, this approach colludes with the myth that all cultures in Canada are equal, despite the power of the dominant culture to shape Canadian norms and values. Although the policy of multiculturalism acknowledges the contribution of Canada's ethnic–racial diversity to everyday life, there are limits to which ethnoracial people can transform the Whiteness of the Canadian landscape. Some people feel that multiculturalism is dividing the country and threatening "Canadian culture" (Mackey, 1996).

In other words, Whiteness remains the underlying dominant mode of understanding embedded within the historical, collective unconscious of Canada. Recognizing this, Homi Bhabha states that the unspoken meaning behind multiculturalism, with its emphasis on difference, is nothing but "a sham universalism that paradoxically permits diversity [and] masks ethnocentric norms, values and interests" (cited in Jordan & Weedon, 1995, p. 485). Such masking, propagated and further supported by multiculturalism and cultural literacy approaches, takes race completely off the social work agenda. With no mention of race, and much talk about ethnicity, diversity in Canada is reduced to a mosaic of cultural practices and traditions; the ability to conceptualize and critically discuss the historical origins of privilege, power, and racial oppression becomes further obscured. Any person who associates race with inequality is accused of propagating the very phenomena discussed. As argued by Proctor and Davis (1994) and reinforced by Tsang and George (1998), a "colour-blind practice assumes equality between client and worker and the acknowledgement of racial difference is seen as racism" (Tsang & George, 1998, p. 75). As well, proponents of a **colour-blind approach** argue that devising solutions from the standpoint of race promotes the polarization of society; however, evading the concept of race denies the extent and degree to which social relationships are, in fact, structured through race. The denial of race oppression promotes the naive belief that, underneath the appearance of differences, everyone is the same and we are all just human. Yet in every instance of interaction, race configures the perceptions of both the observer and the observed and subsequently plays a role in determining the dynamics of the relationship. To deny this reality is to deny that ethnoracial people experience barriers in access to resources and opportunities in daily life and in their interactions and negotiations with institutions.

The conflation of the terms race and ethnicity into mere cultural identities diminishes the potential for social action that would critically interrogate the underlying dominant mode of understanding—a system that benefits White people and supports a structure of inequality. At the same time, ethnoracial groups are easily subsumed into a subordinate role, that of the oppressed, in relation to the dominant culture. Notwithstanding the impact of the **civil rights movements** in the 1960s, the implementation of the policy of multiculturalism in 1971, and the establishment of the **Charter of Rights and Freedoms** in 1982, all of which challenge the power of Whiteness to undermine the rights of ethnoracial communities, there are limits to these multicultural practices. The effectiveness of such social movements and policies must be framed within the context of Whiteness, which maintains its ability to reassert its homogenizing power by seemingly neutral and fair mechanisms and to prevent the dismantling of the larger systemic and institutional forms of discrimination still in place. This is why it is important to recognize that the rights of ethnoracial communities must always be understood in the context of Whiteness; otherwise collusion with Whiteness can too easily occur, with little awareness that this is what is happening.

Anti-racism Approaches

In the 1980s and through the 1990s, critical discourse on the concepts of race and racism created shifts in the literature on cultural diversity. Critical of the multiculturalism approach, many writers (Dei, 1996; Dominelli, 1997; Gilroy, 1987, 1990; Leah, 1995) argued that the problems of race, class, gender, and other forms of oppression are rooted in the historical, social, political, and economic circumstances of people's material, lived experiences. Known as the **anti-racism approach**, some of its key features stand out clearly in opposition to the limitations of the multiculturalism approach. They include an acknowledgement that racism exists in society; that conflict between racial minorities and the dominant group is not due to lack of contact or to cultural misunderstanding between groups, but rather can be traced to power differentials between the dominant group and ethnoracial minorities; and that people's social, political, and economic relationships are racially structured. Dei (1996) defines anti-racism as "[a]n action-oriented strategy for institutional systemic change that addresses racism and other interlocking systems of social oppression" (p. 252). Dei's position is that to bring about change, one must name racism rather than ethnicity and culture as the problem.

Within an anti-racism approach, the concept of race transforms from a descriptive variable to an ideological entity in the context of Western, liberal societies. Western liberalism has two irreconcilable characteristics:

- A strong belief in equality of treatment, regardless of one's race, gender, and class
- The prevalence of discriminatory treatment of people because of race, gender, and class

Much of the anti-racism literature acknowledges the existence of the latter reality by proactively engaging in strategies that dismantle concrete barriers and structures that intentionally or unintentionally exclude ethnoracial people from equal participation in society. As described by Dei (1996), "the antiracism perspective moves beyond acknowledgement of the material conditions that structure societal inequality; it questions White power and privilege and their rationale for dominance. Antiracism questions the marginalization of certain voices in society and the delegitimation/devaluation of the knowledge and experience of subordinate and minority groups" (p. 254). Within this approach, even the positive evaluation of ethnoracial communities and their cultures in social service (for instance, by romanticizing "difference") is harmful because such an evaluation rests against the backdrop of the dominant culture. Ultimately, the dominant culture not only sets the parameters by which ethnoracial communities are understood, it also defines whose voices are heard.

Although many boards of social service agencies encourage ethnoracial representation, tokenism may ensure the domination of White privilege. To expect, for example, a Caribbean-Black person to be representative of all Caribbean-Black people reduces the individual to a particular aspect of his or her social location and, furthermore, implies that people have static social identities. More importantly, to call for greater representation of ethnoracial perspectives in the national culture of Canada, which is dominated by Whiteness, can come across as sounding as though an interest group is speaking. The association of demands for ethnoracial representation with "interest group" politics reveals the power of the White, heterosexual, able-bodied male to be taken as the norm, rather than the interests of the dominant group. An awareness of the marginality of ethnoracial perspectives raises questions about whether the portrayal of the culture of ethnoracial communities can truly be recognized in the context of a White Canada.

A strong backlash has been aimed at the anti-racism perspective. The implementation of an anti-racism perspective in social service agencies failed to gain acceptance by key stakeholders with the power to create change. Naming racism within an agency causes major internal objections. For example, in an evaluation report of a multicultural organizational change project, which is a strategy to help agencies become more culturally accessible to ethnoracial clients, the organization strongly recommended that the word "racism" be completely removed; objection to the use of the word by organizational leaders is not uncommon, since they often see the word as divisive and negative to the organizational culture. Some authors suggest that omission of the word racism is a form of resistance to change (Henry & Tator, 2010, p. 338), yet another political analysis by Humphries (1997) demonstrates how "much of the radical potential of anti-racism has been re-defined and re-situated, *appropriated and accommodated* within a liberal value base" (p. 295; emphasis in original). Once again, the power of Whiteness as an ideological force in Canadian society finds ways to reassert itself and prevent meaningful systemic and structural change, thus perpetuating and maintaining the status quo. In fact, Henry & Tator (2010) highlight the fact that most agencies struggle with creating adequate policies, practices, and models of change within organizational practices that claim a commitment to an anti-racism vision. Perhaps, one could further argue, this is why social service agencies have not moved further ahead in providing culturally appropriate and relevant services to ethnoracial people.

Although an anti-racism perspective aims to tackle the social relations that underlie discriminatory treatment of ethnoracial people, the power of Whiteness refuses to put its own structures and practices under scrutiny; race evasiveness helps to maintain Whiteness. For mainstream agencies to adopt anti-racism and undertake organizational change requires decision makers to challenge the underlying cultural practices of Whiteness that are entrenched in the norms and values of the agency. More problematic for many agencies, such acknowledgement of racism puts into question current forms of multicultural practice, such as educating mainstream service providers about ethnoracial communities, and shifts the focus onto Whiteness as the barrier to fair and equitable outcomes for ethnoracial communities. Examining Whiteness can be threatening, to say the least, but it represents a positive move toward a real sharing of power among those who are privileged and those who are perpetually marginalized.

Strategies on How to Combat Whiteness in Canadian Social Work Practice

Strategies to address Whiteness must begin with the self. This is not a task just for White people, because Whiteness is not simply about race; it is a confluence of interlocking locations that give access to unearned power and privilege. Whatever "race" you are, you are implicated in and are a part of Whiteness. In Case Example 2.2, Gary, who is White, learns about his race privilege.

Case Example 2.2

When Gary was an undergraduate in London, England, he arrived one day at the university he attended to find a crowd bustling at the entrance where Prince Charles was exiting a limousine. The prince walked up the steps to attend a prestigious event, and Gary decided to tag along. The prince shook hands with the university president and said a few words; Gary also shook hands with the president and, mimicking an upper-class accent, said, "Thank you for inviting us." If Gary had spoken with his regular working-class accent he would have been stopped, and perhaps even arrested, but by pretending and passing as a member of the ruling class Gary gained entry. Afterwards, Gary felt pleased with himself for tricking his way into a social space where he did not belong.

Sometime later Gary was travelling in Guyana, South America, and was running to catch a steamer (boat) that was about to sail from Parika to Bartica. Although the steamer had not yet departed, officials closed the Stelling (pier) gates to stop the bustling crowd of latecomers from entering the dock and boarding. Gary, who already knew how to trick his way into places, pushed through the throng and, mimicking an upper-class English accent, ordered the official to let him through, which the official promptly did with a salute. Afterwards, Gary again felt pleased with himself while sitting on the steamer chugging its way up the Essequibo River; until he slowly realized that he had been the only White person in the crowd, and that the official probably did not know the difference between an upper-class and a working-class accent.

In this Case Example, Gary's strategy for addressing his own Whiteness began by recognizing that he was located differently in the two situations above. Gary realized that although he had been marginalized and excluded by class in his early life, he had been gaining entry to places based on other parts of his identity without even realizing it. He now had to think through the extent to which he was implicated in and benefited from Whiteness. To bring about social change, each of us has to go through a similar process and make ourselves a "case study," where we identify, unravel, and name the implications of our own Whiteness. This process never ends, but unless we begin it in ourselves we cannot begin the work of addressing Whiteness in policies or practice. The invisibility of Whiteness in the everdayness of people's actions in positions of power, and how this power is further enforced by institutional structures, is discussed in Case Example 2.3. All institutions are structures that are a part of Whiteness, including social service agencies. To be able to identify how Whiteness operates you must be able to name and identify the behaviours, structures, processes, practices, and policies in place that create and sustain exclusion.

Case Example 2.3

A government ministry designed a new formula for how social service agencies should allocate their funds to programs and services. The new formula was devised by a government-sponsored panel of experts in social policy and organizational management. The panel consulted with academic researchers and senior managers of the agencies concerned; they also solicited input from the public, but very few agency workers and service users attended. The resulting funding formula rearranged and redistributed agency program finances in ways that fully addressed the government's fiscal concerns.

Points to Consider

Can you identify the patterns of behaviour embedded in the social and administrative structure of this organizational culture that produce and reproduce Whiteness?

In Case Example 2.3, Whiteness is operating in the following ways:

1. The decision-making process is clear only to those in power.
2. Those in power make decisions for those without power.
3. Those in power think it is unimportant to understand the viewpoints of those without power.
4. Those without power have difficulty in challenging the new funding formula.
5. Those without power do not know how decisions are made and by whom, yet they are the ones most impacted by the decisions.

The process above carries the practice of Whiteness within a system that recognizes only the power of particular stakeholders, in this case, academic researchers and senior managers. The structures that enable the ministry to behave in this way include the failure of the consultation process to have mechanisms that serve as checks and balances on the ministry's power. In any system that values transparency, equity, and fairness, everyone affected should know who makes the decisions that will impact them directly and also be aware of the different stakeholders' levels of responsibility and authority. However, even those who have authority should be required to include those affected by the decisions so that they are able to share power in that decision-making process.

A major challenge in inviting input from agency workers and service users is that they do not share the same level of power in the decision-making process. One of the myths expounded by capitalism is the government rationale that everyone can participate equitably in the decision-making process. Yet the ministry's current mechanism to seek input fails to recognize that many people experience barriers in being able to participate in the decision-making process. Often, many do not see how institutional structures and the people who work within them are responsible for reinforcing racism and perpetuating colonialist acts upon staff and communities. More specifically, a broader analysis requires us to remember that racism toward staff and communities in systemic forms does, in fact, originate from the internal structures, processes, practices, and policies of institutional structures, including the ministry.

Strategies on how to combat Whiteness within organizational cultures and, specifically, on how to hold the ministry accountable can include the following:

1. Look at how decisions are made within the ministry and create a system and process where different voices can be heard before a decision is made.
2. Make sure those in positions of power have a venue to explain to those to whom they are accountable why particular decisions are made.
3. Demand that decision makers demonstrate how the different viewpoints of those without power were heard and considered in the decision-making process.
4. Ensure that the powerless know that they are allowed to have input in decision making that affects them, and that a venue will be provided where they can hear the rationale for the final decision.
5. Set up systems and processes by which the powerless are able to give input in the decision-making process and are able to confirm how their concerns were heard.

The implications in implementing these strategies for change in combating Whiteness within any system is that a variety of people's perspectives will be heard, rather than only those who hold power.

The critical lesson, especially for those who are committed to social change, is to not underestimate the pervasive power of Whiteness to continually reconstitute itself so that its own structures and power are never dismantled. Within all organizations, tremendous possibilities for change exist, provided we remember the cautionary note that "the master's tools will never dismantle the master's house" (Lorde, 1984, p. 123). Those in positions of power have much at stake in maintaining the status quo, even though they may not be aware of how Whiteness dominates the Other. Discriminatory practices are not always about intent; they are often about how people are socially constructed into positions. This includes social work practitioners who unintentionally participate in the creation of systems that do, in fact, exclude the ethnoracial Other. In fact, everyone is complicitly or explicitly involved in the process of Whiteness, regardless of one's personal social locations of both privilege and oppression. Thus, just because a person socially locates as part of an oppressed group does not necessarily mean that this person is an ally in dismantling the privileged structures of Whiteness. The key issue becomes whether that person's actions proactively demonstrate a dismantling of discriminatory and exclusionary structures, practices, and policies that support a system of privilege and inequality.

Recognizing Whiteness

The importance of recognizing the Whiteness of Canada helps draw linkages between the racial narratives of the Canadian national identity and the taken-for-granted privilege and power of the dominant culture, and to make these linkages visible. Furthermore, to acknowledge the Whiteness of Canada requires a deep understanding of how the particular knowledge production of people's experiences is legitimated and supported by Canada's social, political, and economic institutions.

Unfortunately, many Canadians continue to make comments that attest to the Whiteness of Canada, such as, "Minority/Indigenous peoples' demands for fairness and justice have victimized White people," and "Programs like employment equity and anti-racism policies incorporate authoritarian principles and methods that are antithetical to a liberal democratic society" (Henry & Tator, 2010, p. 360). The first comment assumes that one culture exists in Canada, that of Whiteness, and that the cultures of ethnoracial people threaten the homogeneous power of the dominant culture. The second comment assumes that equal treatment is the goal, when even the Canadian Charter of Rights and Freedoms acknowledges that equal treatment is too simplistic (section 15(2), subsection (1)). Instead, the act allows for affirmative action programs to address historic and ongoing **disadvantage**. In other words, if one does not recognize differences in power, one sees no need to level the playing field.

The perpetuation of myths that work to the detriment of those who are disadvantaged in society is reflected in the sentiments of many Canadians in the discourse of the wider society and, more significantly, reflects the way mainstream agencies provide services to ethnoracial people. We need to develop alternative discourses and methods that introduce new forms of knowledge production to challenge differential power relations by considering "multiple and collective origins of knowledge rather than competing claims to knowledge" (Dei, 1996, p. 254). Spaces for authentic dialogue between members of the dominant culture and ethnoracial communities need to be opened.

Listening to the Oppressed

All knowledge is historically constituted, and Whiteness is a defining component of Canadian history. Contemporary social work practice evolved from specific historical processes that constitute the role of Whiteness in Canada as the determining force in how services can meet the needs of ethnoracial people. A central strategy that focuses on dismantling systems of Whiteness should become the priority of social service agencies. This can occur by facilitating an environment that fosters and supports, as an integral part of the agency's functioning, the practice of listening to the different needs of the oppressed. For example, the establishment of service user committees, which allow ethnoracial groups to partake in the planning, delivery, and evaluation of services, can help democratize the process of ethnoracial participation. Too often the overall system, such as the ministry from Case Example 2.3, claims to know what the community needs and develops programs without adequate consultation with community members. As well, social service providers need an understanding and awareness of the ways in which the entrenched norms and values of the dominant culture may limit and constrain the rights and actions of ethnoracial people.

Beyond Representation

To critique Whiteness without acknowledging the many actions taken by people in positions of power to meet the needs of ethnoracial people runs the risk of essentializing Whiteness, as if it is impervious to change rather than a wily and powerful reactionary force. Put differently, the process of Whiteness can be oversimplified and its full and sometimes contradictory characteristics not grasped. Any measures that attack Whiteness are limited in effect, partly because power structures resist challenge, and partly because those who perpetuate Whiteness may not do so intentionally. This limitation can be overcome by recognizing that those in positions of power cannot dismantle discriminatory practices alone. In fact, one could argue that much multicultural training has been generated and encouraged by people in positions of power (who benefit from Whiteness). If that is the case, does it not make sense to alert these people to issues of Whiteness and expect them to be a key part of developing more critical remedies to discriminatory practice? In other words, before real social change can occur, people must increase their level of awareness and knowledge of how each person socially located within the dominant culture can lay bare the social processes that intentionally or unintentionally discriminate or oppress.

Many agencies focus on increasing the representation of ethnoracial members among staff, volunteers, and board members, but this approach has failed to eradicate systemically entrenched forms of discrimination. Instead, ethnoracial people may experience further oppression as token representatives of the agency. According to Dei (1996), "the question of representation, that is, the need to have a multiplicity of voices and perspectives entrenched (and centred) as part of mainstream social knowledge" is crucial (p. 254). But how can that happen if mechanisms and processes are not in place that enable ethnoracial people to share equal space with the privileged? Again, one cannot expect that the efforts of ethnoracial people to shape Canadian norms and values will come to fruition until the power of Whiteness is confronted directly by those in positions of power. For example, by hiring multicultural outreach workers to address the needs of ethnoracial minorities, some agencies have had limited success in providing services to ethnoracial clients. These staff positions, however, tend to be supported largely by transitional funding on a contract basis and do not operate with the same resources as their mainstream counterparts. This is why mainstream agencies continue to rely heavily on the services of ethno-specific agencies to fill the gaps of their service delivery to ethnoracial clients (Douglas & Casipullai, 2012). But more recently, even ethno-specific agencies who provide support to mainstream agencies have been hampered by severe federal government funding cuts. Since 2011, the federal government has reduced expenditures for immigrant services in Ontario by $31.5 million, despite the fact that the number of immigrants has increased (Elliott & Payton, 2011).

Hopefully, by rendering the invisible visible, a shared consciousness will develop about how Whiteness regulates, defines, and delimits everyone in society, regardless of race, class, or gender oppression and privilege. The goal of eradicating social inequality based on multiple oppressions is a society that successfully sets in place social processes and mechanisms that allow all members to relate to one another in truly authentic ways. This requires that the oppressive forces that subordinate the ethnoracial Other are not reproduced. Thus, authentic social work practice is about legitimating the multiplicity of voices, narratives, and histories of those not from the dominant culture. Yet, bringing the voices from the margin to the centre is not enough. Rather, there needs to be a complete reworking of mainstream practices; a process must occur that acknowledges the impact that various practices have on people who occupy different social locations. This may seem like a utopian goal, but the reason such an approach has not worked in the past was the failure to recognize Whiteness. To fail to engage ethnoracial people in a process with those who hold the power to determine services only marginalizes ethnoracial people, maintains their segregation as separate from the dominant culture, and, more importantly, does not provide the changes that would be of real benefit to the oppressed.

Summary and Conclusion

This chapter has explored how multicultural social work practice can distract social work practitioners from recognizing how Whiteness shapes the norms and values of Canadian society and, in turn, the delivery of social work services. Whiteness is a cultural and social process that gives White structural advantage, assumes its own norms and values as central within institutions, and constitutes a taken-for-granted reference from which to know "Others." By failing to name itself in the process of working across cultural and racial difference, the presence and power of Whiteness is never under scrutiny and, therefore, can maintain its dominance without being questioned.

Whiteness is about more than race; it is a social location that represents multiple sites of advantage and privilege, including race, class, and ability/disability, to name a few. It is from this location that "knowledge" about ethnoracial people in social work practice is produced. A focus on the differences and cultures of the "Other" allows social workers to avoid dealing with the historical and present-day acts of racism found at the individual, cultural, and institutional levels of agency practices. To undo Whiteness, the dominant culture must name itself and confront the racism existing within its institutional practices and structures. Social work that fails to make visible the pervasiveness and power of Whiteness can never fully address the cultural and linguistic needs of ethnoracial communities or lead to emancipation. As Wildman and Davis note:

> Domination, subordination, and privilege are like three heads of hydra. Attacking the most visible heads, domination and subordination, trying bravely to chop them up into little pieces, will not kill the third head, privilege. Like a mythic multi-headed hydra, which will inevitably grow another head if all heads are not slain, discrimination cannot be ended by focusing only on subordination and domination. (1997, p. 317)

The challenge of examining privilege or Whiteness may be especially difficult for White people. Some avoid being associated with Whiteness, because most **liberal Whites** oppose racism and other oppressive isms and the very thought that they could be a part of oppressive processes creates considerable discomfort. One may protest that "Whiteness does not work for me!" This response would not be surprising. Wildman and Davis (1997) suggest that "whites spend a lot of time trying to convince ourselves and each other that we are not racist" (p. 13). Avoiding talking about privilege, however, is counterproductive; the pervasive nature of Whiteness means that nobody escapes having their attitudes shaped by it, especially White people. While we need to be careful not to essentialize the White identity, we should heed Wildman and Davis's contention that "a big step would be for whites to admit we are racist and then consider what to do about it" (p. 318). Indeed, until Whites recognize that racism, and all the other isms associated with Whiteness, is not merely the bigotry of White supremacists and neo-Nazi groups, but a part of everyday society, discriminatory systems, actions, and policies can never be eradicated.

Just as denial often constitutes a White response to being confronted with Whiteness, its opposite—guilt—can also be a common response. Some White people "engage in a form of white self-denigration that expresses itself in conceptualization of non-white cultures as superior to white culture—more authentic, natural and sacred" (Kincheloe, 1999, p. 172). This sort of positive evaluation of the cultures of ethnoracial communities does not constitute an understanding of Whiteness or alter its power, and it essentializes the Others associated with these cultures. Such White self-pity and guilt do not change the dynamics of power and privileged relationships; they merely make these privileges a little more uncomfortable to own.

Denial and guilt are both counterproductive in the deconstruction of Whiteness. Putting aside these defences, social workers on an individual and institutional level must examine how they and their practice are shaped by Whiteness. Identifying Whiteness can be the catalyst needed to transform current social work practice with ethnoracial communities, which is "Other-producing," into forms of liberating practice that effectively deal with oppression. Current social work practice of understanding culture must be modified to reveal rather than rest on the invisible hegemony of Whiteness.

Questions for Review

1. Why does a focus on "culture" help maintain and keep intact oppression and racism at the individual and systemic level?
2. Can you provide an example of an agency practice that demonstrates how Whiteness is a form of hegemony that allows one group to use its power to dominate another group in a position of less power?
3. Do all White people have equal access to the power of Whiteness? Also, can non-White people access Whiteness? If yes, what are the complexities in making these claims?
4. Debate the strengths and limitations of the cultural literacy approach. How do you see it used currently by social service agencies?
5. Can the master's tools be used to dismantle the master's house? What are the dangers in using the master's tools? If you do not use the master's tools, what are the alternatives?
6. What is meant by essentializing Whiteness?

Suggested Readings and Resources

Baskin, C. (2011). *Strong helpers' teachings: The value of Indigenous knowledges in the helping professions.* Toronto, ON: Canadian Scholars Press.

Hart, M., Sinclair, R., & Bruyere, G. (2009). *Wiĭcihitowin: Aboriginal social work in Canada.* Halifax, NS: Fernwood Publishing.

Lawrence, B., & Dua, E. (2005). Decolonizing antiracism. *Social Justice, 32*(4), 120–43.

Levine-Rasky, C. (2000). Framing whiteness: Working through the tensions in introducing whiteness to educators. *Race, Ethnicity & Education,* 3(1), 271–92.

McIntosh, P. (2012). *Beyond whiteness: White privilege—Unpacking the invisible knapsack.* Retrieved from http://www.beyondwhiteness.com/2012/02/18/peggy-mcintosh-white-privilege-unpacking-the-invisible-knapsack

Schick, C. (2012). White resentment in settler society. *Race, Ethnicity and Education, 17*(1), 88–102, doi:10.1080/13613324.2012.733688

Wise, T. (2013). *White privilege, racism, white denial and the cost of inequality* [Video file]. Retrieved from https://www.youtube.com/watch?v=9AMY2Bvxuxc

Yee, J. Y. (2005). Critical anti-racism praxis: The concept of whiteness implicated. In S. Hick, R. Pozzuto, and J. Fook (Eds.), *Social work: A critical turn* (pp. 87–104). Toronto, ON: Thompson Educational Publishing.

References

Akintunde, O. (1999). White racism, white supremacy, white privilege, and the social construction of race: Moving from modernist to postmodernist multiculturalism. *Multicultural Education, 7*(2), 2–8.

Back, L., & Solomos, J. (Eds.). (2009). *Theories of race and racism: A reader* (2nd ed.). London, UK: Routledge.

Blakey, M. L. (1999). Scientific racism and the biological concept of race. *Literature and Psychology, 1*(2), 29–43.

Bonnett, A. (2000). *Anti-racism*. London, UK: Routledge.

Cameron, S., & Wycoff, S. (1998). The destructive nature of the term race: Growing beyond a false paradigm. *Journal of Counseling and Development, 76*(3), 277–85.

Casas, M. J. (1985). A reflection on the status of racial/ethnic minority research. *The Counseling Psychologist, 13*(4), 581–98.

Cournoyer, B. (2014). *The social work skills workbook* (7th ed.). Belmont, CA: Brooks/Cole.

Dei, G. (1996). Critical perspectives in antiracism. *Canadian Review of Sociology and Anthropology, 33*(3), 247–67.

Dominelli, L. (1997). *Anti-racist social work.* London, UK: Macmillan.

Douglas, D., & Casipullai, A. (2012). History of settlement services in Ontario. In S. Pashang (Ed.), *Unsettled settlers: Barriers to integration* (pp. 55–78). Toronto, ON: De Sitter Publications.

Drakes, S. (2000, January 29). Many Canadians are made to feel like strangers in their homeland. *Toronto Star.*

Dumbrill, G. C. (2009). Your policies, our children: Messages from refugee parents to child welfare workers and policymakers. *Child Welfare, 88*(3), 145–68.

Dumbrill, G. C., & Rice-Green, J. (2008). Indigenous knowledge in the social work academic. *Social Work Education: The International Journal, 27*(5), 489–503.

Dyche, L., & Zayas, H. L. (1995). The value of curiosity and naiveté for the cross-cultural psychotherapist. *Family Process, 34*(4), 389–99.

Elliott, L., & Payton, L. (2011, November 25). Immigrant settlement money shuffled among provinces. *CBC News*. Retrieved from http://www.cbc.ca/news/politics/immigrant-settlement-money-shuffled-among-provinces-1.1056453

Fiske, J. (1994). *Media matters: Everyday culture and political change.* Minneapolis, MN: University of Minnesota Press.

Frankenberg, R. (1993). *White women, race matters: The social construction of whiteness.* London, UK: Routledge.

Gabriel, J. (1998). *Whitewash: Racialized politics and the media.* London, UK: Routledge.

Gilroy, P. (1987). *There ain't no black in the Union Jack.* London, UK: Hutchinson.

Gilroy, P. (1990). The end of anti-racism. *New Community, 17*(1), 71–83.

Henry, F., & Tator, C. (2010). *The colour of democracy: Racism in Canadian society* (4th ed.). Toronto, ON: Nelson Education Ltd.

Hepworth, D. H., Rooney, R. H., & Larsen, J. A. (2013). *Direct social work practice: Theory and skills* (9th ed.). California, CA: Brooks/Cole.

Herrnstein, R. (1971). I.Q. *Atlantic Monthly, 228*(3), 43–64.

Humphries, B. (1997). The dismantling of anti-discrimination in British social work: A view from social work education. *International Social Work, 40*(3), 289–301.

Hutchinson, Y. (1992). *Profile of clients in the anglophone youth network: Examining the situation of the black child.* Montreal, QC: Ville Marie Social Service Centre and McGill University School of Social Work.

James, C. E. (Ed.). (1996). *Perspectives on racism and the human services sector: A case for change.* Toronto, ON: University of Toronto Press.

Johnson, J., Rush, S., & Feagin, J. (2000). Reducing inequalities, doing antiracism: Toward an egalitarian American society. *Contemporary Sociology, 29*(1), 95–110.

Jones, J. (1994). Child protection and anti-oppressive practice: The dynamics of partnership with parents explored. *Early Child Development and Care, 102*, 101–14.

Jordan, G., & Weedon, C. (1995). *Cultural politics: Class, gender, race and the postmodern world.* Oxford, UK: Blackwell Publishers.

Kincheloe, J. L. (1999). The struggle to define and reinvent whiteness: A pedagogical analysis. *College Literature, 26*(3), 162–94.

Leah, R. (1995). Anti-racism studies: An integrative perspective. *Race, Gender and Class, 2*(3), 105–22.

Leonard, P. (1997). *Postmodern welfare: Reconstructing an emancipatory project.* London, UK: Sage.

Levine-Rasky, C. (2013). *Whiteness fractured.* Surrey, UK: Ashgate.

Lorde, A. (1984). Age, race, class and sex: Women redefining difference. In *Sister Outsider:*

Essays and Speeches by Audre Lorde. Trumansburg, NY: The Crossing Press.

Mackey, E. (1996). *Managing and imagining diversity: Multiculturalism and the construction of national identity in Canada* (Unpublished doctoral dissertation). Sussex University, Sussex, UK.

Mahtani, M. (2002). Interrogating the hyphen-nation: Canadian multicultural policy and "mixed race" identities. *Social Identities: Journal for the Study of Race, Nation and Culture, 8*(1), 67–90.

McGoldrick, M., Giordiano, J., & Garcia-Preto, N. (2005). *Ethnicity and family therapy* (3rd ed.). New York, NY: Guilford Press.

McIntosh, P. (1998). White privilege: Unpacking the invisible knapsack. In P. Rothenberg (Ed.), *Race, class, and gender in the United States: An integrated study* (4th ed., pp. 165–9). New York, NY: St Martin's Press.

Mercredi, O., & Turpel, M. E. (1993). *In the rapids: Navigating the future of the First Nations*. Toronto, ON: Viking.

Ministry of Industry. (2013). *Immigration and ethnocultural diversity in Canada: National Household Survey*. Ottawa, ON: Statistics Canada.

Moynhihan, D. P. (1965). *The negro family: The case for national action*. Washington, DC: US Department of Labor, Office of Policy, Planning and Research.

Padilla, A. M. (1981). Competent communities: A critical analysis of theories and public policy. In O. A. Barbarin, P. R. Good, O. M. Pharr, & J. A. Siskind (Eds.), *Institutional racism and community competence* (pp. 20–9). Rockville, MD: US Department of Health and Human Services.

Pashang, S. (Ed.). (2012). *Unsettled settlers: Barriers to integration*. Whitby, ON: de Sitter Publications.

Pease, B. (2011). *Undoing privilege: Unearned advantage in a divided world*. London, UK: Zed Books.

Proctor, E., & Davis, L. E. (1994). The challenge of racial difference: Skills for clinical practice. *Social Work, 39*(3), 314–23.

Roger, K. (2000). "Making" white women through the privatization of education on health and well-being in the context of psychotherapy. In A. Calliste & G. J .S. Dei (Eds.), *Anti-racist feminism: Critical race and gender studies* (pp. 123–41). Halifax, NS: Fernwood Publishing.

Rubington, E., & Weinberg, M. S. (1971). *The study of social problems*. New York, NY: Oxford University Press.

Schick, C. (2012). White resentment in settler society. *Race, Ethnicity and Education, 17*(1), 88–102. doi:10.1080/13613324.2012.733688

Swift, K. J. (1995). *Manufacturing "bad mothers": A critical perspective on child neglect*. Toronto, ON: University of Toronto Press.

Tettey, W., & Puplampu, K. (Eds.). (2006). *The African diaspora in Canada: Negotiating identity and belonging*. Calgary, AB: Calgary University Press.

Todd, S. (2011). That power and privilege thing: Securing whiteness in community work. *Journal of Progressive Human Services, 22*, 117–34.

Tsang, A. K. T., & George, U. (1998). An integrated framework for cross-cultural social work. *Canadian Social Work Review, 15*, 73–93.

Twine, F. W., & Gallagher, C. (2007). Introduction: The future of whiteness: A map of the "third wave." *Ethnic and Racial Studies, 1*(31), 4–24. doi:10.1080/01419870701538836

Wildman, S. M., & Davis, A. D. (1997). Making systems of privilege visible. In R. Delgado & J. Stefancic (Eds.), *Critical white studies* (pp. 314–19). Philadelphia, PA: Temple University Press.

Winant, H. (2000). The theoretical status of the concept of race. In L. Back & J. Solomos (Eds.), *Theories of race and racism: A reader* (pp. 181–90). London, UK: Routledge.

Yee, J. Y. (2005). Critical anti-racism praxis: The concept of whiteness implicated. In S. Hick, R. Pozzuto, & J. Fook (Eds.), *Social work: A critical turn* (pp. 87–104). Toronto, ON: Thompson Educational Publishing.

Yee, J. Y., Hackbusch, C., & Wong, H. (2015). An anti-oppression (AO) framework for child welfare in Ontario, Canada: Possibilities for systemic change. *British Journal of Social Work, 45*(2), pp. 474–92. doi:10.1093/bjsw/bct141

Yee, J. Y., Wong, H., & Schlabitz, T. (2014). Beyond inclusion training: Changing human service and public organizations. In M. Cohen & C. Hyde (Eds.), *Empowering workers and clients for organizational change* (pp. 135–55). Chicago, IL: Lyceum Books, Inc.

3 Foundations of Anti-racism and Anti-oppression in Social Work Practice

By Gordon Pon, Sulaimon Giwa, and Narda Razack

Chapter Objectives

This chapter will help you develop an understanding of:

- The foundational significance of Canada as a settler society
- Racism and colonization, especially how they interlock in the preservation of racist and imperialist ideals
- The strengths of and problems encountered in anti-racism social work
- The strengths and limitations of anti-oppression social work
- Rationales for disrupting the discourses of diversity and cultural competency in social work
- The continuing significance of anti-colonial and critical race theory for social work practice and pedagogy

Introduction

In order to understand the foundations of **anti-racism** in Canadian social work, we need first to understand the history of **racism** and White supremacy that underpins a settler society like Canada. This historical understanding is crucial because anti-racism aims to understand and address over 500 years of racism and **colonialism** in Canada. This modern period of racism and colonialism in Canada was first faced by Aboriginal peoples and later included atrocities such as the enslavement of Black people, of which few Canadians remain aware (Cooper, 2006); indenture of Chinese workers (Li, 1998); internment of Japanese Canadians (Oikawa, 2012); and the refusal to allow South Asians aboard the *Komagata Maru* to enter Canada (Johnston, 2014). Few Canadians acknowledge that Canada is a settler society founded on a colonial relationship. Today racism and colonialism continue to manifest in the state refusal to recognize Indigenous sovereignty (although the recently elected 2015 federal government has expressed an interest in conducting an inquiry into the issue), the hundreds of missing and murdered Aboriginal women, racial profiling of Black and Brown men, and the overrepresentation of Black and Aboriginal people in the prison and child welfare systems (Clarke, 2010, 2012; Clarke, Pon, Benjamin, & Bailey, 2015; Contenta, Monsebraaten, & Rankin, 2014; Crichlow & Visano, 2009; Giwa, 2014; Giwa, James, Anucha, & Schwartz, 2014; Henry & Tator, 2010; Pon, Gosine, & Phillips, 2011; Strega & Carrière, 2015).

A colonial relationship can be defined as follows:

> [It is] characterized by domination; that is, it is a relationship where power—in this case, interrelated discursive and non-discursive facets of economic, gendered, racial, and state power—has been structured into a relatively secure or sedimented set of hierarchical social relations that continue to facilitate the dispossession of Indigenous peoples of their land and self-determining authority. (Coulthard, 2010, p. 10, as cited in Simpson, James, & Mack, 2011, p. 293)

White supremacy was central to the establishment of a colonial relationship in Canada and the nation-building projects that followed. According to Thobani (2007), White supremacy refers to exalting Whites as proper nationals (i.e., Canadians) while socially constructing Aboriginal and non-White immigrants in Canada as threats to the nation. Emerging from this White supremacy were explicit legal and social practices that marginalized and excluded persons from the nation-state who were racialized as non-White (Dua, 2007). Canada's first prime minister, John A. Macdonald, made this abundantly clear in his 1867 parliamentary speech, where he declared Canada to be "a White man's country" (Dua, 2007, p. 446).

Yet, despite the systemic and structural racism and colonialism that persist in Canada, most Canadians are extremely averse to speaking about racism. Many tend to assert that racism exists in the United States, but not in Canada. Instead, Canadians embrace the view of Canada as tolerant, benevolent, and multicultural, pointing to how diverse populations are welcomed to Canada and encouraged to maintain their cultural practices and identities (St. Denis, 2011). However, this multiculturalist perspective ignores the fact that Canada is a White settler colony involved in the ongoing expropriation of Indigenous lands and resources (Greensmith & Giwa, 2013; Simpson et al., 2011).

The profession of social work in Canada is not immune from this widespread denial of racism. Social work is a contradictory profession, torn between competing forces—shaped on the one hand by the desire to advance liberation and social justice, while simultaneously being constrained by pressures to enforce state imperatives for social order on the other. Yet social work practitioners, students, and professors alike are often uncomfortable when speaking about issues of racism (Abrams & Gibson, 2007; Razack & Jeffery, 2003; Redmond, 2010). This difficulty is part of a larger societal denial of the existence of racism in Canada and a concomitant clinging to notions of Canadians as benevolent and tolerant (Mahrouse, 2010, p. 169). The emergence of anti-racism in Canadian social work education is thus an important and telling story not only of the modern history of the social work profession in relation to perpetuating racism and colonialism, but also of the continuing difficulty Canadians have in acknowledging and dealing with racism.

In this chapter, we provide an introductory and foundational overview of anti-racism and **anti-oppression** perspectives in social work. (For further discussion on anti-oppression and anti-racism, see Chapter 5 by Douglas Durst.) Our discussion of these two approaches is contextualized in the broader societal context of the persistent denial of racism and colonialism in Canada. This denial manifests itself in social work through discourses of diversity and cultural competency. We assert that anti-oppression in social work has largely replaced anti-racism as the prevailing critical perspective, precisely because the former offers a way to avoid discussions of racism while at the same time appearing to be progressive.

Diversity and Cultural Competency

Diversity and cultural competency have become dominant discourses in Canadian social work practice, which purport to be responsive to the needs of diverse populations including racialized ones. Ahmed (2012) conducted a qualitative study involving educational diversity practitioners in Australia and the United Kingdom. She found that organizations often professed commitments to diversity, but such claims to valuing the diverse often served only to buttress Whiteness. For example, she showed how organizations might use their commitments to diversity to silence and dismiss complaints about racism and to protect Whiteness: "When racism becomes institutional injury, it is imagined as an injury to Whiteness. The claim we would never use the language of racism is a way of protecting Whiteness from being hurt or damaged. Diversity can be a method of protecting Whiteness" (Ahmed, 2012, p. 147). Ahmed argued that organizations use the discourse of diversity management to attack individuals who speak about institutional racism. In her view, organizations often deploy diversity commitments as a response to allegations of racism and to create a climate in which racism is viewed as something that cannot be spoken about. (For further discussion of Whiteness, see Chapter 2 by June Ying Yee and Gary C. Dumbrill.)

Similarly, cultural competency has also been critiqued as a method to secure and protect Whiteness. Numerous scholars have argued that it fails to interrogate Whiteness and in fact uses Whiteness as the standard upon which to judge all other cultures (Baskin, 2011; Pon, 2009; Sakomoto, 2007). Cultural competency asserts that optimum service delivery can be achieved if social workers master knowledge about various cultural groups (Gross, 2000). Once this cultural knowledge is mastered, workers are assumed to be better able to understand and respond to service user needs. But when one contemplates the sheer number of cultures in this world, one can begin to grasp what Gross (2000) describes as the overambitiousness of this model.

Pon (2009) argues that cultural competency operates as a "new racism" (Goldberg, 1993) because it labels people as being abnormally different on the basis of culture and not biology (skin colour). New racism is a shift from racism based on skin colour to discrimination along the lines of culture (Goldberg, 1993). Culture, according to proponents of cultural competency, is understood as rigid, unchanging, and comprising fixed traits or characteristics. This modernist notion of culture fails to understand how cultural identity is, according to Stuart Hall (1996), always in the process of "'becoming' as well as of 'being'" (p. 212)—that is, it is always evolving, changing, or what Yon (2000) calls "elusive." The danger of a rigid and essentialist view of culture is that it resembles the 19th-century racism of proponents of Orientalism and Samuel Huntington's (1996) clash of civilization thesis. Huntington's thesis asserted that war between the United States of America and the Arab world would be inevitable because of vast differences in culture. In Orientalism, a socio-political region of the world was called the *Orient*. This Orient was characterized by a culture of backwardness, perversity, femininity, and cruelty, which was clearly differentiated from the culture of the West (Said, 2003). According to Said (2003), the discourse of Orientalism was promoted by the West to render the Orient ripe for Western, masculinist, imperial conquest and control. Both Orientalism and Huntington's thesis, like cultural competency, rely on understandings of culture that essentialize non-Western cultures (Pon, 2009).

In summary, both diversity and cultural competency discourses operate to buttress Whiteness and hide the racism they actually promote. As such, these discourses are not effective for social work practitioners and educators, who are committed to advancing social justice.

Anti-racism Social Work Theory and Practice

Unlike cultural competency and diversity approaches, anti-racism social work addresses racism, particularly at the structural and institutional levels. Theoretically speaking, anti-racism embraces poststructural conceptions of the discourses of power and difference as central to contemporary forms and manifestations of **racial discrimination** (Dei, 2005; Razack, 1999; Razack, Smith, & Thobani, 2010). Anti-racism adopts postmodern notions of nonessentialist, multiple, and hybrid **identity** categories, while also embracing postmodernism's theoretical eclecticism. More than a theoretical exercise, anti-racism social work addresses the impact of racism on the lives of people of colour by advocating for structural changes to social systems that maintain and reinforce relations of domination and **subordination** (Dei, 2005; Pon et al., 2011; Razack, 2002). For example, anti-racism social work concerns itself with **employment equity** and issues of access and **equity** to education and health services for members of historically marginalized groups. Anti-racism is often understood as consistent with the critical social science paradigm, which has as its goal "the analysis and transformation of power relations at every level of social work practice" (Healy, 2005, p. 172).

Critical social science is characterized by a critique of social structures and a commitment to pursuing the liberation of vulnerable people from **oppression**. Thus, it shares with emancipatory practice theories (such as anti-racism and anti-oppression) a macro-social relational view of structural inequality. For example, a strand of Marxist social thought stresses that capitalism subjugates and exploits workers, creating unequal economic relations between those with the means of production and those without (Badwall & Razack, 2012). Similarly, the social system of androcentrism or patriarchy has been argued by some feminists to negatively affect power relations between men and women, reinforcing women's subordinate status in society (Millett, 1970). Likewise, in response to the repressive function of compulsory heterosexuality, some queerists have challenged heteronormative discourses that fuel phobic attitudes and normalize opposite-sex relationships (Rich, 1980). These distinct yet interconnected elements of injustice help us understand the varying sources of oppression that subject certain individuals and groups to unequal treatment.

Anti-racism social work is differentiated from multicultural and anti-oppression social work approaches by its emphasis on racism as an integral feature of social life (see Chapter 2 by June Ying Yee and Gary C. Dumbrill). It uses race as the primary lens through which to view and understand racism as a constitutive force of interlocking systems of oppression. George Dei (1996) explained that the use of the race lens is a deliberate political stance to counter the persistent denial of racism in Canadian society. Although race is generally understood as a social construction, differential outcomes that result from the processes of **racialization** can and do have material and bodily effects for people of colour (Fanon, 1968; Giwa & Greensmith, 2012).

The Emergence of Anti-racism in Canadian Social Work

From a historical perspective, several factors led to the emergence of anti-racism in Canadian social work, beginning in the 1990s. A powerful influence was the decades of activism by Black-Canadian parents, teachers, students, and community leaders that gave rise to what is called Black education or anti-racism education (Bramble, 2000; Calliste & Dei, 2000; Clarke et al., 2015; Williams, 2005). Ever since the first Blacks were brought to Canada as slaves, Black people in Canada have faced a pernicious form of racism (Deliovsky & Kitossa, 2013). **Anti-Black racism** refers to the particular type of racism that is specifically targeted toward Black people on one hand, and the resistance to this racism on the other (Benjamin, 2003). The tremendous resistance Blacks have exhibited in the face of discrimination is thus a central aspect of anti-Black racism (Benjamin, 2003; Clarke et al., 2015; Pon et al., 2011; Williams, 2005). Anti-Black racism has been at the forefront of valiant and courageous activism for anti-racism and human rights in Canada (Clarke et al., 2015; Williams, 2005), which led to the establishment in the 1980s in Canada of a field of study and practice called anti-racism education (Bramble, 2000; Dei, 1996). Anti-racism education in turn greatly influenced anti-racism in social work (Clarke et al., 2015).

In the United Kingdom in the 1980s, the rise of anti-racism in social work is similarly attributed to the activism of Black social workers and students who struggled to get social work to address structural and systemic forms of racism in welfare agencies. This struggle culminated in the United Kingdom with a recognition by the Central

Council for Education and Training in Social Work of the need for anti-racism training in social work programs (McLaughlin, 2005).

Although some social work scholars in Canada had long drawn attention to this critical issue of racism, it was the report of the Canadian Association of Schools of Social Work (CASSW, 1991) Task Force on Multicultural and Multiracial Issues in Social Work Education that first examined the problem in a systematic way (Clarke et al., 2015).[1] To help transform the observed inequity and racism in schools of social work and beyond, the task force's findings revealed the need for responsive organizational structures. Importantly, the report identified several areas (such as curriculum, faculty representation, and student admission policies and procedures) where the social system of Whiteness reinforced the power of the **dominant cultural group**. In doing so, it highlighted the continuing significance of race and racism for social work practice and education in a society structured along racial lines and other points of difference (Clarke et al., 2015).

In 1997, the Department of Canadian Heritage awarded funding to CASSW to explore anti-racism in the curricula of schools of social work, and provincial teams were organized to conduct the research. After intense discussion, the Ontario team[2] decided to focus on anti-racism, while the other provinces adopted anti-oppression to capture other forms of oppression as well. Findings revealed a beginning discourse of anti-oppression in the curricula where racism was subsumed within the analysis of other forms of oppression. Even though the 1991 study allowed for discussion of anti-oppression, a significant number of schools did not have a core course on anti-oppression and less so one on anti-racism (see Razack & Jeffery, 2003). However, as a result of the task force and the Heritage project, some schools of social work have now expanded the focus of their degree programs to include some anti-discrimination/anti-oppression course offerings at the bachelor and master levels. These offerings are part of an effort to promote inclusive curricula reflecting the diverse population served by the profession, and to prepare graduates to work with people from a wide range of backgrounds (Clarke et al., 2015; Razack & Jeffery, 2003). Anti-racism is still not a prevalent core course in Canadian social work curricula.

The 1990s were a difficult time for the profession and its White and non-White professionals, for different reasons. Social work professors and practitioners from the dominant White racial group were confronted with the reality of their own complicity in perpetuating systems of oppression, as reflected in pedagogical and professional practices that privileged **Eurocentric**/Western knowledge structures (Razack, 1999). Similarly, the few racialized and Aboriginal students and social work professors employed by schools of social work faced the difficult task of negotiating the chilly climate of their fields of practice and academic workplaces, where discussions about racism and other forms of oppression were perceived by some Whites as polemical or provocative (Christensen, 1999; Ferguson, 2012). Christensen (1999) noted that despite the democratic **ideology** professed by the profession, "conflicting belief systems, values and discriminatory behaviours exist[ed] simultaneously" (p. 301). The criticism of discussions about racism as polemics and provocation served a colour-coded function of shutting down difficult but necessary conversations about Whiteness and its exalted subjectivity (Badwall, 2013; Thobani, 2007). Indeed, Whiteness was one of the central concepts that anti-racism social work sought to deconstruct and address. McLaughlin (2005) explained this resistance thus:

> Seeing themselves as working within a caring profession and opposing social injustice, it was noted that many social workers and students found it difficult to come to terms with the possibility that they themselves [might] be perpetrating injustice through racist or sexist practices. (p. 287)

The difficulty experienced by these social workers highlights the deep-seated denial of racism in Canada and the prevailing notion of Canadians as caring, innocent, and benevolent (Jeffery, 2005; Pon, 2009).

White resistance to anti-racism has been evident in the tensions between White women and their racialized counterparts. In their qualitative study of social service providers in Canadian feminist social service agencies, Barnoff and Moffatt (2007) found that White women preferred anti-oppression as a modus operandi, while racialized women favoured anti-racism. White feminist workers alleged that anti-racism created a hierarchy of oppressions in which racism was seen to be the most pressing and deleterious, while some racialized workers believed that anti-oppression was a way for Whites to avoid having to address the issue of racism (Barnoff & Moffatt, 2007). Williams (1999), Pon and colleagues (2011), and Clarke and colleagues (2015) have highlighted how, in settler societies like Canada, anti-oppression discourses are more palatable for Whites in comparison to anti-racism (see also Wagner & Yee, 2011). Clearly much tension and debate has characterized the shift from anti-racism to anti-oppression as the prevailing critical perspective in social work.

Problems Encountered in Anti-racism Work

Sara Ahmed (2012) has reminded us that "there are huge risks in writing or speaking about racism. Even exercising the critical vocabulary of racism can generate a series of defenses such that an exchange ends up being about the defenses rather than about racism" (p. 149). The very mention of the word "racism" in social work settings can cause tremendous aversion among Whites, who see themselves as benevolent and caring professionals (see Badwall, 2013). For racialized individuals, discussions about racism in the social work workplace may cause tremendous unease, since they may fear reprisal and/or termination from their employment. For many workers, particularly those in mainstream social services, speaking out about racism can be perceived as precarious (Gosine & Pon, 2010); it can potentially shut down career advancement opportunities, particularly in organizations and agencies dominated by liberal-minded White men and White women. Open discussion of racism in the workplace can subject racialized social workers to reprisal and retaliation, particularly from White managers and White supervisors who have the backing of their organizational system and structures (Das Gupta, 1996; Hagey et al., 2005). In academia, social work professors, like those working in **mainstream agencies**, may also not feel safe broaching issues of racism and openly supporting anti-racism (Ferguson, 2012).

Sara Ahmed's (2012) research on diversity discourses in institutions reported on newspaper coverage of racial incidents in UK universities. She noted that some victims of racial harassment and violence believed that complaining about the racism they experienced would be heard by the institution as "too much noise" (p. 144). These concerns were validated in public relations statements by university officials who remarked, "we don't have a problem with racism" (p. 145), which in essence made the problem the complainants who alleged racism:

> Racism is heard as an accusation that threatens the organization's reputation as led by diversity. Racism is heard as potentially injurious to the organization . . . but when institutional racism is addressed as accusation, it becomes personalized, as if the organization is "the one" suffering a blow to its reputation. Those who speak about racism become the blow, the cause of injury. (Ahmed, 2012, p. 146)

Thus, individuals who speak candidly about racism, particularly institutional racism, can be viewed as a problem by management and blamed for upsetting a "happy" (Ahmed, 2012, p. 146) organization. This stark reality of reprisals that anti-racism proponents can face represents one of the limitations of incorporating anti-racism social work into pedagogy and practice.

Anti-oppression Social Work Theory and Practice

Anti-oppression social work practice emerged in the 1990s in Canada and was purported to be better and more inclusive than anti-racism (McLaughlin, 2005). Given the tremendous resistance that emerged in the 1980s and 1990s to emergent discussions of anti-racism in social work, it did not take long for anti-oppression to step in, quelling this volatility by supplanting anti-racism as the prevailing critical perspective (Clarke et al., 2015; McLaughlin, 2005; Pon et al., 2011). In doing so, anti-oppression offered White social work professors and practitioners relief from difficult conversations about racism. Rather than using race as the primary lens through which to view intersecting oppressions, this approach adopted a broad view of oppression and discrimination, with the understanding that human experiences are shaped by a multiplicity of social differences (Carniol, 2010; Hick, 2010). Many proponents saw anti-oppression as a way to overcome a hierarchy of oppressions, which allegedly included anti-racism. The goals of anti-oppression were to address the power imbalances between those who have power and those who do not and to eradicate oppressive structures and unequal power relationships (Dalrymple & Burke, 1995).

Emerging from this recognition of the complexities of identity and oppression, an anti-oppression approach to social work practice draws on cross-perspectival insights of other disciplines, including critical theories such as feminism, Marxism, and anti-racism, among others. This suggests the absence of an all-encompassing theoretical base on which anti-oppression can be said to rest (Brown, 2012; Burke & Harrison, 2009; Sakamoto & Pitner, 2005). In a way, the range of theories informing anti-oppression practice enriches an understanding of the structural forces within society that create advantages for some people and disadvantages for others. Consider the case of an individual who, for the sake of discussion, we will call Aduke. She identifies as Black, lesbian, and from a lower socio-economic class. An understanding of Marxist economic theory could help Aduke and others in her situation recognize the material basis of their oppression under a neoliberal global capitalist system. An anti-racism feminist perspective could elucidate how race- and gender-based discrimination factor into the creation of Aduke's and other racialized women's social inequality (Dua & Robertson, 1999). Further awareness of the privileges accorded to individuals in opposite-sex relationships and the persistent legal and social normalization of heterosexuality within public institutions (Collins, 2000) would enhance collective understanding of the enduring violence and oppression experienced by sexual and gender minorities transnationally.

Anti-oppression embraces postmodern and poststructural approaches that emphasize multiple and connected dimensions of identity (Badwall & Razack, 2012; Carniol, 2010; Dominelli, 2002; Healy, 2005; Lundy, 2004; Mullaly, 1997). Such thinking extends to the conceptualization of power as a dynamic factor that cuts across social differences. From a Foucauldian reading and analysis of power, people are simultaneously privileged and oppressed based on the multiplicities of their identities and positions. This view enables the construction of alternative realities and ways of knowing while emphasizing the importance of social contexts, wherein the experiences of oppression are historically and contextually situated in the present. Postmodernism and poststructuralism argue against claims of universal truths that, for example, justified the exploitation and oppression of **racialized Others** based on their assumed inferiority to the White race. In so doing, these theories permit the voice of subaltern groups to be heard at the same time as they critically examine injustices such as slavery, imperialism, and colonialism (Carniol, 2010).

An anti-oppression perspective, as the above point suggests, recognizes the complex structural arrangements that maintain power differentials between social groups. Brown (2012) argues that externalizing the struggles of oppressed and marginalized people acknowledges that everyday experiences of inequalities are rooted in oppressive structures of society that catch individuals and groups as in a web. Thus, the theory avoids pathologizing people because of their problems, while at the same time it seeks to connect systems of oppression and macro-level practices. Barnoff and Coleman's (2007) research on direct service-level strategies employed by feminist practitioners found that anti-oppression theory can also be put into practice to address micro-level oppression. This suggests the need to look beyond the macro-level of oppression when working with service users to make sense of their experiences and transform oppressive social conditions. It is important to understand that neither externalization nor anti-oppression practice encourages the abdication of personal responsibility over one's circumstances. Just the same, not all life challenges and experiences are attributable to macro-level social relations. However, at a direct service level, an understanding of the personal and social dynamic of oppression can inform participatory approaches between workers and service users toward identifying immediate and system-level solutions to pressing problems (Baines, 2007).

Citing Clifford (1995), Burke and Harrison (2009) identified the following key features and underlying assumptions of anti-oppression practice:

- Social difference
- Linking the personal and political
- Power
- Historical and geographical location
- Reflexivity/mutual involvement

A focus on *social difference* views society as divided along major lines of division that include race, class, gender, sexual preference, disability, and age. These dynamic, overlapping identities are assumed to shape individual and group experiences of privilege and oppression. In anti-oppression practice, personal problems are understood as political issues. The notion of *the personal is political* seeks to address collective tendencies to blame individuals or oppressed groups for their circumstances by situating accounts of oppression within the socio-political context from which they arise. For example, the view that survivors of domestic abuse are responsible for not leaving their abusers negates the socialized arrangements of male privilege, including the dominance entrenched in structures and processes of gender relations. These arrangements serve to perpetuate women's abuse and curtail their ability to participate equally in political, economic, and social life. A first step in fighting against oppression and discrimination is to understand how *power* operates to sustain patterns of social inequality. From a practice perspective, social workers must be aware of their professional and personal power, as these can reproduce oppressive relationships. Using these examples, the following questions can help to inform an anti-oppression approach to practice:

- How does a social worker's exposure to or attitude about domestic abuse affect her or his ability to assess the problem and provide appropriate intervention?
- How is the privileging of cultural difference as an explanation for **systemic racism** influenced by one's social location or positionality?
- How is systemic racism and sexism operating here?
- How, if at all, can social workers facilitate power sharing and co-operative or egalitarian relationships with service users across differences?

Along with these questions, the personal biographies of service users must be taken into account to identify structural factors that might be contributing to their differential access to opportunity and power. By focusing on the enactment of power at the personal and structural levels, service users are empowered to overcome the effects of oppression and access resources to meet their needs. The specific time period and physical and geographical context are important to the analysis of inequality in how they locate oppression and discriminatory experiences within the limits of time and place (Mohanran, 1999). Spaces are racialized and also gendered and are critical to the knowledge of how power and exploitation are enacted (Razack, 2009). Concern for *historical* and *geographical* position in response to a problem or situation can support practitioners when working with service users to make meaning out of their struggles against the backdrop of dominant cultural norms, social practice, and history.

Finally, *reflexivity/mutual involvement* emphasizes the importance of self-reflexivity and self-awareness on the part of the social worker (Heron, 2005). When working with oppressed or marginalized service users, social workers must strive to remain conscious of the individual effects of social identity and values on practice. Critical self-reflexivity refers to the process in which individuals critically reflect on their own desires, biases, fears, and practices in an effort to uncover why they do what they do. Critical self-reflexivity can often be a difficult—even excruciating—process to engage in, particularly if it implicates oneself in discriminatory practices such as racism, heterosexism, classism, or sexism. Inextricably linked to this concern is the professional identity of the expert, which plays out in the exercise of power and control over others. Clarke and Wan's (2011) analysis of settlement work with newcomer youth in Ontario suggests that, within anti-oppression social work practice, the service provider's role becomes one of "co-learner, catalyst and ally" (p. 17). Intertwined with the idea of collaborator, likewise, attention must be paid to the formation of participatory agencies whose service users are integral to policy, program, and administrative decision making (Dumbrill, 2003; Strier & Binyamin, 2010). Taken together, anti-oppression practice responds to many aspects of difference, including the wider issues of inequalities and disadvantages. In doing so, it addresses the social effects of oppression, which is ultimately about systems of unequal relations of power (Dominelli, 2002).

The Limitations of Anti-oppression

Notwithstanding the increasing support for anti-oppression in social work practice and professional education, the perspective is not immune to criticism. Pon and colleagues (2011) assert that anti-oppression provides a means for social workers, educators, and managers to avoid discussing racism, particularly anti-Black and anti-Native racism, while seeming to be progressive. This concern for how anti-oppression could serve as a way to silence anti-racism was raised early on by Williams (1999). Seen in this way, anti-oppression does not adequately theorize and address how in settler societies like Canada there is an intense aversion to discussing racism, let alone acknowledging its persistence at the institutional level (Giwa & Boyd, 2014). A cogent example noted by Clarke and colleagues (2015) of the ability of anti-oppression to avoid racism is evidenced in a recent document endorsed by most of the Children's Aid Societies in Ontario, titled "An Anti-Oppression Framework for Child Welfare in Ontario" (Wong & Yee, 2010). In this 52-page document, the word "racism" appears only once in the body of the text, the word "black" occurs only once, and "colonialism" makes no appearance at all. Yet approximately 37 per cent of all the children in the care of Canadian child welfare authorities are Aboriginal, and in one urban centre approximately 65 per cent of all the children in group care are Black (Child Welfare Anti-Oppression Roundtable, 2009). In Toronto, 41 per cent of children in the care of the Children's Aid Society of Toronto are Black, while Black children under the age of 18 make up only 8 per cent of the city's population (Contenta, Monsebraaten, & Rankin, 2014). This example illustrates the discomfort in Canada around talking about race and racism; it demonstrates how anti-oppression can become a discourse that eschews the pressing issues of racism, anti-Black racism, and White supremacy while appearing to be progressive (Clarke et al., 2015; Pon et al., 2011).

In a related example, anti-oppression deflects attention away from the need to hire more social work professors who are from racialized and Aboriginal backgrounds. In fact, one of the recommendations of the CASSW's (1991) Task Force on Multicultural and Multiracial Issues in Social Work Education was the hiring of more racialized and Aboriginal professors. Indeed, the discourse of anti-oppression permits the continued hiring of predominantly White professors in schools of social work; issues of racism and the underrepresentation of racialized professors are not adequately addressed by anti-oppression discourses. In other words, the rise of anti-oppression in social work often silences anti-racism proponents, particularly in relation to concerns of employment equity at the level of the professoriate (Smith, 2010). This silencing is effected by the way in which anti-oppression dovetails with the aversion to speaking about racism in Canadian society. As noted earlier, one of the problems encountered while doing anti-racism work is the risk of reprisal against workers who raise concerns about racism within workplaces. Anti-oppression, in avoiding the explicit engagement with "racism," does little to ameliorate the precarious positioning of workers who raise issues of racism within organizations. By dodging discussions of racism, anti-oppression discourses do not provide social workers or professors with institutional support to broach and address the difficult and volatile topic of racism, including the lack of racialized and Aboriginal faculty. Rather, anti-oppression discourses can be invoked by managers/administrators as emblematic of organizational progressiveness and commitments to a diversity of identities, not just racial ones. These dynamics create a silencing of anti-racism proponents by making the person who raises issues of racism the problem (Ahmed, 2012).

Tester (2003) critiqued anti-oppression practice for its intellectual arrogance and for dismissing human agency. The depths of fortitude and strength people show in coping as well as resisting their subjugation would often be undermined or overlooked by anti-oppression discourses. Scholars such as Collins (2000), Dei (2008), and Razack (2002) have also raised concerns about the anti-oppression practice focus on intersectionality and multiplicity of oppressions, indicating that the complex nature of the problems addressed may give the impression that they are so irreconcilable or diametrically opposed as to be bridged in any meaningful way. Related to this criticism, as an umbrella term covering a range of injustices, anti-oppression practice might erroneously equate various forms of oppression as one and the same (Tester, 2003). In working toward the elimination of oppression, and seeing equity and social justice as its primary goal, the approach does not prioritize one oppression over another (Williams, 2002). In this sense, it assumes that all incidences of oppression are experienced in the same way and can be addressed in similar fashion.

Tester (2003) noted an inescapable reality that arises from subsuming racism, for example, under the banner of anti-oppression: It fuels conflict and confusion, possibly because, for any given category of oppression, the multiple oppression focus of the perspective does not provide a clear nuance and meaning. Stressing this point, de Montigny (2011) noted that the anti-oppression practice invocation of intersectionality and multiple oppressions "elide and avoid the necessary and difficult work of explicating social interaction to the depth of its detail" (p. 14). Connected to these issues, the suggestion that all oppressions might be the same overlooks the different kinds of correction strategies required for their amelioration. For example, the strategy used to fight racism might not be appropriate for combating heterosexist-based discrimination.

Another criticism of anti-oppression practice is its implicit demand for an a priori consciousness of oppression. De Montigny (2011) argues that, rather than rely on empirical observation of people in their daily interactions to inform awareness about enacted social relations, anti-oppression practice encourages, from the outset, an analysis of human social relationships and institutions through the prism of oppression. He warns that this amounts to a disconnection, foreclosing alternative social inquiry and directing attention away from the much-needed focus and engagement with life's myriad complexities. In doing so, it effortlessly recirculates familiar themes of oppression and does not reveal the nuancing of how structures operate to oppress people in day-to-day life. Implicit in his explanation is a call for the suspension of belief and alertness to the discovery of new knowledges that move beyond conventional boundaries and assumptions.

The Importance of Anti-racism in Social Work

Critical approaches to social work education and practice remain a pressing issue today, especially since social work professionals are more likely to come into contact with members from nondominant minority groups. This is the case for reasons including changes to Canada's immigration policy, the adoption of the **Canadian Multiculturalism Act** (1985), the growing influence of neoliberal ideology on social work practice, and the persistence of racial and other structural inequalities that discipline, surveille, and punish racialized individuals and Aboriginal peoples. As a result of these interlocking factors, racialized minorities fare worse on almost every social and economic indicator of well-being in comparison to Whites (Galabuzi, 2006). As noted earlier, Black and Aboriginal people are overrepresented among the prison and child welfare population in Canada (Contenta, Monsebraaten, & Rankin, 2014; Clarke et al., 2015; Henry & Tator, 2010; Pon et al., 2011). The continued legacy of colonial racism, in which colonizing activities are visible, contributes to such outcomes and creates challenges for practitioners in meeting the needs of these groups.

One of the challenges in meeting the needs of racialized and Aboriginal service users is Whiteness in the Canadian social work profession. Historically, missionary activity by White women served as the bedrock for social work activity in the United Kingdom and North America while simultaneously spreading European colonialism and imperialism (See Badwall & Razack, 2012; Dominelli, 2010). Henry and Tator (2010) contend that racialized workers within human services agencies remain concentrated at entry or front-line levels where they have limited power and status. Galabuzi (2006) notes that for key public-sector institutions, racialized groups are significantly underrepresented. Whiteness, racism, and colonialism are implicated in the history of the profession as evidenced in one of its most shameful periods, now infamously referred to as the "60s scoop." Beginning in the 1950s and lasting until the 1980s, record numbers of Aboriginal children were removed from their parents by social workers and placed into non-Aboriginal homes. As such, social workers were directly involved in a colonial practice that reproduced the White supremacy that characterized the nation-state. Consistent with this White settler narrative, which venerated Whites as proper nationals, was the construction of Aboriginal mothers and communities as "Other"—pathological, deficient, and incapable of properly raising children (Pon et al., 2011; Thobani, 2007).

This historical background of Canadian social work alerts us to the precarious roots of our profession and how social workers can readily become complicit with state narratives and be hailed into service as agents of the state. The disciplinary and surveilling nature of social work, as manifested through apprehending Aboriginal and Black children in the name of nation-building, calls attention to the historical and ongoing struggles of social work to deal with Indigeneity, anti-Black racism, and colonialism.

The implication of social work in colonizing Aboriginal families and communities reveals several fault lines in our profession, beginning with the education and training of social workers. An examination of dominant theories that social work students were taught from the 1950s to the 1980s reveals primarily social order perspectives, which basically understand social problems as caused primarily by deficiencies in the family, individual, or subculture (Mullaly, 2010). This perspective fails to grapple with structural and historical factors such as colonialism, poverty, and racism, among other oppressions. For a long time social order perspectives have dominated Canadian social work education (Giwa, 2014; Mullaly, 2010).

In a settler society like Canada, a certain allure or comfort with social order perspectives can be discerned, particularly from the vantage point of those charged with educating future social workers and providing service delivery. Social order perspectives such as psychodynamic or systems theory leave the subjectivity of the practitioner unexamined. These social work approaches see the practitioner as the objective expert; no emphasis is placed on critical self-reflexivity in these perspectives.

A significant challenge to social order perspectives and their lack of critical self-reflexivity emerged in the 1980s—namely, structural social work. This Canadian social work movement was spearheaded by Maurice Moreau, Bob Mullaly, and Ben Carniol, among others. Structural social work challenged the status quo; instead of blaming individuals for their dire circumstances, systemic and structural forms of oppression were identified as the cause of social problems (Baines, 2011; Clarke et al., 2015). Some institutions, including the Carleton University School of Social Work, embraced structural social work as their primary approach to social work education and practice.

A racially representative faculty is vital, especially for social work because our profession deals with some of the most diverse, vulnerable, and marginalized communities in Canada. Schools of social work have struggled with issues of race and racism. For example, hiring a diverse teaching staff has been a long-standing problem in Canadian social work education programs, and most faculties continue to be predominantly staffed by White professors (Henry & Tator, 2009). As noted earlier, the CASSW (1991) task force report recommended the need for a more racially diverse faculty. The combination of anti-racism perspectives that emerged in the 1990s in Canadian social work education, coupled with its important emphasis on self-reflexivity, created and continues to foster a tension-filled, volatile situation because of the unsettling nature of the topic of racism. In the new millennium, issues of race and representation of faculty and students continue to be at stake.

Summary and Conclusion

The discomfort many Canadians feel with speaking about racism is realized in the pedagogical challenges around teaching about anti-racism, particularly in social work (Razack & Jeffery, 2003). Anti-racism in Canadian social work emerged in some schools in the 1990s, but it was a rather short-lived appearance because it was soon replaced by anti-oppression. This was due in large part to anti-oppression being conducive to avoiding discussions of racism in favour of a range of oppressions (Clarke et al., 2015; McLaughlin, 2005; Pon et al., 2011).

Bearing in mind the deep-seated denial of racism in Canada and the need for social work to deal with settler colonialism, alternative theories to anti-oppression are required. Since the introduction of anti-racism in social work education in the 1990s, many research advances have been made in racism and colonialism that may help overcome the limitations of anti-oppression. Two such advances are anti-colonialism and critical race theory.

Anti-colonialism in social work has been recently advanced primarily by Aboriginal social work professors and instructors in Canada such as Billie Allan, Cyndy

Baskin, Gordon Bruyere, Michael Hart, Lynn Lavallée, and Raven Sinclair, among others. Anti-colonialism refers to the political struggle of colonized people against colonialism (Allan, 2006; Ashcroft, Griffiths, & Tiffin, 1995; Greensmith & Giwa, 2013; Hart, 2009; Pon et al., 2011; Sinclair, Hart, & Bruyere, 2009). The approach aims to transform structural inequities and institutional power that promote dominance in settler societies (Hart, 2009). Central to anti-colonialism is decolonizing knowledge production and advancing Aboriginal ways of knowing and being and supporting Indigenous sovereignty. For social work, anti-colonialism encompasses a recognition of Indigenous ways of helping that embrace a holistic understanding of the mind, body, and spirit (Baike, 2009).

Critical race theory (CRT) is another promising perspective that should be increasingly adopted by social work. CRT was first advanced in the 1980s in the United States by racialized legal scholars (Delgado & Stefancic, 2000), who critiqued how legal discourses failed to account for issues of race and racism. Critical race theory rejects the colour-blind approach to law and instead highlights the significant role that institutional racism plays in society (Giwa et al., 2014). CRT values the lived experiences and narratives of oppressed people, while embracing the ways in which law can be used to advance liberation for marginalized populations (Aylward, 1999; Giwa et al., 2014). CRT found proponents in Canada beginning in the 1980s (Aylward, 1999).

In Canada, CRT has influenced the rise over the past 15 years of a movement called *critical race feminism*. Critical race feminism emphasizes the interlocking nature of social relations and how women of colour experience oppressions such as racism and sexism simultaneously (Clarke, 2012; Razack et al., 2010). Critical race feminism also holds at the forefront commitments to an anti-colonial praxis that aims to address continued colonialism and White supremacy in settler societies like Canada (Razack et al., 2010). Given the persistent denial of racism that characterizes Canadian society, we concur with scholars such as Clarke (2012), Clarke and colleagues (2015), and Pon and colleagues (2011) that anti-colonialism and critical race theory are important perspectives that must be foundational to social work education and practice.

Questions for Review

1. What is meant by a "settler society"? Why is this relevant to social work in Canada?
2. What factors influenced the emergence of anti-racism in Canada?
3. What are some main differences between anti-racism and anti-oppression perspectives in social work?
4. How is the profession of social work implicated in historical forms of racism?
5. According to the authors, why are discussions around White supremacy, colonialism, and racism so difficult for many people to engage in?
6. What are the limitations of approaches such as "managing diversity" and "cultural competency"?

7. What are some of the limitations of anti-racism and anti-oppression perspectives?
8. Explain why the authors suggest that critical race theory and anti-colonialism would be useful approaches in Canadian social work.

Suggested Readings and Resources

Abrams, L. S., & Moio, J. A. (2009). Critical race theory and the cultural competence dilemma in social work education. *Journal of Social Work Education, 45*(2), 245–61.

Bartoli, A. (Ed.). (2013). *Anti-racism in social work practice: Critical approaches to social work*. St. Albans, UK: Critical Publishing Ltd.

Canadian Race Relations Foundation. See www.crr.ca

Das Gupta, T., James, C. E., Maaka, R. C. A., Galabuzi, G., & Andersen, C. (Eds.). (2007). *Race and racialization*. Toronto, ON: Canadian Scholars' Press.

Heldke, L., & O'Connor, P. (Eds.). (2004). *Oppression, privilege, and resistance: Theoretical perspectives on racism, sexism, and heterosexism*. New York, NY: McGraw-Hill.

Lavalette, M., & Penketh, L. (Eds.). (2013). *Race, racism and social work: Contemporary issues and debates*. Bristol, UK: Policy Press.

Lawrence, B., & Dua, E. (2005). Decolonizing antiracism. *Social Justice, 32*(4), 120–43.

Ortiz, L., & Jani, J. (2010). Critical race theory: A transformational model for teaching diversity. *Journal of Social Work Education, 46*(2), 175–93.

Sinclair, R., & Albert, J. (2008). Social work and the anti-oppressive stance: Does the emperor really have new clothes? *Critical Social Work, 9*(1). Retrieved from http://www1.uwindsor.ca/criticalsocialwork/social-work-and-the-anti-oppressive-stance-does-the-emperor-really-have-new-clothes

Thomas, W. B. (Ed). (2006). *Fighting for change: Black social workers in Nova Scotia*. Lawrencetown Beach, NS: Pottersfield Press.

Urban Alliance on Race Relations. See http://urbanalliance.ca

Notes

1. The task force was chaired by Carol Christensen and included Akua Benjamin, Wanda Thomas Bernard, Ben Carniol, and Narda Razack, among others.
2. The Ontario team was led by Narda Razack with research assistant Donna Jeffery. Manuscripts include "Anti-Racist Training and Education in Schools of Social Work across Canada: The Ontario Report," Phase 1, and "Developing and Implementing a Core Course on Anti-Oppression in the Social Work Curriculum in Schools across Canada," Phase 2. Canadian Association of Social Workers, 1998–9, Ottawa, ON.

References

Abrams, L. S., & Gibson, P. (2007). Reframing multicultural education: Teaching White privilege in the social work curriculum. *Journal of Social Work Education, 43*(1), 147–60.

Ahmed, S. (2012). *On being included: Racism and diversity in institutional life*. Durham, NC: Duke University Press.

Allan, B. (2006). Remembering, resisting: Casting an anti-colonial gaze upon the education of diverse students in social work education. In G. S. Dei & A. Kempf (Eds.), *Anti-colonialism and education* (pp. 257–70). Rotterdam, NL: Sense Publishers.

Ashcroft, B., Griffiths, G., & Tiffin, H. (1995). *The post-colonial studies reader: The key concepts.* New York, NY: Routledge.

Aylward, C. A. (1999). *Canadian critical race theory: Racism and the law.* Halifax, NS: Fernwood.

Badwall, H. (2013). *Can I be a good social worker? Racialized workers narrate their experiences with racism in every day practice* (Doctoral dissertation). Ontario Institute for Studies in Education of the University of Toronto, Toronto, ON.

Badwall, H., & Razack, N. (2012). Professional approaches: Social work theories, methods and practices. In K. Lyons, M. C. Hokenstad, N. Huegler, & M. Pawar (Eds.), *Handbook of international social work* (pp. 136–49). London, UK: Sage.

Baike, G. (2009). Indigenous-centred social work: Theorizing social work way-of-being. In R. Sinclair, M. Hart, & G. Bruyere (Eds.), *Wícihitowin: Aboriginal social work in Canada* (pp. 42–61). Halifax, NS: Fernwood.

Baines, D. (Ed.). (2007). *Doing anti-oppressive practice: Building transformative politicized social work.* Black Point, NS: Fernwood.

Baines, D. (Ed.). (2011). *Doing anti-oppressive practice: Social justice social work* (2nd ed.). Black Point, NS: Fernwood.

Barnoff, L., & Coleman, B. (2007). Strategies for integrating anti-oppression principles: Perspectives from feminist agencies. In D. Baines (Ed.), *Doing anti-oppressive practice: Building transformative, politicized social work.* Black Point, NS: Fernwood.

Barnoff, L., & Moffatt, K. (2007). Contradictory tensions in anti-oppressive practice in feminist social services. *Affilia: Journal of Women and Social Work, 22,* 56–70.

Baskin, C. (2011). *Strong helpers' teachings: The value of Indigenous knowledges in the helping profession.* Toronto, ON: Canadian Scholars' Press.

Benjamin, A. (2003). *The dialectics of anti-Black racism* (Doctoral dissertation). Ontario Institute for Studies in Education of the University of Toronto, Toronto, ON.

Bramble, M. (2000). Black education in Canada: Past, present and future. In T. Goldstein & D. Selby (Eds.), *Weaving connections: Educating for peace, social and environmental justice* (pp. 99–119). Toronto, ON: Sumach Press.

Brown, C. G. (2012). Anti-oppression through a postmodern lens: Dismantling the master's conceptual tools in discursive social work place. *Critical Social Work, 13*(1), 34–65.

Burke, B., & Harrison, P. (2009). Anti-oppressive practice. In R. Adams, L. Dominelli, & M. Payne (Eds.), *Anti-oppressive practice* (2nd ed., pp. 227–36). Basingstoke, UK: Palgrave Macmillan.

Calliste, A., & Dei, G. J. S. (Eds.). (2000). *Anti-racist feminism.* Halifax, NS: Fernwood.

Canadian Association of Schools of Social Work. (1991). *Social work education at the crossroads: The challenge of diversity.* Ottawa, ON: Author.

Carniol, B. (2010). *Case critical: Social services and social justice in Canada* (6th ed.). Toronto, ON: Between the Lines.

Child Welfare Anti-Oppression Roundtable. (2009). *Anti-oppression in child welfare: Laying the foundation for change.* (Discussion paper). Toronto, ON: Author.

Christenson, C. P. (1999). Multiculturalism, racism and social work: An exploration of issues in the Canadian context. In G.-Y. Lie & D. Este (Eds.), *Professional social service delivery in a multicultural world* (pp. 293–310). Toronto, ON: Canadian Scholars' Press.

Clarke, J. (2010). The challenges of child welfare involvement for Afro-Caribbean Canadian families in Toronto. *Children and Youth Services Review, 33*(2), 274–83.

Clarke, J. (2012). Beyond child protection: Afro-Caribbean service users of child welfare. *Journal of Progressive Human Services, 23*(3), 223–57.

Clarke, J., Pon, G., Benjamin, A., & Bailey, A. (2015). Ethnicity, race, oppression and social work: The Canadian case. *International Encyclopedia of Social and Behavioural Sciences* (2nd ed.), *8,* 152–6.

Clarke, J., & Wan, E. (2011). Transforming settlement work: From a traditional to a critical anti-oppression approach with newcomer youth in secondary schools. *Critical Social Work, 12*(1), 14–26.

Clifford, D. (1995). Methods in oral history and social work. *Journal of Oral History Society, 23*(2), 65–70.

Collins, P. H. (2000). What's going on? Black feminist thought and the politics of postmodernism. In E. A. St. Pierre & W. S. Pillow (Eds.), *Working the ruins: Feminist poststructural theory and methods in education* (pp. 41–73). New York, NY: Routledge.

Contenta, S., Monsebraaten, L., & Rankin, J. (2014, December 11). Just 8% of Toronto kids are black. But 41% of kids in care are black. *Toronto Star*, pp. A1, A33.

Cooper, A. (2006). *The hanging of Angelique: The untold story of Canadian slavery and the burning of old Montreal*. Toronto, ON: HarperCollins.

Coulthard, G. S. (2010). *Subjects of empire? Indigenous peoples and the "politics of recognition" in Canada* (Doctoral dissertation). University of Victoria, Victoria, British Columbia.

Crichlow, W., & Visano, L. (2009). The impact of colour in correcting youths: A program of action. In R. Barmaki (Ed.), *Law and justice: A critical inquiry—A collection of essays* (pp. 107–31). Toronto, ON: APF Press.

Dalrymple, J., & Burke, B. (1995). *Anti-oppressive practice: Social care and the law*. Buckingham, UK: Open University Press.

Das Gupta, T. (1996). *Racism and paid work*. Toronto, ON: Garamond Press.

Dei, G. J. S. (1996). *Anti-racism education: Theory and practice*. Halifax, NS: Fernwood Publishers.

Dei, G. J. S. (2005). The intersections of race, class, and gender in the anti-racism discourse. In V. Zawilski & C. Levine-Rasky (Eds.), *Inequality in Canada: A reader on the intersections of gender, race, and class* (pp. 17–35). Toronto, ON: Oxford University Press.

Dei, G. J. S. (2008). *Racists beware: Uncovering racial politics in contemporary society*. New York, NY: Sense.

Delgado, R., & Stefancic, J. (2000). *Critical race theory: The cutting edge*. Philadelphia, PA: Temple University Press.

Deliovsky, K., & Kitossa, T. (2013). Beyond black and white: When going beyond may take us out of bounds. *Journal of Black Studies, 44*(2), 158–81.

de Montigny, G. (2011). Beyond anti-oppressive practice: Investigating reflexive social relations. *Journal of Progressive Human Services, 22*, 8–30.

Dominelli, L. (2002). Anti-oppressive practice in context. In R. Adams, L. Dominelli, & M. Payne (Eds.), *Social work: Themes, issues, and critical debates* (2nd ed., pp. 3–19). Basingstoke, UK: Palgrave Macmillan.

Dominelli, L. (2010). *Social work in a globalizing world*. Cambridge, UK: Polity Press.

Dua, E. (2007). Exclusion through inclusion: Female Asian migration in the making of Canada as a white settler nation. *Gender, Place & Culture, 14*(4), 445–66.

Dua, E., & Robertson, A. (Eds.). (1999). *Scratching the surface: Canadian anti-racist feminist thought*. Toronto, ON: Women's Press.

Dumbrill, G. (2003). Child welfare: AOP's nemesis? In W. Shera (Ed.), *Emerging perspectives on anti-oppressive practice* (pp. 101–19). Toronto, ON: Canadian Scholars' Press.

Fanon, F. (1968). *The wretched of the Earth*. New York, NY: Grove Press.

Ferguson, R. (2012). *The reorder of things: The university and its pedagogies of minority difference*. Minneapolis, MN: University of Minnesota.

Galabuzi, G.-E. (2006). *Economic apartheid in Canada*. Toronto, ON: Canadian Scholars' Press.

Giwa, S. (2014). Social work practice and people of color. In L. H. Cousins (Ed.), *Encyclopedia of human services and diversity* (Vol. 4, pp. 1230–4), Thousand Oaks, CA: Sage Publications, Inc.

Giwa, S., & Boyd, K. (2014). Discrimination and institutional racism. In L. H. Cousins (Ed.), *Encyclopedia of human services and diversity* (Vol. 4, pp. 383–7), Thousand Oaks, CA: Sage Publications, Inc.

Giwa, S., & Greensmith, C. (2012). Race relations and racism in the LGBTQ community of Toronto: Perceptions of gay and queer social service providers of color. *Journal of Homosexuality, 59*(2), 149–85.

Giwa, S., James, C. E., Anucha, U., & Schwartz, K. (2014). Community policing—a shared responsibility: A voice-centered relational method analysis of a police/youth-of-color dialogue. *Journal of Ethnicity in Criminal Justice*. Advance online publication. doi:10.1080/15377938.2013.837856

Goldberg, D. T. (1993). *Racist culture*. Cambridge, UK: Blackwell Press.

Gosine, K., & Pon, G. (2010). On the front lines: The voices and experiences of racialized child welfare workers in Toronto, Canada. *Journal of Progressive Human Services, 22*(2), 135–59.

Greensmith, C., & Giwa, S. (2013). Challenging settler colonialism in contemporary queer politics: Settler homonationalism, Pride Toronto, and two-spirit subjectivities. *American Indian Culture and Research Journal, 37*(2), 129–48.

Gross, G. D. (2000). Gatekeeping for cultural competence: Ready or not? Some post and modernist doubts. *Journal of Baccalaureate Social Work, 5*(2), 47–66.

Hagey, R. M., Jacobs, J., Turrittin, M., Purdy, R., Lee, A., Braithwaite, C., & Chandler, M. (2005). *Implementing accountability for equity and end racial backlash in nursing*. Toronto, ON: Canadian Race Relations Foundation.

Hall, S. (1996). Cultural identity and cinematic representation. In H. A. Baker Jr., M. Diawara, & R. H. Lindeborg (Eds.), *Black British cultural studies: A reader* (pp. 210–22). Chicago, IL: University of Chicago Press.

Hart, M. (2009). Anti-colonial Indigenous social work: Reflections on an Aboriginal approach. In R. Sinclair, M. Hart, & G. Bruyere (Eds.), *Wicihitowin: Aboriginal social work in Canada* (pp. 25–41). Halifax, NS: Fernwood.

Healy, K. (2005). *Social work theories in context: Creating frameworks for practice*. New York, NY: Palgrave Macmillan.

Henry, F., & Tator, C. (Eds.). (2009). *Racism in the Canadian university: Demanding social justice, inclusion, and equity.* Toronto, ON: University of Toronto Press.

Henry, F., & Tator, C. (2010). Colour of democracy: Racism in Canadian society (4th ed.). Toronto, ON: Nelson Education.

Heron, B. (2005). Self-reflection in critical social work practice: Subjectivity and the possibilities of resistance. *Reflective Practice, 6*, 341–51.

Hick, S. (2010). *Social work in Canada: An introduction* (3rd ed.). Toronto, ON: Thomson Educational Publishing.

Huntington, S. (1996). *The clash of civilizations and the remaking of world order*. New York, NY: Simon and Schuster.

Jeffery, D. (2005). What good is anti-racist social work if you can't master it? Exploring a paradox in anti-racist social work education. *Race, Ethnicity and Education, 8*(4), 409–25.

Johnston, H. J. M. (2014). *The voyage of the Komagata Maru*. Vancouver, BC: UBC Press.

Li, P. S. (1998). *The Chinese in Canada* (2nd ed.). Toronto, ON: Oxford University Press.

Lundy, C. (2004). *Social work and social justice: A structural approach to practice*. Peterborough, ON: Broadview Press.

Mahrouse, G. (2010). Questioning efforts that seek to "do good": Insights from transnational solidarity activism and socially responsible tourism. In S. Razack, M. Smith, & S. Thobani (Eds.), *States of race: Critical race feminism for the 21st century* (pp. 169–90). Toronto, ON: Between the Lines.

McLaughlin, K. (2005). From ridicule to institutionalization: Anti-oppression, the state and social work. *Critical Social Policy, 25*, 283–305.

Millett, K. (1970). *Sexual politics.* New York, NY: Doubleday.

Mohanran, R. (1999). *Black body: Women, colonialism, and space*. Minneapolis, MN: University of Minnesota Press.

Mullaly, B. (1997). *Structural social work: Ideology, theory, and practice*. Toronto, ON: Oxford University Press.

Mullaly, B. (2010). *Challenging oppression and confronting privilege* (2nd ed.). Toronto, ON: Oxford University Press.

Oikawa, M. (2012). *Cartographies of violence: Japanese Canadian women, memory, and the subjects of the internment*. Toronto, ON: University of Toronto Press.

Pon, G. (2009). Cultural competency as new racism: An ontology of forgetting. *Journal of Progressive Human Services, 20*(1), 59–71.

Pon, G., Gosine, K., & Phillips, D. (2011). Immediate response: Addressing anti-Native and anti-Black racism in child welfare. *International Journal of Child, Youth and Family, 2*(3/4), 385–409.

Razack, N. (1999). Anti-discriminatory practice: Pedagogical struggles and challenges. *British Journal of Social Work, 29*(2), 231–50.

Razack, N. (2002). *Transforming the field: Critical antiracist and anti-oppressive perspectives for the human services practicum*. Halifax, NS: Fernwood.

Razack, N. (2009). Decolonizing the pedagogy and practice of international work. *International Social Work, 52*(1), 7–19.

Razack, N., & Jeffery, D. (2003). Critical race discourse and tenets for social work. *Canadian Social Work Review, 19*(2), 257–72.

Razack, S., Smith, M., & Thobani, S. (2010). Introduction. In S. Razack, M. Smith, & S. Thobani (Eds.), *States of race: Critical race feminism for the 21st century* (pp. 1–19). Toronto, ON: Canadian Scholars' Press.

Redmond, M. (2010). Safe space oddity: Revisiting critical pedagogy. *Journal of Teaching in Social Work, 30*(1), 1–14.

Rich, A. (1980). Compulsory heterosexuality and lesbian existence. *Signs, 5*(4), 631–60.

Said, E. (2003). *Orientalism*. London, UK: Penguin.

Sakamoto, I. (2007). An anti-oppressive approach to cultural competence. *Canadian Social Work Review, 24*(1), 105–18.

Sakamoto, I., & Pitner, R. O. (2005). Use of critical consciousness in anti-oppressive social work practice: Disentangling power dynamics at personal and structural levels. *British Journal of Social Work, 35*, 435–52.

Simpson, S. J., James, C. E., & Mack, J. (2011). Multiculturalism, colonialism, and racialization: Conceptual starting points. *Review of Education, Pedagogy, and Cultural Studies, 33*, 285–305.

Sinclair, R., Hart, M. A., & Bruyere, G. (Eds.). (2009). *Wícihitowin: Aboriginal social work in Canada*. Halifax, NS: Fernwood.

Smith, M. (2010). Gender, whiteness and "other others" in the academy. In S. Razack, M. Smith, & S. Thobani (Eds.), *States of race: Critical race feminism for the 21st century* (pp. 37–58). Toronto, ON: Canadian Scholars' Press.

St. Denis, V. (2011). Silencing Aboriginal curricular content and perspectives through multiculturalism: "There are other children here." *Review of Education, Pedagogy and Cultural Studies, 33*, 306–17.

Strega, S., & Carrière, J. (Eds.). (2015). *Walking this path together: Anti-racist and anti-oppressive child welfare practice*. Halifax, NS: Fernwood.

Strier, R., & Binyamin, S. (2010). Developing anti-oppressive services for the poor: A theoretical and organizational rationale. *British Journal of Social Work, 40*(6), 1908–26.

Tester, F. J. (2003). Anti-oppressive theory and practice as the organizing theme for social work education: The case against. *Canadian Social Work Review, 20*(1), 127–32.

Thobani, S. (2007). *Exalted subjects: Studies in the making of race and nation in Canada*. Toronto, ON: University of Toronto Press.

Wagner, A., & Yee, J. Y. (2011). Anti-oppression in higher education: Implicating neo-liberalism. *Canadian Social Work Review, 28*(1), 89–105.

Williams, C. C. (1999). Connecting anti-racist and anti-oppressive theory and practice. Retrenchment or reappraisal? *British Journal of Social Work, 29*(2), 211–30.

Williams, C. C. (2002). A rationale for an anti-racist entry point to anti-oppressive social work in mental health services. *Critical Social Work, 3*(1). Retrieved from http://www1.uwindsor.ca/criticalsocialwork/a-rationale-for-an-anti-racist-entry-point-to-anti-oppressive-social-work-in-mental-health-services

Williams, C. J. (2005). To unnerve and detect: Policing black activists in Toronto. In L. A. Visano (Ed.), *Law and criminal justice: A critical inquiry* (pp. 95–113). Toronto, ON: APF Press.

Wong, H., & Yee, J. Y. (2010). *An anti-oppression framework for child welfare in Ontario*. Toronto, ON: Ontario Association for Children's Aid Societies. Retrieved from http://www.oacas.org/pubs/external/antioppresssive.pdf

Yon, D. (2000). *Elusive culture: Schooling, race, and identity in global times*. Albany, NY: State University of New York Press.

Part II

Social Work in Diverse Settings

Culture entails the shared traditions, beliefs, customs, history, folklore, and institutions of a group of people. Culture can be shared by people of the same ethnicity, language, nationality, lifestyle, socio-economic background, or religion. The idea of a distinctly Canadian culture has been elusive, given the considerable diversity across the country along cultural, ethnic, linguistic, racial, and other dimensions. For many newcomers to Canada, the intricate web of social programs and services overflow with challenges and barriers that could inhibit their full, equitable participation in and use of health and social services.

In Canada, social programs are offered through not-for-profit organizations, public institutions, and for-profit businesses that, together, are often referred to as the three sectors of social welfare. Social welfare services are constantly changing, and it is important for social workers to be current regarding what services are available and to appreciate how issues of identity could impede or be points of access to particular services.

Today, our knowledge base has expanded to include a broader spectrum of populations, and attention is now focused on developing culturally and socially competent practice to more fully encompass the unique needs and considerations of the diverse people with whom we work. This section discusses effective micro- and macro-level social work practice in light of the diverse communities we work within.

Part II Contents

Experiential Phenomenology

Multicultural Social Work in Clinical and Direct Practice Settings

By Marie Lacroix

Chapter Objectives

This chapter will help you develop an understanding of:

- The components of cultural comptence in social work practice
- What ethnorelativism is and how to achieve it
- The significance of using intercultural approaches
- Interventions with individuals and families in contexts of diversity
- Competence areas or areas of possible misunderstandings
- Some of the major communication barriers encountered in intervention
- Major issues to address when preparing group work
- A process toward self-awareness

Introduction

New issues, brought about by the increased mobility of people, massive migrations, and the emergence of a "global village," are challenging old conceptual frameworks and the foundations of our Eurocentric worldview. Within this context what remains unchanged is the mandate of social work, its values, and ethics: Social work has had a long-standing commitment to humanism, egalitarian ideals, and treating people with respect (Mullaly, 1993). Our knowledge base is expanding to include a broader spectrum of populations, and attention is now focused on developing culturally competent practice that considers not only the multicultural and socio-cultural reality of people (Abrams & Moio, 2009; Boyle & Springer, 2001; Chand, 2005; Chau, 1991; Devore & Schlesinger, 1996; Este, 2007; Gallegos, Tindall, & Gallegos, 2008; James, 2003; Maiter, 2010; Ortiz Hendricks, 2003; Rachédi & Pierre, 2007; Thomas Bernard, & Moriah, 2007; Williams, 2006; Yan, 2005) but also the impact of migration, oppression, and marginalization (Mlcek, 2013; Razack, 2002).

Although the multicultural nature of our society and the diversity of our work context have gained some recognition within mainstream social work practice, myths and prejudices still abound about the "other," and often fear of the unknown is at the root of our misconceptions. Major cities such as Vancouver, Toronto, and Montreal, have historically been areas where newcomers have settled. According to Statistics Canada, in 2011 Canada had a foreign-born population of about 6,775,800 people, representing 20.6 per cent of the total population, the highest proportion among the G8 countries. "Between 2006 and 2011, around 1,162,900 foreign-born people immigrated to Canada. These recent immigrants made up 17.2% of the foreign-born population and 3.5% of the total population in Canada" (Statistics Canada, 2011).

Across Canada, however, smaller cities and towns still exist where the population remains relatively homogeneous. Many social work students have therefore been insulated from demographic changes and may have never met people originating from different ethnic or class backgrounds; these students remain "culturally encapsulated" (Ben-David & Amit, 2000). At the same time, immigrants, refugees, and members of other oppressed and minority groups are joining the ranks of the social work profession, raising new issues and bringing forth their worldviews to practice settings. The multicultural nature of practice may also prove to be a new challenge for those who come from more homogeneous and traditional societies.

To address the changing context of practice, social work has evolved. In the 1980s the focus of practice was on cultural sensitivity—being aware of cultural factors that may influence the practice setting. A cultural lens approach was promoted as a way of acknowledging the influence of culture in the intervention process. In the 1990s, **cultural competence** emerged (Lu, Lum, & Chen, 2001) as the concept of diversity took hold to describe the context of practice in our increasingly pluralist societies. Cultural competence is defined by the National Association of Social Workers (2001, p. 11) as a "process by which individuals and systems respond respectfully and effectively to people of all cultures, languages, classes, races, ethnic backgrounds, religions, and other diversity factors in a manner that recognizes, affirms, and values the worth of individuals, families, and communities and protects and preserves the dignity of each."

Cultural competent practice means that diversity transcends all practice settings with all individuals, groups, and families. This includes recognition on the part of the social worker that, in any given context, the client, the worker, and the organizational context may have very different views and points of reference—not only of the world but also of the helping relationship and the role of the social worker. Part of our challenge, then, is to offer tools that will enable students to work with diverse populations.

This chapter introduces the concept of cultural competence and details the intercultural approach as one way to start developing competent practice in a context of diversity. Definitions of culture and cultural competency are first presented. Cultural skill areas are then outlined as a general framework for developing generic skills. Then the most salient issues in practice with individuals, families, and groups are outlined. Concluding remarks offer some fundamental principles to competent multicultural practice.

Culture and Cultural Competency

Any discussion of cultural competency starts with the concept of **culture**. As many authors have noted, culture is not static—it changes and evolves over time. It is inseparable from all conditions affecting an individual's life: economic, political, cultural, religious, psychological, and biological (Kleinman & Benson, 2006; Este, 2007). Culture is a lifelong process (Sue, 2006); it changes and redefines itself through social relations, in a global context, and through migration and integration processes.

Cultural competence is not something to be added on to generic practice. It is a fundamental element that should be included in all practice settings, with all populations (McGoldrick in Sue, 2006). Essentially, cultural competency is about

1. a lifelong process of becoming aware of your own assumptions about values, behaviour, and biases;
2. actively attempting to understand the worldview of others;
3. actively working toward developing culturally appropriate intervention strategies; and
4. understanding the social worker's role in a particular organization and the values reflected by that organization or practice context (see Sue, 2006).

A number of issues arise with the idea of cultural competence. One issue, as pointed out by Kleinman and Benson (2006, p. 1673), is that cultural competence "often becomes a series of 'do's and don't's' that define how to treat a patient of a given ethnic

Case Example 4.1

A medical anthropologist is asked by a pediatrician in California to consult in the care of a Mexican man who is HIV positive. The man's wife died of AIDS one year ago. He has a 4-year-old son who is HIV positive, but he has not been bringing the child in regularly for care. The explanation given by the clinicians assumed that the problem turned on a radically different cultural understanding.

What the anthropologist found, though, was to the contrary. This man had a near complete understanding of HIV/AIDS and its treatment—largely through the support of a local not-for-profit organization aimed at supporting Mexican-American patients with HIV. However, he was a very low-paid bus driver, often working late-night shifts, and he had no time to take his son to the clinic to receive care for him as regularly as his doctors requested. His failure to attend was not because of cultural differences, but rather his practical, socio-economic situation. Talking with him and taking into account his "local world" were more useful than positing radically different Mexican health beliefs.

Source: Kleinman & Benson, 2006, p. 1673.

background." Another issue is that there is a tendency to see everything in a client's life or define his or her situation strictly on a cultural basis, ignoring the context of a person's life.

Cultural competence should be understood as one element in developing an effective and appropriate multicultural social work practice. As will be discussed in other chapters of this book, anti-oppressive and anti-racist approaches constitute other elements that should be integrated into cultural competence. (For more on anti-oppression, see Chapter 2 by June Ying Yee and Gary C. Dumbrill. For more on anti-racism, see Chapter 3 by Gordon Pon, Sulaimon Giwa, and Narda Razack.)

Experiential Knowledge

Moving toward Ethnorelativism

Focus for teaching/learning culturally competent social work practice needs to be on developing skills in the cognitive and affective domains to allow students to move from ethnocentricity to ethnorelativism (Krajewski-Jaime et al., 1996; Garcia & Van Soest, 1999). **Ethnocentricity** is defined as being centred in one's worldview, taking for granted that what we say and think is the only way to be, the one true way of doing things, and assuming that all people behave and think in the same way. **Ethnorelativism**, on the other hand, is defined as "the ability not only to accept and respect cultural differences, but also the empathic ability to shift to another cultural world view" (Krajewski-Jaime, et al., 1996, p. 16). To achieve this, experiential components (LeDoux & Montalvo, 1999; Nakanishi & Rittner, 1992; Weaver, 1998), such as critical incidents (Montalvo, 1999) and intellectual and affective learning (Garcia & Van Soest, 1999; Krajewski-Jaime et al, 1996) are increasingly part of training.

Experiential components aim at putting students in a situation where they confront their prejudices and biases on an emotional rather than strictly cognitive level. In *critical incidents*, for example, a context for intervention is presented through a story. Workers read the story and are asked about its specific salient values. They are then asked to explain their intervention according to the values expressed in the story. Experiential learning enables students to incorporate knowledge and skills relevant to practice in a multicultural context and move from a cognitive level toward affective knowledge to develop a better understanding of immigrant and minority problems—individual, family, and community—that may lead to use of social services (Pigler Christensen, 1992; see Das & Carter Anand, 2014, and Cocea & Dutheil, 2000, for excellent examples of critical incidents).

Among the new ways of learning, some authors are advocating international field placements as "offering the possibility of developing new paradigms of intervention and enhancing understanding of cultural difference and structural oppression" (Lyons, 1999, p. 29; see also Das & Carter Anand, 2014). Multicultural learning is not a linear, orderly process; rather, "it is a process that occurs in complex ways through increasing levels of *cultural self-knowledge* as an integral part of understanding how responses to culturally different persons are manifested" (Nakanishi & Rittner, 1992, p. 29). It is through this process that we become conscious of our own ethnocentricity and apply newly acquired knowledge to practice.

It is important to consider the fact that during an encounter both parties come with their own cultural background and way of seeing the world, and through the relationship they influence each other (Perez-Foster, 1998; Cox & Ephross, 1998; Green, 1999; Cohen-Émerique, 2000). The ultimate goal of practice then, should be "a real collaborative interaction between two human psyches who together are struggling to understand how they impact on each other" (Perez-Foster, 1998, p. 266). As Christensen points out, "If we consider the value perspectives of age, sex role, life-style, socioeconomic status and other special affiliations as cultural, then we may conclude that all encounters in practice are to some extent cross-cultural" (Pedersen, 1978, in Pigler Christensen, 1985, p. 63; see also Vacc, De Vaney, & Wittmer, 1995).

The Intercultural Approach

Hoffman (1999, p. 466) argues that culture "is often reified and essentialized in social analysis." In a practice setting this means that the worker may have a tendency to see but the tip of the iceberg when meeting someone for the first time. The worker may focus on external signs of difference—skin colour, religious symbols, a name, a way of talking, or a way of dressing. The reflex is to put that individual in a category that is fixed: He is Mexican; she is Arab; he is Italian; she is a psychiatric patient; as if these individuals represent a fixed "culture." Developing cultural awareness means recognizing that "culture" is not something fixed in time, unchanged and unchangeable, and the same for everyone in a particular group. To avoid falling into the "cultural" trap and to develop self-awareness of one's own cultural values, the **intercultural approach** offers a process to be used when meeting the "other," whether it is a person from another social class, with a different sexual orientation, from another ethnic or cultural background, or of another gender.

The intercultural approach, dominant in schools of social work in the province of Quebec, puts the emphasis on considering the individual—the subject—rather than his or her personal characteristics (Rachédi & Pierre, 2007). It shifts the focus from "I" versus the "other" to "we," two people engaged in a dialogue. Central to the approach is the fact that it allows one to put oneself in a learning mode. Cocea & Dutheil (2000, p. 3) aptly define the intercultural approach:

> The prefix inter introduces the notion of the other, and as a result an interaction between self and the other. Therefore, the interaction involves both a link and distance between the two entities. The word cultural refers to a system of world views, beliefs, meanings, social practices and structures, produced and reproduced continually by a specific group of humans and constituting a global universe.

> Intercultural, therefore, implies an interaction between two or several cultural universes in a very complex process of linking and distancing, of exchanging and interposing at the personal, community and structural levels (societies and their institutions), as well as at the deepest level of the world view. This interaction presupposes a reciprocity in the exchange and assurance of preserving a continuity in the identity (although transformed) of the partners.

Moving toward ethnorelativism starts with understanding that both the worker and the client come to the counselling relationship with their perceptions, biases, and prejudices about the other. As both engage in the relationship, they influence each other. As Cox & Ephross (1998) point out, all **ethnic groups** distinguish between "us" and "them." To avoid cultural misunderstandings, social workers should be interested not only in facts about the other's culture but also in the client's perceptions (Vacc & Wittmer, 1995). Fulher (1995) argues that we should clearly understand our own cultural/ethnic background/history to move away from the tendency to impose our own values on others, not to limit our intervention/treatment plans, to know when to refer, and to minimize risks of offending clients by our behaviour. It is only through dialogue that our perceptions can become clear. "[P]erhaps the most significant contribution that social work can make to the cultural dialogue is the recognition that it goes on inside all of us" (Martinez-Brawley & Brawley, 1999, p. 29).

The intercultural approach is divided into three important stages that will allow social workers to move from ethnocentricity to ethnorelativism and develop critical self-awareness: decentring, penetrating the other's world, and negotiation/mediation (Cohen-Émerique, 2000, 1993, 1984). Each is addressed below.

Decentring

The first step in an intercultural approach involves a process of **decentring** (Cohen-Émerique, 1980, 2000; see also Furlong & Wight, 2011) from those elements that constitute the foundation upon which our worldview is built. It allows the social worker to find points of entry for good communication and starts the process of reflection and evaluation. Here the worker takes a step back from the situation and takes stock of those elements that make up his or her culture. What are your values? Your position on religion? On equality between men and women? On family? How do you feel in this situation? What are those elements that confront your values or religion? Of course this process involves risks: "recognition of bias can stir feelings of disappointment in oneself, embarassment, guilt and helplessness" (Plionis & Lewis, 1995, p. 181); this is critical self-awareness.

Through the intercultural approach another kind of relationship is established, one that regards "the other's difference as a particular kind of gift, one that has the power to act as a mirror for the practitioner. Meeting with difference gives one the chance to identify, and then to denaturalise, one's location. This location is obviously personal, yet it is also cultural, ideological, and professional" (Furlong & Wight, 2011, p. 49).

Case Example 4.2

You are a 25-year-old single, White, female social worker. You are not religious. You believe women should be autonomous, have a career, and do things for themselves. You have an appointment with a 25-year-old woman from Algeria. When she arrives she is accomompanied by her husband. She is wearing a hijab (veil). She doesn't speak much during the interview, deferring to her husband.

Decentring process

- How do you feel?
- Do you feel this woman is oppressed by her husband because he speaks for her?
- Do you feel her religion may be an impediment to her autonomy?
- Does the hijab symbolize submission to you?
- What are the values you hold dear that may be at play here?

Points to consider

1. What is your definition of "autonomy"?
2. What do you know about Algeria?
3. What do you know about the refugees who have come to Canada from that country?
4. What do you know about this woman:
   - What she believes in, what level of education she has?
   - What her plans for the future are?
   - How long she has been in the country?
5. What do you know about Islam?
6. What do you know about her values regarding equality between men and women?

Case Example 4.3

You are a young, White, female social worker. You are doing a home visit to a family with a newborn in the context of a youth protection agency. No reports of abuse have been made. The young couple lives in a rent-controlled apartment in a poor area of a large metropolitan city. The father, in his early 20s, has tattoos all over his arms and a package of cigarettes tucked into the shoulder of his shirt. The mother is breastfeeding and looks uncomfortable. A public health nurse is also present.

Decentring process

- How do you feel?
- How do you feel as a representative of the state in this case?
- Why do you think the mother looks uncomfortable?

- Do you think this family is "poor"? How so?
- Do you know about the "culture of poverty"?
- Have you ever known someone living in an area such as this one?
- What is your own background? How do you think it may differ from that of this family?

Points to consider

1. Have you ever been poor?
2. How did it feel?
3. How do you think people look at you when you are poor?
4. What would be helpful here in terms of knowledge experience?

Case Example 4.4

You are a young, male, Ghanaian-Canadian social worker. You are meeting with a Chinese family originating from Mainland China. Their young son is sick, and the family seems reticent about the treatment doctors are proposing. You have been asked to make an assessment of the family. Present are the child's parents, grandmother, and someone else who may be an aunt. The members of the family talk among themselves in Cantonese. They are not very responsive to your questions. They look uneasy with your presence. You have heard that Chinese people may be racist.

Decentring process

- How do you feel?
- How does it make you feel when they speak Cantonese and you don't understand?
- Do you feel resistance? How?
- What is it that makes you feel uncomfortable?
- Do you feel your ethnic origin has bearing on what is going on? Why?

Points to consider

1. What does it mean to say "Chinese people are racist"?
2. Who are the "Chinese people"?
3. What do you know about this family's situation? About their beliefs? About what they may be feeling right now?
4. What can you do to make them at ease?
5. What are your assumptions here?

Penetrating the Other's World

Simply put, at this stage the worker enters the other's world. Here the worker tries to understand the world from the client's point of view and to understand the experience of the person, as he or she sees it. As many authors have pointed out, it is impossible to know everything about a culture or every individual's culture within a particular group. Cohen-Émerique (1993) suggests asking questions about an individual's culture, how the family is organized, his or her past, his or her migration trajectory, and what he or she holds dear. Take the time. Although this is often difficult to achieve in institutional contexts where appointments run on a tight schedule, taking the time to ask these questions will improve communication between the worker and the client. Cohen-Émerique suggests ways to enter another's world: travel, read up on different countries, immerse yourself in another culture through movies, dance, literature. As mentioned earlier, international field placements provide an excellent opportunity to learn about other ways of being.

The following discussions continue from the Case Examples on pages 66–67.

Case Examples for Review

Case Example 4.2 Continued

What could you do to know more about Algeria? About the Algerian family in this case? About their immigration experience? How it feels to be a newcomer to a society?

Case Example 4.3 Continued

What could you do to know more about low-income housing? About who the people are who live in rent-geared-to-income housing? Have you ever informally talked with someone who may have less material resources than you have?

Case Example 4.4 Continued

What are some cultural aspects about Chinese culture and how illness is viewed that could be important to know in a hospital context? Is spirituality important when dealing with illness? What are some signs of respect you could show them?

Negotiation/Mediation

This is particularly helpful when working with families in youth protection. Negotiation and mediation acts at the junction of a family/individual and a practice setting often in a context of crisis intervention or when there are serious elements in a situation, such as abuse or neglect reported to youth protection. Intercultural mediation acts as a bridge between individuals and different environments. "Conciliation," "reasonable compromise," and "dialogue" are terms used to define the process (Vatz-Laaroussi, Tadlaoui, & Gélinas, 2013).

Within the social work process, social workers need to be attentive to new areas dictated by the cultural traditions of the client. As we have seen, culture is not static: It is something that evolves and is transformed through time. Culture defines who we are, our beliefs and values, where we come from, and how we see the world. "Cultures shape the understanding of one's self-place in the world, as well as define the threshold and boundaries of connection and communication with others" (Perez-Foster, 1998, p. 258). It should be clear that we never meet "ethnic groups" or "cultures." We meet individuals who may or may not define themselves in the ways we perceive them (Asamoah, Garcia, Ortiz Hendricks, & Walker, 1991). Other issues such as gender or class may override issues of culture and ethnicity in any given situation, as seen with the example of the Mexican man in Case Example 4.1.

Intervention with Individuals and Families

People who come for help do so at times of need and sometimes at great cost to their feelings of self-worth and dignity. The first step in the intervention process is to recognize that social work emerged from a Eurocentric worldview, a Western paradigm (Diller, 1999) with values, beliefs, and approaches specific to Western culture. The following quote offers powerful imagery of what happens when people seek help:

> . . . when the sufferer, trailing a concentrated mix of belief, imagery, and anxiety, appears before an authorized, professional healer [the] disvalued experience is transformed into the clinical "presenting problem." The erupting emotions in one's personal life become "symptoms" to be "managed." Clipboards, file folders, closed doors and modulated voices subdue, at least for the moment, disallowed interpretations of crisis. In the clinics and offices of institutional medicine and counselling, physically and functionally set apart from the client's daily life, the interplay of history, biography, and cultural context is usually subordinant to sympton identification, classification, and assessment. (Green, 1999, p. 54)

Here, "symptom identification," "classification," and "assessment" are concepts rooted in a Western view of the nature of social problems. This is how professionals in the West address social problems, something very foreign to communal societies where family and community are involved in problem-solving processes as part of the culture. At the same time, the notion of process is central and something that may have been lost in our attempt to quantify and apply a "scientific" method to a practice (Green, 1999) that, in the end, is social.

Crucial at the beginning phase of the helping process are a worker's skills for interviewing, information gathering, developing the helping relationship, building rapport, formulating a treatment plan, and applying interventions. Basic facilitative skills such as attending, responding, reflecting, and questioning need to be evaluated to see if they work or not in a multicultural setting (Chau, 1990). Plionis and Lewis (1995), for example, warn that "rephrasing comments actually distorts the original meaning and jeopardizes their integrity because it runs them through the 'filter' of others' life experiences" (p. 185). Social workers need to develop ethno-sensitive listening skills, tuning in to the client's cultural framework (Cox & Ephross, 1998). Goal development should be based on clients' perceptions of needs (Thornton & Garrett, 1995, p. 70). Our asumption of what the problem is may not be accurate. We should strive for the "good fit" (Chau, 1991), understanding clients' perceptions of need. The following categories are representative of some of the major areas social workers should consider when intervening in a multicultural setting.

Types of Services Asked of Social Workers

At the beginning of the intervention process, mutual expectations must be clear for both the client and the worker (Cox & Ephross, 1998). People often come with different notions of daily life in this country, and the reality often falls short of their expectations. Social work is a Western profession, and in many societies problems we consider worthy of social work intervention are dealt with by the family, the community, traditional healers, or religious leaders. This is an area where sensitive clarity of communication is vital. Workers should clarify their role and the limits of what is possible in the practice context, whether institutional or community based.

Culture Shock

Linked to issues of perception are those surrounding culture shock. "'Culture shock' occurs when there is confrontation with a physically remote and dramatically different culture" (Lu, Lum, & Chen, 2001, p. 3). Practice in a multicultural environment can be a confronting experience both for the worker and the client, resulting in culture shock that stems from differing "value systems . . . ways of looking and thinking about things, unconscious images, [and] . . . visions of the world that determines behaviors and actions" (Legault, 1997, p. 52). Legault, who studied the issue among social workers in Montreal, concludes that culture shock "leads to misunderstandings of various kinds and extents and can result in intervention problems if not processed and analysed" (p. 52).

Upon arrival in Canada, immigrants from traditional or hierarchical societies are confronted with new values, ways of thinking, ways of life, family life, and childrearing practices that may precipitate feelings of anxiety, fear, and alienation. Social workers have an important role to play in explaining behaviours, values, daily routines, and expectations, and it takes time and patience. Similarly, issues confronting newcomers that are often mirrored back to us often lead us to question our own values and belief systems. This is an important part of the self-awareness process (see Furlong & Wight, 2011).

Williams (2006, p. 210) points out that "when there are cultural gaps among service systems, practitioners, and clients it contributes to misunderstandings and impasses that prevent effective social work intervention. Miscommunication in a practice setting is often at the root of a failed intervention". The following categories illustrate some of the major areas where cultural misunderstandings often occur[1] in working with individuals, families, and groups.

Competence Areas or Areas of Possible Cultural Misunderstanding

Notions of Time and Space

Whereas in our society time is structured, it may be more fluid in other societies (Al-Krenawi & Graham, 2000). In our society "time is money" and our perception of time may differ from that of other societies, but we often expect people from other cultures to think in the same way. Diller (1999, p. 53) points out that "European Americans view time as compartmentalized and incremental, and as such, being on time and being efficient with one's time are positive values." Furthermore, "lateness is often misinterpreted as indifference, provocative, or symptomatic of a lack of basic work skills" (p. 54). This is one area that can be particularly irritating to social workers, who are often working on very tight schedules. When clients show up late for an appointment or come the next day without an appointment, social workers should be aware that notions of time might be different. Humour is always a good idea to defuse a situation, and flexibility is a skill to be developed. As Al-Krenawi and Graham (2000, p. 5) point out, "Social workers would do well to clearly establish early on what the rules are regarding appointment times, lateness, and missed sessions."

We live in a vast land and we maintain a certain personal distance when speaking to each other—what some call a "bubble," our private space. When someone crosses that line it makes us feel uncomfortable. Proximity of people may make us feel uneasy and lead to misunderstandings. Large numbers of people living in small quarters often challenge our values around appropriate space. Promiscuity may be suspected when adults and children share the same living quarters. This is especially important when child protection services are involved (Legault & Roy, 2000, p. 201). Social workers need to understand these notions and their impact on the relationship with the client and reframe them within a cultural context. "Cultural awareness encompasses knowledge of cultural differences in a vast array of social norms such as nonverbal cues, proxemics, and language" (Fukuyama, 1994, p. 146). In Fukuyama's study on interns in multicultural settings she writes:

> One intern described an incident in which the supervisor seemed to be unaware of cultural-specific norms: "One of my supervisors was very insensitive to my warmth to clients. Hispanics are very warm and caring. He said that I had some countertransference issues." In this case, cultural misunderstandings on "personal space" can be misunderstood. Latin cultures, in general, allow more personal contact in relationships (both nonverbal and verbal) than do Euro-American cultures. (Comas-Diaz, 1989, as quoted in Fukuyama, 1994, p. 146)

Notion of the Person

Generally in our Western societies, the "I" is central to our definition of the person and autonomy of the individual is valued, whereas in many non-Western societies "we" encapsulates the notion of person. The individual does not exist without his or her family and community; a holistic vision of the world prevails, where the "we" feeling overrides the individualist "I" that predominates in Western society (Legault, 1997). Furlong and Wight (2011) point out that "Australian Indigenous languages . . . generally do not have a free-standing word for the 'I'—the individualised single actor. Rather, there is 'I-in-relation-to-a-stranger,' 'I-in-realtion-to-a-male elder,' 'I-in-relation-to-my-land,' and so forth" (p. 40). Language translates a vision of the world and of relationships between people. This is important in practice where, when a meeting is set with an individual, he or she may arrive with members of his or her family. Social workers need to be prepared to meet with family members and forgo, for example, our traditional understanding of privacy and confidentiality.

Notion of the Family

The definition of "the family" in Western societies has become restricted to immediate family members: parents/partners and children. For many societies the definition of family includes the extended family: aunts, uncles, grandparents, cousins, members of the village, or the community. The family may be organized according to a patriarchal structure of power, traditional division of labour, and control over expression of women's sexuality (Cox & Ephross, 1998, p. 64). Al-Krenawi and Graham (2000, p. 12) refer to the patriarchal organization of Iranian families that "is to be acknowledged by addressing fathers first and as the head of the family. The social worker should not attempt to change cultural power hierarchies or role patterns since this will alienate the family." They suggest some techniques in these cases: minimal eye contact and appropriate physical distances. When devising an intervention plan based on our notions of autonomy it is important to consider how this may go against cultural traditions.

Status and the Role of Women within the Family

In many societies the role of women is still confined to her position as wife and mother. Unmarried women often cannot leave the house without being accompanied by a male family member. Social workers need to understand how this configuration often changes through the migratory process. After arriving in Canada women often start working outside the home, upsetting traditional roles within the family. Through family reunification, women may also have joined their husbands after many years of separation. Estrangement, expectations, and dreams are all issues that, at some point, will need to be addressed. (For more on social work and gender, see Chapter 13 by Sarah Fotheringham.)

Childrearing Practices and Punishment

Here emerges the possibility for a strong clash between the Western values of the social workers that focus on individualism, autonomy of the person, and democratic authority and the values of collective and traditional societies (Chiasson-Lavoie & Roc, 2000). Who takes care of the children and the complete authority of the parents over the children are sensitive areas that take on importance in child protection services. How abuse and neglect are defined in Canadian law and how this may contrast with corporal punishment valued in non-Western societies is one of the most controversial aspects of practice with families in a multicultural context (Morneau, 1999). Perceptions of the social worker's role is often a major stumbling block to gaining trust and co-operation from families where abuse is suspected. In these cases, mistrust, anguish, worry, and anger are often at the root of resistance on the part of families to work with social workers. (For an extended example of a suspected case of child abuse, see Chapter 6 by Miu Chung Yan. For a description of the Immigrant Parent Enhancement (IPE) framework, see Chapter 9 by Debashis Dutta and Ross Klein.)

Interpersonal Codes of Behaviour

How people greet each other is an important aspect of our relationship with clients. It is not uncommon to extend one's hand to someone and not have it met. Social workers should not take this as a sign of rudeness. Customs and religion often dictate behaviour, and this is especially salient in relationships between female social workers and male clients. Each situation is different; workers will learn through experience.

Rituals and Beliefs Surrounding Illness, Mental Illness, and Death

This includes folk beliefs, traditional medicine, and those things that are considered a normal part of life and therefore do not require seeking healthcare (Cox and Ephross, 1998; Cohen-Émerique, 2000). For the Western world the medical model is the dominant framework in mental health, leading to a tendency to overpathologize (Ridley, 1995). As a result, social workers may "overlook the possibility that puzzling behavior is a reflection of social pathologies such as racism, discrimination, poverty, [and] inadequate health care" (p. 46).

Rituals surrounding death also need to be understood. Washing of the body, the kind of burrial ceremony, and dying at home may be seen as proper (Cox & Ephross, 1998) and should be considered. In their study with Arab mental health clients, Al-Krenawi and Graham (2000) argue that mental health social workers can learn much from traditional healers, particularly when working with families: "In traditional healing systems, the healer is active, and the client is passive. The healer directs, advises, guides, gives instructions, and suggests practical courses of treatment, such as rituals, incense burning, or visiting saints' tombs" (p. 18).

Religion and Religious Values and Spirituality

This is one emerging area in social work (see Coates, Graham, & Swartzentruber, 2007). Practice has shown us, however, that religion and spirituality often play a central role in people's lives. This may be difficult to understand for those who come from secular societies or from a generation, such as in Quebec today, where people have turned their backs on the Church. "God will provide" may be a sign to some that people have no will of their own or that they have given up the fight. However, religious beliefs and spirituality are often a powerful source of grounding and strength for people, and social workers should strive to accompany people through difficult times by understanding their religious beliefs, offering support, and quietly witnessing. Furthermore, as Al-Krenawi and Graham (2000) point out, social workers should understand not only how people rely on religion but also how it shapes their worldview and actions: "Social workers also should appreciate how a religious outlook could cultivate a conservative approach to family problems, marital problems, family matters, and the education of children. Thus, religious concepts may often be explicitly incorporated in the helping process" (p. 17). (For an in-depth conversation on spirituality, religion, and diversity, see Chapter 11 by Diana Coholic.)

We have addressed general areas of possible cultural misunderstanding. In the following section we address some of the salient areas that constitute barriers to good communication within the intervention process.

Communication Barriers

Social Customs

In our Western society we have a very direct way of approaching people, as seen in our way of greeting and our way of questioning people. During an initial assessment workers may be too direct, asking questions that are seen as very personal, thereby not respecting codes of the culture regarding privacy and taboo subjects. Eye contact, personal distance, and touching are examples of what Fulher (1995) calls "hindrances."

Interpreters

Workers may find themselves in situations where they need to work with an interpreter. This raises issues related to privacy and confidentiality for the client, especially if the interpreter is from the same ethnic group, from a different ethnic group within the same country, or from the same community. Clients may feel uncomfortable speaking freely with an interpreter present, fearing the person knows someone from the family or that word will get around about problems the client may be having. This raises the important issue of stigma. Clients may also feel uncomfortable using a family member as an interpreter, and this may inhibit communication (Chiasson-Lavoie & Roc, 2000). In these cases it is useful to remember to talk to the client and maintain eye contact with the client, not the interpreter, and address the client directly. Short sentences may also ensure that translation is not lost.

The issue of language spoken is also an issue to be considered here. Languages spoken in different countries have variances according to levels of education of the person, social class, regional origin, and rural or urban background. For example, the Spanish spoken by an educated Colombian man is different than the Spanish spoken by an uneducated peasant from Honduras. The same word may also have a different meaning in different countries. To avoid serious miscommunication, this should be considered when choosing an interpreter if one is needed.

Culturally Specific References

Social workers should also be self-conscious of their language (Green, 1999). Jargon and colloquialisms, such as "I'll hit the road now" or "picture it in your head," or references to such things as the CBC, NDG (Montreal), CFL, or culturally specific events, holidays, or special days of the year are all things that are taken for granted in our society. Heart-shaped cards for Valentine's Day and mistletoe at Christmas are not universal practices!

In Fukuyama's (1994, p. 147) study, she recounts another example:

> In another instance, a supervisor used a slang label that offended the supervisee: I remember an incident in which my supervisor called me a "jerk," very innocently and playful, of course. However, I was taken aback because I'd never been called that before. I'm not unfamiliar with name called [*sic*] but jerk is not a term used in my culture.

She concludes that, "The use of slang, even in jest, can be offensive to supervisees regardless of cultural background." In this instance, "it was recounted as inappropriate and shocking to a supervisee whose cultural background did not include such language" (Fukuyama, 1994, p. 147).

Client Communication

Communication styles vary across cultures. For example, in a study on culturally sensitive social work practice with Arab clients, Al-Krenawi and Graham (2000, p. 14) explain that "Arab communication styles are formal, impersonal, and restrained, rather than candid, personal, and expressive." Divulging personal information to someone outside the family or the community may be seen as weak, disloyal, or both. They further state that "Self-disclosure, client affect, and self-exploration are often difficult, particularly if they are perceived as risking damage to family honor. These difficulties should not be constructed as client resistance" (p. 14). In another study, Al-Krenawi and Graham (1997, p. 523) relate the experience of one of the author's clients: "He often revealed his fears and anxiety by quoting Arab proverbs, rather than speaking of his despair outright." It has also been this author's experience that language, what is being said to the worker in words, may not be what is actually meant. There is often a respect or reverence of people in authority such as a social worker: People may say what they think we want to hear. "Yes, yes, I'll come," may mean "I don't think so." In a context of diverse practice, we need to be attentive to body language and nonverbal signs (Cox & Ephross, 1998).

Language of the Client

Lu, Lum, and Chen (2001) present three aspects of language that are important for the client and clinician in the clinical process, as outlined by Lefley & Pederson (1986):

> (1) linguistic aspects or the manifest context of the consciously spoken word or verbal language; (2) idiosyncratic aspects or the quality of the speaker's voice and nonverbal cues such as facial expression, gestures, body movements; and (3) socio-linguistic aspects or a frame of reference, the context within which the message is interpreted and understood.

Green (1999, pp. 119–20) explains that "as does language among social workers, client language defines boundaries, conceals 'inside' information from those who would attempt to penetrate group boundaries, and helps preserve a sense of specialness and dignity among those familiar with the jargon." At times we work with groups or families and people speak among themselves in their own language. At other times we work with people who may come from different countries but speak a common language. At one point, while I was working with a group of men from different African countries, the common language was Swahili, which is not a language spoken by many social workers. It is not easy to step back and allow the group's process to go on without knowing everything being said. The reality is we cannot control all aspects of an intervention at all times. We need to learn to trust our instincts, offer support and guidance when needed, stand back, and give back some control to those we are seeking to empower.

Intervention with Families

The process of **acculturation** is central to intervention with families. Al-Krenawi and Graham (2000) explain that "Acculturation is a central component in conceiving social work services in the West. In providing social work services to an ethnic Arab family in the West, it is essential to consider the level of acculturation and its different effect on families" (p. 12). How long people have been in the country, their level of social and family support, and the degree of religious affiliation are important factors to consider. Takeda (2000) also raises the issue of length of time in the country and social support as factors affecting the adaptation of Iraqi refugees. Al-Krenawi and Graham (2000) further stress that "there is a significant difference . . . between the ethnic Arab who is here as a student and is struggling with issues of sexuality and a middle-aged man who has left his homeland in turmoil and is suffering from a post-traumatic stress disorder" (p. 12). (For further discussion on acculturation, see Chapter 9 by Debashis Dutta and Ross Klein.)

Certain key points should be mentioned about working specifically with families:

- Social workers should be attentive to the migration history of the family and how the family system may have been disrupted by migration (Barudy, 1992), especially in the case of forced migration. As Lum (1996) points out, the immigration process "is an upheaval and disequilibrium of catastrophic proportions which can be considered a crisis. . . . It involves disintegration of the person's intra-familial relationships, loss of social identity, and major shifts in the value system and behavioral patterns" (p. 258–9).
- Social workers should be cognizant of the fact that each individual in the family will have his or her own experience of the migration process, and issues may differ for each member of the family system.
- The ecological systems perspective with families is often appropriate. Here, different systems that constitute the client's environment are taken into account during the intervention process. These include, among others, systems around the community, the family, and the individual.
- Social workers need to assess how each family member's role has been altered by the migration process, considering how the family system is often shattered by the migration experience, where families may be separated for long periods of time because of immigration bureaucracy. Issues related to family separation and family reunification should also be taken into account (see Suarez-Orozco, Todorova, & Louie, 2002; Moreau, Rousseau, & Mekki-Berrada, 1999; Barudy, 1992).
- Social workers should not rush into a situation to change things without understanding the context: family relationships, roles within the family, separation, intergenerational issues, violence that may be due to stress (Lum, 1996), or breakdown of the family system because of migration.
- Social workers should understand the importance of the family and how marriage is looked upon. For example, moving toward ethnorelativism means understanding the Western view of marriage and family. "The constructions and perceptions of marital quality vary across cultures" (Lev-Wiesel & Al-Krenawi, 1999, p. 51). In one study on attitudes toward marriage among Israeli Arabs, it was concluded that children, rather than love or social status, was the primary influence in commitment to marriage. This would explain, in part, "the preference of many Muslim women to suffer a poor marital relationship rather than seek professional intervention" (Lev-Wiesel & Al-Krenawi, 1999, p. 52).
- Social workers should educate themselves regarding family values that may be prominent in different cultures. For example, "The family unit is sacred among Arab peoples, who are raised to depend on it as a continual source of support. Extended family members are valued as well. They are expected to be involved

and are consulted in times of crisis" (Al-Krenawi & Graham, 2000, p. 14). Social workers should therefore expect the family to be involved in the helping process for some clients.

- Groupwork is recommended as the modality of choice in working with families. Cox & Ephross (1998) warn that

> Social workers should be aware that what is expected of "good" clients flies in the face of ethnic group norms and traditions. Finding a way of involving others—family members, other group members, or others whose life experiences and points of view are compatible—is a way to normalize the social work client status for many ethnic group members. (p. 78)

Case Example 4.5

An Algerian woman is the victim of spousal abuse and, with her four children, turns to a shelter for help. After several counselling sessions, the worker, taking a feminist approach, counsels the woman to leave her husband. The woman eventually leaves her husband and the worker is pleased with the outcome.

Repercussions of the intervention

The woman is alienated from her family and friends and the community at large. The father has repudiated his children. The woman finds herself without support in a community she does not trust. The children are having difficulties in school that are compounded by the fact that they are in the process of learning a new language. Values, beliefs, sense of family, and community of the family have been shattered by the intervention.

Case Example 4.6

In another case, a worker from the same community was involved and worked with the family as a group, exploring the issues arising out of the trauma of the migration process. Issues relating to role reversal, status loss of the father who was a professional in his country and is now on welfare, meaning of family, the husband's expectations, and changes in the woman's role were dealt with. Extended family members and members from the community were brought in to support the family in its adaptation to the new country. Support networks were established for the husband and wife, and extra help was given to the children in school.

In Case Example 4.6, use of what Green (1999) calls a "root worker," a person of the same ethnic origin, was helpful and beneficial to the family. In many such cases the worker takes on the role of mediator between the family and the new society, providing guidance and exploring issues relating to the migration process that had not been dealt with.

Groupwork

Groupwork in social work has a long history and increasingly it is used as a particularly effective approach in multicultural practice. It may be especially appropriate for those whose social support networks may be absent or weak (Al-Krenawi, 1996), for example, in the case of immigrant or refugee women in Canada who are separated from their families and communities.

Empowerment

Although some authors consider the group as a natural and universal experience, what is not universal are the different types of groups that are artificially created in this society to offer help to group members within an **empowerment perspective**. Garvin (1997, p. 277) argues that groups "can facilitate empowerment in ways not available to other social work modalities. Empowerment—getting people to do things for themselves—is the focus in group work with marginalized and oppressed people." However, groups we create often emerge out of the concern of social workers, from caseloads, or even out of research interests, and are thus artificial rather than a direct response to needs expressed by clients. Another issue to be considered is the fact that primary networks (family and friends) often fulfill the need for emotional and psychological support with newly arrived immigrants and refugees (Legault & Roy, 2000, p. 189). For this clientele the expressed need is often material. This may determine different expectations of the group process on the part of group members. Setting up a group requires the worker to be sensitive to the fact that group work may be a foreign concept and that needs may be fulfilled by individuals' own communities (see Azmi, 1999). For some communities, however, cultural norms and practices may facilitate a group process.

Groups may be an appropriate approach in rebuilding social networks and social support that may have been lost in migration, thus providing material support and information about individuals' rights, validation that their problems are universal to those in that situation, assistance with particular problems, and organization of self-help groups that will take care of newcomers (Al-Krenawi, 1996).

Barriers to the Group Process

The group process may be influenced by many different factors: age, social class, ethnic origin, immigration status, or political or religious affiliations. It is erroneous to believe that members of one ethnic group constitute a homogeneous mass. For example, refugees coming to Montreal from Bangladesh may be Muslim and fleeing political persecution, or Hindu or Christian and fleeing religious persecution by the Muslim political majority; these are important considerations in terms of group processes and communication. As members of a task-oriented group advocating for the rights of refugees, individuals from these backgrounds may sit together at the same table since the commonality between them is their immigration status and the needs surrounding their particular legal situation, regardless of their ethnic, religious, or political affiliations. However, should the group be focused on trauma or development of self-esteem, resistance to sitting together in the same room or at the same table would be high. The group process and communication between members of the group may be seriously hindered by factors related to ethnic and religious belonging. Originating from societies where the caste system is in place would further impede members from different castes from sitting together in the same room.

Another barrier to the group process is straying from the purpose of the group. In task-oriented groups social workers need to stay focused on the purpose of the group, even though other important issues may arise. Working in a task-oriented group, such as the one mentioned in Case Example 4.6, often means working with the male leaders of the community. Issues such as the social and economic isolation of their wives, domestic violence (as was the case here), lack of social and health services, or trauma suffered in the premigratory process were not addressed. It is up to the worker to devise strategies, often in collaboration with women social workers from those communities, to address these other issues. This may prove to be a difficult situation for women social workers particularly, who have been trained to work toward empowerment, gender equality, and social justice.

Heterogeneity versus Homogeneity of Group

Heterogeneity versus homogeneity of ethnic background, class, age, and gender is one issue on which there is no consensus. The composition of the group is always linked to the objective of the group and the model chosen. Garvin (1997) proposes that when the purpose of the group is not identity or socialization, a heterogeneous group is best.

Case Example 4.7

A support group for women survivors of torture at the Montreal Women's Centre is being set up. Age, ethnicity, immigration status, or social class will not be the major elements to consider in the formative stage since the focus is on a common experience: All members will have experienced some form of torture. This will allow for mutual aid to develop. On the other hand, if the group's goal were to increase women's self-esteeem, age, ethnic background, and immigration status would be important issues to consider.

When considering a heterogeneous group the basic rule should be to ensure that members of the group can relate to each other, either through issues related to ageism, ableism, sexual orientation, social status, oppression, or marginalization. Workers need to ensure that members of the group experience the "mirror" effect, that of finding commonality with other members of the group.

Borrowing from Garvin (1997, pp. 280–1), the following categories reflect information social workers should have for effective groupwork with oppressed populations: communication, habitat, social structure, and group program.

Communication

This refers to the language used by the group members. The common language of group members may be other than French or English. In such a case Garvin (1997) suggests the worker understand the language or, to compensate for not knowing the language, use an Indigenous person as co-facilitator. Language may be a sensitive issue for the worker, and he or she may resent the fact that members of the group cannot speak his or her language. Flexibility and openess on the part of the worker are required in such cases. Immigrants and refugees will often speak one of Canada's official languages, but discussion among themselves may revert to a common language if members are from the same ethnic group. Feelings of being an "outsider" may overwhelm the worker, who feels a loss of control over the group or feels that his or her authority is diminished by the experience. The social worker should understand that this is often part of the process in the group and be open to the fact that there are things the worker will never be privy to.

Habitat

Where the group takes place is an important consideration in planning a group. When setting up a group for Bedouin widows, for example, Al-Krenawi (1996, p. 305) stresses the importance of having the group meet in a medical clinic. "The clinic is a modern institution that Bedouin women can visit without interference from their families and with no breach of cultural norms. The absence of stigma in visiting the health care clinic to attend group sessions was one of the main conditions for developing and maintaining the group."

How we use physical space is another consideration. How a meeting space is arranged, for example, sets the tone and creates an appropriate atmosphere for the group. Our experience in Canada is often to arrange chairs in a circle to ensure that all members of the group see each other, thus facilitating communication patterns. For people coming from hierarchical societies, this is not always customary. For example, a group of Gambian refugees invited to a meeting rearranged the chairs that had been placed in a circle into a more formal setting with rows of chairs and a head table for the leaders.

Social Structure

This refers to the social stratification of the larger oppressed community with which the members identify (Garvin 1997, p. 281). People originating from highly stratified societies will often reproduce the same configurations once they arrive in Canada. In these societies one's place in society defines who speaks to whom and in what context. It may be difficult to engage people in open discussion and engage in a process of mutual aid if they are from different castes, for example. Social workers may use this opportunity, however, to sensitize group members to egalitarian and democratic ideals that are valued in this society.

Group Program

Any program within the group should be thought out carefully. This involves paying attention to issues of stigma, cultural norms (e.g., being knowledgeable about what girls are allowed to do), and customs and rules, and understanding if mixed groups are acceptable and the nature of taboo subjects, such as financial difficulties or problems within the family, which may not be discussed with strangers. Activities involving touching, singing, or involving disclosure may not be culturally appropriate (Cox & Ephross, 1998).

In a multiethnic setting, considering the concept of groupwork with strangers is a major consideration. Careful planning of the group is therefore necessary to ensure members understand the purpose of the group and what is expected of them in terms of participation.

Summary and Conclusion

Social workers are increasingly conscious of the complexity of cultural, situational, political, social, ethnic, and religious factors that intersect with one another and that need to be taken into account in all practice settings. Culturally competent practice is now focusing on this diversity, and social workers will require a specific knowledge base in social diversity and oppression in relation to race, gender, ethnicity, sexual orientation, immigration status, and other attributes.

This chapter set out to develop a better understanding of culturally competent practice. Culturally competent practice is not an add-on to basic practice but should transcend all practice settings with individuals, families, groups, and communities, reflecting an understanding of the client's situation. Through a process of self-knowledge and awareness, the worker moves toward a capacity to understand the other's reality and integrates all aspects of an individual's identity that may be foreign to the worker. The intercultural approach will facilitate the process of moving from ethnocentricity to ethnorelativism and will allow the worker to achieve self-awareness by penetrating the other's world to understand a different worldview.

It is not an orderly or linear process and it takes time, openness, and flexibility. By putting him or herself in a learning mode, the worker comes to an understanding that he or she can learn from any situation. A worker may not be in agreement with the client's beliefs or values, but taking an ethnorelative stance does not mean compromising one's own values—rather, it is about respecting the other's stance, values, and worldview. As Roy (1992) states, many "truths" can coexist. Openness to discovering, within ourselves, what we believe our truth to be is the first step toward understanding what other truths may be. The worker should strive for the "good fit," meaning that practice is adapted to the client's needs within their own cultural context. (For a continued discussion of intercultural approaches in social work, see Chapter 10 by Catherine Montgomery.)

Culturally competent practice should not be seen as a set of barriers to effective social work intervention, nor is it an "add-on" to generic skills specific to social work practice. In all situations social workers encounter they will enter into a relationship based on humanistic, egalitarian, and social justice beliefs and values. Empowerment comes from respecting the people workers encounter through knowledge that is unveiled daily.

In summary, different models and approaches have been developed to work with ethnic and cultural minorities (Green & Watkins, 1998; Cohen-Émerique, 1980, 1993, 2000; Bertot & Jacob, 1991; Dominelli, 1996, 1998; Lum, 1996; Green, 1999; Cox & Ephross, 1998). Whatever the practice model, many writers in this field agree that certain specific knowledge areas are important to multicultural practice. Diller (1999) outlines some major skill areas for social workers to consider:

- Awareness and acceptance of differences in cultures: The ability to recognize how differences may affect the helping process.
- Self-awareness: Workers' ability to recognize that their culture may have an impact on the helping process.
- Dynamics of cultural difference: Workers' capacity to understand that miscommunication can occur because of the meaning different cultures bear; eye contact and shaking hands, for example.
- Knowledge of the clients' culture: Understanding the clients' cultural context, their beliefs, how their world is configured.
- Adaptation of skills: Enhancing generic social work practice with critical self-awareness to accommodate different worldviews.

Questions for Review

1. How do you define your culture?
2. How would you define cultural competency?
3. What makes you uncomfortable when confronted with someone from another culture?
4. What are the three main stages to the intercultural approach? How can you integrate them into your practice?

5. What is the process toward cultural self-awareness?
6. What do you need to do to better your cultural competency? Why?

Suggested Readings and Resources

Bender, K., Negi, N., & Fowler, D. N. (2010). Exploring the relationship between self-awareness and student commitment and understanding of culturally responsive social work practice. *Journal of Ethnic & Cultural Diversity in Social Work, 19*(1), 34–53.

Cocea, M., & Dutheil, F. (2000). *Learning to understand each other. Introduction to the special issues involved in working with an African clientele in the health and social services sectors.* Centre francophone du Toronto Métropolitain.

Colvin, A. (2013). Building culturally competent social work field practicum students through the integration of Campinha-Bacote's cultural competence healthcare model. *Field Scholar, 3*(1). Retrieved from http://fieldeducator.simmons.edu/article/building-culturally-competent-social-work-field-practicum-students-through-the-integration-of-campinha-bacotes-cultural-competence-healthcare-model/

Cox, C. B., and Ephross, P. H. (1998). *Ethnicity and social work practice.* New York, NY: Oxford University Press.

Goodman, D. J. (2013, February 5). Cultural competency for social justice. Commission for Social Justice Educators Blog. Retrieved from http://acpacsje.wordpress.com/2013/02/05/cultural-competency-for-social-justice-by-diane-j-goodman-ed-d/

Potocky-Tripodi, M. (2002). *Best practices for social work with immigrants and refugees.* New York, NY : Columbia University Press.

Sue, D. W. (2001). Multidimensional facets of cultural competence. *The Counseling Psychologist, 29*, 790–821.

Sue, S., Zane, N., Nagayama Hall, G. C., Berger, L. K. (2009). The case for cultural competency in psychotherapeutic interventions. *Annual Review Psychology, 60*, 525–48.

Notes

1. The following discussion is based on the work of Cohen-Émerique (1980) and prepared by G. Aumont for the Montreal Women's Center, date unknown.

References

Abrams, L., & Moio, J. (2009). Critical race theory and the cultural competence dilemma in social work education. *Journal of Social Work Education, 45*(2), 245–61.

Al-Krenawi, A. (1996). Group work with Bedouin widows of the Negev in a medical clinic. *Affilia, 1*(3), 303–18.

Al-Krenawi, A., & Graham, J. (1997). Social work and blood vengeance. *British Journal of Social Work, 27*, 515–28.

Al-Krenawi, A., & Graham, J. (2000). Culturally sensitive social work practice with Arab clients in mental health settings. *Health and Social Work, 25*(1), 9–22.

Asamoah, Y., Garcia, A., Ortiz Hendricks, C., & Walker, J. (1991). What we call ourselves: Implications for resources, policy, and practice. *Journal of Multicultural Social Work, 1*(1), 7–22.

Azmi, S. H. (1999). A qualitative sociological approach to address issues of diversity for social work. *Journal of Multicultural Social Work, 7*(3/4), 147–64.

Barudy, J. (1992). Migration politique, migration écnomique: une lecture systémique du processus d'intégration des familles migrantes, *Santé mentale au Québec, 17*(2), 47–70.

Ben-David, A., & Amit, D. (2000). Do we teach them to be culturally sensitive? The Israeli experience. *International Social Work, 42*(3), 347–58.

Bertot, J., & Jacob, A. (1991). *Intervenir avec les immigrants et les réfugiés.* Montreal, QC: Méridien.

Boyle, D. P., & Springer, A. (2001). Toward a cultural competence measure for social work with specific populations. *Journal of Ethnic and Cultural Diversity in Social Work, 9*(3–4), 53–71.

Chand, A. (2005). Do you speak English? Language barriers in child protection social work with minority ethnic families. *British Journal of Social Work, 35*, 807–21.

Chau, K. (1990). A model for teaching cross-cultural practice in social work. *Journal of Social Work Education, 26*(2), 124–33.

Chau, K. (1991). Social work with ethnic minorities: Practice issues and potentials. *Journal of Multicultural Social Work, 1*(1), 23–39.

Chiasson-Lavoie, M., & Roc, M.-L. (2000). La pratique interculturelle auprès des jeunes en difficulté. In G. Legault (Ed.), *L'intervention interculturelle* (pp. 219–48). Montreal, QC: Gaëtan Morin.

Coates, J., Graham, R. J., & Swartzentruber, B. (2007). *Spirituality and social work: Selected Canadian readings.* Toronto, ON: Canadian Scholars' Press.

Cocea, M., & Dutheil, F. (2000). *Learning to understand each other: Introduction to the special issues involved in working with an African clientele in the health and social services sectors.* Centre francophone du Toronto Métropolitain. Retrieved from http://settlement.org/downloads/apprendre.pdf

Cohen-Émerique, M. (1980). Éléments de base pour une formation à l'approche des migrants et plus généralement à l'approche interculturelle. *Annales de Vaucresson, 17*, 117–38.

Cohen-Émerique, M. (1984). Choc culturel et relations interculturelles dans la pratique des travailleurs sociaux, formation à la methode des incidents critiques. *Cahier de sociologie économique et culturelle, 7*, 183–218.

Cohen-Émerique, M. (1993). L'approche interculturelle dans le processus d'aid. *Santé mentale au Québec, 18*(1), 71–92.

Cohen-Émerique, M. (2000). L'approche interculturelle auprès des migrants. In G. Legault (Ed.), *L'intervention interculturelle* (pp. 161–84). Montreal, QC: Gaëtan Morin.

Cox, C. B., & Ephross, P. H. (1998). *Ethnicity and social work practice.* New York, NY: Oxford University Press.

Das, C., & Carter Anand, J. (2014). Strategies for critical reflection in international contexts for social work students. *International Social Work, 57*(2), 109–20.

Devore, W., & Schlesinger, E. G. (1996). *Ethnic sensitive social work practice.* Boston, MA: Allyn and Bacon.

Diller, J. V. (1999). *Cultural diversity: A primer for the human services.* Wadsworth, CA: Brooks/Cole.

Dominelli, L. (1996). Deprofessionalizing social work: Anti-oppressive practice, competencies and postmodernism. *British Journal of Social Work, 26*, 153–75.

Dominelli, L. (1998). Multiculturalism, anti-racism and social work in Europe. In C. Williams, H. Soydan, & M. R. D. Johnson (Eds.), *Social work and minorities* (pp. 36–57). London, UK: Routledge.

Este, D. (2007). Cultural competency and social work practice in Canada: A retrospective examination. *Canadian Social Work Review, 24*(1), 93–104.

Fukuyama, M. A. (1994). Critical incidents in multicultural counseling supervision: A phenomenological approach to supervision research. *Counselor Education and Supervision, 34*(2), 142–51.

Fulher, J. (1995). Getting in touch with your heritage. In N. Vacc, S. DeVaney, & J. Wittmer (Eds.), *Experiencing and counselling multicultural and diverse populations* (3rd ed., pp. 9–27). Levittown, PA: Taylor & Francis.

Furlong, M., & Wight, J. (2011). Promoting "critical awareness" and critiquing "cultural competence": Towards disrupting received professional knowledges. *Australian Journal of Social Work, 64*(1), 38–54.

Gallegos, J. S., Tindall, C., & Gallegos, S. A. (2008). The need for advancement in the conceptualization of cultural competence. *Advances in Social Work, 9*(1), 51–62.

Garcia, B., & Van Soest, D. (1999). Teaching about diversity and oppression: Learning from the analysis of critical classroom events. *Journal of Teaching in Social Work, 18*(1/2), 149–67.

Garvin, C. D. (1997). *Contemporary groupwork*. Boston, MA: Allyn and Bacon.

Green, J. W. (1999). *Cultural awareness in the human services*. Boston, MA: Allyn and Bacon.

Green, R. R., & Watkins, M. (1998). *Serving diverse constituencies*. New York, NY: Aldine De gruyter.

Hoffman, D. M. (1999). Culture and comparative education: Toward decentering and recentering the discourse. *Comparative Education Review, 43*(4), 464–88.

James, J. (2003). *Seeing ourselves: Exploring race, ethnicity and culture* (3rd ed.). Toronto, ON: Thompson Educational Publishing.

Kleinman, A., & Benson, P. (2006). Anthropology in the clinic: The problem of cultural competency and how to fix it. *PLoS Med, 3*(10), e294.

Krajewski-Jaime, E. R., et al. (1996). Utilizing international clinical practice to build intercultural sensitivity in social work students. *Journal of Multicultural Social Work, 4*(2), 15–29.

LeDoux, C., & Montalvo, F. F. (1999). Multicultural content in social work graduate programs: A national survey. *Journal of Teaching in Social Work, 7*(1/2), 37–55.

Lefley, H. P., & Pederson, P. B. (1986). *Cross cultural training for mental health professionals*. Spring Field, IL: Charles Thomas Publishing.

Legault, G. (1997). Social work practice in situations of intercultural misunderstandings. *Journal of Multicultural Social Work, 4*(4), 49–66.

Legault, G., & Roy, G. (2000). Les difficultés des intervenants sociaux aurprès des clientèles d'immigration récente. In G. Legault (Ed.), *L'intervention interculturelle* (pp. 185–202). Montreal, QC: Gaëtan Morin.

Lev-Wiesel, R., & Al-Krenawi, A. (1999). Attitudes towards marriage and marital quality: Comparison among Israeli Arabs differentiated by religion. *Family Relations, 48*, 41–56.

Lu, Y. E., Lum, D., & Chen, S. (2001). Cultural competency and achieving styles in clinical social work. *Journal of Ethnic and Cultural Diversity in Social Work, 9*(3–4), 1–32.

Lum, D. (1996). *Social work practice and people of color* (3rd ed.). Pacific Grove, CA: Brooks/Cole Publishing.

Lyons, K. (1999). *International social work: Themes and perspectives*. Surrey, UK: Ashgate.

Maiter, S. (2009). Using an anti-racist framework for assessment and intervention in clinical practice with families from diverse ethno-racial backgrounds. *Clinical Social Work Journal, 37*(4), 267–76.

Martinez-Brawley, E. E., & Brawley, E. A. (1999). Diversity in a changing world: Cultural enrichment or social fragmentation? *Journal of Multicultural Social Work, 7*(1/2), 19–36.

Mlcek, S. (2013). Are we doing enough to develop cross-cultural competencies for social work? *British Journal of Social Work, 44*(7), 1–20.

Montalvo, F. (1999). The critical incident interview and ethnoracial identity. *Journal of Multicultural Social Work, 7*(3/4), 19–43.

Moreau, S., Rousseau, C., & Mekki-Berrada, A. (1999). Politiques d'immigration et santé mentale des réfugiés: profil et impact des séparations familiales. *Nouvelles pratiques sociales, 12*(1), 177–96.

Morneau, S. (1999). Réflexions sur l'intervention en maltraitance auprès des groupes culturels minoritaires. *Canadian Social Work Review/Revue canadienne de service social, 16*(2), 219–31.

Mullaly, R. (1993). *Structural social work: Ideology, theory, and practice*. Toronto, ON: McClelland & Stewart.

Nakanishi, M., & Rittner, B. (1992). The inclusionary cultural mode. *Journal of Social Work Education, 28*(1), 27–35.

National Association of Social Workers. (2001). *New standards for cultural competence in social work practice*. Retrieved from http://www.naswdc.org/practice/standards/NASWculturalstandards.pdf

Ortiz Hendricks, C. (2003). Learning and teaching cultural competence in social work. *Journal of Teaching in Social Work, 23*(1/2), 73–86.

Perez-Foster, R. (1998). The clinician's cultural countertransference: The psychodynamics of culturally competent practice. *Clinical Social Work Journal, 26*(3), 253–70.

Pigler Christensen, C. (1985). A perceptual approach to cross-cultural counselling. *Canadian Counsellor/ Conseiller canadien, 19*(2), 63–81.

Pigler Christensen, C. (1992). Training for cross-cultural social work with immigrants, refugees, and minorities: A course model. *Journal of Multicultural Social Work, 2*(1), 79–97.

Plionis, E. M., & Lewis, H. J. (1995). Teaching cultural diversity and oppression: Preparation for risk—the Coverdale Model. *Journal of Teaching in Social Work, 12*(1/2), 175–92.

Rachédi, L., & Pierre, A. (2007). De l'enseignement de la compétence interculturelle à l'université à la promotion des récits de vie. *Canadian Social Work Review/Revue canadienne de service social, 24*(1), 73–80.

Razack, N., & Jeffery, D. (2002). Critical race discourse and tenets for social work. *Canadian Social Work Review/Revue canadienne de service social, 19*(2), 257–71.

Ridley, C. R. (1995). *Overcoming unintentional racism in counseling and therapy*. Thousand Oaks, CA: Sage Publications.

Roy, G. (1992). Devons-nous avoir peur de l'interculturel institutionnalisé? *Nouvelles pratiques sociales, 5*(2), 53–4.

Statistics Canada. (2011). Immigration and ethnocultural diversity in Canada. Retrieved from https://www12.statcan.gc.ca/nhs-enm/2011/as-sa/99-010-x/99-010-x2011001-eng.cfm

Suarez-Orozco, C., Todorova, I. L. G., & Louie, J. (2002). Making up for lost time: The experience of separation and reunification among immigrant families. *Family Process, 41*(4), 625–43.

Sue, D. W. (2006). *Multicultural social work practice*. Hoboken, NJ: John Wiley & Sons.

Takeda, J. (2000). Psychological and economic adaptation of Iraqi adult male refugees: Implications for social work practice. *Journal of Social Service Research, 26*(3), 1–21.

Thomas Bernard, W., & Moriah, J. (2007). Cultural competency: An individual or institutional responsibility? *Canadian Social Work Review/Revue canadienne de service social, 24*(1), 81–92.

Thornton, S., & Garrett, K. J. (1995). Ethnography as a bridge to multicultural practice. *Journal of Social Work Education, 31*(1), 67–74.

Vacc, N. A., De Vaney, S. B., & Wittmer, J. (1995). *Experiencing and counselling multicultural and diverse populations* (3rd ed.). Bristol, PA: Accelerated Development.

Vatz-Laaroussi, M., Tadlaoui, J. E., & Gélinas, C. (2013). *Médiations interculturelles: défis et enjeux pour un meilleur Vivre ensemble*. Centre d'études ethniques des universités montréalaises. Retrieved from http://www.ceetum.umontreal.ca/documents/capsules/2013-enjeux/vatz-tad-gel-enj-2013.pdf

Weaver, H. N. (1998). Teaching cultural competence: Application of experiential learning techniques. *Journal of Teaching in Social Work, 17*(1/2): 65–79.

Williams, C. (2006). The epistemology of cultural competence. *Families in Society: Journal of Contemporary Social Services, 87*(2), 209–20.

Yan, M. C. (2005). How cultural awareness works. An empirical examination of the interactions between social workers and their clients. *Canadian Social Work Review/Revue canadienne de service social, 22*(1), 5–29.

Macro Practice with Diverse Communities

New Challenges for Social Workers

By Douglas Durst

Chapter Objectives

This chapter will help you develop an understanding of:

- Community development, community organizing, and social planning
- The unique knowledge that is required to practise community development in diverse communities
- The specific skills required for community development and organizing in diverse communities
- The appropriate values and attitudes that relate to community practice

Introduction

Approaching most communities in Canada, the traveller is welcomed with a large signpost boldly announcing the name of the village, town, or city, usually in large white letters on a green background. Also included is the community's population. Some metres further along the road, another signpost lists the various religious organizations. Yet another sign lists the numerous community organizations and service clubs—the ubiquitous Lions Club, Elks, and Kiwanis are invariably proudly displayed. This sign is distinctively North American: The idea of service clubs and organizations is a particularly Western phenomenon. Herein lies the caveat for the community organizer in the cross-cultural or multicultural setting.

Canada is a land of immigrants who, because of their personal histories and cultural backgrounds, rarely arrive with the concepts of community service agencies, volunteer organizations, or not-for-profit community-based structures to assist in meeting community needs. For many immigrants, social programs and services do not exist in their native countries in the same manner as they do in Canadian society. In Canada, social programs are offered through not-for-profit organizations, public institutions, and for-profit businesses, often referred to as the three sectors of social welfare. In many poor countries, services for financially or socially disadvantaged people are nonexistent, leaving these citizens to beg, borrow, or steal a marginalized existence, sometimes in the midst of opulence and wealth. The limited services that may be available are provided through some "charitable" religious organizations or government-run institutions. For these new Canadians, the idea that members of the community would collectively apply their financial and personal skills to a social need that is not directly their own is indeed "foreign."

For the most part, behaviours are culturally determined. Each culture has its own values, norms, and expectations that reinforce appropriate behaviour and discourage inappropriate behaviour. An important goal of social work is to enable people to make positive changes in their lives, to facilitate and encourage behaviours that empower individuals, and to allow them to make positive changes as individuals and as members of their community.

In recent decades, the profession of social work has recognized the need to develop models of practice that acknowledge and accommodate **diversity** in race, gender, sexual orientation, and ethnicity (Kirst-Ashman & Hull, 2015). (For more discussion on gender and social work, see Chapter 13 by Sarah Fotheringham.) Social work literature on ethnic-sensitive practice and competence has developed primarily in the clinical field or in direct practice with individuals, families, and groups (Gutierrez & Alvarez, 2000; Harper & Lantz, 1996; Lum, 1992). Dominelli (1988) focuses on racism and promotes anti-racist social work practice. Generally, the area of community development and community organizations has been neglected; however, there are some works found in the American literature (Bradshaw, Soifer, & Gutierrez, 1993; Gutierrez & Alvarez, 2000; Gutierrez & Lewis, 1994; Rivera & Erlich, 1995). Considering the diversity in Canadian society, an emphasis on community development practice with diverse populations, including ethnicity and cross-cultural contexts, is long overdue.

This chapter discusses the knowledge, skills, and values necessary for effective social work practice in the domain of community development and organization in diverse community groups. The chapter is organized into four sections:

- Community development and organizing: definitions, models, and strategies
- Unique knowledge
- Community development skills
- Appropriate values for community work

The first section introduces essential terms and concepts. The second section explores two key types of knowledge necessary for effective community development: self-knowledge and academic/professional knowledge. The third section examines the broad range of skills required by community workers to effectively carry out their many roles as guide, facilitator, educator, and motivator. The final section reviews the values—of the community worker and the client community—that guide behaviour.

In each section, the concepts are discussed first in terms of general community development, where specific considerations for working in multicultural and cross-cultural settings are explored. The knowledge, skills, and values are discussed in the context of the goal of community development: enabling communities to make positive change.

For community workers working in their own culture, cultural knowledge is learned in childhood and may be deeply embedded in their being. The culture is part of the person and is expressed in subconscious ways in everyday life. When working in a cross-cultural environment, community workers must learn about that culture to interact effectively. In a multicultural community or cross-cultural setting, community workers must respect the group's culture: its values, norms, and expectations. This attitude encompasses more than "respect." To be effective, workers must possess an understanding of the history of oppressed or disadvantaged groups and how they have striven to improve their communities (Carlton-LaNey & Burwell, 1996). For example, in the United States the history of civil rights and the efforts of African Americans and others to end discrimination and oppression are essential to understanding and working with African Americans (Munoz, 1989; West, 1990). In Canada, the colonial oppression of First Nations peoples[1] (Bruyere, 2010) and the discriminatory and racist immigration policies that affected new Canadians need to be understood and integrated into the subconscious of the social worker; these must be understood as "given." Multicultural community work is about accepting and embracing cultural and ethnic pluralism, valuing the contributions of all Canadians, and finding ways to enhance their contribution so that Canadian society benefits as a whole. It involves eliminating oppression, racism, and discrimination; removing barriers to social justice; and seeking equality and equity in all sectors of our society (St. Onge, 2013). Finally, the reader must remember that the community worker may not be of the dominant cultural group and may be a member of the disadvantaged or marginalized group.

Community Development and Organizing

Definitions

"Culture" refers to the shared collective norms, values, beliefs, and traditions of a group. Ethnicity does not necessarily determine culture: "Ethnicity refers to sharing a common national origin, race, culture and/or language" (McDonald, Pittaway, & Nahmiash, 1995, p. 9). "Ethnicity is also an abstraction. It refers to the specific aspect of culture of an individual or group that derives from another national cultural heritage" (Herberg, 1993, p. 4). As Fleras and Elliott (1999) state, "Broadly speaking, ethnicity consists of a shared awareness of ancestral differences as a basis for engagement or entitlement. It entails a consciousness about belonging and loyalty to a particular people, homeland or cultural tradition . . . [It] is a statement of affiliation or attachment involving like-minded people in pursuit of a social activity or goal . . . or 'people hood'" (p. 108).

Yet ethnocultural groups are not homogeneous. For example, Aboriginal peoples live in numerous cultural and ethnic groups; all are diverse, with unique cultural systems and historical experiences. First Nations peoples live in all regions of Canada in more than 600 First Nations/Bands with over 60 traditional languages. (For more discussion on social work with Aboriginal peoples in Canada, see Chapter 7 by Raymond Neckoway and Keith Brownlee.) Among Chinese Canadians there are separate groups with several languages and dialects. In addition, the personal experiences of these Canadians vary. Some recent Chinese immigrants come from wealthy and privileged Hong Kong families; others have survived unimaginable horrors in refugee camps. Immigrants may have common cultures and language, and may even have the same extended family, but they may still come out of vastly different environments. The variety of cultural backgrounds and experiences results in differing values, beliefs, and attitudes, which can be quite confusing for the outside community worker. Immigrants who arrived as children will incorporate and develop a new value base from their parents, and the next generation, born and raised in Canada, will create still another cultural mix. "Ethnoculture is a blend of the old culture and new host culture adapted to a specific environment" (Herberg, 1993, p. 4). Like culture, the ethnicity of an individual is not static but alive and ever changing.

Definitions of **community** are also wide and varied (Dasgupta, 1996; Lyon, 1987); an early review by Hillery (1955) found 94 separate uses of the word. Yet most definitions include four components: people, location in a geographic space, social interaction, and common ties (Hick, 2010; Lyon, 1987; Wharf & Clague, 1997). Hence, the term "community" may be used to identify a First Nation of Plains Cree living in Saskatchewan, a group of Vietnamese refugees who settled in Halifax 30 years ago, or a group of Bosnian refugees dispersed across southern Ontario. There can also be communities within communities—for example, a subgroup of entrepreneurial Canadian-born Hong Kong Chinese among the Chinese immigrants originally from the Mainland.

Community development refers to "efforts to mobilize people who are directly affected by a community condition . . . into groups and organizations to enable them to take action on the social problems and issues that concern them" (Rivera & Erlich, 1995, p. 3). Community development is characterized by a dual emphasis on growth of the individual and of the community (Brueggemann, 2014; Ife & Tesoriero, 2006; Lingam, 2013). Rubin and Rubin (1986) state that "community development involves local **empowerment** through organized groups of people acting collectively to control decisions, projects, programs and policies that affect them as a community" (p. 20). The goal of community development for marginalized groups in general, and diverse communities in particular, is to close the gap between needs and resources to improve the condition or social functioning of individual residents who constitute the community.

Models

Many models, approaches, and perspectives frame and direct community development. Rothman's 1974 article "Three models of community organization practice" has become a classic in community and social work literature (Brueggemann, 2014;

Hick, 2010; Wharf & Clague, 1997) and is most frequently used in social work curriculum (McNutt, 1995). Rothman identified 12 characteristics of community work and developed three primary models—locality development, social planning, and social action—based on assumptions about the nature of society, particularly the distribution of power. The three central models are briefly defined below; for a more complete description it is worth reviewing *Strategies of Community Intervention* (Rothman, Erlich, & Tropman, 2001).

- The *locality development model*, commonly referred to as community development, occurs as a result of a community identifying and resolving its problems co-operatively with outside structures. It is based upon co-operation, participation, and coordination of a broad range of participants (Rothman, 1995). It assumes that those in positions of power will support proposals for change from community members and will co-operate in creating change.
- The **social planning**/*policy model* assumes that gathering, presenting, and analyzing facts can resolve problems. It is a logical, rational process that attempts to take a neutral position regarding politics and power. In this model, community development relies on research and a rational approach to problem solving, and on co-operation among community residents but not necessarily their participation. Power is held by the sponsoring or employing agency and decision making is controlled by "elites."
- The **social action model** assumes that some individuals, groups, and communities are disadvantaged or oppressed by existing groups or structures. The disadvantaged group needs to organize and demand change from the broader society in terms of equality in treatment and increased resources. In this model, change (community development) occurs only with a redistribution of power from external sources to the community.

Although useful and practical in most applications, Rothman's three models do not adequately reflect the complexity of community development. In his 1995 chapter, he recognized their limitations and explored the "interweaving of intervention approaches," creating three bimodal mixtures of the three ideal types. These bimodal models expand the application of his theories and better describe and analyze groups and organizations that apply different community development strategies.

Taylor and Roberts (1985) described five models of community work: community development, community liaison, planning, pluralism and participation, and program development and coordination. Expanding on Rothman's original work, Weil and Gamble (1995) listed eight models of community work: neighbourhood and **community organizing**, organizing functional communities, community social and economic development, social planning, program development and community liaison, political and social action, coalitions, and social movements. The two primary characteristics that differentiate the above models are first the roles and strategies used by the community worker, and second the levels of power and decision making at the community level (Hardina, 2000).

Strategies

The specific activities of the community developer should be determined by the community's strategy or long-range goals meant to address the agreed-upon social change. The American community sociologist Roland Warren (1971) identified three strategies that are employed to address the desired change: collaboration, campaign, and contest.

- **Collaborative strategies** seek social change based on negotiation and agreed action. For example, most of the developing First Nations Child and Family Services agencies in Canada are based on tripartite agreements between First Nations Band Councils and the provincial and federal governments (Durst, 2010).
- **Campaign strategies** are persuasive in nature, seeking to change people's or organizations' perspective through education and promotion. In addition to educating, campaign strategies can involve "shocking" or "embarrassing" the more powerful party into some action. For example, television news coverage of the solvent-sniffing children of Davis Inlet, Labrador, shocked the nation and prompted the federal government to take immediate action. Concerns for the health of the individual children portrayed were then expanded to elicit concern about the third-world conditions of the entire community.
- Warren (1971) describes **contest strategies** as confrontation with the intent to pressure the power-based decision-making organizations to implement responses to address the issues of the community.

Generally, community development draws upon consensus and co-operative strategies, and social action applies strategies involving contest and confrontation. Depending on the approach, campaign strategies can be either co-operative/collaborative or confrontational in nature (Warren, 1971). Recent confrontational strategies include First Nations blockages of roads and railways while protesting land claims, resource exploitation, or violations of First Nations rights and treaties.

The orientation that the worker and the community members choose will reflect their understanding of issues of power (Reisch & Thursz, 2013). It will reflect a basic theoretical framework that can be understood and analyzed through sociological theory. Those workers who assume that power is shared and that rational decision making will lead to social improvements may be applying a **social systems framework** (also known as a *functionalist framework*). This assumes that all groups in society have common goals and shared values that can best be achieved through co-operation and collaboration. Those workers who assume that power is not shared and that those in positions of power wish to maintain their power, even at the expense of others, subscribe to a **conflict/feminist/Marxist conceptual framework** (Hick, Fook & Pozzuto, 2005; Ledwith & Asgill, 2007; Ohmer & Brooks, 2013). Many feminists see the oppression and exploitation of patriarchy as central to imbalances of power. African Americans have made significant gains by rejecting past power structures and demanding social change. For these groups, the battle is not over. This, of course, is a rather brief and somewhat superficial summary of how power is understood and reflected in practice; I refer the reader to Strega (2015) for a much deeper discussion.

For the most part, ethnic communities in Canada have been marginalized, but in recent years some groups have become increasingly vocal and active in asserting their wishes. Most Aboriginal communities were traditionally based on egalitarian and co-operative values. Under self-government, many of these communities have seized the autonomy to determine their own needs and the power to develop and carry out plans to meet those needs. The paternalistic practices and policies of the governments of the dominant culture are being relinquished with the recognition of First Nations peoples' inherent right to self-determination and self-government (Durst, 2010).

In Canada, schools of social work vary in terms of their general orientation, but a number of schools publicly espouse a conflict/feminist/Marxist framework. These programs reflect the belief that real social change can occur only if there is fundamental change in the way power and resources are distributed. However, most schools in North America have a functionalist or systems framework with a liberal humanitarian understanding. Faculty tend to teach that permanent social change occurs through a readjustment of resources achieved through collaboration and co-operation. Implicit in this chapter is the belief that each model has a role in community development and that the worker's approach depends on the situation and the wishes of the community.

Many immigrants and new Canadians have struggled, often with great personal sacrifice, to "fit in" and find a comfortable level of social, economic, and sometimes political integration. They have sought to minimize conflict, find harmony and balance, and accept some level of discomfort from discrimination and racism. Adjustment and social integration are found through the collaboration and successful co-operation with all members of society. Some groups, such as Canada's Aboriginal peoples and Black Canadians, have suffered under centuries of oppression, colonialism, discrimination, and blatant racism. Even with efforts of collaboration and co-operation, the experiences of these Canadians have been marked by the continuation and extension of oppression and racism. For many, the most effective response is found in more radical and aggressive tactics for social change (Ohmer & Brooks, 2013). The challenge for the community worker is finding the tactic and style of community development/social action that is appropriate for the community and comfortable for both the community worker and the community members. A community worker who is trained and ready for aggressive strategies in a community that seeks a collaborative style is bound to experience frustration and failure.

Unique Knowledge

> The integration of social workers' perspectives with clients' unique details supplies the concrete and specific knowledge base for each phase of social work. (Krogsrud Miley, O'Melia, & DeBois, 1995, p. 124)

Knowledge is information that is internalized and understood. Problems are identified and resolved through the application of sufficient and appropriate knowledge. Community workers acquire knowledge through personal life experience and through professional education and training. Knowledge of *self* is critical for community workers to understand what motivates and shapes their actions. This intimate knowledge of self allows community workers to recognize how their behaviour influences interactions with others and how they make professional decisions. Professional and academic education and training help workers understand human behaviour and also equip them with the requisite knowledge for specific types of community development initiatives, such as health, economic development, or education.

Self-Knowledge and Personal Life Experience

Community workers are people first and professionals second. Their personal biases, prejudices, strengths, and challenges constitute the foundation upon which the professional is built. To comprehend and influence the behaviour of others, community workers must have a clear and accurate understanding of what directs their own behaviour. All people are biased: We may strive for total objectivity, but as intelligent, sentient creatures people are inherently both intellectual and emotional. Biases—likes and dislikes—develop over a lifetime; they are often unconscious, the product of an individual's cumulative life experiences and influences. Effective community workers know their biases, strengths, and challenges. A successful community worker recognizes that he or she is but one of many resources available to the client; the worker draws on personal strengths and compensates for deficiencies to ensure that clients receive the services and resources they need.

Professional/Academic Knowledge

Knowledge about human behaviour—both the worker's and that of the client community—is essential to the community developer. In addition, the community worker requires general knowledge about human interaction and community intervention, knowledge specific to the particular type of community development initiative planned, and knowledge about the community in which the individual will work.

Social Work Knowledge

Social workers in the community engage in many types of community intervention and development. Depending on the needs identified by the community, social work embraces a wide range of activities: Healthcare, education, economic development, and childcare are but a few examples of the many different needs communities may encounter. Specific knowledge about the topic is required for an effective response to a need. For each area of activity, a body of knowledge has been developed based on the cumulative, collective experiences of thousands of individuals over time. These experiences have been organized into pockets of knowledge that can readily be transmitted by an instructor to students in a classroom setting, and by established community workers to novice colleagues in a practical work environment.

The academic training for a specific discipline provides the theories and foundations, which in turn provide the rationale and structure for interaction and activity. This academic knowledge allows the worker to benefit from the vast experiences, both the successes and the failures, of those who have been working in the field.

In order to influence behaviour, the community worker must know and understand what motivates and constrains human behaviour. Social workers use theoretical knowledge to better understand and predict human behaviour to help foster positive change (Krogsrud Miley, O'Melia, & DeBois, 1995). The disciplines of both social work and psychology focus on human behaviour.

Ethical/Legal Knowledge

In the past, guidelines directing interaction between a researcher or community worker and participants/subjects (human or other animal) were not rigidly regulated. With greater understanding and insight, those working in the fields of human and animal research and interaction have come to recognize the moral obligations of ensuring that study or practice subjects—people and animals—are treated with respect and in such a manner so as to avoid distress or harm. The recognition of this moral obligation is manifested in ethical guidelines or standards. Community workers involved in academic research or clinical activities are expected to adhere to the ethical guidelines applicable to their discipline or institution.

Professional ethics is related to ethical/legal knowledge. Although the community worker may be volunteering, the worker is a "professional," even though he or she may not be a member of the professional association of social workers. Regardless of the worker's status within the profession, the social work profession has established clear and detailed guidelines for ethical practice and ethical decision making. These guidelines provide the foundation for ethical practice and must be adhered to. The national professional associations in Canada and the United States make these standards available on the Internet and in published form. Further discussion on values and ethics is presented in the section below entitled "Appropriate Values for Community Work."

Knowledge of the Community

Before entering a community, workers need to learn about that community—the who, what, where, when, why, and how that shapes and directs community behaviour. Erasmus and Ensign (1991) point out that knowing a community's demographics, history, and culture, and understanding both the formal and informal power systems, helps the community worker identify practical parameters, including barriers or challenges, for community development initiatives.

Knowing whether a community comprises a hundred or a thousand residents has direct implications for the type and scope of possible community development. Geographic location may also have implications in terms of access to resources or issues related to transportation throughout the seasons. Distance and climate are important considerations in planning interventions or development activities, particularly in areas where distances are vast and the climate can be extreme and unpredictable.

Awareness of the community's history and culture helps the community worker understand the forces that shaped the initial development of the community and the beliefs, values, and traditions that shape the community today. Communities with rigid boundaries—that is, communities where there is little interaction between the residents and those outside, particularly with the larger, dominant society—tend to adhere more strongly to traditional values and norms. The social roles and behaviours within the community are shaped according to its specific culture (Cox & Ephross, 1998).

The ability to demonstrate awareness of social and political protocols indicates the community worker is aware of and sensitive to the values and practices that guide social interaction in the community. Acknowledging the importance of these fundamental protocols is the community worker's first step toward building open, trusting relationships with community residents.

The community worker does not work in isolation within the community: Her or his role is to mobilize the community so that residents collectively and co-operatively make positive changes for themselves. This mobilization is facilitated through support of the local political decision-making and service delivery systems. In any group or community there are two systems of power: formal power (authority) and informal power (influence). Community residents have given those in positions of authority, such as elected or appointed representatives, the power to act and make decisions on their behalf. For example, in First Nations communities, the council and head (chief on a reserve, chairperson in a Métis settlement) have the authority to make decisions on behalf of the members within their community. Any initiative designed to have an impact on the community must first be discussed by the Band Council (Erasmus & Ensign, 1991, p. 25). Additionally, there may be individuals or groups who, while not elected representatives, have influence by virtue of possessing a particular skill or are otherwise admired or respected for their demonstrated competence or commitment to community well-being. In First Nations communities, sources of influence may include elders, other community leaders, or friendship centres.

While the community as a whole may wish to work toward its collective betterment, there may not necessarily be consensus on how best to proceed. For example, in attempting to address the problem of violence against women, male band leaders may define the problem and view solutions differently than the women of the community. One of the roles of the community worker is to align the community, including those individuals with authority or influence, so that all members of the community are working co-operatively toward a common goal.

Krogsrud Miley, O'Melia, and DeBois (1995) stress that "only clients know what their history has been, what is currently happening to them, and what they would like their future to hold. They know the challenges they face . . . and have abundant information about their resources" (p. 124). Clearly, the best source of expertise about a community is the community residents; they have intimate knowledge about the problem they wish to address. Their perspective provides essential subjective information that is not available through objective, static reports or other documentation. The community worker needs to discover what the people know about the challenges they wish to address, how they have addressed them in the past, and what similar or other challenges they have successfully resolved in the past. Building on past successes and avoiding repeating past mistakes contributes to positive momentum in achieving goals.

The term "problem" implies a negative situation—it suggests a lack of something or a barrier of some kind. The worker's fresh view of the situation may provide insights into the fundamental nature of the problem that the community wishes to address. The community worker's outside perspective may also help identify the extent of perceived problems. It is important to be aware of the perceived challenges the community faces, which influence how residents respond to the problem or concern.

While negative elements certainly do exist, it is important to focus also on the positive aspects of a situation, particularly the inherent strengths of the community. Drawing from and building on community strengths—current and potential resources (e.g., people, funds, facilities, programs) as well as local and satellite resources—provides at-hand resources and reduces the need to acquire outside resources. Since the goal of community development is to enable communities to make positive changes for themselves, it is imperative that community resources and structures be self-sustaining so that they function effectively and independently in the long term.

Communities experience challenges as the collective needs of their residents change over time. While all residents may agree that a problem exists, it may be difficult to arrive at a consensus about the true nature and scope of the problem. Before any remedial action can be taken, the problem must first be clearly articulated. The community worker must first know what the community has determined the problem to be. Identifying the problem and determining specific goals provide a starting point for research and action. Understanding how community residents perceive the problem, and their perceptions of needs, is the basis for community work (Cox & Ephross, 1998; Durst, McDonald, & Parsons, 1999). The community worker must then make a thorough assessment of the situation. Once this process is completed, the community worker must check for congruence between this personal assessment and the community's perception of the problem. When both the community worker and the community have parallel views about the nature and scope of the problem, then they can begin working together to address it.

When the problem has been clearly defined, the community worker must clarify both his or her role and the community's role in addressing the problem. The worker's role may be defined by the mandate of the institution, department, or discipline that the individual represents; however, the worker's overall role is to help the community help itself. Both the community worker and the community must be clear about their respective roles and responsibilities. Assumptions about role expectations may lead to misunderstandings that compromise or confound goal achievement.

The history in many First Nations communities is one of "outsiders" deciding what is best for the community, a practice that has promoted dependency and passivity (Erasmus & Ensign, 1991). Under these paternalistic practices, community workers coming into a community were expected to "solve a problem," often through an infusion of funds or the implementation of a program developed with no consultation with community residents. As First Nations communities achieve increasing control in determining and addressing their needs, the expectation that the worker will "fix" the problem is giving way to the proactive view of the community worker as a *facilitator*.

Community Development Skills

A "skill" is a demonstrated competence or mastery—a practised ability. A community worker must be competent in a range of skills associated with many and varied roles as guide, facilitator, educator, and motivator. In this chapter, four broad categories of skills are examined: organizational skills, strategic or political skills, communication skills, and analytical skills. Within each of these categories, several specific types of skills are identified and discussed.

Organizational Skills

The goal of community development is to enable communities to solve problems and take action on their own. To accomplish this, communities must establish structures and processes that allow them to communicate about their needs and to act to address them. Many communities have a variety of committees and hold regular meetings to discuss community business. The worker has expertise in identifying additional structures and processes that are suitable for the community's particular needs. This skill is particularly important if community members do not have a history of organizing to meet shared needs; such community members may lack the knowledge and skills required to build and maintain an organization to meet their needs.

The community worker assists the community to identify, coordinate, and activate resources through established or new structures and processes. The community worker aims to build on community strengths so that the community becomes self-sufficient in its problem-solving efforts.

Strategic/Political Skills

A variety of skills are needed to accurately identify a problem, develop a plan of action, and ensure that the plan is implemented. The successful community worker is adept at recognizing the various and often conflicting concerns of community residents, and in working to accommodate these concerns without compromising the community's collective goals.

Residents in a community may have differing views of the problem and how to address it. The role of the social worker is to help residents work toward a consensus so that each member contributes in a co-operative fashion to resolving the problem. An effective worker assists a community to develop a variety of strategies and activities to address the problem; maximum benefit is derived when all groups work concurrently and co-operatively toward a common goal.

Where discrepancies or conflicts exist between groups of residents, the community worker ensures all parties have the opportunity to express their concerns. When all the concerns have been aired, the worker must be flexible and creative in negotiating a compromise that allows all parties to feel they have been heard and treated fairly.

As discussed in the section on knowledge, an important aspect of "getting things done" is engaging the support and co-operation of those with authority or influence. Gaining the co-operation and support of the political decision-making and service delivery systems is an integral component of ensuring that things get done. The community worker must identify both the internal and external sources of authority and influence and work to secure their co-operation.

In First Nations communities, the internal sources of authority include the chief or chairperson and council members. Internal sources of influence might include elders, other community leaders, and community groups, such as friendship centres. External sources of authority include various levels and departments of government. External sources of influence may be individuals, groups, or agencies with expertise or an interest in some facet of the problem. While these people have no direct control over decisions made in the community, they may provide critical information or direction.

Communication Skills

Communication involves information transmission, reception, and exchange. Clear and accurate information is only one component of effective communications. Information must be transmitted in a manner suitable to both the sender and the receiver. Leigh (1998) offers detailed guidelines for culturally competent communication. In this section, several modes of communication—written, electronic, verbal, and nonverbal—are briefly discussed from the community development perspective.

Written Communication

Western culture relies heavily on the written mode of information transmission. Printed and electronic reports and correspondence are used in a wide variety of disciplines and environments. In order for these transmissions to be effective, they must use language that is unambiguous, free of jargon, and at a level appropriate for the intended readers.

Writing is not a traditional mode of communication among some Aboriginal populations. Like other ethnic cultures with strong oral traditions, important information is passed on verbally through story and narrative. These stories are creative and animated, tactics designed to ensure the information is remembered and retold (Graveline, 1998). These elements of story are not part of the so-called factual, objective, linear information transmission of Western culture. For a community worker who is from a Western culture and is working in an Aboriginal community, awareness of the different ways people transmit important information will assist in understanding not only the words but the meanings to be gleaned from spoken dialogue.

Electronic Communication and the Virtual Community

Simple binary communication started with the telegraph—"a dot and a dash"—and developed into digital electronic technology, revolutionizing the way the world communicates. Technological developments have changed the nature of organizations, including how corporations, governments, and community-based organizations function. Lines of communication and styles of communication are much different than even a decade ago; they require new strategies and the adaptation and application of communicating in "cyberspace" (McNutt, 2000). The community organizer can use electronic technology to communicate to agencies and government departments with instantaneous results. Letters, petitions, and proposals can be distributed around the world with the press of a button. Today, many members of provincial and federal legislatures can be reached with individual emails.

This technology can also be used to build the organization (McNutt, 2000). Members of a community group can be contacted and provided with up-to-date information efficiently and effectively. It can become a virtual community existing in cyberspace with no geographic location (Brueggemann, 2014). Sharing information and coordinating events and activities are critical duties for the community worker, and email can greatly facilitate these functions (Brueggemann, 2014). It is easy to develop mailing lists, which can distribute messages, reports, and information quickly and efficiently to group members. In order to recruit members and promote the goals of the organization, a website can be developed that outlines the organization, its goals, and its activities (Grobman & Grant, 1998; Krause, Stein, & Clark, 1998; McNutt, 2000; Zeff, 1996). A website can also stimulate discussion and debate about central ideas and concerns of the group. Social networking and the Web have become essential tools in fundraising, often called e-philanthropy (Hart, Greenfield, & Haji, 2007).

Social networking sites such as Facebook, Twitter, and LinkedIn can build and maintain relationships among community members through online social networking. Users of Facebook and LinkedIn must register and may create a personal profile, add other users as friends, exchange messages, and receive automatic notifications when their friends update their profiles. In community development, users may form interest groups around common issues and share information *around the clock*. Twitter is an online social networking and microblogging site that allows users to send and read short 140-character text messages called "tweets." Registered users can read and post tweets, but unregistered users can only read them. These networks can be created around common issues and concerns (Brueggemann, 2014), which can be local or globalized. For some, face-to-face meetings can be intimidating when conflicting opinions are present, whereas cyber discussions can free individuals to more accurately voice their opinions. However, the brevity of emails and other forms of electronic communication can foster miscommunication that inadequately explains or shares the emotions behind statements. With cyber communication, the concept of "community" is no longer localized but is now global. Meetings are no longer restricted geographically as members can join in through Web-based sites such as WebEx or Skype.

The computer also offers unlimited access to vast amounts of information. Some federal government departments have useful websites with important data and information. Statistics Canada's site (www.statcan.gc.ca) provides data and analysis on numerous social and economic indicators. The material is available 24 hours a day, 7 days a week. For those working on Aboriginal issues, Indigenous and Northern Affairs Canada offers a website with the latest data and past and current publications (see www.aadnc-aandc.gc.ca). Canadian websites are also available for many anti-poverty and welfare rights groups and can be an invaluable resource for advocating against and resisting poverty and oppression.

While knowledge and competency with personal computers is an essential skill, it is also a vast and complicated field of expertise. No community worker can provide all the knowledge and skills useful in computer application, but a basic knowledge is helpful, as is a willingness to find a person who can offer advice or training on computer-related issues. Not unexpectedly, today's generation has grown up with computers and has the expertise to help a community organization with its computer needs. A community developer would be wise to find the right person and "plug them in" to the organization.

Verbal Communication

The verbal transmission of ideas is perhaps the most common mode of information sharing. Yet miscommunication can occur, even between individuals speaking the same language. Effective speaking involves more than using the right words; it involves using both words and tone that are appropriate to the situation. The intimate greeting between family members in public is not appropriate between strangers; similarly, the casual language of an informal setting such as a party is not necessarily appropriate for formal or diplomatic business. Using both the appropriate language as well as the appropriate degree of formality demonstrates respect between those engaged in verbal information transmission.

In all cultures, verbal transmission should be appropriate to the occasion. In particular, the community worker should know and follow the verbal and social protocols associated with ceremonies or spiritual activities. (For an in-depth discussion on spirituality and social work, see Chapter 11 by Diana Coholic.) These protocols vary among communities, and the community worker must remember that what is deemed appropriate in one community may not necessarily be appropriate in another. In Western culture, verbal discourse is often factual, chronological, linear, and direct, which may conflict with the style of other cultures; such directness may seem rude or controlling by other groups. Aboriginal communities have strong oral traditions that create flexible, narrative, and nondirective modes of expression.

Nonverbal Communication

When people engage in conversation, they transmit meaning not only by their words but also by their tone of voice, expressions, gestures, and body position. Effective communication results when there is congruence between the verbal and the nonverbal messages being sent. The individual who says "I am interested in what is being said and I respect what I am hearing," but who is gazing off into space, drumming his or her fingers on the tabletop, and emitting heavy sighs is demonstrating impatience. Such displays indicate that the person believes that his or her time or opinions are more valuable than those of the person who is speaking. This behaviour does not communicate interest and respect.

Like verbal language, the nonverbal elements of communication are, to a large degree, culturally learned. In Western culture, people commonly use direct eye contact and the animated use of one's hands and arms to reinforce the verbal message. This degree of animation and eye contact is not appropriate in all cultures. Aboriginal communities often display a blend of traditional and Western behaviours. Where direct eye contact might be appropriate for the "Westernized" resident, others may view it as a challenge or a sign of disrespect. A non-Aboriginal worker is more effective when aware of appropriate communications behaviours in the community.

In Western culture, listening is a dynamic and often animated practice. Active listening, where the listener nods, makes short verbal affirmations, and maintains direct eye contact with the speaker, is normally considered an indication that the listener is paying attention and understands what is being said. In Aboriginal cultures, members listen intently and nondemonstratively without excessive head nodding or verbal comments or gestures (Graveline, 1998). Aboriginal people have strong connections to the spiritual aspects of their world, and they connect with this spiritual dimension through silence and reflection. For this reason, silence is considered sacred (Graveline, 1998) and is an integral component of communication. The successful community worker is sensitive to these different listening behaviours, interpreting and responding to them appropriately.

Analytical Skills

The role of the community worker is to synthesize information to offer new perspectives on situations and generate options for change (Krogsrud Miley, O'Melia, & DuBois, 1995). This is achieved by using a variety of analytical skills, including observation and interpretation, assessment, development of an action plan, and evaluation of outcomes.

Well-honed observation skills are essential to community workers, who must assess a situation to facilitate the identification of the problem and assist in the development of an action plan. Workers must learn to interpret what they observe as a function of cultural and environmental influences. The person from a tropical country who experiences snow for the first time would likely have difficulty making an accurate conclusion about what they are seeing; if the concept of "snow" is completely unfamiliar, they have no past experience upon which to draw conclusions about the phenomenon.

People use their past experiences to draw conclusions about what they observe. Over time, as similar experiences are repeated, the step from observation to conclusion becomes automatic. In familiar environments, community workers are likely to make accurate interpretations and conclusions about the phenomena that are observed; however, they must be wary of drawing similar conclusions in a new environment. Workers in a cross-cultural community must be particularly diligent about drawing conclusions from observed behaviours or situations. Behaviour is culturally determined and, therefore, cannot be evaluated by the standards or norms of another culture.

To arrive at an accurate conclusion about a situation or behaviour, the community worker must first understand the norms of the culture. Second, the community worker should observe the community from many perspectives. Finally, the worker must verify her or his conclusions by comparing or discussing them with members of the community who are most familiar with their culture.

Using culturally sensitized observation skills, the community worker is ready to assess with the community the nature of the problem or situation. Some years ago I was involved in an assessment of community needs with a Mi'kmaq community in Atlantic Canada (Durst, McDonald, & Parsons, 1999). The problem was violence against women, and many community members believed the solution was some variation of a women's shelter. They had learned about such shelters from television and other media and had envisioned a small facility that would be located in the centre of this community of less than 700 people. With the community, I assisted in completing a needs assessment, which uncovered a variety of issues such as confidentiality, cost considerations, and organizational problems. The assessment concluded that a community-based women's health/education centre was a better plan. In the end, the Band Council approved the centre, which provided a crisis plan to protect women and children in immediate danger but also provided counselling and parenting supports as well as health and social education.

One component of an assessment includes examining the community's past efforts to address the problem. The worker may wish to consider what strategies were successful in the past, what activities were less successful, and what factors apply to the problem that is presently being addressed. Building on past successes reinforces community strengths, and avoiding past mistakes saves time.

With the conclusion of an assessment, the community worker is ready to help the community develop a plan of action to address the problem. The plan should draw from and build on community strengths while accommodating the constraints and challenges of the situation. Drawing on the community's strengths taps into present and future skills and resources that reinforce the community's ability to make and maintain positive changes.

Another important and sometimes forgotten skill is the ability to evaluate outcomes. Although research and evaluation skills are usually low on a worker's priority list, these skills should be included in the community action. They will be valuable in the early assessment of needs and in the determination of goals and objectives of the organization. They are also necessary in determining whether or not these goals and objectives have been achieved. Clearly the community worker cannot be superhuman, but these skills must not be forgotten. If the worker does not possess them, they should be accessed through another person.

Appropriate Values for Community Work

"Values" are the general standards and ideals by which we judge our own and others' behaviour and guide our actions (Kirst-Ashman & Hull, 2015). Every culture has its own set of values that guides the behaviour of its members. Many values, such as honesty, respect, trustworthiness, co-operation, and compassion, are evident in many different cultures but are expressed in different ways. Community workers must be aware of both their own personal and professional values as well as the values of the community. Sometimes these values conflict and compete, creating ethical dilemmas (Reisch & Lowe, 2000). These situations can be difficult to resolve, creating considerable stress for the worker and the community. Reisch and Lowe (2000) offer some helpful guidelines for resolving these dilemmas, including identifying the issues, establishing ethical rules and criteria, and resolving issues of conflict of interest. They also suggest ranking and prioritizing the rules and listing the consequences of various choices.

Community Workers' Personal and Professional Values

Community workers' personal and professional values reflect their commitment to enabling others to make positive changes for themselves. Indispensable to such work are the values of dignity: respect for oneself, for one's clients, and for individual differences, and confidentiality. First, dignity and respect—including self-respect—are fundamental for community workers, helping them to interact in a positive and successful manner with clients and colleagues. Second, while community workers must recognize the collective values of a community's culture, they must also acknowledge and prize the strengths in individual difference. Each person has a unique contribution to make, regardless of education, training, and experience. Finally, personal and professional confidentiality engenders trust and confidence between the community worker and community residents. This trust builds strong, productive relationships that contribute to goal achievement.

Accountability

Accountability—that is, being responsible for the consequences of one's actions—is important in any relationship. It is particularly important in the relationship between the worker and the community members where the worker's actions have such significant and long-term ramifications. Earlier in the chapter we discussed how the orientation of the community worker must fit with the goals and values of the community. The strategies and tactics employed must reflect the value base of both the worker and the community. Community workers must understand that they are accountable for their actions. This raises some questions about civil disobedience and extreme or militant actions.

To achieve shared community objectives, workers may be asked to participate in simple distortions or exaggerations of the truth or in personal attacks. This situation may not be a problem for one community worker but could be a serious ethical decision for another. In a more extreme situation, this same worker may be asked, encouraged, or even pressured into engaging in questionable tactics such as lying, stealing, or vandalizing property (Reisch & Lowe, 2000). The international organization Greenpeace is well known for its extreme measures, including illegal activities, which are justified, in the minds of the activists, as ways to generate publicity and exert political pressure on powerful institutions, both government and corporate. In other cases, one protester in Alberta resorted to bombing oil wells and oil installations to publicize his political message, while others in Quebec have assaulted political and corporate executives with cream pies. The judicial courts have taken these actions seriously, handing down sentences that reflect the belief that such actions cannot be tolerated. Finally, some groups and workers may consider violent activities and even terrorism directed at civilians as justified. Although terrorist acts are rare in Canada, the international community, including the United States, has experienced the horrors of violent terrorism. Ultimately, community workers are accountable for their actions and may need to seriously consider the implications of community action that involves civil disobedience or more extreme acts. Well-respected Canadian scholar Bill Lee expands this discussion and offers some guidelines for making hard choices (Lee, 1999).

Diversity in Values and the Aboriginal Worldview

Many ethnic communities have been exposed to Western values and practices. For practical purposes, some diverse people and communities have adopted Western practices to facilitate interaction with the dominant Western culture. Community workers in cross-cultural communities must keep in mind that the adoption of Western practices does not necessarily mean adoption of Western values.

For example, Lum highlights some of the differences in values between Western culture and that of ethnic minorities, including Aboriginal cultures: "The mainstream society tends to emphasize human control of the environment, future orientation, individual autonomy, competitiveness and upward mobility, and the nuclear family. Ethnic minorities focus on harmony with the environment, reminiscence about the past and pleasure in the present, collectivity, self-discipline and endurance of suffering, and the extended family" (Lum, 1992, p. 86). While Lum's generalizations are rather broad, they do identify some of the key areas in which Western and non-Western values differ regarding issues such as the environment, the community, and the family. With other colleagues, I have explored how Western social work values conflict with Vietnamese values as they relate to social work (Durst, Lanh, & Pitzel, 2010). Vietnamese social workers have very different orientations to the ways in which they understand society. These differences influence and shape social welfare and include cultural views of poverty, empowerment, equality, and self-determination.

Just as each culture has its own norms and values, so too does each community, including each multicultural community. Aboriginal communities do, however, share some fundamental values that arise out of their common worldview. According to Graveline (1998), the Aboriginal worldview was the common sense foundation of early tribal existence. People were dependent on the Earth to provide what they needed for survival; they cherished and nurtured the Earth so it would sustain them physically and spiritually. They cherished and respected all things in the world, including all that is animate and inanimate; visible and invisible; past, present, and future.

Aboriginal values, beliefs, and practices, including immanence and spirituality, interconnectedness, harmony, and holism, arise out of their worldview. This worldview recognizes that each person is intimately and dependently connected with all other forms and forces of life, and that a person is whole and healthy physically, mentally, and spiritually only when that individual is in harmony and balance with the life elements.

While Western culture is increasingly scientific and the rejection of spiritual values is common, many Aboriginal people are rediscovering and revaluing their unique spirituality. Graveline (1998) posits that Aboriginal spirituality is universal and that it coexists in all aspects of life—it resides in the essence of the person, in the community, and among the people. The community worker in an Aboriginal community must recognize the value of this process of spiritual rediscovery and incorporate it into a holistic approach to both Aboriginal personal development and the social work interventions practised in their communities (Feehan & Hannis, 1993).

"Aboriginal Traditionalists have long recognized the link between individual responsibility and community well-being" (Graveline, 1998, p. 57). For Aboriginal people, this link is the foundation of a network with many complex interrelationships and multiple roles that constitute their community. The community is the dominant system; individuals, families, friends, and extended families are interdependent (Feehan & Hannis, 1993). These complex and interdependent relationships must be foremost in any community development initiative. The community worker must ensure that initiatives accommodate and strengthen these relationships, which are the foundation of the community itself.

The Aboriginal worldview perceives life and the world as cyclical and connected. Past, present, and future are infinite and interconnected, not separate, quantifiable, and controllable by people. For Aboriginal people, time is based on a ceremonial and circular understanding of order and harmony (Graveline, 1998). It is more important for an Aboriginal person to be in harmony with self and ritual. This is in direct contrast to the Western attitude toward time as an external, artificial, and often arbitrary construct to be measured, parcelled out, and used to control behaviour.

Summary and Conclusion

The signposts of our villages, towns, and cities are changing. New organizations and community groups are showing their presence in towns and villages that were once "homogeneous" across the nation. These Canadians are expressing themselves and participating in society in new ways through development and organization at the community level, making this nation truly multicultural and multiethnic in ways previously unseen. These changes include new ways of social work practice, including community work.

In this chapter I have argued that successful community development is based on the community worker's ability to understand and influence behaviour to enable community residents to make positive changes for themselves. Community workers must have a thorough understanding of self—what motivates and constrains their own behaviour—before they can effectively influence the behaviour of others. In addition to knowing and understanding human behaviour, community workers must have knowledge of the community as well as academic and professional knowledge specific to the type of community development they will pursue.

Social workers in community development must develop competency in a broad range of organizational, strategic/political, communication, and analytical skills to address their many roles as guide, facilitator, educator, and motivator. Such workers, by virtue of the vocation of working with people, embrace values that respect all people. Successful community workers know and respect the values of the client community, even where those values differ from their own.

Community development and its complexity are essential areas of practice that are often neglected in many schools of social work in Canada. It is normally identified in the mission statements of social programs but often it receives little attention, with student emphasis on working with individuals, families, and groups. This chapter argues for its importance for practice, and with Canada's diverse population it is a critical discussion. Good community practice does not "just happen"; it takes concentrated effort.

In contemporary ethnic communities, much of the members' knowledge of themselves and many of their values are re-emerging from their traditional past, before the disruptive and destructive influences of immigration, forced integration, racism, and, for Aboriginal people, colonialism. For the social worker in a multicultural community, understanding and respecting the self and possessing knowledge, skills, and values of anti-racist and multicultural practice is the foundation for successful community development. Travelling in these new times, it is well worth observing the additions of new groups and organizations that have proudly taken their place on the signposts of each village and town. On leaving, most communities have a proud signpost saying "Come Again."

Questions for Review

1. How can a community be defined by ethnicity and not geography? Can you give an example?
2. There are different models of community practice presented in this chapter. How do they differ from each other?
3. As practitioners, we use strategies to accomplish goals. What three strategies are presented in this chapter and where and when would you use each?
4. Why is knowledge of the community so important to competent and culturally sensitive practice?
5. Electronic technology has changed the way we communicate. Explain how you see this change and what you see for the future.
6. One's values are critical for community practice. In what ways do workers see conflicting and congruent personal and professional values?

Suggested Readings and Resources

Brueggemann, W. G. (2014). *The practice of macro social work* (4th ed.). Independence, KY: Cengage Learning.

Bruyere, G. (2010). The decolonization wheel: An Aboriginal perspective on social work practice with Aboriginal peoples. In K. Brownlee, R. Neckoway, R. Delaney, & D. Durst (Eds.), *Social work and Aboriginal peoples: Perspectives from Canada's rural and provincial norths* (pp. 1–11). Thunder Bay, ON: Centre for Northern Studies. Lakehead University.

Lingam, L. (2013). Development theories and community development practice. In M. Weil (Ed.), *The handbook of community practice* (2nd ed., pp. 195–213). Thousand Oaks, CA: Sage Publications, Inc.

Ohmer, M. L., & Brooks III, F. (2013). The practice of community organizing: Comparing and contrasting conflict and consensus approaches. In M. Weil (Ed.), *The handbook of community practice* (2nd ed., pp. 233–48). Thousand Oaks, CA: Sage Publications, Inc.

Reisch, M., & Thursz, D. (2013). Radical community organizing. In M. Weil (Ed.), *The handbook of community practice* (2nd ed., pp. 361–82). Thousand Oaks, CA: Sage Publications, Inc.

Rothman, J., Erlich, J. L., & Tropman, J. E. (Eds.). (2001). *Strategies of community intervention* (6th ed.). Itasca, IL: F.E. Peacock Publisher, Inc.

Note

1. For the purpose of this report, the term "First Nations peoples" is used to describe persons who are status Indians as defined by the Indian Act. The phrase "Aboriginal peoples" is a broader term used to define all those who identify as being of Aboriginal ancestry and may be of mixed background. The term is used to include status and non-status Indians, Métis, and Inuit persons.

References

Bradshaw, C., Soifer, S., & Gutierrez, L. (1993). Toward a hybrid model for effective organizing in communities of color. *Journal of Community Practice, 1*(1), 25–42.

Brueggemann, W. G. (2014). *The practice of macro social work* (4th ed.). Independence, KY: Cengage Learning.

Bruyere, G. (2010). The decolonization wheel: An Aboriginal perspective on social work practice with Aboriginal peoples. In K. Brownlee, R. Neckoway, R. Delaney, & D. Durst (Eds.), *Social work and Aboriginal peoples: Perspectives from Canada's rural and provincial norths* (pp. 1–11). Thunder Bay, ON: Centre for Northern Studies, Lakehead University.

Carlton-LaNey, I., & Burwell, N. Y. (Eds.). (1996). *African American community practice models: Historical and contemporary responses.* New York, NY: Haworth Press.

Cox, C. B., & Ephross, P. H. (1998). *Ethnicity and social work practice.* New York, NY: Oxford University Press.

Dasgupta, S. (1996). *The community in Canada: Rural and urban.* Lanham, MA: University Press of America, Inc.

Dominelli, L. (1988). *Anti-racist social work: A challenge for white practitioners and educators.* London, UK: Macmillan.

Durst, D. (2010). A turbulent journey: Self-government of social services. In K. Brownlee, R. Neckoway, R. Delaney, & D. Durst (Eds.), *Social work and Aboriginal peoples: Perspectives from Canada's rural and provincial norths* (pp. 70–88). Thunder Bay, ON: Centre for Northern Studies. Lakehead University.

Durst, D., Lanh, T. H., & Pitzel, M. (2010). A comparative analysis of social work in Vietnam and Canada: Rebirth and renewal. *Journal of Comparative Social Work, 2,* 1–12.

Durst, D., McDonald, J., & Parsons, D. (1999). Finding our way: A community needs assessment on violence in Native families. *Journal of Community Practice, 6*(1), 45–69.

Erasmus, P., & Ensign, G. (1991). *A practical framework for community liaison work in Native communities.* Brandon, MB: Justin Publishing.

Feehan, K., & Hannis, D. (1993). *From strength to strength: Social work education and Aboriginal people.* Edmonton, AB: Grant MacEwan Community College.

Fleras, A., & Elliott, J. L. (1999). *Unequal relations: An introduction to race, ethnic, and Aboriginal dynamics in Canada* (3rd ed.). Toronto, ON: Prentice Hall/Allyn Bacon.

Graveline, F. J. (1998). *Circle works: Transforming Eurocentric consciousness.* Halifax, NS: Fernwood Press.

Grobman, G. M., & Grant, G. B. (1998). *The nonprofit Internet handbook.* Harrisburg, PA: White Hat Communications.

Gutierrez, L., & Alvarez, A. R. (2000). Educating students for multicultural community practice. In D. Hardina (Ed.), *Innovative approaches for teaching community organization skills in the classroom* (pp. 39–56). New York, NY: Haworth Press.

Gutierrez, L., & Lewis, E. (1994). Community organizing with women of color: A feminist approach. *Journal of Community Practice, 1,* 23–44.

Hardina, D. (Ed.). (2000). *Innovative approaches for teaching community organization skills in the classroom.* New York, NY: Haworth Press.

Harper, K. V., & Lantz, J. (1996). *Cross-cultural practice: Social work with diverse populations.* Chicago, IL: Lyceum Books.

Hart, T., Greenfield, J. M., & Haji, S. D. (2007). *People to people fundraising: Social networking and Web 2.0 for charities*. Hoboken, NJ: John Wiley & Sons, Inc.

Herberg, D. C. (1993). *Frameworks for cultural and racial diversity: Teaching and learning for practitioners*. Toronto, ON: Canadian Scholars' Press.

Hick, S. (2010). *Social work in Canada: An introduction*. Toronto, ON: Thompson Educational Publishing, Inc.

Hick, S., Fook, J., & Pozzuto, R. (2005). *Social work: A critical turn*. Toronto, ON: Thompson Educational Publishing, Inc.

Hillery, G. A., Jr. (1955). Definitions of community: Areas of agreement. *Rural Sociology, 20*, 779–91.

Ife, J., & Tesoriero, F. (2006). *Community development: Community-based alternatives in an age of globalization* (3rd ed.). Frenchs Forest, NSW: Pearson Education Australia.

Kirst-Ashman, K. K., & Hull, G. H., Jr. (2015). *Understanding generalist practice* (7th ed.). Stamford, CT: Cengage Learning.

Krause, A., Stein, M., & Clark, J. (1998). *The virtual activist: A training course*. Netaction. Retrieved from www.netaction.org/training

Krogsrud Miley, K., O'Melia, M., & DuBois, B. L. (1995). *Generalist social work practice: An empowering approach*. Boston, MA: Allyn and Bacon.

Ledwith, M., & Asgill, P. (2007). Feminist, antiracist community development: Critical alliance, local to global. In L. Dominelli (Ed.), *Revitalising communities in a globalising world* (pp. 107–22). Hampshire, UK: Ashgate Publishing Limited.

Lee, B. (1999). *Pragmatics of community organization* (3rd ed.). Toronto, ON: Commonact Press.

Leigh, J. W. (1998). *Communicating for cultural competence*. Needham Heights, MA: Allyn and Bacon.

Lingam, L. (2013). Development theories and community development practice. In M. Weil, (Ed.), *The handbook of community practice* (2nd ed., pp. 195–213). Thousand Oaks, CA: Sage Publications, Inc.

Lum, D. (1992). *Social work with people of color: A process-stage approach*. Pacific Grove, CA: Brooks/Cole.

Lyon, L. (1987). *The community in urban society*. Chicago, IL: Dorsey Press.

McDonald, L., Pittaway, E., & Nahmiash, D. (1995). Issues in practice with respect to mistreatment of older people. In M. J. Maclean (Ed.), *Abuse and neglect of older Canadians: Strategies for change* (pp. 5–16). Ottawa, ON: Canadian Association on Gerontology.

McNutt, J. (1995). The macro practice curriculum in graduate social work education: The results of a national study. *Administration in Social Work, 19*, 59–74.

McNutt, J. (2000). Organizing cyberspace: Strategies for teaching about community practice and technology. In D. Hardina (Ed.), *Innovative approaches for teaching community organization skills in the classroom* (pp. 95–109). New York, NY: Haworth Press.

Munoz, C. (1989). *Youth identity and power: The Chicano movement*. London, UK: Verso.

Ohmer, M. L., & Brooks III, F. (2013). The practice of community organizing: Comparing and contrasting conflict and consensus approaches. In M. Weil (Ed.), *The handbook of community practice* (2nd ed., pp. 233–48). Thousand Oaks, CA: Sage Publications, Inc.

Reisch, M., & Thursz, D. (2013). Radical community organizing. In M. Weil (Ed.), *The handbook of community practice* (2nd ed., pp. 361–82). Thousand Oaks, CA: Sage Publications, Inc.

Reisch, M., & Lowe, J. I. (2000). Of means and ends revisited: Teaching ethical community organizing in an unethical society. In D. Hardina (Ed.), *Innovative approaches for teaching community organization skills in the classroom* (pp. 19–38). New York, NY: Haworth Press.

Rivera, F. G., & Erlich, J. L. (1995). *Community organizing in a diverse society* (2nd ed.). Needham Heights, MA: Allyn and Bacon.

Rothman, J. (1995). Approaches to community intervention. In F. Cox, J. Erlich, J. Rothman, & J. Tropman (Eds.), *Strategies of community organization* (4th ed., pp. 26–63). Itasca, IL: F. E. Peacock Publisher, Inc..

Rothman, J., Erlich, J. L., & Tropman, J. E. (Eds.). (2001). *Strategies of community intervention* (6th ed.). Itasca, IL: F. E. Peacock Publisher, Inc.

Rubin, H. J., & Rubin, I. (1986). *Community organizing and development*. Columbus, OH: Merrill Publishing.

St. Onge, P. (2013). Cultural competency: Organizations and diverse populations. In M. Weil (Ed.), *The handbook of community practice* (2nd ed., pp. 425–44). Thousand Oaks, CA: Sage Publications, Inc.

Strega, S. (2015). The view from the poststructural margins: Epistemology and methodology reconsidered. In L. Brown & S. Strega (Eds.), *Research as resistance: Critical, Indigenous, & anti-oppressive approaches* (2nd ed., pp. 119–52). Toronto, ON: Canadian Scholar's Press.

Taylor, S. H., & Roberts, R. W. (Eds.). (1985). *Theory and practice of community social work*. New York, NY: Columbia University Press.

Warren, R. (1971). Types of purposive social change at the community level. In R. Warren (Ed.), *Truth, love, and social change* (pp. 134–49). Chicago, IL: Rand McNally.

Weil, M., & Gamble, D. (1995). Community practice models. In R. L. Edwards (Ed.), *Encyclopedia of social work* (19th ed., pp. 577–94). Washington, DC: National Association of Social Workers.

West, G. (1990). Cooperation and conflict among women in the welfare rights movement. In L. Albrecht & R. Brewer (Eds.), *Bridges of power: Women's multicultural alliances* (pp. 149–71). Philadelphia, PA: New Society Publishers.

Wharf, B., & Clague, M. (Eds.). (1997). *Community organizing: Canadian experiences*. Toronto, ON: Oxford University Press.

Zeff, R. (1996). *The nonprofit guide to the Internet*. New York, NY: Wiley.

Part III

Social Work with Diverse Populations

Today's world requires social workers to be able to understand diversity and to work with it effectively to deliver more comprehensive and inclusive services. Social workers need to be able to understand their own identities and those of their clients. The nature of differences varies from one situation to the next; people are never utterly alike even if they come from the same or even a similar socio-cultural community.

This section guides the reader through these vital matters of diversity of race, language, ethnicity, sexuality, spirituality, and social status and illustrates the connections these socio-cultural characteristics have with social category, social identity, and social position, while also considering the impact of our own social positions on providing social work practice within Canada.

Part III Contents

Multiple Positionality and Intersectionality

Toward a Dialogical Social Work Approach

By *Miu Chung Yan*

Chapter Objectives

This chapter will help you develop an understanding of:

- Key concepts such as social category, social position, positionality, and intersectionality and their relevance to social work with diversity
- The complexity of clients' social positions and the intersectional effects of these positions on their predicament and the social work process
- Your own social positions and their intersectional effects, particularly on your relationship with clients and the social work process
- How to rethink the ideas of dialogical and reflexive social work practice

Introduction

When someone asks us, "Who are you?" our minds may come up with many possible answers. Instead of telling the inquirer all the possible answers that may be in our minds, often we tell them only a couple of things that we think are useful for the purpose of and are relevant to the context in which the inquirer asked the question. For instance, when I make a restaurant booking for dinner with friends, I will probably tell the inquirer that I am Mr Yan. However, if the booking is for business, I may tell them I am Professor Yan from the UBC School of Social Work. In both cases, it would be strange if I were to tell the inquirer my gender, age, class status, sexual orientation, (dis)ability, citizenship (or immigrant) status, and so on, all of which are some of the possible answers in my mind that I might use to tell people who I am. Each of these answers also constitutes a label that we use to identify who we are.

Naming ourselves by using these labels is an **identification** process through which we disclose our **social identity**. Meanwhile, the label also serves as a signifier of our membership in a group of people who share the same **social category**. In our daily lives, we always categorize things, people, phenomena, and ideas. However, social categorization is not just a banal act done to help organize the messy everyday encounters of numerous things, people, phenomena, and ideas. In particular, social categories that we use to classify people are products of a social construction process through which people are included or excluded from a certain categorical collective. The word "social" implies a shared understanding of the meaning among not only members classified in the same category, but also people of the larger society that employ this social category to divide people into groups.

Furthermore, by placing or being placed in a certain social category, we position ourselves or are set in a particular **social position**. Sociologically speaking, not all social positions are equal. Instead, they are structurally distributed within a hierarchy of social power that determines people's access to social, political, and economic resources. For instance, referring to myself as either Mr Yan or Professor Yan may place me into two different categories: just a regular patron or a member of a prestigious profession at a respectable educational institution. The latter one positions me in a higher social status and may secure me a better table. However, in both cases the inquirer will also classify me as a member of the Chinese immigrant group based on my last name Yan (and probably my thick Chinese accent). In other words, among all the social positions that we have, some are more privileged and advantageous, and others are more deprived and oppressed.

Analytically we can separate each social category to examine its meaning and impact on an individual who classifies himself or herself or is classified in a particular category. However, such an analysis is problematic for at least two interrelated reasons. First, each person has multiple social identities, each of which locates the person in a specific social position. Except for a very small group, most people will have a mix of privileged and disadvantaged social positions. In other words, we are privileged in some ways but deprived in others. Second, although we can analytically examine the nature and meaning of each social identity (and its positional effect) that we have had, in our everyday lives they are not always separable and isolated from each other. Instead, they **intersect** each other and generate an **interlocking** effect, for good and for bad, shaping our life conditions and interactions with others.

Going back to my story, the actual table to which I end up being assigned may depend on many factors, some of which may simply be practical ones, such as the availability of tables. While I think that telling the inquirer that I am a professor may secure me a better table, being classified as a member of the Chinese immigrant group may deprive me of this "advantage." Meanwhile, among all the factors, who the inquirer is and how he or she perceives my social identities is also crucial. After all, it is the inquirer who decides which table I will have. He or she is also someone who has multiple identities that locate him or her in different social positions. In other words, even in a simple table booking situation, it is not just a straightforward conversation between two people. Behind the conversation is an interplay of multiple social positions embodied in the speakers and possibly also a **strategic exchange** of social power embedded in their multiple social positions.

Social Position, Understanding, and Social Work

Among all the helping professions, the social work professional tends to be positioned as a gatekeeper and distributor of social resources. Thus, these concepts—social identity, social category, social position, and intersectionality—are critical to social work practice, particularly in a **superdiverse society** like Canada in which the influx of culturally and racially different immigrants has made people more conscious of both their and others' "plurality of affiliations" to different social groups and "the coexistence of cohesion and separateness" among and between them (Vertovec, 2007). It is important for social workers to be critically aware of how the intersection of their own social positions may affect their intervention and relationship with their clients who also embody a dynamic set of social positions. From a social justice perspective, a lack of reflexivity regarding how our and our clients' multiple social positions have an impact on our interaction with each other may deprive our clients' access to social resources and reinforce the unjust social positions in which our clients are being trapped.

Meanwhile, interpretive social work scholars (e.g., Goldstein, 1986; Saleebey, 1994), who articulate the social work process as a meaning-generating process, have long argued that the social work process always involves *at least* two human beings. To them, social work intervention is a collaborative project between social workers and their clients, through interaction and mutual interpretation, "in pursuit of understanding and meaning that is relevant to the client's life" (Goldstein, 1986, p. 355). The generation of meaning process can be understood as a **self-indication process** in which the engaging actors will symbolically, constantly, and mutually interpret, evaluate (define), and respond to each other (Blumer, 1969). However, the questions we are concerned with are how two human beings who come with a set of intersecting social identities located in different social positions can work together to generate this shared meaning, and how do the multiple social positions of a social worker and his or her client influence the self-indication process of an effective social work intervention? To answer these questions and to ground the discussion of these concepts in social work practice, an actual case is used to help illustrate their meaning and implication for social work practice. This case is a modification of a real story of a child protection worker.

Case Example 6.1

A teacher of a 10-year-old immigrant boy, Y, suspected that Y was being physically abused by his father. His face was swollen with signs of having been slapped. The teacher reported this case to the child protection agency. Kate, who identified herself as a local-born woman, 25 years old, lesbian, single, White Anglo-Saxon, non-Protestant, and without any disability, was a child protection worker in one of the metropolitan cities of Canada. She was assigned to this case.

Kate met with Y and his father, Mr X, at the school. The mother was not present. She had been visiting her family in her home country for a few months because her father was ill. When Kate met with Y alone, he begged her not to charge his father, whom he respected and loved. The boy told her sincerely that, although his father occasionally would use some minor corporal punishment such as hitting with his palm, his father would never have beaten him so seriously if he had not lied about his homework so many times. His father always wanted him to study hard and be successful.

Kate found it extremely difficult to start her investigation because Mr X would not answer her questions. Instead, Mr X, who was in his early 40s, questioned Kate about her age, marital status, and if she had any children. Mr X also claimed that corporal punishment was normal in the culture of the Asian country from which they migrated to Canada. Kate did not feel there was any immediate threat to Y. She arranged a home visit the next day to investigate the situation further.

After the first meeting, Mr X heard from his friends that the police might become involved and the social worker, Kate, also had the power to remove Y, the only *child* of the X family, if Mr X did not co-operate with her. Mr X thought that it would be detrimental to his family if the police became involved. Mr X and his family came to Canada three years ago and still had only permanent resident status. Given the recently tightened immigration policy, he worried that a successful charge might imply a repatriation of him and his family back to their home country. During Kate's home visit, Mr X had changed his attitude and became very co-operative. Later, Kate found out that Mr X did in fact physically punish Y, who had lied to his father several times by saying that he had done all his homework when he had not. She also found out that prior to moving to Canada, Mr X had been a senior engineer of a large factory in his home country. He was now working as a server in the meat section of an ethnic supermarket and financially supporting his wife's family in his home country.

Social Identity, Social Category, and Social Dimension

To simplify our discussion, I will focus mainly on the two major actors in this case, Kate and Mr X, both of whom have multiple social identities. In Table 6.1 I have listed eight possible identities that we will find useful in this particular discussion (although there are many more than just eight). After a quick glance at these identities, we may see that they are organized along eight different **social dimensions.** In each social dimension, there is a specific axis of social power that divides people into at least two different but intertwined asymmetrical social categories that allow one social group to exert control over another to secure its position of dominance in the system (Weber, 1998). For instance, the axis of social power in the social dimension of gender is a form of patriarchal power that traditionally privileges men and subjugates women to men's authority.

Table 6.1 List of Social Identities

Social Dimension	Social Category	
	Kate	**Mr X**
Gender	Female	Male
Ethnicity	Canadian with Anglo-Saxon heritage	Asian*
Race	White	Visible minority
Class	Middle class (professional)	Lower class (manual worker)
Citizenship status	Citizen of Canada	Permanent resident in Canada
Sexual orientation	Homosexual	Heterosexual
Age	Younger	Older
Organizational status	Child protection worker	Suspected child abuser

*Asian is not an ethnic label. It is used here only for discussion purposes.

This axis of social power not only divides people into different social groups but also creates a boundary between these groups that includes and excludes people from each one, and thus from each other—majority versus minority, dominant versus marginalized, oppressor versus oppressed. On one hand, the boundary generates a sense of "we versus others," differentiating between ourselves and others (Yuval-Davis, 2006), and on the other hand the boundary homogenizes members of each social group within some collective attributes (Anthias, 2013b).

Thus, a social category is not just a tool for selecting, sorting, and ordering people into different social groups (Staunaes, 2003). It also has a political–economic function to differentiate and position people hierarchically into different classes in the socio-economic system of a society (Anthias, 2013b, p. 7). This differentiation is therefore political. In different historical situations, this axis of social power in each social dimension differentiated the degree of access people in separate social categories would have to economic, political, and cultural resources (Yuval-Davis, 2006). Along the axis of social power in each social dimension, some people are marginalized into a disadvantaged social category. **Marginalization** is a form of oppression that isolates disadvantaged people from useful participation in the socio-economic system and even potentially leaves them in extreme poverty (Young, 1990).

Throughout history, people have used different means to validate the unequal differentiation of social power between different social groups. Perhaps the most powerful means is by naturalizing the power difference and unequal conditions between groups. Learning from Foucault (1980), we can argue that often this is done by a discursive practice that naturalizes the domination of a particular social category (or group) by making its socio-cultural norms and practices the normative standard. As Staunaes (2003) observes, a social category is made and sustained by the daily interaction of both people who are classified inside and outside that category "in relation to normative conceptions of in/appropriateness" (p. 11) within a particular situation. The normative "conception of in/appropriateness" is naturalized as a hegemonic form of mutual knowledge that informs our social interaction.

Social Identity, Mutual Knowledge, and Normalcy

Identifying with or being identified as a member of a social category indicates our taking up of a social identity. When taking up a social identity, we subscribe to or are assumed by others to subscribe to a set of mutual knowledge inscribed to members of a particular social category. As some social psychologists (e.g., Burk & Stets, 2009) argue, a social identity bears two mutually reinforced functional characteristics: (1) "knowledge of belonging" to a social group, and (2) "emotional and evaluative signification" caused by being a member of this group (Deschamps & Devos, 1998, p. 5). This knowledge informs us of what will be expected of us as a member of that social group, what norms we need to follow, and how we should perform appropriately as a member of that social group. Like cultural tools (Swindler, 1986), it provides resources for people to make sense of their situations and make their social environment predictable (Burk & Stets, 2009). (For more on social identity and social work, see Chapter 12 by Christine A. Walsh, Carey Mulligan, and Gio Dolcecore.)

This set of mutual knowledge is often used in an unconscious manner, which Giddens (1984) calls "practical consciousness." As he argues, humans are inherently knowledgeable beings who have acquired a fund of mutual knowledge that is needed for them to function in a particular historical and spatial context in a particular social position. Hidden in our memories, unconscious knowledge becomes the "practical consciousness which consists of all the things which actors know tacitly about how to 'go on' in the contexts of social life without being able to give them direct discursive expression" (Giddens, 1984, p. xxiii). Consequently, during interactions with others, individuals, who can monitor their own acts as ones being expected, also "expect others to do the same for their own; they also routinely monitor aspects, social and physical, of the contexts in which they move" (Giddens, 1984, p. 5). Actors may not be fully aware of why they have acted in a certain way before the action is done, but they are always capable of providing reasons why they did so afterwards.

Indeed, by repeating their activities in a form of routinization, individuals will have a sense of predictability, structure, and security (Giddens, 1984). Members of a social group impose or forge the shared meanings of a group in terms of "the shared cultural forms, social situation, and history that group members know as theirs," which partially constitutes individuals by forming their sense of history, affinity, and separateness, and even their mode of reasoning, evaluating, and expressing feeling (Young, 1990, pp. 44–5). In other words, this set of mutual knowledge is also useful for our psychological well-being.

Yet this set of unconscious knowledge is not only a resource for manoeuvring ourselves in different social situations. It also has a regulative function that defines what is *intelligible* (Butler, 2006), *normative,* and *legitimate* (Brah, 1996) for the members of the social group to do or not to do (and even to think or not to think) when they are interacting not only with other members of the same group but also, more importantly, with nonmembers in the greater social context. Indeed, the manifestation of our social identity (a membership in a social group) is often in relation to the actual or imagined presence of an "other" (Bhabha, 1994; Ropers-Huilman & Winters, 2010) who is categorically different from us. The other is not just an individual. He or she is also a part of a collective of people classified in the same way *but* into a social category that is physically, socially, or culturally different from ours. Both the other and we ourselves are located in different social positions, and our interaction is regulated by the power difference between us. As a form of practical consciousness, we tend to subscribe to this power difference along with the naturalized and hegemonic discourse that differentiated us.

At different moments in history and in different societies, different social categories have been identified as having a prominent marginalizing effect. Returning to the case example, I selectively highlighted eight social dimensions that are particularly noticeable in Canada. In Canada, the Canadian Charter of Rights and Freedoms (1982) has explicitly given protection to people who are disadvantaged because of their "race, national or ethnic origin, colour, religion, sex, age, mental disability and physical disability" (Section 15(2)) and later in 1998 the Supreme Court added sexual orientation to this list. In other words, in Canada the public discourse agrees and recognizes that these are some social dimensions in which people can be divided into advantaged or disadvantaged social groups.

Based on what we know, we sort and place Kate and Mr X in different pairs of intertwined social categories along the eight social dimensions. Each identity pairing also signifies their different social position located on a social power axis. In a simplistic way, we can say that Kate is privileged and powerful in terms of her ethnicity and race while Mr X is better off in his gender and sexual orientation. Also, as a middle-class social work professional representing a formal institution, Kate is more powerful than Mr X, a manual service worker who is also suspected to be a child abuser. However, is this binary and additive–subtractive analytical model useful to Kate in analyzing her work with Mr X and reaching a shared understanding with Mr X in this suspected child abuse incidence?

Intersectionality

Before we answer this question, we need to problematize the assumption that social categories are independent from each other and can be separated for analytical purposes. So far we have argued that in each social dimension the axis of social power asymmetrically divides people into *at least* two categories: one privileged and one marginalized. However, critical race feminists have questioned if this kind of static, binary, and singular analysis is enough for us to understand the predicament of many non-White women. For instance, in the United States, based on the experiences of low-income Black women, Collins (1990) argues that the oppression they experience cannot be understood by a separate analysis of how each of the social categories (woman, poor, and black) works. Instead, the power axis of gender, class, and race are connected in an interlocking manner to form a matrix of domination that leads to the predicament of many low-income Black women in the United States.

Following a similar analytical methodology, Crenshaw (1991) coins the term **"intersectionality"** to explain how gender and race intersect in shaping the understanding of violence against women in different social domains, including social welfare, political and judicial systems, and the mass media. This concept of intersectionality has become "a fast traveling concept" (Knapp, 2005, cited in Anthias, 2013a, p. 125) that has been extended to not only the intersection of gender and race but many other social dimensions, such as class, age, sexual orientation, (dis)ability, and so on.

Recently, the transformational nature of the intersectionality approach has also received attention in social work literature (e.g., Hulko, 2009; Mehrotra, 2010; Mullaly, 2010; Murphy, Hunt, Zajicek, Norris, & Hamilton, 2009). As members of a profession that has a high commitment to social justice, social workers require an analytical tool for understanding the multiple forms of oppression challenging their clients and to inform their practice, which should aim at transforming, instead of perpetuating, social injustice. This approach prompts anti-oppressive social work practitioners to critically examine their own assumptions of how oppression operates. As Murphy et al. (2009) suggest, the intersectionality approach offers a holistic analytic framework of oppression that is both broad enough to cover the multifaceted dimensions of human experience and deep enough "to capture both the structure and dynamic consequences of the interaction between two or more axes of subordination" (Crenshaw, 2000, quoted in Murphy et al., 2009, p. 2).

Intersectionality is not about social categories but the axis of power that shapes them. From an intersectionality point of view, Crenshaw (1991) rejects the "vulgar constructionist" (p. 1241) logic that social power embedded in each social dimension is exercised simply through a process of categorization and generates social and material consequences unique to that very dimension. As Brah and Pheonix (2004) suggest, intersectionality signifies the "complex, irreducible, varied, and variable effects which ensue when multiple axis of differentiation—economic, political, cultural, psychic, subjective and experiential—intersect in historically specific contexts" (p. 76). As such, the experience and practice of our social lives and conditions are mutually constituted by all interrelated social categories and their underlying social power.

The mutual constitution is not simply an addition to or a subtraction from the social power of the different social categories that we bring into the intersectional analysis. For instance, Kate is not just White + middle class + social worker + Canadian – woman – lesbian – younger. Indeed, these social categories are often related to each other in multiple ways: reinforcing, supporting and catalyzing, or contradicting and conflicting. Proponents of intersectionality have tried different analytic models to explain methodologically how intersection works (Mehrotra, 2010; Walby, Armstrong, & Strid, 2012). McCall (2005) summarizes them into three major approaches to understanding how intersectionality works.

The first approach is "anti-categorical complexity," which tends to destabilize and challenge the fixedness of all social categories. Being skeptical of any use of categories in a simplistic way to capture the complexity of people's lived experiences, the focus of proponents of this approach is on the social processes of categorizing and drawing social boundaries with others. As McCall (2005) suggests, the problem with this approach is that it turns everything into a social discourse that may lack a foundation in reality. The fluidity and instability of categories also makes practical analysis difficult, if not impossible.

The second approach is "intracategorical complexity." This approach shares the former one's skepticism, but instead of abandoning social categories in their analysis, proponents of this approach focus on the "neglected points of intersection—ones that tend to reflect multiple subordinate locations as opposed to a dominant or mixed location" (McCall, 2005, p. 1780). At these neglected points of intersection we can reveal the complexity of the lived experiences of people positioned in these categories. This approach is criticized for its potential displacement of focus from the larger social forces and processes that cause the inequalities to personal stories of misfortune.

The third approach, which is the one McCall favours, is called "intercategorical complexity." This approach does not reject existing social categories being used as tools to analyze and "document relationships of inequality among social groups and changing configurations of inequality among multiple and conflicting dimensions" (McCall, 2005, p. 1773). In this approach relationships of inequality among social groups are not just a factor for analysis but are the focus of the analysis. Applying this approach to examine wage inequality by gender, class, and race in four cities, each of which has a different economic environment, McCall demonstrates that inequalities exist not only between categories but also within them when they are situated in different larger social structures that generate inequality (Walby et al., 2012).

The economic environment that McCall includes in her analysis highlights the importance of "context" in the intersectionality approach. Although the power axis of many social dimensions such as race, gender, class, and so on, are persistent throughout history, their social significance and their power dynamic related to each one and to their interactions with each other also undergo constant change "as part of new economic, political, and ideological processes, trends, and events" (Weber, 1998, p. 16). They are contingent on the time and space in which these social categories are constructed and applied in terms of actual forms of domination in social structure and everyday practice (Hulko, 2009).

For instance, in a superdiverse society like Canada, where *all* people, not just immigrants, are globally connected and mobile, time and space are not only local. In other words, many people live in a *translocal* condition in which they maintain an active connection and interaction with people living in different socio-geographical locations. Thus, we also need to take a "translocational" perspective to analyze how the intersections of different social structures and processes work (Anthias, 2013a). For instance Mr X, while being a highly skilled immigrant who is trapped at the bottom of the local Canadian labour market, is also a respectable senior engineer of his home country. In some developing societies, people who migrate to a developed country are often placed in an admirable position by the friends and families who stay behind. Thus being charged with child abuse in his host country may have a huge negative translocal impact on Mr X and his family both here and back home.

Case Example 6.1 *continued*

As a child protection worker Kate's concern is the welfare of the child. However, before she makes any recommendation she will need to understand what triggered this incident, how it happened, and if it is necessary to remove the child or to keep him at home with Mr X, particularly when his wife is away. Among all the family members, conditions, and issues that she needs to assess, Mr X, the suspected abuser, is perhaps the most critical. She probably will assess not only Mr X's personality and temperament, but from an anti-oppressive perspective she will also need to examine any social conditions in which he and his family (including those in his home country) are situated that might trigger this sort of incident.

Taking an intersectionality approach, Kate may recognize that Mr X has multiple social identities: male, middle aged, Asian, visible minority, immigrant, low class (service worker). While each of these identities locates Mr X in different social positions along different axes of social power, some intersect. For instance, in Canada the intersection of race and immigrant status have marginalized and disadvantaged many visible minorities in the economic domain (Yssaad, 2012). Despite having a higher level of education, many immigrant men who are also visible minorities, like Mr X, face numerous incidents of discrimination against not only their qualifications, credentials, and foreign experience (Sakamoto, Chin, & Young, 2011), but also their accent (Creese & Kambere, 2003) and non-European names (Oreopoulos, 2009). The intersectional effect of these multiple forms of oppression against Mr X might be the cause of his bad temperament and what triggered the abusive act.

Furthermore, Mr X's immigrant and racial positions also intersect with his ethnicity and gender positions. Mr X's ethnic identity signifies his adherence to a culture (Jenkins, 1996) that may privilege the man in the family and accept the use of corporal punishment as a means to discipline children. This culture is different from the mainstream Canadian one. Thus, by imposing a dominant universalized meaning from Canadian society as a norm on people who have a different cultural affiliation, we may undervalue or even oppress their culture.

Meanwhile, it has also been found that visible minority immigrant youth tend to have higher enrolment rates in higher education along with higher educational aspirations

continued

(Krahn & Taylor, 2005) and educational attainment (Davies & Guppy, 1998). To many immigrant parents, the high expectations they have for their children's success in school is not only a cultural norm that they adhere to but also a measure by which they hope to uplift the marginalized social status of their family in the future. (For more discussion on immigrant parenting tendencies, see Chapter 9 by Debashis Dutta and Ross Klein.) The abusive act of Mr X might be a response to his high expectations of Y's education caused by his marginalized immigrant status.

The above analysis has by no means exhausted all the possible intersections of Mr X's multiple identities nor justified any form of cruelty against children and male domination. But it may at least help Kate better understand Mr X and his family and their existing situation. Indeed, Mr X's situation is not uncommon to many immigrant families involved in the child protection system. As Stalker, Maiter, and Alaggia (2009) found in their study, immigrant families involved in the child protection system tend to face numerous challenges: "loneliness, financial struggles, language struggles, struggles to provide for the family, and sense of betrayal and hopelessness" (p. 34). Many of these are consequences of the multiple forms of oppression that immigrants like Mr X experience. (For more discussion on the socio-economic stresses faced by immigrants, see Chapter 9 by Debashis Dutta and Ross Klein.)

As an analytical tool that helps promote social justice and social change (Dill & Zambrana, 2009), intersectionality has contributed greatly to the analysis of how different social categories mutually reinforce the power of some dominant groups that solidify the unequal conditions of marginalized groups. However, this approach is not without limitations. McCall (2005) has already pointed out some methodological challenges for an empirical examination of how intersectionality works. Meanwhile, as formulated and advocated by critical race feminist scholars, the intersectionality approach has been prototypically applied to the experiences, predicaments, and actions of racial minority women from lower economic classes (Nash, 2008). Recently, this concept has also been applied to the analysis of oppressive conditions of other groups of people. For instance, in this case Mr X, as a heterosexual, middle-aged, able-bodied man, can be placed in a position of being a victim of intersecting forms of oppression based on his immigrant status, race, culture, and class.

Meanwhile, as Chang and Culp note, "it's one thing to say that race, gender, sexuality, class, and nation operate symbiotically, co-synthetically, multi-dimensionally, or interconnectedly. The next step is to be able to *prescribe or imagine points of intervention*" (quoted in Nash, 2008, p. 5, emphasis added), which is a core concern of social work practice. The intersectionality approach has no doubt offered social workers an analytical tool to understand how marginalization and social inequalities work. However, as Nash (2008) points out, serving as a tool for the analysis of exclusion, the intersectionality approach lacks recognition and analysis of the ways in which "positions of dominance and subordination work in complex and intersecting ways to constitute subjects' experience of personhood" (p. 10) and "has yet to contend with whether its theory explains or describes the processes and mechanisms by which subjects mobilize (or choose not to mobilize) particular aspects of their identities in particular circumstances" (p. 11).

The idea of "subject" is important to social work practice. From an interpretive perspective, an effective social work intervention requires a mutual understanding of the meaning and experience of the marginalization process between the worker and the client as subjects. Without a proper articulation of the role of the subject in intersectionality, an important question is raised for social workers who try to understand the multiple oppressions challenging their clients through the lens of intersectionality: If reaching a mutual understanding is key to successful social work intervention, then how do the privileges and oppressions (and their intersection) of two subjects—social worker and client—affect their understanding of each other? Here we will turn to the concepts of *positionality* and intersubjectivity to search for promising insights into how we understand intersectionality in social work practice.

Subject, Positionality, and Role

In brief, a social identity is a marker for locating a person, as a member of a social category, in a position on the asymmetrical axis of social power within a particular social dimension. To catch the dynamics of the locating process, we may need to turn to the concept of **positionality** that, in a nutshell, is about a person's ability to position him or herself and his or her inability to avoid being positioned by others. Simply put, positionality bears at least two interrelated connotations. The first one is the temporal–social position that an individual socially or organizationally occupies (Burk & Stets, 2009). Social location is often used as a conceptual label to signify the *positional* aspect of one's social identity in order to serve a particular analytical purpose. For instance, Anthias (2013a) uses social location to signify how a *specific* social identity is tied to a particular social and historical context. In Anthias's words, a social location inhabits "a 'real time and place' context" (p. 130). In social work, some use social location as a spatial metaphor to indicate a "snapshot" (Carniol, 2004, p. 158) of "the result of this (social) interaction in terms of privileges and disadvantages and functions at more of a practical or everyday level" (Hulko, 2009, p. 45).

Seen through the intersectionality lens, a social position is situated on the axes of power differentiation within a particular spatial–temporal context as forces of domination and marginalization. While social location is a useful analytical tool for examining the temporal–spatial snapshot of an intersection, it does not mean that we always passively and co-operatively accept the destiny and the storyline imposed on us by the script inscribed on the social position in which we are "located". Thus we should not lose sight of the subjective process of locating and being located. The fact that we embody multiple social positions that are compatible, mutually reinforcing, conflicting, and competitive all at the same time indicates that we cannot be passive respondents to our social positions.

The subjective process of locating and being located points exactly to the second connotation of positionality, and perhaps a more important one, which is **positioning**, that is, "the discursive process whereby people are located in conversations as observably and *subjectively* coherent participants in *jointly produced storylines*" (Davies & Harre, 1999, p. 37, emphasis added). To compensate for the shortcomings of the concept of intersectionality that underplay the notion of the actor as a subject (Nash, 2008; Staunaes, 2003), the concept of positioning helps reinstate the actors as "the subjects" who are capable, albeit not without limitation, of co-constructing a story (or shared meaning of an event).

From a Foucauldian perspective, the idea of the human actor as a subject is twin-faced, which represents the dual nature of positioning: to position and to be positioned. On one side, the *agency*, or ability, of a subject "to act purposefully and reflectively" (Frie, 2008, p. 1) allows us to act upon contextual conditions, while on the other side we are being subjected to the same contextual conditions (Hall, 2004; Staunaes, 2003). In other words, people are not rigidly tied to a social position or an intersection of different positions or both. As a subject of his or her own story, human actors are actively engaged in negotiating (and, if necessary, strategically shifting) his or her different aspects of social positions in particular circumstances.

Case Example 6.1 *continued*

In the case study, when Mr X questioned Kate about her age, marital status, and if she had any children, and also claimed that corporal punishment was part of his ethnic culture, he intentionally (or unintentionally) shifted his subjugated social position of "child abuser" to other social positions that place him on different axes of power between Kate and himself.

Like Mr X, in our everyday social encounters we also position ourselves strategically in different contexts, reflexively corresponding to "actual and comprehensible discourses, practices and distributions of power, as well as the composition of actors" (Staunaes, 2003, p. 104). In this process, we turn our social position into a *subject position.* Mediated by our own personal histories and informed by our everyday lived experiences and based on "our emotions, our own reading of the situation and our own imaginative positioning of ourselves in the situation" (Davies & Harre, 1999, pp. 42–3), we generate multiple and often contradictory *interpretations* of contexts and possible social discourses (of the social positions in which we are located). Based on these interpretations, we not only discursively but also behaviourally "'refuse' or accept the nature of the discourse through which a particular conversation takes place" (Davies & Harre, 1999, pp. 42–3).

The idea of shifting the position of the subject highlights the "agency" function of human actors. To position or be positioned in a particular context requires actors in the situation (or the interaction) to engage in a self-indication process, a process of mutual interpretation in which individuals will symbolically, constantly, and mutually interpret, evaluate (define), and respond to each other (Blumer, 1969). Such self-indication is closely related to how the individuals in the social process perceive their own roles. Hewitt (1983) defines role as "a cluster of duties, rights, and obligations associated with a particular *social position*" (p. 77, emphasis added). In other words, when people are located in a social position, they are expected to play a certain role that comes with a set of knowledge, abilities, and motivation as well as expectations (LaRossa & Reitzes, 1993). This is the mutual knowledge we discussed above.

The concept of role is crucial to social work practice. In social work, it has been widely accepted that most people perceive and define their problems in terms of a "current transaction between themselves and others in specific social roles" (Perlman, 1968, p. 199). For instance, both Kate and Mr X are human actors who take up certain social roles (i.e., social worker and client) in the social work process. To symbolic interactionists, the concept of role not only explains how an individual is constrained but also offers a way for people to grasp how situations are structured (Hewitt, 1983). The self-indication process may end up with a set of symbols (e.g., a co-constructed storyline) that stands for commonly agreed-upon meanings that we use to communicate, think, and perform or indicate a plan of action (Meltzer, 1972).

Defined by a social position, role is situation specific. People are active agents in defining the situations in which their social position is located and, according to their definition of the situation, they take up their expected roles (Thomas, 1972). We also make up our roles by constructing "activity in a situation so that it fits the definition of the situation" (Hewitt, 1983, p. 61). Therefore, no role is fixed; each role has a "career" that denotes the possibility of changing the definition of that role to help a person adjust to a *situational* shift (Goffman, 1959; LaRossa & Reitzes, 1993).

This does not mean that people can elevate themselves from their social positions and be immune to their structural limitations and constraints. Instead, it does point to the possibility that people can rupture the scripts of their roles and negotiate different storylines to retell their stories. However, due to the differences in roles, the definition of the problem will inevitably lead to tension among the actors and competition for control of the definition of the situations in everyday life (Goffman, 1959). To do so, both actors will need to figure out a way in which they can take the role of another, and then develop an appropriate storyline for further action. (For further discussion on structural restraints and oppression, see Chapter 5 by Douglas Durst.)

For instance, in order for Mr X and Kate to understand each other better, Mr X will need to engage in Kate's role and its inscribed responsibilities and mandates as a child protection worker, while Kate is stepping into Mr X's position as a newcomer struggling to settle in Canada. As human actors, we are not only subjected to a storyline inscribed on our social position but are also a subject that we can shift and co-construct as an alternative storyline together with other actors in each situation. In other words, the self-indication process is also an *intersubjective* process in which active subjects try to exercise their agency to make sense of the context in which they are co-situated and the discourse to which they are co-subjected.

Intersubjectivity and Power

Crossley (1996) argues that **intersubjectivity** is the fabric of social becoming. Borrowing Giddens's structuration theory (Giddens, 1984), we can argue that the routine recurrence of intersubjective interaction among social actors creates and sustains the very social structure that structures the actors and their interaction. A social category is, indeed, a social structure, mostly in a discursive and ideological form, created by the recurring interaction among actors who position themselves or are positioned in asymmetrical power relations. In return it offers resources (such as cultural tools and performance scripts) that facilitate as well as constraints that regulate the intersubjective process among the actors.

However, Matusov (1996) challenges the traditional concept that intersubjectivity is "a process of a coordination of participants' contributions in joint activity" through agreement (p. 25). Instead he argues that since, in most situations, the roles of actors are not necessarily equal and are often even competitive, the dialectic relationship between understanding and misunderstanding may result in disagreement. In the intersubjective process, the engaging actors not only make and take roles, but also refuse those roles that are less powerful to balance out the power. As in our case study, while playing down the role of child abuser, Mr X tried to take up his role as a member of an ethnic group that prefers corporal punishment to justify his position and prelude doubts about his act. Therefore, in this process the social power embedded in the asymmetric social positions between the actors is no longer just a power of oppression; rather, it allows the actors to change the power relations by switching their subject position from the disadvantaged one (e.g., child abuser) to the privileged one (e.g., member of an ethnic group) and vice versa (Staunaes, 2003).

In other words, the intersubjective process is also a political process. Crossley (1996) argues that the asymmetrical power of a social category is "parasitic upon" the intersubjective relationship among actors—"it needs intersubjectivity and draws upon intersubjectivity to create its effects" (p. 127). In asymmetrical social dimensions, as Foucault (1980) suggests, the social power domination (and marginalization) tied to different social categories is exercised through subtle mechanisms (e.g., an ideology of education, an ideology of citizenship, and an ideology of welfare, to name a few). These mechanisms evolve and are organized and put into circulation through different "apparatuses of knowledge" (p. 102), such as methods of observation, techniques of registration, and procedures for investigation and research. This apparatus produces disciplinary knowledge that normalizes the formal and informal codes of a role and the social scripts for how people perform them.

Young (1990) has warned professionals, including social work practitioners, that the power embedded in disciplinary knowledge privileges us in terms of the acquisition of specialized knowledge through education, autonomy to make discretionary judgment, and respect expected by others. As Freud (1999) critically reminds us, the professional knowledge of social work is a means to construct normalcy. Thus, taking up the role as professionals, social workers consciously or unconsciously perpetuate the axis of social power between the professionals who help and the clients who are to be helped.

To Foucault, power and resistance coexist and are enacted recursively by "multiple persons located at multiple points within a network" (Keenan, 2004, p. 541). Seen through the lens of intersectionality, different forms of these powers interweave to form a network of power. In other words, in its discursive form social categorical power is everywhere. We are all sorted and placed in different social positions in this network according to who we biophysically and/or socio-politically are. Each of these positions is also a point of interaction with others. However, how power plays out in the interaction of a particular social position is not predetermined. It depends on the mutual knowledge of how that particular social position is interrelated with others within the social context (Crossley, 1996, p. 142).

The logic is that human beings are inherently interdependent and have a desire for recognition from others (Crossley, 1996, p. 97). It is due to the latter that we strategically respond to people's exercise of power over us. It varies depending on what we wish to achieve in the situation. Therefore our acceptance or rejection of the social power exerted on us can be a *strategic exchange* in the intersubjective process. For instance, if you remember, Mr X first tried to refuse to co-operate with Kate, but later, after learning that she might have the power to remove his son and involve the police, he changed his attitude. In sum, in the intersubjective process the subjects do not just passively respond to their predetermined power positions. As Gillespie (2012) suggests, intersubjectivity enables us to reflexively go beyond our own social position "to either take the perspective of others upon themselves, thus mediating their own activity, or to identify with others, and thus act on their behalf" (p. 45).

Social Work Practice with Differences

Let's go back to the two questions we started with: How can two human beings who come with a set of intersecting social identities located in different social positions work together to generate this shared meaning? And how does the intersection of the multiple social positions of a social worker and her or his client impact the self-indication process in an effective social work intervention? Answering these questions requires us not only to acknowledge the exclusionary and marginalizing effects of the network of powers, but also to recognize the possibility of collaboration within the network because of the logic inherent in the concept of intersubjectivity, as Crossley (1996) argues, which makes "practices of collaboration, support, solidarity, and human development" possible within the network of power (Keenan, 2004, p. 541). This collaborative understanding of the networks of power may sound counterintuitive, but it offers the powerless hope and the people who aspire to social justice, like social workers, the possibility for creative change (Keenan, 2004); it also creates a possible strategy for transformative practice (Bishop, 2002). (For further in-depth discussion on social work and difference, see Chapter 16 by Natalie Blake-Noel.)

We summarize four principles for transformative social work practice that aim to build solidarity among people who are located in multiple and different social positions. As Young (1990) reminds us, solidarity among differences is not built upon homogenizing or essentializing people into one unified group. Therefore, the first principle is to recognize and politicize difference as a terrain of political struggle for social justice. Encompassed in this struggle is a desire for equality.

The second principle is that the understanding of difference should not simply serve as a conceptual and analytical function for explaining how dividing, otherizing, and excluding opposition works. The relational meaning of difference should be used to question under what conditions, for what purpose, and with whom we are engaging (Sin & Yan, 2003). In other words, the understanding of difference should be specific, situational, various, and heterogeneous. We need to break the inertia that tends to assume that people's perception of and adherence to their social positions are unalterable.

The third principle is to recognize that among people belonging to the same social category there are differences in values and social positions in other social dimensions. As Young (1990) sharply points out, by positioning *ourselves* and being positioned in a social category we may risk creating pressures toward homogenization among members of the category. Homogenization goes hand in hand with essentialization. Together they build an impermeable categorical border between oneself and others, silence the minorities within the minority, and create new privileges and exclusion among them.

The fourth principle is to engage people of different positions in a dialogue to achieve an intersubjective outcome—that is, a shared understanding. Indeed, a genuine dialogue is liberating, particularly in a Freirean sense. Through dialogue, people come to feel like masters of their thinking by discussing the ideas and views of the world that are explicitly or implicitly manifest in their own suggestions and those of their comrades (Freire, 1997). Also, through a genuine dialogue with people of different position, we can learn from each other in a complementary way and expand our understanding of the world (Young 1997).

Dialogical Practice

Conceiving social work to be a form of dialogue is becoming popular. However, the late Iris Marion Young (1997) has critically pointed out that when people of differential positions engage in dialogue, their relationships and contributions are *asymmetrical*. She first explains that people enter the dialogue with "the specificity of position." Therefore, to achieve a genuine dialogue we should recognize that the engaging actors are subjects who are actively engaging in a self-indication process by curiously and strategically negotiating the similarities and dissimilarities between them, despite their irreducible and irreversible positions.

Second, she explains that each individual engaging in the dialogue has his or her own temporality. Elaborated in her own words, "Each person brings to a communication situation the particular experiences, assumptions, meanings, symbolic associations and so on that emerge from a particular history, most of which lies as background to the communicating situation" (Young, 1997, p. 51).

Third, the asymmetric nature of dialogue is also situation specific. For social work practice, the situation means a specific organizational context that is the microcosm of and is influenced by the larger social system, and the context of people's engagement is also defined by organizational mandates and social functions. In an organizational context, tensions among different actors are inevitable (Yan, 2008). Since the salience of our many different social positions is situational, the positions of the subject(s) within a particular context in which interaction takes place is often more influential in shaping the dialogues between us and others.

In brief, people strategically pick and choose from their inexhaustible history (lived experience) to retell their story to others in different situations. Therefore, we should not be surprised to know that people retell the same story differently to different people for different purposes.

Case Example 6.1 ***continued***

In our case study, the dialogical engagement between Kate (with the subject position of a social worker) and Mr X (in a subject position of a suspected child abuser) is within an organizational context of child protection that is shaped by the social ideology and the relevant legislation of the society.

Reflexive Reflection

When the worker and the client pick and choose how to share and what parts of his or her lived experience are to be shared and not shared in a social work dialogue, they both are engaging in an intersubjective self-reflecting process (Yan & Wong, 2005). To understand how intersubjective self-reflection works, we may first need to turn to the symbolic interactionist notion of self as a continuous process of interplay between "I" and "me" (Blumer, 1969). The symbolic interactionism notion of self emphasizes the interplay between the "'I', the spontaneous self, and the 'me', the social constraint within the self" (Ritzer, 1983, p. 312).

According to Hewitt (1983), the self as a process involves two phases. In the "subject" phase, "I's" respond as acting subjects to objects or to the particular or generalized others in their situations (Hewitt, 1983, p. 72). The concept of "I" denotes its immediate, spontaneous, and impulsive aspects, which are open to change (LaRossa & Reitzes, 1993). In other words, the "I" is also the subject, having the human agency to interpret the situation in which one is positioned or wants to position his or herself. The "I," however, will need to interpret the meaning of the situation by referring to "me."

In the "object" phase, in which people operate at the "me" level, people view themselves as objects that are subjected to a **generalized other** that is "a collective whole, which transcends the idiosyncratic features of its [society's] individual members" (Baert, 1998, p. 70). A generalized other represents the norms, expectations, and regularities that are inscribed onto a role and align the performance of the occupant of the role with the role's meaning held by others (LaRossa & Reitzes, 1993). For instance, the role of child protection worker or the role of child abuser are the two key "generalized others" that Kate and Mr X refer to when they try to reflect on themselves in the engaging process. The "me" is the identity marker of the otherness of ourselves from which we understand how we relate to others. The object phase is, therefore, a self-reflective process; it refers "to the ability of individuals to reflect upon their own circumstances, on the meaning and effects of their own (imaginary, possible or real) actions, on their beliefs about themselves, and on their beliefs about their beliefs" (Baert, 1998, p. 69). An extension of this reflection is the ability to exert self-control and self-monitoring, which ensures that action is directed as indicated in the self-reflection.

However, critical theorists (e.g., Crossley, 1996; Young, 1990) have recently pointed out that the symbolic interactionist understanding of self-reflection as an internal dialogue between our "I" and "me" is inadequate in at least two senses. First, the mirroring function of "generalized other" is not impartial. Returning to our analysis of social categories, the generalized other, in a hegemonic form, is inherently political because of its embedded asymmetrical categorical power. Uncritical acceptance of the generalized other in a given role of a particular social position sustains and reinforces the positional injustice that members of marginalized groups suffer and privileges the seemingly neutral standard of the dominant group (Crossley, 1996; Young, 1990). In turn, the generalized other serves as an internalized negative reference for one's self and produces an internalized devaluation of members of marginalized groups.

Second, the "I" is not transcendental. It has been argued that to reflect on a subject critically demands the subject to be reflexive, which, as Kondrat (1999) argues, means that we also need to place the "I" in a positional analysis. Young (1997) suggests that, like the "me," the "I" is also positional and is subjected to and limited by the partiality of the *situationally* salient subject position from which the "I" gazes at the "me."

Case Example 6.1 continued

When Kate reflexively reflects on herself as a woman, a White person, and so on, she is not gazing on these "object–me's" as a transcended human being. Instead, she is situated at the subject position of a social worker when she searches for the meaning and possible impact of the "me's" on her engagement with Mr X.

Meanwhile, the "subject–I" is not invisible. It is embodied in a physical and materialistic body—for example, Kate's White, young, female-looking body, the visibility of which may affect her engagement with others' (Mr X's) imagination and the association of some "object–me's" of which the "subject–I" (Kate) may not be conscious.

This engaging of others' imagination and association, which may be triggered by past lived experiences unknown to the "subject–I," can lead to unexpected emotional, behavioural, or verbal reactions from the engaged other. These reactions may have a chain-reaction effect on how the "subject–I" understands him or herself in the situation (Kogler, 2012).

Case Example 6.1 continued

When Mr X challenged Kate as a young White woman who did not know about his culture, what he saw was not a social worker but an objectified body signifying not only the "Whiteness" of Kate but also her affiliation with a group of people who treated him unfairly. In response, his challenges may shift Kate's subject position (e.g., from that of a social worker to that of a White woman) to reflect on herself.

As Young (1997) suggests, reflexive reflection enlarges our understanding of the interworld where our reflective partners are situated, and of "those relations that are unavailable to any of them from their own perspective alone" (p. 59). Therefore, Keenan (2004) suggests that, similar to a backstitch in sewing, we need to turn back the "I or I'*s*" to examine it or them from where it or they are standing, and examine under what conditions and for what purposes which "subject–I" is gazing at which "object–me or –me'*s*."

Miehls and Moffatt (2000) proposed that reflexive self-reflection in a dialogue is "a search for ways to interact with the other which opens the relationship for new possibilities of discourse" (p. 342). By reflexively reflecting on both the "I'*s*" and "me'*s*," one can "work on oneself so that one creates new strategic possibilities for relationships" (p. 343). As Falzon (1998) suggests, to generate a genuine dialogue with people positioned in disadvantageous positions with respect to ourselves, we need to accept that in the process we may expose ourselves and our positions to the possibility of being challenged. These challenges may make it possible for us to be transformed by others and to reach a better mutual understanding with others. However, reflexive self-reflection does not guarantee agreement among the actors in the dialogical process (Falzon, 1998; Matusov, 1996). After all, because of the positional power difference among speakers, a dialogical process is itself an asymmetrical process.

Summary and Conclusion

In this chapter we have discussed the meaning of social dimension, social category (or group), social identity, and social position. Structurally, people are differentiated into interrelated social categories in different social dimensions. Identifying ourselves as a member of a particular social category gives us a social identity that locates us in a particular social position. Social classification is divided along an asymmetrical power axis embedded in each social dimension in different historical and spatial contexts. Power, in the form of disciplinary and normalized norms, codes, and knowledge, discursively and ideologically privileges one group's control and domination over the other by informing and limiting the recurring interaction among actors positioned in competitive positions.

These concepts are useful analytical tools for helping us understand how inequality, oppression, and social injustice are discursively and ideologically justified by classifying people structurally into different social categories based on their biophysical and socio-political attributes. However, no one social category operates separately and independently from others. Instead they often intersect with each other. Since people have multiple social identities, we are also subjected to multiple and intersecting (or even interlocking) axes of power that work to differentiate us from each other. The intersecting effect can further marginalize people who are members of multiple and interrelated denigrated social groups. As a force for marginalization, the intersection or interlocking of multiple denigrated social categories fortifies the oppressive conditions of people who are, unwillingly or willingly, positioned in these categories.

Despite the ubiquitous nature of social classification, people are not solely an object of a social position as defined by their membership in a social category. Indeed, the power of the social category is exercised through an intersubjective process. We, as autonomous subjects, can choose and reject, albeit to a limited extent, a social position and shift among the multiple positions that we embody when interacting with other people whose social positions are similar or different from ours. We are intersubjectively capable, albeit not without limits, of engaging in strategic exchanges of positions to satisfy our desires.

To conclude, recognizing the specificity of position and the temporality and situation of each engagement, social workers should metaphorically treat each social work encounter as a dialogue between them and their clients. This chapter does not end with a definitive answer to how Kate should work with Mr X. (For discussion of a strengths-based appreciation of challenges faced by immigrant families, see the

Immigrant Parent Enhancement (IPE) framework in Chapter 9 by Debashis Dutta and Ross Klein.) Although dialogue does not guarantee results, through reflexively reflecting on our own positions in the dialogical process we can gain knowledge of our client's perception and reaction to their social positions and transform our own self-understanding. From an interpretative perspective, hopefully we can generate a shared understanding (a storyline) with our clients that can help both of us creatively and strategically move the working process forward. After all, from an intersubjective perspective, one's understanding of oneself and others is infinite; it is always relational, situational, contingent, and strategic. It requires us, as social work practitioners, to be reflexive and dialogical when working with our clients.

Questions for Review

1. Using the eight dimensions listed in Table 6.1, list your own social identity in each of these dimensions. Then critically examine your own power position in each of these dimensions and how these dimensions intersect with each other. What impacts do the intersections have on you as a member of Canadian society?
2. Have you had the experience of shifting a social position when interacting with people whose positions are different from yours? Why did you shift your position and *how did you do it*?
3. Imagine you are the social worker working with Mr X. Consider how your own social positions may influence your work with Mr X.
4. So far, most of our discussion has been about the social worker, Kate. What do these social identities mean to Mr X in front of a younger White woman who has the power to break up his family? How will he use his multiple social positions to interpret and respond to Kate and to you?
5. Assume now that it is Mr X, an Asian immigrant, who is the child protection worker, and Kate is a young, White, single mother who is suspected of abusing her child. How will their social positions change the dynamic of their interaction?

Suggested Readings and Resources

Freire, P. (1997). *Pedagogy of the oppressed* (Rev. 20th anniversary ed.). New York, NY: Continuum.

Gillespie, A. (2013). Identity, intersubjectivity and methodology [Video file]. Retrieved from http://www.youtube.com/watch?v=zIMJFLFGAyw

Haggis, P. (Director). (2004). *Crash* [Motion picture]. Yari Film Group.

International Literacy Institute. (2009). Paulo Freire—An incredible conversation [Video file]. Retrieved from http://www.youtube.com/watch?v=aFWjnkFypFA

Keenan, E. K. (2004). From sociocultural categories to socially located relations: Using critical theory in social work practice. *Families in Society, 85*(4), 539–48.

McCall, L. (2005). The complexity of intersectionality. *Signs, 30*(3), 1771–800.

PSA: Intersectionality. (2012). [Video file] Retrieved from http://www.youtube.com/watch?v=VKN7e5vz1SI

Reckless Tortuga. (2009). Racism in the elevator: Alternate version [Video file]. Retrieved from http://www.youtube.com/watch?v=EHCqz-J51IU

Young, I. M. (1990). *Justice and the politics of difference*. Princeton, NJ: Princeton University Press.

References

Anthias, F. (2013a). Hierarchies of social location, class and intersectionality: Towards a translocational frame. *International Sociology, 28*(1), 121–38.

Anthias, F. (2013b). Intersectional what? Social division, intersectionality and levels of analysis. *Ethnicities, 13*(3), 3–19.

Baert, P. (1998). *Social theory in the twentieth century*. New York: New York University Press.

Bhabha, H. (1994). *The location of culture*. New York, NY: Routledge.

Bishop, A. (2002). *Becoming an ally: Breaking the cycle of oppression in people* (2nd ed.). Halifax, NS: Fernwood Publishing.

Blumer, H. (1969). *Symbolic interactionism: Perspective & method*. Englewood Cliffs, NJ: Prentice Hall.

Brah, A. (1996). *Cartographies of diaspora*. New York, NY: Routledge.

Brah, A., & Phoenix, A. (2004). Ain't I a woman? Revisiting intersectionality. *Journal of International Women's Studies, 5*(3), 75–86.

Burk, P., & Stets, J. E. (2009). *Social identity*. New York, NY: Oxford University Press.

Butler, J. (2006). *Gender trouble* (2nd ed.). New York, NY: Routledge.

Carniol, B. (2004). Analysis of social location and change: Practice implications. In S. Hick, J. Fook, & R. Pozzuto (Eds.), *Social work: A critical turn* (pp. 153–65). Toronto, ON: Thompson Educational Publishing Inc.

Collins, P. H. (1990). *Black feminist thought: Knowledge, consciousness, and the politics of empowerment*. New York, NY: Routledge.

Creese, G., & Kambere, E. N. (2003). What colour is your English? *Canadian Review of Sociology & Anthropology, 40*(5), 565–73.

Crenshaw, K. (1991). Mapping the margins: Intersectionality, identity politics, and violence against women of color. *Stanford Law Review, 43*(6), 1241–99.

Crossley, N. (1996). *Intersubjectivity: The fabric of social becoming*. London, UK: Sage Publications.

Davies, B., & Harre, R. (1999). Positioning: The discursive production of selves. In R. Harre & L. van Langenhove (Eds.), *Positioning theory: Moral contexts of intentional action* (pp. 32–52). Oxford, UK: Blackwell Publishers Ltd.

Davies, S., & Guppy, N. (1998). Race and Canadian education. In V. N. Satzewich (Ed.), *Racism and social inequality in Canada* (pp. 131–56). Toronto, ON: Thompson Educational Publishing.

Deschamps, J.-C., & Devos, T. (1998). Regarding the relationship between social identity and personal identity. In S. Worchel, J. F. Morales, D. Paez, & J.-C. Deschamps (Eds.), *Social identity: International perspective* (pp. 1–12). Thousand Oaks, CA: Sage Publications.

Dill, B. T., & Zambrana, R. E. (Eds.). (2009). *Emerging intersections: Race, class, and gender in theory, policy, and practice*. Piscataway, NJ: Rutgers University Press.

Falzon, C. (1998). *Foucault and social dialogue*. New York, NY: Routledge.

Foucault, M. (1980). *Power/knowledge: Selected interviews & other writings 1972–1977*. C. Gordon, L. Marshall, J. Mepham, & K. Soper (Trans.). New York, NY: Pantheon Books.

Freire, P. (1997). *Pedagogy of the oppressed* (Rev. 20th anniversary ed.). New York, NY: Continuum.

Freud, S. (1999). The social construction of normality. *Families in Society: The Journal of Contemporary Human Services, 80*(4), 333–9.

Frie, R. (2008). Introduction: The situated nature of psychological agency. In R. Frie (Eds.),

Psychological agency: Theory, practice, and culture (pp. 1–32). Cambridge, MA: MIT Press.

Giddens, A. (1984). *The constitution of society*. Berkeley, CA: University of California Press.

Gillespie, A. (2012). Position exchange: The social development of agency. *New Ideas in Psychology, 30*, 32–46.

Goffman, E. (1959). *The presentation of self in everyday life*. Garden City, NY: Doubleday Anchor Books.

Goldstein, H. (1986). Toward the integration of theory and practice: A humanistic approach. *Social Work, 31*, 352–7.

Hall, D. E. (2004). *Subjectivity*. New York, NY: Routledge.

Hewitt, J. P. (1983). *Self and society*. Newton, MA: Allyn and Bacon.

Hulko, W. (2009). The time- and context-contingent nature of intersectionality and interlocking oppressions. *Affilia, 24*(1), 144–55.

Jenkins, R. (1996). Ethnicity etceteras: Social anthropological points of view. *Ethnic and Racial Studies, 19*(4), 807–22.

Keenan, E. K. (2004). From sociocultural categories to socially located relations: Using critical theory in social work practice. *Families in Society, 85*(4), 539–48.

Kogler, H.-H. (2012). Agency and the other: On the intersubjective roots of self-identity. *New Ideas in Psychology, 30*, 47–64.

Kondrat, M. E. (1999). Who is the "self" in self-aware: Professional self-awareness from a critical theory perspective. *Social Service Review, 73*(4), 451–77.

Krahn, H., & Taylor, A. (2005). Resilient teenagers: Explaining the high educational aspirations of visible-minority youth in Canada. *Journal of International Migration and Integration, 6*(3/4), 405–34.

LaRossa, R., & Reitzes, D. C. (1993). Symbolic interactionism and family studies. In P. G. Boss, W. J. Doherty, R. LaRossa, W. R. Schumm, & S. Steinmetz (Eds.), *Sourcebook of family theories and methods: A contextual approach* (pp. 135–63). New York, NY: Plenum Press.

Matusov, E. (1996). Intersubjectivity without agreement. *Mind, Culture, and Activity, 3*(1), 25–45.

McCall, L. (2005). The complexity of intersectionality. *Signs, 30*(3), 1771–800.

Mehrotra, G. (2010). Toward a continuum of intersectionality theorizing for feminist social work scholarship. *Afflilia: Journal of Women and Social Work, 25*(4), 417–30.

Meltzer, B. N. (1972). Mead's social psychology. In J. G. Manis & B. N. Meltzer (Eds.), *Symbolic interaction: A reader in social psychology* (2nd ed., pp. 4–22). Boston, MA: Allyn and Bacon.

Miehls, D., & Moffatt, K. (2000). Constructing social work identity based on reflexive self. *British Journal of Social Work, 30*, 339–48.

Mullaly, B. (2010). *Challenging oppression: A critical social work approach*. Toronto, ON: Oxford University Press.

Murphy, Y., Hunt, V., Zajicek, A. M., Norris, A. N., & Hamilton, L. (2009). *Incorporating intersectionality in social work practice, research, policy and education*. Washington, DC: National Association of Social Workers.

Nash, J. C. (2008). Re-thinking intersectionality. *Feminist Review, 89*, 1–15.

Oreopoulos, P. (2009). Why do skilled immigrants struggle in the labour market? A field experiment with six thousand resumes. NBER Working Paper No. 15036. National Bureau of Economic Research. Retrieved from http://www.nber.org/papers/w15036

Perlman, H. H. (1968). *Persona: Social role and responsibility*. Chicago, IL: University of Chicago Press.

Ritzer, G. (1983). *Sociological theory*. New York, NY: Alfred A. Knopf.

Ropers-Huilman, R., & Winters, K. T. (2010). Imagining intersectionality and the space in between: Theories and processes of socially transformative knowing. In M. Sarin-Baden & M. C. Howell (Eds.), *New approaches to qualitative research: Wisdom and uncertainty* (pp. 37–48). New York, NY: Routledge.

Sakamoto, I., Chin, M., & Young, M. (2011). Canadian experience, employment challenges, and skilled immigrants: A close look through tacit knowledge. *Canadian Social Work, 12*(1), 145–52.

Saleebey, D. (1994). Culture, theory, and narrative: The intersection of meaning in practice. *Social Work, 39*(4), 351–9.

Sin, R. W. C., & Yan, M. C. (2003). The margin as the center of a theory of social inclusion: Searching for a point of departure for integrative anti-racist social work practice in Canada. In W. Shera (Ed.), *Emerging perspectives on anti-oppressive practice*. Toronto, ON: Canadian Scholarly Press.

Stalker, C., Maiter, S., & Alaggia, R. (2009). The experiences of minority immigrant families receiving child welfare services: Seeking to understand how to reduce risk and increase protective factors. *Families in Society, 90*(1), 28–36.

Staunaes, D. (2003). Where have all the subjects gone? Bringing together the concepts of intersectionality and subjectification. *Nordic Journal of Feminist and Gender Research, 11*(2), 101–10.

Swindler, A. (1986). Culture in action: Symbols and strategies. *American Sociological Review, 51*, 273–86.

Thomas, W. I. (1972). The definition of the situation. In J. G. Manis & B. N. Meltzer (Eds.), *Symbolic interaction: A reader in social psychology* (2nd ed., pp. 331–6). Boston, MA: Allyn and Bacon.

Vertovec, S. (2007). Super-diversity and its implications. *Ethnic and Racial Studies, 30*(6), 1024–54.

Walby, S., Armstrong, J., & Strid, S. (2012). Intersectionality: Multiple inequalities in social theory. *Sociology, 46*(2), 224–40.

Weber, L. (1998). A conceptual framework for understanding race, class, gender and sexuality. *Psychology of Women Quarterly, 13*(32), 12–32.

Yan, M. C. (2008). Exploring cultural tensions in cross-cultural social work practice. *Social Work, 53*(4), 317–28.

Yan, M. C., & Wong, Y. L. R. (2005). Rethinking self-awareness in cultural competence: Toward a dialogic self in cross-cultural social work. *Families in Society: The Journal of Contemporary Social Services, 86*(2), 181–8.

Young, I. M. (1990). *Justice and the politics of difference*. Princeton, NJ: Princeton University Press.

Young, I. M. (1997). *Intersecting voices: Dilemmas of gender, political philosophy, and policy*. Princeton, NJ: Princeton University Press.

Yssaad, L. (2012). The immigrant labour force analysis series: The Canadian immigrant labour market. Statistics Canada. Retrieved from http://www.statcan.gc.ca/pub/71-606-x/71-606-x2012006-eng.pdf

Yuval-Davis, N. (2006). Intersectionality and feminist politics. *European Journal of Women's Studies, 13*(3), 193–209.

Social Work with Aboriginal Families

A Traditional and Urban Dialectic

By Raymond Neckoway and Keith Brownlee

Chapter Objectives

This chapter will help you develop an understanding of:

- Aboriginal families and how they are portrayed in the literature, including comments about children, parents, grandparents, and extended family
- The medicine wheel and how it is used to teach specific values important to Aboriginal parents
- The role of the naming ceremony for Aboriginal children and their parents
- The struggles of urban Aboriginal parents who tried to base their childrearing practices on traditional parenting methods
- How the incorporation of Aboriginal parent voices and the challenges and transformations that they have had to confront is a powerful way to reflect on hegemonic thinking about parenting

Introduction

Social work with Aboriginal families requires workers to understand Aboriginal parenting realities. Unfortunately, the literature on this topic is limited, especially in regard to Aboriginal parents living in an urban setting (Weaver, 2012). When examining Canadian Aboriginal perspectives and practices on parenting, the challenge is not only in identifying ideas rooted in Aboriginal traditions and culture, but also in recognizing how they are being transformed because of new circumstances not encountered by previous generations. As with most modern parenting realities, Aboriginal parenting has evolved in concert with the continuous and gradual development of society. However, several authors draw attention to the devastating loss of traditional Aboriginal parenting knowledge and attribute it to pernicious decisions made outside of Aboriginal cultures, including colonization (Castellano, 2002), the hegemony of the Euro-Western views of parenting (Hand, 2006), and the deliberate invalidation and eventual destruction of traditional parenting (Lavell-Harvard & Corbiere-Lavell, 2006).

One example where the charge of colonization has been identified by Aboriginal peoples is in the child welfare arena (Blackstock, Trocmé, & Bennett, 2004). Child welfare courts are one of the most visible and contentious domains where Aboriginal peoples' perspectives on families and children confront a Euro-Western system. In one court case involving the adoption of two Aboriginal children to two separate non-Aboriginal families, Justice Mesbur acknowledged that she did not have an understanding of Aboriginal families (*A.[...] (First Nation) v. Children's Aid Society of Toronto*, 2004), yet believed that the bonding of the children to their foster parents was a better indicator of their future than releasing them to their home community with extended family. This type of child welfare court decision is reflective of the historical experience of Aboriginal peoples, with courts choosing to ignore Aboriginal preferences and realities (Zylberberg 1991; Blackstock, 2014). An Aboriginal child welfare agency in northern Manitoba, familiar with the above court decisions, expressed its desire to implement historical and traditional values rather than those imposed on them through child welfare laws (Awasis Agency of Northern Manitoba, 1997; AMR Planning and Consulting, 2015). American Indians encounter similar obstacles with institutional bias (Crofoot & Harris, 2012).

Closely related to colonization is the hegemony of Euro-Western worldviews. In today's information age, with increasingly complex, multicultural, and diverse populations, the aim for theorists on parenting is to develop ideas that can incorporate as many circumstances as possible. To accomplish this, many theories are abstracted to universal human motivations, values, or functions. However, these theories do not take into account the context or history of a specific people group where they are applied (Gray, Coates, & Yellowfeather, 2010). For example, the culture and personality movement in the early to mid-20th century generated a portion of literature examining Aboriginal parenting and explanations of child development (Boggs, 1958; Caudill, 1949; Landes, 1937). They sought cultural explanations of parenting and its consequences for the child: a personality constructed by the culture. A central criticism of the culture and personality movement was its oversimplification of the concepts of culture and personality (Levine & Norman, 2001). The culture and personality movement reflects the historical practice of academics studying specific Aboriginal groups or Aboriginal peoples. Researchers come with predetermined concepts or theories and fail to take into consideration the worldview of the parents (White, Maxim, & Beavon, 2003). Thus, the Aboriginal group being researched is silenced as academics observe, record, interpret, and leave. The parenting theory that was being developed is then applied to Aboriginal families. Rogoff (2003) uses the term "imposed-etic" to describe the process where ideas developed outside the culture are applied uncritically and are inconsistent with the understandings and contexts of the people being helped. For this reason, knowledge of Aboriginal parenting is required to restrain the imposed-etic by those outside Aboriginal cultures.

In response to the challenges of an imposed-etic, Aboriginal leaders and academics advocate the return to and promotion of traditional parenting and childrearing practices (Aboriginal Healing Foundation, 2006; Fathers Involvement Research Alliance, 2008).

The promise of using parenting knowledge, values, and practices reflective of Aboriginal culture(s) is the difference between appropriateness and consistency versus the experience of continued colonization and cultural hegemony (Battiste, 2002; Castellano, 2002; Hart & Rowe, 2014).

In this chapter we examine the available literature on the organization and structure of Canadian Aboriginal families. First we describe the organization of Aboriginal families and the roles of children, parents, and extended family, including grandparents. We review the role that cultural teachings and ceremonies have on Aboriginal parents. Then we discuss the experiences and perspectives of Canadian Aboriginal parents as they apply their traditions in an urban context. We end with ideas on how parents manage their culture in an urban environment.

Descriptions of Aboriginal Families

Aboriginal cultures arrange their family systems specific to their geographic contexts and social networks (RCAP, 1996). Although it is widely recognized that there are differences between and within each Aboriginal culture in terms of parenting and goals of development, there are, nevertheless, some consistently reported regularities based upon observations and shared experiences (Brown & Brightman, 1988; Dhooper & Moore, 2001; Mihesuah, 2003).

Traditionally, among the Aboriginal cultures in Canada the roles of parents, families, extended families, and kinship systems were relatively stable for hundreds of years (Black-Rogers, 1967; Hallowell, 1946). Each person had an expected role and contribution to the functioning of the community according to the context: agrarian, hunting/gathering, or primarily fishing. Failure to learn and practice the tasks and lessons of survival could bring dire consequences to the whole family. Therefore, adults were role models for the children and mentored them into required roles for the community.

Rapid changes brought about changes in the family systems through displacement from territory, loss of traditional lifestyles, and government interventions, which affected parents and the roles played by individuals (Preston, 2002). Aboriginal families throughout Canada experienced disruption that negatively affected their ability to perform simple acts of parenting. For example, competition with settlers and restrictions placed by governments for land, fish, and animals made it difficult to provide the basic necessities of life. The resulting change from a nomadic to a sedentary lifestyle eliminated many of the traditional roles expected of adults in the community. All of this had a disruptive effect on all members of the family and the role of the extended family.

Children

Cultures collectively develop their understandings and explanations of children's development, which they pass on to successive generations of parents. These understandings and explanations inform parents about their child's needs and the responses that will meet those needs. Cultures evolve and are affected by the environment and interactions of people from other cultures through the exchange of ideas. This phenomenon has led to the tendency of those seeking explanations of childhood to seek universal features among children, regardless of specific cultural influences. The search for universals among children tends to focus on the biological, psychological, and physical development of children. Universals in parenting can obscure the boundary between commonalities and unique parenting perspectives and practices. Context, culture, and other significant factors affect a universal theory's ability to describe, explain, and predict in a particular situation or with a particular child (Stairs & Bernhard, 2002). The overreliance on universalizing theories, such as children's development, have led some to rediscover the contemporary child and not one that is abstracted beyond the immediate context. Aboriginal children need to be understood from their past as well as their present conditions.

Aboriginal children have had a qualitatively different experience than Canadian children in general. Several generations have endured the legacy of the residential school era, where children were separated from their parents for prolonged periods of time with the aim of undermining their culture. Over time, these children became parents who were products of these institutions (Aboriginal Healing Foundation, 2008), and did not have the traditional ceremonies or teachings to refer to as previous generations did. The systematic governmental effort to assimilate Aboriginal people into the dominant Euro-Canadian culture meant important beliefs and practices around parenting were devalued, disparaged, or lost. The policy of assimilation also meant an assault on the very identity of the Aboriginal person, to the point where some despised being in his or her own body and were ashamed of their Aboriginal heritage. Theories of child development were applied without consideration of this historical context and the devastating results of assimilation policies.

Aboriginal writers and cultural teachings often characterize Aboriginal infants as transitioning from the spirit realm to inhabit a physical body; as such, they are gifts from the Creator (Goodluck & Short, 1980; RCAP, 1996). There are, therefore, obligations and responsibilities on the parents and community to provide an environment to entice the "spirit" to stay within the infant and grow into adulthood. One contemporary Aboriginal writer (Anderson, 2006) describes the Ojibwa practice of keeping infants away from negative energy for the first 40 days of life. The concern is that if the infant is made aware of negativity in this world he or she may decide to return to the spirit world. There are similar parenting practices within Aboriginal cultures that are spiritually informed.

A related theme to the spiritually based view is the common Aboriginal understanding that the destiny of individuals is influenced through rituals and ceremonies beginning in infancy (Eastman, 1980). The belief is that children have a destiny, and parents participate in the process through the discernment of their child's spiritual journey (Angell, 1997). The consequence for Aboriginal parents is that children are allowed to make many of their own decisions because they are considered a person with destiny and are free to explore and influence their own environment (McPherson & Rabb, 2001). Parents create or expose their children to a nurturing environment, which enables children to develop at their own pace and discover their unique personalities. Once this is established, parents can then take a long-term view as their child's destiny unfolds (Bopp, Bopp, Brown, & Lane Jr., 1984; Goulet, Bell, Tribble, Paul, & Ariella, 1998). The belief that the child's destiny has been decided is reflected in Aboriginal parents' preferring nonverbal teaching and learning styles where they monitor their children's behaviours rather than try to shape them (Letourneau, Hungler, & Fisher, 2005; MacDonald & Boffman, 1995).

Children were expected to assume the roles and responsibilities of a community member as their development allowed. This was initially accomplished by listening, watching, and taking on tasks when and where appropriate (Fournier & Crey, 1997). Fournier and Crey are repeating a common assertion made among Aboriginal leaders (Aboriginal Head Start, 2006; Report of the Aboriginal Committee, 1992; Report of the First Nation's Child and Family Task Force, 1993); but this tradition of preparing children, by involving them as soon as practical, is seldom explored for its continued practice. The traditional educational system of obligations and responsibilities of Aboriginal parents and community toward infants and children was fairly straightforward because of the small (15–20 people), subsistent, nomadic groupings of families and their relative isolation from other cultures. These groupings of families have been altered by the consolidation of Aboriginal peoples onto lands set aside as reserves.

The geographical changes imposed upon Aboriginal peoples has meant that families are less likely to go out onto the land because of several challenges like mobility, sedentary life, and competition for scarce lands for hunting and trapping near the settlements. This, in turn, affects the mentoring of infants and children on land-based living and its associated teachings (Ohmagari & Berkes, 1997). For many contemporary Aboriginal families, teaching their children about the land occurs later in life, if at all. What is not clear from the literature is the transition some Aboriginal parents make in teaching and mentoring their children from land-based living to acquiring knowledge and marketable skills for urban life. Parenting and child development knowledge exist in Aboriginal communities. Therefore, acquiring Aboriginal perspectives on children needs to be examined through those primarily responsible for them—the parents and grandparents.

Parents

In an increasingly complex, interconnected world where cultural boundaries overlap, parents nevertheless implicitly refer to and apply their culture's customs and knowledge of parenting practices (Harkness & Super, 2006). This preference does not mean that parents from one culture are homogeneous; rather, they use their culture as the foundation in which to consider other cultures' knowledge and practices of parenting. Aboriginal peoples in Canada reflect, by their experiences, intracultural and intercultural differences in their parenting based on the multiple influences they are exposed to—that is, the union of parents from other cultural groups, the effects of assimilation policies, and the choices of parents to raise their children according to their priorities that may be separate from their culture's priorities. Largely, the literature on Aboriginal parenting reflects historical and traditional practices as representative of a cultural foundation (Densmore, 1970; Hilger, 1951; Jennes, 1935).

Perhaps the most devastating impact on Aboriginal parenting to date has been the residential school era, where four to five generations of children were removed from families to be educated by church-operated and federally financed schools (ChrisJohn, Young, & Maraun, 1997; Fournier & Crey, 1997). One consequence of having been raised in residential schools has been the change from traditional, nurturing roles of parenting to being bewildered about parenting (RCAP, 1996). Residential school experiences of regimentation, lack of emotional closeness, and negation of culture and language dominated many children's experiences from the age of 5 until they were 18 (Schissel & Wotherspoon, 2003). Children raised in residential schools, when they became adults and started their own families, did not benefit from having their parents as role models and, as a result, did not learn appropriate parenting skills (Johnston, 1988; Knockwood, 2001). This made the challenging task of parenting that much more difficult. Many parents found themselves replicating their negative childhood experiences of residential school in their orientation to their children, such as harsh, punitive discipline, and were unable to express nurturing emotions with their children (Aboriginal Healing Foundation, 2008).

Testimonies at the Royal Commission on Aboriginal Peoples (1996) revealed that once the residential school era was over, the child welfare era began. Large numbers of Aboriginal children became involved with children's aid societies because of neglect and other protection concerns (Timpson, 1995). In addition, the migration of more than 50 per cent of the Aboriginal population to urban centres (Norris & Clatworthy, 2011) forced the re-examination of traditional roles and functions of parents. The increasingly diverse living conditions of Aboriginal mothers reveals that there isn't a universal experience that informs Aboriginal parenting (Lavell-Harvard & Corbiere-Lavell, 2006). This understanding makes generalizations of Aboriginal parenthood a cautious undertaking because of the varied experiences and priorities of parents.

Aboriginal cultures throughout Canada are trying to heal from the negative impacts of colonization, residential schools, and child welfare involvement by re-examining their cultural identity. One of the top priorities toward developing a strong nation is to develop healthy parenting skills (Pintarics & Sveinunggard, 2005). (For a further discussion on culture, race, and intersectional identities, see Chapter 1 by Alean Al-Krenawi, John R. Graham, and Nazim Habibov.) The task of eliminating negative parenting roles, modifying traditional roles, or adopting new ones has been different for each Aboriginal culture because of their unique history with colonization, residential schools, and cultural priorities. One response has been to revive historical roles through the incorporation of **kinship** or **clan** systems (Neckoway, Brownlee,

Jourdain, & Miller, 2003). These systems draw upon traditional teachings, specified roles, and a social network of individuals to help in parenting.

Other Aboriginal groups or individuals try to walk both worlds by incorporating ideas of parenting from outside the culture with traditional notions (Ball & Pence, 2001; Carriére & Thomas, 2014; Lavell-Harvard & Corbiere-Lavell, 2006). There is an acknowledgement of some commonality between cultures where ideas on parenting can be shared and borrowed. Some Aboriginal parents try to adopt new parenting roles in light of the changed context from traditional patterns to ones that fit the urban setting (Weaver & White, 1997). There is recognition that traditional parenting roles occur within a context and, without that context to support those roles, Aboriginal parents have to adapt. This challenge usually occurs when families move from a relatively homogeneous community to a larger urban centre where the Aboriginal population is fairly small (Weaver, 2001).

In most Aboriginal communities, parenting is rarely an isolated task because of the presence of family, extended family, and friends. The role of family and extended family has changed from living off the land and travelling with the seasons to a sedentary life based in one community with several groupings of families. In addition, the movement of Aboriginal people into urban centres has reduced extended family involvement in parenting and passing along information on childrearing. This has changed the historical roles and reach of the social network of family in influencing parents and children. The use of the extended family network by all family types is not known in urban centres nor is the kind of support the extended family can give over long distances.

Extended Family

The extended family has been identified as the pivotal influence in Aboriginal societies (RCAP, 1996). The role and importance of the extended family system has been widely reported in the literature (Castellano, 2002; RCAP, 1996; Report of the First Nation's Child and Family Task Force, 1993). Extended family means lineage and bloodlines are important, but it also encompasses a wider view where clans, kin, and **totems** can include elders, leaders, and communities (Hallowell, 1955; Red Horse, 1980b). When the extended family functions at its best all members share a collective responsibility for the caring and nurturing of the child (McShane & Hastings, 2004) and keep a watchful eye on young children in the community (Lame Deer & Erdoes, 1994). The extended family socializes children into cultural expectations and guides them throughout their formative years.

Eastman (1980) describes the layers of assistance the new mother can access within her community and surroundings. These include her mother and grandmother, the accepted rules from her people, and lessons from observing nature. The cultural, social, and spiritual orientation of Aboriginal families does not put pressure on the sole relationship between mother and infant (Report of the Aboriginal Committee, 1992; Weaver & White, 1997). The child who lives in this extended family network would have multilayered relationships rather than a dyadic one (Brendtro & Brokenleg, 1993; Gfellner, 1990). The common feature of the "nuclear" family of mother, father, and children is considered a household within the larger extended family (Red Horse, 1980a). Those outside the culture who fail to understand the extended family system can interpret this type of parenting as having a lack of bonding between biological parents and children (Stremlau, 2005).

Another facet of the network of extended family relationships occurs through customary adoption by grandparents, which is a time-honoured practice among most Aboriginal cultures (Awasis Agency of Northern Manitoba, 1997). The reasons for grandparent involvement in Aboriginal communities are similar to those in mainstream culture—that is, death of a parent, alcohol abuse or violence in the child's birth family, or the grandparent's availability while the parents work (Jendrek, 1994). Hayslip and Kaminski (2005) in their literature review of grandparents note how grandparents take on several roles, such as caregivers, financial aid, safety net, and a second chance for their own parenting. However, they do not address some of the important roles Aboriginal grandparents play, such as passing down cultural teachings and an Aboriginal language, teaching skills for subsistence living, and communicating traditional values. In essence, what the grandparents are doing is transmitting an Aboriginal culture to another generation.

The extended family system within Aboriginal cultures has been strained by the outmigration of approximately 50 per cent of the members of **First Nations** communities to major urban centres in Canada (Alderson-Gill & Associates, 2005; Statistics Canada, 2008). Many youth and families relocate to pursue education, employment, housing, and opportunities for their children, or medical services that are not available in their communities (Statistics Canada, 2011). Because of leaving the extended family system, many youth and young families have a difficult time adjusting to their new urban surroundings. The Royal Commission on Aboriginal Peoples (1996) identified the transition from a family-centred perspective to an individualistic, urbanized, and somewhat alienating context as a source of difficulty. Because of the inherent tension, many chose to return home because of the isolation and homesickness they experienced (Yellow Horse Brave Heart, 2001). However, some youth and families are able to establish new relationships and create support structures that act as an extended family in an urban setting. Another source of support for families that relocate is the revitalization of traditional teachings and practices.

Cultural Teachings and Ceremonies Relevant to Families and Parenting

Childhood ceremonies that were historically practised in most Aboriginal cultures were banned by the federal government in the early part of the 20th century but are experiencing a renaissance with many Aboriginal parents. Some of these teachings, values, and ceremonies identify and prioritize infant's needs and what is expected of parents. The details of who implements the specific obligations and responsibilities that exist between parents, families, and their community are embedded within the teaching, values, or ceremony (Bopp et al., 1984; Hart, 2002).

Aboriginal cultures vary in their teachings on the timing of the first influences on a person's life. Some teachings predict or discern a destiny beginning at pregnancy up to the first days of life (Beck, Walters, & Francisco, 1995). For example, one Mohawk midwife describes the process of discerning the baby's life path during the birthing process (Anderson, 2006). A midwife discerning and interpreting the appropriate "signs" during childbirth prescribes characteristics or destiny to the child. The identified characteristics can be developed throughout childhood by the common teaching tool of the medicine wheel. The medicine wheel describes desired behaviours and explains internal processes from infancy to old age (Swinomish Tribal Mental Health Project, 1991).

Medicine Wheel

The medicine wheel is a symbolic teaching tool. Hart (2002) uses the medicine wheel as a tool that gives information on developmental tasks to be accomplished by a person throughout his or her life, beginning with infancy/childhood. The medicine wheel arranges interrelating concepts into groups of four. These groups, for example, include the four directions, the four stages of life, the four aspects of personhood, the four races of people, and the four primary elements. Each direction, stage of life, and aspect of personhood has developmental tasks appropriate for the person in the present. The goal is to achieve wholeness and balance in life, which is a lifelong task, periodically and momentarily achieved.

A medicine wheel explanation of childhood would begin in the eastern direction, which is the place for all beginnings: of birth, a symbol for renewal, innocence, and spontaneity. Bopp and colleagues (1984) provide a list of 33 qualities/values attributed to the east (p. 72). Parents using the medicine wheel perspective would be informed of this array of personal qualities and values, which reveals a combination of inherent qualities of the child as well as those that need to be developed. It is the parents' responsibility to implement the medicine wheel perspective, which depends upon the qualities or values their child needs to develop. For example, the value of "uncritical acceptance of others" may not be displayed in the child's life, so the parents may arrange social occasions where their child is able to meet and play with a variety of children in order to develop this quality. Since there is no possibility of exhausting the development of these qualities or values in a person's life, there is a continual return to the eastern direction.

What is learned in the east must be balanced with the qualities and values associated with the other three directions. The direction of the south is the place of summer: fullness, youth, physical strength, and vigour. Inherent in the development of the south is the discipline required in the newfound abilities. Therefore, the east and the south must be balanced with the other two directions. The west is a place of testing. It is also a place of prayer and meditation. It is the blending of the idealism and goals of youth with the spiritual understanding of the west. The north is the dwelling place of true wisdom; it is a place to think, to synthesize, and to interpret hidden meanings. The north is a place of completion and fulfillment, where the gifts from the other directions reach their highest point (Bopp et al., 1984). In the medicine wheel perspective, individuals are whole when they incorporate the teachings of the four directions in their life (Graveline, 1998). The four directions, therefore, allow a parent who is familiar with the teachings of the medicine wheel to reflect on their child's needs and how they should orientate to their child to facilitate their optimal future growth and development.

Values

Brant (1990), a Mohawk psychiatrist, refers to childrearing values and beliefs of Aboriginal cultures to explain behaviours of Aboriginal parents and children. He believed that these were adaptive to the contexts in which Aboriginal peoples originally lived—that is, small groupings of families numbering 15 to 20 individuals who spent six to eight months in close proximity because of living off the land. These living arrangements emphasized values and relationship characteristics that ensured the survival and productivity of the group. Despite the passage of time and the changed context in which they originated, these values have been slow to change and continue to play a role in social relationships and parenting (Bedard, 2006).

Brant (1990) identified several ethics of traditional childrearing that were significant for the existence of the family. The ethic of noninterference, sometimes called the value of noninterference, has gained widespread acceptance among social scientists (Portman, 2001; Sue, 2003) as representing American Indian or Canadian Aboriginal reality. Noninterference has a high degree of respect for individual independence, which leads Aboriginals to resist giving instructions, coercing, or even persuading another person to do something uninvited. This is reflected in childrearing practices that have children learn through modelling and natural consequences, and for parents to appear to outsiders as permissive rather than in control of their child's behaviour. A common experience where this ethic is played out among many Aboriginal families is letting the child decide, for example, whether they want to go to school or whether they want to go to the dentist. To most outsiders it would be incomprehensible to allow a child to possess such decision-making power. According to the ethic of noninterference, these types of occurrences reflect the application of the value of noninterference (Ross, 2006).

Brant (1990) also observed the practice of emotional restraint among family members. He attributed this practice to the context of isolated settings where anger must not be shown because displays of vexation could jeopardize the voluntary co-operation essential to the survival of closely knit groups. The restraint on the direct expression of the emotion of anger meant that parents rarely, if ever, expressed this emotion toward their children (Hay, 1973). Parents had to use other means to express their reaction to an anger-producing situation.

Other childrearing values mentioned by Brant (1990) are the values of excellence and gratitude. These are demonstrated through the nonverbal expression of praise and the withholding of expressions of gratitude because of the pre-existing expectations of high standards of behaviour. Praise and expressions of gratitude are reserved for exceptional accomplishments. One of the implications of this value is that children are reluctant to try something they feel they will not do well at. The common parental teaching method is based on modelling rather than shaping. This is expressed primarily through the child observing until they are ready to put into practice what they have learned. This preferred method replaces discussions or presentations.

Possibly one of the most frustrating expressions of a value that confronted Brant was the conservation-withdrawal reaction of psychic and physical resources as an adaptive reaction to stress. Children withdrew into themselves, became uncommunicative and basically tried to be "invisible" to the person or situation that was producing the stress, much like a grouse that depends on its camouflage to hide from predators.

When parents and children were in natural, subsistence settings, this reaction to a common stressor, usually danger, worked because of the life-and-death situations that confronted them. Parents who continue to emphasize the conservation-withdrawal reaction to stress may not prepare their children for the expected stressors of school and other common stressors of daily activities in Canadian society. The relevance of such Aboriginal childrearing values might need to be examined to see if it would be preferable to replace them with other values to enable parents and children to thrive in an other-than-subsistent context. Brant and Patterson (1990) note that Aboriginal parents who wish to follow their traditions in an urban setting, where none exist or exist minimally, are not likely to find it easy to sustain their endeavours.

Naming Ceremony

Several Aboriginal parenting practices incorporate traditional ceremonies that take place soon after birth and up to two years of age. Beck, Walters, and Francisco (1995) provide detailed practices of various Aboriginal tribes that have ceremonies for infants and toddlers. Ceremonies for infants helped in setting the direction for their lives through the assignment of a namesake, a prophecy indicating a future condition or role, or the confirmation of membership into the community (Landes, 1969). Since the infants were oblivious to these early ceremonies, it was the responsibility of the parents, extended family, and community to remind the person throughout their lives of these early events (Landes, 1937). The naming ceremony has enjoyed a renaissance as more Aboriginal parents explore the role of this ceremony in their parenting and reclaim some of their cultural practices. When the name is conferred onto the infant, an identity is received and the person can take his or her place as a member of the community. References to the future role or condition of the child are made with miniature "guns" or "bows and arrows" and other objects that are hung over the infant's cradleboard (Densmore, 1970). The infant's older siblings, parents, and grandparents refer to these throughout the first years of life, serving as constant reminders about fulfilling the requirements of his or her name until the message is incorporated as his or her own. Landes (1969) also mentions the introduction of one-day fasts for children beginning at eight years of age where they are to receive their visions or dreams related to their names. Some of the names given to children are patrons from the spirit world, who the child can petition for guidance and help and who are acknowledged by the community (Landes, 1969). Parents socialized their children to participate in the chores of daily life but also isolated their child for periods of time to receive their vision/dreams.

Unfortunately for Aboriginal cultures, most traditional childhood ceremonies were outlawed by the Canadian government in the early 1900s (RCAP, 1996). Childhood ceremonies were replaced with Christian ceremonies like baptism and baby dedications. For many Aboriginal cultures, traditional childhood ceremonies have dwindled in practice as the knowledge disappears with the elders who knew the teachings associated with them. Despite the widespread absence of many of the traditional ceremonies performed for infants and children, the spiritual values associated with such practices have remained in the consciousness of Aboriginal peoples. As stated earlier, the belief among many Aboriginal parents that children are gifts from the Creator or come from the spirit world is still widely held despite the attempt to eradicate these beliefs. These beliefs are reported in the literature: many, ironically, through government reports (Report of the Aboriginal Committee, 1992; Report of the First Nation's Child and Family Task Force, 1993; Truth and Reconciliation Commission of Canada, 2012). These reports confirm the existence of certain Aboriginal beliefs about children, but they have not been examined for their application to an urban setting.

Parents' Perceptions of Factors Influencing Parenting

What follows below is an exploration of a number of Aboriginal parents' comments on parenting realities in an urban context. We interviewed 20 Aboriginal parents in 2009 who have tried to base their childrearing practices on traditional parenting methods in an urban setting. Parents originated from 15 First Nation communities in northwestern Ontario and consisted of 11 mothers and 9 fathers. Of the 20 parents, 12 had children under 5 years of age, and 8 had children over 18 years of age. Parents' experiences and perspectives were compared to the literature to highlight the personal impact of historical and contextual factors.

Historical Factors Affecting Parenting

Historical experiences have conditioned Aboriginal people to be guarded against solutions offered by government and those outside the culture who act on behalf of their interests. The parents were cognizant of the historical factors affecting them and their relations with the government of Canada. Several parents noted the changes in their lifetime from a nomadic, subsistence lifestyle to a more sedentary one. These changes continue to have an impact on how they identify with their culture without using the subsistent lifestyle as one of the foundations. As this way of life is decreasing, other identifying features or practices that represent Aboriginal people are emerging in contemporary conditions. Some of these features or practices include practising traditional spirituality, pow-wow dancing, espousing a particular value, or having art or craft products representing Aboriginal culture. (For a continued in-depth discussion on cultural spirituality, religion, and diversity, see Chapter 11 by Diana Coholic.)

The literature and participant comments reveal the impact of the government intervention that colonized Aboriginal peoples in Canada (RCAP, 1996; Truth and Reconciliation Commission of Canada, 2012). Colonizers conferred upon the colonized an inferior status, which paved the way to "speaking to" Aboriginal peoples in terms of what is in their best interests rather than Aboriginal peoples "speaking for" themselves. The silencing of Aboriginal people marginalized much of their existing knowledge, which included parenting. The dominant discourse of colonization permeated interactions between the newcomers and the Aboriginal population.

The literature on Canadian Aboriginal realities cited numerous attempts by the federal government to eliminate several aspects of Aboriginal culture, such as speaking their languages, gatherings at pow-wows or potlatches, and traditional parenting styles (Awasis Agency of Northern Manitoba, 1997; Hamilton & Sinclair, 1991; RCAP, 1996; Swinomish Tribal Mental Health Project, 1991). This was commented on by most of the parents, who mentioned experiencing first-hand the damaging effects of these government assimilation policies for their communities and for their own parents, including the significant impact of residential schools on the family.

In response to historical (and some would say contemporary) factors, there is a collective wariness toward the government of Canada because of its role in attempting to destroy many aspects of Aboriginal cultural identity. This circumstance has forced Aboriginal parents to focus on cultural survival through emphasizing cultural practices, values, beliefs, traditions, and identities as part of their parenting practices. The parents we interviewed stressed various aspects of Aboriginal culture in their parenting because they do not want to be absorbed by Canadian mainstream culture. Though they cannot model a subsistence lifestyle in an urban centre, many parents referred to using various cultural teachings and traditions as a way to ensure their child has knowledge and experience of Aboriginal culture.

Several parents appealed to traditional Aboriginal culture, prior to European contact, as the approach to restore what has been lost to assimilation. One parent imagined that, historically, Aboriginal families met the qualities of sharing, respect, and several other espoused parenting values. Reference to historical conditions to emulate is commendable, on the one hand, because it is a source of inspiration and motivation to continually strive to achieve positive qualities. On the other hand, the historical conditions and contexts that created the development of particular parenting values cannot be reproduced in contemporary society to the same degree. Those who use culture, in the historical sense, as a source of inspiration/motivation face the impossibility of reproducing the conditions that spawned particular values. Thus, in the long run, Aboriginal people can reach only marginal levels of historical parenting practices. Thus, while the parents referred to using Aboriginal culture to inform them on several aspects of parenting, they pointed out that they still have to contend with the impacts of the urban context on their parenting.

Contextual Factors Affecting Parenting

Contexts are important for situating behaviours and grasping social and cultural importance (Dey, 1993). As stated earlier, Aboriginal cultures arrange their family systems to align with their geographic contexts and social networks (RCAP, 1996). The parents described the childhood context of their First Nation territory and the lifestyle that was prevalent. Various members of the community were expected to contribute to the functioning of family and community. For many of the parents, this meant engaging in hunting and gathering activities. The presence of family and extended family meant that roles and tasks of parenting were distributed among a group of people.

Many of the parents commented that they were the first in their family to relocate to an urban centre and deal with the challenges that arise as part of this new context. During their upbringing, parents experienced relative cultural and social homogeneity in their home community. When in their First Nation community, questions of their ethnicity, social behaviour, or cultural practices were rarely raised. The change to an urban context rendered them unfamiliar with the norms of urban life and required them to reconsider their taken-for-granted parenting assumptions and practices. Parents revealed their struggles in coming to terms with their inability to replicate for their children their own childhood experiences of freedom in the First Nation community, as well as the presence of and access to extended family and land-based activities.

When the parents compared their upbringing to the urban context, they described limits to the freedom of movement and sense of space. Parents' childhood memories were of playing with friends and freely visiting extended family scattered throughout the community. In contrast, some described the confining nature of urban life by always having their child physically close to them when in public. They also discussed the enclosing nature of their house or backyard when used as play areas for the child. However, if their child has only known urban life, then the urban context may not be as stifling as parents imagine.

Urban life is full of strangers to those who were used to knowing, and being known by, practically everyone in the community. The descriptions of their First Nation communities as extended family meant that constant attention of children was not needed because parents came to rely on family, friends, and neighbours to keep watch over their children and could be counted on to contact parents or intervene if necessary. The expectation and reliance on others meant that parents were probably not aware of minor incidents their child was involved in because someone else resolved the matter, with or without the parent's knowledge. In contrast, urban life means that parents are usually in close physical proximity to their children and are more aware of what transpires with their child throughout a given day. Activities are structured for the child rather than unfolding according to the rhythm of community life.

The majority of parents participated in land-based activities during their childhood. Land-based activities included camping, fishing, trapping, hunting, and harvesting berries or herbal medicines. Several parents commented that their involvement in these activities did not occur until they went back to their First Nation territory, which was usually once or twice a year. For some, the increased effort to locate and participate in traditional and cultural activities in an urban centre meant these activities were reduced to a few days per year, if at all. Both situations limit the amount of time parents have to pass on to their children the skills and knowledge of land-based activities, and to build relationships through these activities as well as foster in their children a connection to the culture and the land.

Cultural Factors Affect Parenting

Parents who relocate to an urban centre change more than their physical location—they also become exposed to other cultures. The parents made the observation that they are exposed to opportunities to acquire other parenting knowledge and practices, which may not be congruent with some features of Aboriginal culture. Kluckhohn and Strodtbeck (1961), who studied Native American tribes, identified this phenomenon as *cultural variation*, where individuals are expected to reflect their dominant intracultural features and yet exhibit characteristics that vary from their culture because of being exposed to new environmental or social forces. Most parents had to select which aspects of the Aboriginal culture to implement in their new surroundings.

The internal struggle for the parents was seen as coming from the phenomenon of implicitly referring to and applying their culture's customs and knowledge of parenting practices onto a context that does not fully support them (Harkness & Super, 2006). In light of this urban challenge, the literature on Aboriginal parenting largely reflects a subsistent lifestyle and assorted traditional practices as representative of a cultural foundation. The subsistent lifestyle of working off the land in family groupings and the perspective that arises from it (i.e., knowledge of animal patterns, weather, and suitable clothing) has provided solutions to the challenges previous generations of parents have faced (Densmore, 1970; Hilger, 1951; Jennes, 1935). However, parents' urban circumstances created new lifestyle demands that their parents had not encountered, and historical solutions were not informative to the new conditions. This made parenting a dynamic enterprise, where previous information and strategies coexist with the new ones being developed. (For further discussion on the importance of intergenerational culturism in social work, see Chapter 9 by Debashis Dutta and Ross Klein.)

Despite the changes in parenting behaviour in an urban centre, all the parents personally identified with their cultural heritage. The parents referred to their cultural heritage as a source of strength and pride. Parents used their culture as a basis to teach their children their identity and about living a spiritual life and cultivating values toward themselves and others. A consistent theme from the parents as well as the literature is a focus on values and beliefs, the naming ceremony, and the role of extended family and grandparents. These themes are discussed in more detail below.

Values and Beliefs

The caveat to the dynamic nature of culture, at the behavioural level, is the slower pace of change at the internal level—that is, cultural values and beliefs. Brant (1990) wrote about the values and beliefs that inform Aboriginal parents and described them as adaptive to the subsistent context, namely, small family constellations seldom greater than 20 individuals who relied on the land and natural resources as a means of sustenance. These living arrangements emphasized enduring values and the qualities of relationships that safeguarded the continuing survival of the group. Even with considerable transformations of the social contexts, these values have been slow to change and continue to play a role in relationships and parenting.

Those who have migrated to urban settings have left part of their cultural heritage behind; however, a physical move off the land or from the First Nation community does not automatically shed Aboriginal culture and its values and beliefs. Comments from the parents revealed the Aboriginal culture's emphasis on sharing, respect, helping those who need it, and valuing family. Parenting according to these cultural values would include teaching and modelling them throughout the child's life. Despite the changed parenting behaviours in the urban context, there remains an attitude or disposition toward parenting that reflects historical values developed from a subsistent lifestyle. These values and beliefs also considered the subtlety of relationships and of maintaining favourable orientations among one another.

In the urban setting, where such stark contrasts of life and death are not considered when deciding to share or help others, it is not known how these cultural values are maintained and exercised by Aboriginal parents. The urban centre is generally based on a sedentary lifestyle, a wage economy, and the acquisition of material goods and the availability of social programs and services. In contrast, the subsistent economy is based upon a nomadic lifestyle that depended on the skills and labour of every individual in the group and minimal acquisition of material possessions. Sharing, helping those in need, and valuing the importance of family take on a different meaning when implementing historical Aboriginal cultural values in an urban setting.

Many of the parents recognized the inherent wisdom of Aboriginal cultural values, for example, strengthening relations among those around you, sharing, or cultivating a spiritual understanding. However, the parents pointed out that some of these values are taking on different expressions from previous generations because of the changed conditions.

One expression of the value placed on infants and children that has been affected historically is Aboriginal childhood ceremonies. Most Aboriginal ceremonies were prohibited from public expression as part of the assimilation strategy to introduce

European practices. This meant that those who wanted to maintain Aboriginal ceremonies had to practise them in secret and with limited numbers of parents.

Naming Ceremony

In relation to children and their development, cultures collectively build on their understandings and explanations of children's optimal development, which they pass on to successive generations of parents. These understandings and explanations inform parents about their child's needs and behaviours and the ceremonies that will meet those needs. A common practice with many cultures is the recognition and initiation of the newborn into the community in which they belong. These various practices convey information about the child and some of the responsibilities of the parents, family, and community. One example of a cultural belief among Aboriginal peoples is the naming ceremony.

The historical significance of the government of Canada and Christian denominations stopping the naming ceremony from being practised created a state of confusion for the first generation of Aboriginal parents impacted by this decision. Parents who oriented their childrearing activities according to the Aboriginal name of the child no longer had their familiar foundation to build upon. Instead, Aboriginal parents were told to obtain "Christian names," which meant European names. The Christian names would not have had the same effect as the child's Aboriginal name because they did not convey a direction for the child or identify certain characteristics and a future condition/role for the child.

The naming ceremony's approach to children is different from conventional parenting understandings. The naming ceremony identifies several characteristics of the person before they are shaped by personality or experience. Perhaps this explains what looks like permissive parenting, to outsiders, because the parent believes that key characteristics of the child have already been identified. This perspective is at odds with many child development or parenting theories that prescribe specific actions for parents and its predicted positive consequence. Conventional parental understanding refers to experience and personality as ongoing developments in the child's life, and parents mould and shape what the person is to become rather than facilitate who the child already is.

Some parents mentioned that their child's characteristics were identified through the naming ceremony. For example, one parent stated that his daughter was going to be a strong, confident, and assertive person when she became an adult because that was what the elder told him. This parent saw some of these developing characteristics displayed in his daughter's personality and behaviours, since the elder revealed them to him. This father will emphasize the characteristics related to the Aboriginal name and presumably pay less attention to characteristics that do not. He approached parenting with key features identified and consciously oriented toward the fulfillment of certain characteristics of his daughter. At this point in the child's life (less than five years old), the father is referring to himself and his wife in implementing the naming ceremony characteristics.

For many parents, using the child's Aboriginal name to inform parenting is relatively new, that is, none of the parents had yet parented their children from birth to adulthood using the child's Aboriginal name as a guide. It remains to be seen what influence this type of parenting has on those children who are oriented to this perspective.

Another example of an Aboriginal parenting role is using the Aboriginal name as an antidote to being teased at school. One parent reminded his child that regardless of the names they were being called at school, their Aboriginal name was the true reflection of who they were. The Aboriginal name of the person can play a powerful role in annulling negative experiences or labels. During childhood, the person has to be reminded of its significance by those who know their Aboriginal name. However, daycare workers, teachers, or social workers that come into contact with the Aboriginal child in an urban setting may not be familiar with this parenting strategy and cannot join with or reinforce Aboriginal parents. This is one of the limitations of using a cultural strategy to parenting when the strategy is not well known and therefore cannot be reinforced by cultural outsiders. Demographically, Aboriginal people are a minority in an urban context and are spread throughout the city; therefore they cannot readily educate daycare workers, teachers, or others that play a role in the child's life. Aboriginal parents who participated in the naming ceremony did not allude to the psychological phenomenon called the Pygmalion effect (or the self-fulfilling prophecy), where certain characteristics of the child are identified by a respected person and parents expect those characteristics to be prominent and act upon them. Instead, parents believed that the elder who gave the Aboriginal name to their child had heard from the spirit world regarding the child's destiny.

The characteristics identified in the naming ceremony remain with the person throughout his or her life. The characteristics are initially developed by the parents, then endorsed by the family and community, and eventually by the bearers of the respective names as they progress through life and new dimensions are discovered.

Parents did not elaborate on whether their child can fulfill the destiny of their Aboriginal name in a non-Aboriginal context, which all parents were living in at the time of being interviewed. Parents did not give examples of roles and responsibilities in an urban centre that their child would assume as part of the fulfillment of the name given. Historically, the origin of the ceremony linked the name to being fulfilled in an Aboriginal community or context. Contemporary writers describing the naming ceremony have not made this aspect of the person's destiny clear (Lavell-Harvard & Corbiere-Lavell, 2006; Warren, 1984)

Parents did not comment on the urban context as limiting the expression or fulfillment of the child's Aboriginal name. They did comment on the significance of receiving their Aboriginal name. The most common feature was the sense of belonging/identity it conveyed for the person—that they were rooted in their culture and their culture was rooted in them. Most parents obtained their Aboriginal name when they were adults rather than the usual pattern of parents initiating the ceremony during infancy. Parents describe receiving their Aboriginal name as answering a fundamental question of who they are. In turn, they sought out an elder to conduct the naming ceremony for their children. Parents indicated that they would convey the significance of the name to their children as they grew up.

The people who reminded the child of their name throughout their lifetime were usually extended family members, primarily the grandparents because of proximity and access to the child. The beliefs and teachings associated with childhood naming imply benefits of parental involvement. In the naming ceremony, parents learn of the child's destiny through the name given and focus on preparing the infant for his or her journey in life. This practice offers substantial motivation for parents, families, and the community to ensure their continuation.

Extended Family and Grandparents

The literature review identified the extended family as a pivotal component in the structure of the Aboriginal family, and the nuclear family as a subsystem of it (RCAP, 1996; Red Horse, 1980b). Although not unique to Aboriginal societies, extended families are an important feature of support and socialization for Aboriginal people. Furthermore, most of the interviewed parents experienced the full range of what an extended family is, which includes their aunts, uncles, grandparents, cousins, and ultimately the community. The parents had interconnecting relationships with their extended family and were nurtured and supported by them throughout their childhood.

The influence of parents' extended family is restricted in an urban context in two ways. First, parents' comments were in the past tense, indicating they no longer had the same level of relationship with extended family as they had in the past. Second, parents visit their First Nation community once or twice a year, which means that the exposure of their children to extended family is limited and the ability to transmit cultural knowledge and practices are reduced significantly.

The function of the extended family was drastically reduced for those who had moved to an urban centre. Parents could not replicate the functions and relationships of the extended family with their children. Most parents keep regular contact by phone, mail, or email with family, friends, and extended family and are able to receive some support, advice, and guidance this way.

In an urban centre, the absence of extended family creates an emphasis on the nuclear family model where both parents carry full responsibilities of parenting rather than distributing the tasks of parenting to several family members. For many of these parents, they are the first generation to live the exclusive nuclear family model without being surrounded by extended family, friends, and their First Nation community. Several parents missed the presence of extended family and the multiple roles it played in their lives (cultural and familial continuity, babysitting, and several other forms of support and tangible aid). In light of this new circumstance, parents had to create a network of relationships with co-workers, parents from the same school their children attended, or clubs, associations, or church groups. These new relationships were based on common features of their lives (i.e., work, school, or leisure activities). The transition of relationships has been a difficult process.

The new form of extended family in the urban centre does not have the same ease as those back in their community. One mother commented that she had to remind her daughter not to go to the kitchen to help herself to a drink or food when visiting friends. There were degrees of etiquette or formality observed with those considered friends or acquaintances versus family. Some parents taught their child to know the difference between the two.

It is not known by parents' comments and through the literature the extent that new relationships created in the urban context parallel the features of an extended family. One key feature would be the ethnicity of individuals, because one of the primary roles of the extended family is the transmission of cultural knowledge and identity. Though healthy, nurturing relationships can be developed in an urban centre that mirror many aspects of extended family, those relationships may not be able to contribute in cultural ways that are important to Aboriginal parents. Several of the Aboriginal mothers with young children echoed this sentiment when they compared their parenting style with peers from their First Nation community. The mothers with young children enjoyed the friendships developed with other mothers in urban areas, and the effect of this relationship was to parent like them rather than family and friends back home. Parents had to seek out Aboriginal cultural activities or develop relationships with other Aboriginal people in the urban centre for their child to be exposed to their culture.

What was not clear from the parents' responses was whether the new network of friends in the urban centre shared the same values or beliefs deemed important to Aboriginal people or whether they reflected a reordering of values because of the influence of new relationships and cultures. The values and beliefs identified by parents were sharing, respect, helping those who need it, the importance of family, respecting the land, and being aware of their spiritual nature. None of the parents mentioned whether their non-Aboriginal peers shared these values and beliefs. Parents with children who were over 18 years of age continued to ascribe to Aboriginal cultural values and beliefs in a greater way than their younger counterparts. The passage of time will reveal whether younger parents will be influenced to modify or change their current values and beliefs.

Among extended family members, grandparents were mentioned the most by parents because of the parental roles they assumed from their adult children and for imparting cultural knowledge. The parents described grandparents' roles of taking them out on the land, ensuring they spoke the Aboriginal language, and passing down familial, cultural, and communal history. Some grandparents took on parental roles when it was necessary.

For those in First Nations communities, grandparents continue many of these practices, while Aboriginal parents in urban centres do not have access to this cultural resource. Urban parents, who do not have a safety net of grandparents or extended family, rely on formal services like daycare, children's aid societies, and numerous parenting or children's programs. However, these are time-limited services and there are no expectations of continuing relationships between worker and client.

The absence of grandparents from the parents' lives made them aware that their recourse if things went awry was the formal services offered in the city. Some parents received parenting education soon after their child was born and were grateful for the service. Those who received the service did not comment whether the information and skills they received were objectionable to Aboriginal worldviews. The parenting advice dealt with practical matters of feeding, discerning types of cries, and establishing a routine for the baby. Some of these young mothers did not have basic knowledge about raising an infant and therefore did not object to the service they received.

The loss of the role of grandparents' is similar to that of the larger extended family, since the service provided by professionals are generic in nature and do not cater to the individual's cultural preference. Aboriginal values, beliefs, and cultural teachings do not form part of parenting programs offered in an urban centre. In these circumstances, Aboriginal parents find that parenting knowledge is not supported by traditional teachings or informing mothers of the role of their child's Aboriginal name. The usual practice is to focus on the physical, mental, or emotional nature of the child based on theories or models that have been developed outside of Aboriginal culture. The spiritual nature, which is considered pre-eminent among Aboriginal peoples, is rarely referred to by service providers in the city and especially not in respect to infancy.

Historical and contextual forces affect how parents focus on their role and what they emphasize with their children. For Aboriginal people, protecting further erosion of their culture is a priority after a century of assimilation policies by the federal government. Many features of parenting in a First Nations community could not be replicated in an urban centre, which left parents searching for alternative means to pass on cultural knowledge and practices to their children. A primary difference is that Aboriginal parents in an urban centre have to be intentional and explicit in cultivating an Aboriginal culture, while their counterparts in their First Nation community can rely on grandparents, extended family, and the cultural context to transmit many aspects of the culture.

Parents are aware of the ease in which they drifted into and out of extended family homes as they were growing up in their First Nation community. Extended family and grandparents offered them numerous opportunities to learn Aboriginal cultural knowledge and activities. The absence of this network and safety net in the urban centre puts the onus on parents to seek alternative networks that are not based on pre-existing relationships or sharing the same cultural perspectives or practices.

Case Example 7.1

After a breakup with her partner, Bernadette relocated from her First Nation community to a city many hundreds of kilometres south with her three children. Bernadette did not have any family relations or friends who lived in the new city. With this transition to an urban centre Bernadette moved from an extended family context to a nuclear family situation.

continued

Points to Consider

1. What type of support do you think Bernadette might require now that she has made this move?
2. How do you think the support in the urban environment would feel different from relying on her extended family?

Case Example 7.2

Cathy is living with her grandmother in a major city. Cathy moved in with her grandmother when Cathy and her children moved from her First Nation community. Cathy is currently attending a parent-training group that her daughter's school referred her to because her youngest daughter is having behaviour problems in the classroom. Cathy has been learning some positive reinforcement strategies, which she has been encouraged to try at home. This has caused some conflict between her and her grandmother, who regards these strategies as spoiling her children when using a reward system and not following the Aboriginal way of parenting.

Points to Consider

1. Assuming the grandmother follows traditional parenting practices such as permissive parenting, discuss the dilemma or issues this family would be facing.

Case Example 7.3

A school counsellor working with Delores has suggested that she should be more proactive with her oldest child, Andy, who is in Grade 5 and is refusing to attend school regularly. Andy has been staying up late at night to watch hockey and is often tired in the morning. On these occasions he complains of being too tired for school, and when he does this Delores lets him stay home for the day. After a few weeks no change has taken place. When the counsellor speaks to Delores she finds out that it is difficult for Delores because it goes against her values to force Andy to go to school.

Points to Consider

1. How should the counsellor approach this situation?

Summary and Conclusion

Aboriginal cultures are not monolithic or homogeneous. Instead, there is recognition of a dynamic variability in individual and collective expressions of Aboriginal culture. For example, the culture is not practised identically today as in historical periods, there are different influences on those Aboriginal parents living in urban centres from those who live in a First Nation community, and individuals adhere to some Aboriginal cultural values and meaning systems and not to others. At the individual level, there are increased variations in cultural expressions, while collectively there are recognizable, shared understandings and practices of Aboriginal culture.

As long as Aboriginal peoples were separate from mainstream Canadian society on their First Nations territories, they could be characterized or stereotyped as a homogeneous culture. The recent outmigration of half the Aboriginal population from their First Nation territories into Canadian urban communities has challenged the primary descriptions the literature reflects about Aboriginal peoples. There is a gap from the present experiences of Aboriginal parents and what is reported in the academic literature. Part of this gap in the literature is attributed to the limited amount of scholarship being written about contemporary Aboriginal parents.

Aboriginal tribes know by experience the damage of their knowledge being devalued. Aboriginal peoples are in the process of reclaiming their knowledge that had been ignored, devalued, misunderstood, or prohibited. The foundation of Aboriginal knowledge exists in their culture, which affects what happens in practice.

The literature describes several features of Aboriginal parenting based on the cultural practice of subsistent living off the land, the important role of family and extended family, and adhering to various cultural teachings and traditions. The parents we interviewed were living in an urban centre, and their childhood experience reflected much of what the literature states. However, their new location prevented the continuation of some aspects of their traditional life. Therefore, they acquired additional parenting perspectives and practices that their counterparts in their First Nations communities did not. For example, First Nation parents do not have to be as vigilant of their children because of the presence of family, extended family, and friends in the home or in the community, whereas similar layers of support do not surround urban Aboriginal parents. The context, therefore, altered parents' traditional, cultural parenting expressions in some areas and significantly reduced it in other areas.

The urban context created tension in terms of the parents being unfamiliar with social norms, having to change their parenting style, and experiencing cultural dissonance. Being first to relocate to an urban centre or to complete a postsecondary degree or diploma meant that circumstances arose that their family members did not have to negotiate. Therefore, family members could not equip the person with prior required knowledge. Further, because of the urban context parents could not replicate their childhood environment and had to learn new ways of parenting. They had to transition from their familiar perspectives and practices to new ones.

However, their First Nations communities continue to play a role as repositories of their Aboriginal heritage, for example by imparting knowledge about living off the land, maintaining their Aboriginal language, and various cultural teachings and practices. Although some elements of Aboriginal culture were forced into the background because of the new context, other elements came to the foreground. This is most readily acknowledged in access to and participation in land-based activities. Aboriginal parents are also affected by the absence of family and extended family in the urban centre. Friends and service providers have been able to replace some of the roles family or extended family play in the lives of Aboriginal parents, but the one area that cannot be readily replaced is the impartation of cultural perspectives and practices, including the Aboriginal language. Therefore, the Aboriginal community continues to play a role in parents' lives.

This chapter suggests that there are unique features to Aboriginal parenting that are not reflected in mainstream Canadian parenting. To protect further erosion of their parenting knowledge and practices, Aboriginal people have to affirm their own practices and knowledge about parenting. This can take the form of doing their own research or using political and legal means to challenge externally imposed theories and the policies and practices that emanate from them.

Questions for Review

1. What conditions generate the desire for universal theories to be developed?
2. What role does context and experience play in forming parenting beliefs, values, and behaviours?
3. What role does the naming ceremony have for parents?
4. How does context influence which parenting strategies are used?
5. How does colonization or hegemony affect parenting information?
6. What challenges do parents who relocate from a First Nation context into an urban centre encounter?
7. What would be considered a "successful" transition of a First Nation parent moving to an urban centre?

Suggested Readings and Resources

Ball, J., & Simpkins, M. A. (2004). The community within the child: Integration of Indigenous knowledge into First Nations childcare process and practice. *The American Indian Quarterly*, *28*(3), 480–98.

Benzies, K. M. (2014). Parenting in Canadian Aboriginal cultures. In H. Selin (Ed.), *Parenting across cultures* (pp. 379–92). Netherlands: Springer.

Eni, R., & Rowe, G. (2011). Understanding parenting in Manitoba First Nations: Implications for program development. *Family & Community Health*, *34*(3), 221–8.

Griffiths, J. (2014). *Family futures: 2014—Twentieth anniversary of the International Year of the Family*. Tudor Rose: UK.

Menzies, P., & Lavallee, L. (Eds.). (2014). *Journey to healing: Aboriginal people with addiction and mental health issues: What health, social service and justice workers need to know*. Toronto, ON: CAMH Publications.

Tremblay, M., Gokiert, R., Georgis, R., Edwards, K., and Skrypnek, B. (2013). Aboriginal perspectives on social-emotional competence in early childhood. *The International Indigenous Policy Journal, 4*(4). Retrieved from http://ir.lib.uwo.ca/iipj/vol4/iss4/2

References

A.[...] (First Nation) v. Children's Aid Society of Toronto. (2004). CanLII 34409 (ON SC). Retrieved from http://canlii.ca/s/q1q8

Aboriginal Healing Foundation. (2006). *A healing journey: Vol. 1. Reclaiming wellness*. Ottawa, ON: Author.

Aboriginal Head Start. (2006). *Aboriginal Head Start in urban and northern communities: Program overview.* Ottawa, ON: Public Health Agency of Canada.

Aboriginal Healing Foundation. (2008). *From truth to reconciliation: Transforming the legacy of residential schools*. Ottawa: ON: Author.

Alderson-Gill & Associates Consulting Inc. (2005). *Urban Aboriginal strategy pilot projects, formative evaluation: Final report*. Ottawa, ON: Indian and Northern Affairs Canada.

AMR Planning and Consulting (2015). *Options for action: An implementation report for the legacy of Phoenix Sinclair*. Retrieved from http://www.gov.mb.ca/fs/childfam/pubs/options_for_action.pdf

Anderson, K. (2006). New life stirring: Mothering, transformation and aboriginal womanhood. In D. M. Lavell-Harvard & J. Corbiere-Lavell (Eds.), *Until our hearts are on the ground: Aboriginal mothering, oppression, resistance and rebirth*. Toronto, ON: Demeter Press.

Angell, B. G. (1997). Madness in the family: The Windigo. *Journal of Family Social Work, 2*(2), 179–96.

Awasis Agency of Northern Manitoba. (1997). *First Nations family justice: Mee-noo-stah-tan Mi-ni-si-win*. Thompson, MB: Author.

Ball, J., & Pence, A. (2001). *Program evaluation report: Strengthening community capacity for early childhood care and development*. Victoria: BC: University of Victoria.

Battiste, M. (Ed.). (2002). *Reclaiming indigenous voice and vision* (2nd ed.). Vancouver, BC: UBC Press.

Beck, P., Walters, A. L., & Francisco, N. (1995). *The sacred*. Tsaile, AZ: Navajo Community College Press.

Bedard, R. (2006). An Anishinaabe-kwe ideology on mothering and motherhood. In D. Lavell-Harvard & J. Corbiere Lavell (Eds.), *Until our hearts are on the ground: Aboriginal mothering, oppression, resistance, and rebirth*. Toronto, ON: Demeter Press.

Black-Rogers, M. (1967). *An ethnoscience investigation into Ojibwa worldview*. Stanford, CA: Stanford University Press.

Blackstock, C. (2014). Mosquito advocacy: Change promotion strategies for small groups with big ideas. In H. Weaver (Ed.), *Social issues in contemporary Native America: Reflections from Turtle Island*. Burlington, VT: Ashgate Publishing.

Blackstock, C., Trocmé, N., & Bennett, M. (2004). Child maltreatment investigations among Aboriginal and non-Aboriginal families in Canada. *Violence against Women, 10*(8), 901–16.

Boggs, S. T. (1958). Culture change and personality of Ojibwa children. *American Anthropologist, 60*, 47–58.

Bopp, J., Bopp, M., Brown, L., & Lane Jr., P. (1984). *The sacred tree*. Lethbridge, AB: Four Worlds International Institute for Human and Community Development.

Brant, C. (1990). Native ethics and rules of behaviour. *Canadian Journal of Psychiatry, 35*, 534–9.

Brant, C., & Patterson, P. G. R. (1990). Native child rearing practices: Their role in mental health. Unpublished paper, in C. Brant, *A Collection* (pp. 99–118), Trent University Archives (TUA). Peterborough, Ontario.

Brendtro, L. K., & Brokenleg, M. (1993). Beyond the curriculum of control. *Journal of Emotional and Behavioural Problems, 1*(4), 5–11.

Brown, J., & Brightman, R. (1988). *The orders of the dreamed: George Nelson on Cree and Northern Ojibwa religion and myth, 1823.* Winnipeg, MB: University of Manitoba Press.

Carriére, J., & Thomas, R. (2014). Indigenous children and state care: The dark underside of citizenship. In M. Moosa-Mitha & L. Dominelli (Eds.), *Reconfiguring citizenship: Social exclusion and diversity within inclusive citizenship practices* (pp. 117–26). London, UK: Ashgate Publishing.

Castellano, M. B. (2002). *Aboriginal family trends: Extended families, nuclear families, families of the heart.* The Vanier Institute of the Family. Retrieved from http://www.vanierinstitute.ca/include/get.php?nodeid=1142

Caudill, W. (1949). Psychological characteristics of acculturated Wisconsin Ojibwa children. *American Anthropologist, 51*, 409–27.

ChrisJohn, R., Young, S., & Maraun, M. (1997). *The circle game.* Penticton, BC: Theytus Books Ltd.

Crofoot, T., & Harris, M. (2012). An Indian child welfare perspective on disproportionality in child welfare. *Child and Youth Services Review, 34*(9), 1667–74.

Densmore, F. (1970). Chippewa customs. Minneapolis, MN: Minnesota Historical Society Press.

Dey, I. (1993). *Qualitative data analysis: A user friendly guide for social scientists.* New York, NY: Taylor & Francis.

Dhooper, S., & Moore, S. (2001). *Social work practice with culturally diverse people.* Thousand Oaks, CA: Sage.

Eastman, C. A. (1980). *The soul of the Indian.* Lincoln, NB: Bison Books.

Fathers Involvement Research Alliance. (2008). Research clusters: Indigenous fathers. Retrieved from http://www.fira.ca/page.php?id=24

Fournier, S., & Crey, E. (1997). *Stolen from our embrace.* Vancouver, BC: Douglas & McIntyre.

Gfellner, B. M. (1990). Culture and consistency in ideal and actual child-rearing practices: A study of Canadian Indian and white parents. *Journal of Comparative Family Studies, 21*(3), 413–23.

Goodluck, C. T., & Short, D. (1980). Working with American Indian parents: A cultural approach. *Social Casework, 61*(8), 472–5.

Goulet, C., Bell, L., Tribble, D. S.-C., Paul, D., & Ariella, L. (1998). A concept analysis of parent-infant attachment. *Journal of Advanced Nursing, 28*(5), 1071–81.

Graveline, F. J. (1998). *Circle works: Transforming Eurocentric consciousness.* Halifax, NS: Fernwood Publishing.

Gray, M., Coates, J., & Yellowfeather, M. (Eds.). (2010). *Indigenization and indigenous social work around the world: Towards culturally relevant social work education and practice.* London, UK: Ashgate Press.

Hallowell, A. I. (1946). *Some psychological characteristics of the north eastern Indians: Vol. 3.* Andover, MA: Papers of the Peabody Foundation.

Hallowell, A. I. (1955). *Culture and experience.* Philadelphia, PA: University of Pennsylvania Press.

Hamilton, A. C., & Sinclair, C. M. (1991). *Report of the Aboriginal Justice Inquiry of Manitoba: The justice system and Aboriginal people.* Aboriginal Justice Implementation Commission. Retrieved from http://www.ajic.mb.ca/volume.html

Hand, C. (2006). An Ojibwe perspective on the welfare of children: Lessons of the past and visions for the future. *Children and Youth Services Review, 28*, 20–46.

Harkness, S., & Super, C. M. (2006). Themes and variations: Parental ethnotheories in Western culture. In K. Rubin (Ed.), *Parenting beliefs, behaviours, and parent-child relations: A cross-cultural perspective.* New York, NY: Taylor & Francis.

Hart, M. A. (2002). *Seeking Mino-Pimatisiwin: An Aboriginal approach to helping.* Halifax, NS: Fernwood Publishing.

Hart, M., & Rowe, G. (2014). Legally entrenched oppressions: The undercurrent of First Nations peoples' experiences with Canada's social welfare policies. In H. Weaver (Ed.), *Social issues in contemporary Native America: Reflections from Turtle Island*. Burlington, VT: Ashgate Publishing.

Hay, T. H. (1973). A technique for formalizing and testing models of behavior: Two models of Ojibwa restraint. *American Anthropologist, 75*, 708–30.

Hayslip, B., & Kaminski, P. (2005). Grandparents raising their grandchildren: A review of the literature and suggestions for practice. *The Gerontologist, 45*(2), 262–9.

Hilger, S. I. M. (1951). *Chippewa child life and its cultural background*. Bulletin 146. Washington, DC: Smithsonian Institution: Bureau of American Ethnology.

Jendrek, M. (1994). Grandparents who parent their grandchildren: Circumstances and decisions. *The Gerontologist, 34*(2), 206–16.

Jennes, D. (1935). *The Ojibwa Indians of Parry Island, their social and religious Life: Vol. 78*. National Museums of Canada.

Johnston, B. (1988). *Indian school days*. Norman, OK: University of Oklahoma.

Kluckhohn, F., & Strodtbeck, F. (1961). *Variations in value orientations*. Evanston, IL: Row, Peterson.

Knockwood, I. (2001). Out of the depths. Lockeport, NS: Roseway Publishing.

Lame Deer, J. F., & Erdoes, R. (1994). *Lame deer: Seeker of visions*. New York, NY: Washington Square Press.

Landes, R. (1937). The Ojibwa of Canada. In M. Mead (Ed.), *Cooperation and competition among primitive peoples* (pp. 87–126). Boston, MA: Beacon Press.

Landes, R. (1969). *The Ojibwa woman*. New York, NY: AMS Press

Lavell-Harvard, D. M., & Corbiere-Lavell, J. (2006). *Until our hearts are on the ground: Aboriginal mothering, oppression, resistance and rebirth*. Toronto, ON: Demeter Press.

Letourneau, N. L., Hungler, K. M., & Fisher, K. (2005). Low-income Canadian Aboriginal and non-Aboriginal parent-child interactions. *Child: Care, Health and Development, 31*(5), 545–54.

Levine, R. A., & Norman, K. (2001). The infant's acquisition of culture: Early attachment re-examined in anthropological perspective. In C. C. Moore & H. F. Mathews (Eds.), *The psychology of cultural experience* (pp. 83–104). Cambridge, UK: Cambridge University Press.

MacDonald, N., & Boffman, J. (1995). Mother-child interaction among the Alsakan Eskimos. *Journal of Obstetric, Gynecological and Neonatal Nursing, 24*(5), 450–7.

McPherson, D. H., & Rabb, J. D. (2001). Indigeneity in Canada: Spirituality, the sacred and survival. *International Journal of Canadian Studies, 23*, 57–79.

McShane, K. E., & Hastings, P. D. (2004). Culturally sensitive approaches to research on child development and family practices in First Peoples communities. *First Peoples Child and Family Review, 1*(1), 38–44.

Mihesuah, D. A. (2003). *Indigenous American women: Decolonization, empowerment, activism*. Lincoln, NB: University of Nebraska Press.

Neckoway, R., Brownlee, K., Jourdain, L. W., & Miller, L. (2003). Rethinking the role of attachment theory in child welfare practices with Aboriginal people. *Canadian Social Work Review, 20*(1), 105–19.

Norris, M., & Clatworthy, S. (2011). Urbanization and migration patterns of Aboriginal populations in Canada: A half century in review (1951–2006). *Aboriginal Policy Studies, 1*(1), 13–77.

Ohmagari, K., & Berkes, F. (1997). Transmission of indigenous knowledge and bush skills among the Western James Bay Cree women of subarctic Canada. *Human Ecology, 25*(7), 197–222.

Pintarics, J., & Sveinunggard, K. (2005). Meenoostahtan Minisiwin: First Nations family justice, pathways to peace. *First Peoples Child and Family Review, 2*(1), 67–88.

Portman, T. (2001). Sex role attributions of American-Indian women. *Journal of Mental Health Counseling, 23*(1), 72–84.

Preston, R. (2002). *Cree narrative* (2nd ed.). Montreal and Kingston: McGill-Queen's University Press.

Royal Commission on Aboriginal Peoples (RCAP). (1996). *The Report of the Royal Commission on Aboriginal Peoples*. Ottawa, ON: Aboriginal Affairs and Northern Development Canada.

Red Horse, J. G. (1980a). American Indian elders: Unifiers of Indian families. *Social Casework, 61*(8), 490–3.

Red Horse, J. G. (1980b). Family structure and value orientation in American Indians. *Social Casework, 61*(8), 462–7.

Report of the Aboriginal Committee. (1992). *Liberating our children: Liberating our nations*. Vancouver, BC: Community Panel Family and Children's Services Legislation.

Report of the First Nation's Child and Family Task Force. (1993). *Children first: Our responsibility: Assembly of Manitoba Chiefs*. Winnipeg, MB: Department of Indian and Northern Affairs.

Rogoff, B. (2003). *The cultural nature of human development*. New York, NY: Oxford University Press.

Ross, R. (2006). *Dancing with a ghost: Exploring Indian reality*. Toronto, ON: Penguin Books.

Schissel, B. W., & Wotherspoon, T. (2003). *The legacy of school for Aboriginal people*. Toronto, ON: Oxford University Press.

Stairs, A. H., & Bernhard, J. (2002). Considerations for evaluating "good care" in Canadian Aboriginal early childhood settings. *McGill Journal of Education, 37*(3), 309–30.

Statistics Canada. (2008). Aboriginal peoples in Canada in 2006: Inuit, Métis, and First Nations. 2006 Census (No. 970558-XIE). Ottawa, ON: Ministry of Industry.

Statistics Canada. (2011). National Household Survey: *Aboriginal peoples in Canada: First Nations people, Métis, and Inuit*. Retrieved from http://www12.statcan.gc.ca/nhs-enm/2011/as-sa/99-011-x/2011001/tbl/tbl03-eng.cfm

Stremlau, R. (2005). To domesticate and civilize wild Indians: Allotment and the campaign to reform Indian families, 1875–1887. *Journal of Family History, 30*(3), 265–86.

Sue, D. W. (2003). *Overcoming our racism: The journey to liberation*. San Francisco, CA: Jossey-Bass

Swinomish Tribal Mental Health Project. (1991). *A gathering of wisdoms*. LaConner, WA: Swinomish Tribal Community.

Timpson, J. (1995). Four decades of literature on native Canadian child welfare: Changing themes. *Child Welfare, 74*(3), 525–46.

Truth and Reconciliation Commission of Canada. (2015, March 17). *Truth and Reconciliation Commission of Canada: Interim report*. Retrieved from http://www.myrobust.com/websites/trcinstitution/File/Interim%20report%20English%20electronic.pdf

Warren, W. (1984). *History of the Ojibway people*. St. Paul, MN: Historical Society Press.

Weaver, H. N. (2001). Organization and community assessment with First Nations people. In R. Fong & S. Furuto (Eds.), *Culturally competent practice*. Boston, MA: Allyn & Bacon.

Weaver, H. N. (2012). Urban and Indigenous: The challenges of being a Native American in the city. *Journal of Community Practice, 20*(4), 470–88.

Weaver, H., & White, B. J. (1997). The Native American family circle: Roots of resiliency. *Journal of Family Social Work, 2*(1), 67–80.

White, J. P., Maxim, P. S., & Beavon, D. (Eds.). (2003). *Aboriginal conditions: Research as a foundation for public policy*. Vancouver, BC: UBC Press.

Yellow Horse Brave Heart, M. (2001). Culturally and historically congruent clinical social work assessment with Native clients. In R. Fong & S. Furuto (Eds.), *Culturally competent practice*. Boston, MA: Allyn & Bacon.

Zylberberg, P. (1991). Who should make child protection decisions for the Native community? *Windsor Yearbook of Access to Justice, 11*, 74–103.

The Franco-Ontarian Community

From Resistance to New Social Solidarities and Economic Challenges

By David Welch

Chapter Objectives

This chapter will help you develop an understanding of:

- How the Franco-Ontarian community has developed over the years, beginning in the mid-19th century, while still retaining strong links to French-speaking Quebec
- How Franco-Ontarians have spread across Ontario, gradually evolving into a diverse community of over 650,000 people
- How Franco-Ontarians have developed original means of resistance when confronted with opposition to their language and schooling rights that remain part of their historical memory
- How the economic forms of the community are linked to the development of social and health measures that have evolved over the generations, with new social economic projects that are more adapted to contemporary realities

Introduction

The purpose of this chapter is not to present an exhaustive study of the Franco-Ontarian community, but rather to highlight some of the elements that contribute to an understanding of the social construction of the community and the development of some of its social practices. During this process, we discuss some of the main socio-economic transformations of this community that, in turn, have transformed social practices that led to new ways in which the community sees and defines itself.

The historical patterns of settlement are examined first, followed by the development of some of the community's social practices and institutions, most notably those in social and health services and, to a limited extent, schooling. Emphasis in terms of the examination of social services is placed on developments in the last 45 years.

It is important to keep in mind that Franco-Ontarians have not been passive objects in the development of their community and Ontario; they have been active participants who have made particular social and economic choices. These choices have permitted the Franco-Ontarian family and community to survive and, in turn, have helped to assure its continual development.

The Early Development of Social Institutions and Practices in French-Speaking Ontario

Early French-Canadian Settlement in Ontario

The earliest permanent French-speaking settlement in Ontario was established in 1749, when French Canadians settled near a Huron, or Wendat, village along the south shore of the Detroit River across from Fort Detroit (now the city of Detroit, Michigan), which had been founded in 1701. To avoid harming the lucrative fur trade and draining population away from the scattered settlements along the St. Lawrence River, agriculture was developed only enough to feed the local garrison and fur traders. Consequently, the number of families was small and the population relatively mobile.[1] This early population gradually increased and took up new lands along the south shore of Lake St. Clair. As new settlers arrived from Quebec in the 1840s, the French-Canadian population increased: By 1871 there were about 14,000 French Canadians in this region in Kent and Essex counties (Brodeur, 1979).

The Ottawa Valley lumber industry brought the first French Canadians into eastern Ontario. As seasonal workers, thousands of young French-Canadian men worked in the woods in the winter and on the timber rafts down the Ottawa and St. Lawrence rivers in the spring, returning to Lower Canada (Quebec) in the summer (Greening, 1972). By the 1840s, French Canadians began taking up land in the counties of Prescott and Russell, the low, flat, swampy lands between the Lower Canadian border and the emerging city of Bytown, later called Ottawa. The region's proximity to Lower Canada, the union of Upper and Lower Canada into the province of Canada in 1841, and the common economic forms within the French-Canadian community all helped to transform the community into a single social and economic entity on both sides of the Ottawa River. Furthermore, in founding the diocese of Ottawa in 1847, the Catholic Church included territory from what would become in 1867 Ontario and Quebec. By the 1880s, the majority of the population in Prescott-Russell was French Canadian (Choquette, 1984; Gaffield, 1987).

From its beginnings, Ottawa, which was founded in 1827 at the time of the construction of the Rideau Canal, was always at least 25 per cent French Canadian, a segment of the population that was concentrated in Lower Town around the market. This working-class population, whose men laboured in the local lumber mills, quickly founded its own parishes and social, health, and educational institutions (Brault, 1942; Vallières, 1980).

Further French-Canadian settlement in Ontario occurred in 1828, when the British military base on Drummond Island was moved to Penetanguishene, on the shores of Georgian Bay. Many French-Canadian and Métis voyageurs followed, to be joined in the 1840s by settlers from Lower Canada. Some of the new arrivals took up land, while others worked in the expanding lumber mills along Georgian Bay (Marchildon, 1984).

The building of the Canadian Pacific Railway (CPR) in 1882–3 brought the first French Canadians to northeastern Ontario (Brandt, 1979). Thousands of French Canadians from Quebec and eastern Ontario worked on the construction gangs. Encouraged by the CPR (which wanted to sell land along the railway) and the Catholic Church (which was seeking to stop the exodus of French Canadians to the New England cotton mills), families took up land in the region. Later, as mines were opened and new towns situated around the sawmills were founded, more French Canadians moved into the region. By 1901, there were 15,000 French Canadians, constituting about 42 per cent of the population (Brandt, 1976). Although the northeastern part of the province was settled at different times, from the 1880s until the 1930s the various French-Canadian agricultural settlements, being generally homogeneous, followed quite closely the familiar patterns seen earlier in eastern Ontario and Quebec, with life centred around the parish.[2]

The National Policy of 1879 promoted industrial development in Canada and led to the migration of thousands of French Canadians to the emerging industrial centres of Ontario, stanching, to some extent, the flow to the New England states. By 1881 there were 2,230 French Canadians in Toronto (Trudelle & Fortier, 1987); in 1931 there were 4,846 in Cornwall, concentrated in the textile industry (Scheinber & McIntosh, 1995; Sylvestre, 1984). Much the same process occurred in Welland during World War I (Schneiderman, 1972; Trudel, 1982). As in the more rural areas, the population tended to settle around their own French parishes and schools and often chose to work in factories where French Canadians were concentrated, thus assuring the daily use of the French language in spite of their minority status.

The Beginnings of French-Language Social Services

One of the earliest examples of social organization within the Franco-Ontarian community was the volunteer work done by women, both in the cities and the rural areas. Women worked as midwives or healers and they organized community services. As well, the community established various charitable institutions—hospitals, orphanages, and shelters for the aged—usually under the direction of women's religious congregations. Situated mainly in Ottawa and Sudbury, these institutions remain even today prominent in the larger community. For instance, the Hôpital général d'Ottawa was founded in 1845 to serve the Catholic community, which was largely French Canadian. In the same city, St. Joseph's orphanage was founded in 1865 and the St. Charles home for the aged in 1871 (Brault, 1942). Later, similar institutions were founded in northeastern Ontario. The development of and interaction between these community social practices laid the foundation for today's French-language social services in Ontario.

By the beginning of the 20th century, women had begun to set up their own autonomous (i.e., independent from male organizations) organizations to better deliver social services to the community. One of the most important organizations was the

Fédération des femmes canadiennes françaises (FFCF), founded in 1914 by Almanda Walker-Marchand (Desjardins, 1991). Though its initial mission was to assist in the war effort, very quickly the FFCF expanded to the various parishes across French Canada outside of Quebec and began to diversify its work to the larger social service field (Brunet, 1992). For instance, in 1916 and 1921 the FFCF gave relief to many of the victims of the devastating forest fires that raged across northeastern Ontario. The FFCF was, to a large extent, a national organizaton, and in 1923–4 it affiliated with the Canadian Council on Child Welfare. Later, in the 1930s, the FFCF became active in the struggle of the Dionne family to regain custody of their quintuplets. It also worked to ensure that the girls received Catholic and French-language schooling (Welch, 1994–5).

In 1937 the Union catholique des fermières de l'Ontario (UCFO) was founded with the expressed aim of increasing social services, especially in rural areas. Not unlike the FFCF, the UCFO was one of many Franco-Ontarian women's groups that remained closely linked to the Catholic Church, with the mission of providing social services to the poorest sectors of the community.

There were also volunteer organizations that had both social and economic objectives. The Saint Vincent de Paul Society, founded in Ottawa by French Canadians in 1860, was responsible for giving help to the poorest families in Lower Town, a largely French-Canadian neighbourhood of Ottawa. In 1874, members of the society asked for meat from the local butchers and heating wood from the local sawmills and farmers to ensure that the poorest survived the winter (Brault, 1942). During the economic crisis of 1875–80, along with the Soeurs de la Charité, the Saint Vincent de Paul Society organized a community kitchen for the poor.

To help combat unemployment during the Great Depression of the 1930s, the Franco-Ontarian elite and its main umbrella organization, the Association canadienne-française d'éducation de l'Ontario (ACFEO), founded the Oeuvre des Chômeurs, an early form of unemployment centre for young men. The centre offered direct financial aid, housing for those most in need, and counselling to help the unemployed find work. It hoped that its activities within the Franco-Ontarian working class would counterbalance whatever influence the Communist Party might have with young unemployed men (Gravel, 1980). At the same time, the ACFEO began looking at ways to create a youth centre for young Franco-Ontarians to counterbalance the YM/YWCA, which was seen as a Protestant, anglophone organization. In 1957, the Patro St. Vincent was founded as a sport and recreation organization for young boys.

In the mid-19th century, under the leadership of both lay and religious elites, Franco-Ontarians began setting up co-operatives. One of the first was a mutual aid society called the Union Saint-Joseph (later Union du Canada, which declared bankruptcy in February 2012 after 149 years of existence), which was initially founded by French-Canadian workers in 1863 in Ottawa. In its early years, the society had only about 700 members; however, by 1910 its membership had increased to around 8,000 and it had 145 local councils around the province. The insurance policies covered from 50,000 to 60,000 people out of a total Franco-Ontarian population of about 203,000 (Comeau, 1982).

The Union Saint-Joseph, in spite of its co-operative spirit and its aim to furnish not-for-profit services, rejected all social and economic practices that might have been seen as promoting state intervention. Although it was ready to defend the identity interests of Franco-Ontarians, the union rejected any state intervention on social issues as being too socialistic or communistic (Grimard & Vallières, 1986). This narrow social and economic vision would best be summed up in a book published in 1939. The author, Charles Leclerc, wrote that "la Saint Joseph s'inscrit en faux contre les doctrines entachées de socialisme, qui demandent à l'État de se constituer en une sorte de providence, qui veulent faire peser sur tous les citoyens indifféremment le poids de la subsistance d'un certain nombre, qui veulent tuer l'initiative individuelle, et entraver la compétition. . . . Plutôt que de verser, même modérément, dans les théories à saveur socialiste, elle rappelle que le Christ a dit qu'il y aurait toujours des pauvres et que c'est eux qu'il a aimés"[3] (Leclerc, cited in Grimard & Vallières, 1986, p. 195).

The same vision of Franco-Ontarian self-reliance was present in the founding of the first caisses populaires, a form of parish credit union. The ones in Ontario were established on much the same model as those in Quebec; indeed, Alphonse Desjardins, who had founded the first caisses populaires in Quebec, resided in Ottawa for many years. The caisses, which grew quickly in number after World War II (a period when Franco-Ontarians were able to save, seeing prosperity, often for the first time), allowed community members to save and borrow, thereby ensuring that money stayed in the community. Today, the various caisses populaires in French-speaking Ontario have over $4 billion in deposits.

From the 18th century onwards, French Canadians established their own autonomous schools. As restrictions were placed on these schools in the 1880s and later, especially between 1912–27, Franco-Ontarians undertook large-scale campaigns of civil disobedience. This resistance to state oppression allowed the French-speaking Catholic Church to become far more active in the social and economic life of the community, over time becoming, in a sense, the main governing institution (Choquette, 1984). At the same time, there was some resistance to educational models imposed on the community by the Church, especially when this led to higher taxes on the largely impoverished population (Welch, 1995, 2005). As a result of continual resistance by the community against state educational policies, the provincial government was forced over time to recognize the language rights of Franco-Ontarians and, thereby, certain limits to its own state power.

In contrast to their relative autonomy in educational matters, Franco-Ontarians had little control over health and social services, and most of these services that developed in Ontario, other than those administered by French-speaking religious congregations and charitable organizations, were unilingual English. Often these services were administered by not-for-profit organizations such as children's aid societies and functioned almost entirely in English, regardless of their funding sources, even in cities such as Ottawa and Sudbury that had large Franco-Ontarian minorities. French-language services became increasingly marginalized as new state-funded services were organized; the most vulnerable were particularly affected by this marginalization of French-language services (Carrière, 1995; Pettey & Ouimet, 1988; Welch 2005).

This indifference to francophone needs can be understood when one remembers that French Canadians remained excluded from positions of economic and political power. In the industrial workforce, francophones never rose above the level of foremen; they forever remained the subsistence farmers, the lumberjacks, the servants, the semi-skilled railway workers, and the surface workers for the mines. The inequalities of capitalism along with hostility against French Canadians excluded them from positions of any influence over the wider socio-political institutions of the province.

During the 1930s and the 1940s, contrary to the situation in Quebec where the state supported many of the initiatives that emerged out of civil society, the Ontario government, closely linked to the interests of capital, gave far less support to various co-operative projects, and even less to those of the Franco-Ontarians. Thus the social and economic projects of the community, whether of the private or public sector, were born and nurtured on the margins of the activities of the dominant English-speaking society. In spite of their limits, these various initiatives showed Franco-Ontarians that they were capable of organizing themselves and of creating and managing new organizations that were a reflection of their own community.

From this brief outline of Franco-Ontarian settlement patterns and the creation of distinct social institutions, certain conclusions can be drawn. From the beginning of permanent European colonization in Ontario during the 18th century, Franco-Ontarians have played an active role in the economic and political development of the province (Jaenen, 1993; Welch, 1999, 2005). Founding relatively homogeneous villages throughout eastern, northeastern, and southwestern Ontario, the French Canadians who moved to Ontario managed to preserve many of their unique cultural forms. Their social and economic strategies allowed them to survive—"continuing to live when others have disappeared or perished"—even though they were "on the frontier of the dominant economic system" (Berger, 1979, pp. 196–9). In many regions there were enough Franco-Ontarians to establish schools, parishes, social organizations, and later co-operatives and caisses populaires. Many of these same patterns were reproduced in the urban centres of Ottawa, Cornwall, Hawkesbury, Sudbury, Toronto, and Welland. These first initiatives, whether in schooling or the social and health services, were marked by the large-scale mobilization of women, farmers, and workers. Working together, usually as volunteers, they founded a multitude of self-help and pressure groups that led to new social and economic forms such as co-operatives.

The autonomous institutions that were created laid the basis for a Franco-Ontarian civil society that, over time, gave the community a distinct social life and the means to distribute resources within the community. Although they were a minority within the province, Franco-Ontarians continued to see themselves as being part of a larger French-Canadian society, with links to French Canadians elsewhere, including the Franco-Americans of New England.

Many of the organizations founded by Franco-Ontarians, and under the leadership of the emerging middle class, had a very conservative moral vision. Their aim was to help the less fortunate without questioning the underlying social and economic inequalities that existed. In spite of the limits of their actions, their strategies built on a belief in social solidarity that assured the survival of Franco-Ontarians as a distinct community in a larger society that was undergoing rapid change.

Accelerated Urbanization and Transformations in Franco-Ontarian Institutions

The period during and after World War II, with its rapid industrial expansion, saw the complete transformation of the economic and socio-cultural face of Ontario. The province completed its transformation to industrial capitalism, becoming more and more integrated into the North American economy. These changes had an important impact on the Franco-Ontarian community. In the space of only a few years, the community went through a massive population displacement from the countryside to the regional cities of the north, and from the north to the industrial cities of the south. Parallel to these demographic changes, thousands of Québécois and Acadians settled in the manufacturing cities of southern Ontario and in some of the mining and pulp and paper cities in the northern part of the province (Vallières, 1980).

This increased proletarianization led to new identities, embodied, for example, in unions, which led to new social relationships within the community and to frequent conflicts between the expanding working class and the various elites, who had differing class interests. Frequently, the traditional Franco-Ontarian elite did not support miners and lumber workers as they fought to improve their working conditions; in some cases they openly supported the mine owners (Arnopolous, 1982; Pelletier, 1987). To help temper these social and economic changes, Franco-Ontarians established new institutions (schools, caisses populaires, recreation centres) that were better adapted to the urban environment.

It is important to note that many Franco-Ontarians experienced a rapid improvement in their standard of living and general working conditions after they abandoned subsistence agriculture and forestry. In the mines and the pulp mills, in construction, in the factories, and in the ever-expanding service sector, wages increased far more quickly than the cost of living. However, the transition did not improve the economic situation of all Franco-Ontarians. Unionization had led to better wages for many, but there remained a segment of the population without the skills to profit from postwar prosperity, living in either rural or urban poverty and forming a kind of economic underclass. Many Franco-Ontarians, along with the Québécois and Acadians who had left the rural areas of their respective provinces for Ontario cities, continued to feel the effects of over a hundred years of economic subsistence. Often with few of the necessary skills and with high rates of illiteracy, they found it difficult to profit from the economic opportunities offered by the city, regardless of the region. For these people, being French Canadian continued to mean a life of poverty and misery, perpetuating in the city the historic conditions of the countryside. In a sense, the country had followed them to the city.

With greater industrialization and urbanization, and with the disappearance of subsistence agriculture and forestry, Franco-Ontarian women had a lesser role to play in direct economic production, giving them less recognition and status within the family. Even on the remaining farms, mechanization resulted in less need for the farm work of the wife and children. The gap between the public world of waged work and the private lives of women, organized primarily around childrearing and domestic labour, widened (Proulx, 1982, p. 5). Women were limited to the home and the constant care of children, leading to their greater social isolation. The state gradually took over many of the tasks of the social services formerly provided informally by women, and it now demanded credentials that most women did not have to work there. In northeastern Ontario the best-paying jobs were in the mining and lumber industry, both of which excluded women, limiting them to low-paying service jobs and making them even more financially dependent on men. Thus, urbanization and better wages, though improving the situation of Franco-Ontarian men, in many cases did little in the short term to change the situation of Franco-Ontarian women. As families migrated to the cities and their children became even more exposed to the dominant Anglo-Canadian culture, the tasks of women, who were seen as the principal defenders of the language and culture, became even more demanding. Many experienced feelings of guilt when, in some cases, their children lost use of the French language.

Urbanization and industrialization increased the dangers of assimilation. As they became more urbanized, Franco-Ontarians tended to use the social and health services of the majority, which operated almost solely in the English language. Schooling fared somewhat better: in the north and the east, Franco-Ontarians frequently dominated the separate (Catholic) school boards. In the south, new schools were created only after strong opposition from the existing English-speaking Catholic boards.

The Franco-Ontarian Community and New Relationships with the State

In the 1960s, the Ontario government became far more interventionist in almost all sectors of socio-economic life, as did the governments of the other provinces. In the name of reform and the improvement of society, the Ontario government spent millions of dollars to transform educational, social, and health services across the province. The 1960s also brought about greater recognition of Franco-Ontarian rights, most notably through new legislation that allowed the establishment of solely French-language elementary and secondary schools. The federal Official Languages Act (1969), following the recommendations of the Royal Commission on Bilingualism and Biculturalism, also helped to increase the bilingual presence in federal government institutions, especially in the Ottawa area. These reforms coincided with the breakdown of what had been referred to as French-Canadian society, a sense of a common identity across French Canada that was constructed around the Catholic Church and a common language (Martel, 1997; Welch, 2005). During the 1960s, people began to see themselves differently, identifying more with their province and seeing themselves as Québécois, Franco-Ontarians, Franco-Albertans, and so on.

These changes over the course of the 1960s led to a historical transformation in the attitudes of the Franco-Ontarian elite toward the state, especially at the provincial level. Traditionally, the religious and secular elites had turned to the family and to religious institutions for the protection of Franco-Ontarian identity as well as for the development of educational, social, and health services. Secularization and greater state intervention increased the distance between the elites and their community, and people looked outside the community for resources (Carrière, 1993; Juteau & Séguin-Kimpton, 1993). In the future, the rights won from the state, and the responsibilities delegated by it, would increasingly determine the power and influence of the Franco-Ontarian elite and the degree of autonomy the community would retain.

Even with the right to new schools, struggles between Franco-Ontarian community organizations on one side and many English-speaking Ontarians and the government on the other continued for another 15 years before a relatively complete network of French-language secondary schools was established across the province. These struggles—in places such as Kapuskasing, Penetanguishene, Iroquois Falls, Sturgeon Falls, Windsor, and Mattawa, to name only a few locales—led, in turn, to many divisions within the Franco-Ontarian community during vicious fights over the control of ever-decreasing resources (Welch, 1991–2). Moreover, it took over 25 years to establish three French-language community colleges in the province.

In the arena of social services, it was only in the 1970s in eastern Ontario and in the early 1980s in northeastern Ontario that the provincial government began to allocate funds for French-language services. Because there were no obligations to provide services in French, both government agencies and private state-subsidized organizations did little to increase services to the French-speaking population (Carrière, 1995). The Franco-Ontarian community remained dependent on the limited French-language services offered on a voluntary basis and, decreasingly, by religious institutions. Yet more and more of the old French-language or bilingual hospitals, usually in areas with a concentrated Franco-Ontarian population, were being replaced by new facilities that, while providing better services, tended to function far more in English than in French. Thus in some cases, in the name of modernity, Franco-Ontarians lost control of institutions that they had managed for generations.

Franco-Ontarians also lost control of their neighbourhoods. For example, in the name of urban renewal and in spite of large-scale opposition, large parts of Lower Town in Ottawa, once about 80 per cent French speaking, were demolished. The establishment of low-rent housing brought in non-francophone people; other renovations brought in a wealthier English-speaking population. Lower Town is now only about 40 per cent francophone. In the process, the social fabric of the neighbourhood was destroyed, eliminating many of the collective self-help projects. The same process happened in the Moulin à Fleur neighbourhood in Sudbury and in the Sacré-Coeur parish in the Cabbagetown area of Toronto. In the new suburbs of Ottawa, Sudbury, and Toronto, it became difficult to re-create a similar community life: There was now greater dispersion of the population and greater distances between schools and community centres. New social practices tended to be centred on middle-class interests, leaving less for the original working-class culture that once flourished in the inner cities.

In some ways, the French Language Services Act (1986) was an important step forward for the Franco-Ontarian community. A victory for the community after years of pressure, it assured that, in certain designated areas of the province, provincial government services would be provided in both English and French. Its application showed a somewhat increased respect for the 550,000 Franco-Ontarians in the province and had, as a secondary effect, the creation of hundreds of jobs for community members in public and semi-public services. However, all municipal services were excluded from the act, and nongovernmental agencies receiving government funding were left to decide for themselves if they wanted to apply for bilingual service designation (Carrière, 1994). In cities such as Ottawa, which has never declared itself officially bilingual, services for the francophone population are often not clearly defined and are left to the goodwill of public servants. Frequently, given the cutbacks of the past 20 years, designated positions remain unfilled by bilingual personnel, or they are filled by people speaking very little French.

New Visions, New Social Practices

New social practices emerged out of the many reforms that directly affected the Franco-Ontarian community since the 1960s. As the state was pushed to grant greater recognition and space to the Franco-Ontarian community, many Franco-Ontarians turned away from the more traditional elite to a more "modern" one, advocating the importance of working with the government to bring about what were perceived as needed reforms. Others went even further and sought French-language services distinct from, but parallel to, those offered in English (based in part on the New Brunswick model of services), rather than spending huge amounts of energy on attempting to make existing English-language services bilingual.

Out of these various mobilizations, some social practitioners went beyond the historical demands for French-language services. They began advocating for the establishment of totally new services that were not simply translations of English-language services with all their "professionalism" and lack of citizen participation. These advocates proposed original, more democratic social practices that reflected the culture and needs of the community, especially its more vulnerable members (C'est le temps, 1981, p. 112; Tissot, 1981, p. 95). This process re-enforced a break with the traditional leadership, who frequently remained far more preoccupied with increasing the number of educational institutions and who tended to ignore the importance of developing social services (Coderre & Dubois, 2000). It was as if the elite perceived social services to be solely for "the less fortunate" or "those with problems," an attitude that demonstrated a difficulty in understanding that new daycare centres or shelters for women were real community needs that touched all sectors of the community.

Some of the most dynamic alternative projects have come out of various women's organizations, who recognized the need for better daycare, shelters for battered women, and immigrant information services for women. In some cases new organizations were created—for example, Ontaroises de l'Est, Franco-femmes in the northern part of the province, and the Réseau des femmes du Sud de l'Ontario in the south (Cardinal & Coderre, 1990). In other cases some of the more traditional women's organizations restructured their activities, integrating new perspectives and objectives.

Other community practitioners became directly involved in economic as well as social issues. They actively supported striking forestry workers during the Elk Lake mill strike of 1980 in northeastern Ontario and the AMOCO textile strike of 1981 in eastern Ontario (Andrew, Archibald, Caloren, & Denis, 1986). They also supported striking Union du Canada office workers, although this went against the tradition of not striking against the co-operative movement. These actions were new attempts to link social issues with the basic economic realities of many of the community members, even when this meant coming into conflict with the more traditional leadership.

In the 1970s and 1980s, social activists recognized the importance of the welfare state in financing the multitude of projects that were cropping up in French-speaking Ontario. Franco-Ontarians were not only trying to "catch up" to the anglophone majority, but were proposing new ways of looking at and doing things. Although such reassessments led to frequent tensions among Franco-Ontarians as to what should be prioritized, few people questioned the greater reliance of the community on the financial resources of the provincial government. Some raised the issue that large numbers of the most active people in the Franco-Ontarian community were enticed into jobs with state agencies, thereby creating a "brain drain" away from groups in the not-for-profit sector in various regions and toward government ministries in Toronto. Even those who continued to work independently frequently found themselves dependent on the government for continued funding of their activities, making them vulnerable to cutbacks (Welch, 1995, 2005).

Owing in part to the relative openness of the David Peterson Liberal and the Bob Rae NDP governments to French-language services in the 1980s and 1990s, few questioned the tendency of the provincial government to impose conditions on the forms these services might take. This facilitated an increase in government power to define what might be considered proper boundaries for Franco-Ontarians and to determine, to a certain extent, what were and were not acceptable practices. This greater dependency, which some characterized as co-opting, made it more difficult for Franco-Ontarians to work out their own compromises or to adapt to rapid changes within and outside their community, and in turn to create their own collective solutions (Welch, 1995). Most of the demands of the community did little to question established notions of the social, economic, and political order.

Neoconservatism and Its Effects on the Franco-Ontarian Community

The election of the Mike Harris Progressive Conservative (PC) government in Ontario in June 1995, with its cutbacks in social programs and transfer of government programs to the private sector, had at the time extremely negative effects on Franco-Ontarian social and educational institutions as well as community-based projects. Even after the defeat of the PCs by the Liberals in 2003, many of the effects of the cutbacks can still be felt. The policies of the PC government put people on the defensive in an attempt both to retain what has already been won and to achieve further reforms. Neoconservative notions that one succeeds or fails on one's own ability, hard work, risk taking, and personal initiative (Browne, 2000) and that there is no civil society, only individual enterprise and self-reliance, are attitudes that go against the historical understanding of many Franco-Ontarians, who believe that the "social" does indeed exist and that society cannot be reduced to simple self-interest. They have learned over the years that the state's attempts to redistribute national wealth and assure a greater respect for minorities have generally benefited the community. People have discovered by trial and error that civil society, in spite of its limitations, has benefited the majority within the community and that the private sector has little interest in the limited benefits to be won from the social or educational needs of the Franco-Ontarian community.

On a number of levels, Franco-Ontarians remain vulnerable. Although the vast majority of Franco-Ontarians are urbanized, many remain isolated and dispersed in small towns, far from the main networks of services and living with the effects of closing pulp and paper mills and layoffs in the manufacturing south. As is the case for other minorities, overall schooling costs for Franco-Ontarians have tended to be higher than those for the English-speaking majority, though their budgets have often been smaller. Because francophone students are relatively dispersed, transportation eats up a significant part of Franco-Ontarian educational budgets. French-language books are more expensive than their English-language counterparts, and schools tend to be smaller, leading to higher per capita costs. Any cuts in government funding can potentially be very harmful.

Franco-Ontarian social service institutions, which have been established more recently and are less wealthy than those of the majority, have had fewer reserves to cope with cutbacks. At times, such as shelters for battered women, one French-language institution must provide services to a very large area. If this sole service is cut, the French-speaking population is left with only English-language services.

When cutbacks occur, the seniority rules and bureaucratic organization of many social services mean that, unless a position is designated as French language, French-speaking employees, who often have less seniority than their English-speaking counterparts, have been laid off or transferred and replaced by employees who speak only English. The ability to speak French and to have an understanding of some cultural aspects of the local community is often overridden by other considerations.

The trend of the provincial PC government had been to cut overall funding and then leave the decisions on what to cut to the local communities.[4] This in turn led to divisions within the community. People were forced to ask—and answer—difficult questions. Do we cut salaries or jobs? Which services should be kept and which should be dropped? Since many of the parallel services established in recent years by Franco-Ontarians were relatively small, such decisions led to some bitter divisions among social practitioners, particularly in smaller communities.

Financial cutbacks have not been the only means by which to marginalize a community, or at least certain sectors of it. Closely linked to the actual cutbacks has been a vicious neoconservative discourse—that continued up until recently with the federal Conservatives led by Stephen Harper—that tends to present all demands that are contrary to a particular narrow view of society as being from a "special interest group." This leads to a situation where any commitment to discuss policy with large sectors of civil society and accommodate their concerns is seen as scorning the intermediary role that social organizations have historically played in Ontario and elsewhere. For instance, in June 1996 the government abolished without warning the 25-year-old Conseil de l'éducation franco-ontarienne, a Franco-Ontarian advisory agency on all matters pertaining to schooling, including postsecondary education. This leads to the government in power giving legitimacy to some groups and not to others, especially those seeking greater equality, notably for women, children, the low-income population, people with disabilities, and visible minorities. Because so many Franco-Ontarians have worked directly or indirectly for state-funded institutions with the mandate of providing French-language services, family incomes can be left extremely vulnerable to cutbacks and the consequent layoffs.[5] In this context, it is important to keep in mind that not all Franco-Ontarians were and continue to be affected by cutbacks in the same way: important class, gender, racial, occupational, and regional differences exist.

Given its other destructive policies, it may at first seem surprising that the provincial PC government did not seek to reform the French Language Services Act. Yet why change something that already has so many exceptions to it? A more effective way was simply to limit funding and to allow services to wither. An example of this trend was the 35 per cent cut in March 1996 of the annual budget for l'Office des affaires francophones, the government commission whose mandate is the protection of gains made under the French Language Services Act. Another danger for the community was the tendency of the leadership to concentrate its energies on the protection of the French Language Services Act, while the PC government cut welfare, education, social housing, community services, transfers to municipalities, and so on, thereby affecting the most vulnerable in the Franco-Ontarian community.

The cutbacks certainly led to an initial feeling of hopelessness within the Franco-Ontarian community. Franco-Ontarian social interventionists began voicing their opposition to government policies by refusing to participate in the government's dirty work of deciding who and what would be cut.[6] However, many community spokepeople, with the exception of certain women's groups, tended to be low-key in their criticism, as if their silence would lead to Franco-Ontarians remaining unnoticed and therefore being less affected by the cuts! One notable exception ended up being one of the largest mobilizations within the Franco-Ontarian community since restrictions on French-language schooling in the early 20th century. A rally in Ottawa in March 1997 brought together over 10,000 people opposed to the closing of Montfort Hospital, the only French-language university hospital outside of Quebec. This mobilization and the subsequent court decision resulted in the survival and continued development of the hospital in recent years (Gratton, 2003, Martel, 2005).[7]

Other Franco-Ontarians at the time and since then have continued to propose that, instead of trying to catch up to the majority by re-creating the same services in French, the community should begin looking at alternative solutions that depend less on government control and funding and more on community creativity and resources. Based on years of involvement in the Franco-Ontarian community they have begun to pose new questions. Are some alternative projects less vulnerable to government cutbacks than others? What role should the state play in the continued development of the Franco-Ontarian community?

Franco-Ontarian Alternatives in the Social Service Sector

Over the past 30 years those who have been seeking new alternatives in social practices base their thinking on two premises. First, many have criticized the tendency of government to be too paternalistic, bureaucratic, and top-down in its dealings with the social sector. The welfare state has been shown to have important weaknesses and limitations. Second, some believe that, though the state has played a role in supplanting or absorbing some of the activities that had previously been the responsibility of the volunteer sector, it should be kept in mind that government policies and financial support have led to the formation of many new social practices (Browne, 2000; Welch, 2005). By studying the changing role of the state and how civil society is changing its social and economic role, we can better grasp the role of new approaches to social and community development and how this role might change over time.

Contrary to what neoconservatives proclaim, many social interventionists and professionals have not been blind defenders of the status quo in education and social services. On the contrary, they have been critical of the increasing bureaucratization and dehumanization of the state and its actors, be they teachers, community activists, or social workers. At least since the 1970s, some Franco-Ontarian social activists have been critical of the welfare state, not limiting their criticisms to issues of weaknesses in the provision of French-language schooling and services. Yet while criticizing government as being too rigid, hierarchical, and impersonal, these activists have continued to defend the notion that the state has an important role to play in providing, through the system of taxation and disbursement, the financial means for organizations to provide services as defined democratically by the community.

Over the past 20 years, these advocates have been supporting the struggle for lesser government control but, at the same time, have rejected the transfers of service provision to the private sector. Many Franco-Ontarians have realized that the private sector, with its notions of profit, makes many of the vital services needed in the community economical only to the wealthiest. Consequently, they have defended the idea that, although funding and overall regulation should be provided by the state, these funds should be transferred to community-based groups that can better mobilize volunteer efforts while providing the necessary services. In practice this can lead to a greater number of options, since the community-based groups would be alternatives to state agencies, thereby being more adaptable to changing conditions. As pointed out above, Franco-Ontarian community service providers would also provide services that better respect both the language and culture of the community. It remains an attempt to link present-day practices with those of the past, urban practices with those of the rural areas, and social issues with those that are more economic in nature. This means that the state must respect the autonomy of organizations within civil society so that they can continue to be strengthened with a diversified presence and with a recognized legitimacy to participate in problem solving. In the end, respect for this autonomy becomes a means of strengthening both citizenship and democracy (Ninacs, 1998).

When we speak of "civil society," we are referring to the multitude of social spaces, groups, and organizations that have been created by citizens outside the formal arena of the state and the market sector and that might, at times, appear to be a form of "creative chaos" (Powell & Guerin, 1997, p. 25). As has been shown earlier in this chapter, civil society that goes back to the beginnings of the Franco-Ontarian community has remained one of the key building blocks of this community. Over time, this presence of an active civil society has resulted generally in increasing trust and co-operation, leading to relatively high levels of social cohesion within the community. In these times of rapid social change, some Franco-Ontarians regard their community organizations or civil society as the means by which they can not only win back some of the social, economic, and even political power they have lost, but as instruments to building new social and economic means. In a sense, people have recognized that democracy has permitted the growth of civil society and that, in turn, civil society has permitted the development of a more effective and more inclusive democracy—one that, in spite of its limits, has benefited Franco-Ontarians.

At the same time, it is important to keep in mind that civil society remains a terrain of struggle that is mined with frequently undemocratic power relations and many different forms of exclusion. As we have attempted to show in this chapter, Franco-Ontarians have, at times, lived the contradiction where different people with opposing interests within the community can all sing the praises of civil society without recognizing unequal power relationships. Many strong advocates of civil society can also be defenders of the status quo or can have conservative views about any notion of bottom-up democracy.

In different parts of the province, Franco-Ontarians continue to look for new socio-economic strategies and practices and develop new alternatives. In Hearst, a city in northeastern Ontario, a women's co-operative tree nursery, La Maison Verte, was founded in 1981 under the direction of a local women's group called Parmi-Elles.

Starting up with some federal funding, the project has provided eight full-time and about 35 part-time jobs. The participants are now growing millions of tree seedlings and garden plants and are building new greenhouses to grow tomatoes for the local market. In 2012, La Maison Verte's greatest success lay in the fact that they celebrated their 30th year in business. Although the organization has seen many changes over the last 30 years, it has demonstrated its ability to adapt to a fluctuating and declining forest sector and to diversify its operations to survive.[8]

On a larger scale, Franco-Ontarian women participated in the organization of the International Women's March that was held throughout the world in October 2000. In collaboration with anglophone groups, Franco-Ontarian women's groups sought to unite their struggles with others across the world in the struggle against poverty and violence against women (Gérôme, 2000).

New Socio-Economic Practices in the Past 10 Years

As globalization has taken an even greater place in all economic and social spheres, Franco-Ontarians, as with many other Canadians, are living with the consequences. Pulp and paper mills have closed in Sturgeon Falls (2002) and Smooth Rock Falls (2006), whereas any new mines have been opening with fewer workers. Likewise existing mines can remain productive using far few miners. In southern Ontario, the automobile industry employs far fewer workers, whereas layoffs in the "rust belt" has led to the closing of factories such as Atlas Steel in Welland (2007), where once up to 2,000 people worked, many of them Franco-Ontarians. In turn young people are not only leaving northeastern Ontario, but are also leaving eastern Ontario for Ottawa, gradually turning the region into part of the extended suburbs of largely English-speaking Ottawa. Agriculture has remained dominated by dairy farming that allows fewer outlets for younger farmers.

It is in this context of economic decline that the new socio-economic solutions have been developed in the past 10 years. In this section we will give examples of a few of these interesting projects and how they are helping develop new economic alternatives (Welch, 2005; Thériault, 2007; Forgues, 2007). What is striking is how many of these economic projects are linked to food production or consumption. A good example has been the recent establishment in Moonbeam, a town in northeastern Ontario, of a community food co-operative. After the only commercial food store closed, rural families would have had to travel long distances to buy food. A local group of families seeking co-operative members recruited about 400 families. By 2012 more than enough money had been raised to start the co-operative. Many of the subscribers were people who had left the region but remained loyal to their town of origin.

In eastern Ontario food security has become an important consideration. Since dairy quotas are extremely expensive, some Franco-Ontarians have been encouraging new forms of local production in food. First started in 2010, the Foire gourmande Outaouais—Est ontarien has permitted a unique form of co-operation between the

Quebec side of the Ottawa River and the Ontario side regarding food. Because meat products that are processed in provincial slaughterhouses cannot be transported from one province to another for sale, during the festival people who visit one side can cross over the river in a special ferry boat to sample food in the other province. Held over two days, the festival allows people to be exposed to local food production, mostly with some form of value added, and it brings together people from both provinces. It has assured that Franco-Ontarian food production has become far better known, permitting a new generation of younger farmers to get involved in an economically viable way (Fox, 2012).

An example of local private enterprise was the founding of Beau's All Natural Brewing Company in 2006 by Steve and Tim Beauchesne, when father and son realized that their leather tannery could not compete with production in the developing world. Starting as a small micro brewery, it uses only natural or organic products. Renowned for its natural brew, it sells throughout eastern Ontario and employs about 125 people in the area around Vankleek Hill. In turn it gives financial support to the Franco-Ontarian Festival and other local fundraising efforts. It has become a sort of unofficial beer of choice for Franco-Ontarians in eastern Ontario (Fox, 2012).

When the award-winning St-Albert Cheese Co-operative, in existence since 1896, burnt down in the winter of 2013, the communities rallied and made it possible for the co-operative to open a new factory that, since February 2015, has been operating with the potential to triple production. The provincial government has given $1 million to train the workers. One of the most moving aspects of the disaster was when cheese co-operatives in Quebec made space so the famous St-Albert curds could continue to be produced, thus saving jobs.

The most recent example of community solidarity was in March 2014, when the University of Guelph announced that it was closing the Collège d'Alfred in eastern Ontario, the only French-language agricultural postsecondary institution in Ontario, along with the English-language agricultural college in Kemptville for cost-saving measures. Within two days, after an outcry of anger in the Franco-Ontarian community, both the Cité collégial (Ottawa) and the Collège Boréal (Sudbury) promised that all courses would continue on the Alfred campus. In May 2015 it was agreed that the college would be the administered by the Cité collégiel.

One of the more original work-creation projects has been closely tied to the social service sector. In 2004 the Groupe Convex was established with the aim of creating work for people with developmental disabilities in Prescott-Russell. Since then nine projects have been set up, giving work to over 120 people, most with intellectual disabilities who previously had been considered "unemployable." The projects include recycling cardboard, two cafés, and a carpentry and furniture-building company that makes high-quality products out of western red cedar. The trained employees are now looking to export outdoor furniture to France. Convex refuses to be seen as a charity, but rather as a not-for-profit business with specific aims, all the while contributing to the larger community. It is a positive example of solidarity between private businesses, public agencies, and nine social enterprises to create wealth, good jobs for marginalized people, and provide market opportunities. Convex has received some funding to document its practices and approaches as a replicable model capable of creating decent jobs in a rural context.

All these examples show that the institutions of the Franco-Ontarian community, not unlike those in many other communities in Ontario and elsewhere in Canada, are up to the challenge of providing new forms of services and even job creation. Although they have recognized the importance of government funding and sought its assistance, they have attempted to avoid the overprofessionalization of state agencies by starting from grassroots initiatives. At the same time, they have been confronted with the challenge of avoiding these same tendencies within their own organizations—of becoming too bureaucratic, too professionalized, and in the end anti-democratic. New forms of social practice have permitted these organizations to reach populations that have often been neglected, notably francophone immigrants (especially women), those with relatively little schooling, those living in isolated regions, and those who live with intellectual disabilities.

These various alternatives have helped to rekindle self-confidence in communities that, over the years, have suffered losses in population (especially younger people), and local actions have reinforced sentiments of social solidarity, as could be seen around the threat to close Montfort Hospital (Benoît, Bouchard, Garcieau, & Leis, 2012) and more recently the Collège d'Alfred. As had often happened in the past, new practices have helped reinforce existing French-language institutions and have helped to create new ones that are often better adapted to new needs in the communities (Coderre & Dubois, 2000; Bagaoui & Dennie, 1999; Welch, 2005; Forgues, 2007). A final challenge has been the need to avoid becoming inward-looking, thereby developing other forms of intolerance and exclusion, and to find new ways of uniting their actions with those in other communities who have common interests. It has become a "struggle between very different values; the logic of competition versus the logic of community; the logic of machines and machine efficiency versus the logic of people trying to make a life for themselves and participate meaningfully in their society" (Menzies, 1996, p. xv). In the end it becomes a question of whether "the local [will] be an extension of global uniformity, or the global [will] be an extension of local diversity" (Menzies, 1996, p. 19).

Summary and Conclusion

The different social practices in the past and those of today have played a vital role in the survival and development of the Franco-Ontarian community. Although the early leaders of the community did not question the socio-economic status quo to any degree, they developed practices that permitted self-help and the means to help others in need. They aided in overcoming deficiencies in some basic needs such as housing, health, and schooling, to name only a few areas. But these practices also answered community preoccupations with retention of cultural identity, community recognition, and fostering a sense of community. In time, this sense of identity led to the creation of networks and the grounding of practices, customs, and traditions.

As government began intervening far more within the community in the 1960s and the welfare state was reaching its peak, many Franco-Ontarians began to recognize the importance that the state had in the development of new social projects. Social practitioners spent much of their energy in creating new French-language social services and educational institutions to answer the needs of their communities. Others went further, seeking to develop services that went beyond a question of language and questioning the objectives and practices of more traditional social services. Such goals led to frequent conflicts with more traditional practitioners and with community leaders.

With the crisis of the welfare state and the rise of neoconservatism, new practices have been developed by practitioners who seek greater autonomy from the state while recognizing that the state has an essential role to play in developing overall policy around social issues and in the continued financing of the social services. These new social practices promote the notion that, although services are still financed by the state, they can be administered in a way that is more democratic and inclusive. Historically, Franco-Ontarians have been part of a frequently excluded minority, but they have continued to develop their creativity as a community. It is certainly not coincidental that many of the recent and most original social and economic practices have come from low-income Franco-Ontarians, immigrant women, and those living in relatively isolated regions. It is out of these common yet diverse efforts that new ways of seeing and doing will continue to emerge, allowing new forms of social and economic practices to be developed.

All these new actions lead one to ask how individuals can unite the new practices within the Franco-Ontarian community with those elsewhere. A start might be the formation of new alliances, such as with the Aboriginal movement, Idle No More, to develop alternatives to the wealthy minority who control an ever-greater part of the world's wealth and whose greed is leading the world to environmental and human destruction. As they have done in the past, Franco-Ontarians must continue to create alternative centres of power at the grassroots level, and they must continue to be preoccupied with greater gender equality, the struggle against poverty, and a concern for the environment that will permit the long-term sustainability of local communities and the active participation in decision making by local communities (Langdon, 1999). For Franco-Ontarians, this focus entails making choices, as they have throughout their history, based on the options available and, in turn, fulfilling these choices to bring about changes. In the end, Franco-Ontarians retain a collective understanding that they have something to share together and with others—a desire to build a certain social consensus between people on what kind of world they want.

Addressing environmental, cultural, social, and economic issues, communities and not-for-profit Franco-Ontarian organizations continue to demonstrate social innovation by developing their entrepreneurial capacity, empowering themselves, creating wealth in the community, and revitalizing neighbourhoods, rural communities, and villages.

Questions for Review

1. When studying the history of the Franco-Ontarians in what ways has their history been somewhat different from the Québécois?
2. What are some of the particular roles that women have played in the development and struggles of the Franco-Ontarian community, especially in the social and health sectors?
3. Discuss some of the principal changes and social practices that have occurred within the community since the 1960s.
4. How has the notion of cultural diversity played out within the community, especially in more recent years?
5. Why do you think that community economic development or the social economy have played an increased role in the overall development of the Franco-Ontarian community?
6. Based on what you learned, where would you say the Franco-Ontarian community is heading in the next 25 years?

Suggested Readings and Resources

Bouchard, L., & Leis, A. (2008). La santé en français. In J. Y. Thériault, A. Gilbert, & L. Cardinal (Eds.), *L'espace francophone en milieu minoritaire au Canada: nouvelles mobilisations* (pp. 351–81). Montreal, QC: Editions Fides.

Forgues, E., in collaboration with Beaudry M., & de Varennes, H. (2007). The Canadian state and the empowerment of the francophone minority communities regarding their economic development. *International Journal of the Sociology of Language, 185,* 163–86.

Gérôme, M. (2000). La marche mondiale des femmes en l'an 2000 en Ontario français. *Reflets: Revue ontaroise d'intervention sociale et communautaire, 6*(1), 192–6.

Gratton, M. (2003). *Montfort—La lutte d'un peuple.* Ottawa, ON: Centre franco-ontarien de ressources pédagogigue.

Pilote, A. M. O. (2012). La construction identitaire des jeunes francophones en situation minoritaireau Canada: Négociation des frontiers linguistiques au fil du parcours universitaire et de la mobilité géographique. *Canadian Journal of Sociology, 3*(2), 169–95,

Welch, D. (1994–5). The Dionne quintuplets: More than a showcase—Five Franco-Ontarian children. *Revue d'études canadiennes, 29*(4), 36–64.

Welch, D. (2005). La collectivité franco-ontarienne: une persective historique liée à son développement socio-économique. *Francophonie d'Amérique 20,* 123–32.

Notes

A special thanks should be given to Ethel Côté who has been involved in the economic, social, cultural, and environmental sectors for over 30 years. Presently she works with the Canadian Centre for Community Renewal as a social enterprise practitioner and developer. Her comments on the later part of this chapter were most helpful.

1. By 1786, the population on both sides of the Detroit River was about 2,000. Although the majority of the population was French Canadian, a significant new population was developing owing to the frequent marriages between French-Canadian men and Aboriginal women, thereby creating a particular symbiotic relationship between Aboriginal women and the French-Canadian fur traders. By the late 18th century in the Great Lakes region, a new nation, known as the Métis, was emerging—a people who were neither French Canadian nor Aboriginal, but who spoke French as well as Aboriginal languages, were Catholic, and worked for the fur companies (Peterson, 1985). Penetanguishene, founded by Métis and French-Canadian voyageurs, is another example of these permanant French-Canadian and Métis settlements (Marchand, 1989).
2. It was in this environment that the Dionne quintuplets were born. Their grandparents had come from Quebec in the 1890s to settle in the region around Corbeil. Out of the 104 families in Corbeil, 102 were French Canadian (Welch, 1994–5).
3. "The Saint Joseph condemns those ideologies that are tainted with socialism, for they demand that the State act as a kind of providence by imposing on all citizens the duty of looking after a certain number. These ideologies seek to destroy all individual initiative and prevent competition . . . rather than fall, even moderately, into the trap of socialistic theories. One must remember that Christ said that there would always be the poor among us and it is them that he has loved most of all" [author's translation].
4. The effects of downloading responsibilities on local municipalities with fewer resources was seen in May 2000 in Walkerton, Ontario, when seven people died and thousands became ill after drinking water contaminated with *E. coli* bacteria. The province had closed its own water-testing labs, forcing municipalities to rely on private labs that charged twice as much. Regular inspections were stopped after a large number of employees from the Ministry of the Environment were laid off. Lab reports were no longer sent to either the Ministry or the local district health council. In the end, to save money, Walkerton, along with many other municipalities, simply cut corners—in this case with fatal results.
5. It has been estimated that, in the mid-1990s, about 32.5 per cent of Franco-Ontarians (as opposed to 25.4 per cent of Anglophones) worked in the public and para-public sectors (Grenier, 1996).
6. For instance, in March 1996 a representative from the Social Services Department of the Regional Municipality of Ottawa–Carleton came to speak to a group of French-speaking community workers about what role they might play within the context of the Harris government's plans regarding workfare for those receiving social assistance. The community representatives angrily made it clear that they were unwilling to do the government's work and betray the very population with whom they had been working for years. They made it clear that, with regard to workfare or any other program perceived to be coercive, the regional government was on its own.
7. The optimism of the community was dashed when, in December 1999, the provincial government decided to appeal a divisional court decision that ordered that the Montfort Hospital be kept open to prevent the assimilation of Franco-Ontarians. The government appeal stated that it had no obligation to prevent Franco-Ontarian assimilation and that the lower court decision

distorted the Canadian Constitution. The Ontario Court of Appeal that gave its decision in December 2000 rejected the appeal of the Ontario government by stating that the government had not given "serious consideration to the importance of Montfort to the survival of the Franco-Ontarian minority." In February 2002 the provincial government announced that it would not appeal to the Supreme Court.

8. Although there are many new social practices being developed in French-speaking Ontario, in the past they have often not been documented. Since 1995, a new journal called *Reflets: Revue ontaroise d'intervention sociale et communautaire* is being produced jointly by the schools of social work at Laurentian University and the University of Ottawa. Because researchers and social activists are thus being encouraged to write articles, more of these new practices are being documented and studied. For instance, an article by Coderre and Dubois (2000) documented a number of creative projects in low-income Franco-Ontarian neighbourhoods in Ottawa.

References

Andrew, C., Archibald, C., Caloren, F., & Denis, S. (1986). *Une communauté en colère: La grève contre. AMOCO Fabrics à Hawkesbury.* Hull, QC: Éditions Asticou.

Arnopoulos, S. M. (1982). *Hors du Québec point de salut?* Montreal, QC: Libre Expression.

Bagaoui, R., & Dennie, D. (1999). Le développement économique communautaire: Nouveau départ pour le mouvement associatif Franco-Ontarien? *Reflets: Revue ontaroise d'intervention sociale et communautaire, 5*(1), 75–94.

Benoît, M., Bouchard, L., Garceau, M. L., Leis, A. (2012). "Les inégalités sociales de santé chez les communautés francophones en situation minoritaire au Canada." *Reflets, 18*(2).

Berger, J. (1979). *Pig earth.* London, UK: Writers and Readers Publishing Cooperative.

Brandt, G. (1976). *J'y suis, j'y reste: The French Canadians in Sudbury, 1883–1913.* Unpublished doctoral dissertation, York University.

Brandt, G. (1979). The development of French Canadian social institutions in Sudbury Ontario, 1883–1920. *Revue de l'Université Laurentienne, 11*(2), 5–12.

Brault, L. (1942). *Ottawa, capitale du Canada de son origine à nos jours.* Ottawa, ON: Éditions de l'Université d'Ottawa.

Brodeur, R. (1979). *Villages et visages de l'Ontario français.* Toronto, ON: TV Ontario.

Browne, P. L. (2000). The neo-liberal uses of the social economy: Non-profit organizations and warfare in Ontario. In E. Shragge & J.-M. Fontan (Eds.), *Social economy: International debates and perspectives.* Montreal, QC: Black Rose Books.

Brunet, L. (1992). *Almanda Walker-Marchand (1868–1949): Une féministe.* Ottawa, ON: L'interligne.

Cardinal, L., & Coderre, C. (1990). Les francophones telles qu'elles sont: Les Ontaroises et l'économie. *La revue du Nouvel-Ontario, 12,* 151–81.

Carrière, F. (1993). La métamorphose de la communauté franco-ontarienne, 1960–1985. In C. J. Jaenen (Ed.), *Les Franco-Ontariens* (pp. 305–40). Ottawa, ON: Les Presses de l'Université d'Ottawa.

Carrière, R. (1994, November). La loi 8 et les services sociaux destinés aux familles francophones. Paper presented at the Colloque familles francophones: Multiples réalités, Sudbury, ON.

Carrière, R. (1995). La loi 8 et les services sociaux destinés aux familles francophones. In C. Bernier, S. Larocque, & M. Aumond (Eds.), *Familles francophones: Multiples réalités* (pp. 279–91). Sudbury, ON: Institut franco-ontarien.

C'est le temps (1981). Se prendre en main. *Revue du Nouvel-Ontario, 3,* 110–14.

Choquette, R. (1984). *L'Église catholique dans l'Ontario français du XIX siècle.* Ottawa, ON: Édition de l'Université d'Ottawa.

Coderre, C., & Dubois, M. (2000). Solidarité et citoyenneté: Initiatives pour contrer la pauvreté chez les francophones dans Ottawa-Carleton. *Reflets: Revue ontaroise d'intervention ssociale et communautaire, 6*(2), 61–86.

Comeau, G. (1982). *The role of the Union Saint Joseph du Canada in the organization of the association canadienne-française d'Ontario.* Unpublished master's thesis, University of Montreal, QC.

Desjardins, M. (1991). *Les femmes de la diaspora canadienne-française: Brève histoire de la FNFCF de 1914 à 1991.* Ottawa, ON: Fédération nationale des femmes canadiennes-françaises.

Forgues, E., in collaboration with Beaudry M., & de Varennes, H. (2007). The Canadian state and the empowerment of the francophone minority communities regarding their economic development. *International Journal of the Sociology of Language, 185,* 163–86.

Fox, J. (2012). *Comment aller au-delà de l'agriculture traditionnelle. Un regard des alternatives alimentaires locales de Prescott et Russell.* Mémoire de maitrise, QC: l'Université d'Ottawa.

Gaffield, C. (1987). *Language, schooling, and cultural conflict.* Montreal and Kingston: McGill-Queen's University Press.

Gérôme, M. (2000). La marche mondiale des femmes en l'an 2000 en Ontario français. *Reflets: Revue ontaroise d'intervention sociale et communautaire, 6*(1), 192–6.

Gratton, M. (2003). *Montfort—La lutte d'un peuple.* Ottawa, ON: Centre franco-ontarien de ressources pédagogigue.

Gravel, J. (1980). *Quelques aspects de la vie des franco-ontariens durant les années de la Grande Dépression (1930–1939).* Unpublished master's thesis, York University, Toronto, ON.

Greening, W. E. (1972). The lumber industry in the Ottawa Valley and the American market in the nineteenth century. *Ontario History, 62,* 134–6.

Grenier, G. (1996, April 26). Analyse de la performance économique de la population franco-ontarienne. Paper presented at the Colloque l'Ontario français, valeur ajoutée? Ottawa, Université d'Ottawa.

Grimard, J., & Vallières, G. (1986). *Travailleurs et gens d'affaires canadiens-français en Ontario.* Montreal, QC: Éditions Études Vivantes.

Jaenen, C. J. (Ed.). (1993). *Les Franco-Ontariens.* Ottawa, ON: Presses de l'Université d'Ottawa.

Juteau, D., & Séguin-Kimpton, L. (1993). La collectivité franco-ontarienne: Structuration d'un espace symbolique et politique. In C. J. Jaenen (Ed.), *Les Franco-Ontariens* (pp. 265–304). Ottawa, ON: Presses de l'Université d'Ottawa.

Langdon, S. (1999). *Global poverty, democracy and north-south change.* Toronto, ON: Garamond.

Marchand, M. (1989). *Les voyageurs et la colonisation de Pénétanguishene (1825–1871): La colonisation française en Huronie.* Sudbury, ON: La Société historique du Nouvel-Ontario.

Marchildon, D. (1984). *La Huronie.* Ottawa, ON: Le Centre franco-ontarian de ressources Pedagogiques.

Martel, M. (1997). *Le Deuil d'un pays imaginé: Rêves, luttes et déroute du Canada français. Les rapports entre le Québec et la francophonie canadienne (1867–1975).* Ottawa, ON: Presses de l'Université d'Ottawa.

Martel, M. (2005). Usage du passé et mémoire collective franco-ontarienne: le souvenir du Règlement 17 dans la bataille pour auver l'hôpital Montfort. *Mens: revue d'histoire intellectuelle de l'Amérique française, 6*(1), 64–9.

Menzies, H. (1996). *Whose Brave New World?* Toronto, ON: Between the Lines.

Ninacs, W. A. (1998). *A practitioner's perspective on the social economy in Quebec.* Victoriaville, QC: Human Resources Development Canada.

Pelletier, J. (1987). *Le conflit minier.* Toronto, ON: TV Ontario.

Peterson, J. (1985). Many roads to Red River: Métis genesis in the Great Lakes region, 1680–1815. In J. Peterson & J. S. H. Brown (Eds.), *Being and becoming Métis in North America.* Winnipeg, MB: University of Manitoba Press.

Pettey, D., & Ouimet, R. (1988). *Quand je suis malade, je ne suis pas bilingue.* Ottawa, ON: Association canadienne pour la santé mentale, Section d'Ottawa-Carleton.

Powell, F., & Guerin, D. (1997). *Civil society and social policy: Voluntarism in Ireland.* Dublin: A. & A. Farmer.

Proulx, P. (1982). *La part des femmes il faut la dire.* Ottawa, ON: La Fédération des femmes canadiennes-françaises.

Scheinber, E., & McIntosh, R. (1995, August). *The mills of Cornwall: Family, work and ethnicity in a late nineteenth century Ontario town.* Paper presented to the Canadian Historical Association, Montreal, QC.

Schneiderman, E. (1972). *A community profile of Welland, Ontario's French-speaking population.* Unpublished master's thesis, University of Buffalo, Buffalo, NY.

Sylvestre, P. (1984). *Cornwall.* Ottawa, ON: Le Centre franco-ontarien de ressources pédagogique.

Thériault, J. Y. (2007). Pas d'exception culturelle sans exceptionnalisme politique: un défi pour la francophonie in *Faire société: Société civile et espaces francophones* (pp. 321–31). Sudbury, ON: Collection Agora Prise de parole.

Tissot, G. (1981). L'auto-détermination. *Revue du Nouvel-Ontario, 3,* 91–6.

Trudel, C. (1982). *Welland.* Ottawa, ON: Association des enseignants franco-ontariens.

Trudelle, C., & Fortier, P. (1987). *La paroisse du Sacré-Coeur: Toronto se raconte.* Toronto, ON: La société d'histoire de Toronto.

Vallières, G. (1980). *L'Ontario français par les documents.* Montreal, QC: Éditions Études Vivantes.

Welch, D. (1991–2). La lutte pour les écoles secondaires franco-ontariennes. *Revue du Nouvel-Ontario, 13–14,* 109–31.

Welch, D. (1994–5). The Dionne quintuplets: More than a showcase—Five Franco-Ontarian children. *Revue d'études canadiennes, 29*(4), 36–64.

Welch, D. (1995). The Franco-Ontarian community and the provincial educational state: A relationship for greater self-autonomy or a new Trojan horse? *Canadian Ethnic Studies, 27*(2), 145–65.

Welch, D. (1999). L'économie social en Ontario français: analyse historique, pratiques actuelles et recherche de sens. *Reflets: Revue ontaroise d'intervention sociale et communautaire, 5*(1), 54–74.

Welch, D. (2005). La collectivité franco-ontarienne: Une persective historique liée à son développement socio-économique. *Francophonie d'Amérique, 20,* 123–32.

Adaptation and Acculturation among New Canadians

Implications for Intergenerational Relations and Social Work Practice

By Debashis Dutta and Ross A. Klein

Chapter Objectives

This chapter will help you develop an understanding of:

- The historical influences of Canada's immigration policies and practices being rooted in exclusion and discrimination
- The concepts, processes, and models around acculturation
- The various stresses associated with immigration, such as employment, financial stability, identity and status, family separation, and intergenerational conflict
- The factors that support coping and resiliency for immigrant families
- How to apply the Immigrant Parent Enhancement (IPE) framework to immigrant parents and their families

Introduction

From its early days, social work has focused on issues that result from the movement of people from place to place, in terms of both cause and impact of migration. People's search for a better life has always inspired adventurous moves for the sake of discovering new lands and exploring other cultures; however, more pressing causes such as fleeing persecution and seeking better opportunities also motivate people to migrate.

The effect of migration was noted initially in the field of anthropology with significant contributions from psychology. Indeed, the adjustment of the "stranger in a strange land" is well documented in history, literature, and film. In addition to attention paid to the challenges an immigrant faces with regard to adjusting to new customs, social rules, foods, workplace cultures, and education systems, the significant adjustment on the family also requires recognition. While family is the primary socializing agent for children, the impact of acculturation on parents and in turn children requires attention, understanding, and care.

The purpose of this chapter is to explore the parenting-related stresses and successes of immigrants to Canada. It will address the gap of resiliency factors in immigrant parenting and how this relates to acculturation. First, an overview of Canadian immigration history will provide context, followed by theories of acculturation with an analysis of the process of acculturation, acculturative stress, and coping. Second, the chapter will examine traditional social work approaches to immigration and acculturation. Third, the chapter will introduce the Immigrant Parent Enhancement (IPE) framework. The final part of the chapter will consider the processes discussed and implications for social work practice.

Canadian Immigration Policy: Historical Influences and Sentiments

> We in Canada have certain more or less clearly defined ideals of national well-being. These ideals must never be lost sight of. Non-ideal elements there must be, but they should be capable of assimilation. Essentially, non-assimilable elements are clearly detrimental to our highest national development, and hence should be vigorously excluded (Woodsworth, 1909, p. 232).

Early Beginnings

The history of post-European contact settlement in Canada is well documented (Avery, 1995; Kelley & Trebilcock, 2010; Knowles, 1997)—it has not always been kind to those wanting to relocate here. Before the 1400s, Irish monks and Viking whalers made brief visits to what is now Newfoundland and Labrador, creating collaborative relationships with Aboriginal inhabitants; the first colonies were established by French explorers: Cartier in 1534 and de Champlain in 1603 (Wallace, 1930). The fur trade, farming, lumber, and fishing provided prolific opportunities for business and trade, which necessitated the need for labour. With increased infusion of immigrants, the Canadian Immigration Service was formed in 1820. As the British and French immigrants capitalized on economic development, they also attempted to civilize and "Christianize" the Aboriginal peoples (Frideres & Gadacz, 2008), a theme that marked the overarching ideology of Canada's immigration policies. Fear, inferiority, and presumed failure were and continue to be prevailing areas of social thought that have influenced immigration sentiment. (For discussion on contemporary social work and policy with Canadian Aboriginal peoples, see Chapter 7 by Raymond Neckoway and Keith Brownlee.)

Throughout the 1800s and into the 20th century, Canada appeared to resemble Britain-inspired anti-immigration sentiment toward non-White, non-Christian populations, which was rooted in attitudes of ethnoracial superiority (Walker, 2008). Immigrants who did not bear a similarity to British people were perceived to harbour disease, be physically weak, and maintain uncivilized socio-political thought. For example, fears of racial mixing resulted in the 1885 amendment to immigration policy that imposed head taxes to discourage the Chinese from coming to Canada and required Asian immigrant women to marry only within their own race (Dua, 2007). In the mid- to late 1800s, Jewish, Icelandic, Russian, Hungarian, German, and Ukrainian immigrants were permitted to settle in the West, mainly because they were stereotyped to be pacifist and hard working (Woodsworth, 1909). Canada admitted White soldiers from the American Civil War, but denied entry to freed Black/African American slaves because of the perception that they could not tolerate the harsh Canadian climate (Stewart, 2004). In 1907, Canada imposed limits on Japanese and Chinese immigrants, denying them the opportunity to bring their families. Primarily, Canada permitted these immigrants to work on the railways. The result was significant emotional separation between families. Canada also enacted the Continuous Journey Clause (1908) directed toward South Asians, legislation that denied entry to Canada if the ship they travelled on made any stops along the way (La Brack, 1988). Usually, steamers at the time would travel from Asia to Vancouver with a stop in Hawaii. Most notably, this clause was challenged by the Japanese steamship *Komagata Maru*, carrying 376 Indian passengers in 1914. The ship was hired by an Indian entrepreneur who argued that Indian citizens were British subjects and therefore could not be denied entry to another British colony. The ship made stops in Hong Kong, Singapore, and Japan before landing in Vancouver Harbour where it was held. Two months passed before the ship and its passengers were sent back to India.

The Influence of the World Wars

World War I incited new fears about "aliens" from "enemy" countries; those suspected were people from Germany and Eastern European countries (Russia, Estonia, Latvia, Hungary, Czechoslovakia, and Romania), thereby halting immigration (Kelley & Trebilcock, 2010). There was limited increase in immigrants from these countries post-World War I, but the Great Depression of the 1930s once again curtailed immigration, and "foreigners" incurred bigotry because they were perceived to have taken jobs away from Canadians (Avery, 1995). In the later 1930s, as Nazism prevailed in parts of Europe, Canada promoted anti-Semitism by barring Jewish immigrants to Canada, an attitude conveyed by an immigration officer who, when asked how many Jews Canada should permit entry to, replied: "None is too many" (Abella & Troper, 1983).

The Japanese attack on Pearl Harbour resulted in Canada incarcerating tens of thousands of Japanese residents in concentration camps and eventually deporting many. Germans living in Canada also faced persecution as Canada became skeptical about "enemy states" and intolerant of refugees and immigrants. World War I and World War II essentially divided the world into "good" and "evil," thereby transforming the fear of difference to paranoia about being obliterated by evil (Strange & Loo, 1997). However, after World War II Canada relaxed its immigration rules because there was a growing need for skilled and unskilled labour. Essentially, the war brought with it advances in technology, industry, and commerce that required a capable and willing workforce. This, combined with the horrors of the war, inspired Canada's social conscience and it gained a reputation for being sympathetic to immigrants and refugees (Kelley & Trebilcock, 2010).

From Tolerance to Openness to Reluctance

In 1947, immigration policy sought to balance population growth and avoid overtaxing the economy while maintaining Canada's British character (Knowles, 1997). In 1951, Canada signed agreements with India, Pakistan, and Ceylon (now Sri Lanka) limiting the numbers of South Asian immigrants (Avery, 1995). The Immigration Act of 1952 simplified immigration processes but relied on racist rationale to deny immigrants' entry to Canada based on ethnic group, occupation, lifestyle, unsuitability with Canada's climate, and the perceived inability to assimilate into Canadian society. Legislation in 1962 finally eliminated racial discrimination from immigration policy. As long as immigrants could support themselves in Canada, no one could be denied admission because of race, heritage, or ethnic background. However, only European immigrants could bring their families and relatives; four years later, the clause was removed.

In 1966 the Department of Manpower and Immigration was formed, which essentially merged immigration with employment: Canada's approach to immigration would be directed by the immigrant's ability to find work. The points system was introduced in 1967, which allotted points for what potential immigrants would bring to Canada. During the 1970s the backlog of applications for landed immigrant status and citizenship increased, and there was mounting evidence that immigration laws were being abused. Despite a government Green Paper in 1975 cautioning against high immigration because of the hidden costs of social strain (Grady & Grubel, 2011), Canada decisively became a country of immigration, while realizing that it could not afford an open-door immigration policy. The Immigration Act of 1976 established annual limits and categories for landed immigrant status (family class, humanitarian class, independent class), and the revisions to the points system emphasized practical training and experience (Kelley & Trebilcock, 2010). The removal of race-based restrictions facilitated an increase of qualified immigrants from countries such as the West Indies, Guyana, Haiti, Hong Kong, India, the Philippines, and Indochina. Most recently, immigrants from non-European countries have surpassed the number of European immigrants as their numbers have increased and European immigration has decreased (Riddell-Dixon, 2008).

The 1980s saw Canada grapple with worldwide refugee issues and poverty in the developing world. Advances in technology raised hope for people escaping oppressive regimes, but also caused an ever-widening gulf between rich and poor countries. The economic recession complicated Canada's willingness to accept refugees and immigrants. The increase in illegal immigrants was the catalyst for the Refugee

Deterrence and Detention Bill in 1988, which placed restrictions on refugees coming to Canada. It also created the "investor" class of immigrants, awarding more points to immigrants who financed Canada's economy. Immigration policy was becoming increasingly driven by economics and less by family reunification and humanitarianism. This continued into the 1990s with clearer movement toward the independent and investor classes and with stricter controls on family class immigrants. Refugees were fingerprinted, faced public hearings, placed in harsher detention conditions, and deported without a hearing (Wallace, 1995), echoing sentiments from the fear-based intolerance of the past.

The 21st century holds additional challenges and obstacles for immigrants. Landing fees for immigrants continue to increase, reminiscent of the discriminatory head taxes from 100 years ago, making Canada more accessible to a wealthier class of immigrants. Globalization, technological advances, and the emergence of poor countries into competitive countries shape immigration practice and ideology (Valtonen, 2008). The tension of post-9/11 fears about terrorism have prompted governments to increase security and embrace racial/ethnic profiling. Revised notions of "alien" and "enemy" permeate current discourse on immigration, multiculturalism, and nationalism (Kim, 2009).

However, the anti-immigration sentiment that marks Canada's overall approach to newcomers is also tempered by a statement by Kellor (1921) who was sympathetic toward the plight of immigrants, which may still hold true today:

> The alien comes here in good faith, ignorant of the existing laws and discrimination against him. He makes no special appeal to our sympathy or interest. He is changed with most of our economic if not political evils. He is an outcast. He is a source of revenue and the victim of all sorts of swindles by some of the immigrants who came before him. He is a lonely figure. (p. 41)

Canada has tended to presume failure of immigrants to assimilate into Canada because of their own inherent weakness. In the 1880s, the mayor of Toronto believed that immigrants were unsuited to live and work there (Cross, 1974) because of the cold and the British, urban lifestyle. Van Kooten (1959) stated, "By the grace of God, the immigrant too must know and rule his own spirit, rather [than] try to beat down the citadels about him" (p. 31). Additionally, nationalistic concerns of Americanization or **assimilation** in Canada required a discouraging of the immigrants to talk too much of the old country (Abbott, 1926). This pervasive attitude of blaming the immigrant for his or her own failure to adjust continues the theme of Canada's assimilationist approach. As such, Canada must acknowledge these overarching sentiments while addressing barriers to successful **integration** in the face of issues such as the lack of recognition of credentials, gender differences, income disparities, discrimination, and a lack of access to settlement services. These issues contribute to immigrants' stress as they move from their home country to the host country.

Case Example 9.1 New Immigrant Challenges

Juanita immigrated to Montreal from Colombia. She settled into a lower income area in the city that has a mix of recent and long-standing immigrants. Employment opportunities vary, so some in the neighbourhood work full time while others cobble together several part-time jobs or temporary jobs to make ends meet. Juanita's husband works in construction and has long days. Her two children (8 and 10 years of age) are adjusting to school. Juanita works part time in a store but wishes to obtain education to become a nurse. She is hesitant, however, because she does not know where to start to get this information. She is also unsure about whether her high school marks from Colombia will be accepted in Canada and is very concerned about her accent and lack of language skills. While she has been told that to get a job in nursing in Canada she needs to brush up on her English, Juanita has also heard that people tend not to hire "Hispanics" because of stereotypes of gang activity, violence, and poverty.

Acculturation and Its Impact on the Immigrant

The fear and reluctance that marks the history of immigration is countered with successful immigrant outcomes in terms of high educational achievement, strong occupational attainment, and positive integration in mainstream society (James, 2010). However, the processes by which immigrants integrate, though quite widely researched, are not adequately recognized in dominant society. This section will provide background information on acculturation, examine the impact of acculturation on the **identity** of the immigrant, and summarize the literature on stress and coping as a primary contributor to immigrant acculturation.

What Is Acculturation?

The concept of **acculturation** was first referred to in 1880, with clearer definitions from anthropology and sociology in 1936 and 1951, respectively. The earliest definition follows:

> Acculturation comprehends those phenomena which result when groups of individuals having different cultures come into continuous first-hand contact, with subsequent changes in the original culture patterns of either or both groups . . . under this definition acculturation is to be distinguished from culture change, of which it is but one aspect, and assimilation, which is at times a phase of acculturation. It is also to be differentiated from diffusion, which while occurring in all instances of acculturation, is not only a phenomena which frequently takes place without the occurrence of the types of contact between

> peoples specified in the definition above, but also constitutes only one aspect of the process of acculturation. (Redfield, Linton, & Herskovits, 1936, p. 149)

From the field of organizational sociology, Firth (1951) states that "Terms such as 'acculturation' were introduced to express the way in which new patterns of behaviour or types of relationship were acquired and incorporated into a primitive system" (p. 81). Interestingly, in 1953 acculturation implied that a primitive community was in the process of being acculturated to the West. The 1954 Social Sciences Research Council (SSRC) Summer Seminar defined acculturation as follows:

> . . . culture change that is initiated by the conjunction of two or more autonomous cultural systems . . . Its dynamics can be seen as the selective adaptation of value systems, the processes of integration and differentiation, the generation of developmental sequences, and the operation of role determinants and personality factors. (p. 974)

From sociology and anthropology, Graves (1967) introduced psychological acculturation as "changes in an individual who is a participant in a culture contact situation." Berry (1980) stated that acculturation is multifaceted and falls into four classifications: nature, course, level, and measurement. He believed that the nature of acculturation necessitated the contact of two or more cultural groups that resulted in change. The course of acculturation included phases of contact, conflict, and adaptation. The two levels were the group and the individual, with the range of impact affected by individual and personality factors. Measurement required an examination of purpose, history, and persistence of cross-cultural contact. This led to his development of a bi-dimensional, four-cell model for acculturation outcomes.

Kundu and Adams (2005) asserted that cognitive elements such as expectations, attitudes toward the new culture and members, cultural identity, perception, attribution, and change in values played a role in acculturation. The concept of acculturation is closely related to "adaptation," which connotes change or modification. Marin and Gamba (2003) suggested that such adaptations take place through processes of "culture shedding" (the process through which the immigrant lets go of aspects of their culture that may not be as relevant or useful in adjusting) and "culture learning" (the process by which the immigrant acquires the knowledge and skills necessary to be able to fit in); however, these also result in culture conflict and **acculturative stress** (Berry, Phinney, Sam, & Vedder, 2006).

Early theories on acculturation and stress were influenced by medicine and psychiatry; the notion of pathology associated with acculturation and change was prominent. Subsequent stress and coping theories moved away from pathologically based "culture shock" toward recognizing adaptive coping mechanisms that drew on personality strengths and emphasized skill learning and acquisition. In this context, Sam and Berry (2010) updated Berry's earlier definition to include change as a result of the meeting of cultures, stressing the mutually impactful processes of one culture making contact with another (Crisp & Hewstone, 2006).

Acculturation theories have also been classified over time. Initially, Redfield et al. (1936) suggested that assimilation was not the only form of acculturation. The SSRC (1954) definition implied increasing complexity around assimilation that required a multifaceted perspective. Marin and Gamba (2003) described three perspectives on acculturation: (1) *assimilation*—a move toward the host culture, requiring a relinquishing of identity; (2) *integration*—the maintenance of original cultural integrity while moving toward the host society; and (3) *rejection*—a self-imposed or forced move away from the host society. Finally, Portes and Rivas (2011) classify acculturation theories into culturalist (emphasizing the assimilation of immigrants into the mainstream) and structuralist (examining the immigrants' place in socio-economic hierarchies).

Models of Acculturation

The development of definitions of culture, ethnicity, and assimilation has influenced the evolution of acculturation models. Gordon (1964) proposed a linear/bipolar model with seven types of assimilation: culture, structure, marital, identity, attitude, behaviour, and civic. These types assumed that the immigrant largely moved away from his or her culture of origin and into that of the host country. Also inherent in this model is the assumption that cultures are static. In addition, Gordon suggested that while people could acculturate into another society, assimilation was not always possible. Suggesting ownership and choice over the outcome of acculturation, a linear model of acculturation was offered by Szapocznik, Scopetta, and King (1978), where acculturation was a function of the amount of time one spent in the host culture. They stated that this varied across age and sex and that there was a difference between the behavioural things we do and our values.

Another approach is proposed by Berry (1980, 1990). He suggests a bicultural framework of acculturation with four end-states based on two continua: cultural maintenance, which is the extent to which individuals maintained their original cultural identity, and contact-participation, which is the extent to which individuals sought out contact with those outside their cultural group. The four end-states or outcomes of acculturation are as follows:

- *Integration*, where individuals maintain their identity with their home culture but also take on some characteristics of the new culture
- *Assimilation*, where individuals do not keep their identity from their home culture but prefer to take on all of the characteristics of the new culture
- *Separation*, where individuals separate themselves from the dominant culture
- *Marginalization*, where individuals do not want anything to do with either the new culture or the old culture

These initial theories examined acculturation as an individual phenomenon, thus ignoring family and group changes (Santisteban & Mitriani, 2003) as well as structural influences on acculturation (Kim, 2009). Matsumoto (2006) defined culture "as a shared system of socially transmitted behavior that describes, defines, and guides people's ways of life, communicated from [one] generation to the next" (p. 220). Thus, acculturation is more a process of cultural learning that changes over time. The application of this definition also suggests acculturation is not limited to the four outcomes suggested by Berry. Bourhis, Moïse, Perreault, and Senécal (1997) presented the interactive acculturation model, which established acculturation along structural (government and political) environments. The relativistic theory is based on

1. the acculturation strategies of immigrants according to culture;
2. the majority attitudes toward immigrants' acculturation; and
3. the relational outcomes by combining these two areas.

The two macro-level factors that provided structural influence are whether the state ideology on immigration is pluralist or ethnist, and the relative position of immigrant groups in the host society. The combination of host and minority community orientations then resulted in one of three acculturation processes: consensual, problematic, or conflictual.

Like Berry, Rivera-Sinclair (1997) introduced a bicultural model where the immigrant's acculturation is assessed on continua of cultural involvement-marginality and monoculturalism-biculturalism. Castro (2003) adds complexity to acculturation strategies by suggesting that group-level and individual-level factors affect acculturation. Group-level factors include the context of the society of origin, the attitudes and policies of the host society, and the predisposing characters of the acculturating group. Individual-level factors include pre-immigration characteristics, and conditions and factors that arise during acculturation.

There are other additions to theories for understanding acculturation. Tajfel's (1981) addition of social identity theory expanded acculturation to include the influence of social categorization and social comparison on group membership, group perception, and interaction between groups and individuals. Hermans and Kempen (1998) introduced the idea of the dialogical self in which the intertwining of self and culture requires social interaction, thereby encouraging a narrative perspective of acculturation. This idea of cultural synergy emphasizes the efforts made by both the immigrant group and the host society in understanding one another. This is encapsulated by Ward, Bochner, and Furnham (2001) who incorporate societal-level with individual-level variables and examine the processes of transitions, stress, strategies, responses, and eventual outcomes for acculturation. The model permits the multidimensionality of acculturation while maintaining a nondeterministic outcome. An expanded multidimensional model that adds notions of collectivism, familism, individualism, and interdependence was proposed by Schwartz, Unger, Zamboanga, and Szapoczni (2010).

The discussion of models of acculturation requires addressing the notion of **reacculturation**. Onwumechili et al. (2003) succinctly define reacculturation processes "as involving a 'stranger's' attempt to readjust upon reentry to the homeland" (p. 46). Nato (2010) found that Berry's model for acculturation could be used to understand the processes and potential outcomes for reacculturation. In other words, when immigrants return to their country of origin, they endure much of the same challenges, identity shifts, and acculturative stresses as they do when they leave their country of origin and adjust to a new country.

Impact of Acculturation and Acculturative Stress

Acculturation models provide perspectives on the outcomes for immigrant adjustment and the influences they contend with as they acculturate. The impact of acculturation requires exploration to better contextualize the immigrant experience. This section will track how socio-economic differences influence the status of the immigrant, which leads to role stress, and how this shapes acculturative stress for the immigrant family.

Structural Influences

From a macro perspective, larger structural issues of the host country influence and shape the experience of the acculturating individual. For example, barriers to gainful employment (Balgopal, 1999; Ontario Human Rights Commission, 2013) lead to stresses associated with underemployment and unemployment. These barriers are often structurally perpetuated forms of racism that contribute to economic differences between cultural groups, which in turn leads to overall differences in the abilities of certain immigrant groups (e.g., Mexicans and African Americans) to achieve financial stability and upward mobility (Portes & Rumbout, 1996; Ortega & Peri, 2013).

Financial and employment instability subsequently lead to acculturation issues related to status for the immigrant. While immigrants may eventually improve their financial status from what it was in their home country, they may lose social status in terms of status according to cultural standards, power in the extended family, becoming religious minorities when in Western countries, and particularly parental authority as children acculturate more quickly than their parent(s) (Atkhar, 2011). Immigrant minorities also lose status as they face the daily hassles of discrimination (Abouguendia & Noels, 2001). Additionally, while ethnic-minority and immigrant students endure the same developmental challenges (career choices, educational attainment, individuation, and role conflict) as native-born students, they concurrently face the challenge of adapting to another culture, which places them in a lower status position to their peers (Morrison & James, 2009). Ngo (2006) states that Southeast and South Asian American students dealing with the "model minority myth"—a belief that people from Asia generally fit into dominant society and experience success, thereby making them the ideal minority who will assimilate without any issue (Bhattacharya,

2000; Trytten, Lowe, & Walden, 2012) face an increased risk of marginalization from American and Canadian society. This search for status or "fit" is a challenge to the immigrant child's identity.

Impact for Immigrants and Families

The impact of losing status or searching for status because of acculturation is closely related to role stress and loss of self-esteem for the immigrant. The cost of immigration is loss in the form of familial guidance, cultural continuity, and environmental supports. These losses add stress on how immigrants negotiate their own cultural identities as they adapt and cope with their new home—this stress is often greater for parents than for children who more easily adapt to their new social environment. Additionally, strife, war, and conflict from the country of origin for some immigrants result in uprooted lives and associated feelings of failure, grief, and depression (Warr, 2010). Especially for fathers, this can lead to a loss of confidence and self-esteem (Shimoni, Este, & Clark, 2003). Children of immigrant parents negotiate between two cultures: They experience the shame of having "different" parents and are forced into the role of having to teach their parents. Parents are stressed with high cultural expectations, which increases family stress (Akthar, 2011).

An additional stress for many immigrant men is the role reversal that takes place when their female partners or wives have to work, resulting in a loss of self-esteem at failing to be the provider for the family (Shimoni et al., 2003). Similarly, immigrant women tend to experience a multiplicity of structural vulnerabilities related to their gender, their ethnoracial status, and increased chances for poverty. Additionally, in many non-Western countries of origin, joint and extended families provide mutual care for members of intergenerational families; upon immigration, women maintain similar responsibilities without the additional, extended kinship support, thereby creating additional stress.

The aforementioned issues of socio-economic differences, status, and stress play out in four key aspects related to the context of the family:

1. The acculturation gap between parents and their children
2. The difference in values between the host and home cultures
3. The resulting concerns about separation of the family
4. Intergenerational conflict

Since children of immigrants are more interested in immersion into the dominant culture of their peers, they tend to integrate more rapidly than their parents, thereby increasing the acculturation gap (Farver, Narang, & Bhandha, 2002). The gap is furthered as the child of the immigrant turns to people from the dominant culture for support, while the parents have lost their support from extended family (Merz, Özeke-Kocabas, Oort, & Schuengel, 2009).

The difference in values between host and home cultures is another family context for acculturative stress. Whereas most immigrants come from countries with a generally collectivistic orientation, most receiving countries are associated with an individualistic orientation. The values of co-operation and interdependence associated with collectivistic cultures are diametrically opposed to individualistic notions of competition and independence. For example, from a Southeast Asian perspective, there are two dimensions of acculturation style: traditionalism (maintenance of original cultural identity) and participation (involvement in the dominant cultural [Western] group) (Atzaba-Poria, Pike, & Deater-Deckard, 2004; Suinn, 2010). For Arab immigrant parents, acculturation is influenced by parallel processes of their openness to the host culture and the degree to which they perceive their native culture as important (Henry, Biran, & Stiles, 2006; Safdar, Dupuis, Lewis, El-Geledi, & Bourhis, 2008). These differences then weave their way into relationships between parents and their children. For fathers from Chinese and Mexican ethnic origins, the more acculturated they are the more likely they are to be involved with their children (Capps, Bronte-Tinkew, & Horowitz, 2010). Portuguese immigrant families to Canada place high importance on honour, respect, goodness, and trust (Morrison & James, 2009); families stay together for the sake of maintaining family honour.

The third key family context for acculturative stress culminates in the potential separation of family members. Immigrant families are inherently disadvantaged because the family members tend to experience distance because of variations in values and acculturation rates (Kwak, 2003). Children of most immigrant parents internalize stress more than externalize it, which coincides with the values of deference and obedience in collectivistic cultures (Aroian, Hough, Templin, Kulwicki, Ramaswamy, & Katz, 2009); the exposure to individualistic values of self-expression challenges the children's notions of discretion, which distances them from traditional family values (Sapru, 2006). "Acculturative dissonance" refers to conflict that occurs when parent and youth cultural systems clash because of the differential acculturation rates. Some youth cope with the separation by turning to manipulation, outside influences, and rebelliousness. Since immigrant families from collectivistic cultures tend toward multigeneration family dynamics, fathers and mothers grieve the lack of extended family support and presence (Inman, Howard, Beaumont, & Walker, 2007). The lack of guidance and cultural continuity from extended family also represents a separation between family members.

Case Example 9.2 Intergenerational Stressors

Assad has come to a cross-cultural immigrant support agency because he is heavily disheartened. He immigrated to Toronto 17 years ago from Pakistan. His children, aged 16, 13, and 10, were born in Toronto. He recalls that "back home" he was a manufacturing engineer with master's degrees in engineering and business. He worked in a senior management position in a prominent company in Pakistan. Upon his arrival to Toronto, he had no success in finding work in his field. To support his family, Assad has taken jobs in factory-line work and recently in quality assurance. He reminisces about being respected when he was in Pakistan, where he loved his work and could provide for his family. In Toronto, employers always ask for Canadian experience, but "no one will give me the chance in my field." He has had difficulty encouraging his daughters and son to adhere to religious and cultural teachings, but finds he does not have the control he would have if they had remained in Pakistan. He complains to his wife about these issues, but also feels a sense of grief at losing so much. In addition to feeling like he is losing control of his children, Assad feels like a failure because his wife has to work so they can make ends meet. He also deeply misses his parents and siblings and believes that if they were nearby there would be more family support, "people who understand us and those who can be a family for my children."

Finally, the family provides the forum for intergenerational conflict because family is the primary unit for socialization of children. As such, ethnic families are encumbered with dual and competing processes of acculturation (Tsai-Chae & Nagata, 2008). Within the context of a new host culture, the natal ethnicity is subject to critical evaluation by both parents and their children as well as the host society. This evaluation problematizes the utility, applicability, and significance of the natal culture in the face of the host culture, which contributes to intergenerational conflict. Since collectivistic cultures emphasize interdependence and deference to authority, intergenerational conflict tends to be muted and therefore more subtle than in individualistic cultures. For example, Gupta, Johnstone, and Gleeson (2007) find that intergenerational conflicts are subtly manifested in the change in gender roles, the issue of respect versus individual assertiveness, the change from collective family power to individual members, conflict over differences in lifestyle, the incorporation of grandparents, the concerns about Westernization, and the overall social context of immigration. Similar to other cultures, children of Indian immigrant parents adapt and embrace the new culture readily and are more apt to assume the behaviours, attitudes, and values of the dominant culture. This contributes to parent–child conflict because of the stress associated between what parents want for their children and what children want for themselves (Baptiste, 2005). Conflict for immigrant Indian families increases as hierarchies are challenged, resulting in lower levels of connectedness (Dwairy & Dor, 2009).

Alongside the above-noted concerns and the stressful effects of immigration and acculturation, there are strengths within the immigrant family that can be maintained and enhanced. Shimoni, Este, and Clark (2003) found that immigrant fathers perceive that immigration to Canada brought them the gift of time to interact with their children, play with them, and instruct them in cultural practices and their ethnicities. Kim's

(2009) study on residential group patterns of immigrants found that geographic proximity to members of the same ethnic group promoted increased integration of immigrants into mainstream society. As such, ethnic enclaves like "Chinatown" and "Little India" provide a sense of continuity of the home culture, which makes the impact of immigration easier to bear. As educational success and integration are sought-after goals for immigrant parents, the educational system in the host country is valued and appreciated. Since education is perceived as the vehicle to economic success, integration in the education system represents the immigrant's goal of providing a better life and opportunities for their children (Shimoni et al., 2003). For the children of immigrants, Kwak (2003) found that immigrant teens have a healthy self-construct and are generally well adapted into academic settings. The value of maintaining close intergenerational family relations allows for closer monitoring of children's activities, discouraging delinquent behaviour, instilling the value of higher education and the retention of a minority language (Abada & Tenkorang, 2009). These factors are also seen as buffering effects of acculturation and immigration. Chen and Tse (2010) find strength in the process of acculturation for Chinese children in prolonging cohabitation before marriage and a low divorce rate, thereby demonstrating that traditional values play a protective role during acculturation.

Coping with Immigration and Acculturation

Since the transition of immigration and acculturation is a stressful life event, the issue of coping with this stress requires attention. Initial concepts around stress and adaptation came from biology and ecology, which led to pathology-based notions of stress and coping where, if a person was not able to cope with stress or adapt to a stressful situation, he or she was somehow incapable, weak, or inept. This led to the ego-psychology–based model, emphasizing unconscious cognitive processes such as denial, repression, suppression, and intellectualization. Lazarus (1966) developed a cognitive model of stress and coping that placed emphasis on the individual's appraisals of stressful situations. With Folkman, Lazarus developed the transactional life stress model that identified four types of coping: problem solving, positive appraisal, confrontive coping, and distancing (Folkman & Lazarus, 1988).

Increasing attention to environmental and situational factors that contribute to stress and coping resulted in augmentation of the original model. The "broaden and build" model (Frederickson, 1998) emphasized that as a person copes, he or she draws upon already existing internal resources and uses these as leverage to increase his or her competence in coping with the stressful situation. The learning and acquisition of coping strategies can then be drawn upon in future stressful situations. Notions of communal and prosocial coping are also introduced as a way to counter the highly individualistic nature of stress and coping and to draw on religion, shared experience, and community. In other words, the importance of voluntary sharing, valuing co-operation, and recognizing that stresses are common to those who experience them helps facilitate a mutual and collective approach to stress reduction. Further, this type of sharing promotes interdependence and resiliency while reducing isolation.

Current thought emphasizes the interplay between coping and positive emotions. Folkman and Moskowitz (2000) found that coping had a number of key converging issues: coping regulates distress, appraisal processes influence coping, coping is also influenced by personality, and social resources affect coping. Frydenberg (2004) suggested that three coping domains (solving the problem, reference to others, and non-productive coping) can be drawn on to articulate specific teachable skills around coping. Folkman and Moskowitz (2000) also examined the notion of meaning-focused coping, which generates positive emotions and appraisals of stressful situations. It taps into benefit finding, benefit reminding, adaptive goal processes, reordering priorities, and infusing ordinary events with positive meaning. These have significance in terms of contributing to resiliency and inherent strength.

For immigrants, a significant aspect of coping has to do with the stress of racism. As this also impacts identity and self-concept, support-seeking strategies are important to assess to enhance emotional stability. Liang, Alvarez, Juang, and Liang (2007) found that women of East Asian origin experience less deleterious impacts of racism than men because they seek advice from others about their experiences. Daniels, Harris, and Briner (2004) suggest that in the workplace employees ought to tap into their own histories to cope with stress at work. This ignores the nature of management–employee relations and inherent oppressions of many workplaces and hierarchies.

Researchers have examined other elements of coping that are important to consider. Khan and Watson (2005) found that Pakistani immigrant women in Toronto encountered excitement, grieving, shock, and hardship. However, they used hope, religion, community, and family in order to cope. For Somali immigrants and refugees, underlying anxieties, anger, frustration, and loss were masked, and the emphasis on education, safety, and connecting to the community became important coping activities (Silveira & Allebeck, 2001). Chinese-American immigrants drew from culturally held notions of suffering, faith, and religion as they coped with immigration (Lee & Chan, 2009). The use of resiliency factors, strengths-based notions, and wellness activities activate coping factors of salvation, trust, inner peace, humility, harmony, and mutuality.

In their study of immigrants from Russia to Israel, Markovitzky and Mosek (2005) examined the use of symbolic resources such as landscape, climate, literature, and music to maintain one's ethnic identity and ease the process of acculturation. For South Asian women immigrating to Toronto, contemporary hopes for the present and future tempered the perceived loss of tradition from the past (Naidoo & Davis, 1988). In order to cope, these women remained rooted to deeply held symbolic notions of home, faith, and women's roles, while at the same time seeking opportunities for equality and success. This dualistic coping is reminiscent of the duality inherent in Hindu religion and Indian culture.

Poulsen, Karuppaswamy, and Natrajan (2005) examined the meaning-making of immigration and acculturation, especially as it relates to women's coping, and found that themes of choice and control over immigration, experience of the primary social network, level of emotional attachment to and investment in the host country, and ongoing relationships with the home country were salient in drawing on coping strategies. For Chinese and Somali immigrants to Canada, the importance of finding instrumental resources such as daycare, transportation, and employment were important ways to cope with acculturation (Stewart et al., 2008) and added to successful integration. Hispanic immigrants to the United States relied heavily on faith and concepts of destiny (Strug, Mason, & Auerbach, 2009). For Turkish immigrants, optimism and proactive coping were indicators of well-being that assisted in coping with acculturative stress (Uskul & Greenglass, 2005). As well, marriage and the ability to rely on family and educational success were indicators of positive coping. Similarly for youth, academic integration and persistence were found to be strong indicators of coping (Zea, Reisen, Beil, & Caplan, 1997). Roesch, Weiner, and Vaughn (2002) examined the big five personality traits (openness, conscientiousness, extraversion, agreeableness, neuroticism) and coping for Korean immigrants to the United States and concluded that highly acculturated individuals were able to cope better because they minimized negative feelings, were more agreeable to social support, assertively made plans for the future, and were somewhat more extraverted. These sorts of coping contributed to the meaning-making that immigrants used to reconcile acculturation difficulties. As can be seen, while there are commonalities across cultures, there are also unique differences based on the family's natal culture and the characteristics they bring to acculturation to Canada.

The Immigrant Parent Enhancement (IPE) Framework

This section will synthesize a number of models of parenting, acculturation, and identity formation and combine this with the resiliency enhancement model (Greene 2007), resulting in the Immigrant Parent Enhancement (IPE) framework. Following the description, the framework's convergence with several social work orientations will be provided.

Elements of the IPE Framework

In explaining parental coping as it relates to immigration and acculturation, several models have been examined so far (i.e., Berry, 1980, 1990; Baumrind 1966, 1991; Maccoby, 1992; Ragg, 2011; Mana, Orr, & Mana, 2009; Akthar, 2011). As all are four-cell or four-outcome based models, they can be placed in a four-quadrant framework. The key question is, "How do immigrants cope with acculturation and their role as parents?" Greene's (2007) resiliency enhancement model can then be placed in the centre of this framework as the unifying construct for acculturation, coping, and parenting. Greene (2007) uses six wellness concepts in her model: self-acceptance, positive relations, autonomy, environmental mastery, purpose in life, and personal growth. The socio-cultural influences in Ragg's (2011) parent empowerment model are considered as conditions of change that the parent mediates through resilience and his or her four parenting functions (guidance, discipline, nurturing, and accessibility) and are recategorized to fit the framework. The assumptions are (1) parents strive toward a balance (culturally influenced and personally defined) in their parenting functions; (2) as immigrant parents acculturate, they contend with socio-cultural factors from the home and the host culture; and (3) immigrant parents strive toward their children's successful parenting by tapping into their strengths and resiliency factors. Four new categories of immigrant parental "tendencies" are proposed:

1. Unified-restorative
2. Abandoned-providential
3. Partitioned-austere
4. Deprecated-detached

The *unified-restorative* parenting tendency suggests that immigrant parents are successful in resolving cultural conflicts between the host and home cultures. They are able to strike a balance between raising their children in the dominant society while maintaining their cultural values and assisting their children in "taking the best from both worlds." This parent is assumed to provide a recuperative function whereby they are able to support their children in developing a bicultural identity, thereby mediating losses and challenges.

The *abandoned-providential* tendency fits the parent who values the dominant/host culture over his or her own and tends toward a significant "letting go" of original culture traits such as language, religion, mores, and behaviours in favour of those of the dominant culture. The parent is rather liberal and permissive, allowing their children to participate fully in the dominant culture with few restrictions or limits.

Parents who tend toward the *partitioned-austere* quadrant place greater value on their original culture over that of the host society. They expect their children to adhere to strongly held cultural values, beliefs, and behaviours, emphasizing the importance and superiority of these over that of the dominant culture. This leads to increased separation from the dominant society and a very regulated and rigid parenting approach.

Finally, the *deprecated-detached* parental tendency is characterized by an overall uninvolved, self-denounced approach toward children. Not only do these parents separate from the dominant culture, they also separate from their children. The assumption of mental health issues is prevalent in this tendency. Table 9.1 provides a depiction of the parental tendencies and the models from which they are constituted. The framework's orthogonal, four-cell quadrant depiction (see Figure 9.1) is not intended to minimize or celebrate any one particular approach. The use of the word "tendency" suggests the parent may not be fixed in any of the quadrants—they may gravitate toward one or may draw from a few tendencies depending on their propensity, inclination, and socio-cultural environment.

The socio-cultural environment that shapes parenting includes (1) values, (2) experiences of difference, (3) permission for abstractness in thought, (4) sanctions for

Table 9.1 Immigrant Parental Tendencies

	Unified-Restorative	**Abandoned-Providential**	**Partitioned-Austere**	**Deprecated-Detached**
Societal approach to immigration (Berry, 1980)	Multiculturalism	Melting pot	Segregated	Exclusion
Immigrant approach to acculturation (Berry, 1990)	Integration	Assimilation	Separation	Marginalization
Four parental functions (Ragg, 2011)	Balance of discipline, guidance, nurturing, and accessibility	Focus on nurturing and accessibility	Focus on discipline and guidance	All functions are "muted"
Parental styles (Baumrind, 1966, 1991; Maccoby, 1992)	Authoritative	Permissive	Authoritarian	Disengaged
Immigrant identity statuses (Mana, Orr, & Mana, 2009)	Extended identity	Secluded identity	Rivalry identity	Identity loss
Children's ethnic identity status (Akthar, 2011)	Bicultural identity	Hyper-assimilated identity	Ethnocentric identity	Alienated identity

Source: Adapted from Berry, 1980, 1990; Baumrind, 1966, 1991; Maccoby, 1992; Ragg, 2011; Mana, Orr, & Mana, 2009; Akthar, 2011; Greene, 2007.

behaviours, (5) tapping resources, (6) an orientation to a collectivistic versus individualistic society, and (7) an understanding of roles and expectations (Ragg, 2011). These seven factors are socio-culturally based and shape the overall approaches to parenting. Ragg (2011) states that the influence of these socio-cultural factors then determines the balance between four parental functions: guidance, discipline, nurturing, and accessibility. With immigration and acculturation, parents are faced with different and often competing socio-cultural factors that in turn influence how they carry out their parental functions. Changes in adjustment to the new culture will then result in a new balance according to the parental tendencies introduced above.

The unifying construct for the IPE framework comes from Greene's (2007) risk and resiliency model. Specifically, it draws from a wellness perspective (Ryff & Singer, 2002) with six domains of wellness: self-acceptance, positive relations with others, autonomy, environmental mastery, having a purpose in life, and personal growth. Applied to

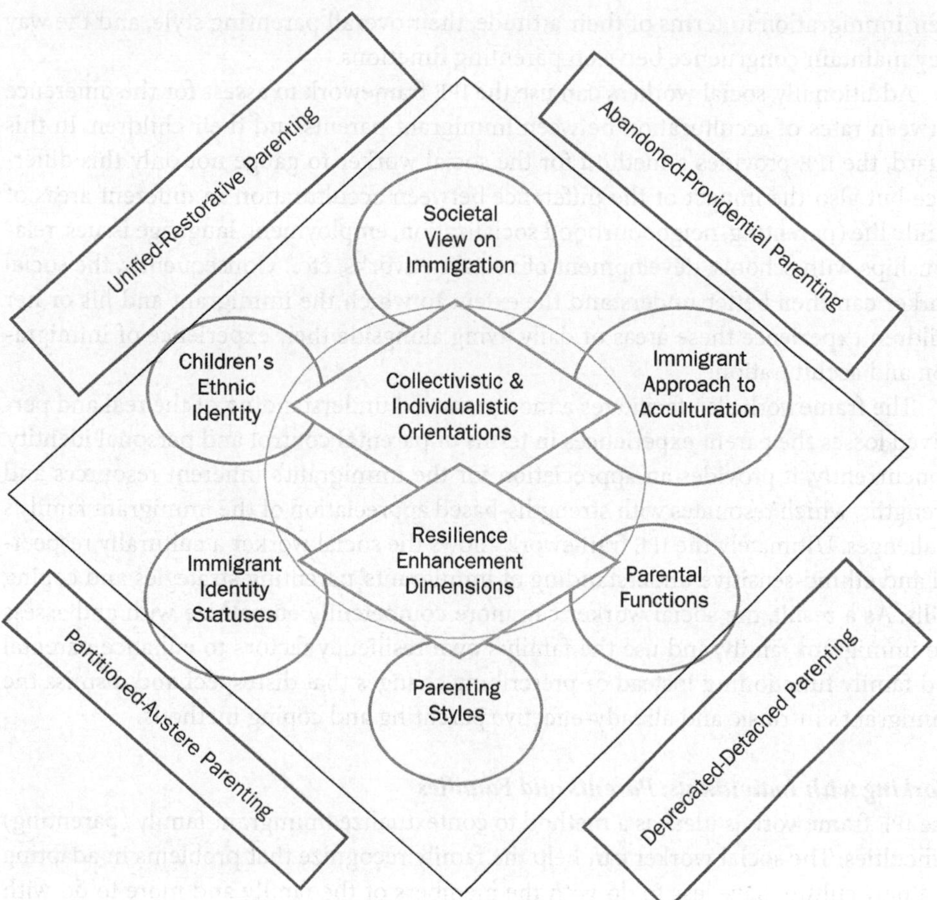

Figure 9.1 Immigrant Parent Enhancement Framework

Source: This framework is adapted from materials as per Table 9.1 (Berry, 1980, 1990; Baumrind, 1966, 1991; Maccoby, 1992; Ragg, 2011; Mana, Orr, & Mana, 2009; Akthar, 2011; Greene, 2007).

the IPE framework, these domains can be drawn upon to examine how to mediate the change in socio-cultural factors (Ragg, 2011) for immigrant parents (see Figure 9.1).

Implications for Social Work Practice

The IPE as an Assessment Tool

Social workers can employ the IPE framework as a comprehensive tool to assess the stability and acculturation of immigrant families. Specifically, the IPE framework assesses the parent's balance between maintaining familiar cultural parenting and adapting newer approaches. Recognizing the immigrant's likelihood to parent from one of the four tendencies, the social worker uncovers how parents have approached their immigration in terms of their attitude, their overall parenting style, and the way they maintain congruence between parenting functions.

Additionally, social workers can use the IPE framework to assess for the difference between rates of acculturation between immigrant parents and their children. In this regard, the IPE provides a method for the social worker to gauge not only this difference but also the impact of the difference between acculturation in different areas of family life (parenting, neighbourhood socialization, employment, language issues, relationships with schools, development of social networks, etc.) Consequently, the social worker can then better understand the extent to which the immigrant and his or her children experience these areas of daily living alongside their experience of immigration and acculturation.

The framework also facilitates a more nuanced understanding of the real and perceived losses the parent experiences in terms of parental control and personal identity. Concurrently, it provides an appreciation for the immigrant's inherent resources and strengths, which resonates with strengths-based appreciation of the immigrant family's challenges. Ultimately the IPE framework allows the social worker a culturally respectful and ethnic-sensitive understanding of immigrants' parenting strategies and coping skills. As a result, the social worker can more competently empathize with and assess the immigrant family, and use the family's own resiliency factors to enhance parental and family functioning instead of prescribing changes that disrespect and dismiss the immigrant's intrinsic and already-effective parenting and coping methods.

Working with Individuals: Parents and Families

The IPE framework is ideal as a method to contextualize immigrant family (parenting) difficulties. The social worker can help the family recognize that problems in adapting to a new culture have less to do with the members of the family and more to do with the experience of immigration and acculturation. In essence, as the social worker externalizes the issue of immigration, he or she can more accurately empathize with the losses, fears, and frustrations that the family members are experiencing. With regard to parents, the social worker can help parents voice their feelings about adapting to the rules and norms of a new culture. As the social worker works toward a trusting helping relationship, the parents can be engaged to take a more critical look at their parenting strategies—what worked "back home" may not be easily translated in the host country. The social worker needs to tread carefully in suggesting alterations to overall parenting techniques to avoid cultural imperialism.

Issues of parent–child conflict and intergenerational tensions can be exacerbated by the experiences of immigration and acculturation. Social workers can engage the IPE framework by helping parents alter some of their parenting strategies to encourage communication between their children and themselves. Such communication could be directed at encouraging family members to articulate their challenges in acculturating more overtly, but more so their needs. As a result, the IPE framework can be used in a way that helps family members support one another through their individual changes and adjustments while maintaining strong family cohesiveness. Acts that family members perform that contribute to cohesiveness can then be drawn upon as examples of minimizing conflict, working through challenges, and maintaining family togetherness. In this way, social workers can assist the family in developing ways of constantly raising, addressing, and resolving intergenerational relationship issues that cause conflict. This in turn creates opportunities for the social worker to encourage a healthier and more intentional acculturation experience.

For example, a social worker can also assist parents in discussing how their approach to immigration is impeding or facilitating adjustment to the host society: The social worker must pay particular attention to initial reasons for immigrating, areas of excitement, anticipatory anxiety, and immigrant hopes and dreams. The social worker must also be able to assist the parent in raising the issue of identity change. In other words, the social worker can address the question, "How has coming to this new country changed you as a person?" which leads to the question, "How have your changes influenced how you parent your children?" Such approaches then allow for a greater exploration of immigrants' cultural and ethnic influences on their self-identity and their worldviews on how children ought to be raised versus how they are being raised in the new culture.

Following along with the approach to immigration is the social worker's ability to capitalize on resiliency. Social workers can help clients name specific culturally based strengths and resiliency factors that can be drawn upon to validate immigrants' experiences, assist in the narrative around immigration challenges and successes, and solidify immigrants' inherent strengths. Through these methods, the social worker can then support the immigrant in reaching toward competencies, and instead of denying or dismissing them, use them in an ethnic-sensitive way to adapt more effectively to the host culture.

Case Example 9.3 The IPE as a Tool

Andrea is a social worker at the immigrant support agency. She determines a number of factors that contribute to Assad's feeling of being disheartened. As they talk, Andrea assesses that while Assad is frustrated at his own perceived "failures" as a parent and provider, his parenting strategies are not overly controlling. She finds that he does indeed rely on his faith and extended family for support and mutual care. She discovers that Assad and his family are generally well-connected to the Pakistani community and attend many of the cultural and religious functions. Even as his children are somewhat defiant with Assad and his wife, they maintain good relations with family friends. Andrea also takes into account that Assad has been in Canada for close to 20 years, has established a livelihood, and is able to (along with his wife) provide for his family.

continued

In terms of parenting, Andrea assesses that despite his challenges, stresses, and losses, Assad is likely to fit into the unified-restorative tendency. However, she believes that he could be at risk of leaning toward the partitioned-austere or even the deprecated-detached tendencies, but she sees opportunities to help maintain and even enhance Assad's coping, confidence, and dignity.

She and Assad develop a plan where they uncover his strengths in terms of perseverance in work, his faith in religion, his willingness to be somewhat flexible with his children, their willingness to be close to family friends, and his own strong connections in his cultural community. They also work toward acknowledging that despite the challenges he has experienced, Assad has indeed maintained his ultimate goal for immigration—to ensure better opportunities for his children. Andrea connects Assad to employment services and a business-mentorship program to explore opportunities for Assad to find work in his field.

An important facet of the IPE framework in parental and family work with immigrants lies in its intrinsic use of culturally respectful ideas. While the framework explicitly refers to terms that are normally associated with cultural competence and ethnic-sensitive practice, it positions itself to draw from the immigrant client's own experiences and strengths and invites the client to tell his or her story while the worker highlights the strengths. In this regard, the social worker can individualize service that respects the client's cultural orientation, acknowledges the various adjustment issues around immigration and the impact on family, and support changes in the family to encourage acculturation.

Working with Groups: Parents and Children

The IPE framework lends itself well to social group work applications. Traditional parent support groups can be adapted to meet immigrant parents' common needs. The group work format allows members to share common concerns and find support in one another. Group activities and discussions can easily be formulated to reflect the primary components of the IPE framework, namely parenting styles, the immigrants' approaches and attitudes to their acculturation and the host society, parental functions, and identity statuses. A structured group work approach for immigrant parents can provide a psycho-educational component to acculturation while engendering some therapeutic benefits.

While the group work approach would employ the IPE framework quite well, social workers should be cautious about group formation and membership. Even if the immigration adjustment issues and subsequent challenges associated with parenting are similar across cultural groups, social workers must remember that different ethnic groups have their own specific histories, values, strategies, and practices. As such, immigrants should not be "lumped" into a one-size-fits-all approach. Cross-cultural differences can be significant enough to distract away from the overall purpose of the group and cause more conflict than support. There is more value in running groups with members whose immigration histories are similar and whose cultural, ethnic, and religious backgrounds have common threads. (For a further discussion on understanding diverse ethnocultural groups through religious and spiritual lenses, see Chapter 11 by Diana Coholic.)

Children of immigrants tend to acculturate at a higher rate than their parents, and because their primary venue for socialization is the school setting, a specific group for coping with immigration may not be easy to develop. Nevertheless, the children's identity status as noted in the IPE framework offers ways in which the children can be engaged in groups to discuss acculturation issues that conflict between them and their parents. At the same time, multiple-family group work could be more promising so long as it is done with similar principles in mind as parent groups (i.e., keeping membership to similar immigrant groups). Multiple-family group work could incorporate activities that engage whole families to address pertinent overall relational issues as well as to determine common problem-solving methods.

The use of co-leadership can enhance group work with immigrants, especially where one or both leaders are members of the immigrant group. This allows for role-modelling, an additional professional for group members to consult, and the opportunity for professional self-reflection for the leaders. Experienced group leaders who are a part of the immigrant group can provide the members with a sense of hope as well as a recognition that immigration does not equate with total loss of ethnic identity; rather, it shows the nature of an evolving identity in the face of acculturation.

Group work with immigrants can also easily use the resiliency factors highlighted in the IPE framework. Social workers can identify these factors and engage members in the group in discussions about the ways in which they are resilient, the resources they gather and use, and the methods they rely on to succeed as they acculturate. Sharing resiliency experiences in group settings promotes more resiliency among members of the group.

Summary and Conclusion

The purpose of this chapter is to provide an understanding of how Canada's immigration history has shaped the way in which immigrant families cope with inherent stresses associated with coming to Canada and adjusting to a new culture. Elaborating on acculturative stresses and coping strategies helps underline challenges that immigrant families face. Universally, parents play the roles of leader, guide, teacher, disciplinarian, and protector for their children. However, immigration complicates and challenges these roles because parents and children may encounter different rates of acculturation, experience differing forms of stress, and rely on different forms of coping. This may compromise the role and influence of the immigrant parent.

The chapter introduced the Immigrant Parent Enhancement (IPE) framework as a way to assess overall parental tendencies, draw upon inherent and newer parental and family strengths, and enhance resiliency for parents and their children. The framework focuses on cultural competence and anti-oppression and on a narrative-constructivist framework drawing on empowerment, resiliency, strength, and solutions. (For a more in-depth discussion on the importance of considering narrative constructions when working with diverse groups, see Chapter 10 by Catherine Montgomery.) Concepts in Canada that fill the gap of extended family and build on resiliency are "community" and "neighbourhood"; social workers can encourage immigrant families to connect with existing ethnic communities in their city and to develop relationships in their neighbourhoods. This raises the potential to connect immigrants to members of their ethnic community to draw on collective self-determination and collective motivation. The emphasis on socio-centrism, collective responsibility, and the reduction of cultural conflict strengthens cultural identity, self-concept, and social support and enhances resilience.

The literature informing this chapter and the IPE framework clearly shows that immigration and acculturation comprise multiple layers and complex processes combining both internal psychosocial dynamics for the immigrant and societal-structural undercurrents from the external environment. While there is a difference between the rate of acculturation between immigrant parents and their children, the acculturative stresses resulting from loss of the old and adjustment to the new impacts all family members and the dynamics between them. Particularly for immigrant parents, the amendments to their role in their children's lives requires shifts in personal identity and coping strategies. Acculturation is not an outcome but a process that changes according to the immigrant family's challenges and successes at any given time in their lives.

The IPE framework provides social workers with a structure in which to better assess a family's acculturation processes. While it focuses on the balance between maintaining important aspects of the home culture and learning the new, it also places particular emphasis on resiliency, wellness, and inherent strengths that members of the family bring. In this regard, the IPE framework brings less of a prescriptive approach to working with immigrant families ("here's what you need to do to fit in to this country and culture") to more of a collaborative perspective ("let's draw on what you already have to help you cope with immigration").

Questions for Review

1. Discuss how the history of Canada's immigration attitudes, policies, and practices shape the way in which we treat immigrant families.
2. What are the primary stressors that immigrant families face?
3. Discuss the significant losses that immigrant families address.
4. How does acculturative stress create problems for immigrant parents?

5. As social workers, how can we draw upon immigrants' strengths and capacities to help them cope?
6. How do we as social workers extrapolate and build upon resiliency factors of immigrant parents while not dismissing their losses and challenges?

Suggested Readings and Resources

Canadavisa.com Immigration Forum. (2010). Topic: Tips on adjusting to a new life in Canada for newcomers. Retrieved from http://www.canadavisa.com/canada-immigration-discussion-board/tips-on-adjusting-newlife-in-canada-for-newcomers-t59514.0.html

Centre of Excellence for Research on Immigration and Settlement. http://ceris.ca

Government of Canada. (2010). Adjusting to life in Canada. Retrieved from http://www.cic.gc.ca/english/newcomers/after-life.asp

Immigrant Services Association of Nova Scotia. http://www.isisns.ca

Meléndez, L. (2005). Parental beliefs and practices around early self-regulation: The impact of culture and immigration. *Infants & Young Children*, *18*(2), 136–46.

Polycultural Immigrant & Community Services. http://www.polycultural.org

Quilt of Belonging. http://www.invitationproject.ca/home.htm

Rose, E. (2013, February 4). Raising a Canadian: Immigrant children develop different views. Canadian Immigrant. Retrieved from http://canadianimmigrant.ca/family/raising-a-canadian-immigrant-children-develop-different-views

Walters, D., Phythian, K., & Anisef, P. (2006). The ethnic identity of immigrants in Canada. CERIS Working Paper Series #50. Retrieved from http://ceris.ca/wp-content/uploads/virtual-library/Walters_et_al_2006a.pdf

YWCA Immigrant Settlement Services. http://www.ywcaprincealbert.ca/settlement-services-refugees-immigrants--newcomers.html

References

Abada, T., & Tenkorang, E. Y. (2009). Pursuit of university education among the children of immigrants in Canada: The roles of parental human capital and social capital. *Journal of Youth Studies, 12*(2), 185–207.

Abbott, E. (1926). *Historical aspects of the immigration problem: Select documents*. Chicago, IL: University of Chicago Press.

Abella, I., & Troper, H. (1983). *None is too many: Canada and the Jews of Europe, 1933–1948*. Toronto, ON: Lester and Orpen Dennys.

Abouguendia, M., & Noels, K. A. (2001). General and acculturation-related daily hassles and psychological adjustment in first- and second-generation South Asian immigrants to Canada. *International Journal of Psychology, 36*(3), 163–73.

Akthar, S. (2011). *Immigration & acculturation: Mourning, adaptation and the next generation*. Lanham, MD: Jason Aronson.

Aroian, K., Hough, E. S., Templin, T. N., Kulwicki, A., Ramaswamy, V., & Katz, A. (2009). A model of mother–child adjustment in Arab-Muslim immigrants to the U.S. *Social Science & Medicine, 69*(9), 1377–86.

Atzaba-Poria, N., Pike, A., & Deater-Deckard, K. (2004). Do risk factors for problem behavior act in a cumulative manner? An examination of ethnic minority and majority children through an ecological perspective. *Journal of Child Psychology and Psychiatry, 45*(4), 707–18.

Avery, D. H. (1995). *Reluctant host: Canada's response to immigrant workers, 1896 to 1994.* Toronto, ON: McClelland and Stewart.

Balgopal, P. R. (1999). Getting old in the U.S.: Dilemmas of Indo-Americans. *Journal of Sociology and Social Welfare, 26*(1), 51–68.

Baptiste, D. A. (2005). Family therapy with East Indian immigrant parents rearing children in the United States: Parental concerns, therapeutic issues, and recommendations. *Contemporary Family Therapy: An International Journal, 27*(3), 345–66.

Baumrind, D. (1966). Effects of authoritative parental control on child behavior. *Child Development, 37*(4), 887–907.

Baumrind, D. (1991). The influence of parenting style on adolescent competence and substance use. *Journal of Early Adolescence, 11*(1), 56–95.

Berry, J. W. (1980). Acculturation as varieties of adaptation. In A. Padilla (Ed.), *Acculturation: Theories, models and findings* (pp. 9–25). Boulder, CO: Westview.

Berry, J. W. (1990). Psychology of acculturation. In J. Berman (Ed.), *Cross-cultural perspectives: Nebraska symposium on motivation* (pp. 201–34). Lincoln, NE: University of Nebraska Press.

Berry, J. W., Phinney, J. S., Sam, D. L., & Vedder, P. (2006). Immigrant youth: Acculturation, identity and adaptation. *Applied Psychology, 55*(3) 303–32.

Bhattacharya, G. (2000). The school adjustment of South Asian immigrant children in the United States. *Adolescence, 35*, 77–85.

Bourhis, R. Y., Moïse, L., Perreault, S., & Senécal, S. (1997). Towards an interactive acculturation model: A social psychological approach. *International Journal of Psychology, 32*(6), 369–86.

Capps, R. C., Bronte-Tinkew, J., & Horowitz, A. (2010). Acculturation and father engagement with infants among Chinese and Mexican-origin immigrant fathers. *Fathering: A Journal of Theory, Research, & Practice about Men as Fathers, 8*(1), 61–92.

Castro, V. S. (2003). *Acculturation and psychological adaptation.* Westport, CT: Greenwood Press.

Chen, X., & Tse, H. C. H. (2010). Social and psychological adjustment of Chinese Canadian children. *International Journal of Behavioral Development, 34*(4), 330–8.

Crisp, R. J., & Hewstone, M. (2006). Multiple social categorization context, process, and social consequences. In R. J. Crisp & M. Hewstone (Eds.), *Multiple social categorization: Processes, models and applications* (pp. 3–23). New York, NY: Psychology Press.

Cross, M. S. (Ed.). (1974). *The working man in the nineteenth century.* Toronto, ON: Oxford University Press.

Daniels, K., Harris, C., & Briner, R. B. (2004). Linking work conditions to unpleasant affect: Cognition, categorization and goals. *Journal of Occupational and Organizational Psychology, 77*(3), 343–63.

Dua, E. (2007). Exclusion through inclusion: Female Asian migration in the making of Canada as a white settler nation. *Gender, Place & Culture: A Journal of Feminist Geography, 14*(4), 445–66.

Dwairy, M., & Dor, A. (2009). Parenting and psychological adjustment of adolescent immigrants in Israel. *Journal of Family Psychology, 23*(3), 416–25.

Farver, J. A. M., Narang, S. K., & Bhandha, B. R. (2002). East meets west: Ethnic identity, acculturation, and conflict in Asian Indian families. *Journal of Family Psychology, 16*(3), 338–50.

Firth, R. (1951). *Elements of social organization.* London, UK: Watts & Co.

Folkman, S., & Lazarus, R. S. (1988). Coping as a mediator of emotion. *Journal of Personality and Social Psychology, 54*(3), 466–76.

Folkman, S., & Moskowitz, J. T. (2000). Positive affect and the other side of coping. *American Psychologist, 55*(6), 647–54.

Fredrickson, B. L. (1998). What good are positive emotions? *Review of General Psychology, 2*(3), 300–19.

Frideres, J. S., & Gadacz, R. R. (2008). *Aboriginal peoples in Canada* (8th ed.). Toronto, ON: Pearson Prentice Hall.

Frydenberg, E. (2004). Coping competencies: What to teach and when. *Theory into Practice, 43*(1), 14–22.

Gordon, M. M. (1964). *Assimilation in American life*. New York, NY: Oxford University Press.

Grady, P., & Grubel, H. (2011). *Immigration and the Canadian welfare state, 2011*. Toronto, ON: The Fraser Institute.

Graves, T. D. (1967). Acculturation, access and alcohol in a tri-ethnic community. *American Anthropology, 69*(3–4), 306–21.

Greene, R. R. (2007). *Social work practice: A risk and resiliency perspective*. Belmont, CA: Nelson.

Gupta, V., Johnstone, L., & Gleeson, K. (2007). Exploring the meaning of separation in second-generation young South Asian women in Britain. *Psychology & Psychotherapy: Theory, Research & Practice, 80*(4), 481–95.

Henry, H. M., Biran, M. W., & Stiles, W. B. (2006). Construction of the perceived parental acculturation behaviors scale. *Journal of Clinical Psychology, 62*(3), 293–7.

Hermans, H. M., & Kempen, H. G. (1998). Moving cultures: The perilous problems of cultural dichotomies in a globalizing society. *American Psychologist, 53*(10), 1111–20.

Inman, A. G., Howard, E. E., Beaumont, R. L., & Walker, J. A. (2007). Cultural transmission: Influence of contextual factors in Asian Indian immigrant parents' experiences. *Journal of Counseling Psychology, 54*(1), 93–100.

James, C. E. (2010). *Seeing ourselves: Exploring race, ethnicity and culture* (4th ed.). Toronto, ON: Thompson Educational Publishing.

Kelley, N., & Trebilcock, M. (2010). *The making of the mosaic: A history of Canadian immigration policy* (2nd ed.). Toronto, ON: University of Toronto Press.

Kellor, F. (1921). *The federal administration and the alien: A supplement to immigration and the future*. New York, NY: George H. Doran.

Khan, S., & Watson, J. C. (2005). The Canadian immigration experiences of Pakistani women: Dreams confront reality. *Counselling Psychology Quarterly, 18*(4), 307–17.

Kim, A. H. (2009). *The social context of residential integration: Ethnic groups in the United States and Canada*. El Paso, TX: LFB Scholarly Publishing.

Knowles, V. (1997). *Strangers at our gates: Canadian immigration and immigration policy, 1542–1997*. Toronto, ON: Dundurn Press.

Kundu, S., & Adams, G. R. (2005). Identity formation, individuality, and connectedness in East Indian and non-East Indian female Canadian emerging adults. *Identity: An International Journal of Theory and Research, 5*(3), 247–60.

Kwak, K. (2003). Adolescents and their parents: A review of intergenerational family relations for immigrant and non-immigrant families. *Human Development, 46*(2), 15–136.

La Brack, B. (1988). Evolution of Sikh family form and values in rural California: Continuity and change 1904–1980. *Journal of Comparative Family Studies, 19*(2), 287–309.

Lazarus, R. S. (1966). *Psychological stress and the coping process*. New York, NY: McGraw-Hill.

Lee, E. O., & Chan, K. (2009). Religious/spiritual and other adaptive coping strategies among Chinese American older immigrants. *Journal of Gerontological Social Work, 52*(5), 517–33.

Liang, C. T. H., Alvarez, A. N., Juang, L. P., & Liang, M. X. (2007). The role of coping in the relationship between perceived racism and racism-related stress for Asian Americans: Gender differences. *Journal of Counseling Psychology, 54*, 132–41.

Maccoby, E. E. (1992). The role of parents in the socialization of children: An historical overview. *Developmental Psychology, 28*, 1006–17.

Mana, A., Orr, E., & Mana, Y. (2009). An integrated acculturation model of immigrants' social identity. *Journal of Social Psychology, 149*(4), 450–73.

Marin, G., & Gamba, R. J. (2003). Acculturation and changes in cultural values. In K. M. Chun, P. B. Organista, & P. Marin (Eds.), *Acculturation: Advances in theory, measurement and applied research* (pp. 83–94). Washington, DC: American Psychological Association.

Markovitzky, G., & Mosek, A. (2005). The role of symbolic resources in coping with immigration. *Journal of Ethnic & Cultural Diversity in Social Work, 14*(1), 145–58.

Matsumoto, D. (2006). Culture and nonverbal behavior. In V. Manusov & M. L. Patterson (Eds.), *The SAGE handbook of nonverbal communication* (pp. 219–35). Thousand Oaks, CA: SAGE.

Merz, E., Özeke-Kocabas, E., Oort, F. J., & Schuengel, C. (2009). Intergenerational family solidarity: Value differences between immigrant groups and generations. *Journal of Family Psychology, 23*(3), 291–300.

Morrison, M., & James, S. (2009). Portuguese immigrant families: The impact of acculturation. *Family Process, 48*(1), 151–66.

Naidoo, J. C., & Davis, J. C. (1988). Canadian South Asian women in transition: A dualistic view of life. *Journal of Comparative Family Studies, 19*(20), 311–27.

Nato, F. (2010). Re-acculturation attitudes among adolescents from return Portuguese immigrant families. *International Journal of Intercultural Relations, 34*, 221–32.

Ngo, B. (2006). Learning from the margins: The education of Southeast and South Asian Americans in context. *Race, Ethnicity, and Education, 9*(1), 51–65.

Ontario Human Rights Commission. (2013). *Policy on removing the "Canadian experience" barrier.* Retrieved from http://www.ohrc.on.ca/sites/default/files/policy%20on%20removing%20the%20Canadian%20experience%20barrier_accessible.pdf

Onwumechili, C., Nwosu, P. O., Jackson, R. L., II., & James-Hughes, J. (2003). In the deep valley of mountains to climb: Exploring identity and multiple reacculturation. *International Journal of Intercultural Relations, 27*(1), 41–62.

Ortega, F., & Peri, G. (2013). The effect of income and immigration policies on international migration. *Migration Studies, 1*(1), 47–74.

Portes, A., & Rivas, A. (2011). The adaptation of migrant children. *Future of Children, 21*(1), 219–46.

Portes, A., & Rumbout, R. G. (1996). *Immigrant America: A portrait* (2nd ed.). Berkeley, CA: University of California Press.

Poulsen, S., Karuppaswamy, N., & Natrajan, R. (2005). Immigration as a dynamic experience: Personal narratives and clinical implications for family therapists. *Contemporary Family Therapy, 27*(3), 403–14.

Ragg, D. M. (2011). *Developing practice competencies: A foundation for generalist practice.* Toronto, ON: John Wiley & Sons.

Redfield, R., Linton, R., & Herskovits, M. J. (1936). Memorandum for the study of acculturation. *American Anthropologist, 38*(1), 149–52.

Riddell-Dixon, E. (2008). Assessing the impact of recent immigration trends in Canadian foreign policy. In D. Carment & D. Bercuso (Eds.), *The world in Canada: Diaspora, demography, and domestic politics* (pp. 31–49). Montreal and Kingston: McGill-Queen's University Press.

Rivera-Sinclair, E. A. (1997). Acculturation/biculturalism and its relationship to adjustment in Cuban-Americans. *International Journal of Intercultural Relations, 21*(3), 379–91.

Roesch, S. C., Weiner, B., & Vaughn, A. A. (2002). Cognitive approaches to stress and coping. *Current Opinion in Psychiatry, 15*(6), 627–32.

Ryff, C. & Singer, B. (2002). From social structure to biology. In C. R. Snyder & S. J. Lopez (Eds.), *Handbook of positive psychology* (p. 541–55). New York, NY: Oxford University Press.

Safdar, S., Dupuis, D. R., Lewis, R. J., El-Geledi, S., & Bourhis, R. Y. (2008). Social axioms and acculturation orientations of English Canadians toward British and Arab Muslim immigrants. *International Journal of Intercultural Relations, 32*(5), 415–26.

Sam, D. L., & Berry, J. W. (2010). Acculturation: When individuals and groups of different cultural backgrounds meet. *Perspectives on Psychological Science, 5*(4), 472–81.

Santisteban, D. A., & Mitrani, V. B. (2003). The influence of acculturation processes on the family. In K. M. Chum, P. B. Organista, & P. Marin (Eds.), *Acculturation: Advances in theory, measurement and applied research* (pp. 121–36). Washington, DC: American Psychological Association.

Sapru, S. (2006). Parenting and adolescent identity: A study of Indian families in New Delhi and Geneva. *Journal of Adolescent Research, 21*(5), 484–513.

Schwartz, S. J., Unger, J. B., Zamboanga, B. L., & Szapocznik, J. (2010). Rethinking the concept of acculturation: Implications for theory and research. *American Psychologist, 65*(4), 237–51.

Shimoni, R., Este, D., & Clark, D. E. (2003). Paternal engagement in immigrant and refugee families. *Journal of Comparative Family Studies, 34*(4), 555–68.

Silveira, E., & Allebeck, P. (2001). Migration, ageing and mental health: An ethnographic study on perceptions of life satisfaction, anxiety and depression in older Somali men in East London. *International Journal of Social Welfare, 10*(4), 309–20.

Social Science Research Council (SSRC) Summer Seminar on Acculturation. (1954). Acculturation: An exploratory formulation. *American Anthropologist, 56*, 973–1002.

Stewart, M., Anderson, J., Beiser, M., Mwakarimba, E., Neufeld, A., Simich, L., & Spitzer, D. (2008). Multicultural meanings of social support among immigrants and refugees. *International Migration, 46*(3), 123–59.

Stewart, P. E. (2004). Afrocentric approaches to working with African American families. *Families in Society, 85*(2), 221–8.

Strange, C., & Loo, T. (1997). *Making good: Law and moral regulation in Canada, 1867–1939.* Toronto, ON: University of Toronto Press.

Strug, D. L., Mason, S. E., & Auerbach, C. (2009). How older Hispanic immigrants in New York City cope with current traumatic stressors: Practice implications. *Journal of Gerontological Social Work, 52*(5), 503–16.

Suinn, R. M. (2010). Reviewing acculturation and Asian Americans. *Asian American Journal of Psychology, 1*(1), 5–17.

Szapocznik, J., Scopetta, M., & King, O. (1978). Theory and practice in matching treatment to the special characteristics and problems of Cuban immigrants. *Journal of Community Psychology, 6*(2), 112–22.

Tajfel, H. (1981). *Human groups and social categories: Studies in social psychology.* New York, NY: Cambridge University Press.

Trytten, D. A., Lowe, A. W., & Walden, S. E. (2012). "Asians are good at math. What an awful stereotype": The model minority stereotype's impact on Asian American engineering students. *Journal of Engineering Education, 101*(3), 439–68.

Tsai-Chae, A., & Nagata, D. K. (2008). Asian values and perceptions of intergenerational family conflict among Asian American students. *Cultural Diversity and Ethnic Minority Psychology, 14*(3), 205–14.

Uskul, A., & Greenglass, E. (2005). Psychological wellbeing in a Turkish-Canadian sample. *Anxiety, Stress & Coping, 18*(3), 269–78.

Valtonen, K. (2008). *Social work and migration: Immigrant and refugee settlement and integration.* Surrey, UK: Ashgate Publishing.

Van Kooten, T. C. (1959). *Living in a new country: A study on the integration of immigrants into the life of their new country.* Hamilton, ON: Guardian Publishing.

Walker, B. (2008). *The history of immigration and racism in Canada: Essential readings.* Toronto, ON: Canadian Scholars' Press.

Wallace, W. S. (1930). *A history of the Canadian people.* Toronto, ON: Copp Clark Company.

Ward, C., Bochner, S., & Furnham, A. (2001). *The psychology of culture shock* (2nd ed.). New York, NY: Routledge.

Warr, S. (2010). Counselling refugee young people: An exploration of therapeutic approaches. *Pastoral Care in Education, 28*(4), 269–82.

Woodsworth, J. S. (1909). *Strangers within our gates.* Toronto, ON: University of Toronto Press.

Zea, M. C., Reisen, C. A., Beil, C., & Caplan, R. D. (1997). Predicting intention to remain in college among ethnic minority and nonminority students. *Journal of Social Psychology, 137*(2), 149–60.

10 Narratives as Tools in Intercultural Intervention with Immigrant and Refugee Populations

By Catherine Montgomery

Chapter Objectives

This chapter will help you develop an understanding of:

- The evolution of intervention models for working with immigrant and refugee populations
- The use of narrative techniques for understanding migration trajectories and integration processes
- The use of narrative techniques for encouraging practitioner reflexivity

Introduction

Forces of globalization, increasingly accessible means of transportation, and new technologies of communication have contributed to the growing mobility of world populations. The International Organization for Migration estimated that international migrants worldwide numbered approximately 214 million persons in 2010 (IOM, 2010). Migration patterns have also changed dramatically over the past century. Migration is often thought of as a relatively permanent or long-term life transition. Traditionally, it has been thought of as a linear process in which people leave one country to establish themselves in another and, in this process, go through various stages of adaptation by modifying past values and practices to fit new life situations. However, migration today is rarely linear. People may transit through several countries over a lifetime. They are often connected through transnational networks and maintain regular contact with families and friends through information technologies such as the Internet, email, or webcam applications. Many of these same people have travelled, studied, or worked in other countries. Other more temporary forms of mobility are also increasingly characteristic of diverse societies. These mobilities may include international students, temporary foreign workers, precarious status migrants, internationally mobile career professionals, diplomats, and tourists. These new forms of mobility, both long and short term, lead us to question our classic understandings of diversity and the intervention models that we use to work in intercultural contexts.

Often, intervention models have considered immigration to be a sort of radical break in which the migrant's past is completely dissociated from his or her present. Expressions such as "starting over again" imply that migrants start out in a new country without histories and without pasts. Past cultural values were either to be replaced by new ones in the process of adaptation or seized upon as archaic artifacts belonging to primitive traditions. However, the increasing mobility of populations and the interconnectedness enabled by new technologies of information makes it possible for migrants to think of their lives in ways that are not reliant on fixed cultural models from either the country of origin or the host country. Instead, their experiences and sense of belonging draw from a variety of sources and references. (For a continued conversation on immigration, multiculturalism, and intersection of identities in Canada, see Chapter 1 by Alean Al-Krenawi, John R. Graham, and Nazim Habibov.)

This chapter proposes considering the intervention relationship as a space where stories—those of migrant populations and of the practitioners who work with them—are exchanged, negotiated, understood, and sometimes misunderstood. More specifically, we will look at the way in which narratives and narrative approaches can become tools for social intervention with immigrant and refugee populations. To set the stage for the discussion of these approaches, the chapter will begin with a brief look at early intercultural intervention models and some of the presuppositions that they make with respect to working with migrant populations. We will then look at more recent work on intercultural intervention and, more specifically, the role of narrative approaches in intercultural intervention for working with migrants in the community and as tools for encouraging reflexivity for social practitioners.

Early Intervention Models and the Trappings of Culturalism

Early conceptions of intercultural intervention emerged mostly in practical field applications rather than as academic models taught in university or college settings (Cohen-Émerique, 2011). Practical field applications were originally associated with international peace initiatives meant to reconstruct a new world order in the wake of World War II. Central to these interventions was the idea of dialogue between nations and peoples for the preservation of international peace (Tournès, 2002; UNESCO 1980). During this period, international development programs were largely based on an understanding of developing countries as socio-geographical areas defined as culturally homogeneous groupings of countries and peoples. This homogeneous "**Other**" was conceived in very broad and standardizing terms that left little place for understanding the complexity of local social realities or the way in which personal and professional identities of development workers and their organizations influence the process of intervention. (For further discussion of multicultural intervention in social work, see Chapter 4 by Marie Lacroix.)

Another example of early practical applications of intercultural intervention can be found in the work of Edward T. Hall (1990, 1989; Leeds-Hurwitch, 1990, 2013). An anthropologist, Hall worked for the American Foreign Service in the 1950s, developing training programs for Foreign Service Officers who were to be posted overseas. As Hall suggests, the officers were not interested in complicated theoretical models about culture or intervention. Instead, they wanted clear-cut recipes that would tell them how to work with people in different countries in which the American Foreign Service was involved. In Hall's later work, he would develop cultural guides for business people working overseas (Hall & Reed-Hall, 1990). However, like the development work mentioned above, these guides were based on generalized conceptions of culture, proposing stereotypical portraits of peoples and countries in rather static and essentialist terms.

Models based on generalized conceptions of culture also dominated social intervention practices throughout the 1980s and are still present, though contested, in many intervention contexts today. From a culturalist perspective, social intervention practice with immigrants was structured around the idea that immigrant groups have cultural values and traits that are easily identifiable and considered to be distinct from one community to another (Cohen-Émerique, 2011; Legault & Rachédi, 2008; Cognet & Montgomery, 2007). Training programs were set up to encourage social practitioners to learn about the cultural specificity of identified groups, leading to an understanding that intervention practices should be organized around objectified categorizations. Cohen-Émerique (2011), reflecting on her own experiences as an intercultural trainer in the 1990s, recalls the way in which practitioners tended to group migrants into generalized ethnic categories with little regard to individual life experiences or trajectories, as if their entire identity could be reduced to ethnic markers.

Since the 1990s, culturalist models have been increasingly called into question. This is mostly due to the static way in which culture was defined, as a sort of objective set of categorizations that tended to ignore variations within groups, patterns of interaction, minority–majority relations, and subjective ways in which individuals and groups identify themselves (Cuche, 2010). These critiques also serve as a reminder that there are no clear-cut recipes in social intervention practice with immigrant communities, or any other population for that matter. Overall, the idea was not so much to dispense with the notion of culture altogether, but rather to work toward a more dynamic and complex understanding of the intervention relationship as being the product of multiple determinants.

More recent work in the field of intercultural intervention places greater emphasis on the dynamic nature of **identity** construction in which identity markers, cultural beliefs, and values are conceived of as being products of social processes that evolve across time and according to different contexts (Maalouf, 2001; Cuche, 2010). (For further discussion on positionality, intersectionality, and identity construction, see Chapter 6 by Miu Chung Yan.) Consequently, the defining characteristics of any given individual or community are not considered to be fixed, but rather malleable over time and according to interaction contexts. For social intervention practice, this means understanding individuals and groups not only in terms of a strictly ethnic or cultural identity, but also in terms of their **social location** within other forms of social relations, according to socio-economic status, age, sex, professional or educational background, and so on. From this point of view, a person's cultural baggage, the mainstay of culturalist intervention models in the 1980s, becomes just one contributing factor among others in understanding the intervention relationship. Intervention should instead reflect an all-embracing, multidimensional understanding of the social situations experienced by immigrants and refugees throughout their integration process, taking into account the complexity of their life experiences.

This work also draws attention to the relational dimension of all types of intervention practice, emphasizing the reciprocal nature of the relationship between practitioner and client. Reciprocity is based on trust and respect, both essential dimensions of any form of professional relationship. Independent of individual world visions or cultural, linguistic, or other differences, trust is achieved through countless little gestures, empathy, and a healthy curiosity with respect to life experiences. The acknowledgement of the interactional dimension of intercultural intervention places emphasis not only on the Other (the client, the immigrant), but also on the practitioner. It is in the interaction between the two actors that the term **"intercultural"** takes on its full meaning. Both actors bring to the intervention relationship their respective life histories, including cultural and social markers such as age, gender, generation, migration, professional and social status. All of these forms of belongingness become the backdrop for intervention in intercultural contexts, which makes it necessary to assess the positioning of all actors in the intervention setting rather than only that of the migrant. In earlier culturalist models, the practitioner was conceived of as a relatively neutral actor. It was their job to find out about the culture of the Other, but their own positioning was left relatively unquestioned. Social practitioners need to be aware of the way in which their personal, social, and professional histories play into the intervention relationship, thus ensuring that their own group memberships do not interfere in the intervention process (Legault & Rachédi, 2008).

Figure 10.1, based on the work of Cohen-Émerique (2011), illustrates the interplay of practitioner and client frames of reference. While the column to the left identifies different elements of the practitioner's frame of reference, the column on the right identifies similar elements from the perspective of the client. These frames of reference become "filters" for understanding the intervention problem and potential avenues for acting on it and colour the way in which each of the actors perceives the situation. Cohen-Émerique identifies three interrelated steps that can help practitioners and clients come to a mutual understanding during the course of an intercultural intervention.

In the first stage, "decentering," social practitioners are invited to reflect on the way in which their own filters may influence their understanding of the intervention relationship, revealing potential stereotypes, conflicts of values, or ethnocentrism. In the second stage, "exploration of the client's frame of reference," the practitioner is invited to ask questions that elicit the client's filters and his or her comprehension of the

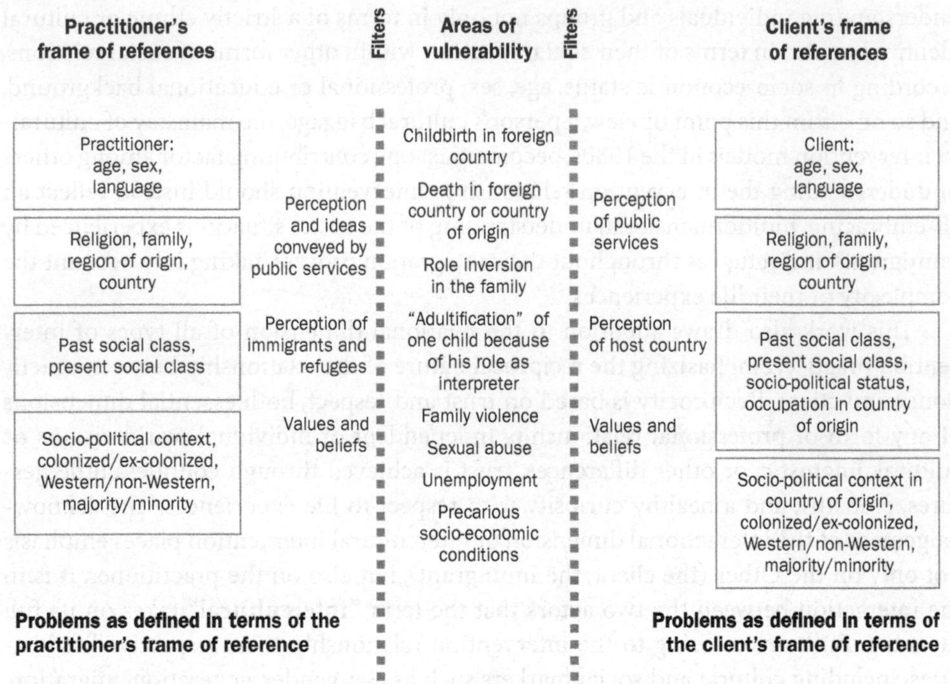

Figure 10.1 Practitioner and Client Frames of Reference

Source: Adapted from Roy, G. (2000). Le protocole de discussion de cas, et "Les modèles de pratique." In G. Legault (Ed.), *L'intervention interculturelle* (pp. 131–58). Montreal: Gaëtan Morin Éditeur. Based on the work of Morris, 1991 and Cohen-Emerique, 1984.

intervention problem. In the final stage, "negotiation and mediation," the practitioner and the client negotiate a common ground between their respective filters and frames of reference, thus enabling them to arrive at a mutual understanding of the intervention problem or issue.

In Figure 10.1, interaction between social practitioners and clients necessarily draws on the capacity of both actors to express in words their personal histories, perceptions of belongingness and difference, and their comprehension of the intervention problem. This capacity of expression is all about using personal subjectivity to reduce communication barriers in the intervention relationship.

Introducing Subjectivity in Social Intervention

Introducing subjectivity in intercultural practice is not without challenges. One of these challenges is embedded in the increasing institutionalization of social intervention practices. Growing caseloads and bureaucracies, pressure toward shorter intervention times, and the move toward standardized practices, procedures, and policies are changes that have radically affected all forms of social intervention. As Roscoe (2009) has noted, there is increasing pressure for intervention approaches to be functional and time efficient to the detriment of more creative approaches in which the care relationship is adapted to the specificities of client profiles, needs, and life histories. With this process of rationalization comes an obsession for producing best practices and statistics as hard facts that structure the intervention relationship by categorizing people and groups into tidy, neat, and homogeneous packages. Indeed, it would be practical to eliminate difference in social intervention practice, but the fact is that difference exists. Sometimes cases that stand apart—the exceptions to the rule—are viewed with suspicion or even frustration because they are perceived as being resource-heavy and a waste of precious intervention time. The fact of the matter is that immigrant and refugee populations rarely fit into predetermined boxes and checklists. They may share many things in common with other clienteles, but they are also characterized by the specificity of their migration statuses and personal life histories.

Client diversity is by no means unique to work with immigrant populations. People are not machines. The acknowledgement of difference calls for the need to be particularly attentive to personal stories and the way in which they are intertwined with societal, family, and community stories. This attention to detail calls for a greater emphasis on the role of subjectivity in the intervention relationship. Subjectivity defies so-called objective facts and standardized classifications by placing emphasis on the way in which people give meaning to their experiences, the situations they face, and the potential solutions to their problems. Over the past two decades, there has been a renewed interest in personal stories and subjectivity, which some have referred to as the "narrative turn" in the social sciences (Czarniawska, 2004). To paraphrase Thurlow (2004), narrative approaches open themselves to the chaos, joys, and discomforts of everyday life, however unruly that might be. Thurlow encourages us to reject what he calls the "positivist impulse" in the social sciences and to accept the anecdotal as a kind of understanding that places particular emphasis on the specificity of lived experience, rather than fearing subjectivity because it may bring us to think and act outside of the box.

In **social intervention** more specifically, narrative approaches are a logical choice for many reasons. As Graitson & Neuforge (2008) have noted, subjectivity and individual stories are the "stuff" of which social intervention is made. This is not to exclude structural conditions and inequalities—poverty, social exclusion, discrimination, migration status—which impact on individual life stories, but rather to suggest that social intervention acts on the intersection between the structural and the individual through personal constructions of meaning and understanding. From this perspective, social intervention is all about turning words and stories into action. Narrative approaches invite individuals to construct meaning around their experiences while encouraging a broader reflection on the conditions for making change, whether on an individual, family, or collective basis. They provide tools for enabling people to think back on specific events relating to migration or social integration, while rearranging the diverse elements of their stories to re-create new meanings and interpretations. It is precisely this subjective dimension that makes narratives an interesting tool for social intervention, since they enable the narrator to revisit the past all while giving them the possibility to reinterpret key elements of their life story linked to the intervention issue. Breckner (2002) proposes that the lives of individuals who have migrated are best understood when explored within a biographical context. By understanding the meaning that is ascribed to the migration experience, it is possible to develop more effective interventions.

Narratives in Intervention with Immigrant and Refugee Populations

Migrant narratives can tell the story of specific immigration trajectories, integration in transnational and local networks, capacity or incapacity to mobilize resources in times of crises and, even more importantly, the ability to understand and give meaning to their stories. Chamberlayne (2002) suggests that narrative approaches can contribute to intervention with migrant populations in several ways, such as

- opening up a space for talking about their migration stories,
- helping individuals identify personal, family, and community strengths,
- acknowledging the shared nature of their situation with other immigrants and refugees, and
- identifying role models and meaningful relationships.

Placing emphasis on biographical strengths, rather than deceptions and disillusions, can help recent immigrants see themselves as resilient actors who have played an active role in the *mise en scène* of their life trajectories. In this sense narratives may enable individuals to renegotiate their relationship to the past by revisiting their stories in a nonstigmatizing way, identifying strengths and coping mechanisms used in the past that could be appropriate for their current situations, and giving them the possibility to express concerns and doubts, thoughts, and questions.

Understanding Migration Trajectories

As a basic tool in the social intervention toolbox, narrative techniques can be used simply for eliciting information about migration histories in general. Migration stories reveal personal projects and aspirations and, in this sense, are unique to each individual. At the same time, however, these stories also reveal logics that extend beyond the individual. Not only are they embedded in family and community dynamics, but they are also rooted in the specific social and political contexts of the home country at any given point in time. The interconnectedness of these different dynamics can be useful to the practitioner for establishing a global understanding of the intervention issue or problem. Generally speaking, intervention practices in intercultural settings tend to focus on immediate needs and requests, such as basic necessities (food security, housing, or employment), accompaniment for administrative reasons (papers relating to immigration, medical exams, or school admission), or specific psychosocial needs (parent–child relationships, family crises, migration, or other losses). Response to these needs is often disconnected from the overall life history of the individual, which could lead to a fragmented understanding of intervention issues and problems. This fragmentation of social practice is by no means limited to intervention in intercultural settings. As mentioned earlier, it is symptomatic of the bureaucratization of social services more generally. What is specific to intercultural intervention, however, is the migration story itself:

- The premigratory period and context of departure
- The impact of immigration status on living conditions in the postmigratory phase
- The capacity to mobilize support networks, whether transnational or local
- The disillusions and deceptions surrounding migration

Introduced early in the intervention setting, narrative approaches can be helpful in developing mini-stories around these themes as a means of contextualizing other intervention issues (Roy & Montgomery, 2003; Montgomery, Xenocostas, Le Gall, Hamez-Spy, Vatz Laaroussi, & Rachédi, 2009; Montgomery & Lamothe-Lachaîne, 2012). While not exhaustive, Table 10.1 provides themes that could be used for the elaboration of such mini-stories. One or several themes may be developed, ranging in length from a few minutes per theme to more elaborate stories, depending on the objectives and constraints of the intervention setting (time, objectives, mandate of organization, etc.). The mini-stories may be shared orally or put into written form.

Themes such as the ones outlined in Table 10.1 can be useful to the practitioner for identifying elements of individual stories that may contribute to a more global understanding of a client's migration story. Not only can this understanding be useful for contextualizing intervention issues, but also for establishing a solid relationship of confidence between practitioner and client.

Narrative Approaches for Negotiating Continuity between the Past and the Present

Migration creates what Breckner (2002) has referred to as "biographical discontinuities." Like other major life transitions, migration is often accompanied by uncertainty and a sense of disconnectedness. In academic literature, uncertainty is often described in terms of loss and mourning of the past which, particularly in the initial stages following migration, may seem to be incompatible with new life experiences, as if the past had to be put aside to pursue life in another country (Diminescu, 2006; Montgomery, Xenocostas, Racine, Alexandre, & Hamisultane, 2012). From an intervention perspective, it is worthwhile to shift the focus from discontinuity to elements of continuity that

TABLE 10.1 Elaborating Mini-Stories about the Migration Process

Migration Period	Potential Themes for Elaborating Stories
Premigration context	Tell me a little bit about your country and your life there. • Socio-political and family contexts in country of origin • Work, studies, leisure activities What caused you to leave your country? • Motivations or context leading to the migration project • Perceptions, dreams, and aspirations about the migration project (prior to immigrating) • Constraints and facilitators in relation to the migration project (family, peers, country, or personal situation) Have you lived/travelled to other countries before? Could you tell me about these experiences? Do you have friends/family in other countries with whom you correspond regularly? When did you immigrate to Canada? What was your initial immigration status? Did you know anything about Canada before coming here? What did you imagine it would be like?
Period of arrival following migration	What was your first impression upon arriving in Canada? Has your impression changed since your arrival? Did you know friends or family members already living in Canada? Tell me a little bit about your first weeks in Canada—difficulties faced and overcome?
Social networks (friends, family, neighbours, work colleagues)	Tell me a little bit about the people you feel closest to, those who give you advice and support when needed. These people may live in Canada or elsewhere. In the latter case, you may maintain contact with them through transnational networks of communication, such as the telephone, Internet, email, webcam, or regular visits between countries. Who are these people? Are they family members, friends from your country of origin, people who you've met here (friends, colleagues, employers, acquaintances, association volunteers, professionals)? What types of activities do you do together, what types of help do you get from them? Additional questions may be asked to help the person think of concrete situations of support. For instance, you can ask questions about help received during events such as • the birth of a child; • illness or death in the family; • the initial period of establishment in Canada; • employment, school, or professional training; or • health.

Source: Adapted from Montgomery, C. & Lamothe-Lachaîne, A. (2012).

link the premigratory and postmigratory experiences. Continuity enables individuals to conceive of their trajectories not only in terms of what has been left behind, but also on the movement toward new life situations that build on past experiences. From this point of view, migration can be considered an important turning point rather than a radical break or rupture.

Narrative approaches can be used as tools to encourage migrants to look back on their stories and put into words not only losses but also strengths and strategies that have been mobilized at different moments in their lives and that can contribute to a more nuanced understanding of the migratory experience. This understanding allows us to break away from pathologizing or paternalizing discourses in which migrants are thought of as passive victims of a world gone wrong. Instead, emphasis is placed on **agency** and the capacity of actors to observe, understand, and capitalize on their situations by acting on them. As Chamberlayne (2002) has suggested, narratives are useful in linking disparate elements of the life trajectory into a coherent story in which uncertainties are negotiated:

> A particular feature of biographical interpretation lies in identifying shifts in self-understanding over time, and going beyond the self-perception of the narrator. In many instances, we felt that our method of interviewing was helping our interview subjects to organise their thoughts, giving them the space to think emotionally. For those whose lives were manifestly stuck, the interview might nudge them towards seeking out further opportunities for such emotional work, as in counselling or various forms of therapy. (p. 276)

Two research action projects undertaken in Montreal can serve as an illustration of the use of narrative approaches for working on the movement from discontinuity to continuity in migration histories. Known as the "Family Novel" projects,[1] the studies explored the ways in which family stories, anecdotes, and memories could be used to identify family strengths and coping mechanisms that could help them adapt to their life experiences in a new country. The idea of the "novel" was used as a metaphor to invite families to revisit their stories, put them into words and, through this process, give new meaning to them (Montgomery et al., 2009, 2012).[2] During the course of the projects, the participating families met with the team members over two or three sessions to elaborate narratives around their family and migration histories. These sessions were tape recorded and, in addition to oral testimony, used other media, such as genograms, photos, drawings, poetry, and significant family objects, to complete the stories. The idea of the "novel" also took on a more concrete meaning in these projects. The oral testimonies and other support materials were combined as a published "novel" and given to the participating families at the end of the narrative process as a token of their participation and a concrete trace of their histories. Table 10.2 contains a brief description of the types of activities proposed in these projects, but the families were free to

TABLE 10.2 Summarized Version of Themes Addressed in the Family Novel Project

- Activity 1. Drawing the family's past: You may draw a picture or use words to describe your family's past.
- Activity 2. Describing memorable events, anecdotes, and important family figures: You may choose to describe particular events, memories, or anecdotes relating to your family's past.
- Activity 3. Creating a genogram: You may create what we call a "genogram." A genogram is a chart or diagram that represents your family's history. Today we will draw the genograms on paper, but they will later be printed in your family novel.
- Activity 4. What's in a name? We all have names: first names, last names, name diminutives (nicknames), and other surnames that have been attributed over time. In this activity we would like to look at the meanings of these names.
- Activity 5. Family events, values and traditions: In this activity we will look at important family events and how significant values and traditions are passed on between generations.
- Activity 6. Changing countries: Immigration is an important event in a family's history, both for parents and children. Although it is a period of adjustment, it is also a period of new beginnings. This activity tells the story of your migration.
- Activity 7. Dreams and projects for the future: This activity looks at the future. Obviously it is impossible to know what the future holds for any of us. What we are interested in here are your "dreams" for the future, your aspirations, and your projects.
- Activity 8. Going to school (for youth): This activity is specifically designed for youth and looks at perceptions of schooling and differences between educational values in the country of origin and in Quebec.
- Activity 9. Personalized theme or topic (choice of participant): Perhaps you would like to include another theme or topic in your family novel that is important to your family but hasn't been covered in the topics proposed in the guide. Please feel free to add any other theme of your choice and we will include it in your novel.
- In addition to activities, you are invited to add other supports to your family novel, such as photos, drawings, texts, and so on. Materials will be scanned and all originals will be returned to their owners in a short time frame.

Source: Adapted from Montgomery, C. & Lamothe-Lachaîne, A. (2012).

choose the themes they wanted to work on or to add other themes that they considered to be particularly relevant to their stories.

Case Example 10.1 is a summarized narrative provided during the Family Novel projects. Narratives such as these can also be used as illustrations for exploring elements of continuity that characterize the migration process. Questions such as the following could be used to orient discussions around the narratives:

- What are the principal elements of the migration story?
- What types of intervention issues can be identified in the narrative?
- What types of resources were used by the narrator in the immediate period following arrival in Canada?
- What types of strengths and coping mechanisms are revealed in the narrative?

Case Example 10.1 Anissa's Story

Anissa was born and raised in Morocco, where she worked for over 10 years as an electrical technician in a small industrial town. Married, she submitted her immigration application while she was pregnant with her first child. Several friends and acquaintances of the couple had already immigrated to Canada and encouraged them to do the same, especially given Anissa's training and work experience, which they suggested would facilitate the procedure. Friends also recommended that they hire a lawyer who would help them with the application. That was the first mistake. In retrospect, they realized that he had charged an exorbitant price and taken advantage of them. He also made a critical mistake that would cost them dearly. The lawyer advised the couple that Anissa should make an application alone, claiming only the recently born first child as a dependent and leaving her husband's name off the application. He argued that her qualifications were stronger than those of her husband and that their chances of acceptance might be weakened if his name was included on the form. The lawyer told them that the husband's name could be added at a later time, once the initial selection interview was over. He advised her to sign a declaration stating that she was currently separated from her husband. That was the second mistake.

While the immigration procedure was underway, the couple had a second child. The selection interview went well and her application was accepted, but the couple then learned that the husband's name could not be added on the now-approved immigration application. She would have to make a separate application to sponsor her husband when she arrived in Canada. One of the conditions of sponsorship was that she could not accept welfare. She would have to have paid employment in Canada, all the while living as a single parent with two young children. After much discussion, the couple decided to go ahead with the immigration procedure anyway, so Anissa left with the two children with plans to have her husband follow later once the sponsorship papers were in order.

With two children under the age of four, Anissa set off for Canada where, upon her arrival, she had hoped to be greeted by a friend living here. The friend, however, had troubles of her own and only reluctantly gave Anissa and the children a place to sleep for one night. The next day Anissa was obliged to find an apartment and move in, without furniture, blankets, or food. She was alone, anxious, and responsible for two young children. Things were very bad at first, but then, suddenly, they began to take a turn for the better.

A compatriot living in the same building put Anissa in contact with a community organization for newcomers. With two young children and few resources at her disposable, Anissa was considered a priority case for the organization. They first took care of her immediate material needs: food stamps; donations of furniture, clothing, and kitchen utensils; and a debit card for a local grocery store and a local food bank. They

continued

also assigned a legal aid lawyer to plead her case for making a sponsorship application. With the help of the new lawyer, she had to prove that she had been a victim of fraud by the original lawyer in Morocco and that she had never been separated from her husband, despite the declaration that she had signed. The fact of having had a second child during the immigration process was a key component in her defence. The community organization also found a daycare placement for her youngest child and opened the doors for Anissa's first job in a school where she served lunch to children. Both daycare and a job were necessary for Anissa to meet the sponsorship criteria. She soon found additional sources of income: as an assistant in a daycare centre and cleaning houses for middle-class families. During this period she also made contact with public-sector social workers, who helped her find a summer camp for her older child and provided her with additional resources for food and clothing. She had also met other women in similar situations, and they organized a pool for taking their children to and from school and daycare so that each woman would have some mornings and afternoons off.

Throughout this period Anissa had her ups and downs, but she realizes how far she has come in such a short time. As a participant in the Family Novel project, her narrative also constitutes a reflection on personal and family strengths that she was able to mobilize as coping mechanisms in this initial period of settlement. Her narrative places specific emphasis on family and religious values. From her parents she retains the importance of strong family ties, illustrated in her narrative through regular contact with her husband, parents, and siblings through Skype. These contacts constituted an important source of moral support and encouragement throughout this period. Aside from these regular contacts, she also talks about how her parents have been important role models for her. It is from them, she suggests, that she learned the courage to always move forward and never be afraid. She specifically remembers similar situations faced by her parents and their capacity to resolve problems without panicking. Religion and religious values are also an important source of comfort for Anissa. Since her arrival in Montreal, she regularly attends a local mosque. Not only does she find solace in spirituality, but the mosque is also an important social meeting place where she has met other compatriots who have given her a helping hand when needed.

Above all, Anissa realizes that her most important strength lies in herself. As a young woman in Morocco, she was already a fighter. She was athletic as a young girl and always enjoyed pushing the limits and testing fate. As a trained electrical technician, she was also a woman in a male-dominated field. She considers herself to be unconventional and realizes that she is a strong woman who is capable of confronting adversity. Although her initial period of settlement was incredibly trying and she would not want to repeat it, she is proud of what she was able to accomplish. This accomplishment, she realizes, was also made possible by the strong social network that surrounded her in her first year in Canada, a strength she acknowledged by inscribing on the front page of her family novel "A heartfelt thank you to my Québécois friends." As for the future, at the time of our meeting with Anissa her husband had received his visa and was to arrive in Montreal within a short period of time. The children are happy in school and daycare, and Anissa looks forward to passing to a new phase. Throughout, her motto has been to take advantage of what life has to offer.

Source: Family Novel project.

Narratives and the Refugee Determination System: Accompanying Asylum Seekers

Narratives can also serve more specific purposes in the intervention process, such as accompanying asylum seekers in the refugee determination process. Unlike people in the independent and family immigration categories, refugee claimants[3] have to present their stories before an administrative tribunal known as the Immigration and Refugee Board (IRB). The IRB is designed to determine the eligibility of asylum claims in accordance with the provisions of the Geneva Convention on the Status of Refugees.[4] During this process, refugee claimants have to submit what is known as a "Basis of Claim Form," or BOC. In part the BOC is used to collect personal information relating to the claimant, such as identity, nationality, language, and membership in ethnic, racial, religious, or other relevant social groups. The primary purpose of the BOC, however, is to document the reasons for the refugee claim and, more specifically, to provide proof of their fear of persecution if they return to their country of origin, the events leading to flight from their country of origin or other countries of transit, their family history, and the reasons why they cannot seek protection from authorities in their home country. The information contained in the BOC must be defended orally before the IRB.

An important role for social practitioners is to accompany asylum seekers through this process by helping in the preparation of their narrative, their oral defence, and in some cases by accompanying the individual to the hearing setting itself. Léonard, a social practitioner and trained lawyer in Belgium, describes how she uses narrative techniques in her work with young refugees who have been separated from their families (Montgomery, Léonard, & Defert, 2011). Her work consists primarily in preparing the youth for their passage before the tribunal. Through a series of individualized interviews that are approximately one hour in length, she invites them to tell their stories, encouraging them to talk about their family and country history, the reasons and events leading up to their departure, as well as any traumatic experiences they may have faced. Since beginning this type of narrative accompaniment with the youth, Léonard has noticed an increase in the youths' acceptance rates for refugee status, a result that she attributes in part to the one-on-one accompaniment offered to them and, consequently, to the quality and the coherence of their asylum stories. A coherent narrative, though, is only one of the advantages noted by Léonard, who also comments on the important role that the narratives play in developing the self-confidence of the youth and in fostering a healthy intervention relationship based on trust.

The narratives developed specifically for the refugee determination process are nonetheless significantly different from other forms of narratives because of their administrative nature. The BOC has a strictly instrumental purpose—it is the primary tool used to establish a person's right to pursue their life in Canada. Not only must the BOC document elements of the life story in support of the refugee claim, but this story must be coherent, complete, and convincing. It is also a story that is passed through strict scrutiny. Indeed, the treatment reserved for asylum stories in the determination process illustrates the ambiguous positioning of the refugee tribunal, which oscillates between a gatekeeper role based on the control of immigration and a humanitarian role based on compassion and the protection of human rights. Showler's (2006) collection of stories in the *Refugee Sandwich* provides a compelling analysis of the way in which this ambiguity is revealed in the tribunal setting, leading to what he refers to as the "illusion of meaningful communication." This illusion is revealed in his presentation of 13 stories written from the perspectives of various actors in the refugee determination process, such as asylum seekers, lawyers, interpreters, and board members. Although these stories are fictitious accounts, they draw on his personal experience as a past board member of the Immigration and Refugee Board. Showler writes:

> [T]here are invariably moments in every hearing where the profound gap between the realities of the claimant and the Board member suddenly becomes apparent. Illusions of meaningful communication are momentarily shattered. The best of the Board members and lawyers find ways to bridge those gaps. Others, because of indifference or hardened world views, founder in them, usually to the detriment of the claimant. (Showler, 2006, p. xiv)

Others have also commented on the discursive treatment of refugee narratives in the determination process, demonstrating the way in which these stories are scrutinized and tested for lies and contradictions through the use of intimidating questions and interrogation techniques (Barsky, 2001; Rousseau & Foxen, 2006; Montgomery & Pälsson, 2009). In the words of one young refugee, "I used to think these people [immigration officials] enjoy playing God, you know, you can have it, you can't" (Tiffany, in Montgomery, 2002, p. 59). The refugee determination process can be a dehumanizing experience. Through the interrogatory techniques used by the members of the tribunal, the refugee narrative is treated with mistrust. It becomes a contested story.

Other types of narrative approaches can also be used with refugees as a means of countering the more negative effects of the official narrative used for administrative purposes before the tribunal. This was another objective of the first Family Novel project described in the previous section, which was undertaken with recently accepted refugee families. The project was designed to create a space for giving accepted refugees another avenue in which to formulate their stories than that which is imposed on them during the refugee determination process (Montgomery et al., 2009). Twelve families who had already been accepted as refugees participated in the project, which aimed to construct individual and family narratives that were not only focused on the painful memories of flight or reasons for persecution. Instead, by encouraging a greater flexibility with respect to the form and content of their narratives, the project was intended to create a space for reframing their stories around other types of memories, such as positive elements of family stories, significant role models, rites, and traditions.

The brothers in Case Example 10.2 suggested that the Family Novel project had brought them a form of closure and a new sense of legitimacy regarding their stories: "The project brings out segments that would otherwise remain unknown to every member of the family. On the one hand, it gave value to our narrative ... official almost" (Montgomery et al., 2009). This type of counternarrative, focused on positive elements of the migration story, can thus be used as a technique for helping refugee populations negotiate the more negative effects associated with the administrative narrative elaborated for the IRB.

In intercultural intervention, the use of narrative approaches is not limited to migrants and refugees. As discussed earlier, intervention takes place in an interactive space between practitioners and clients. Intervention is thus not only about "them," the Other, "the migrant," but also very much about "us" as social or community practitioners and the way in which personal and professional stories influence the direction and outcome of interventions. The next section looks at narratives from a practitioner perspective.

Case Example 10.2 The Story of Mohammed and Rafic

The story of Mohammed and Rafic, two brothers from the Middle East, provides a good example of how narratives can be used in this respect. In their narrative for the Family Novel project, they describe the way in which their adolescent years were marked by conflicts that marred the political landscape of their country for decades. They experienced bombings, school closings, family separation, and anxiety caused by separation. Like most asylum seekers, the experience of the refugee determination process had been difficult for them. Their refugee determination narratives were centred on painful memories that they would rather have put behind them. Throughout the determination process, the "truthfulness" of their stories was constantly called into question and contested, and they had the distinct impression that the board members did not believe them. They also had the impression that they had "sold their souls" to the system and, in so doing, had been dispossessed of their stories. Their participation in the Family Novel project enabled them to reconstruct their stories around other types of themes, focusing on significant family memories that they told with a sense of pride.

Source: Family Novel project.

Reflexivity in Action: Intercultural Practice and the Social Location of the Practitioner

Over the past two decades, there has been increasing interest in professional practice and the use of narrative approaches for exploring the interaction between personal and professional biographies (Graitson & Neuforge, 2008; Grobman, 2005; Lainé, 2004). While professional neutrality is important in intervention, absolute neutrality is an ideal. Personal histories, beliefs, and values may well influence the way in which practitioners perceive immigrant clients, define intervention issues, or structure intervention strategies. In intercultural practice, social practitioners may be confronted with situations that may be difficult to assess in terms of their own life experiences. The ability to step back from day-to-day practice and reflect critically on questions such as these has been referred to by Schön (1983) as reflexivity in action. This reflexivity enables practitioners to reflect on what has been labelled "implicit" or "practical" knowledge; that is, forms of expertise that emerge from personal and field experience rather than knowledge learned strictly through formal training programs or models (Schön, 1983; Roy, 2001; Racine, 2000, 2007). In the rush of day-to-day routine, there is little time available to reflect on the role played by personal and professional histories in orienting practice. This is where narrative approaches can play a particularly interesting role. Integrated in the professional training of social practitioners, these approaches open up a space for them to become aware of their social location as practitioners and to reflect on the ways in which this positioning may influence their practice with diverse populations (Graitson & Neuforge, 2008; Lainé, 2004; Grobman, 2005).

Unlike the clinical relationship, in which the client is generally thought of as being the subject of the intervention, in training approaches using professional narratives it is the practitioner who becomes the subject (Lainé, 2004). This role reversal invites practitioners to act as the biographers of their own stories. Kanouté, Hohl, Xenocostas, & Duong (2007) use a reflexive approach in training sessions offered to practitioners working with immigrant populations in Montreal. During the two-day training workshops, case studies and interactive exercises are used to encourage practitioners to think about the different dimensions of their own identities that they draw on in their interactions with clients, such as important identity markers, personal cultural and religious values, perceptions of otherness, social class and gender differences, and perceptions regarding services and institutional norms. Overall, the objective of the workshops is to create an awareness of how personal frames of reference, which are often implicit rather than explicit, colour their perceptions of intercultural intervention.

Personal migration stories may also contribute to the ways in which a practitioner perceives intercultural practice. Rachédi (2008), for instance, describes how the migration history of her own family influenced her decision to become a social practitioner and to work with immigrant families. Similarly, Saillant, Châteauneuf, Cognet, & Charland (2009) and Cloutier (2011) examine the intermingling of personal, family, and professional identities in their respective studies of social practitioners working with immigrant and refugee populations in the community sector. Many of the practitioners who participated in these studies had migrated themselves and described how they were drawn to this type of work because they could identify with the immigrant experience and wanted to help others overcome the barriers that they had faced personally. Cloutier (2011) also mentions the desire that these practitioners had to give back to the organizations that had helped them during the migratory process. The studies also draw attention to the fact that some practitioners in intercultural settings may place less emphasis on formal models of intervention and rely more extensively on their personal experience of migration as a guide to helping clients.

The use of narratives as professional training tools may take on a variety of forms, using combined individual and group settings, written or oral forms, and ranging from short sessions of a couple of hours to longer sessions over a period of several weeks or months. They may be used in the university classroom as techniques for training future social practitioners or in intervention settings as a form of continuing education for experienced practitioners. The **identity exam** is a technique that is easily adaptable to different professional settings. The idea of an identity exam is inspired by the work of Amin Maalouf (2001) in his book entitled *In the Name of Identity: Violence and the Need to Belong*:

> I sometimes find myself "examining my identity" as other people examine their conscience. As you may imagine, my object is not to discover within myself some "essential" allegiance in which I may recognize myself. Rather the opposite: I scour my memory to find as many ingredients of my identity as I can. I then assemble and arrange them. I don't deny any of them. (p. 16)

An identity exam could be done in two steps, as represented in Tables 10.3 and 10.4. The first step invites practitioners to explore their personal reflections on the principal elements that they consider to be important to their identity (Table 10.3). This exercise reflects the way in which they see themselves and can be called their "self-identity" (*identité affirmée*) (Cuche, 2010).

Table 10.3 My Identity Exam (Self-Identity)

Length: 10–15 minutes
Material: Index cards (3 × 5). Only one side is used for this exercise.
Participation: This exercise could be done individually or in pairs, with one person acting as "interviewer" and the other as "interviewee."
Themes to be noted on the index card:

- What are the principal elements or values that define my identity?
- How would I define my culture?
- What are the types of situations that confront me most in my values?
- Do I present my identity or culture differently according to circumstances, such as the context of the interaction or the person with whom I am interacting? Provide examples.

At the end of the first exercise, the participants present their cards to the group. The ensuing discussion should address themes relating to differences and similarities in the ways in which the participants present themselves, prioritize certain values over others, and how their perceptions of identity may change according to the interaction context. A second related exercise looks at another dimension of identity, referred to as assigned identity (*identité assignée*); that is, the ways in which others may perceive us (Table 10.4) (Cuche, 2010).

In the group discussion that follows this exercise, participants should assess the differences between self-identity and assigned identity. The objective of the two exercises is to explore how identities are expressed and adapted according to the point of view of the individuals in interaction with each other and according to the setting. They enable participants to reflect on the idea that others may perceive them differently than they perceive themselves, both as individuals and as professionals, and that generalized stereotypes may play an important role in this perception. These exercises enable participants to reflect on their personal frames of reference, but it is also worthwhile to anchor these reflections in the day-to-day experiences that make up intercultural intervention.

Another complementary narrative technique that can be used for this purpose is the "practitioner narrative" (*récit de pratique*). This type of narrative technique is structured around concrete intervention experiences encountered in intercultural settings that have caused practitioners to think about their practice in a different light or inspired them to make changes to the way they interact in intercultural settings (Tilman, 1996; Desgagné, 2005). These experiences may refer to challenging cases or to those considered to be success stories. They may refer to cases in which everything went just right or instead to cases gone awry. In either case, the objective of the narratives is to use a ground-up approach to reflect on ways in which professional expertise is adapted in response to

Table 10.4 My Identity as Seen by Others (Assigned Identity)

Length: 10–15 minutes
Material: Index cards (3 × 5). Use the opposite side of the index card used for the first exercise.
Participation: This exercise could be done individually or in pairs, with one person acting as "interviewer" and the other as "interviewee."
Themes to be noted on the index card:

- To begin, identify a group that is "culturally" distant from your own. This could be a community often encountered in the intervention setting or that is present in your region/city. It could also be defined from an international setting; for instance, "Imagine that you are temporarily living or travelling in X (name a country)."
- How would members of this group identify my culture and my identity?
- What are the principal identity markers that they would put forward if they had to describe me?
- What are the stereotypes or biases that they might have toward me because of (1) my origins or (2) my professional role as a social practitioner?

the specific circumstances and constraints of concrete cases. This knowledge formed in action (Schön, 1983) is the result of a negotiation that takes place between formal models of practice and challenges met in the field.

These types of narratives can be used in any type of intervention setting, but have found specific application in intercultural intervention, particularly in the education and community sectors (Audet, 2011; Cloutier, 2011; Montgomery et al., 2013). Used in group settings, these narratives can be used to identify key issues in intercultural intervention, reflect on perceptions and stereotypes, and explore different strategies for managing challenging situations. Overall, they enable practitioners to distance themselves from the immediacy of daily practice and, through the analysis of specific cases, to better understand the interplay between practitioner positioning and the intervention relationship. Table 10.5 provides some basic guidelines for developing this type of narrative, which could be structured around short oral presentations prepared directly in the classroom (15–20 minutes is allowed for the preparation of the narratives individually or in pairs, followed by group discussion) or longer written narratives (2–4 pages) prepared at home and later used for group discussion in the classroom.

Table 10.5 Practitioner Narratives: Reflecting on Intercultural Situations

The objective of your narrative is to describe an intervention situation that you consider to be particularly significant in terms of the intercultural issues encountered. The intervention situation may refer to a meeting with a client or a project or activity that made you question or adapt the way in which you intervene in intercultural practice. It may be a case that was particularly challenging for you or that you are particularly proud of, or any other type of situation that you consider to have influenced the way in which you work with immigrant and refugee populations. Your narrative can be written as a story that describes the context of the intervention situation, the issues or challenges encountered, the adaptations made along the way, and the result or outcome of the intervention situation. The following questions may help you structure your narrative:

- What is the history or context of the intervention situation that you have selected?
- What specific issues or challenges were encountered in this situation?
- Who were the people involved?
- How did you adapt, modify, or reorient your intervention strategy?
- Describe any professional or personal challenges met in relation to this intervention situation.
- What are the intercultural issues addressed in this story? What strategies or solutions were adopted to address these issues?
- What lessons did you learn from this story that could be useful to other practitioners working in intercultural settings?

Source: Activity adapted from Montgomery, Racine, Xenocostas, Rhéaume, and Labescat, 2013. The production of this guide was made possible through a SSHRC research grant (2010–12) directed by the author, entitled *Pratiques d'intervention novatrice dans les organismes d'aide aux nouveaux immigrants: Expérimentation d'une démarche réflexive de récits de pratique*. The research team was comprised of Montgomery, Racine, Rhéaume, Xenocostas, and Labescat.

Case Example 10.3 is a shortened version of a practitioner narrative that relates an experience encountered during the social work training of an undergraduate student.[5] Discussion around this narrative could touch on a number of themes. What types of assumptions are behind the practitioner's original response to the intervention relationship? What is the intercultural significance of these assumptions? How do they reflect the practitioner's social location and discomfort? How and why are these assumptions modified over time? What lessons can be learned from the narrative?

Narrative approaches such as these enable practitioners to step back from the intensity of everyday practice. By placing emphasis on practitioner intuition and the capacity to transform personal experience into learning experience, these approaches

Case Example 10.3 When Assumptions Influence Action

I had been working with a family whose son had some language development problems. The members of the family are devout Muslims and, in our meetings, I tended to communicate mostly with the father, since he made the initial request for the service, speaks English well, and I felt more comfortable speaking with him rather than with his wife. I was hesitant about speaking with the mother, because I didn't know the proper rules of interaction with Muslim families, particularly concerning relationships between men and women. As a male social practitioner, I wasn't sure if I could shake her hand or know how to include her in the discussions about her child. As a result, I had much more difficulty involving the mother in the intervention plan.

I soon realized that this wasn't the best solution. During the day, she cared for the children and, by excluding her, I didn't have access to her perception of the family situation or her ideas for the intervention plan. After a while I started feeling more comfortable in my response to this family. I also realized that I had to make more of an effort to involve the mother in the discussions. At first she seemed surprised when I asked her to join in conversations with her husband, but she didn't seem to be uncomfortable with the request.

Overall, I think that my lack of knowledge created uncertainty as to how I should interact with the family. I felt uncomfortable, not knowing if my actions were adequate or not. I was afraid of the unknown and afraid to make mistakes. In retrospect, I think that my uncertainty led me to adopt false assumptions about the family. These types of assumptions can create ambiguous situations, such as the one described above, and can even jeopardize the intervention relationship. It wouldn't be realistic to study in detail the characteristics of all cultures. Instead, I think we have to question our assumptions and take the time to verify whether they are right or wrong.

Source: This narrative was collected as part of a research action project undertaken with social work students in Montreal, Quebec. Montgomery, Xenocostas, Racine, Alexandre, & Hamisultane, 2012. This project was made possible through seed funding from the METISS research team (2012).

also enable us to observe the ways in which practice can be adapted to the reality of concrete intervention experiences.

Summary and Conclusion

This chapter has explored the notion of subjectivity in intercultural intervention and, more specifically, the way in which narrative approaches can be used as tools for working with migrants in the community and for developing the professional reflexivity of social practitioners. The first section examined the evolution of intercultural intervention models and their ability to take into account the multidimensionality of the migrant experience. It also called for the necessity of addressing the reciprocal nature of the practitioner–client relationship by taking into account the social location of both client and practitioner when considering intercultural intervention. The second section looked at social intervention as a form of practice that is necessarily based on the way in which clients construct meaning around their experiences. The third section explored the ways in which narrative approaches can be used to better understand the migratory process from the perspective of migrants by drawing attention to the global context of their life stories to identify biographical strengths and resources and to accompany specific populations, such as refugees and refugee claimants. And finally, the last section of the chapter looked at how narratives can be an important tool for exploring the personal and professional frames of reference that practitioners bring into the intervention setting and that may have an influence on the intervention relationship.

In intercultural settings, practitioners are confronted with complex, multidimensional realities. They must negotiate between the ideals of what *should be* and the reality of *what is*, the greatest challenge being their capacity to integrate and make sense of values, norms, and practices, which may be quite different from their own. Preconceived categorizations relating to refugee and immigrant populations are ill-adapted to everyday practice, because they do not allow for the complexity of personal and migration stories. By placing subjectivity—that of practitioners and clients—at the forefront of intercultural intervention, narrative approaches can be particularly useful in working in the margins between preconceived cultural categories and real-life experiences.

Narrative approaches build on the basic function of making sense of the world around us through the telling of stories based on the personal, family, and collective contexts that shape migration and intercultural practice. From the migrant's point of view, narratives can help individuals identify biographical strengths, acknowledge the shared nature of their experiences, and contribute to new models of understanding. From the point of view of practitioners, narratives are particularly useful in developing reflexivity around intercultural practices. This reflexivity contributes to an understanding of the way in which personal and professional filters may influence the intervention relationship, both positively and negatively, while at the same time revealing the mechanisms at work in the adaptation of practice to specific clienteles such as refugees and immigrants. Overall, the basis for action in intercultural intervention is grounded in the acknowledgement of difference and openness toward diverse values. Not only do narrative approaches provide an opportunity for strengthening collaboration in the intervention relationship, but they also participate in reducing communication barriers by providing a means for achieving mutual understanding.

Questions for Review

1. The chapter proposes that intercultural intervention models have changed over time. What types of changes can be observed between the 1980s and the present? How do these changes reflect the way in which migrant populations are viewed by social practitioners?
2. Drawing on the arguments outlined in the chapter, explain why subjectivity can be important to intercultural intervention. What types of institutional constraints are identified that may limit the way in which subjectivity can be introduced in social intervention?
3. Why are narrative approaches particularly well-suited to working in intercultural contexts? How can they contribute to a more global understanding of migration and integration processes?
4. Breckner (2002) suggests that narrative approaches can be useful for understanding "biographical discontinuities" linked to migration. What does she mean by the term "biographical discontinuity"? What role can narrative approaches play with respect to discontinuity in intercultural intervention?
5. What are the specificities of using narrative approaches with refugee populations? How do these narratives differ from the other forms discussed in the chapter?
6. What is meant by the term "reflexivity in action" used by Schön (1983) and referred to in the chapter? In what way can practitioner narratives contribute to this reflexivity?

Suggested Readings and Resources

Chamberlayne, P., Rustin, P., & Wengraf, P. (Eds). (2002). *Biography and social exclusion in Europe: Experiences and life journeys.* Bristol, UK: The Policy Press.

Grobman, L. (Ed.). (2005). *Days in the lives of social workers.* Harrisburg, PA: White Hat Communications.

Maalouf, A. (2001). *In the name of identity: Violence and the need to belong.* New York, NY: Penguin Books.

METISS research group in Montreal, Quebec. See www.equipemetiss.com. METISS is an interdisciplinary research group specializing in questions relating to intercultural intervention in the health and social services. The research group is funded by the Quebec funding agency for research on culture and society (FRQSC: Fonds de recherche Québec—Société et Culture).

Montgomery, C., & Lamothe-Lachaîne, A. (2012). *Histoires de migration et récits biographiques. Guide de pratique pour travailler avec des familles immigrantes.* Montreal: CSSS de la Montagne. Retrieved from http://www.sherpa-recherche.com/wp-content/uploads/2013/10/histoires_de_migration_et_recits_biographiques_en_ligne.pdf

Montgomery, C., Le Gall, J., & Stoetzel, N. (2010). Les familles maghrébines au Québec: mobilisation des liens transnationaux et cycle de vie. *Lien social et politiques, 64*, 79–93.

Montgomery, C., Xenocostas, S., Le Gall, J., Hamez-Spy, M., Vatz Laaroussi, M., & Rachédi, L. (2009). *Intergenerational transmissions in refugee families: The Family Novel project.* Montreal: CSSS de la Montagne. Retrieved from http://www.sherpa-recherche.com/wp-content/uploads/2013/10/Maintaining_continuity.pdf

Nakayama, T., & Halualani, R. (2013). *The handbook of critical intercultural communication.* West Sussex, UK: Wiley-Blackwell.

Roscoe, K. (2009). Critical social work practice, a narrative approach. *International Journal of Narrative Practice, 1*(1), 9–18.

Schön, D. A. (1983). *The reflective practitioner.* New York, NY: Basic Books.

Showler, P. (2006). *Refugee sandwich: Stories of exile and asylum.* Montreal and Kingston: McGill-Queen's University Press.

Thurlow, C. (2004). Relating to our work, accounting for ourselves: The autobiographical imperative in teaching about difference. *Language and Intercultural Communication, 4*(4), 209–28.

Notes

1. The projects were funded by the Social Sciences and Humanities Research Council (SSHRC). The first project, *Transmissions intergénérationnelles. Roman familial et jeunes réfugiés* (Montgomery, 2005–7), was undertaken in collaboration with a community organization offering housing and settlement services to recently arrived refugees. The second project, *Parcours d'insertion et roman familial. Le cas de jeunes familles immigrantes nouvellement arrivées au Québec* (Montgomery, 2007–10) was put into place in 2007 with families from North Africa (Algeria, Tunisia, and Morocco) who had arrived in Quebec as economic immigrants. Both projects were directed by the author and undertaken in collaboration with a multidisciplinary team of researchers, including Spyridoula Xenocostas, Lilyane Rachédi, Jacques Rhéaume, Josiane LeGall, Cécile Rousseau, Michèle Vatz Laaroussi, and Miriam Hamez-Spy. Amel Mahfoudh, Nadia Stoetzel, Sara Sultan, and Maris Feo were the principal research assistants.
2. Drawing on de Gaulejac's work, the "Family Novel approach" is generally undertaken in group settings in the form of interactive seminars (de Gaulejac, 1999; Rhéaume, Chaume, & Poupart, 1996). In our projects, however, we met with each of the families separately for the construction of their narratives. The participants in our projects, particularly the refugee families, were reluctant about telling their stories in a public space and preferred a more private setting.
3. In Canada, a distinction is made between refugee claimants and accepted refugees. A refugee claimant is a person who has made a claim for protection as a refugee, but whose claim has not yet been accepted by the

Canadian government. An accepted refugee is a person whose claim has already been heard and accepted by the administrative tribunal of the Immigration and Refugee Board.

4. According to the Convention relating to the Status of Refugees (1951), also known as the Geneva Convention, a refugee is a person who is "outside of his or her home country and who has a well-founded fear of being persecuted for reasons of race, religion, nationality, membership in a particular social group or political opinion" (UNHCR, 2011).

5. This narrative was collected as part of a research action project undertaken with social work students in Montreal, Quebec. Montgomery, Xenocostas, Racine, Alexandre, & Hamisultane, 2012. This project was made possible through seed funding from the METISS research team (2012).

References

Audet, G. (2011). Composer avec la diversité culturelle en classe de maternelle: Résultats d'une analyse de récits de pratique enseignante. *Revue de l'intégration et des migrations internationales/Journal of International Migration and Integration (RIMI/JIMI), 12*(1), 43–60.

Barsky, R. (2001). *Arguing and justifying: Assessing the convention refugee choice of moment, motive and host country*. Burlington, VA: Ashgate.

Breckner, R. (2002). Migrants: A target-category for social policy? Experiences of first-generation migration. In P. Chamberlayne, M. Rustin, & T. Wengraf (Eds.), *Biography and social exclusion in Europe: Experiences and life journeys* (pp. 213–28). Bristol, UK: The Policy Press.

Chamberlayne, P. (2002). Second-generation transcultural lives. In P. Chamberlayne, M. Rustin, & T. Wengraf (Eds.), *Biography and social exclusion in Europe: Experiences and life journeys* (pp. 229–45). Bristol, UK: The Policy Press.

Cloutier, G. (2011). Savoirs de femmes immigrantes en milieu communautaire: Une contribution à l'intervention. *La valorisation des savoirs de femmes immigrantes en milieu communautaire*. Montreal, QC: Richard Vézina éditeur.

Cognet, M., & Montgomery, C. (2007). *Éthique de l'Altérité. La question de la culture dans le champ de la santé et des services sociaux*. Quebec, QC: Presses de l'Université Laval.

Cohen-Émerique, M. (2011). *Pour une approche interculturelle en travail social: Théories et pratiques*. Rennes, FR: Presses de l'EHESP.

Cuche, D. (2010). *La notion de culture dans les sciences sociales*. Paris, FR: La Découverte.

Czarniawska, B. (2004). *Narratives in social science research*. Thousand Oaks, CA: Sage publications.

De Gaulejac, V. (1999). *L'histoire en héritage. Roman familial et trajectoire sociale*. Paris: Desclée de Brouwer.

Desgagné, S. (2005). *Récits exemplaires de pratique enseignante. Analyse typologique*. Quebec, QC: Presses de l'Université du Québec.

Diminescu, D. (2006). Genèse d'une figure de migrant. *Cosmopolitiques, 70*, 63–72.

Graitson, I., & Neuforge, E. (2008). *L'intervention narrative en travail socia: Essai méthodologique à partir des récits de vie*. Paris, FR: L'Harmattan.

Grobman, L. (Ed.). (2005). *Days in the lives of social workers*. Harrisburg, PA: White Hat Communications.

Hall, E. T. (1989). *Beyond culture*. New York, NY: Anchor Books. (Original work published 1976).

Hall, E. T. (1990). *The silent language*. New York, NY: Anchor Books. (Original work published 1959).

Hall, E. T., & Reed-Hall, M. (1990). *Understanding cultural differences: Germans, French and Americans*. Boston, MA: Intercultural Press.

International Organization for Migration (IOM). (2010). *World migration report 2010: The future of migration*. France: Author.

Kanouté, F., Hohl, J., Xenocostas, S., & Duong, L. (2007). Les mots pour le dire et pour intervenir. In M. Cognet & C. Montgomery (Eds.), *Éthique de l'altérité. La question de la culture dans le champ de la santé et des services sociaux* (pp. 241–60). Quebec, QC: Presses de l'Université Laval.

Lainé, A. (2004). *Faire de sa vie une histoire. Théories et pratiques de l'histoire de vie en formation.* Paris, FR: Desclée de Brouwer.

Leeds-Hurwitz, W. (1990). Notes in the history of intercultural communication: The Foreign Service Institute and the mandate for intercultural training. *Quarterly Journal of Speech, 76,* 262–81.

Leeds-Hurwitz, W. (2013). Writing the intellectual history of intercultural communication. In T. Nakayama & R. Halualani (Eds.), *The handbook of critical intercultural communication* (pp. 21–33). West Sussex, UK: Wiley-Blackwell.

Legault, G., & Rachédi, L. (Eds.). (2008). *L'intervention interculturelle.* Montreal, QC: Gaëtan Morin.

Maalouf, A. (2001). *In the name of identity: Violence and the need to belong.* New York, NY: Penguin Books.

Montgomery, C. (2002). *Seeking asylum: Separated youth in the Quebec context.* Montreal, QC: Publications du CLSC Côte-des-Neiges.

Montgomery, C., & Lamothe-Lachaîne, A. (2012). *Histoires de migration et récits biographiques. Guide de pratique pour travailler avec des familles immigrantes.* Montreal: CSSS de la Montagne. Retrieved from http://www.sherpa-recherche.com/wp-content/uploads/2013/10/histoires_de_migration_et_recits_biographiques_en_ligne.pdf

Montgomery, C., Léonard, S., & Defert, F. (2011). Favoriser la parole par le récit. Expériences d'intervention et de recherche auprès de demandeurs d'asile. *Politiques sociales, 3–4,* 27–40.

Montgomery, C., & Pälsson, P. (2009). Determining refugee status: The case of young refugees separated from their families. *Cahiers METISS, 4*(1).

Montgomery, C., Racine, G., Xenocostas, S., Rhéaume, J., & Labescat, G. (2013). *Récits de pratiques d'intervenants dans des organismes d'aide aux nouveaux immigrants. Guide d'animation.* Retrieved from http://www.sherpa-recherche.com/wp-content/uploads/2013/10/recits_de_pratique.pdf

Montgomery, C., Xenocostas, S., Le Gall, J., Hamez-Spy, M., Vatz Laaroussi, M., & Rachédi, L. (2009). *Intergenerational transmissions in refugee families: The family novel project.* Retrieved from http://www.sherpa-recherche.com/wp-content/uploads/2013/10/Maintaining_continuity.pdf

Montgomery, C., Xenocostas, S., Racine, G., Alexandre, J.-M., & Hamisultane, S. (2012). *Analyse des pratiques en contexte pluriethnique.* Montreal: CSSS de la Montagne.

Racine, G. (2000). *La production de savoirs d'action chez des intervenants sociaux.* Paris, FR: L'Harmattan.

Racine, G. (2007). De la production du silence aux invitations à l'échange de savoirs: Le cas des pratiques en travail social. In H. Dorvil (Ed.), *Problèmes sociaux.* Montreal: Presses de l'Université du Québec.

Rachédi, L. (2008). Des histoires de migration aux assignations identitaires: Éloge de l'imposture pour le travail social. *EMPAN, 3*(71), 85–91.

Rhéaume, J., Chaume, C., & Poupart, D. (1996). Roman familial et trajectoires sociales: le groupe comme outil d'implication et de recherche. *Revue Intervention,* 83–90.

Roscoe, K. (2009). Critical social work practice, a narrative approach. *International Journal of Narrative Practice, 1*(1), 9–18.

Rousseau, C., & Foxen, P. (2006). Le mythe du réfugié menteur: Un mensonge indispensable? *Évolution psychiatrique, 71,* 505–20.

Roy, G. (2001). Le praticien réflexif: un pied dans la marge. *Intervention, 114,* 82–5.

Roy, G., & Montgomery, C. (2003). Practice with immigrants in Quebec. In A. Al-Krenawi & J. Graham (Eds.), *Multicultural social work in Canada* (pp. 122–146). Toronto, ON: Oxford University Press.

Saillant, F., Châteauneuf, D., Cognet, M., & Charland, M. (2009). L'intervention auprès des réfugiés. Accueil, proximité, transformation. In. M. Clément, L. Gélineau, & A.-M. McKay (Eds.), *Proximités. Lien, accompagnement et soin* (pp. 41–64). Quebec, QC: Presses de l'Université du Québec.

Schön, D. A. (1983). *The reflective practitioner.* New York, NY: Basic Books, Inc.

Showler, P. (2006). *Refugee sandwich: Stories of exile and asylum*. Montreal and Kingston: McGill-Queen's University Press.

Thurlow, C. (2004). Relating to our work, accounting for ourselves: The autobiographical imperative in teaching about difference. *Language and Intercultural Communication*, *4*(4), 209–28.

Tilman, F. (1996). Comment parler de sa pratique pour la faire partager? *Courrier du CETHES*, *35*, 18–28. Retrieved from http://www.meta-educ.be/textes/parler-de-sa-pratique.pdf.

Tournès, L. (2002). La diplomatie culturelle de la fondation Ford. Les éditions Intercultural Publications (1952–1959). *Presses de Sciences Po*, *4*(76), 65–77.

UNESCO. (1980). *Introduction aux études interculturelles. Esquisse d'un projet pour élucidation et la promotion de la communication entre les cultures: UNESCO 1976–1980*. Paris, FR: Author.

United Nations High Commissioner for Refugees (UNHCR). (2011). The 1951 Convention relating to the Status of Refugees and its 1967 protocol. Retrieved from http://www.unhcr.org/4ec262df9.html

Spirituality, Religion, and Diversity

By Diana Coholic

11

Chapter Objectives

This chapter will help you develop an understanding of:

- How social work has conceptualized and defined spirituality and religion
- How spiritually sensitive social work practices are defined
- What spiritually sensitive social work practices and methods look like in practice
- Rationales and reasons for incorporating spiritually sensitive methods into social work practices
- Strategies for including spirituality or religion in social work

Introduction

I have been teaching social work theory and practice to fourth-year social work students for over 10 years. In general, when I introduce the topic of spirituality students express a variety of opinions and experiences. Some students have never contemplated that a spiritual dimension could be part of social work practice, so they are initially surprised that the topic is being introduced. Others might have a rich spiritual or religious life themselves but view this as separate from their social work professional self and identity. Some students have had negative experiences with religion and are wary about discussing spirituality and religion, or they have a strong emotional reaction when the topic is raised. Finally, there are students for whom these discussions resonate and are meaningful, and who are searching for places to have these conversations.

Most social workers trained in Canada are skilled at conducting multidimensional assessments and work from a generalist perspective. Krogsrud Miley, O'Melia, and DuBois (2013) describe generalist social work practice as an integrated and multilevel approach that can be applied in work with individuals, families, groups, neighbourhoods, communities, and societies to maximize human system functioning. Generalist practitioners use multilevel assessments and interventions, drawing on multiple theories depending on a client's needs. Along these lines, many of us work from a systemic and holistic perspective that could be described as a bio-psycho-social-spiritual approach (the spiritual dimension is added here to the traditional bio-psycho-social model). At the very least, a holistic approach should include inquiries about a client's spiritual or religious viewpoints and connections (or the lack thereof), particularly during an assessment.

Indeed, the people that we work with often have rich connections with spiritual or religious communities and groups that can offer much support and a sense of belonging, or religious affiliation might be an important part of their familial or cultural background, comprising one of their social locations. In fact, as will be discussed in this chapter, spirituality is often understood as an important aspect of coping and resilience (Farley, 2007). Resilience is a concept that has been studied for over 40 years. Dr Michael Ungar, who is a social worker and co-director of the Resilience Research Centre (RRC; see: http://resilienceresearch.org) explained that while "resilience is often understood as a person's ability to overcome adversity and continue their normal development, a more ecological and culturally sensitive definition emphasizes a system's responsibility to provide relevant and meaningful resources" (RRC, 2014). The RRC defines resilience as follows:

> In the context of exposure to significant adversity, resilience is both the capacity of individuals to navigate their way to the psychological, social, cultural, and physical resources that sustain their well-being, and their capacity individually and collectively to negotiate for these resources to be provided in culturally meaningful ways. (RRC, 2014)

The reality is that no matter what your perspective and experience is regarding spirituality and religion, you will most likely encounter clients, groups, and communities in your social work practice for whom spirituality and religion are important and relevant to understanding and resolving the issues that have brought you together. Some obvious examples of contexts and situations where it would be difficult to avoid thinking about or discussing spirituality include working in a hospice and within the field of palliative care, working with elderly clients who adhere to religious traditions and beliefs, and working with a variety of cultures that are inextricably linked with spiritual or religious beliefs and practices. In my own practice experiences, I have included discussions about spirituality and religion in work with clients who have been sexually abused by religious clergy, with clients who had a profound fear of death but were not dying, and when serious trauma such as childhood abuse or disasters such as fires and accidents had occurred in a person's life. Included in this chapter are two case studies that provide a more in-depth look at how spiritual and religious matters might be relevant in micro-social work, which is the background of my social work experience.

In this chapter, I provide a brief overview of spirituality and religion within social work and briefly describe how social work has conceptualized spirituality and religion as being related but also different. Then I discuss how most social workers understand spiritually sensitive practices and some of the rationales for including spirituality or religion into one's social work practice, noting that it is increasingly difficult, if not impossible, to avoid clients' spiritual/religious beliefs in our work. Specifically, I consider how spirituality can be an aspect of arts-based approaches, social justice activities, and the process of helping clients cope and make meaning of life events. Transpersonal theory, which is grounded in spiritual perspectives and experiences, and mindfulness, which is a holistic practice and philosophy, are also examined.

History of Social Work

While the roots of social work are based in religious organizations and practices, as the profession has developed it has became secularized. (For a review of the influence of spiritual values and religious thought in early social work, as well as the influence of early key thinkers to the profession's development, please see Graham & Shier, 2012, and Graham, Coholic, & Coates, 2006.) As Graham and Shier (2012) explain, the profession sought to rid itself of its religious roots once it became part of an academic setting and claimed to be a professional and scientific discipline. In the foreword to a book titled *Spirited Practices*, Richard Hugman also noted that as modern society became secularized, spirituality was marginalized or denied as a legitimate knowledge. Additionally, he points out that helping professionals are conscious of their power over the people they work with. Thus, spiritual or religious matters were avoided to eschew the threat of imposing our own beliefs and values onto our clients (Hugman, 2007).

Suffice it to say that because of this historical process of professionalization and modernization, as well as other priorities like the development of social work theory, in today's context some people become concerned when religion and spirituality are introduced as topics for consideration within professional discourse. Some practitioners worry that they will be viewed as unprofessional or as proselytizers. Some have had negative experiences with spirituality or religion and thus do not think to include these dimensions of life into social work. Still others are unsure of how to talk with clientele about spirituality and religion, are not familiar with the literature in this area, or they believe that they lack the appropriate training or knowledge to do so. As Baskin (2007) recounts, outside of Indigenous communities discussions about spirituality are often met with "silence and a lowering of the eyes" (p. 191).

Certainly, when I began my doctoral studies in 1998, in which I was exploring spiritually sensitive practice within feminist social work theory and practice (Coholic, 2003), I encountered many social workers who expressed these concerns but who were also very interested in places where they could openly discuss spiritually sensitive social work. For many of them it was already something that was part of their practice, whether or not they shared that with their colleagues (it was often something they kept to themselves).

Many of you probably came to study social work out of a sincere desire to help others, improve society, and change the world, and for some of you these aspirations rested on spiritual or religious values and beliefs. In turn, these values and beliefs may strongly converge with social work values. For example, the idea that showing compassion for other people is relevant and important can be both a social work and spiritual or religious value. Canda and Furman (2010) discuss this idea of compassion in their book and state that social workers are often "called to service"; through this call, which they describe as a "spiritual journey of growth," we are also helped to grow and develop (p. 11).

Perhaps this call to service explains in part the growing interest in considering spirituality within social work. Despite persistent and legitimate concerns and beliefs that spirituality is "fuzzy" and religion is not within our practice domain, there has been a steady increase in the Canadian scholarship in this area over the past 14 years. In 2001 the Canadian Association for Spirituality and Social Work was formed, which is now known as the Canadian Society for Spirituality and Social Work (CSSSW). The people that spearheaded CSSSW have helped to organize annual national and international conferences that have brought together researchers, practitioners, and students interested in spiritually sensitive social work. The international conferences have been planned in co-operation with our American colleagues and their Society for Spirituality and Social Work.

Definitions of Spirituality and Religion

Dr Edward Canda was one of the first Western social workers to take on the task of developing a definition of spirituality for social work. The conceptualization he developed was based on common themes found in five perspectives (Zen Buddhism, Christianity, Existentialism, Judaism, and Shamanism; Canda, 1988). Much of the spirituality and social work scholarship has used Canda's definition as a foundation. It is important to note that much of the social work scholarship focuses on spirituality and delineates a difference between spirituality and religion. Generally speaking, within social work **spirituality** is understood to include "one's search for life purpose and meaning, and connection with self, others, the universe, and a self-defined higher power; either with or without a particular faith orientation" (Groen, Coholic, & Graham, 2012, p. 2). For example, Canda and Furman (2010) define spirituality as "a universal quality of human beings and their cultures related to the quest for meaning, purpose, morality, transcendence, well-being, and profound relationships with ourselves, others, and ultimate reality" (p. 5). Spirituality is necessarily self-defined. This means that for me to understand what spirituality means to you, I need to understand how you make sense of it and experience it in your life.

There is certainly an all-encompassing nature to spirituality that includes a variety of experiences, embraces a diversity of beliefs, and reflects the complexity of spirituality. This is not to say that religion is not complex, but **religion** is generally understood to comprise both individual and collective relationships, belief systems, and practices. While spirituality and religion can be fused for some people, spirituality is typically defined in ways that help us understand individual experiences or cognition. To summarize, as Sheridan (2002) states, "spirituality refers to a search for purpose, meaning and connection between oneself, others, and ultimate reality, experienced within a religious or nonreligious framework, while religion refers to a set of beliefs, practices, and traditions experienced with a specific social institution" (pp. 567–8). Conceptualizing spirituality and religion as being related but different has occurred in part because spirituality is more acceptable for social work practitioners and it is viewed as being more inclusive of diverse belief systems and consistent with professional social work values that honour people's interpretations of their experiences, strengths, and cultures (Groen, Coholic, & Graham, 2012). However, we should keep in mind that for some people, such as members of non-Western cultures, separating spirituality and religion will not make a lot of sense. Similarly, Hodge and McGrew (2005) make the point that one's faith tradition likely affects how one defines spirituality and religion.

In discussions at scholarly conferences, I have heard researchers criticize social work's focus on spirituality as being divorced from religion. Some of these arguments point out that the focus on spirituality is really just humanism and humanist values. Indeed, as Payne (2005) has argued, because social work became secularized, it became associated with humanism instead of religion. It is true that social work values align nicely with the secular philosophy of humanism, which is concerned with people and their needs and values compassion and human agency. A glance at humanist organizations around the world illustrates that humanists advocate for the use of reason and respect for others; finding meaning and joy in life without a need to believe in an afterlife; the use of critical thinking and science; and empathy and compassion to make the world a better place (see, for example, Humanist Canada, http://humanistcanada.ca). As you read this chapter, you should keep in mind that the concepts discussed, such as meaning-making (finding meaning in life), do not have to be conceptualized or experienced as spiritual processes to be effective, and many people may not experience these processes as spiritual or religious, which is perfectly fine. However, many others will experience these processes as spiritual or religious, and for these people it may be beneficial if we understand their experience and make space for the spiritual part of it to enter into our work in appropriate ways when it is relevant to do so.

Spirituality and Religion in Social Work Practice

Dr David Hodge has conducted much research on spiritual assessment, including the use of spiritual life maps (Hodge, 2005) and spiritual ecograms (Limb & Hodge, 2011), advocating that this will make our services more effective (Hodge, 2003). More recently, he argued for an implicit approach (avoiding the use of traditional spiritual/religious language) in assessing a client's spirituality with clients who might be reluctant to discuss spirituality/religion overtly (Hodge, 2013). For example, a social worker can ask a person, "What helps you get through times of difficulty?" to assess the relevance of spirituality/religion in that individual's life (p. 227).

In my experience, if we do not inquire about this area of people's lives they may not think to share it with us. Sometimes clients do not think that we would be open to hearing about their spiritual or religious beliefs. A good friend of mine engaged for quite some time with a social work psychotherapist and never discussed spirituality with him, even though when we talked about the issue that brought her to therapy she clearly identified the matter as "spiritual." She explained that she did not think he would be open to the discussion. Thus, it is important for us as social workers to provide space for these discussions to emerge if they are relevant, and this is why it is important to ask about it during an assessment. Otherwise there is a chance that we will fail to thoroughly understand a person's life and experiences and how they are making meaning of their experiences.

Similarly, I find the same can be said for dreams. Often a client will have vivid dreams or recurring dreams, and unless I ask about this I will never know it is occurring. Dreams can be such a rich device for assisting people to understand themselves better and develop their self-awareness, and for some people dreams are intimately connected with their spiritual beliefs. Indeed, since the beginning of time many cultures have regarded dreams as having some special power that transcends the past, present, and future; many believe that dream messages are a vehicle through which God can speak (France, 2002). As Jung (1964) argued, dreams are linked to spiritual life and can be inspired by transcendental forces.

For example, in an arts-based group we facilitated with women who were having substance use problems, a woman reported that it was a dream that led her into treatment—she believed the dream was a message from God letting her know that she had to address her substance use (Coholic & LeBreton, 2007). (Arts-based or creative methods can include a variety of activities, such as drawing, painting, collaging, sculpting with clay, writing, using music or sand, and participating in experiential games.) Dreams can also be a source of distress. For example, I recently worked with a middle-aged man who was a first responder suffering with post-traumatic stress disorder. He had recurrent dreams of tragic events he had witnessed over the course of his career, which left him feeling anxious and distressed. It was important for us to discuss these dreams to understand the meaning of these events and how they had affected and changed him.

Rice and McAuliffe (2009) explain that while there are differing opinions on what constitutes spiritually influenced interventions, they are considered to be those practices that practitioners believe have been informed or adapted from religious or spiritual practices/ideas or are considered to directly engage with the spiritual aspect of a client's life. Within social work, this often includes the topics of helping people make meaning or sense of significant life events and assisting people to cope. Sheridan (2009) found that students and practitioners are using spiritually sensitive interventions to a large degree in (1) conducting assessments, (2) supporting aspects of a client's spirituality identified as a coping resource and strength, (3) referring clients to appropriate spiritual helpers and programs, and (4) helping clients address issues that require deep reflection or meaning-making, such as loss and death.

Spirituality and Social Justice

Before we consider the topic of coping, it is important to note that spiritually sensitive social work also has to do with social activism toward the betterment of communities, society, and the world. You will notice that there is emphasis in this chapter on social work that could be described as more clinical or micro-social work and pertaining to mental health. It is important to remember that social workers who recognize the relevance of spirituality and religion, and who conduct micro types of practice, do not abandon their anti-oppressive, critical, feminist, and structural values and approaches. Thus spirituality within social work is not some new-age individualistic endeavour that people embark upon to access individual desires. Rather, as Baskin (2007) argues, spirituality is about resistance and connects us to the work of social change. She states that we all have a responsibility to apply our spirituality to affect change and create a better world. (For a further discussion on the importance of competence in diversity in micro-level practice, see Chapter 4 by Marie Lacroix.)

For an example of how spiritual and religious viewpoints can inform social justice practice, Todd (2004) discusses how a small group of feminist community organizers' secular practices were informed and shaped by stories about religion and spirituality. She examined the possibility that religious affiliations and spiritualities shape commitments to social justice and ethical relations with others. Also, in discussing social justice and spirituality, Consedine (2002) argues that we need an alternative vision of life and that linking spirituality to social justice is an important part of human movement for social change. His contention is that a just, more inclusive, and spiritually sound future can be attained if we focus on the common good, which includes (1) the principles of solidarity and the protection of human rights, (2) sustainability, (3) wisdom, which is the accrued insights gathered through experience and knowledge and retained for the benefit of the common good, and (4) holistic spirituality, wherein spirituality is integrated into daily life.

Similarly, social work scholars such as Besthorn (2002, 2012) and Coates (2003b, 2004) discuss the need for a spiritually influenced social activism pertaining to the environment. John Coates (2003a, 2012) argues that to avoid continued environmental destruction, we need to embrace a new narrative, set of beliefs, and values that address the questions "Why are we here?" and "What is the proper human–earth relationship?" As he explains, these are spiritual questions concerning our ultimate meaning and purpose that call for a new consciousness. A holistic worldview demands awareness of our interdependence with each other and with the world we live in.

Coping

Some—perhaps many—people cope with life events and stresses by drawing on their spiritual resources and beliefs. Researchers have found that spirituality can be important in helping people construct positive meanings from a crisis (Gockel, 2009). (The second case study in this chapter illustrates how Susan did this concerning an unplanned pregnancy.) Spirituality has also been noted to be important for client well-being and the recovery process within mental health (Sullivan, 2009). Others have found that spiritual and religious resources can help people accept change and use adversity, such as serious illness and substance abuse or poverty, as an opportunity for growth (Banerjee & Canda, 2009; Carlson & Larkin, 2009; Ka'opua, Gotay, & Boehm, 2007).

In some cultures, spirituality/religion and cultural practices cannot be divorced when the issues of coping and meaning-making are considered. Gilbert, Harvey, and Belgrave (2009) discuss how spirituality is one value that, together with other values such as collectivism, have been found to create significant change across a number of important areas in practice with African Americans; they have called for an Africentric paradigm within social work. Other researchers examined how spirituality aided in resettling after leaving one's country as a refugee (Sossou, Craig, Ogren, & Schnak, 2008). Al-Krenawi and Graham (2000) wrote an informative paper outlining mental health practice guidelines with Arab peoples that is still useful for practice today. They explained that ethnic Arab peoples view helping and health practitioners as professionals who discount religious values and fail to see these as sources of healing, thereby making it difficult to establish a trusting helping relationship. Furthermore, Arab peoples consider religion as an important context within which problems can both be constructed and resolved; for instance, mentally ill people may be considered to be associated with the supernatural realm.

Working on being a culturally competent practitioner is an ongoing process and an important one within social work, where we value anti-oppressive and critical approaches to practice and aim to work collaboratively with people, groups, and communities. Thus as social workers we need to continually build knowledge about the best ways to approach and work with clients from cultures where religion, spirituality, and culture are intimately connected. It can already be complex to work with someone from a culture different from our own, and spirituality and religion add another intersecting layer of a person's identity to consider. Maintaining the values of respect and open-mindedness, working with people in nonhierarchal ways and in collaboration, and applying good critical thinking skills can assist us to become competent as these values and skills form a solid foundation for the building of knowledge.

One of the ways I have developed my own professional knowledge regarding Aboriginal spirituality and practice was to work closely with a traditional healer and elder. Early in my social work career I worked in an agency that had an Aboriginal elder on staff. We shared several clients, in that I would address a client's trauma in more "mainstream" or traditional/global ways according to recognized theories and approaches, and the Aboriginal elder would meet with the client to conduct healing ceremonies and to discuss Aboriginal culture and spirituality, using local knowledge. Sometimes he would invite me to participate in a ceremony with a client. From participating in these ceremonies and our discussions about clients, I learned a lot from this elder about Aboriginal culture and healing. This was an ideal situation, having the opportunity to work so closely together and to draw upon both global and local knowledge. That being said, social workers should consider referring to traditional healers when relevant (Al-Krenawi & Graham, 2000). Similarly, I have referred clients to their pastor or priest when they raised religious issues in our work that I was not qualified or prepared to address.

Specifically regarding Aboriginal peoples in Canada, Schiff and Pelech (2007) studied the effects of a Sweat Lodge ceremony, which is an Indigenous ceremony aimed at restoring a balance of spiritual, emotional, mental, and physical well-being. They concluded that this ceremony may help people increase their sense of spirituality and connection to each other. Along with Aboriginal colleagues, I conducted research exploring the use of arts-based mindfulness group methods to improve self-awareness and self-esteem in Aboriginal women living in our local community (Coholic, Cote-Meek, & Recollet, 2013). Unsurprisingly, many if not most of the discussions of the arts-based creations and the group processes were linked with spirituality. In fact, one of the women discussed how taking part in the group enabled her to contemplate her relationship with the Creator. Women discussed how the natural world helped them maintain their spirituality and was spiritual itself—for instance, the healing essence of nature and the spirits in the trees. Women also discussed how the Creator, ancestors, and spirit guides helped them on their healing journeys. We pointed out that in working with Aboriginal women, practitioners need to be comfortable listening to and exploring spiritual beliefs when they arise while also understanding that not all Aboriginal peoples will share spiritual beliefs and experiences: It is important not to essentialize people from a shared cultural background. In this manner, arts-based methods can be useful in that they provide ways to explore thoughts and feelings while supporting a diversity of viewpoints and experiences.

This discussion about culture, coping, and spirituality points out that whether we are prepared or not to address spiritual and religious issues with our clients, these matters may arise and necessitate our attention and skill. At other times, spirituality and religion are an important aspect underlying the reason a client has come to see you. The case study described next (Case Example 11.1) has to do with a situation in which a client left his religion and the challenging consequences for him as a result of this decision.

Meaning-Making

Strongly related to coping is the matter of meaning-making and making sense of one's life experiences. This can include developing an understanding of why something has occurred and using this understanding to make peace with a situation, accept it, or deal with it. As described in the case study above, Peter had to learn to cope with his current life situation, but ultimately he may also want to make meaning of his life situation by trying to understand why his parents made the decision they did to exclude him from their lives. Certainly this process is often ongoing, so the meaning Peter makes of his life situation may change as he ages through life.

Case Example 11.1

When I first met with Peter he was in his early 30s. He was referred to me by his family physician because he was "depressed." Peter presented a painful familial issue in which he was shunned by his parents because of his decision to leave his family's fundamentalist religious tradition. The term "fundamentalist" is used here to describe movements that profess to be upholding some kind of orthodoxy or right practice, with members of these movements often living separate from mainstream society. Peter had struggled for a long time with the religious beliefs and practices he was raised with, and he described some painful incidents from his childhood in which he was made to feel embarrassed in church and among the congregation. He described his family as working class and told me that his stay-at-home mother had always been unhappy and on medication for depression for as long as he could remember. In the past year, Peter had become involved with a woman who was not of this faith, and they were recently married. This relationship propelled him to finally leave the religion and stop attending church, which led to the shunning; Peter's parents would not speak or meet with him unless he re-embraced the religion.

The family dynamics were inextricably linked with the religious viewpoints, so it was not possible to separate these in our work together. This type of complex situation leads to many emotions that can all exist at the same time. Peter felt sad and guilty about leaving his faith, and he also believed that something was inherently wrong with him. He felt angry and frustrated about the loss of relationships with both his family and the religious community. Also, this situation is something that Peter will have to deal with on an ongoing basis over the course of his life because if his parents do not find a way to have contact with Peter, they will be absent from many of his life's milestones, such as graduation and having a relationship with future grandchildren.

Peter was brought up with many rigid rules and no encouragement to express and identify his own feelings and needs. Many of the religious ideas and beliefs he was raised with were negatively affecting him in his current life. For example, he was encouraged to believe that it was wrong to desire or pursue success. Thus his decision to pursue a career caused him to feel as if he was doing something wrong. He also had a lot of difficulty making decisions, even what we might consider to be small decisions such as where to buy clothes, because he was never encouraged to identify his own feelings and needs. This in turn created some conflict in his current relationship, because his wife felt frustrated by

You have probably heard some people state that "everything happens for a reason." This is one way to make meaning of events, although a person has to search for the "reason" if he or she adheres to this tenet. Perhaps you have heard someone dealing with cancer or another serious illness state that the illness "was the best thing that ever happened to me." While this may be difficult for some of us to understand, in this type of his lack of decision-making ability. Additionally, he struggled with his self-esteem in part because he did not receive unconditional love growing up in his family. One received "love" when one followed the rules and lived according to the religious beliefs. Peter's sense of self and his understanding of who he was in the world were not clear to him. In situations such as Peter's, there is an added complexity in that Peter believed not only the negative messages about himself received from his parents, but also that God was displeased with him and that he was doing something wrong by not living according to what he was raised to believe were God's wishes.

Peter's "depression" was a symptom of all of the emotions (many of which were unconscious) pertaining to his life situation that were accumulating. These included feelings of sadness, anger, confusion, frustration, guilt, and anxiety. Peter's goals were to feel better about himself and to cope more effectively with his life situation. Thus, I used a variety of approaches with Peter, including a strengths-based approach that affirmed his strengths and helped him recognize his abilities and skills. It took a lot of courage to leave his religious beliefs and community behind. Also, cognitive-behavioural theory and tools such as thought records assisted him to identify and change his negative and judgmental beliefs about himself. It was also relevant for Peter to develop his self-awareness and to understand how his past experiences were affecting his current feelings, thoughts, and behaviours; he needed to improve his ability to express his feelings. To this end, using insight-oriented approaches and learning about and practising mindfulness in his day-to-day life helped Peter to become more self-aware and to connect the dots between his past and his present experiences. This in turn led to more effective expressions of emotion with his wife, which improved the communication and understanding of each other within their marital relationship.

Importantly, throughout our work together I strove to be nonjudgmental and curious about the religious beliefs we discussed. We explored these together, assessing what was relevant for him and what was not. For instance, the belief that one should not strive for success was related to the notion that one should not aim to be "better" than other community members. It was important to explore this idea, contemplating its purpose and analyzing the benefits and drawbacks to it as well as how it had affected him and his family members. In this manner, Peter created a new narrative about himself and his life that enabled him to move forward in positive, healthy ways.

situation people might be communicating how the illness forced them to rethink their priorities in life and focus on what really matters. We could imagine how someone who attributed an illness to being a workaholic might realize how the focus on work had harmed his or her health and familial relationships. Consequently, after the illness this person might focus more time on his or her marriage and children rather than work.

Have you ever had something awful happen to you that resulted in you wondering "Why me?" For some people, coming up with answers to this type of question can become an existential crisis or dilemma. I have worked with many adults who, upon reaching middle age, begin to reflect on the meaning of their life: Are they happy with their life? Are they doing something meaningful with their life? Are they where they want to be (or where they thought they would be) in their life at this time? What is the purpose of their life? Understanding suffering and making meaning of it has long been the domain of existentialist philosophy (Krill, 2011). Relevant to our discussion is the fact that some researchers argue that a major route to finding meaning in life is through religion and spirituality (Milam, 2006). Indeed, definitions of spirituality for social work typically include the human quest for a sense of meaning and purpose (Nelson-Becker & Canda, 2008).

Making meaning of life events has long been a rationale for the incorporation of spirituality in social work practice, because for many people spiritual beliefs and experiences will be integral in this process. For example, Cadell, Janzen, and Haubrich (2007) explored the spiritual experiences in people who had cared for someone who had died of AIDS-related complications. Many of these caregivers were also HIV positive themselves. They found that the participants' spirituality grew so that they were able to create meaning in their lives from the death of the person they cared for but also in facing their own mortality. Many of the participants shifted the focus in their lives to what was really important to them so that they experienced a greater participation in and appreciation for life.

We do not have to share our clients' spiritual or religious beliefs to work with and consider these beliefs in assisting them to make meaning. For instance, a client recently reported to me that after her mother died she and her father went to see a psychic who claimed to be able to communicate with people who had died. What the psychic told her father appeared to bring great comfort to him in his grief. I was not able to identify any harm in what they were told by the psychic, so this belief was not something for me to challenge. However, I can use my client's beliefs to explore her viewpoints and how these are helping her (or not) to cope and make sense of the situation. The following case study (Case Example 11.2) describes a situation where a client used her religious faith and beliefs to make meaning and sense of an unexpected event in her life.

It is important to note that it is a complex task to directly incorporate religious language or teachings into social work practice unless there are shared beliefs, traditions, practices, and language between practitioners and clients and the client is interested in drawing on this shared experience. Doherty (2009) developed a useful model for using clinical, moral, and spiritual language in therapy. Among other things, he argued that we should avoid the use of spiritual language such as asking someone if they are praying over their problem if we do not know the client's beliefs. We should also be careful about self-disclosing our own beliefs so that we do not abuse our position of power. Also, he explained how we can incorporate spiritual language and concepts if we are familiar with the client's spiritual language and if the client is interested in using this language in the process, for example, clarifying with a person that he or she is seeking

Case Example 11.2

I met Susan when she was 41 years old. She had a stable and supportive 15-year marriage and three children, aged 10, 11, and 13 years. Her family was financially stable and secure, and she identified no atypical issues with her children, who were doing well in school and who were involved with a variety of sport activities. Her family also had support from extended family who lived in the same city and from the church they belonged to. She came to see me because she was emotionally and psychologically struggling with recently finding out that she was pregnant.

Susan and her husband were not trying to conceive a child, and her pregnancy came as a surprise and a shock to both of them. Susan was at that stage of her life where her three children were growing increasingly independent. Having been a stay-at-home mom for many years, in the past year she had returned to full-time work. She had a career that she really enjoyed and found fulfilling, and she was also involved with her church, participating in several committees with other members. She and her husband had begun to consider their future retirement, as they both wished to retire early in their lives.

Susan identified as a Christian, and because of her faith she explained that having an abortion was not an option for her, although she had briefly thought about it. Susan expressed feeling angry, disappointed, stressed, and conflicted about the pregnancy given her stage of life. Having a baby would signify dramatic changes. She expressed that she did not want to return to the days of changing diapers, breastfeeding, being sleep deprived, and so forth; she was done with that part of her life and had moved on. In fact, she discussed how she really enjoyed being able to do activities with her children now that they were older. Also, she was disappointed in what this would mean for her career plans, not to mention her and her husband's future retirement plans. Furthermore, she worried about her age and the possibility of having a high-risk pregnancy or a child with a disability. Also, she was very worried about thinking in this manner and what effect that might be having on her developing baby and on the type of mothering she would be able to provide. She expressed worries that the baby would somehow know how she currently felt.

Susan's goal was to change her thinking and her feelings about the pregnancy so that she could cope better with it and prepare to welcome the baby into the world with love and happiness. Thankfully, from a strengths perspective, Susan had lots of resources and supports in her life, and she had many skills and coping abilities that helped her tackle all of the issues she raised with me. Clearly, there were lots of matters that Susan needed to discuss and many feelings to process so that she could accomplish the change she desired. To this end, I used many methods to help her express her thoughts and feelings, including journaling exercises and arts-based activities such as creating collages and drawings of her feelings. The therapeutic process provided a

continued

place for Susan where she could express herself honestly, including her feelings of frustration at God.

A feminist social work perspective was also a useful theory to guide our work together because feminist social work draws attention to the implications of gender in people's lives. (For a continued discussion on the implication of gender in social work, see Chapter 13 by Sarah Fotheringham.) Through this lens, Susan was assisted to develop an analysis of how our society constructs "good" mothers, for example, the idea that a "good" mother sacrifices her own needs/desires for the sake of her children. This analysis helped Susan process her own thinking and decisions around her work outside the home, and helped her understand and address her feelings of resentment related to mothering and her career. Understanding that she could be a good mother while still working opened up new possibilities for her and helped to lessen her feelings of resentment. Also, it helped her talk to her husband about his role in parenting and how they could parent more equally. Ultimately, Susan had to make meaning of her pregnancy. Why her and why now? Susan's faith was integral to this process of making sense of why another child was coming into her life.

forgiveness from God. He provides a useful example of how he used scripture to challenge a Christian couple's notion that they had to disown their son because he came out as gay. He was able to do this because he shared this couple's faith and was knowledgeable about the religious beliefs and values.

While the use of religious language is not a regular occurrence or practice for me (nor I suspect for most social workers), I have worked with several people for whom their Christian faith and practice were very important. For example, I recently worked with a middle-aged Christian woman who struggled with her self-esteem. She grew up with a father who was an alcoholic and a mother who parentalized her and inappropriately used her to meet her own emotional needs. Knowing a little about Christianity and knowing that this was very important to my client, I asked her in a session if she thought God created people who were not equal to others or who were not as "worthy" as others (knowing that this was not what she believed). This was a way for me to demonstrate to her that I understood the importance of her faith to her, and it also encouraged her to use her own religious beliefs to challenge her judgmental thinking about herself; she believed that she was "not as good as" other people, which was in direct contrast to her religious beliefs and values.

Post-Traumatic Growth

Related to the topic of meaning-making is the construct and process of post-traumatic growth, which is the idea that people can grow and transform from experiences of suffering and trauma. Post-traumatic growth (PTG) is considered different from resilience in that PTG includes growth and transformation, not just a return to functioning after a crisis. Pertinent to our discussion is the fact that spiritual and religious change is considered to be part of PTG (Calhoun & Tedeschi, 2006). Kilmer and colleagues (2009) examined PTG in children impacted by Hurricane Katrina. They noted that the children reported the most growth on the spirituality items on the Revised Posttraumatic Growth Inventory for Children. These items included the questions "I understand how God works better than I used to" and "My faith (belief) in God is stronger than it was before" (p. 253). The authors noted that this result may be a reflection of where the children lived—a region high in religiosity. Also, the children's parents may have encouraged faith-based explanations for the hurricane experience. However, as Calhoun and Tedeschi (2006) point out, while a religious component may not always be relevant to PTG, considering existential questions about life's purpose is often important for people coping with major life crises and disasters.

Viktor Frankl (2006) was a well-known psychiatrist who wrote the bestselling book *Man's Search for Meaning* (originally published in 1959) based on his experiences as a prisoner in a concentration camp during the Holocaust. His existential theory and practice (logotherapy) advocated that life has meaning even in the most horrible of conditions and suffering. This being said, it is important for us to note that spirituality and religion can be both a source of positive change and growth but also a source of struggle with trauma, for example, wondering how a loving God could let horrific tragic events occur (like the Holocaust) (Pargament, Desai, & McConnell, 2006). It is not difficult to imagine how a parent who loses a child or a person who suffers a devastating natural disaster might lose his or her faith in the Creator, a God, or the Universe.

So far in this chapter we have explored how spirituality and religion can be important aspects of clients' lives. Social workers can also experience changes to their spiritual or religious viewpoints as a result of their work. For instance, we could consider the opposite of post-traumatic growth to be secondary traumatic stress (STS) (Bride, Robinson, Yegidis, & Figley, 2004), compassion fatigue (CF) (Adams, Figley, & Boscarino, 2008), or vicarious trauma (VT) (Pearlman & Saakvitne, 1995). The concepts of STS, CF, and VT encapsulate the damaging effects on social workers who bear witness to the experience of another person's trauma but are not direct targets of that trauma. For instance, as a result of repeatedly listening to and empathizing with clients' narratives of being psychologically tormented, sexually assaulted, or physically attacked and controlled, one can begin to experience increased sensitivity to reports of violence, feelings of helplessness, hypervigilance with children, altered sexual relations, and reduced tolerance for others, among many other effects. While these terms refer to similar processes and effects, Robinson-Keilig (2014) explains that "vicarious trauma" is the terminology used when referring to changes in a practitioner's thoughts, beliefs, and interpretations about one's self, others, and the world; these are known as one's cognitive schemas and include ideas about safety, trust, esteem, and intimacy. "Secondary traumatic stress" is the terminology used when referring to arousal symptoms, avoidance, and intrusive thoughts; STS is thought to mirror symptoms of post-traumatic stress disorder. The term "compassion fatigue" has been used to describe STS, and both STS and CF include experiences such as nightmares and intrusive thoughts. However, CF is a unique occupational hazard for those working with victims of trauma (Thompson, Amatea, & Thompson, 2014).

Specific to spirituality and religion, Pearlman and Saakvitne (1995) explain how the effects of VT can encompass changes in spirituality, for instance, feeling anger toward God and having one's religious beliefs challenged. In a study I conducted with a colleague several years ago, wherein we explored sexual assault workers' experiences working in northern Ontario contexts, we found similar results. For instance, some of the women reported that they experienced secondary trauma (encompassing effects related to STS, CF, and VT, as noted above) that challenged their faith in traditional institutions like the church, and some withdrew from participation in organized religious practices. Others described effects to their spirituality and experienced their work as "wearing their soul out" and "draining their spirit" (Coholic & Blackford, 2003).

Personally, I can relate to these women's experiences, having worked in the area of trauma (primarily sexual assault and abuse) for many years. I can recall, early in my career, walking home from work feeling like I "hated" people. When you are exposed to the dark side of humanity, even vicariously, it can challenge your faith in humanity. If you have beliefs in a just God or Universe, these beliefs can also be challenged. To survive and thrive, we need to understand what is happening to our worldview, we require support from knowledgeable colleagues and supervisors, and ultimately we need to find meaning in our work. For me, practising mindfulness (which is discussed later in this chapter) made the difference and enabled me to sustain and develop my practice and my well-being. As Dombo and Gray (2013) discuss, meditation and contemplation can be spiritual practices that can help a social worker find meaning beyond the self, in relationships, and in clinical practice. Others will create meaning and contribute to their well-being through religious rituals and practices such as attending church or praying.

Working with people who have experienced traumatic experiences such as sexual abuse can involve helping the person to cope, make meaning, heal, and even experience post-traumatic growth. In my experience, dealing with the effects of abuse sometimes feels like very "deep" work because the person has been affected on levels that seem to go beyond personally identified aspects of the self. It is sometimes difficult to encapsulate in words these experiences because they are experiential. Perhaps you can identify with this in contemplating a close relationship you have with someone significant in your life that you feel deeply connected to. While this experience of depth does not have to be conceptualized as spiritual it can feel that way, and I have worked with many survivors of abuse who, through the course of our work together, have identified that they have been wounded on a soul or spiritual level. Transpersonal theory can help us understand this because it is concerned with the most profound aspects of human experience, such as personal transformation and expansive states of consciousness, and offers a conceptual framework for considering spirituality in social work practice.

Transpersonal Theory

Braud and Anderson (1998) explain that transpersonal theory focuses on understanding the language and development of the spiritual dimension in life—that which lies beyond the personal or ego level. There is a belief that there is a higher or inner self, which is distinct from the personal ego. Thus, there is a focus on an expanded theory of human consciousness. Transpersonal theory also includes and is interested in the human potential for creativity and communion, the process of self-actualization, and experiences of spiritual growth (Robbins, Chatterjee, & Canda, 2006). Transpersonal theory builds on the work of many well-known psychologists such as Carl Jung, Abraham Maslow, Ken Wilber, Erich Fromm, and Viktor Frankl, to name just a few, and it is influenced by many fields such as medicine, consciousness studies, philosophy, religion, yoga, and the creative arts. Canda and Smith (2001) point out that transpersonal theory has been growing steadily within psychology and philosophy since the 1960s but is not a strong influence within social work, which still holds true today. Within social work, transpersonal theory has been discussed in relation to suffering in the face of death, levels of consciousness and their relationship to mental health, themes in living with a disability, exploring linkages with deep ecological philosophy, client self-determination and growth, and hospice care. Robbins, Chatterjee, and Canda (2006) argue that social work has a great deal to contribute to the transpersonal theory movement by bringing knowledge about the social environment and social justice movements that can help transpersonal theory incorporate political and ecological concerns.

While transpersonal theorists and practitioners have long been interested in meditative practices, mindfulness-based meditation and practices are increasingly becoming part of current helping and health practices. Social work has taken up mindfulness in a more holistic manner compared to other professions such as psychology and medicine.

Mindfulness

Mindfulness is a holistic philosophy that is known as an element of the Buddhist tradition; one of its original intentions was to assist people in dealing with suffering (Chiesa, 2013). According to Weiss (2004), mindfulness was meant to help people see clearly and understand themselves and others better so that a more fulfilling and joyful life could be lived. Jon Kabat-Zinn (1990) was one of the first practitioners to develop a mindfulness-based program for use in North America: the Mindfulness-Based Stress Reduction (MBSR) program. As a result, his conceptualization of mindfulness is widely used by practitioners and researchers who have used his work as a foundation. Kabat-Zinn (1990, 1994) defined mindfulness as activity that encourages awareness to emerge through paying attention on purpose, in the present moment, and nonjudgmentally to the unfolding of experience moment by moment. It has to do with exploring ourselves, questioning our perspectives and our place in the world, and cultivating an appreciation for the fullness of each of life's moments.

Within Western helping and health professions, mindfulness is most often conceptualized as part of a cognitive-behavioural therapy (CBT) approach. Commonly taught forms of this type of mindfulness practice are mindfulness-based stress reduction (MBSR) and mindfulness-based cognitive therapy (MBCT) (Segal, Williams, & Teasdale, 2002). In general, these programs include practices such as sitting, walking, and eating meditations; breathing meditations; guided body awareness and scans; light yoga; psychoeducation; and cognitive-behavioural techniques. Both the research and popular literature in this field have grown considerably over the past decade, and several systematic reviews of this scholarly work have been completed. A few examples include Chiesa and Serretti (2014), who report that mindfulness-based interventions (MBIs) can reduce the consumption of substances such as alcohol, cigarettes, and opiates, and that MBIs are associated with reductions in cravings. There is also evidence that MBSR improves mental health and reduces symptoms of stress, anxiety, and depression, and MBCT prevents depressive relapse in recurrently depressed people (Fjorback, Arendt, Ornbol, Fink, & Walach, 2011). Regarding anxiety, researchers found MBIs to be associated with reductions in symptoms of anxiety (Vollestad, Birkeland Nielsen, & Hostmark Nielsen, 2012). Also, a systematic review of MBSR for breast cancer patients found evidence of its effectiveness in decreasing symptoms of depression and anxiety (Cramer, Lauche, Paul, & Dobos, 2012).

My own research has explored the benefits of an arts-based mindfulness program for improving aspects of resilience and self-concept in vulnerable children. Ten years ago mindfulness with children was a virtually unexplored area (Ott, 2002; Semple, Reid, & Miller, 2005). It is still an emerging area in the literature, but overall conclusions indicate that interventions are acceptable and well tolerated by children (Burke, 2010). Researchers found that mindfulness holds promise as an intervention for anxiety (Semple et al., 2005), that mindfulness training helped adolescents with attention and impulsivity problems to achieve goals, develop better attention, feel happier, and develop mindful awareness (Bogels, Hoogstad, van Dun, de Schutter, & Restifo, 2008), as well as improve optimism, social competence, self-concept, and emotional resilience (Schonert-Reichl & Lawlor, 2010; Semple, Lee, Rosa, & Miller, 2010). Greco, Baer, and Smith (2011) argue that mindfulness is associated with quality of life, academic competence, social skills, and fewer internalizing symptoms and externalizing behaviour problems. We found that our arts-based mindfulness program helped children feel happier and develop skills such as paying attention and emotion regulation (Coholic, 2011b; Coholic & Eys, 2013).

Mindfulness within social work has been taken up in a different way compared to psychology and health. Most social workers approach mindfulness and MBIs in a more holistic manner, being cognizant of the holistic nature and history of mindfulness philosophy and practice, which reflects social work values and practices. For instance, as Hick (2009) explains, social work is using mindfulness in unique ways, including community work and social justice practice. A holistic mindfulness might be more creative, attuned to people's specific needs and goals, and open to discourse that is spiritual/holistic and existential (Gause & Coholic, 2010). In a paper that I wrote with a doctoral student, we described how in a mindfulness-based group with adult women, discussion arose that was connected to spiritual and existential themes such as life after death, suffering, and meaning-making. Mindfulness does not have to be a spiritual practice, but for some people, such as the group participants in this example, learning mindfulness helped them express their spiritual viewpoints and experiences by providing them with a daily practice. One woman stated that becoming mindful of what brought meaning to her life was a "spiritual awakening" (Gause & Coholic, 2010, p. 13).

Similarly, in the arts-based mindfulness groups we conducted and studied with vulnerable children and youth, we made room for spirituality to enter the discourse (Coholic, 2010). For example, on one occasion a girl stated that something "touched her soul." The facilitators then asked the other group members what the "soul" meant to them. Examples of responses were "Your soul is the inner you or something"; "It's basically what makes us who we are . . . boring in this world if we were like everyone else"; and "I don't know . . . If we had no soul, then we wouldn't be who we are. It's hard to explain, but if you sell your soul then . . . it's like you're not living" (Coholic, 2011a, p. 201). In this manner, conversations, even with children, can incorporate spiritual themes. You might be surprised at the conversations you will have with the people you work with if you make room for spirituality and religion to enter into the discourse.

Finally, most of my applied research has studied holistic group work methods. Certainly mindfulness is usually taught and facilitated by way of groups. Other researchers have also studied the benefits and effectiveness of spiritually sensitive practices by way of group work, which lends itself well to comparing spiritually sensitive interventions with other modalities. For example, researchers found that a spiritually sensitive group intervention for clients with eating disorders helped to reduce depression and anxiety, relationship distress, social role conflict, and eating disorder symptoms. The spiritually sensitive group used a workbook that included spiritual readings about identity, forgiveness, and meditation (Richards, Berrett, Hardman, & Eggett, 2006). Antle and Lott Collins (2009) studied a breast cancer support group among African American breast cancer survivors and found that the women who participated in a spiritually based group reported higher levels of satisfaction and benefits. For some of these women, the illness strengthened their faith and belief that they were going to be fine.

Summary and Conclusion

This chapter provided a brief overview of how spirituality and religion have been considered within contemporary Western social work. We began by exploring how the modern social work profession has conceptualized spirituality and religion as being related but also different. Overall, spirituality is understood to include a search for purpose, meaning, and connection between oneself, others, and ultimate reality, which can be experienced within a religious or nonreligious framework. Religion generally refers to a set of beliefs, practices, and traditions experienced with a specific social institution.

Social work has come to this understanding because spirituality is viewed as more inclusive of diverse belief systems and consistent with professional social work values. It is important to understand that for some of the people and communities we work with, this separation of spirituality and religion will not resonate.

Spiritually sensitive social work practices have largely been adapted from religious or spiritual practices and ideas, or are considered to directly engage with the spiritual or religious aspect of a client's life. Spiritually sensitive topics and processes often include helping people to cope and make meaning of events, because for many people their spiritual or religious values will be important in these processes. Spirituality can also be part of conducting a holistic assessment, working with clients' cultures, and in social activism and social justice practices. Increasingly, social workers are encountering diverse clientele, and for some people their culture is inextricably connected with their spiritual and religious beliefs, so it is difficult, if not impossible, to avoid these beliefs in our practices. Indeed, sometimes the issues that people want to address are spiritual in nature or are bound up with their religious beliefs and experiences. Also, many social workers come to the profession as a result of their spiritual or religious values, and these values sustain them in their work.

It is vitally important to be open-minded and nonjudgmental in our social work practices. Being a social worker is a privilege in that we are continually offered opportunities to learn and grow from professional knowledge but also from our clients by way of their experiences and the relationships we form with them. Certainly we need to be open to learning from our clients, particularly when it comes to their spiritual or religious perspectives and traditions. To be effective practitioners, we also need to analyze our own biases with regard to religion and spirituality, just as we do with other diversities and social locations such as race and gender (Sheridan, 2002).

If you are interested in exploring spirituality and religion in social work further, the recommended resources will help you develop your knowledge in this area. You should keep in mind that all of the topics that were introduced and discussed in this chapter have a rich knowledge base and we really only "skimmed the surface" in this chapter.

Questions for Review

1. How does social work define spirituality and religion?
2. What are some common spiritually sensitive social work practices?
3. What are some situations when it would be appropriate to include discussions about spirituality or religion with clients?
4. What do we need to keep in mind when having discussions about spirituality or religion with clients?
5. What do we need to keep in mind regarding spirituality and religion when working with clients from diverse cultures?
6. What are some theories and philosophies that incorporate spirituality?

Suggested Reading and Resources

Canadian Society for Spirituality and Social Work; www.stu.ca/~spirituality

Canda, E., & Furman, L. (2010). *Spiritual diversity in social work practice: The heart of helping* (2nd ed.). New York, NY: Oxford University Press.

Coates, J. (2003). *Ecology and social work: Toward a new paradigm*. Black Point, NS: Fernwood Publishing.

Coates, J., Graham, J., Swartzentruber, B., & Ouellette, B. (Eds.). (2007). *Spirituality and social work: Selected Canadian readings*. Toronto, ON: Canadian Scholars' Press Inc.

Coholic, D. (2010). *Arts activities for children and young people in need: Helping children to develop mindfulness, spiritual awareness and self-esteem*. London, UK: Jessica Kingsley Publishers.

Council on Social Work Education. (n.d.). Religion and spirituality educational resources. Retrieved from http://www.cswe.org/CentersInitiatives/CurriculumResources/50777/58508.aspx

Groen, J., Coholic, D., & Graham, J. (2012). *Spirituality in social work and education: Theory, practice and pedagogies*. Waterloo, ON: Wilfrid Laurier University Press.

Hick, S. (Ed.), (2009). *Mindfulness and social work*. Chicago, IL: Lyceum Books Inc.

Journal of Religion and Spirituality in Social Work: Social Thought; http://www.tandfonline.com/toc/wrsp20/current#.Uxnse1z-Jg0

Society for Spirituality and Social Work; http://societyforspiritualityandsocialwork.com

Walsh, F. (Ed.), (2009). *Spiritual resources in family therapy* (2nd ed.). New York, NY: The Guilford Press.

References

Adams, R. E., Figley, C., & Boscarino, J. (2008). The compassion fatigue scale: Its use with social workers following urban disaster. *Research on Social Work Practice, 18*(3), 238–50.

Al-Krenawi, A., & Graham, J. (2000). Culturally sensitive social work practice with Arab clients in mental health settings. *Health and Social Work, 25*(1), 9–22.

Antle, B., & Lott Collins, W. (2009). The impact of a spirituality-based support group on self-efficacy and well-being of African American breast cancer survivors: A mixed methods design. *Social Work & Christianity, 36*(3), 286–300.

Banerjee, M., & Canda, E. (2009). Spirituality as a strength of African-American women affected by welfare reform. *Journal of Religion & Spirituality in Social Work: Social Thought, 28*(3), 239–62.

Baskin, C. (2007). Circles of resistance: Spirituality and transformative change in social work education and practice. In J. Coates, J. Graham, B. Swartzentruber, & B. Ouellette (Eds.), *Spirituality and social work: Selected Canadian readings* (pp. 191–204). Toronto, ON: Canadian Scholars' Press Inc.

Besthorn, F. (2002). Expanding spiritual diversity in social work: Perspectives on the greening of spirituality. *Currents: New Scholarship in the Human Services, 1*(1).

Besthorn, F. (2012). Deep ecology's contributions to social work: A 10-year retrospective. *International Journal of Social Welfare, 21*, 248–59. doi:10.1111/j.1468-2397.2011.00850.x

Bogels, S., Hoogstad, B., van Dun, L., de Schutter, S., & Restifo, K. (2008). Mindfulness training for adolescents with externalizing disorders and their parents. *Behavioural & Cognitive Psychotherapy, 36*(2), 193–209.

Braud, W., & Anderson, R. (Eds.). (1998). *Transpersonal research methods for the social sciences: Honouring human experience.* London, UK: Sage Publications.

Bride, B., Robinson, M., Yegidis, B., & Figley, C. (2004). Development and validation of the secondary traumatic stress scale. *Research on Social Work Practice, 14*(1), 27–35.

Burke, C. A. (2010). Mindfulness-based approaches with children and adolescents: A preliminary review of current research in an emergent field. *Journal of Child and Family Studies, 19,* 133–44.

Cadell, S., Janzen, L., & Haubrich, D. (2007). Engaging with spirituality: A qualitative study of grief and HIV/AIDS. In J. Coates, J. Graham, B. Swartzentruber, & B. Ouellette (Eds.), *Spirituality and social work: Selected Canadian readings* (pp. 175–90). Toronto, ON: Canadian Scholars' Press Inc.

Calhoun, L., & Tedeschi, R. (2006). The foundations of posttraumatic growth: An expanded framework. In L. Calhoun & R. Tedeschi (Eds.), *Handbook of posttraumatic growth: Research and practice* (pp. 3–23). New York, NY: Lawrence Erlbaum Associates.

Canda, E. R. (1988). Conceptualizing spirituality for social work: Insights from diverse perspectives. *Social Thought, 14*(1), 30–46.

Canda, E. R., & Furman, L. (2010). *Spiritual diversity in social work practice: The heart of helping* (2nd ed.). New York, NY: Oxford University Press.

Canda, E. R., & Smith, E. (Eds.). (2001). *Transpersonal perspectives on spirituality in social work.* New York, NY: The Haworth Press Inc.

Carlson, B., & Larkin, H. (2009). Meditation as a coping intervention for treatment of addiction. *Journal of Religion & Spirituality in Social Work: Social Thought, 28*(4), 379–92.

Chiesa, A. (2013). The difficulty of defining mindfulness: Current thought and critical issues. *Mindfulness, 4,* 255–68.

Chiesa, A., & Serretti, A. (2014). Are mindfulness-based interventions effective for substance use disorders? A systematic review of the evidence. *Substance Use & Misuse, 49,* 492–512.

Coates, J. (2003a). *Ecology and social work: Toward a new paradigm.* Halifax, NS: Fernwood Publishing.

Coates, J. (2003b). Exploring the roots of the environmental crisis: Opportunity for social transformation. *Critical Social Work, 4*(1).

Coates, J. (2004). From ecology to spirituality and social justice. *Currents: New Scholarship in the Human Services, 3*(1).

Coates, J. (2012). Prisoners of the story: A role for spirituality in thinking and living our way to sustainability. In J. Groen, D. Coholic, & J. Graham (Eds.), *Spirituality in social work and education: Theory, practice, and pedagogies* (pp. 57–76). Waterloo, ON: Wilfrid Laurier University Press.

Coholic, D. (2003). Incorporating spirituality in feminist social work perspectives. *Affilia, 18*(1), 49–67.

Coholic, D. (2010). *Arts activities for children and young people in need: Helping children to develop mindfulness, spiritual awareness and self-esteem.* London, UK: Jessica Kingsley Publishers.

Coholic, D. (2011a). Exploring how young people living in foster care discuss spiritually sensitive themes in a holistic arts-based group program. *Journal of Religion & Spirituality in Social Work: Social Thought, 30*(3), 193–211.

Coholic, D. (2011b). Exploring the feasibility and benefits of arts-based mindfulness-based practices with young people in need: Aiming to improve aspects of self-awareness and resilience. *Child and Youth Care Forum, 40*(4), 303–17.

Coholic, D., & Blackford, K. (2003). Exploring secondary trauma in sexual assault workers in northern Ontario locations: The challenges of working in the northern Ontario context. *Canadian Social Work, 5*(1), 43–58.

Coholic, D., Cote-Meek, S., & Recollet, D. (2013). Exploring the acceptability and perceived benefits of arts-based group methods for Aboriginal women living in an urban community within Northeastern Ontario. *Canadian Social Work Review, 29*(2), 149–68.

Coholic, D., & Eys, M. (2013, May 8–12). *Evaluating the effectiveness of a 12-week arts-based mindfulness group program for the improvement of resilience and self-concept in vulnerable populations*. Paper presented at the First International Conference on Mindfulness, Sapienza Universita Di Roma, Rome, Italy.

Coholic, D., & LeBreton, J. (2007). Working with dreams in a holistic arts-based group: Connections between dream interpretation and spirituality. *Social Work with Groups, 30*(3), 47–64.

Consedine, J. (2002). Spirituality and social justice. In M. Nash & B. Stewart (Eds.), *Spirituality and social care: Contributing to personal and community well-being* (pp. 31–48). London, UK: Jessica Kingsley Publishers Ltd.

Cramer, H., Lauche, R., Paul, A., & Dobos, G. (2012). Mindfulness-based stress reduction for breast cancer: A systematic review and meta-analysis. *Current Oncology, 19*(5), 343–52.

Doherty, W. J. (2009). Morality and spirituality in therapy. In F. Walsh (Ed.), *Spiritual resources in family therapy* (2nd ed., pp. 215–28). New York, NY: The Guilford Press.

Dombo, E., & Gray, C. (2013). Engaging spirituality in addressing vicarious trauma in clinical social workers: A self-care model. *Social Work and Christianity, 40*(1), 89–104.

Farley, Y. (2007). Making the connection: Spirituality, trauma and resiliency. *Journal of Religion & Spirituality in Social Work: Social Thought, 26*(1), 1–15.

Fjorback, L., Arendt, M., Ornbol, E., Fink, P., & Walach, H. (2011). Mindfulness-based stress reduction and mindfulness-based cognitive therapy: A systematic review of randomized controlled trials. *Acta Psychiatr Scand, 124*, 102–19.

France, H. (2002). *Nexus: Transpersonal approach to groups*. Calgary, AB: Detselig Enterprises Ltd.

Frankl, V. (2006). *Man's search for meaning*. Boston, MA: Beacon Press.

Gause, R., & Coholic, D. (2010). Mindfulness-based practices as a holistic philosophy and method. *Currents: New Scholarship in the Human Services, 9*(2), 1–23.

Gilbert, D., Harvey, A., & Belgrave, F. (2009). Advancing the Africentric paradigm shift discourse: Building toward evidence-based Africentric interventions in social work practice with African Americans. *Social Work, 54*(3), 243–52.

Gockel, A. (2009). Spirituality and the process of healing: A narrative study. *International Journal for the Psychology of Religion, 19*, 217–30.

Graham, J., Coholic, D., & Coates, J. (2006). Spirituality as a guiding construct in the development of Canadian social work: Past and present considerations. *Critical Social Work, 7*(1).

Graham, J., & Shier, M. (2012). Religion and spirituality in social work academic settings. In J. Groen, D. Coholic, & J. Graham (Eds.), *Spirituality in social work and education: Theory, practice, and pedagogies* (pp. 35–56). Waterloo, ON: Wilfrid Laurier University Press.

Greco, L., Baer, R., & Smith, G. T. (2011). Assessing mindfulness in chidren and adolescents: Development and validation of the child and adolescent mindfulness measure (CAMM). *Psychological Assessment, 23*(3), 606–14.

Groen, J., Coholic, D., & Graham, J. (Eds.). (2012). *Spirituality in social work and education*. Waterloo, ON: Wilfrid Laurier University Press.

Hick, S. (Ed.). (2009). *Mindfulness and social work*. Chicago, IL: Lyceum Books Inc.

Hodge, D. (2003). *Spiritual assessment: Handbook for helping professionals*. Botsford, CT: North American Association of Christians in Social Work.

Hodge, D. (2005). Spiritual lifemaps: A client-centered pictorial instrument for spiritual assessment, planning, and intervention. *Social Work, 50*(1), 77–87.

Hodge, D. (2013). Implicit spiritual assessment: An alternative approach for assessing client spirituality. *Social Work, 58*(3), 223–30.

Hodge, D., & McGrew, C. (2005). Clarifying the distinctions and connections between spirituality and religion. *Social Work & Christianity, 32*(1), 1–21.

Hugman, R. (2007). Foreword. In F. Gale, N. Bolzan, & D. McRae-McMahon (Eds.), *Spirited practices: Spirituality and the helping professions* (pp. v–vii). Crows Nest, NSW, Australia: Allen & Unwin.

Jung, C. (1964). *Man and his symbols*. New York, NY: Dell.

Kabat-Zinn, J. (1990). *Full catastrophe living: Using the wisdom of your body and mind to face stress, pain and illness*. New York, NY: Delta.

Kabat-Zinn, J. (1994). *Wherever you go, there you are: Mindfulness meditation in everyday life*. New York, NY: Hyperion.

Ka'opua, L., Gotay, C., & Boehm, P. (2007). Spiritually based resources in adaptation to long-term prostate cancer survival: Perspectives of elderly wives. *Health & Social Work, 32*(1), 29–39.

Kilmer, R., Gil-Rivas, V., Tedeschi, R., Cann, A., Calhoun, L., Buchanan, T., & Taku, K. (2009). Use of the Revised Posttraumatic Growth Inventory for children. *Journal of Traumatic Stress, 22*(3), 248–53.

Krill, D. (2011). Existential social work. In F. Turner (Ed.), *Social work treatment: Interlocking theoretical approaches* (5th ed., pp. 179–204). New York, NY: Oxford University Press.

Krogsrud Miley, K., O'Melia, M., & DuBois, B. (2013). *Generalist social work practice: An empowering approach* (7th ed.). Upper Saddle River, NJ: Pearson Education.

Limb, G., & Hodge, D. (2011). Utilizing spiritual ecograms with Native American families and children to promote cultural competence in family therapy. *Journal of Marital and Family Therapy, 37*(1), 81–94.

Milam, J. (2006). Positive changes attributed to the challenge of HIV/AIDS. In L. Calhoun & R. Tedeschi (Eds.), *Handbook of posttraumatic growth: Research and practice* (pp. 214–24). New York, NY: Lawrence Erlbaum Associates.

Nelson-Becker, H., & Canda, E. (2008). Spirituality, religion, and aging research in social work: State of the art and future possibilities. *Journal of Religion, Spirituality & Aging, 20*(3), 177–93.

Ott, M. J. (2002). Mindfulness meditation in pediatric clinical practice. *Pediatric Nursing, 28*(5), 487–90.

Pargament, K., Desai, K., & McConnell, K. (2006). Spirituality: A pathway to posttraumatic growth or decline? In L. Calhoun & R. Tedeschi (Eds.), *Handbook of posttraumatic growth: Research and practice* (pp. 121–37). New York, NY: Lawrence Erlbaum Associates.

Payne, M. (2005). *Modern social work theory* (3rd ed.). Chicago, IL: Lyceum Books Inc.

Pearlman, L. A., & Saakvitne, K. W. (1995). Vicarious traumatization: How trauma therapy affects the therapist. In L. A. Pearlman & K. W. Saakvitne (Eds.), *Trauma and the therapist* (pp. 279–94). Los Angeles, CA: Norton and Company.

Resilience Research Centre. (2014, May 21). What is resilience? Retrieved from http://resilienceresearch.org/about-the-rrc/resilience/14-what-is-resilience

Rice, S., & McAuliffe, D. (2009). Ethics of the spirit: Comparing ethical views and usages of spiritually influenced interventions. *Australian Social Work, 62*(3), 403–20.

Richards, P. S., Berrett, M., Hardman, R., & Eggett, D. (2006). Comparative efficacy of spirituality, cognitive, and emotional support groups for treating eating disorder inpatients. *Eating Disorders, 14*, 401–15.

Robbins, S., Chatterjee, P., & Canda, E. (2006). *Contemporary human behavior theory: A critical perspective for social work* (2nd ed.). New York, NY: Pearson Eduction.

Robinson-Keilig, R. (2014). Secondary traumatic stress and disruptions to interpersonal functioning among mental health therapists. *Journal of Interpersonal Violence, 29*(8), 1477–96.

Schiff, J., & Pelech, W. (2007). The sweat lodge ceremony for spiritual healing. *Journal of Religion & Spirituality in Social Work: Social Thought, 26*(4), 71–93.

Schonert-Reichl, K., & Lawlor, M. (2010). The effects of a mindfulness-based education program on pre- and early adolescents' well-being and social and emotional competence. *Mindfulness, 1*, 137–51.

Segal, Z., Williams, J., & Teasdale, J. (2002). *Mindfulness-based cognitive therapy for depression: A new approach to preventing relapse*. New York, NY: Guilford Press.

Semple, R., Lee, J., Rosa, D., & Miller, L. (2010). A randomized trial of mindfulness-based cognitive therapy for children: Promoting mindful attention to enhance social-emotional resiliency in children. *Journal of Child and Family Studies, 19*, 218–29.

Semple, R., Reid, E., & Miller, L. (2005). Treating anxiety with mindfulness: An open trial of mindfulness training for anxious children. *Journal of Cognitive Psychotherapy: An International Quarterly, 19*(4), 379–92.

Sheridan, M. (2002). Spiritual and religious issues in practice. In A. Roberts & G. Greene (Eds.), *Social workers' desk reference* (pp. 567–71). New York, NY: Oxford University Press.

Sheridan, M. (2009). Ethical issues in the use of spiritually based interventions in social work practice: What are we doing and why. *Journal of Religion & Spirituality in Social Work: Social Thought, 28*, 99–126.

Sossou, M., Craig, C., Ogren, H., & Schnak, M. (2008). Qualitative study of resilience factors of Bosnian refugee women resettled in the southern United States. *Journal of Ethnic & Cultural Diversity in Social Work, 17*(4), 365–85.

Sullivan, P. (2009). Spirituality: A road to mental health or mental illness. *Journal of Religion & Spirituality in Social Work: Social Thought, 28*(1/2), 84–98.

Thompson, I., Amatea, E., & Thompson, E. (2014). Personal and contextual predictors of mental health counselors' compassion fatigue and burnout. *Journal of Mental Health Counseling, 36*(1), 58–77.

Todd, S. (2004). Feminist community organizing: The spectre of the sacred and the secular. *Currents: New Scholarship in the Human Services, 3*(1).

Vollestad, J., Birkeland Nielsen, M., & Hostmark Nielsen, G. (2012). Mindfulness- and acceptance-based interventions for anxiety disorders: A systematic review and meta-analysis. *British Journal of Clinical Psychology, 51*, 239–60.

Weiss, A. (2004). *Beginning mindfulness: Learning the way of awareness*. Novato, CA: New World Library.

Social Work and Sexual Diversity

A Review

By Christine A. Walsh, Carey Mulligan, and Gio Dolcecore

Chapter Objectives

This chapter will help you develop an understanding of:

- The history of the LGBTQ movement in Canada
- The discourse of sexuality and gender
- Structural, cultural, and individual levels of oppression for LGBTQ
- Theoretical perspectives to frame social work practice with LGBTQ
- LGBTQ counselling guidelines
- Violence within LGBTQ relationships
- How to be an ally or advocate for the LGBTQ community

Introduction

Lesbian, **gay**, **bisexual**, **transgender**, and **queer** (LGBTQ) are a vibrant and diverse population, accounting for approximately 5 per cent of the Canadian population (Forum Research Inc., 2012). While LGBTQ rights in Canada are touted as some of the most advanced in the world, these gains have been fought within a context of historical oppression, which included in its most severe form the death penalty for same-sex activities. Social work practice with the LGBTQ population needs to adopt a strengths-based perspective that is responsive not only to the evolving diversity inherent within the community, but also with an understanding of the contexts and consequences of historical and current micro, mezzo, and structural levels of oppression. This chapter introduces the concept of sexuality to foreground an introduction of LGBTQ culture and developments in relationship to social work professional practice. Topics in this chapter include the LGBTQ movement and discourse surrounding sexuality and gender in relationship to structural oppression within the legal, education, employment, and healthcare sectors.

Intersectionality theory and queer theory are offered as theoretical applications, although they must be couched within counselling guidelines and contemporary issues within LGBTQ culture. The issue of interpersonal violence is provided as one example of a site for social work intervention. Intimate partner violence in queer relationships (QIVP) is examined as a means of dismantling possible assumptions regarding violence in these relationships. The roles of ally and advocate for LGBTQ individuals, groups, and communities are outlined for LGBTQ and heterosexual identified social workers. By the end of this chapter, you will have a better understanding of the intricacies of working with the LGBTQ population.

Discourses of Sexuality and Gender

Sexuality, other than the act of reproduction, has been a taboo subject for the past 300 years. Modern rendering of sexuality is rooted in Freud's theory of repression, which asserts that human beings repel their sexual desires from consciousness and subdue them in their unconscious (Huffer, 2012). Foucault (1978) questioned the imperative of suppressing a part of one's identity that, he suggested, was a consequence of societal rejection. Social rejection, in Foucault's rendering, includes those individuals who fall outside what is culturally considered "acceptable" as dictated by dominant structures such as government, religious, and traditional customs, including LGBTQ individuals and others marginalized based on race, ethnicity, culture, age, (dis)ability, income, and gender. Foucault (1978) proposed that there is no true happiness unless a person fully understands who she or he is and is able to express all aspects of her or his identity—that is, to be more sexual, more open, and most importantly to enjoy one's sexuality.

Western society has ascribed to a dualism of "accepted" and "unaccepted" sexualities (Sedgwick, 1990). Discourses around sexuality are not neutral; they are foundational with how we understand and comprehend ourselves and the world (Kolmar & Bartkowski, 2010). These discourses are socially constructed, structured by dominant institutions, and reinforced by cultural practices that are designed to maintain the power of dominant groups while assigning others to minority statuses (Bishop, 2002). They are also entrenched within cultural practices, resulting in the negative attitudes, behaviours, prejudice, and discrimination being sanctioned as normative. For example, historically LGBTQ identities were viewed as an abomination, resulting in LGBTQ individuals having to choose between asserting their sexual identity in the face of socially sanctioned prejudice and discrimination or hide or repress their identity to adopt privilege and avoid oppression (Stryker, 2009). (How members of the LGBTQ experience some of these prejudices and discriminations is illustrated in a case example in Chapter 16 by Natalie Blake-Noel.) Oppression, which exists on structural, cultural, and personal levels (Bishop, 2002), is defined as

> the social act of placing severe restrictions on an individual, group or institution. Typically, a government or political organization that is in power places

> these restrictions formally or covertly on oppressed groups so that they may be exploited and less able to compete with other social groups. The oppressed individual or group is devalued, exploited and deprived of privileges by the individual or group which has more power. (Barker, 2003, pp. 306–7)

Structural Level Oppression

The largest level of oppression is structural, and it is manifested through social institutions such as government, the law (including correctional institutions), educational systems, and healthcare systems (Bishop, 2002). Oppression on this level is enacted by discourses that create a dualist society of "right" and "wrong" identities, such as the criminalization of homosexuality. The following sections describe the experience of LGBTQ people in Canada within four major systems: legal, educational, employment, and healthcare. (A complementary discussion on inequality and structural level oppression can be found in Chapter 3 by Gordon Pon, Sulaimon Giwa, and Narda Razack.)

The Legal System

Prior to the 1970s, homosexuality was a criminal offence in Canada, with those accused of homosexual activities charged as sex offenders and, if convicted, sentenced to lengthy prison terms. Currently discrimination on the basis of sexual orientation in Canada is illegal (see Canada's Criminal Code, 2007, and the Charter of Rights and Freedoms, 1982), and rights of marriage have been extended to same-sex couples (Bill C-38, the Civil Marriage Act, 2005).

The justice system in North America and the Western world, however, has been criticized for its failure to adequately recognize the safety and psychological well-being of incarcerated LGBTQ individuals (Arkles, 2009). The disproportionately high risk of being assaulted and becoming a victim of crime while in prison (Arkles, 2009), and for transgendered individuals the inappropriate gender housing and the absence of any cases of gender reassignment surgery while in prison (Howell & Windsor, 2010) are noteworthy.

Although Canada has been an international leader in progressive human rights protection laws, internationally LGBTQ individuals are rarely protected by legislation (Balzer, Hutta, Adrian, & Hyndal, 2012); instead they are frequently subjected to harsh measures, including imprisonment and death.

The Educational System

Educational systems impact the optimum development of LGBTQ children. Without safe schools, LGBTQ children face an array of psychological consequences (Darwich, Hymel, & Waterhouse, 2012), including school disengagement, poor academic attainment, and early school leaving (Biegel & Kuehl, 2010). Sexual minority youth in Canada report lower feelings of belonging to their school community (Taylor et al., 2011) and are at much higher risk of experiencing physical and sexual abuse, harassment, and victimization at school or in the community (Saewyc, Konishi, Rose, & Homma, 2014; Taylor et al., 2011) compared to their non-LGBTQ peers. Sexual minority identities are also vulnerable to poor mental health; 28 per cent of LGB students in Grades 7 to 12 in British Columbia attempted suicide compared to 4 per cent of heterosexual youth (Saewyc et al., 2007), and 47 per cent of transgender youth in Ontario reported having seriously considered suicide in the previous year while 19 per cent attempted suicide (Trans PULSE, n.d., 2010).

Educational systems need to develop a safe space (Buzuvis, 2011) and support equality (Watson, 2005) for LGBTQ students through inclusive practices that legitimize and normalize LGBTQ identity. This could include curricula on gender fluidity and diverse affectional or romantic orientations to combat stigmas, prejudice, and discrimination and promote inclusion and equity.

Several provinces in Canada have formally endorsed gay–straight alliances (GSA), which are "school-based, student-led groups that promote welcoming, caring, respectful, safe, inclusive learning environments for sexual and gender minority students and their allies" (Alberta Government, 2013, p. 1). GSAs have also been found to reduce suicide ideation and attempts for LGB students and suicide ideation and attempts were reduced for heterosexual boys (Saewyc et al., 2014).

Employment

Work environments are not always safe spaces for LGBTQ individuals. Although the vast majority of employed LGB adults in Canada describe their employer's attitude as tolerant (93 per cent) and most (72 per cent) report improvements over the past five years, some (34 per cent of gay men and 40 per cent of lesbians) report experiencing discrimination during their professional lives and 28 per cent of respondents have not **"come out"** at their workplace because of perceived negative outcomes (Angus Reid Public Opinion Poll, 2011). The report concluded that

> a sizeable proportion of LGBT people who are not "out" in the workplace are concerned about social exclusion, ridicule, harassment and being passed over for a promotion—all factors that could negatively affect both an employee's sense of belonging and productivity. (p. 3)

The transgendered population faces higher rates of workplace discrimination than other sexual minorities, with low rates of employment—37 per cent were employed full time and 15 per cent were employed part time—and high rates of reported discrimination—18 per cent had been turned down for a job and 13 per cent reported being fired or constructively dismissed for being transgender, according to a 2011 Ontario survey (Bauer, Nussbaum, Travers, Munro, Pyne, & Redman, 2011).

Marginalization in workplace directly impacts workers' income. In Canada, "gay men have significantly lower personal incomes than similarly situated straight individuals, and lesbians have significantly higher personal incomes than straight women. Differences in labour force participation and intensity can explain some—but not all—of these differences" (Carpenter, 2008, p. 27). The relationship between sexual orientation and income in Canada has been described as "significant and complex" and requires further research (Carpenter, 2008, p. 27).

Although human rights campaigns in Canada and internationally have contributed to building awareness of the diversity of employees and the protection against discrimination based on gender and sexuality, individuals within work settings are not always protected. LGBTQ employees are often marginalized, and many fear losing their status as an employee or being treated unequally if their identities were discovered (Balzer et al., 2012). The experience of LGBTQ individuals within workplace environments also varies depending on multiple marginalized social locations (Crenshaw, 1991; McCall, 2005). Termed "intersectionality," this refers to the interrelationship of race, class, gender, and other status markers that results in systemic inequities (Choo & Ferree, 2010). For instance, a worker who identifies as LGBTQ who is an immigrant or racialized experiences oppression differently than a White, Canadian-born LGBTQ person. Compounding this problem, employment sensitivity training does not always attend to the diversity within the LGBTQ community, especially transgender individuals who are not always incorporated into sexuality diversity training (Bell, Özbilgin, Beauregard, & Sürgevil, 2011). (For a continued discussion on the unique challenges associated with intersectionality, see Chapter 1 by Alean Al-Krenawi, John R. Graham, and Nazim Habibov.)

The Healthcare System

In 2010, the National Institutes of Health convened an expert panel to assess the current state of knowledge about the health of LGBT people (Institute of Medicine, 2011). The panel concluded that LGBT individuals

> . . . experience unique health disparities . . . [and] there are subpopulations based on race, ethnicity, socioeconomic status, geographic location, age, and other factors. Although a modest body of knowledge on LGBT health has been developed, these populations, stigmatized as sexual and gender minorities, have been the subject of relatively little health research. (p. 1)

There is limited Canadian data on the health of LGBTQ populations. A large-scale national probability survey (the Canadian Community Health Survey [CCHS]), with data from the 2003 and 2005 cycles, found that patterns of healthcare needs and service utilization differed according to sexual identity (Tjepkema, 2008). Among those who identified as gay, lesbian, or bisexual (n = 346,000), lesbians reported lower rates of consulting family physicians and were less likely to have had a Pap test, and bisexuals reported more unmet healthcare needs than the majority population.

The CCHS found that GLB individuals were more inclined to consult mental health service providers, which was attributed to either a positive norm for using mental health services in the LGBTQ community (Tjepkema, 2008) or the fact that minority stress issues (the stress faced by individuals who belong to a stigmatized social category) could trigger seeking this type of care (Cochran, Sullivan, & Mays, 2003; Meyer, 2003). An intersectional approach is useful in understanding the interplay of health status and minority stress of LGBTQ individuals (Institute of Medicine, 2011).

The designation of LGBTQ as a population of special interest in the healthcare system means that LGBTQ patients (specifically trans individuals) are seen as an anomaly (Flores, Gee, & Kastner, 2009), and the failure of many healthcare centres to create space for LGBTQ individuals and families through inclusive policies contributes to systemic oppression (Spicer, 2010). Documentation that acknowledges same-sex couples uses fluid rather than binary gender categories, and settings that provide open and safe spaces that allow patients to be in control of self-disclosure, without judgment and prejudice regarding their identity, are more inclusive practices. Medical professionals with expertise in servicing the community are limited, which results in a scarcity of resources, prolonged waiting times, and travel, particularly in regard to transgender healthcare (Steever, Francis, Gordon, & Lee, 2014; Spicer, 2010).

Cultural Level Oppression

Oppression can be manifested culturally through dominant attitudes and beliefs that separate one group from the dominant group (Bishop, 2002). The intolerance from dominant groups, such as governing bodies and social groups, manifest oppression by encouraging practices that "other" sexual minorities (Markman, 2011). (For a continued discussion on the concept of the "other," see Chapter 2 by June Ying Yee and Gary C. Dumbrill.) Informal practices that discriminate against those who do not follow normative behaviour cater to traditional sexual and gender expectations, which separate LGBTQ individuals from the majority. This is referred to as "othering" and results in particular minority populations feeling unsafe, misunderstood, and separated from the community at large (Bishop, 2002). The othering of LGBTQ individuals results from promoting heteronormative and cis-normative identities, which assign those who fall into traditional gender and sex categories as normal and those who are gender nonconforming or sexually nonconforming as the other (Flores et al., 2009). Oppression through social, political, and institutional systems is termed **homophobia** or **transphobia**, although the use of these two words can be contradicting. "Phobia," defined as a fear, does not appropriately categorize the prejudice and discrimination directed at LGBTQ individuals or communities.

Hate crimes are an example of oppression enacted at the cultural level. Although limited, international official statistics and figures from nongovernmental monitoring suggest hate crimes directed at LGBTQ are increasing and constitute serious physical violence (Stahnke, Grekov, Petti, McClintock, & Aronowitz, 2008). Jeltova and Fish (2005) highlight that LGBTQ individuals have an increased risk of violence and a disproportionate risk for severe hate crimes within their daily lives compared to individuals who are heterosexual. In North America there have been numerous cases of LGBTQ individuals being victimized by physical forms of violence fuelled by discrimination and prejudice (Pepler & Craig, 2011). According to 2012 police-reported incidents in Canada, approximately 13 per cent of all reported hate crimes were motivated by sexual orientation (Allen, 2014).

Individual Level Oppression

Oppression that occurs at the personal or individual level "comprises those thoughts, attitudes, and behaviours that depict a negative pre-judgment of a particular subordinate group experience of both oppression and privilege" (Mullaly, 2002, p. 49). Individual forms of oppression are evidenced by attitudes, beliefs, and behaviours enacted at the interpersonal level. Adopting a micro view can assist in identifying the ways in which discrimination and prejudice manifest through social customs, personal beliefs, and attitudes (Bishop, 2002).

Bullying of sexual minority youth is an example of this form of oppression. The first national climate survey on homophobia, biphobia, and transphobia in Canadian schools found that 70 per cent of the more than 3,700 students surveyed reported hearing homophobic and transphobic comments in school, and LGBTQ students reported high rates of verbal, physical, and sexual harassment and feeling unsafe at school (Taylor et al., 2011).

Gay Liberation

Starting in the late 1950s and early 1960s, the Royal Canadian Mounted Police (RCMP) began an extreme anti-gay/anti-lesbian security campaign in an effort to stop "sexual abnormalities," which included, among other activities, a series of bathhouse raids in Toronto (Kinsman, 1995, p. 134). In the 1970s, gay rights organizations were formed throughout Canada. Prominent incidents included the Ottawa Sex Scandal, in which 18 men were charged and publicly identified following a police raid, and protests were held in Montreal in response to the "clean up" of the gay village prior to the 1976 Olympics. The gay liberation movement in Canada is recognized as truly beginning on 5 February 1981, when more than 150 members of the bathhouse were charged for operating a "bawdy house." The following day 3,000 protestors took to the streets and mobilized against discriminatory arrests (Adam, Duyvendak, & Krouwel, 1999; Warner, 2002).

An important distinction of the first Canadian liberation was the dedication to diversity; those who took to the streets in protest represented individuals of colour, transgender, and an array of other diverse groups. Furthermore, the Toronto Bathhouse Riots marked an event where the existence of large numbers in one situation, geographical concentration, identified opposition, social positioning, and intellectual leadership were all available and used to produce a political community (Duggan, 2003).

Gay liberation should be understood as a movement to change the system. Duggan (2003) states that the LGBTQ social movements began as visible demonstrations to call attention to the inequalities of the LGBTQ community as a public issue rather than a minor private issue. Through the transformation of social attitudes, the liberation movement was committed to eradicating fixed notions of femininity and masculinity that would liberate other oppressed groups that did not fall in the normative constructed roles (Duggan, 2003).

In 1981, the first documented Dyke March took place in Vancouver (Burgess, 2012). The event attracted over 200 identified lesbians who gathered and took part in a protest march. Since then, annual Dyke Marches take place nationwide a day or two prior to annual pride events to demonstrate against lateral oppression within the LGBTQ community. This means specific community members who are not represented by the dominant White, able-bodied, gay male are made visible and celebrated. Women continue to struggle under forms of inequality even within the LGBTQ community. These struggles include gay male dominance in LGBTQ spaces and feminine inclusion within lesbian spaces (Burgess, 2012).

It wasn't until 2004 that annual Trans Marches began to take place to bring recognition to the violence and discrimination faced by transgender and gender nonconforming individuals. Trans Marches demonstrate a political action for equality and equal civil rights, and aim to dismantle stereotypes, discrimination, and violence by increasing acceptance and respect.

Theoretical Perspectives

Queer Theory

The term **"queer"** is more than a derogatory term for members of the LGBTQ community (Sedgwick, 1990). It points to an underlying challenge to view sexually diverse identities as a minority group compared to **cis-gendered** and heterosexual identities. Queer is defined within political, sexual, and gender categories. Politically it references the radical position in favour of gender and sexual fluidity and the performance of both in a "homonormative" fashion (Browne & Nash, 2010). Butler (1999) defined **homonormative** as the assimilation of heterosexual normalities, or the constructs given to gender and sexual appropriation.

The queer movement began in the 1990s when Act Up, a grassroots activist group, began political protests and formed a collective movement called homonationalism (Butler, 1988). **Homonationalism** is the collective energy of political movements that coexist together and strive toward equality for queers and other minority populations (Butler, 1999). The queer movement was supported by the early queer theorists (i.e., Butler, 1999; Foucault, 1978; and Sedgwick, 1990) who adopted a radical approach to community development through broadening a minority population by focusing on political action. Early movements, Butler (1999) argued, paid attention to hierarchies of responsibility, movement through overlapping and widely disparate structures, and the dynamics of power and control between minorities and the majority.

Post-queer theory has taken a paradigm shift with added focus on the intersection of social status and social location of individuals (Halperin, 2003). Queer theory also shifted its viewpoint on gender and sexuality from critically exploring the dynamics between identity and performance to examining the relationships of identity to various structures, systems, and forms of oppression. Post-queer theory is sensitive to the discursive production of sexual identities and mindful of the oppressive relationships that act as fundamental building blocks of self-development. This means that instead of viewing sexuality and gender as individual units of analysis, like contemporary queer theorists would, post-queer theorists view the intersection of self, environment, and the influences of relationships. Green (2002) conceptualized four changes to queer theory since the start of the millennium. First, that sexuality should be viewed as sexual power embodied in different levels of social life. Sexuality is expressed differently based on environment, the boundaries felt by individuals, and the binary dividers or structural forms of discrimination. Second, identity is always viewed as uncertain ground, as a consequence of the constant transformation people go through as they experience life and self-develop. Third, instead of viewing a rejection of civil rights strategies, post-queer theory stresses the transgression parody. "Transgression" is a term used when referring to politics and the deconstruction, re-envisioning, and projecting of an anti-assimilationist stance. Finally, post-queer theory interrogates areas that normally would not be seen as relating to sexuality and stresses the value of incorporating queer into anything that explores humanity. For instance, queer theorists push for LGBTQ recognition in research pertaining to domestic violence, parenting, and health studies, all of which typically exclude specific references to queer individuals.

Intersectionality

The term "intersectionality," conceptualized by Kimberlé Crenshaw (1991), is rooted in a social constructionist framework, which asserts that social categories are constructed depending on cultural and social circumstances and history. While race and gender are two aspects of identity, other elements such as class, age, (dis)ability, religious affiliation, sexual orientation, ethnicity, Aboriginal status, and other social categories are also relevant. (For further discussion on intersectionality, see Chapter 6 by Miu Chung Yan.)

Identity politics were born out of intersectionality because of the emphasis on barriers, which inhibit individuals from moving up the social ladder. Thus, the main objective of intersectionality is to interrogate groups and how individuals within them identify uniquely. When attempting to create policies, intersectionality creates an opportunity to evaluate how various subgroups may be affected.

One of the critiques of intersectionality is that it does not take into account the multiple subjectivities of marginalized individuals' lives based on location (Nash, 2008).

For example, a professional Aboriginal woman who is queer and disabled may experience systemic barriers, but she may also have privilege based on her class and age and by residing in an urban setting, while someone with many of the same identity characteristics may have different experiences. Therefore, when applying an intersectional lens in social work, there also needs to be consideration of an individual's subjective experience in living their multiple identities, rather than having their identity be a determinant of their lived reality.

Anzaldua (1987), who was a major contributor to intersectionality through queer and feminist theory, discusses the topic of clashing aspects of identity, which moves beyond a binary way of thinking into a new conceptualization of self. This concept of "The New Meztiza" refers to a person who is aware of how his or her multiple identities intersect and conflict and uses this standpoint as a way to challenge hegemonic binary constructs. This notion allowed for culture to be woven into our understanding of identity politics wherein multiple facets could be seen as empowering rather than mystifying. Intersectionality can be used by social workers as a tool to understand identity politics with their clients who present as having complex and fluid positions.

Counselling Practice with Sexual Minorities

Gay Affirmative Practice and Coming Out Models within Social Work

Gay affirmative practice (GAP) is an approach within the social work and counselling professions that "affirms a lesbian, gay, or bisexual identity as an equally positive human experience and expression to heterosexual identity" (Davies, 1996, p. 25). GAP aligns with other social work models, including person in environment, strengths perspective, and cultural competency models (Crisp & McCave, 2007). GAP is not a therapy but a set of guidelines for practitioners, within which social workers demonstrate warmth, unconditional positive regard, and empathy when hearing about discrimination, injustice, and complexity within client stories. Along with performing key interviewing skills, being knowledgeable with regard to LGBTQ issues is pivotal in moving forward with the counselling process. Practitioners must take the initiative to secure this knowledge to understand how clients are affected by internalized homophobia, social rejection and isolation, identity conflicts, as well as other manifestations of oppression (Langdridge, 2012).

"Conversion therapies" are not condoned by the National Association of Social Workers because of the lack of evidence-based research showing positive outcomes (Bieschke, Paul, & Blasko, 2007). A recent position statement from the Pan American Health Organization (PAHO, 2012) noted that "services that purport to 'cure' people with non-heterosexual sexual orientation lack medical justification and represent a serious threat to the health and well-being of affected people" (para. 1).

GAP can be used with a client who is **coming out**, which describes the cognitive and behavioural effects individuals may be experiencing in sexual identity development (Hill, 2009). Bilodeau and Renn (2005) summarized the history of models of identity development for non-heterosexuals. They noted that early models, based primarily on the experience of gay adolescents, proposed a linear model of identity development of gay men (i.e., Cass, 1979, 1984; Fassinger, 1991; Savin-Williams, 1988, 1990; Troiden, 1979, 1988). Moving from these early stage paradigms, "lifespan" models of sexual orientation development were proposed that accounted for social contexts and intersectionality (D'Augelli, 1994).

The medical and psychiatric models of LGBTQ identity development use the criteria of the Diagnostic and Statistical Manual (DSM) of psychiatric disorders (American Psychiatric Association [APA], 2000) to render transgendered identity as a disorder (Bilodeau & Renn, 2005). Similar to activist success in removing homosexuality as a mental illness from the 1973 edition of the DSM (Carter, 2000), activism by the transgendered community has resulted in the category "Gender Identity Disorder" being replaced in 2013 by "Gender Dysphoria," defined as emotional distress over "a marked incongruence between one's experienced/expressed gender and assigned gender" (APA, 2013).

Feminist, postmodern, and queer theorists present significant alternatives to medical and psychiatric perspectives on gender identity, suggesting that gender identity is not necessarily linked to biological sex assignment at birth, but is created through complex social interactions and influenced by the dynamics of institutionalized power inequalities (Butler, 1990, 1993; Halberstam, 1998; Wilchins, 2002).

In these conceptualizations of identity development, initially there will be an acknowledgement of dissimilarity from the heterosexual norm. In order to further understand one's sexuality, a person may continue to experiment sexually with members of the same gender and thus become more conscious of his or her orientation. Afterwards there may also be feelings of alienation from heterosexuals caused by nonconformity with heterosexual norms. In the next stage there is a suspected mutual identification with nonheterosexual counterparts while clarifying one's LGBTQ identity. Thus, a person may partake in her or his first queer relationship, recognize the feeling of being "othered," or begin to feel pride associated with her or his newly defined self. Within the last stage individuals begin to feel more at peace with their communities and begin to live within a space where they must navigate both heterosexual and nonheterosexual customs.

While there are models that describe the stages of identity development, clinicians must be aware that clients will not necessarily go through all stages in a linear fashion. Rather, they have their own unique experience of working through each stage. These models reflect primarily the experiences of gay, White, able-bodied, cis-gendered men living within the Western world and thus exclude queer individuals who do not fall into this spectrum (Bilodeau & Renn, 2005; Haldeman, 2000). Additionally, these models promote an individualistic framework, excluding the experiences of LGBTQ newcomers in Canada from collectivist cultures and others whose experiences of war, trauma, and displacement are not adequately captured (Fassinger & Arseneau, 2007).

Case Example 12.1

Faye, a 20-year-old White woman, was seen at the counselling centre intake regarding concerns of ongoing anxiety and the recent loss of her grandmother. During the first session she explained that her partner of two years had recently come out as transgender. Faye described this revelation as "shocking" and further explained that she was now left with many questions and feelings as to where she stood on the matter as well as her own sexual identity. When they first met her partner identified as a lesbian woman and Faye identified as a straight woman. Faye's current issues were grief and loss as a result of her grandmother's recent death and concerns about the nature of her sexual identity and her relationship.

When Faye first came out as lesbian two years ago, she described feeling the loss of her heterosexual identity as well as feeling uncertainty as to how she wanted to identify. Now Faye was asking herself, "What does my partner's transition mean for my own sexual identity?" "Will I be attracted to them if they choose to fully transition?" "What will my family and friends think of my partner's transition?" and "How will I explain this to other people?"

In response the counsellor validated Faye's thoughts, feelings, and concerns while also supporting, normalizing, and empathizing with her. It is important for social workers to reinforce the normalcy of the client's experience as well as to try to understand the circumstances that the client is facing.

The counsellor also determined with Faye that what was most concerning for her at this moment in time was her sexual identity. Faye noted that she felt as though she was at a crossroad where she could no longer identify as lesbian because of her partner's gender now being male. In addition Faye questioned her attraction to other cis-gendered males.

The counsellor also provided psycho-education pertaining to identity and orientation by identifying their differences and providing an open and safe space for further exploration. Furthermore, the options of queer, questioning, and bisexual were also introduced. Faye stated that bisexual and questioning were not something she felt described her identity entirely but rather limited her expression. The term "queer," however, was one she had not considered before and as a result wanted to do more research. The counsellor encouraged and supported Faye in her search for a term that she felt suited her, while also suggesting that it would be OK if Faye did not endorse a specific identity label.

During Faye's subsequent visit she revealed that she and her partner had decided to use the term "queer" to see if it worked for them. Faye explained that the term provided her with the option to remain fluid with the understanding that her sexuality and orientation could change over time. The counsellor reaffirmed Faye's identity by supporting her decision to identify as queer. The counsellor also provided a support group for LGBTQ individuals who had partners going through transition. Faye and the counsellor continued their work together, navigating the new relationship Faye was choosing to continue with her partner at that time.

Social Workers' Role as an Advocate

Social workers are required to act as both allies and advocates for LGBTQ communities in their professional roles according to codes of ethics. When advocating for an individual, the fundamental premise is to ensure equality is attained based on access to resources, services, and prospects (Watkinson, 2001). Human rights and social justice are key goals of advocacy. Advocacy should be a central facet in social work practice whether in policy, clinical work, research, or leadership employment.

Case Example 12.2

Sixteen-year-old newcomer Jadon has recently come out as LGBTQ and as a result has been asked to leave his home. He has come to your youth-serving agency for housing services. He experiences multiple intersecting forms of oppression: structures of poverty, racism, sexism, and heterosexism or cis-sexism all influence this individual's current circumstances and create or exacerbate his existing vulnerabilities. Although in your position as social worker you determine that meeting his basic needs for shelter, food, healthcare, financial resources, and clothes are imperative, you also recognize that accounting for Jadon's experiences of homophobia, transphobia, or biphobia must be understood to provide optimum care and to advocate effectively for him.

Initially you conduct an assessment of the client's situation. The focus of the assessment is to identify issues and sources of the current problem. It is important that you identity the kind of change Jadon is seeking. In some cases clients will not know what services and supports they are entitled to, and if this is the case with Jadon you need to be able to inform him of his rights and the types of resources your agency can provide. In the assessment phase, as a practitioner you also need to review available resources in terms of not only what your agency offers but also explore opportunities to develop further collaborations to meet the needs of this youth.

Once a goal is established such as "attaining housing," the process can move forward into developing a plan for advocacy for Jadon and youth who experience similar issues on a broader level. When devising the plan consider who needs to be contacted and in what time frame while collecting the resources needed to achieve the tasks outlined. Tasks to consider in creating an advocacy agenda include raising awareness about navigating systems, writing letters and meeting with key stakeholders, lobbying, using media, and mobilizing for effective programming and policy within agencies and government.

Once the plan for advocacy is developed it will need to be initiated or acted upon. It may need to be readjusted or re-evaluated depending on the outcomes of the actions taken (Family Services of Ottawa, 2008).

Social workers need to advocate for LGBTQ identified individuals based on the levels of oppression they experience enacted through an intersectional framework; sexual minorities are more than their sexual or gender orientation.

Social Workers' Role as an Ally

The word **ally**, used in many social justice initiatives, has different interpretations. According to Reynolds (2011), an ally is someone who is part of a privileged group yet works with other marginalized groups to dismantle various systems and structures of oppression that inhibit equality. Reynolds describes the position of ally to be fluid—in constant flux—where aspects of identity change based on the circumstances. For example, someone who presents as male may change his gender status in the future. Thus, while allies have privilege in some instances the canvas of oppression and privilege is able to transform over time.

Beginnings of theorizing oppression and privilege began in the late 1980s. McIntosh (1989) used the analogy of an "Invisible Knapsack" to illustrate how her unearned privilege as a White woman played out in her daily interactions within a racist, classist, and sexist society. This same concept can be applied to members of the LGBTQ community. Responsive practice in this context means that social workers should analyze their own social location and reflect upon areas of oppression and privilege. For example, if you are someone who identifies as heterosexual, what types of privilege do you possess? Or if you identify as LGBTQ what particular privileges do you possess within your own community that other members may not?

Areas of oppression that ought to be considered when exploring how one may be privileged are heterosexism and cis-sexism. Heterosexism, the belief system that reinforces the notion that heterosexuality is the norm, is illustrated when it is believed or assumed that others are heterosexual rather than queer in social interactions (Matthews, 2007). Cis-sexism is also a belief system that reinforces the notion that biological or assigned natal sex is one-dimensional (Mention, 2013). An example of cis-sexism is when someone fails to address a transgender individual by their preferred pronoun rather than their natal sex. Reflecting on one's cis-gender and heterosexual privilege as a social worker leads to a better understanding of what members of the LGBTQ community experience frequently and supports the social worker's goal of becoming a strong ally. This type of reflection may cause conflict or resentment; most individuals have a tendency to personalize unearned privilege. However, these forces are a consequence of larger systems and structures that have given rise to injustice and inequities. This does not mean, however, that those who possess privilege do not have a responsibility to work with the oppressed to build a more equitable future for all (Bishop, 2002).

Becoming an ally with the LGBTQ community requires listening to and developing an awareness of the issues considered important by the community. Adopting this stance also builds trust and facilitates the development of a deeper understanding of the community and your role as an ally. Speaking to friends, family members, or others who are queer identified may be a useful starting point. Additionally, forms of education such as attending information sessions, visiting LGBTQ community centres, reading LGBTQ materials, or searching the Internet for LGBTQ content offer opportunities to learn about and interact with the LGBTQ community.

While social workers cannot take responsibility for historical oppressive events experienced by members of sexual minorities, they can recognize the role of their profession in contributing to historical oppression and move toward developing more effective ally and advocacy roles for LGBTQ identified individuals, groups, and communities.

Contemporary Issues among Sexual Minorities

Queer Intimate Partner Violence (QIPV)

The literature on intimate partner violence (IPV) in heterosexual relationships is vast. In contrast, there is a marked lack of research specifically on violence in queer partnerships. This gap in research can result in misrepresentation of violence in queer relationships because of the misappropriation of readily available heterosexual studies of IPV. Relying on such research, in which heteronormative dynamics are assumed and expected, to understand queer intimate partner violence QIPV is problematic. To combat these dynamics, social work practitioners must refer to the literature on QIPV and be aware of their own biases and understandings of IPV, including gender dynamics.

IPV is abuse (physical, emotional, psychological, financial, spiritual, and sexual) that occurs between individuals in an intimate relationship. Although there is some debate, it is estimated that QIPV occurs at a similar rate among the LGBTQ community as does IPV among heterosexuals (Murray, Mobley, Buford, & Seaman-DeJohn, 2007). A 2015 meta-analytic review of self-identified lesbians found a mean lifespan prevalence rate of IPV of 48 per cent, the majority of which was psychological or emotional abuse (Badenes-Ribera, Frias-Navarro, Bonilla-Campos, Pons-Salvador, & Monterde-i-Bort, 2015).

Risk factors for QIPV can be as diverse as the individuals who compose the queer community. For Black lesbian women, poverty, substance use, history of trauma, and mental health symptoms are risk factors that enhance the probability of experiencing QIPV (Hill, Woodson, Ferguson, & Parks, 2012). QIPV in lesbian partnerships may be thought of as virtually nonexistent by mainstream society because of hegemonic gender assumptions that women are not inherently violent. Tactics that are used in QIPV with women include intimidation, isolation, threats, manipulation, and humiliation. Arising from the dual stigma of their sexual minority status and IPV exposure, sexual minority mothers face formal helping systems that invalidate their relationship, so they may rely instead on informal support networks (Hardesty, Oswald, Khaw, & Fonseca, 2011).

In the case of QIPV with men who have sex with men, it is suggested that there is a higher probability for physical violence (Gillis & Diamond, 2006); however, this may be a result of gender stereotyping with the application of a heterosexist lens. Queer men who have HIV are at higher risk of being victims of QIPV (Siemieniuk, Krentz, Miller, Woodman, Ko, & Gill, 2013). Further, abusive intimate partners may threaten to disclose the illness to friends, family, or other members of the community to control men who are not out about their HIV status.

Similar to IPV, QIPV is a serious social determinant of health, which has multiple acute and chronic impacts on the person being abused (Klostermann, Milletich, Kelley, Mignone, & Pusateri, 2011; Badenes-Ribera et al., 2015). QIPV, however, is more complex because of the social context in which it occurs. For example, mainstream services may not have the necessary resources or training, and victims may be isolated if they are not being open or fear reporting because of homophobia or heterosexism.

Summary and Conclusion

Throughout the past few decades the LGBTQ community has gone through many political changes and affirmations within the public realm. Liberation is most commonly understood as an event that has advanced human rights law and reduced homophobia and discrimination against queers in Canada. Nonetheless, in contemporary society there are still many issues that plague the LGBTQ community, including the protection of transgender persons in correctional facilities, availability of gender-neutral bathrooms, lack of services for sexual minorities experiencing IPV, discrimination within health-care settings, hate crimes, and protections within the workplace. As social workers it is crucial that in our practice we recognize how these problems affect LGBTQ members on individual, community, and systemic levels. Without this understanding we are limited in providing effective social work practice and in research and policy initiatives. This chapter provides only a glimpse into the diversity of the LGBTQ community through a critical social work lens. Thus, we actively encourage students to continue acquiring and deepening their knowledge regarding diversity and sexual minorities. If you yourself are part of the community, then it is also necessary to reflect on your position and how it may influence working with members of the community.

With regard to theory and practice, whether in research, policy initiatives, clinical applications, or community building, social work has a variety of theories to choose from. In this chapter we have outlined two dominant theories—queer theory and intersectionality—both of which can be useful when working with the LGBTQ community. These theories take a postmodern constructivist approach to working with sexual minorities, which recognizes identities as fluid, complex, contextualized, and dependent on social interactions. When combining theory with GAP, practitioners are better able to validate, support, empathize with, and normalize the client's experience. These theories can assist in critically examining the many structures, systems, and aspects of oppression with the end goal of social justice.

Heteronormativity and cis-sexism promote socially constructed dominant understandings of gender and sexual orientation. These can be resisted by reflecting on one's own privilege as well as taking action to educate others. Furthermore, homophobia, transphobia, and biphobia are an unfortunate but integral part of the lives of sexual minorities. Social workers have a role to play in advocating for LGBTQ to reduce these oppressive forces and promote their well-being. Recently, the term "ally" is used to outline the role of social workers in supporting marginalized groups while recognizing that they themselves are privileged. As a social worker engaged in social justice initiatives, having a thorough understanding of the structures and intersecting systems of oppression is necessary. It is our hope that this chapter has helped you as a student and future social work practitioner gain more insight into your own developing practice as well as inspired you to become more involved with this particular area of diversity.

Questions for Review

1. How does understanding the history of LGBTQ rights contribute to effective social work practice with sexual minority individuals or groups?
2. How are sexual minorities affected by structural, cultural, and individual forms of oppression? Provide five examples of this.
3. If you were to incorporate GAP into a support session with an LGBTQ identified individual, family, or group, what steps would you take? How would you evaluate the effectiveness of your intervention?
4. What unique tactics can be used in QIPV that may not be found in heterosexual partnerships? How would you tailor your intervention to address these unique tactics?
5. How does the concept of minority stress inform your work with a LGBTQ client?
6. How is queer theory relevant to social work practice? How can it be used to understand LGBTQ individuals, families, or groups?
7. When developing new policy or practice initiatives within your organization for elder LGBTQ Aboriginal individuals, how can intersectionality be helpful when considering this population?
8. Imagine that you are conducting a study in collaboration with the LGBTQ community. What are some biases or assumptions you would have at the beginning of the process and how would you mitigate them throughout the research process?

Suggested Readings and Resources

EGALE. (n.d). Discrimination and hate crimes. Retrieved from http://egale.ca/category/discrimination-and-hate-crimes

Fish, J. (2009): Invisible no more? Including lesbian, gay and bisexual people in social work and social care practice. *Social Work in Action, 21*(1), 47–64.

Haldeman, D. C. (1994). The practice and ethics of sexual orientation conversion therapy. *Journal of Consulting and Clinical Psychology, 62*(2), 221–2.

The International Gay and Lesbian Human Rights Commission. (2014). Information by country. Retrieved from http://iglhrc.org/content/information-country

Janoff, V. D. (2005). *Pink blood: Homophobic violence in Canada*. Toronto, ON: University of Toronto Press.

Morrow, S., & Beckstead, A. (2004). Conversion therapies for same-sex attracted clients in religious conflict: Context, predisposing factors, experiences, and implications for therapy. *The Counseling Psychologist, 32*, 641–50.

PFLAG Canada; http://www.pflagcanada.ca/en/about-e.html

Reynolds, V. (2011). Resisting burnout with justice-doing. *International Journal of Narrative Therapy and Community Work, 4*, 27–45.

References

Adam, B. D., Duyvendak, J. W., & Krouwel, A. (Eds.). (1999). *The global emergence of gay and lesbian politics: National imprints of a worldwide movement*. Philadelphia, PA: Temple University Press.

Alberta Government. (2013). *Creating welcoming, caring, respectful, safe learning environments: Gay-straight alliances in schools*. Retrieved from http://education.alberta.ca/media/7869893/gay-straight%20alliances%20in%20schools.pdf

Allen, M. (2014). Police-reported hate crime in Canada, 2012. *Juristat, 34*(1), 1–30. Statistics Canada catalogue no. 85-002-X. Retrieved from http://www.statcan.gc.ca/pub/85-002-x/2014001/article/14028-eng.pdf

American Psychiatric Association (APA). (2000). *Diagnostic and statistical manual of mental disorders* (4th ed., text rev. [DSM-IV-TR]). Washington, DC: Author.

American Psychiatric Association (APA). (2013). Gender dysphoria. Retrieved from www.dsm5.org/Documents/Gender Dysphoria Fact Sheet.pdf

Angus Reid Public Opinion Poll. (2011). *Canadian LGBT survey*. Retrieved from http://www.angusreidglobal.com/wp-content/uploads/2011/11/2011.11.15_LGBT.pdf

Anzaldua, G. (1987). *La conciencia de la mestiza:* Towards a new consciousness. In W. K. Kolmar & F. Bartkowski (Eds.), *Feminist theory: A reader* (3rd. ed., pp. 362–8). New York, NY: McGraw Hill.

Arkles, G. (2009). Safety and solidarity across gender lines: Rethinking segregation of transgender people in detention. *Temple Political & Civil Rights Law Review, 18*(2), 515–60.

Badenes-Ribera, L., Frias-Navarro, D., Bonilla-Campos, A., Pons-Salvador, G., & Monterde-i-Bort, H. (2015). Intimate partner violence in self-identified lesbians: A meta-analysis of its prevalence. *Sexuality Research and Social Policy, 12*(1), 47–59).

Balzer, C., Hutta, J. S., Adrian, T., & Hyndal, P. (2012). Transrespect versus transphobia worldwide: A comparative review of the human-rights situation of gender-variant/trans people. *Transgender Europe (TGEU), 6*. Retrieved from http://www.transrespect-transphobia.org

Barker, R. (2003). *The social work dictionary* (5th ed.). Washington, DC: NASW Press.

Bauer, G., Nussbaum, N., Travers, R., Munro, L., Pyne, J., & Redman, N. (2011, May). We've got work to do: Workplace discrimination and employment challenges for trans people in Ontario. *Trans PULSE e-Bulletin, 2*(1). Retrieved from http://www.transpulseproject.ca

Bell, M. P., Özbilgin, M. F., Beauregard, T. A., & Sürgevil, O. (2011). Voice, silence, and diversity in 21st century organizations: Strategies for inclusion of gay, lesbian, bisexual, and transgender employees. *Human Resource Management, 50*(1), 131–46.

Biegel, S., & Kuehl, S. J. (2010). Safe at school: Addressing the school environment and LGBT safety through policy and legislation. Retrieved from https://escholarship.org/uc/item/6882f656#page-1

Bieschke, K. J., Paul, P. L., & Blasko, K. A. (2007). Review of empirical research focused on the experience of lesbian, gay, and bisexual clients in counseling and psychotherapy. In K. Bieschke, R. Perez, & K. DeBord (Eds.), *Handbook of counseling and psychotherapy with lesbian, gay, bisexual, and transgender clients* (2nd ed., pp. 293–316). Washington, DC: American Psychological Association.

Bilodeau, B. L., & Renn, K. A. (2005). Analysis of LGBT identity development models and implications for practice. *New Directions for Student Services, 111*, 25–39.

Bishop, A. (2002). *Becoming an ally: Breaking the cycle of oppression* (2nd ed.). Halifax, NS: Fernwood.

Browne, K., & Nash, C. (Eds.). (2010) *Queer methods and methodologies: Intersecting queer theories and social science research.* London, UK: Ashgate.

Burgess, A. H. (2012). *It's not a parade, it's a march! Subjectivities, spectatorship, and contested spaces of the Toronto dyke march* (Doctoral dissertation, University of Toronto). Retrieved from http://hdl.handle.net/1807/31701

Butler, J. (1988). Performative acts and gender constitution: An essay in phenomenology and feminist theory. *Theatre Journal, 40*(4), 519–31.

Butler, J. (1999). *Gender trouble.* New York, NY: Routledge.

Buzuvis, E. (2011). Transgender student-athletes and sex-segregated sport: Developing policies of inclusion for intercollegiate and interscholastic athletics. *Western New England University School of Law Legal Studies Research Paper Series, 11*(2), 1–59.

Carpenter, C. S. (2008). Sexual orientation, work, and income in Canada. *Canadian Journal of Economics, 41*(4), 1239–61.

Carter, K. A. (2000). Transgenderism and college students: Issues of gender identity and its role on our campuses. In V. A. Wall & N. J. Evans (Eds.), *Toward acceptance: Sexual orientation issues on campus.* Washington, DC: American College Personnel Association.

Cass, V. C. (1979). Homosexual identity formation: A theoretical model. *Journal of Homosexuality, 4*, 219–35.

Cass, V. C. (1984). Homosexual identity formation: Testing a theoretical model. *Journal of Sex Research, 20*, 143–67.

Choo, H. Y. & Ferree, M. M. (2010). Practicing intersectionality in sociological research: A critical analysis of inclusions, interactions, and institutions in the study of inequalities. *Theory and Society, 28*(2), 129–49.

Cochran, S. D., Sullivan, J. G., & Mays, V. M. (2003). Prevalence of mental disorders, psychological distress, and mental health services use among lesbian, gay, and bisexual adults in the United States. *Journal of Consulting and Clinical Psychology, 71*(1), 53–61.

Crenshaw, K. (1991). Mapping the margins: Intersectionality, identity politics, and violence against women of color. *Stanford Law Review, 43*, 1241–99.

Crisp, C., & McCave, M. L. (2007). Gay affirmative practice: A model for social work practice with gay, lesbian, and bisexual youth. *Child and Adolescent Social Work Journal, 24*, 403–21. doi:10.1007/s10560-007-0091-z

Darwich, L., Hymel, S., & Waterhouse, T. (2012). School avoidance and substance use among lesbian, gay, bisexual, and questioning youths: The impact of peer victimization and adult support. *Journal of Educational Psychology, 104*(2), 381–92.

D'Augelli, A. R. (1994). Identity development and sexual orientation: Toward a model of lesbian, gay, and bisexual development. In E. J. Trickett, R. J. Watts, & D. Birman (Eds.), *Human diversity: Perspectives on people in context* (pp. 312–33). San Francisco, CA: Jossey-Bass.

Davies, D. (1996). Towards a model of gay affirmative therapy. In D. Davies & C. Neal (Eds.), *Pink therapy: A guide for counselors and therapists working with lesbian, gay and bisexual clients* (pp. 24–40). Philadelphia, PA: Open University Press.

Duggan, L. (2003). *The twilight of equality? Neoliberalism, cultural politics, and the attack on democracy.* Boston, MA: Beacon Press.

Family Services of Ottawa. (2008). *Advocacy series handbook: A guide to being your own advocate*, 1–61.

Fassinger, R. E. (1991). The hidden minority: Issues and challenges in working with lesbian women and gay men. *Counseling Psychologist, 19*(2), 157–76.

Fassinger, R. E., & Arseneau, J. R. (2007). I'd rather get wet than be under that umbrella: Differentiating the experiences and identities of lesbian, gay, bisexual, and transgender people. In K. J. Bieschke, R. M. Perez, & K. A. DeBord (Eds.), *Handbook of counseling and psychotherapy with lesbian, gay, bisexual, and transgender clients* (2nd ed., pp. 19–49). Washington, DC: American Psychological Association.

Flores, G., Gee, D., & Kastner, B. (2009). The teaching of cultural issues in US and Canadian medical schools. *Academic Medicine, 75*(5), 451–5.

Forum Research Inc. (2012, June 28). One twentieth of Canadians claim to be LGBT. News release. Retrieved from https://www.forumresearch.com/forms/News%20Archives/News%20Releases/67741_Canada-wide_-_Federal_LGBT_(Forum_Research)_(20120628).pdf

Foucault, M. (Ed.). (1978). *The history of sexuality* (Vols. 1–3). New York, NY: Random House Inc.

Gillis, J. R., & Diamond, S. (2006). Same-sex partner abuse: Challenges to the existing paradigms of intimate violence theory. In R. Alaggia & C. Vine (Eds.), *Cruel but not unusual: Violence in Canadian families* (pp. 127–44). Waterloo, ON: Wilfrid Laurier University Press.

Green, A. I. (2002). Gay but not queer: Toward a post-queer study of sexuality. *Theory and Society, 31*(4), 521–45.

Halberstam, J. (1998). *Female masculinity.* Durham, NC: Duke University Press.

Haldeman, D. (2000). Gender atypical youth: Social and clinical issues. *School Psychology Review, 29*(2), 216–22.

Halperin, D. M. (2003). The normalization of queer theory. *Reflections: Queer Theory and Communication, 45*(2–4), 339–43.

Hardesty, J. L, Oswald, R. F., Khaw, L., & Fonseca, C. (2011). Lesbian/bisexual mothers and intimate partner violence: Help seeking in the context of social and legal vulnerability. *Violence Against Women, 17*(1), 28–46. doi:10.1177/1077801209347636

Hill, N. (2009). Affirmative practice and alternative sexual orientations: Helping clients navigate the coming out process. *Clinical Social Work Journal, 37*, 346–56.

Hill, N. A., Woodson, K. M., Ferguson, A. D., Parks Jr., C. W. (2012). Intimate partner abuse among African American lesbians: Prevalence, risk factors, theory, and resilience. *Journal of Family Violence, 27*(5), 401–13.

Howell, A., & Windsor, A. (2010). Comparison of the treatment of transgender persons in the criminal justice systems of Ontario, Canada, New York, and California. *Buffalo Public Law Journal International, 133*(28), 133–210.

Huffer, L. (2012). Foucault and Sedgwick: The repressive hypothesis revisited. *Foucault Studies, 14*(1), 20–40.

Institute of Medicine (IOM). (2011). *The health of lesbian, gay, bisexual, and transgender people: Building a foundation for better understanding.* Washington, DC: The National Academies Press.

Jeltova, I., & Fish, M. C. (2005). Creating school environments responsive to gay, lesbian, bisexual, and transgender families: Traditional and systemic approaches for consultation. *Journal of Educational and Psychological Consultation, 16*(1-2), 17–33.

Kinsman, G. (1995). Character weaknesses and Fruit machines: Towards an analysis of the anti-homosexual security campaign in the Canadian civil service. *Labour/Le Travail, 35*, 134–61.

Klostermann, K., Milletich, R. J., Kelley, M. L., Mignone, T., & Pusateri, L. A. (2011). *Partner violence and alcoholism: The issue of gender symmetry.* Washington, DC: American Psychological Association.

Kolmar, W. K., & Bartowski, F. (Eds.). (2005). *Feminist theory: A reader* (2nd ed.). Boston, MA: McGraw Hill.

Langdridge, D. (2012). *Existential counselling and psychotherapy*. London, UK: Sage.

Markman, E. R. (2011). Gender identity disorder, the gender binary, and transgender oppression: Implications for ethical social work. *Smith College Studies in Social Work, 81*(4), 314–27.

Matthews, C. R. (2007). Affirmative lesbian, gay, and bisexual counseling with all clients. In K. J. Bieschke, R. M. Perez, & K. A. DeBord (Eds.), *Handbook of counseling and psychotherapy with lesbian, gay, bisexual, and transgender clients* (2nd ed., pp. 201–19). Washington, DC: American Psychological Association.

McCall, L. (2005). The complexity of intersectionality. *Signs, 30*(3), 1771–800.

McIntosh, P. (1989). White privilege: Unpacking the invisible knapsack. *Peace and Freedom, 7*, 1–8.

Mention, A. (2013). Who is woman enough for feminism? Dialogue and conversation around inclusivity and exclusivity in feminism. *The LAS Student Research Journal, 6*, 146–54.

Meyer, I. I. (2003). Prejudice, social stress, and mental health in lesbian, gay, and bisexual populations: Conceptual issues and research evidence. *Psychological Bulletin, 129*(5), 674–97.

Mullaly, R. P. (2002). *Challenging oppression: A critical social work approach*. Toronto, ON: Oxford University Press.

Murray, C. E., Mobley, A. K., Buford, A. P., & Seaman-DeJohn, M. M. (2007). Same-sex intimate partner violence: Dynamics, social context, and counseling implications. *Journal of LGBT Issues in Counseling, 1*(4), 7–30.

Nash, J. C. (2008). Re-thinking intersectionality. *Feminist Review, 89*(1), 1–15.

Pan American Health Organization (PAHO). (2012, May). Latest news. Retrieved from http://www.paho.org/hq/index.php?option=com_content&view=article&id=6803&Itemid=1

Pepler, D., & Craig, W. (2011). Promoting relationships and eliminating violence in Canada. *International Journal of Behavioral Development, 35*(5), 389–97.

Reynolds, V. (2011). The role of allies in anti-violence work. *Ending Violence Association of BC Newsletter, 2*, 1–4.

Saewyc, E., Konishi, C., Rose, H., & Homma, Y. (2014). School-based strategies to reduce suicidal ideation, suicide attempts, and discrimination among sexual minority and heterosexual adolescents in Western Canada. *International Journal of Child, Youth & Family Studies, 5*(1), 89–112.

Saewyc, E. M., Poon, C., Wang, N., Homma, Y., et al. (2007). *Not yet equal: The health of lesbian, gay, & bisexual youth in BC*. Vancouver, BC: McCreary Centre Society.

Savin-Williams, R. C. (1988). Theoretical perspectives accounting for adolescent homosexuality. *Journal of Adolescent Health, 9*(6), 95–104.

Savin-Williams, R. C. (1990). Gay and lesbian adolescents. *Marriage and Family Review, 14*, 197–216.

Sedgwick, E. (Ed.). (1990). *Epistemology of the closet: Updated with a new preface*. Berkley, CA: University of California Press.

Siemieniuk, R. A., Krentz, H. B., Miller, P., Woodman, K., Ko, K., & Gill, M. J. (2013). The clinical implications of high rates of intimate partner violence against HIV-positive women. *Journal of Acquired Immune Deficiency Syndromes, 64*(1), 32–8.

Spicer, S. S. (2010). Healthcare needs of the transgender homeless population. *Journal of Gay & Lesbian Mental Health, 14*(4), 320–39.

Stahnke, T., LeGendre, P., Grekov, I., Petti, V., McClintock, M., & Aronowitz, A. (2008). *Violence based on sexual orientation and gender identity bias: 2008 hate crime survey*. Human Rights First.

Steever, J., Francis, J., Gordon, L. P., & Lee, J. (2014). Sexual minority youth. *Primary Care, 41*(3), 651–69. doi:10.1016/j.pop.2014.05.012

Stryker, S. (2009). *Transgender history*. Berkley, CA: Seal Press.

Taylor, C., Peter, T., Schachter, K., Paquin, S., Beldom, S., Gross, Z., & McMinn, T. L. (2011). *Youth speak up about homophobia and transphobia: The first national climate survey on homophobia in Canadian schools. Phase one report*. Toronto, ON: EGALE Canada Human Rights Trust.

Tjepkema, M. (2008). Health care use among gay, lesbian and bisexual Canadians. *Health Reports, 19*(1), 43–64. Retrieved http://www.statcan.gc.ca/pub/82-003-x/2008001/article/10532-eng.pdf

Trans PULSE. (2010). Ontario's trans communities and suicide: Transphobia is bad for our health. *Trans PULSE e-Bulletin, 1*(2).

Troiden, R. R. (1979). Becoming homosexual: A model of gay identity acquisition. *Psychiatry, 42*, 362–73.

Troiden, R. R. (1988). Homosexual identity development. *Journal of Adolescent Health Care, 9*, 105–13.

Warner, T. (2002). *Never going back: A history of queer activism in Canada*. Toronto, ON: University of Toronto Press.

Watkinson, A. M. (2001). Human rights laws: Advocacy tools for a global civil society. *Canadian Social Work Review, 18*(2), 267–86.

Watson, G. (2005). The hidden curriculum in schools: Implications for lesbian, gay, bisexual, transgender, and queer youth. *Alternate Routes: A Journal of Critical Social Research, 21*(1), 18–39.

Wilchins, R. A. (2002). *Queerer bodies*. In J. Nestle, C. Howell, & R. A. Wilchins (Eds.), *Genderqueer: Voices from beyond the sexual binary* (pp. 33–46). Los Angeles, CA: Alyson.

13 Reviving and Reshaping Gender in Social Work

By Sarah Fotheringham

Chapter Objectives

This chapter will help you develop an understanding of:

- Some of the prominent ideas and theories about gender
- The strengths, weaknesses, and implications of these ideas and theories
- How these ideas about gender permeate our daily lives
- The relationship between social work and gender
- Future directions of social work and gender
- How to begin thinking critically about gender and integrating gender into practice as a social worker

Introduction

When I mentioned to my friend that I was writing a chapter on gender for a social work and diversity textbook, she quipped, "That should be easy; 'Men are from Mars, Women are from Venus'!" Her comment was in reference to the popular *Men Are from Mars, Women Are from Venus: The Classic Guide to Understanding the Opposite Sex* by John Gray, a 1992 publication that has sold a remarkable 50 million copies worldwide. The book is predicated on the belief that men and women are so fundamentally unalike that we might as well be from different planets. Our communication styles, modes of behaviour, and emotional needs differ to such an extent that we require instruction, advice, and counselling to learn how to overcome our differences and coexist. The title of the book has become a popular symbolic representation about men and women, and its premise continues to dictate mainstream thinking about gender.

In truth however, gender is not so straightforward. As will be shown, gender is an incredibly multifaceted and theoretically dense idea spanning numerous disciplines, including biology, anthropology, sociology, psychology, history, and social work. Both within and across these fields, assorted theories and perspectives intertwine and sometimes contrast, creating a complex yet fascinating concept.

Outside of academia, issues related to gender bombard our daily news headlines and social media sites. Recent gender-related news topics range from "Gone but Not Forgotten: Documenting Canada's Missing and Murdered Aboriginal Women" (CBC Radio, 2014), "282 Join RCMP Sexual Harassment Class-Action Lawsuit" (*CBC News*, 2013), and "Did Sexism Play a Role in [Premier] Alison Redford's Downfall?" (Gedds, 2014) to daily reports on sexual assaults and domestic homicides. Additionally, growing mainstream attention toward transgender issues is also making headlines. Examples of these include "Transgender Woman Avery Edison Finally Moved to Female Jail after Being Locked in Male-Only Facility" (*National Post*, 2014b), "Miss Universe Disqualifies Transgender Finalist" (*Huffington Post*, 2012), and "School Violated Transgender Student's Human Rights by Refusing to let Fifth-Grader use Girls' Bathroom: U.S. Court" (*National Post*, 2014a). These are put forth to illustrate that issues of gender permeate our daily lives.

What's more, gender also shapes us as social workers. It influences us as students and professionals, affects our clients (McPhail, 2008), and is integrated into the very institution of social work (Cavanagh & Cree, 1996). Dealing with gender is therefore unavoidable, regardless of whether we work with clients, organizations, communities, or policy. Engaging in critical thinking about gender, reflecting on our own beliefs and assumptions and how these affect our practice, and providing gender-sensitive service models are essential aspects of ethical social work practice. This chapter provides a respectable start to meeting several of these objectives. It begins with an overview of a number of perspectives in answer to the question, "What is gender?" It then examines the social work literature on the topic, closing with a section dedicated to social work practice with gender. Throughout the chapter several case examples are presented to encourage critical thinking about gender.

What Is Gender?

This question does not have a simple answer. In popular discourse, **sex** is defined as being biologically male or female (Muehlenhard & Peterson, 2011; Nelson, 2006) and **gender** is used to describe the cultural characteristics of males and females (Connell, 2009; Kessler & McKenna, 1978; Muehlenhard & Peterson, 2011; Nelson, 2006). In the academic literature, however, there is no agreed upon definition (Hawkesworth, 1997; Muehlenhard & Peterson, 2011; Nelson, 2006). Sometimes the terms "gender" and "sex" are used interchangeably (Nelson, 2006), are not defined at all (Wood & Ridgeway, 2010), or vary widely in their meaning across publications (Muehlenhard & Peterson, 2011). Nelson (2006), for example, explains gender simply as "all expected and actual thoughts, feelings, and behaviours associated with masculinity and femininity" (p. 2), whereas Connell's (2009) definition is much more complex: "The structure of social relations that centres on the reproductive arena, and the set of practices that bring reproductive distinctions between bodies into social process" (p. 11). Even more advanced is West and Zimmerman's (2002) explanation of gender as "[t]he activity of managing situated conduct in light of normative conceptions of attitudes and activities appropriate for one's sex category" (p. 43). The following discussion will deconstruct this thinking and explore some of the theoretical ideas and areas of contention, ultimately examining the question, "What is gender?"

Gender Is Biologically Based

The first idea explored here is the idea that gender is biologically based. A biological reading of gender would maintain that a combination of genitalia, reproductive processes, chromosomes, and hormones dictate one's gender (Connell, 2009; Hawkesworth, 1997; Kessler & McKenna, 1978). In other words, an individual with a penis and testicles, reproductive organs that produce sperm, XY chromosomes, and testosterone would become male and masculine. This idea is often referred to as *biological determinism*—the standpoint that biological sex determines whether one will be masculine or feminine (Nelson, 2006).

Biologically based theories centre on two main constructs: *dichotomy* and *difference*. These are two of the most established themes in the gender literature, suggesting the continued superiority of biologically based ideas (Burdge, 2007; Connell, 2009; Hawkesworth, 1997; Markman, 2011; Nelson, 2006; Ridgeway & Correll, 2004). Dichotomy, the separation of two things, presupposes that any person can be identified and placed within one of two mutually exclusive categories: in regard to gender, this is either the male or female category (Burdge, 2007; Nelson, 2006). Importantly, within dichotomous thinking there is no room for ambiguity; a person must be one or the other (Markman, 2011).

From the notion of dichotomy emerges the significance of difference. Nelson (2006) explains, "Dichotomies are integral to the *dualism* that characterizes the predominant patterns of Western thought. Dualism is the doctrine that in any domain of reality there are two separate and distinct underlying principles representing opposition and difference" (p. 2). According to Nelson, dualism creates an "either/or" dichotomy that is intrinsically rooted in difference. In terms of gender, this means one is either male or female (dichotomy), and what males are, females cannot be, and vice versa (difference). This is the basis of gender difference.

On account of an emphasis on dichotomy and difference within biologically based theories, there is a long history of research focusing on the behavioural and biological differences between men and women (Deaux, 1999; Hyde, 2005; Kimball, 2001; Shields & Dicicco, 2011). In his book *The Gendered Society*, Michael Kimmel (2013) provides a thorough discussion on early biological explanations of the sexes and the role of science in advancing the idea that women were naturally inferior to men. Claims of smaller brain size, weaker dispositions, emotional fragility, and delicate reproductive systems were used as reasons to deny women a range of rights such as the right to vote, access to education, and work outside the home. Kimmel provides several examples of books and publications illustrating this history, including those written by notable people like Charles Darwin.

This early scientific research appeared to "prove" that men were naturally superior to women, subsequently resulting in the acceptance of women's **subordination** (Hawkesworth, 1997; Kessler & McKenna, 1978; Kimmel, 2013; Nelson, 2006). Kimmel describes, "no sooner had the biological differences between women and men been established as scientific fact than writers and critics declared all efforts to challenge social inequality and discrimination against women to be in violation of the '*laws of nature*'" (2013, p. 23, emphasis in original). Thus, not only was it acceptable that women were inferior, it was also believed to be natural; as such, there was no one person or system to hold accountable for women's inequality (Kimmel, 2013).

Early scientific research about women's natural inferiority has been widely discredited (women do not have smaller brain sizes when compared to their body size, for example) yet the underlying premise that men and women are profoundly different (think *Men Are from Mars, Women Are from Venus*) continues to prevail. What's more, this emphasis on difference upholds a gender hierarchy where men and male characteristics continue to be regarded as superior and systems of gender **oppression** endure (Burdge, 2007; Hyde, 2014; Nagoshi & Brzuzy, 2010; Risman, 2004; West & Zimmerman, 1987).

Just as an emphasis on gender difference lingers, so too does the belief in gender dichotomy. The story of Avery Edison, a transgender woman from the United Kingdom, illustrates how these prevailing ideas are embedded in our institutions. Upon entering Canada, it was found that Edison had issues related to her travel status. Members of the Canada Border Services Agency consequently jailed her in a male-only facility despite her declaration of being female and her passport identifying her as female. *CBC News* reported "Canadian law states that where a person is detained or imprisoned depends on his or her genitals" (*CBC News*, 2014, para. 10). Because Edison had male genitalia, she was identified as male. This was the sole factor in determining her gender. In biologically based explanations of gender, a person is either male or female and is identifiable simply by genital examination (Hawkesworth, 1997).

Gender Is Socially Constructed

The perspective that gender is socially constructed directly contrasts with biological determinism. A social construction perspective advances the idea that gender does not exist as a reality or in one's biology; instead gender is created from our ideas and emerges from our actions (Payne, 2005). Kimmel (2013) offers the following explanation:

> Our identities are a fluid assemblage of the meanings and behaviors that we construct from the values, images, and prescriptions we find in the world around us. Our gendered identities are both voluntary—we choose to become who we are—and coerced—we are pressured, forced, sanctioned, and often physically beaten into submission to some rules. (p. 114)

By way of explanation, not only is gender socially constructed through ideas and actions, we are also simultaneously active and passive in its social construction. We are active in the sense that we contribute to how gender is understood through our daily actions, but passive in the sense that society dictates and reinforces acceptable gender conduct (Kimmel, 2013). This is the circular nature of social construction, where individual ideas and behaviours actively construct gendered institutions while these same gendered institutions determine how individuals should think and behave (Payne, 2005).

The evidence for the social construction of gender is strong. Stanley (2002) summarizes it within three themes:

- Gender variations between cultures
- Gender variations in one culture over time
- Gender variations in one culture at one point in time

The first, gender variations between cultures, is based in anthropological work. It contends that what constitutes masculinity and femininity significantly differs across cultures (Connell, 1998; Deaux, 1999; Deaux & Stewart, 2001; Kessler & McKenna, 1978; Nelson, 2006). Kimmel (2013) offers several examples, including Dominican *pseudo-hermaphrodites* who are raised as the opposite gender and are permitted to

Case Example 13.1

Kelly is a soldier in the Canadian military. She is a White woman and a mother of two school-aged children. Her husband is the primary caregiver of the children when Kelly is away on deployment. Kelly recently returned to Canada after serving eight months in Afghanistan. She is struggling with nightmares, feelings of isolation, depression, and anxiety. You have an appointment with Kelly to discuss support options and provide information.

Points to Consider

- What is your reaction to Kelly being a woman and a soldier? A mother?
- What are your assumptions about women, men, femininity, and masculinity in the context of the military?
- What could Kelly be experiencing as a woman in the military? As a female soldier returning home to her family?
- How could this differ if Kelly were male?
- What if Kelly were a Chinese woman? How do you think her experiences would be different?
- How could your beliefs and assumptions about women in the military affect how you respond to Kelly?

transition to the other sex, the *two-spirited* person in some Indigenous cultures where an individual belongs to one biological sex yet assumes the gender of the other, and the *muxe*, considered a third gender in Indigenous parts of Mexico. If gender were strictly biologically based, there would be an absence of cultural variation.

The second type of evidence advanced by Stanley (2002) is gender variations in one culture over time. Here Stanley emphasizes history and the economic and social changes brought about by capitalism that resulted in new roles for men and women. For example, Kimmel (2013) explains that it was not until the 1950s when "traditional" gender roles were established. During this time, men were persuaded to be the breadwinners and women were informed their proper place was in the home. The women's movement of the 1960s and 1970s challenged these traditional beliefs and resulted in new conceptualizations about the roles of men and women. Femininity and masculinity look different today than they did in the 1950s. Ideas of appropriate gender behaviours have varied over time (Connell, 1998; Deaux & Stewart, 2001; Nelson, 2006), adding further support to the social construction of gender and the rejection of a biological basis.

Finally, according to Stanley (2002) the third theme supporting the idea that gender is socially constructed is due to the account of variations in one culture at one point in time. She claims that doubt has been raised about the belief of a strict biological distinction between males and females, insisting instead that such boundaries are actually quite blurred. She states, "women and men are not always nor emphatically distinguished from one another either biologically or psychologically, though social structures may treat people as though they must be distinguished from one another in sharp and discontinuous ways" (p. 34). The existence of **intersexed** individuals and transgendered persons are further confirmation of this position (Connell, 2009; Kessler & McKenna, 1978; Kimball, 2001; McPhail, 2008; Stanley, 2002). Biologically based explanations would view these people as unnatural and work toward placing them in the appropriate category. Kimball (2001) describes the common reaction of the medical profession to this natural ambiguity, which is to assign the child a male or female gender and then physically alter the child with the appropriate matching genitalia. In contrast, social construction–based perspectives view transgendered and intersexed people and the wide variation of masculinity and femininity as further affirmation that gender is not biologically determined.

Gender Is Not What One Is, but What One Does

In 1987, West and Zimmerman, feminist sociologists, proposed a new social constructionist approach to gender. Entitled "doing gender," this theory is regarded as one of the most significant writings in the field. "Doing gender" conceptualizes gender as an outcome of everyday regular activities: "we argue that gender is not a set of traits, nor a variable, nor a role, but the product of social doings of some sort . . . gender itself is constituted through interaction" (p. 129). They offer the following example: "The man 'does' being masculine by, for example, taking the woman's arm to guide her across a street, and she 'does' being feminine by consenting to be guided and not initiating such behavior with a man" (p. 135). Gender is therefore not what one is, but what one does (West & Zimmerman, 2002) and is continually practised in social interactions, both large and small (Shields & Dicocco, 2011). It is thus a process that simultaneously constructs its own meaning.

One of the main principles of "doing gender" is the creation of difference. Gender is socially constructed by "creating differences between girls and boys and women and men, differences that are not natural, essential, or biological. Once the differences have been constructed, they are used to reinforce the 'essentialness' of gender" (West & Zimmerman, 2002, p. 13). If men are doing dominance and women are doing subordination, for example, and these doings are interpreted as reflective of the natural social order, then the gender hierarchy is supported and legitimated (West & Zimmerman, 2002).

"Doing gender" aligns with the perspective that gender is a social construction. In some respects, when people are "doing gender" they are creating their own gender, but they are not free to conceive of gender in any way they choose (Connell, 2009). People are instead constrained by the prevailing gender order and held accountable for their gendered behaviour in relation to dominant and acceptable ideas about masculinity and femininity. The "allocation of power and resources not only in the domestic, economic, and political domains but also in the broad arena of interpersonal relations" are at risk if someone fails to do gender appropriately (West & Zimmerman, 2002, p. 21). This is the social constructionist aspect of the theory.

Gender Is about Women's Oppression

Feminism is one of the most significant influences on our contemporary understanding of gender. The movement emerged from a rejection of the biological argument that women were physically and emotionally inferior to men (Connell, 2009; Hawkesworth, 1997; Nagoshi & Brzuzy, 2010; Shields & Dicicco, 2011). In the 1970s a feminist psychologist, Rhoda K. Unger (1998), disputed the term "sex" due to the biological implication that women were naturally different than men and instead promoted the use of the word "gender" in psychological research. Indeed, this turned into a widespread shift as feminists appropriated the term "gender", using it to "distinguish culturally specific characteristics associated with masculinity and femininity from biological features" (Hawkesworth, 1997, p. 650). Feminism thus separated the term "gender" from "sex," rendering sex to biological territory and gender to the social arena (Connell, 2009; Hawkesworth, 1997; Muehlenhard & Peterson, 2011; Scott, 1986, 2010).

Feminism also forwarded the idea that the "personal is political" within discussions about gender. This refers to the argument that issues and experiences that a woman may endure are not a result of individual inadequacies (as biological determinism would suggest) but are grounded in political and social structures (McPhail, 2008). **Patriarchy**, a concept reflecting male power and privilege, was the chief structure feminists identified as problematic and became the core issue feminism worked to oppose (Kemp &

Brandwein, 2010). Thus, feminism sought to politicize women's subordinate treatment by challenging patriarchal structures that upheld men's power over women.

Sameness versus Difference

While the main objective of early feminism was to uproot ideas about biological determinism and establish women's equality, debate about how this should be achieved ensued. One significant area of tension was whether difference or sameness should be emphasized as the route to equality (Kimball, 2001; Shields & Dicicco, 2011). Kimball (2001) offers the example of the early suffrage and temperance movements in North America as illustration. Suffrage organizations, Kimball observes, advanced the idea that women were the same as men and could share in public responsibilities and political equality. Obtaining the right to vote, on par with that of men, was an important goal of the suffrage movement. In contrast, the temperance movement emphasized differences between men and women in an attempt to affirm women's power in traditional roles and among certain social issues like prohibition.

A more contemporary example, which used difference to promote equality, was Carol Gilligan's classic work *In a Different Voice* (1982). Through interviews with women undergraduates, Gilligan documented differing criteria for moral decision making. Many women, she argued, think in an "ethic of care," signifying intimacy, connectedness, and relation. Men, in contrast, reflect an "ethic of justice," stressing objectivity and rationality. Importantly, Gilligan strictly objected to these differences on the grounds they were hierarchical. Her main intention was to challenge the norm of male development and the associated assumptions of women's moral deficiency. Kimmel (2013) explains that Gilligan's position invoked heated debate among feminists, as it seemed to be advancing the idea that women and men were fundamentally different—a step back to biological determinism. He reports that groups who sought to discriminate against women used Gilligan's evidence to support their claims. Gilligan's work has since been disconfirmed through meta-analysis (Hyde, 2005); researchers now report there is no difference in moral reasoning between men and women (Kimmel, 2013). Despite this, these ideas continue to threaten women today; military branches and certain fire departments have been known to use the differences argument to justify the exclusion of women (Kimmel, 2013).

On account of difference being used to legitimate women's oppression, some feminists have rejected this stance as a means of promoting women's equality, turning instead to a focus on similarities, much like that of the early suffrage movement (Kimball, 2001). Hyde (2005) advances a gender similarities hypothesis, which posits that males and females are more similar than they are different. Hyde reviewed results from 46 meta-analyses on psychological gender differences. She found support for her hypothesis in that most psychological gender differences were in the "close-to-zero or small range" (p. 581). Hyde (2014) later reconfirmed her similarities hypothesis when she again found mostly trivial to small gender differences in cognitive performance, personality, social behaviours, and psychological well-being.

The sameness versus difference route to women's equality has long been a debate in feminist theory. Some have affirmed women are different than men—different, not less than—as a way of promoting and valuing unique characteristics of women. Others have advanced that women are the same as men and therefore deserve the same rights as men. Contemporary research supports the sameness argument. As it turns out, women and men are more alike than they are different. In fact, "the broad psychological similarity of men and women as groups can be regarded, on the volume of evidence supporting it, as one of the best-established generalizations in all the human sciences" (Connell, 2009, p. 65). Many now assert that there is greater variation *among* men and *among* women than there is *between* them (Connell, 2009; Kimball, 2001; Kimmel, 2013; Shields & Dicicco, 2011).

Using Gender as an Analytic Category

In addition to using the concept of gender to separate cultural influences from biological sex, early feminists also constructed the idea of "women" as one cohesive group.

Case Example 13.2

Cindy has been an RCMP officer for five years. She was recently transferred to a small town detachment after a senior RCMP officer retired. Four other officers, all men, are stationed at this location along with Cindy. They have worked together for close to 10 years and don't appreciate someone new or someone female coming to work with them.

During the first week of her new job, the men began making comments on her appearance—her long hair, her breasts, and how she "wiggles" when she walks. Cindy is very uncomfortable with these types of comments but tries to be a good sport by laughing along with them. The comments have lately become worse—they have begun to speculate about Cindy's virginity, her sex life, and whether she is gay. During one particular event, Gerald, a senior RCMP officer, propositioned her while the two were alone working a night shift.

Cindy is finding it harder and harder to come to work. She feels humiliated and ashamed and doesn't feel she could trust her fellow officers if she were in danger. Cindy finds out that several women have launched a lawsuit against the RCMP for sexual harassment. She is surprised to learn that almost 300 women from across Canada have come forward with stories of sexual harassment and sexual assault.

Points to Consider

- What is it about institutions like the RCMP that has resulted in numerous claims of sexual harassment from women?
- Why is it important to talk about this as a gender issue?
- What if Cindy were an Aboriginal woman? How would her experiences be different? How could race and gender intersect here?

Connell (2009) refers to this as the "categorical approach" to gender, where feminists grouped all women into the category of "female." In doing so, feminists stressed the commonalities and shared experiences among women while minimizing difference (McPhail, 2004a). This represents a second area of tension in feminist theory.

Like the difference/similarity argument presented above, feminists have also debated the merits of using a categorical approach to achieving women's equality. On one side, the use of categories for analysis and political purposes have, in many respects, served to bring important issues such as violence against women to the forefront. Feminists have used the categorical approach in a political manner; it became an important means to conduct gender analysis (McPhail, 2004a), demonstrate women's unequal treatment (Scott, 1986), and challenge the so-called naturalness of difference (Hawkesworth, 1997). McPhail (2004a) aptly notes the success of feminism's use of the categorical approach toward gender:

> Feminists who use gender as a unit of analysis have challenged male **bias**, privilege, and gender role stereotypes while placing the issues of women front and centre on the national agenda. Reforming discriminatory practices, building centers to serve abused and sexually assaulted women, and opening up new economic and occupational opportunities can almost entirely be attributed to the success of the women's movement. (p. 14)

Indeed, cataloguing the names and details of the 500 plus missing and murdered Aboriginal women in Canada, for example, demonstrates how the categorical approach can still bring both public and political attention to serious social issues. The 282 women currently involved in sexual harassment claims against the RCMP (*CBC News*, 2013) is another of many suitable examples where women as a group face oppression.

On the other side of the debate, Connell (1985) critiques this approach, citing its alignment with biological determinism. If feminism arose in objection to the prevailing belief that women and men were different because of biology, Connell indicates, then using the same biological argument to divide men and women into two **binary** categories is a contradiction. Connell states, "If 'all men' are seriously to be taken as a political category, about the only things they actually have in common are their penises. The biological fact of maleness thus gets attached to the social fact of power . . . conversely, the biological fact of femaleness becomes the central way of defining the experience of women" (1985, p. 265).

Like that of Connell, one of the strongest criticisms about feminism's use of the "women" category is from women of colour. Several notable Black feminists have charged that the mainstream feminist movement largely reflects the ideas of White, middle-class women and as such has largely excluded the ideas and experiences of non-White and low-income women (Collins, 2006; Dill & Zambrana, 2009; hooks, 1984). (For more in-depth discussion on White privilege, see Chapter 2 by June Ying Yee and Gary C. Dumbrill.)

The method of categorizing women as one fixed group assumes that all women experience gender oppression in the same manner—that all women are equally oppressed under male domination. In truth, this stance **essentializes** women (Brah & Phoenix, 2004; Crenshaw, 1991). hooks (1984) claims the certainty of a "common oppression" hides the "true nature of women's varied and complex social reality. Women are divided by sexist attitudes, racism, class privilege, and a host of other prejudices" (1984, p. 44). Yet by and large early feminist leaders largely rejected calls to examine issues of racism and classism embedded in White feminism (hooks, 1984), and the Western media concentrated on the experiences and voices of White, middle-class feminists in the United States (Dominelli, 2002). (For further discussion on social work and issues of racism in Canada, see Chapter 3 by Gordon Pon, Sulaimon Giwa, and Narda Razack.)

The idea of a common oppression thus took hold among those in power and, consequently, much of the feminist agenda reflected those who dominated the movement: White, middle-class, privileged women. **Intersectionality** theory is derived from these feminist critiques and is an important theme within the gender literature (Connell, 2009; Deaux & Stewart, 2001; Hawkesworth, 1997; Hyde, 2014; Kimball, 2001; Ridgeway & Correll, 2004; Risman, 2004; Shields & Dicicco, 2011; West & Fenstermaker, 2002). (For continued discussion on intersectionality, see Chapter 6 by Miu Chung Yan.)

How to respect difference while using the categorical approach for political purposes is one of the current debates in feminism (West & Fenstermaker, 2002). Gringeri, Wahab, and Anderson-Nathe (2010) explain:

> Of particular concern to some feminist scholars on difference is how to explore and work with differences in a way that does not rely on essential notions and categories of difference (such as race, class, gender, sexual orientation, and age) but, rather, recognizes the complexities of multiple, competing, fluid and intersecting identities. (p. 394)

Recognizing and respecting differences and intersecting identities is essential to many feminists, yet so too is the preservation of categorical analysis for political objectives. McPhail (2004a) worries, "taking away that collectivity engenders fears that it will lead back to invisibility, lack of recognition, and powerlessness" (p. 14), and "[a]lthough the categories themselves may be fluid and constructed, the reactions to them, violence, discrimination, and hate, are very tangible" (p. 15).

Gender Is Also about Men and Masculinity

Often when gender is theorized, it is done so in relation to women (Gringeri, 2005; McPhail, 2008). Men and masculinities, however, are also an essential part of the gender discourse. In fact, one of the most prominent ideas in the gender literature today relates to men and the theory of **hegemonic masculinity**. Principally shaped by feminist ideas about patriarchy, Black feminist critiques that reject the essentialization of gender, and core concepts of gay liberation such as power and difference (Connell & Messerschmidt, 2005), hegemonic masculinity is based on a model of multiple masculinities and analyses of power relations (Carrigan, Connell, & Lee, 1985). Simply put, hegemonic masculinity represents the dominant form of masculinity (among many masculinities) in a particular culture at a given time (Connell, 1998, 2002, 2005, 2009). It is the cultural ideal of men, a model from which many measure their manhood (Correia & Bannon, 2006).

In Western society, hegemonic masculinity typifies a White, heterosexual, and professional male who has characteristics of authority, competition, independence, control, aggressiveness, and the capacity for violence (Messerschmidt 2000, as cited in McPhail, 2008). This central construction of masculinity is largely reflected in society's fantasy figures such as film actors (Sylvester Stallone, Arnold Schwarzenegger, and Dwayne Johnson, a.k.a. "The Rock.") and sports heroes (Connell, 2002). An important component of hegemonic masculinity is the recognition that the majority of men do not fit the cultural ideal, but it remains the model many men aspire to (Connell, 1998).

Hegemonic masculinity exists in relation to hierarchy and exclusion (Connell, 1998). As the leading ideal, all other forms of masculinity are constructed as subordinate (Connell & Messerschmidt, 2005; Messerschmidt, 2012). Groups such as gay men, non-White men, and low-income men, like that of women, are subjected to exclusion, oppression, discrimination, and violence (Carrigan et al., 1985; Connell, 2002, 2005; Correia & Bannon, 2006). The power relations between subordinated masculinities and hegemonic masculinity is the crux of this theory.

Case Example 13.3

John is a 16-year-old Black male. He loves to play video games, listen to hip-hop music, and watch movies and sports. His favourite sport to watch is mixed martial arts. He found himself in trouble a few months ago when he was caught skipping school, stealing, and getting into fights. John lives with his mother in a rental apartment. She works three jobs just to pay the bills and is not around very much. His father left when he was a little boy and there are no other family members in his life. A teacher at school encouraged John to get involved with the local Boys and Girls Club. You are a social worker at the Boys and Girls Club, and John is in several of your programs.

Points to Consider

- What are your thoughts about the theory of a dominant masculinity?
- How could the presence of a dominant masculinity in a society affect someone like John?
- How could it affect John's relationships with other men? With women?
- If you are a male social worker, how could you work to demonstrate other ways of being masculine?
- If you are a female social worker, how could you support other ways of being masculine?

Gender Is a Fluid Concept

The final idea explored in this chapter is the conceptualization of gender as fluid. Queer theory has largely advanced this idea, rejecting rigid identity categories and the gender binary (Connell, 2009). **Heterosexism** and sexuality are significant elements here (Butler, 1990; Connell, 1985; McPhail, 2008). As such, this idea will only be briefly mentioned, as it is covered extensively in the chapter on sexual diversity (see Chapter 12 by Christine A. Walsh, Carey Mulligan, and Gio Dolcecore).

One of the iconic writings of these ideas was Judith Butler's *Gender Trouble* (1990) (Connell, 2009), a feminist work that challenged the very basis of the male/female binary. Yet, unlike some of the other perspectives presented in the biological section of this chapter, Butler extends her theory to include sexuality. She states that within the biological discourse it is assumed that both gender *and* sexuality result from one's biological sex. In other words, the male sex becomes the masculine gender, which results in heterosexuality. Butler dismisses the theory of a causal link between biology, gender, and sexuality, instead advancing the argument that both gender and sexuality are socially constructed. She further asserts that the means to challenging these prevailing constructions is not through the common feminist practice of solidifying women as a political category, but by subversive acts that destabilize sex categories and gender norms.

An example of someone who works to disrupt sex categories and gender norms is English singer/songwriter Boy George. On 12 February 2014 Boy George gave a television interview with Piers Morgan (CNN Live, 2014). He appeared with the top half of his face adorned in glittery makeup and carefully sculpted eyebrows—much like that of a woman celebrity. On the bottom half of his face however, was a full-grown goatee. If one covered the bottom half of his face, most would have identified him as a woman. If the top half of his face were covered, most would have identified him as a man. Butler would applaud this move. In using his appearance, Boy George challenges our dominant conceptions about what constitutes masculinity and femininity, demonstrating instead a more fluid, blended version.

Another gender-related story to illustrate gender as a fluid concept is from Facebook, one of the leading social media sites worldwide. Facebook now allows users in the United States to customize their gender identity on their Facebook page. The *Toronto Sun* reported that "some of the new options include **two-spirit, gender variant**, gender fluid, gender **questioning**, trans, and transgender" (Shah, 2014, para. 4). Boy George and Facebook are two of many examples of people and organizations embracing the idea of gender as a fluid and malleable concept.

Social Work and Gender

The first section of this chapter presented an overview of some of the leading ideas about gender. The concepts introduced represent some of the many varied and sophisticated ideas present in the literature. This section focuses on the literature on social

Case Example 13.4

Gina is a transgendered woman who was recently detained in an all-male facility by the Canada Border Services Agency when she tried to enter Canada three months ago on an expired visa. Gina has made an appointment with you at your resource centre. She arrives at the appointment wearing a dress, jewellery, and makeup. You notice she has a deep voice and some stubble on her chin. She is looking for support and information related to immigration.

Points to Consider

- What are your beliefs and assumptions about transgendered people?
- How could these beliefs and assumptions affect the way you treat Gina?
- How could you make sure Gina feels respected and included?
- What could Gina have experienced while detained in the male facility?
- What kind of support could Gina be looking for?
- If Gina were a transgendered man, what assumptions would you have?
- What would he have experienced if he were detained in an all-female facility?
- How could experiences differ between transgendered men and transgendered women?

work and gender. It begins with a review on the gendered nature of the profession, followed by a discussion of the influence of feminism. The section then closes with an examination on men and masculinities in social work.

Social Work: A Male-Dominated Profession

Social work has long been known as a female-dominated profession; the field employs large numbers of women compared to that of men. Sakamoto, Anastas, McPhail, and Colarossi (2008) reported that up to 79 per cent of social workers registered with the National Association of Social Workers in the United States are women. Similar trends are found across North America, the United Kingdom, and Australia (Bent-Goodley & Sarnoff, 2008; Christie, 1998, 2001; McLean, 2003; Pease, 2011).

Yet these large numbers of female social workers are predominately delegated to the poorly paid front-line positions, while male social workers hold the majority of posts in social work management and academia (Cavanagh & Cree, 1996; Christie, 2001; Cree, 2001; Dominelli, 2002; Kemp & Brandwein, 2010; McLean, 2003; McPhail, 2004b; Payne, 2005; Sakamoto et al., 2008). In addition to this, women social workers, on average, earn less than their male counterparts (Anastas, 2007; Bent-Goodley & Sarnoff, 2008; Koeske & Krowinski, 2004). In the most recent research to date, Anastas (2007), for example, reported that the National Association of Social Workers in the United States found a 14 per cent wage gap (approximately $7,000) between men and women in 2004, while controlling for other factors such as age, race, geographical location, and education. Sakamoto and colleagues (2008) indicate that even though Canada's national social work body, the Canadian Association of Social Workers, does not collect data on gender differences within the profession, comparable trends are also evident in Canada.

Due to the above realities, McPhail (2004b) takes issue with social work being labelled a "female-dominated" profession, arguing instead it is more truthfully a "female-majority, male-dominated" profession. In other words, while the number of women in the profession far outweighs the number of men, males are more likely to be in positions of authority. As such, some regard the profession as under male control (Dominelli, 2002; Lazzari, Colarossi, & Collins, 2009; Orme, 2009; Pease, 2011) where women are relegated to second-class status (Sakamoto et al., 2008).

Feminism and Social Work

The relationship between feminism and social work has been a fluctuating one. Kemp and Brandwein (2010) appropriately describe it as a "complex spiral, with multiple, intersecting dimensions and ongoing dialectic between continuity and change" (p. 342). From the time feminism entered social work's lexicon some 40 years ago until today's contemporary debates, the two have had a wavering connection.

Initially, social work was slow to integrate feminist ideas into the profession (Kemp & Brandwein, 2010). It "remained relatively unresponsive to emerging issues concerning women's changing roles and needs" and widely resisted integrating feminist ideas (Barretti, 2001, p. 268). Moreover, the feminist movement was likewise distrustful and critical of the social work profession in the early years as it was seen as an institution that upheld women's oppression and blamed women for their social problems (Orme, 2009). Payne (2005) adds, "It is widely accepted that the history of social work and its role in surveillance on behalf of the patriarchal welfare state means that women remain socially oppressed and social work does not do much to alter that" (p. 257).

Nevertheless, individual social workers were heavily shaped by the feminist movement (Gringeri et al., 2010; Kemp & Brandwein, 2010; Payne, 2005; Valentich, 2010, 2011b). These feminist social workers were instrumental in documenting women's inequalities such as poverty and violence (Orme, 2002), founding women's shelters and rape crisis centres (Valentich, 2011a), and were among the first social workers to critique women's problems in relation to their limited social position and traditional gender roles (Dominelli, 2002). Feminist social workers also objected to the androcentric and sexist nature of early social work interventions, promoted women-centred models, challenged structural oppression, and directly served women through community organizations (Cavanagh & Cree, 1996; Dominelli, 2002; Kemp & Brandwein, 2010; Payne, 2005). Over time, feminism has had a remarkable influence on the social work profession, widely shaping areas of practice including clinical models, social service structures, service provision, research, and policy (Cavanagh & Cree, 1996; Dominelli, 2002; Orme, 2009; Pease, 2011; Philips, 2007; Valentich, 2011b).

Yet despite feminism's known influence on the profession since the 1970s, many are now citing its decline (Barretti, 2011; Grise-Owens, 2002; Lazzari et al., 2009; Valentich, 2011a, 2011b). One point of weakening appears to be in social work education, where content related to gender, feminism, and sexism is quickly decreasing (Figueira-McDonough, Netting, & Nichols-Casebolt, 1998; Grise-Owens, 2002; McPhail, 2008). Orme (2003), Philips (2007), Valentich (2011b), and Hyde and Deal (2003) highlight that many social work students now consider feminism outdated and express a lack of awareness about feminist values and ideology.

A second area of decline is within academic publications (Barretti, 2001, 2011; Grise-Owens, 2002; Kemp & Brandwein, 2010). Barretti (2001, 2011) has been reviewing key social work journals to determine their content and coverage related to women since the 1970s. In 2001 she noted a "gradual improvement in coverage over [the last 10 years], but the coverage was still disappointingly low" (p. 288). Ten years later, Barretti found a more troubling pattern: There was sharp downturn in both women's and feminist content in academic journals compared to the previous 10-year period. Her reviews reveal that women's content and feminist perspectives in academic literature relating to social work has primarily been considered "as supplemental, not central—a special interest" (p. 265).

Social work curriculum and academic publications are two fundamental pieces of the social work profession where gender and feminism are losing ground. Furthermore, only certain areas of practice, such as work with violence against women, promote feminist analysis and ideology; in other areas, little feminist discourse is present (Valentich, 2011a). Payne (2005) states the profession as a whole has always resisted the full integration of feminism, relegating it to "a matter of special interest, rather than a general critique of social ideas and practice" (p. 257). This, in addition to the "male-dominated, female-majority" nature of the profession discussed above, has led some social work scholars to regard the profession as perpetuating gendered practices and patriarchal ideology (Lazzari et al., 2009; McPhail, 2008; Orme, 2009; Pease, 2011).

Subsequently, numerous social work writers are calling on the profession to reinvigorate gender and feminism in social work, noting its importance to critical thinking, anti-oppressive practice, and achieving aims of social justice (Dominelli, 2002; Gray & Boddy, 2010; Gringeri & Roche, 2010; Hyde & Deal, 2003; Kemp & Brandwein, 2010; McPhail, 2008; Pease, 2011; Philips, 2007). Furthermore, persistent gender-based issues such as intimate partner violence, sexual assault, sex trafficking, and poverty continue, adding fuel to the argument that feminist frameworks are still relevant (Kemp & Brandwein, 2010; Valentich, 2011a).

This declaration for renewal will also need to include a meaningful integration of contemporary scholarship from third-wave feminism, sociology, and queer and transgender studies. Unlike feminist theory, feminist social work study has largely failed to examine these newer ideas to any wide extent (Burdge, 2007; Gray & Boddy, 2010; Gringeri et al., 2010; Kemp & Brandwein, 2010; McPhail, 2008). Exceptions include recent articles on intersectionality (Mehrotra, 2010), transnational feminism

(Moosa-Mitha & Ross-Sheriff, 2010), postcolonial feminism (Gray & Boddy, 2010), and transgender theory (Burdge, 2007; Markman, 2011; McPhail, 2004a; Nagoshi & Brzuzy, 2010), but much more is needed.

Academic feminist social workers have begun to explore similar debates as those found in general feminist theory around solidarity, essentialization, and recognition of diversity and difference. In response to essentialization critiques (as presented above), some scholars have advocated for a more central position—one that respects difference and diversity while simultaneously protecting the feminist idea of solidarity. Kemp and Brandwein (2010), for example, state:

> Pressing reminders of women's continuing experiences of oppression, small and large, local and global, underscore the need for feminist frameworks that are capable of sustaining a dynamic commitment to solidarity and shared action in concert with deeply attentive recognition of difference. (p. 358)

Dominelli (2002) adds that social work is particularly poised to conduct practice in an anti-essentialist manner. She asserts, "As a profession, social work is committed to the uniqueness of every individual within his or her social situation. The opportunity to respond without essentialising the person or treating them as a member of a homogeneous category is unparalleled" (p. 8) and "feminist social workers seek to bridge gaps amongst women by examining the commonalities they share with each other alongside the specificities of the particular positions" (p. 9). The tension between conceptualizing how gender is used as a fundamental means of organizing society and distributing resources and power while respecting differences among women represents an area in need of continued examination in feminist social work (Orme, 2009).

Men and Masculinities in Social Work

Men and masculinities is an area that is receiving greater attention in social work. This is a relatively new development, as men have remained largely "invisible and genderless" in the social work literature (Cavanagh & Cree, 1996; Dominelli, 2002; Christie, 2001; Furman, 2010; McPhail, 2008, p. 40). One theme under exploration in the last decade is whether men should be engaged in social work. Predominately focused in Britain, this contentious debate resulted from several child sexual abuse allegations against male social workers that triggered a wider discussion about men, violence, and social work (Christie, 1998, 2001; McLean, 2003; Pringle, 2001). Keith Pringle (2001), for example, provides a provocative discussion on the issue of men employed in social work juxtaposed with sexual violence committed by men. He advances the argument that men's inclusion in social work is particularly valuable because of men's responsibility to challenge patriarchal ideas and benefits of male power, and "try to broadly change the ways they live their masculinity" (p. 46). Pringle maintains, however, that any discourse on men and social work needs to include a wider analysis of men's violence.

Rich Furman (2010), agreeing with Pringle, advocates that for women to be safe, men must engage in deconstructing and changing the behaviours of men and structures that reinforce violence against women. Christopher Hall (2007) shares this stance but grounds it in a place of ethics. He asserts that male social workers have an ethical responsibility to confront patriarchy and women's oppression: "unlike many men, as male social workers, we have a unique view into the world of oppression and power because we so closely see its effects and the toll it has taken on our female clients. We are therefore ethically bound to share that view with other power holders in society" (p. 221).

These pro-feminist ideas forwarded by male social workers are shared with a number of feminist social work scholars who also advocate for the participation of both men and women in ending women's oppression (Cavanagh & Cree, 1996; Cree, 2001; Dominelli, 2002; McPhail, 2008). For Gringeri (2005), "women and men live within and are shaped by systems of gender . . . limiting 'gender' to women really misses the boat: We would fail to see how social systems shape masculinities and femininities and the ways in which we are all influenced by them" (p. 399). Cavanagh and Cree (1996) fear that by excluding men an anti-feminist agenda would ensue, as illustrated in work by Kosberg (2002). In his writing, Kosberg advocates the position that social work has focused too long on women and gay men, neglecting the needs of heterosexual men. Pease (2011) identifies this type of effort as a backlash against feminist social work that fails to understand male privilege and power.

A second but related theme in the social work literature is hegemonic masculinity. Like that of the gender literature presented in the first section, much of the writing on men and masculinities in social work also centres on this theory (Furman, 2010; McLean, 2003; Orme, Dominelli, & Mullender, 2000; Pease, 2011). Pease (2011), for instance, underscores the need for male social workers who are critical of hegemonic masculinity and recognize male privilege. Christie (2001) adds that without male social workers questioning dominant forms of masculinity, male privilege becomes embedded in social work as an institution and established in social work practices.

For many of these writers, engaging in discussions about hegemonic masculinity and social work demands reflection on gender privilege and anti-sexist practice (Christie, 1998; Hall, 2007; Pringle, 2001; Pease, 2011). As observed by Christie (2001), "men social workers are expected to reflect on their gendered privilege and the gendered nature of their work (alongside issues of 'race', class, sexuality and disability)" (p. 2). Reflection on positions of privilege and anti-oppressive practice are fundamental aspects of social work for everyone (Dominelli, 2002), so exploring sexism and hegemonic masculinity should be easy to accommodate in social work curricula.

The final theme explored here is social work literature on men as clients. Exploring the dominant cultural ideal of masculinity in social work presents "a new lens through which to view men and boys. How would interventions change if social workers recognized men and boys' emotional and physical vulnerabilities as well as their strengths?" (McPhail, 2008, p. 41). Furman (2010), in his book *Practice with Men at Risk*, further discusses issues related to men seeking and accessing social work services. He notes

Case Example 13.5

You are a male social worker who has just been hired to oversee several programs at the YWCA. Most of your staff are women, as are the majority of your clients.

Points to Consider

- What are some gendered issues you should be aware of in regard to your female staff? Your female clients?
- How might you be perceived?
- How could you create a respectful and safe environment?

You are a female social worker who has been hired at a homeless shelter that predominately serves men.

Points to Consider

- What might you experience from the male clients?
- If you were working a night shift on the floor, would the presence of homeless men make you feel unsafe? Do you think a male social worker would feel the same?
- Why is there a difference between men and women?

that men traditionally do not ask for help, are at risk of being misunderstood because of difficulties with expressing feelings, and are commonly pathologized. He states:

> Because traditional male cultural norms make it difficult for many men to seek and receive help, the often not-so-subtle message that men are the problem, or are not wanted as clients, serves only to exacerbate matters . . . many men need help, and making services appealing, accessible, and effective for men is in everyone's best interest. (p. 6)

Furman specifies particular populations that are predominantly male and could potentially be social work clients, such as men as victims of violent crime, incarcerated men, and veterans, and presents practice guidelines for social work with men. Feminist scholars Cavanagh and Cree (1996), Orme et al. (2000), and Dominelli (2002) also discuss the importance of work with men as clients, detailing how to do so from a feminist perspective.

Social Work Practice

This final section moves the theoretical ideas into the practice realm by presenting a summary of seven ideas synthesized from the literature examining how to work critically with gender in social work:

1. **Understand/familiarize oneself with various theories, perspectives, and explanations about gender** (McPhail, 2008). Theories are explanations about why something is happening or where something comes from. Theories are inherently value laden and political; they inform our social work practice, interventions, and policy. It is therefore important for social workers to understand the various perspectives on gender, their respective strengths and weaknesses, and how these ideas compare to those of other social workers, organizations, and clients (McPhail, 2008). Further, social workers need to be able to identify their own personal beliefs, assumptions, and positions of privilege or oppression with respect to gender since it will affect how one responds in a particular situation or with a particular issue. If a social worker believes in the biological basis of gender, for example, he or she may react in a different way to a transgendered person or to a military woman than someone who holds a social constructionist view of gender. If you have read this chapter in its entirety, you have already started to explore and understand the various viewpoints. Further reading and self-reflection are recommended.
2. **Continue learning and integrating new ideas into practice** (Burdge, 2007; Gray & Boddy, 2010; Gringeri et al., 2010; Kemp & Brandwein, 2010; McPhail, 2004a, 2008). Part of the competency of the social work profession is a commitment to ongoing learning. Further, as we saw in the review of social work and gender literature, there are several emerging ideas that warrant social work attention. Intersectionality, various third-wave feminisms, men and masculinities, and transgender theories are all bringing different ideas to social work and gender. Certainly academic theoretical reading is important here, but supplementary forms of information can also prompt critical thinking. Following activists, institutions, and groups on Twitter, Facebook, and TED Talks, for example, also provide interesting debates in the public arena. A few websites are suggested at the end of the chapter as a starting point.
3. **Think critically** (Burdge, 2007; McPhail, 2004a; Nagoshi & Brzuzy, 2010; Payne, 2005). Critical thinking is a hallmark of social work (Payne, 2005). This flows nicely from the point above: We need to be open to new material and new ideas and continually ask questions of others and ourselves. Consider these questions:

   a. What implications does this idea/news story/opinion have on women/men/transgendered people?
   b. Who does the idea/news story/opinion serve?
   c. How is power involved?
   d. What perspective (or theory) does this idea/news story/opinion fit with?
   e. How does this idea/news story/opinion challenge my belief system?
   f. How does this idea/news story/opinion affect the way I would respond in a social work situation?
   g. Where can I explore these ideas further?

Critical thinking is an essential skill in social work across all domains. It requires us to actively analyze, synthesize, and evaluate information as it relates to social work practice.

4. **Self-reflection** (Christie, 1998; Dominelli, 2002; Hall, 2007; Hyde & Deal, 2003; Pease, 2011; Pringle, 2001). All social workers need to engage in self-reflection about privilege and areas of oppression. In terms of gender, this was most seen in the literature regarding men in social work and sexism, but can also include those who work with people who may not identify as either male or female. Self-reflection also involves assessing one's assumptions about behaviours, motivations, and attitudes based on stereotyped gender categories (McPhail, 2008) and identifying ways in which we may perpetuate oppressive ideas (Burdge, 2007).
5. **Use frameworks** (Dominelli, 2002; McPhail, 2008; Nagoshi & Brzuzy, 2010; Norman & Wheeler, 1996; Payne, 2005). Dominelli (2002) offers a feminist social work framework for clinical practice; McPhail (2008), Norman and Wheeler (1996), and Figueira-McDonough et al. (1998) present curriculum-based gender frameworks; Nagoshi and Brzuzy (2010) offer transgender theory as a framework for working with individuals with multiple and oppressed identities; and Furman (2010) provides ideas for working with men. Using practice frameworks developed by scholars can tremendously assist social workers in the field.
6. **Language** (Burdge, 2007; Nagoshi & Brzuzy, 2010). Language can be a key area of change in social work practice. Burdge (2007) states that social workers can challenge rigid categorizations of gender by referring to people in the manner they prefer and using gender inclusive language. Nagoshi and Brzuzy (2010) add that gendered pronouns such as "sir" or "madam" should be avoided, and McPhail (2004a) advances the use of continuums of gender rather than traditional male/female categories in diagrams and models. Language involves our verbal communication, but it also includes written materials. When clients come to an organization, are they filling out forms where they have to identify as either male or female? These are the types of questions social workers can pose in regard to language, gender, and social work practice.
7. **Advocacy/social justice** (Burdge, 2007; Dominelli, 2002; Markman, 2011; McPhail, 2004a; Nagoshi & Brzuzy, 2010). Social justice is a core concept of social work and a central tenet of feminism (Dominelli, 2002). Both share beliefs and values about the worth and dignity of people, diversity, social justice, social change, and **empowerment** and are concerned with person-in-environment analyses (Barretti, 2001; Gringeri, 2005; Gringeri & Roche, 2010; Lazzari et al., 2009). Nagoshi and Brzuzy (2010) prioritize advocacy as an important role for social workers working with transgendered people, specifically in relation to the pathologizing of transgenderism. Similarly, Burdge (2007) underscores social work's role in advocating for gender rights, challenging gender stereotypes, educating the public about gender diversity, and challenging the gender dichotomy.

By incorporating all seven actions into one's social work practice, you have begun to engage critically with gender. Through continued learning, reflection, engagement

Case Example 13.6

According to the Child Care Advocacy Association of Canada (2014), universal childcare is a system that is publicly funded through tax dollars. It is available to anyone who wants or needs childcare. Access is independent of income or other criteria. Examples of other publicly funded, universal programs are schools, hospitals, and fire halls.

In Canada, Quebec is the only province that offers universal childcare at $7 per day for everyone. The rest of Canada is based on a user-fee system where parents pay fees directly to the childcare provider. As a result, childcare is often expensive and difficult to access for many families.

Points to Consider

- What is the issue that a universal childcare policy tries to address?
- What are the assumptions in this policy about men and women?
- How would the implementation of a universal childcare policy affect women in Canada?
- Are there certain groups of women who would be affected differently? If so, how?
- How would the policy affect men?
- Why does this policy have different effects on men and women?
- What other issues are involved with this policy?

with theory, critical thinking, attention to language, advocacy, and use of already established frameworks, social workers are well poised to begin to interrogate how gender affects their practice.

Summary and Conclusion

Several prominent ideas in the gender literature have been presented in this chapter, examining the question, "What is gender?" Some of the viewpoints reviewed include (1) gender is biological; (2) gender is socially constructed; (3) gender is not what one is, but what one does; (4) gender is about women's oppression; (5) gender is also about men and masculinities; and (6) and gender is a fluid concept. It is important for social workers to comprehend and critique the various versions of gender, understanding how they affect individuals and institutions. As seen, biologically based ideas that centre on difference and dichotomy continue to prevail in popular culture, despite ample evidence for gender being socially constructed.

The profession of social work itself is also strongly influenced by issues of gender. As a female-majority, male-dominated profession, social work has an implicit connection with gender and a tendency toward male privilege. The strong but wavering influence of feminism on social work is significant, while so too is the appeal for a regendering of the profession. The academic literature and the social work education system are key areas where this can occur. Social workers can strive toward greater awareness and sensitivity about gender by engaging in critical thinking, reflecting on personal beliefs and assumptions and how these affect practice, and providing gender-sensitive service models. Areas of future engagement include the integration of third-wave feminist ideas, intersectionality theory, thought on men and masculinities, and queer and transgender theories.

Ultimately, social work is concerned with issues of social justice and inequality. Since gender is a foundational element that is used to organize society and distribute power and resources it cannot be ignored. Social work as a profession and individual social workers must be educated and informed about various gender issues, theories, interventions, and practice. Gender, together with race, ethnicity, religion, and sexuality, for example, are essential aspects of a well-rounded, ethical, anti-oppressive social work practice.

Questions for Review

1. What are some of the various perspectives about gender?
2. What are some of the strengths and weaknesses of each perspective?
3. How do these ideas affect individual people? Institutions? Policy?
4. What does social work have to say about gender?
5. What are your assumptions about gender? Have any of these changed after reading this chapter? If so, how?
6. How will you integrate your learnings about gender into your social work practice?

Suggested Readings and Resources

The Brown Boi Project; http://www.brownboiproject.org

Christie, A. (2001). *Men and social work*. New York, NY: Palgrave Macmillan.

Dominelli, L. (2002). *Feminist social work theory and practice*. New York, NY: Palgrave.

Everyday Feminism; http://www.everydayfeminism.com

Furman, R. (2010). *Social work practice with men at risk*. New York, NY: Columbia University Press.

hooks, b. (1984). *Feminist theory: From margin to center*. Cambridge, MA: South End Press.

Jhally, S. (Director), & Katz, J. (Featured). (1999). *Tough guise: Violence, media and the crisis in masculinity* [Documentary film]. Northampton, MA: Media Education Foundation. Available at www.mediaed.org.

McPhail, B. A. (2008). Re-gendering the social work curriculum: New realities and complexities. *Journal of Social Work Education, 44*(2), 33–52.

Men Can Stop Rape; http://www.mencanstoprape.org

Nelson, A. (2006). *Gender in Canada*. Toronto, ON: Pearson Education Canada.

References

Anastas, J. W. (2007). Theorizing (in)equity for women in social work. *Affilia, 22*(3), 235–9. doi:10.1177/0886109907302282

Barretti, M. (2001). Social work, women, and feminism: A review of social work journals, 1988–1997. *Affilia, 16*(3), 266–94. doi:10.1177/088610990101600302

Barretti, M. (2011). Women, feminism, and social work journals 10 years later, 1998–2007. *Affilia, 26*(3), 264–77. doi:10.1177/0886109911417688

Bent-Goodley, T. B., & Sarnoff, S. K. (2008). The role and status of women in social work education: Past and furture considerations. *Journal of Social Work Education, 44*(1), 1–8. doi:10.5175/JSWE.2008.334812008

Brah, A., & Phoenix, A. (2004). Ain't I a woman? Revisiting intersectionality. *Journal of International Women's Studies, 5*(3), 75–86.

Burdge, B. J. (2007). Bending gender, ending gender: Theoretical foundations for social work practice with the transgender community. *Social Work, 52*(3), 243–50. doi:10.1093/sw/52.3.243

Butler, J. (1990). *Gender trouble: Feminism and the subversion of identity*. New York, NY: Routledge, Chapman & Hall, Inc.

Carrigan, T., Connell, B., & Lee, J. (1985). Toward a new sociology of masculinity. *Theory and Society, 14*(5), 551–604. doi:10.1007/BF00160017

Cavanagh, K., & Cree, V. (1996). *Working with men: Feminism and social work*. New York, NY: Routledge.

CBC *News*. (2013, June 11). 282 join RCMP sexual harassment class-action lawsuit. Retrieved from from http://www.cbc.ca/news/canada/british-columbia/282-join-rcmp-sexual-harassment-class-action-lawsuit-1.1346440

CBC *News*. (2014). Transgender woman Avery Edison moved to women's jail after outcry online. Retrieved from http://www.cbc.ca/news/canada/toronto/transgender-woman-avery-edison-moved-to-women-s-jail-after-outcry-online-1.2532392

CBC Radio. (2014, February 19). Gone but not forgotten: Documenting Canada's missing and murdered Aboriginal women. *The Current.* Retrieved from http://www.cbc.ca/thecurrent/episode/2014/02/19/gone-but-not-forgotten-documenting-canadas-missing-and-murdered-aboriginal-women/

Child Care Advocacy Assocation of Canada. (2014). What do we mean by universality and accessibility? Retrieved from http://ccaac.ca/canadian-childcare-resources

Christie, A. (1998). Is social work a "non-traditional" occupation for men? *British Journal of Social Work, 28*(4), 491–510.

Christie, A. (2001). Introduction: Themes and issues. In A. Christie (Ed.), *Men and social work: Theories and practices* (pp. 1–7). Basingstoke, UK: Palgrave.

CNN Live (Producer). (2014, March 24). Boy George talks with Piers Morgan about coming out [Video file]. Retrieved from http://www.youtube.com/watch?v=O1FJygLf_kY

Collins, P. H. (2006). The politcs of black feminist thought. In E. Hackett & S. Haslanger (Eds.), *Theorizing feminisms: A reader* (pp. 51–61). New York, NY: Oxford University Press.

Connell, R. W. (1985). Theorising gender. *Sociology, 19*(2), 260–72. doi:10.1177/0038038585019002008

Connell, R. W. (1998). Masculinities and globalization. *Men and Masculinities, 1*(1), 3–23. doi:10.1177/1097184X98001001001

Connell, R. W. (2002). Hegemonic masculinity. In S. Jackson & S. Scott (Eds.), *Gender: A sociological reader* (pp. 60–2). New York, NY: Routledge.

Connell, R. W. (2005). *Masculinities*. Berkeley, CA: University of California Press.

Connell, R. W. (2009). *Gender: In world perspective* (2nd ed.). Cambridge, UK: Polity Press.

Connell, R. W., & Messerschmidt, J. W. (2005). Hegemonic masculintiy: Rethinking the concept. *Gender and Society, 19*(6), 829–59. doi:10.1177/0891243205278639

Correia, M. C., & Bannon, I. (2006). Gender and its discontents: Moving to men-streaming development. In I. Bannon & M. C. Correia (Eds.), *The other half of gender: Men's issues in development* (pp. 245–60.). Washington, DC: The International Bank for Reconstruction and Development/The World Bank.

Cree, V. (2001). Men and masculinities in social work. In A. Christie (Ed.), *Men and social work: Theories and practices* (pp. 147–63). Basingstoke, UK: Palgrave.

Crenshaw, K. (1991). Mapping the margins: Intersectionality, identity politics, and violence against women of color. *Stanford Law Review, 43*(6), 1241–99.

Deaux, K. (1999). An overview of research on gender: Four themes from three decades. In W. B. Swann, J. H. Langlois, & L. A. Gilbert (Eds.), *Sexism and stereotypes in modern society: The gender science of Janet Taylor Spence* (pp. 11–33). Washington, DC: American Psychological Association.

Deaux, K., & Stewart, A. J. (2001). Framing gendered identities. In R. K. Unger (Ed.), *Handbook of the psychology of women and gender* (pp. 84–97). New York, NY: John Wiley & Sons.

Dill, B. T., & Zambrana, R. E. (2009). Critical thinking about inequality: An emerging lens. In B. T. Dill & R. E. Zambrana (Eds.), *Emerging intersections: Race, class, and gender in theory, policy and practice* (pp. 1–21). Piscataway, NJ: Rutgers University Press.

Dominelli, L. (2002). *Feminist social work theory and practice.* New York, NY: Palgrave.

Figueira-McDonough, J., Netting, E. F., & Nichols-Casebolt, A. (1998). *Toward a gender-integrated knowledge in social work.* New York, NY: Garland Publishing Inc.

Furman, R. (2010). *Social work practice with men at risk.* New York, NY: Columbia University Press.

Gilligan, C. (1982). *In a different voice.* Cambridge, MA: Harvard University Press.

Gedds, L. (2014, March 20). Did sexism play a role in Alison Redford's downfall? *Global News.* Retrieved from http://globalnews.ca/news/1221870/did-gender-politics-play-a-role-in-alison-redfords-downfall

Gray, M., & Boddy, J. (2010). Making sense of the waves: Wipeout or still riding high? *Affilia, 25*(4), 368–89. doi:10.1177/0886109910384069

Gringeri, C. E. (2005). Naming our work. *Affilia, 20*(4), 397–400. doi:10.1177/0886109905279807

Gringeri, C. E., & Roche, S. E. (2010). Beyond the binary: Critical feminisms in social work. *Affilia, 25*(4), 337–40. doi:10.1177/0886109910384194

Gringeri, C. E., Wahab, S., & Anderson-Nathe, B. (2010). What makes it feminist? Mapping the landscape of feminist social work research. *Affilia, 25*(4), 390–405. doi:10.1177/088610991034072

Grise-Owens, E. (2002). Sexism and the social work curriculum: A content analysis of the journal of social work education. *Affilia, 17*(2), 147–66. doi:10.1177/088610990201700202

Hall, J. C. (2007). Perceptions of need and the ethicality of the male social work practice. *Families in Society, 88*(2), 214–22. doi:10.1606/1044-3894.3619

Hawkesworth, M. (1997). Confounding gender. *Signs, 22*(3), 649–85. doi:10.1086/495188

hooks, b. (1984). *Feminist theory: From margin to centre* (2nd ed.). Brooklyn, NY: South End Press Classics.

Huffington Post. (2012, March 24). Miss Universe disqualifies transgender finalist. Retrieved from http://www.huffingtonpost.ca/2012/03/24/transgender-miss-universe_n_1377147.html

Hyde, C. A., & Deal, K. H. (2003). Does gender matter? Male and female participation in social work classrooms. *Affilia, 18*(2), 192–209. doi:10.1177/0886109903251404

Hyde, J. S. (2005). The gender similarities hypothesis. *American Psychologist, 60*(6), 581–92. doi:10.1037/0003-066X.60.6.581

Hyde, J. S. (2014). Gender similarities and differences. *Annual Review of Psychology, 65*, 373–98. doi:10.1146/annurev-psych-010213-115057

Kemp, S. P., & Brandwein, R. (2010). Feminisms and social work in the United States: An intertwined history. *Affilia, 25*(4), 341–64. doi:10.1177/0886109910384075

Kessler, S. J., & McKenna, W. (1978). *Gender: An ethnomethodological approach.* New York, NY: John Wiley & Sons.

Kimball, M. M. (2001). Gender similarities and differences as feminist contradictions. In R. K. Unger (Ed.), *Handbook of the psychology of women and gender* (pp. 66–83). New York, NY: John Wiley & Sons.

Kimmel, M. (2013). *The gendered society* (5th ed.). New York, NY: Oxford University Press.

Koeske, G. F., & Krowinski, W. J. (2004). Gender-based salary inequity in social work: Mediators of gender's effect on salary. *Social Work, 49*(2), 309–17. doi:10.1093/sw/49.2.309

Kosberg, J. I. (2002). Heterosexual males: A group forgotten by the profession of social work. *Journal of Sociology & Social Welfare, 29*(3), 51–70.

Lazzari, M. M., Colarossi, L. G., & Collins, K. S. (2009). Feminists in social work: Where have all the leaders gone? *Affilia, 24*(4), 348–59. doi:10.1177/0886109909343552

Markman, E. R. (2011). Gender identity disorder, the gender binary, and transgender oppression: Implications for ethical social work. *Smith College Studies in Social Work, 81*(4), 314–27. doi:10.1080/00377317.2011.616839

McLean, J. (2003). Men as minority: Men employed in statutory social care work. *Journal of Social Work, 3*(1), 45–68. doi:10.1177/1468017303003001004

McPhail, B. A. (2004a). Questioning gender and sexuality binaries: What queer theorists, transgendered individuals, and sex researchers can teach social work. *Journal of Gay & Lesbian Social Services, 17*(1), 3–21. doi:10.1300/J041v17n01_02

McPhail, B. A. (2004b). Setting the record straight: Social work is not a female-dominated profession. *Social Work, 49*(2), 323–6. doi:10.1093/sw/49.2.323

McPhail, B. A. (2008). Re-gendering the social work curriculum: New relaities and complexities. *Journal of Social Work Education, 44*(2), 33–52. doi:10.5175/JSWE.2008.200600148

Mehrotra, G. (2010). Toward a continuum of intersectionality theorizing for feminist social work scholarship. *Affilia, 25*(4), 417–30. doi:10.1177/0886109910384190

Messerschmidt, J. W. (2012). *Gender, heterosexuality, and youth violence: The struggle for recognition*. Plymouth, UK: Rowman & Littlefield Publishers, Inc.

Moosa-Mitha, M., & Ross-Sheriff, F. (2010). Transnational social work and lessons learned from transnational feminism. *Affilia, 25*(2), 105–9. doi:10.1177/0886109910364366

Muehlenhard, C. L., & Peterson, Z. D. (2011). Distinguishing between sex and gender: History, current conceptualizations, and implications. *Sex Roles, 64*(11), 791–803. doi:10.1007/s11199-011-9932-5

Nagoshi, J. L., & Brzuzy, S. (2010). Transgender theory: Embodying research and practice. *Affilia, 25*(4), 431–43. doi:10.1177/0886109910384068

National Post. (2014a, January 30). School violated transgender student's human rights by refusing to let fifth-grader use girls' bathroom: U.S. court. Retrieved from http://news.nationalpost.com/2014/01/30/na0131-tba-a2

National Post. (2014b, February 11). Transgender woman Avery Edison finally moved to female jail after being locked in male-only facility. Retrieved from http://news.nationalpost.com/2014/02/11/transgender-woman-moved-to-ontario-female-correction-facility-after-internet-uproar

Nelson, A. (2006). *Gender in Canada*. Toronto, ON: Pearson Prentice Hall.

Norman, J., & Wheeler, B. (1996). Gender-sensitive social work practice: A model for education. *Journal of Social Work Education, 32*(2), 203–13. doi:10.1080/10437797.1996.10778451

Orme, J. (2002). Social work: Gender, care and justice. *British Journal of Social Work, 32*(6), 799–814. doi:10.1093/bjsw/32.6.799

Orme, J. (2003). It's feminist because I say so! Feminism, social work and critical practice in the UK. *Qualitative Social Work, 2*(2), 131–53. doi:10.1177/1473325003002002002

Orme, J. (2009). Feminist social work. In M. Gray & S. A. Webb (Eds.), *Social work theories and methods* (pp. 65–75). Thousand Oaks, CA: Sage Publications.

Orme, J., Dominelli, L., & Mullender, A. (2000). Working with violent men from a feminist social work perspective. *International Social Work, 43*(1), 89–105.

Payne, M. (2005). *Modern social work theory* (3rd ed.). Chicago, IL: Lyceum Books.

Pease, B. (2011). Men in social work: Challenging or reproducing an unequal gender regime? *Affilia, 26*(4), 406–18. doi:10.1177/088610991142428207

Philips, R. (2007). The place of feminism in contemporary social work education in Australia. *Advances in Social Work and Welfare Education, 9*(1), 54–68.

Pringle, K. (2001). Men in social work: The double-edge. In A. Christie (Ed.), *Men and social work: Theories and practices* (pp. 35–48). Basingstoke, UK: Palgrave.

Ridgeway, C. L., & Correll, S. J. (2004). Unpacking the gender system: A theoretical perspective on gender beliefs and social relations. *Gender & Society, 18*(4), 510–31. doi:10.1177/0891243204265269

Risman, B. J. (2004). Gender as a social structure: Theory wrestling with activism. *Gender & Society, 18*(4), 429–50. doi:10.1177/0891243204265349

Sakamoto, I., Anastas, J. E., McPhail, B. A., & Colarossi, L. G. (2008). Status of women in social work education. *Journal of Social Work Education, 44*(1), 37–62. doi:10.5175/JSWE.2008.200600103

Scott, J. W. (1986). Gender: A useful category of historical analysis. *American Historical Review, 91*(5), 1053–75. doi:10.2307/1864376

Scott, J. W. (2010). Gender: Still a useful category of analysis? *Diogenes, 57*(1), 7–14. doi:10.1177/0392192110369316

Shah, M. (2014, February 13). New Facebook gender options lauded. *Toronto Sun*. Retrieved from http://www.torontosun.com/2014/02/13/facebook-adds-news-gender-options

Shields, S. A., & Dicicco, E. C. (2011). The social psychology of sex and gender: From gender differences to doing gender. *Psychology of Women Quarterly, 35*(3), 491–9. doi:10.1177/0361684311414823

Stanley, L. (2002). Should sex really be gender—or gender really be sex? In S. Jackson & S. Scott (Eds.), *Gender: A sociological reader* (pp. 31–41). New York, NY: Routledge.

Unger, R. K. (1998). *Resisting gender: Twenty-five years of feminist psychology*. Thousand Oaks, CA: Sage.

Valentich, M. (2010). Finding one's own identity as a feminist social worker. *Canadian Social Work Review/Revue canadienne de service social, 27*(2), 221–37.

Valentich, M. (2011a). Feminist theory and social work practice. In F. J. Turner (Ed.), *Social work treatment: Interlocking theoretical approaches* (5th ed., pp. 205–24). New York, NY: Oxford University Press.

Valentich, M. (2011b). On being and calling oneself a feminist social worker. *Affilia, 26*(1), 22–31. doi:10.1177/0886109910392523

West, C., & Fenstermaker, S. (2002). Doing difference. In S. Fenstermaker & C. West (Eds.), *Doing gender, doing difference: Inequality, power, and institutional change* (pp. 55–80). New York, NY: Routledge.

West, C., & Zimmerman, D. (1987). Doing gender. *Gender & Society, 1*(2), 125–51. doi:10.1177/0891243287001002002

West, C., & Zimmerman, D. (2002). Doing gender. In S. Fenstermaker & C. West (Eds.), *Doing gender, doing difference: Inequality, power, and institutional change* (pp. 3–24). New York, NY: Routledge.

Wood, W., & Ridgeway, C. L. (2010). Gender: An interdisciplinary perspective. *Social Psychology Quarterly, 73*(4), 334–9. doi:10.1177/0190272510389005

Working with Individuals with Disabilities and Their Families

14

By Irene Carter

Chapter Objectives

This chapter will help you develop an understanding of:

- Disability and education about disability
- The social model of disability
- The history of disability
- Disability and independent living
- Disability and working with individuals and families
- Disability and promoting access to education and employment
- Disability and advocacy

Introduction

The purpose of this chapter is to look at how we might prepare social work graduates to be equipped to work with individuals with disabilities and their families. Definitions of disability are followed by the consideration of the need for education about the study of disability in social work. Research indicates that too many young people with disabilities face enormous difficulties transitioning from adolescence to adulthood (Lewis-Fleming, 2007; Milsom & Hartley, 2005), increasing the necessity for social and educational institutions to address the needs of persons with disabilities. Despite policy and legislative gains in recent decades (e.g., the Canadian Charter of Rights and Freedoms, 1982), many individuals with disabilities lack the social supports, training, or postsecondary education to secure employment. Canada needs to improve its record as far as people with disabilities are concerned, and this chapter helps address the need for social work students to know more about disability from the perspective of education on disability, models of disability, the history of disability, approaches to service delivery, the direction and tasks required for further accessibility in education and employment, and the role of advocacy.

The chapter is organized around what social work students need to know to successfully work with individuals with disabilities. Models of disability are explored with an emphasis on the social model of disability and the independent living model. The independent living movement is discussed with respect to the importance of maintaining independence. The history of disability is presented as essential to understanding the obstacles that were overcome through the work of activists, community organizations, academics, and the civil rights movement, which has resulted in the development of legislation (Canadian Human Rights Act, 1977; Canadian Charter of Rights and Freedoms, 1982; Ontarians with Disabilities Act, 2001; Accessibility for Ontarians with Disabilities Act, 2005). How family members can help with achieving greater accessibility is revealed through parental efforts to have children with disabilities grow with their peers in school and the community. The steps needed to increase accessibility in education and employment for people with disabilities is followed by a discussion that considers the role of advocacy in achieving positive outcomes.

Defining Disability

The International Classification of Functioning, Disability and Health (ICF) defines **disability** as "an umbrella term for impairments, activity limitations and participation restrictions" (World Health Organization, 2015). This definition takes into consideration that disability is the interaction between an individual's health condition, such as autism or depression, and the related personal and environmental factors, such as inaccessibility and limited social supports. The World Health Organization estimates that about 1 billion people, or 15 per cent of the world's population, has a disability, with 110 million, or 2.2 per cent, experiencing significant difficulties in functioning. Moreover, disabilities are increasing because of aging populations and increases in chronic conditions.

The 2012 Canadian Survey on Disability (CSD) (Statistics Canada, 2015) used the World Health Organization's ICF framework in defining disability as the relationship between body function and structure, daily activities and social participation, and environmental factors. The survey population comprised all Canadians aged 15 or older as of 10 May 2011, excluding the institutionalized population. The survey indicated that 3.8 million adult Canadians, or 13.7 per cent of the adult population, reported being limited in their daily activities because of a disability. The CSD definition of disability included those who reported sometimes, often, always, or rarely being limited in activities of daily living because of a long-term condition or health problems.

Statistics on people with disabilities imply there is as much variation and complexity among people with disabilities as among people in general. Being defined as having a disability does not automatically mean dependency or a loss of potential, productivity, social contribution, value, capability, or ability. Learning how to work with individuals with disabilities is to realize that disability is a natural part of life and is influenced by social factors.

The Study of Disability

The study of disability developed as a result of a movement by international individuals with disabilities. It is global and transdisciplinary, and it analyzes the politics of human variation from a variety of viewpoints and disciplines (Goodley, 2011). An interdisciplinary perspective challenges us to overcome "deeply ensconced professional and cultural responses to significant disability" (Kliewer, Biklen, & Kasa-Hendrickson, 2006, p. 169). Viewing the study of disability as a scholarly convergence of the humanities and social sciences, Kliewer, Biklen, and Kasa-Hendrickson suggest it displaces "traditional, reductionistic, psychological and medical orientations with their emphases on defect, impairment, and abnormality" (p. 188).

An interdisciplinary program of **disability studies** employs the arts and humanities to help students develop understanding, acceptance, and meaning. No single discipline is able to know and adequately understand the range of areas of information and knowledge needed to understand disabilities. The study of disability requires an interdisciplinary approach because of the complexity of life experienced by people with disabilities. Individuals with disabilities often need to adapt to the physical, technological, emotional, intellectual, economic, and social aspects of life.

Greater interdisciplinary activity allows students to become fully aware of injustices and continuing barriers for people with disabilities. For example, an interdisciplinary approach that combines the study of disability and social work results in the inclusion of disability in social work's critical analysis of gender, race, and class (Meekosha & Dowse, 2007). Such a process aligns social work with the rising development of disability studies. An interdisciplinary framework for the study of disabilities explores the realities of oppression and how we address it (Goodley, 2011), allowing for new forms of disability activism and new possibilities for research. The promotion and evolution of disability studies will depend on access to and alliance with courses, faculty, and research in other disciplines, as well as consultation with people with disabilities and community disability organizations.

Disability and the Social Work Curriculum

By 2020 there is expected to be a 38 per cent increase in demand for community-based services for people with disabilities (Laws, Parish, Scheyett, & Egan, 2010), making the likelihood of social workers working with a person with a disability in some capacity very high. With an aging population, many more of us will be affected by disability issues, whether for ourselves or an immediate family member, thus making the promotion of accessibility crucial. Russo-Gleicher (2008) suggests social workers need to be better prepared to work with the disabled population, indicating the need for curriculum development and further training. In its commitment to better the lives of marginalized groups, social work can play a more prominent role in confronting disability **stigma** (Gormley & Quinn, 2009). Further, social work education can take a leading role in embracing anti-discriminatory practice initiatives through its aim to achieve social justice, beginning by demystifying disability issues (Covarrubias & Han, 2011).

The study of disability has not, until recently, been introduced to the field of social work. Less than 40 per cent of social work practitioners with a master's degree recalled content on disability in their social work training (Tower, 2003). Although professionals are familiar with issues of gender, race, and class, there is an educational gap with regard to issues about disability (Meekosha & Dowse, 2007). Dunn, Hanes, Hardie, Leslie, and Macdonald (2008) suggest the need for enhancement; despite some improvements, they found obvious barriers to the inclusion of those with disabilities in terms of social work recruitment, admissions, accommodations, retention, graduation, employment, curriculum, hiring faculty and staff with disabilities, and university relations and resources. Courses that promote an inclusive environment and accessibility, using an interdisciplinary approach, need to be incorporated into the social work curriculum. Increasing student participation in the study of disability calls for a rise in the number of courses on disability and placement sites that promote knowledge about disability and **advocacy** skills related to **accessibility**.

Rees and Raithby (2012) used a longitudinal study to explore the attitudes of students toward working with persons with disabilities and how curriculum impacts these attitudes. Their findings reveal a lack of understanding about disability issues among social work students. For example, only 58 per cent of the subjects thought persons with disabilities experienced discrimination. Further lack of understanding was evidenced in students' responses where most did not consider people with depression or schizophrenia as having a disability. Rees and Raithby found some students were critical of having disability course content infused into the curriculum because it detracted from other specialized areas of social work, while other students thought that the disability material enhanced their needed knowledge of disability. Overall, their study suggests a lack of interest and preparation in working with persons with disabilities.

Recently, Canadian social work academics have joined with their US counterparts "in highlighting the importance of increased disability-related curriculum, disability-specific research, greater inclusion of people with disabilities both as students and faculty, and better preparation of social work students to work with people with disabilities" (Hanes, Carter, MacDonald, McMurphy, & Skinner, 2014, p. 5). Although there is a growing demand for services for individuals with disabilities, research suggests that social work students have minimal opportunities to obtain the knowledge necessary to feel as though they are competent to work in the field of disability. The study of disability encourages social work students to engage in finding effective ways to remove barriers for people with disabilities. Students need opportunities to join social workers and disability activists who work to address the growing societal demand to include those with disabilities in the larger culture.

Learning about the History of Disability

Studying the history of disability develops an understanding of the degree of historical injustice experienced by people with disabilities who were labelled with negative stereotypes, forced into dependency, and cut off from the rest of society. Brown, Radford, and Percy (2007) explain that our ancestors believed the reasons for disabilities were a result of possession by demons, sins by the parents, or omens or warnings from the gods. Recorded information on the early history of persons with disabilities is rare because of the high rate of mortality among children with disabilities, the tendency to ostracize or kill people with disabilities, and the likelihood that mild disabilities were not recorded. The Industrial Revolution brought the categorization and recorded descriptions of people with differences and the rise of the asylums, a huge social and economic investment that was intended to care for and train people with disabilities. Institutionalization influenced the public immensely in viewing the inmates as unable, unworthy, or unfit to make a contribution to society. Institutionalization ended over a period of decades because of the lack of progress shown by inmates, failed experimentations on patients, overcrowding, use of drugs, reduced public interest in funding, improved community conditions, increased interest in equality and human rights, and the cessation of support for the eugenics movement (Brown, Radford, & Percy, 2007).

In North America, optimism emerged in the mid-18th century about improving possibilities for persons with disabilities, which lasted until the 1920s (Neufeldt, 2003) when it was affected negatively by the eugenics movement. The ideas about eugenics stem from thoughts about the burden of disability, the danger of increasing numbers of disabled people, and the cost to society for their care (Shakespeare, 2008). The era of eugenics was characterized by social fear that if inferior specimens failed to die and reproduced, the lower classes might eventually predominate over superior beings (Shakespeare, 2008). Such thoughts, prevalent with the development of the belief in natural selection, were highly inaccurate and based on prejudice. By 1945, following the knowledge of the crimes committed by the Nazis, the idea of eugenics was largely rejected.

The modern Canadian approach to disability surfaced after World War II, when returning veterans were unhappy with the treatment they received and formed the Canadian Paraplegic Association in 1945 (Neufeldt, 2003). Mothers who advocated for group homes, education, and employment preparation and training formed the Canadian Association for Community Living (CACL), an early and continuing important Canadian disability organization (Stienstra, 2012). In the 1950s and 1960s, community-based treatment in North America began when more effective psychotropic drugs became available and policymakers became increasingly aware of the costs, substandard living conditions, and inadequate level of care in psychiatric institutions. Deinstitutionalization occurred without the provision of adequate supports, resulting only in modest benefits. Due to poverty, those discharged from hospital commonly secured substandard housing, which led to a worsening of their mental health condition, often resulting in readmission to institutionalized care. In the 1970s, large disability social movements surfaced that resulted in a change in public policy and the development of the consumer movement for independent living and school inclusion (Prince, 2009).

Case Example 14.1 Gerry Realizes He Is Not the Problem

When a social worker, Amanda, first met Gerry, who was diagnosed with paraplegia, he was living in a poorly kept one-bedroom apartment located in a medium-sized Canadian city in an area where illegal drug activity and prostitution frequently occurred. Despite a disability pension and access to the local food bank, Gerry was often without food or appropriate physical supports. He appeared depressed, lonely, and resigned to the thought that he was unable to improve his present circumstances. Prostitutes and homeless people used his apartment as a drop-in centre, eating his food, using his kitchen and bathroom, borrowing money that was never returned, and sharing sad stories that he could not mend. Gerry was overwhelmed and confined to his apartment because his wheelchair needed repairs. Gerry telephoned his physician for help. The nurse gave him the number for a continuing care agency, the office at which Amanda worked.

Gerry told Amanda he was raised by several foster mothers with whom he had lost contact. Gerry believed his mother was unable to care for him when he was left with limited use of his lower limbs following his experience with polio. Gerry was placed in a children's rehabilitation residence and discharged at age 18. Amanda formed a therapeutic alliance with Gerry, noting his strengths despite his physical barriers and social circumstances. Amanda helped Gerry approach the landlord about changing the locks to his apartment, made a referral to a physiotherapist, and arranged for repairs to Gerry's wheelchair. Amanda also assisted Gerry with applying for financially supported, accessible housing and recommended weekly visits for household maintenance and meal preparation and a gym membership to aid in strengthening Gerry's upper body.

Amanda promoted the idea that Gerry's disability was not his fault by having Gerry come to the realization that the way people and society viewed him was the problem and that all he needed was a few supports to live as others do. Gerry's shame left him as he accepted that others had taken advantage of him only because they felt desperate. Gerry grew stronger mentally as well as physically. Within two years Gerry met Chelsea, a neighbour, who was diagnosed with cerebral palsy. They applied for an accessible two-bedroom apartment. Gerry explained to Amanda that although Chelsea's parents were apprehensive about their decision to marry, he was hopeful they would eventually view it as a positive development. He asked Amanda if she knew of any programs that could help him finish school so he could eventually secure paid employment.

Points to Consider

- As a person with a disability, what physical and social obstacles does Gerry face?
- How did society react to Gerry as a person with a disability as a child? As an adult?
- As an adult, what social and economic barriers does Gerry face?
- What did Gerry have to do to obtain and maintain the supports he needed?

The Social Model of Disability

People with disabilities have been viewed through a **medical model of disability** in which the individual has a condition or deficit that is unwanted. The medical model has been criticized for viewing disability as an illness (Oliver, 1990). One of the fundamental problems with the medical model is that it blames the "victim," judging people as "sick" or "unemployable" on the basis of their ability to function as a "normal" person does. Moreover, in the medical model the professional is the one who makes the decisions to help the person who is sick recover. In the United Kingdom, the United States, and other Western countries, including Canada, the focus on medical rehabilitation became inadequate with the realization that social, cultural, political, and environmental barriers are more disabling.

The **social model of disability** was created by "a small but influential group of disabled activists" in the United Kingdom in the late 1960s and early 1970s (Shakespeare, 1998, p. 72). The social model of disability presented a view of people with disabilities as an oppressed, marginalized, nonethnic minority that is caused by society's failure to provide appropriate services (Oliver, 1990). The social model offered a means to address "environmental and social barriers which exclude people with perceived impairments from mainstream society" (Shakespeare, p. 78). Morris (2001) explains that personal experiences of being denied opportunities is not explained by bodily limitations but rather by disabling social, environmental, and attitudinal barriers. As with issues of gender and race, a change in thinking enabled disability to be viewed as a natural occurrence that does not lessen a person's access to a normal life (Silverstein, 2001; Mackelprang & Salsgiver, 2015). Viewing people with disabilities as an oppressed minority awakens us to the realization that people with disabilities face discrimination when they are confronted with architectural, sensory, attitudinal, cognitive, and economic barriers. The social model brought with it the realization that "it is the environment that creates and perpetuates the disabling condition, not the individual" (Rothman, 2003, p. 12).

The social model of disability emphasizes that negative social factors—not the disability—restrict participation, and that progressive social policy can alleviate and address oppression. The social model of disability resulted in legislation and laws that outlawed discrimination based on a person's characteristics and expected public agencies to provide programs and services that also meet the needs of individuals with disabilities. Progressive social policy somewhat reduced and addressed oppression (Goodley, 2000). To date, the accomplishments made possible by the social model of disability include policies to relieve oppression (Prince, 2004), promotion of accessibility for persons with disabilities through necessary support (Roeher Institute, 2003), and the philosophical foundation for the study of disability in postsecondary institutions.

The social model of disability continues to evolve as it strives to address the challenges faced by persons with cognitive disabilities and chronic illnesses, areas that have been less focused on while identifying structural barriers to persons with physical disabilities. The social model of disability is criticized for not paying enough attention to personal experience and feelings regarding the impact of impairment on individual lives: Even if all the barriers were removed, we would still have impairments (Oliver, Sapey, & Thomas, 2012). The social model of disability distracts from compensation for individual circumstances while it directs policies to alleviate oppression. To become involved in society as equals, many people with disabilities must not only have access to and means of gaining services, but they must also have the necessary supports (Roeher Institute, 2003, pp. 5, 9, & 19). Thus, the social model must continue to evolve by taking into account particular disabling impairments that require unique **social support**. Although public beliefs and a lack of awareness continue to contribute to limited policy reform and social adjustments (Prince, 2004), the social model remains influential because it allows others to see disabled people as "people" and not as a "disability."

Implications of the social model for social work training and practice include the need for social workers to collaborate with disability scholars in addressing issues that concern people with disabilities. Carter, Hanes, and MacDonald (2014) view "social work as a profession that needs to embrace a progressive, social justice perspective on disability, which broadens our understanding of the barriers faced by people with disability and of the options for moving toward a fully accessible and inclusive society" (p. 4). Schools of social work need to assist with the evolving orientation of disability from a medical to a social model that reflects the intent of the disability movement and progressive legislation. By studying the social model of disability, students are able to consider the consequences and dynamics of systemic barriers that compromise or exclude the participation of people with disabilities in social, economic, and political processes. Studying the social model of disability helps students build commitment to social change by committing, collectively, to accessibility for persons with disabilities.

The Independent Living Model

Independent living involves the management of one's own finances and care independently with programs that provide social and medical services, such as the modification of homes to allow accessibility. The independent living model regards the person with a disability as a responsible decision maker who is in charge of his or her care requirements. It stems from a philosophy that states people with disabilities should have the same civil rights and choices as do people without disabilities. Independent living organizations have conceptualized disability as a social pathology and advocated that empowerment and self-direction were the keys to achieving equality (Rioux & Samson, 2006). Stienstra (2012) writes that the independent living movement has shown that independence is "about being able to achieve goals and have control of one's own life" (Stienstra, 2012, 104).

The independent living movement mobilized "people with disabilities into disability organizations at the grassroots, national and international levels" (Rioux & Samson, 2006, p. 129). It was pioneered by the Canadian Paraplegic Association, founded in 1945 by World War II veterans with spinal cord injuries (Tremblay, 2003). World War II veterans rejected a philosophy of special services for the disabled and sought to participate fully in everyday society. People with disabilities continued to question the organization of services, and in many countries they began to demand a role in the management of these services (Rioux & Samson, 2006). People with disabilities began to organize services independently in independent living centres. Phillips (2003) describes how the Canadian Association of Independent Living Centres (CAILC), as a national umbrella organization, grew to consist of more than 24 local and autonomous independent living resource centres (ILRCs) that focused on self-advocacy.

The independent living model offers people with disabilities the opportunity to control their lives and to live independently in their communities, with independence defined as freedom to make one's choices. Thus, the independent living model de-emphasizes the disability and highlights the supports needed for the individual to succeed in his or her environment. This model portrays people with disabilities as experts in knowing their needs and aiming to adapt the environment to meet those needs.

Independent living is challenged by the controlling attitudes on the part of professionals and others, inadequate support services, and attitudinal, architectural, sensory, cognitive, and economic barriers. For example, Hauch (2014) writes that service provision tends to focus on specific clinical criteria, noting that "while more IL-based services, such as attendant outreach services and self-administered Direct Funding may be cost-effective on a per capita basis for hours provided, recent Governments have proven wary of expanding those services due to broad eligibility criteria" (p. 52). Services provided by the government are said to vary, but range from professional services, such as nursing and physiotherapy, to personal support and homemaking (Kuluski, Williams, Berta, & Laporte, 2012, p. 439). It is clear to Hauch that personal support workers and professional services are not provided in a manner conducive to the independent living philosophy. He writes that potential exists to deliver services with more of an independent living approach, pointing out that "the IL philosophy holds that people with disabilities should be granted control over their lives, including the physical assistance services that enable them to live in the community" (p. 53).

The independent living model exposes students to multiple issues that involve the actions of consumer leaders, activists, and professional managers in the design and delivery of support models for people with disabilities. It encourages students to analyze power, inequality, issues of access and related policies and practices, and to build strategies for actions. Students learn to appreciate how opportunities are needed to lead dignified lives and to exercise greater personal choice, control, and independence. It considers how people with disabilities access societal and community resources, engage socially, and take part in policy development and implementation. Self-advocacy and outcomes chosen by the person with a disability are viewed as solutions.

Students who study service delivery systems like the independent living model grow to understand how to put the social model of disability and the independent living models into practice, as evident in the case of Gerry in Case Example 14.1. Gerry's success in overcoming personal and social barriers is attributable to the development of empowerment and self-advocacy that the independent living model encourages. Gerry's story represents how much one can accomplish when acting independently, which is evident in Gerry's increased physical independence and his confident attitude in being able to access further social support.

Case Example 14.2 Shelly Learns to Advocate with Her Son

Shelly had been married for two years when her son, Adam, was born. Shelly and her husband, John, both worked, and nearby grandparents provided daycare. When Adam was about two years old, Shelly noticed that he did not appear to be developing as progressively as her sister's and friends' children were. Adam avoided eye contact and preferred to engage in repetitive play by himself. John insisted Adam would grow out of it. Initially, her family physician advised Shelly her son was only taking a bit longer to develop; however, at Shelly's insistence he referred Adam to a pediatrician who diagnosed Adam with a mild form of autism. Shelly was devastated, and the pediatrician arranged for an appointment with Beverly, a social worker, the same day.

When Shelly met with Beverly she began to cry uncontrollably, explaining that her baby was diagnosed with autism, her husband was in denial, and that she was overwhelmed with guilt and worry. Beverly acknowledged how much Shelly loved her son, Adam. They talked about how they could relieve some of Shelly's stress, allowing her to enjoy her son without so much worry by initially arranging for the supports that Adam and she needed. Together they developed a plan to apply and advocate for services, such as speech therapy and behavioural therapy. Shelly agreed to join a parental self-help group for autism to gain more information and support. Most importantly, Beverly and Shelly affirmed how the diagnosis did not lessen the joy Shelly would experience in parenting Adam. Over several meetings, they discussed how society has historically viewed disability and how a brighter future was likely possible for Adam. Shelly began to develop a circle of support around her son and hoped John would be encouraged by her actions.

Shelly's sense of guilt faded and was replaced by a feeling of commitment and empowerment gained by sharing her concerns with other parents. She learned about the benefits of inclusion at daycare and school. She joined an advocacy committee that focused on acquiring improved supports for all children with disabilities. Rather than viewing her son as someone who needed a cure, she began to view society as unable to adapt to people with disabilities. Confidently, she helped Adam achieve greater accessibility. Using collaborative efforts, she created an educational pilot project for autism in Adam's school. Shelly remained concerned about issues such as stigma, higher education, and employment. As Adam grew older Shelly led an advocacy group that focused on teaching self-advocacy to young people with disabilities. Although there were numerous obstacles, Adam completed high school and entered a computer-related program at his local college.

Points to Consider

- Why is the diagnosis of a child with autism viewed as a tragedy?
- How does the history of disability contribute to Shelly's fear for her son's future?
- Why would a doctor suggest that Adam's symptoms would eventually disappear?
- How did joining a parental support group help Shelly?
- How might you teach self-advocacy to a group of young people with disabilities?

Working with Families

One of the most important factors contributing to the development of the supports for people with disabilities has been the vision and courage of people with disabilities and their families. Particularly mothers, "who identified the impact of discriminatory practices on the exclusion of their child" (Panitch, 2003, p. 273), spurred the development of advocacy for persons with disabilities. Following World War II, parents of children with disabilities raised awareness as a group about the needs of their children. They promoted accessibility for their children in the areas of education, group homes, and employment preparation and training. The advocacy of mothers of people with intellectual disabilities resulted in the Canadian Association for Community Living (CACL), which introduced an early and continuing plan of comprehensive, community-based services (Stienstra, 2012). The efforts of these parents continued through the 1970s and 1980s in large disability social movements. Presently, parents continue to question the quality of social supports provided for children with disabilities. Parents remain a potent influence in shaping legislation (Trainor, 2010) by identifying deficiencies in environments rather than individuals.

Although family members continue to engage in both structural analysis and social and political change, many fear what might happen to their child based on how people with disabilities were treated in the past. The lack of knowledge about disability and legislated disability rights remains high, as illustrated in Case Example 14.2, where Shelly feared sharing her son's disability with co-workers. Moreover, many parents do not feel qualified or welcomed to collaborate with school professionals about their children's disability. Some parents report an atmosphere of power differentials in which they experience intimidation that could further be complicated by language barriers (Carter, Park, & Cragg, 2015).

Parents with children with disabilities who had immigrated to Canada were eager to gain formal supports for their children but found themselves unaware of services because of language barriers (Lo, 2010). Unlike Shelly in Case Example 14.2, Lo found it was difficult for Chinese-speaking parents to locate preferred, Chinese-speaking disability support groups that were crucial for Chinese parents of children with disabilities who found their extended families to be judgmental and unsupportive. In some cases, the extent of stigma about having a child with a disability made parents hesitant to seek or accept help. For example, Turkish parents rated negative societal attitudes highest among daily stressors, which could lead to anxiety, isolation, and problems receiving services (Uskun & Gundogar, 2010). Despite cultural differences, parents of children with disabilities, as a group, experience high levels of parenting stress (Phetrasuwan & Miles, 2009; Lopez, Clifford, Minnes, & Ouellette-Kuntz, 2008; Manor-Binyamini, 2010), often resulting in pessimism about services and their children's futures. Social workers need to be prepared to help parents by being aware of community resources and services that offer translations and other multicultural services for new Canadians. (For further discussion of the importance of the family unit in relation to diversity and equality within Canada, see Chapter 7 by Raymond Neckoway and Keith Brownlee and Chapter 9 by Debashis Dutta and Ross Klein.)

A major concern of parents with children with disabilities is their child's future care; social workers can work with parents while their child is at an early age to discuss various options in creating a plan of care. Parents with children with disabilities, particularly those new to Canada, often require assistance in navigating the social system in search of resources and supports for their children. As preparation to work with families, it is recommended social workers increase their knowledge and competency related to disability, including various cultural perspectives of disability.

Promoting Accessible Education and Employment

The commitment to accessibility, diversity, social justice, and equality is reflected in legislation that recognizes Canadian society is strengthened by including all its citizens (Canadian Human Rights Act, 1977; Canadian Charter of Rights and Freedoms, 1982; Ontarians with Disabilities Act, 2001). The Canadian Human Rights Act protects people in Canada from discrimination when they are employed by or receive services from the federal government. Section 3 of the Canadian Human Rights Act makes it illegal for federally regulated employers and service providers to discriminate against people or treat them unfairly based on race, national or ethnic origin, colour, religion, age, sex, sexual orientation, marital status, family status, disability, or a conviction for which they have been granted a pardon. There are many similarities between the Canadian Human Rights Act and provincial and territorial human rights laws. Section 15 of the Canadian

Charter of Rights and Freedoms contains guaranteed equality rights and is part of the Canadian Constitution. Rights under Section 15 of the Charter include racial equality, sexual equality, mental disability, and physical disability. Section 15 states that

> Every individual is equal before and under the law and has the right to the equal protection and equal benefit of the law without discrimination and, in particular, without discrimination based on race, national or ethnic origin, colour, religion, sex, age or mental or physical disability.

In Ontario, the 2001 Ontarians with Disabilities Act was intended to improve the identification, removal, and prevention of barriers faced by persons with disabilities. The intent of this legislation was to create a barrier-free society for people with disabilities related to employment, public transit, education, provincial and municipal government services and facilities, and other goods, services, and facilities offered to the public. The Ontarians with Disabilities Act Committee asked the government to revisit the act, and in 2005 the Ontario government passed the Accessibility for Ontarians with Disabilities Act (AODA), which sets as a goal the removal of all barriers to full participation in Ontario by the year 2025.

Stienstra (2012) makes the point that the reality for people with disabilities differs from how their rights are presented in the Charter of Rights and Freedoms. Despite the advancements in disability rights, people with disabilities still live in poverty, without work, isolated from the community, and often exposed to abuse and violence. Stienstra challenges Canadians to incorporate the rights of people with disabilities as written in existing legislation by suggesting that Canadians can increase access for people with disabilities with approaches such as universal design, income support, and social support.

Improving Higher Education Practices

With respect to higher education at college or university, "diversity has become a fact of life" (Burgstahler & Cory, 2008, p. 4). Burgstahler and Cory note that what used to be a campus of White, young, able-bodied males is now represented by students from other racial/ethnic groups (25 per cent), women (over 50 per cent), older students, and students with disabilities (6 per cent or more). Moreover, there will likely be students requiring diverse methods of teaching and learning. To achieve accessibility, students require the principles of universal design to be uniformly applied to instruction (Burgstahler & Cory). Universal design ensures products and environments, such as the car and roadways, are usable by all people, as much as possible, without the need for adaptation (Hebdon, 2007). The application of universal design in education seeks to create educational processes, learning environments, and teaching strategies that are usable by the greatest diversity of people possible (Samuels, 2007). One of the dimensions within universal design in education is the application of this perspective to teaching practices and processes, called **universal**

instructional design (UID) (Burgstahler & Cory). Principles of UID are equitable, flexible, and simple to use; require low physical effort; consider size and space for appropriate use; create a community of learners; and promote an inclusive environment. The potential needs of all learners are considered, while removing unnecessary barriers to teaching and learning (Burgstahler & Cory).

In Case Example 14.1, Gerry resided in a children's rehabilitation centre until he reached the age of 18, when he was discharged to the community. Although capable of doing so, Gerry did not have the opportunity to access a high school education that would have better prepared him for employment, whether through postsecondary education or supportive job training programs. Consequently, he has to manage on a restricted government-based disability income and is left questioning how he can secure employment. In Case Example 14.2, Adam, through advances in legislation and educational practices and help from family advocates, obtained a Grade 12 education that prepared him to enter postsecondary education. Adam's success will depend on the support provided by an accommodation status provided by the student disability office; however, Adam fears asking for an accommodation status because of the associated stigma. These examples indicate that there remains a need to improve inclusive practices and accessibility in the educational process that normalizes student diversity (Embry, Parker, McGuire, & Scott, 2008).

The support for students with disabilities in higher educational institutions is "based on the premise that students will disclose their disability to the institution's disability services office" (Thompson-Ebanks, 2014). However, students in social work, nursing, and education found that disclosure is risky for students seeking to practice professionally (Stanley, Ridley, Harris, & Manthrope, 2011, as cited in Thompson-Ebanks, 2014). Research indicates that only a small percentage of students who qualify for accommodations actually disclose, register, request, and receive disability services and accommodations (Matthews, 2009). Thompson-Ebanks makes the point that non-disclosure or delaying disclosure places students at risk, because students with non-disclosed disabilities were three-and-a-half more times likely not to graduate in six years than those who formally did so. Reasons that students give for concealing their disability include stigmatization, risks to identity and integrity, negative perceptions of peers and faculty, regrets with previous disclosures, fear of discrimination, and loss of access to opportunities.

Legislation that requires accommodation in education is not enough. Issues in accommodation need to be examined to develop an understanding of ways to promote greater student participation. For example, in Ontario, accommodation is required to enhance participation of persons with disabilities in society's educational institutions. As part of the AODA (2005), universities are required to develop an annual accessibility plan that identifies any barriers to full accessibility to universities by people with disabilities. Yet research indicates that students are often unaware of available supports or how to access them (Goode, 2007). Although progress has been made with recent legislative developments, Goode predicts that significant long-term cultural changes both outside and inside institutions of higher education will be challenging to achieve. While legislative changes have resulted in the development of more inclusive environments, further steps need to be taken to ensure implementation of progressive disability-related policies that challenge universities and colleges to move beyond minimum legislated standards. Social work students can contribute to the goal of transforming social work education into an accessible environment through studying disability and strategies to affect change, helping to ensure educational barriers are removed in institutions of higher learning.

Creating Accessible Employment

In Ontario, there are concerns that we are not making the progress we should be regarding the creation of a barrier-free society, especially with respect to employment opportunities for people with disabilities. David Lepofsky, a lawyer, disability activist, and volunteer chair of the AODA Alliance, asserts that there are concerns that Ontario is not on track to make the 2025 goal of an accessible society (TV Ontario, 2015). David Onley, Ontario's lieutenant-governor from 2007 to 2014, supports David Lepofsky by adding that over 50 per cent of Canadians are affected by a disability if they take into account family members affected by a person with a disability. Lepofsky and Onley stress that employment for people with disabilities is crucial, emphasizing that people with disabilities make excellent employees, counter to existing myths.

Despite protective legislation, many problems remain for individuals with disabilities. In both Case Examples 14.1 and 14.2, employment is an issue for Gerry, as an adult male planning to marry, and Adam, a young adult with autism who will be looking for employment following graduation from college. Income for Gerry is government subsidized and will be for Adam once he finishes school if he is unsuccessful in finding employment. In fact, Adam may enter another stage of overwhelming challenges as he experiences the lack of social support that is dominated by social exclusion and isolation without employment.

The document "Rethinking DisAbility in the Private Sector: Report from the Panel on Labour Market Opportunities for Persons with Disabilities" (Employment and Social Development Canada, 2015) provides some hope for Gerry and Adam as it explains the need for society to employ people with disabilities in greater numbers and explains how people with disabilities are a good investment as employees. This report indicates there are approximately 795,000 working-aged Canadians with disabilities whose disability does not prevent them from working, half of which have postsecondary education. In this report, about 200 Canadian employers shared their opinions on the subject of employing people with disabilities. These employers indicated that in 57 per cent of cases accommodation was not required, and in the cases where accommodation was required the average amount spent to create accommodation was $500. Two of the major employers advised that they used the AODA as a guide. The employers implemented a policy of asking what accommodation each new employee would require, effectively removing some of the stigma attached to requesting accommodation. Comparing the performance of people with and without disabilities, the company representative indicated job performance was similar in both groups. The report indicates that progress can be made by breaking down barriers for people with disabilities in the workplace through matching the job to the person and providing accommodation, including the use of mentors.

The report indicates that we cannot afford to exclude people with disabilities from the workplace as our population ages and disability rates increase (Employment and Social Development Canada, 2015). This report reminds us to focus on attitudes, ability rather than disability, and leadership. Social work education that focuses on these characteristics will enable social workers to collaborate with organizations that promote employment for people with disabilities. As in Case Example 14.1, part of the plan to help Gerry find employment would be ensuring that he is prepared with the skills that the employer requires. As recommended by the report, post–job placement support would be critical to ensure employment success for Gerry. Social workers can play a role in promoting an inclusive workplace for Gerry by being informed of supportive employers who believe people with disabilities contribute to their overall success.

Advocacy and Disability

Advocacy practice takes "action in a systematic and purposeful way to defend, represent, or otherwise advance the cause of one or more clients at the individual, group, organizational, or community level in order to promote social justice" (Hoefer, 2012, p. 3). With respect to disability, advocates target stigma, education, employment, transportation, and telecommunications in bringing about inclusion for all Canadians (Stienstra, 2012). Once the social worker has identified barriers to full participation in society's social, economic, and political institutions, they require additional skills in advocacy to work with clients with disabilities. In preparing the client to advocate, students can use case examples to explore professional intervention strategies that promote full participation and equality for people with disabilities. For example, in Case Example 14.1, the social worker encourages Gerry to be creative in increasing his "personal, interpersonal, socio-economic and political strength to develop influence toward improving" his circumstances (Barker, 2009). Case Example 14.2 illustrates how a key role for the social worker is to help engage the client in continuous learning about disability rights through collaboration with others and to appreciate the role of self-advocacy in building strategies for action.

Self-Determination and Choice

In supporting disability rights and self-advocacy organizations, the social worker respects self-determination and choice as exercised by individuals with disabilities. Case Example 14.1 illustrates the importance of recognizing client self-determination and choice as well as empowerment when Gerry explains how he and Chelsea are putting steps in place to marry and how Chelsea' s parents would eventually see it as a positive development. Gerry recognizes the importance of family to Chelsea, and thus considers the family's views but does not let the family's wishes take precedence over what he and Chelsea have decided will be their future. The term **"empowerment"** represents the belief that one can change one's environment. Social workers and clients begin to understand empowerment when they realize how exclusion is constructed and make use of their skills to analyze how society has created such barriers to inclusion. Empowerment necessitates that the social worker view the client as the expert, recognize the power differential between the social worker and the client, encourage user involvement, see the client's strengths, and develop hope that inequality can be addressed.

Therapeutic Approaches

Where clients with disabilities feel oppressed, social workers can apply therapeutic approaches to address feelings of being oppressed, personally and culturally. For example, the racial/cultural identity development (R/CID) model (Sue & Sue, 2013) is applicable in addressing issues of oppression with respect to gender and disability when assessing where individuals are in their cultural identity. (For a continued conversation on gender, oppression, and social work, see Chapter 13 by Sarah Fotheringham.) The social worker can use the R/CID model to assist the client in moving through five stages:

- Conformity (preference for dominant culture)
- Dissonance (challenges previously held beliefs)
- Resistance and immersion (endorses minority views and rejects dominant values)
- Introspection (experiences conflict of resistance and immersion as unhealthy)
- Integrative awareness (balances a sense of one's culture and other cultures)

Where the client currently falls in the model is the starting point for the intervention. The goal of intervention is to assess the degree of oppression caused by oppressive social structures and to help the client understand and address such oppression.

Stigma

Advocacy is used to address stigma, the most formidable obstacle to progress for people with disabilities that results in systemic oppression and increases with multiple disabilities (Encinares & Golea, 2005). Stigma affects the ability to achieve an education, secure healthcare or housing, or keep a full-time job. Social workers use strengths-based approaches to reduce social isolation and promote empowerment, focusing on client skills and competencies as opposed to limitations. Social workers identify the need for access to adequate education, health, transportation, housing, and employment services, and encourage client(s) whenever appropriate and possible to advocate independently for such services. As noted in Case Example 14.1, the social worker, Amanda, is prepared to assist Gerry with professional intervention strategies that he determines are necessary.

Advocacy Training

In Case Example 14.2, the social worker, Beverly, must align the needs of the parent, Shelly, with the needs of the client wherever possible. When Shelly seeks services for her son, Adam, who has autism, Beverly needs to consider the implications of the views and experiences of family members as well as Adam's right to make choices. For example, Adam may not agree with his mother's preference that his autism be treated with intensive behavioural therapy to change or modify some of Adam's behaviours. Social workers need to differentiate the needs of the client with disabilities as described by themselves from the client's needs as described by others. For example, Carter and Wilson (2011) found that although parents viewed social skills training as a priority for their children, youth with autism remained skeptical about the purpose of group involvement. Expressing concern about communication challenges, the youth viewed opportunities for friendship and companionship as their primary needs. In addition to noting the varying viewpoints between parents and youth with disabilities, a social worker familiar with disability issues sees an opportunity for young people to learn how to engage in self-advocacy.

Advocacy can initially represent a daunting task for an individual with a disability and his or her family members. When individual and collective advocacy goals are not achieved, there is a risk that the disappointment can lessen confidence and create ambivalence about participating in advocacy. Training in advocacy creates confidence. For example, in a six-session, co-facilitated support group regarding advocacy and self-efficacy of parents coping with a child's diagnosis, Banach, Iudice, Conway, and Couse (2010) found that the average mean scores on the Family Empowerment Scale increased. Parents who have learned to advocate are, in turn, helpful to other parents who are unaware of their children's rights. For example, the Volunteer Advocacy Project (VAP) trains advocates and parents to assert their rights, promote parent–school collaboration, and improve transition and outcomes after high school (Taylor, 2014). The VAP is an intensive, 40-hour special education advocacy training curriculum that covers topics such as individualized education plan (IEP) meetings, interventions, assistive technology, least restrictive environment, discipline provisions, and advocating for legislative change. Graduates of the program reported significant gains in their perceived advocacy skills.

Activism

Prince (2012) suggests that most Canadian disability activism takes place within conventional political structures and works by creating incremental change. In this environment, social workers can advocate alongside clients as disability advocates by approaching advocacy in stages (Hoefer, 2012). The first step is to understand the issue and to get involved. During this stage, Hoefer suggests the advocate consider what they want and who can get them what they want. Next, during the middle stage of planning, the advocate considers when they should act and how they should act, producing long- and short-term goals. In the final step, Hoefer suggests the advocate assess what action to take. To be helpful in the above advocacy steps, social workers need training as policy advocates (Jansson, 2011) in efforts to improve or change policies in legislative, agency, and community settings.

Summary and Conclusion

Although 158 countries adopted the 2006 UN Convention on the Rights of Persons with Disabilities with an understanding that all people with impairments have a right to be educated, to work, and to live without segregation, much needs to be done (Zavirsek, 2014). Social work education everywhere needs to ensure it is based on social activism with the goal of eliminating social inequality for people with disabilities. The study of disability should explore models of disability and critically examine assumptions that have shaped traditional responses, and highlight people, events, and legislation that have affected disability rights. For example, the study of disability should analyze power and inequality and include the eugenics movement, the civil rights movement, efforts to achieve accessibility and inclusion, and encourage a team approach with people with disabilities and community leaders.

In recent decades Canadian schools of social work have increasingly developed courses in disability and supported access to interdisciplinary disability studies programs. Developing disability content in the social work curriculum reflects social work's commitment to social justice and accessibility by involving people with disabilities and the disability community as well as social work and disability scholars, supporting diversity in the local community, and demonstrating a Canadian government human rights approach. In promoting the study of disability, social work and disability scholars continue to shape education for the future by providing leadership and focusing on engaging all students through instruction, services, information technology, and physical spaces. In Canada, the Canadian Centre for Disability Studies, the Canadian Disability Studies Association, and the Canadian Association for Social Work Education present scholarly work on disability and disseminate this work through annual conferences, journals, and websites.

The study of disability will continue to evolve as disability scholars and social workers share, exchange, and integrate information between community organizations and academic institutions, leading the way to collaborative community initiatives through practice, education, and research. Although a rehabilitative and medically focused perspective still exists in some schools of social work, there is a growing awareness in social work to emphasize progressive change in accessibility that is promoting change, especially in the areas of education and employment that is supported by individuals with disabilities and organizations from local and global communities. (For continued discussion on equality and community organization, see Chapter 5 by Douglas Durst.) People with disabilities who are educated are prepared to be employed. Accessing employment will depend on the capacity to see ability rather than disability and to collaborate with employers who recognize that people with disabilities are productive employees. The ability to use advocacy strategies will continue to address barriers to accessibility in the areas of stigma, health, transportation, education and technology, and employment.

Questions for Review

1. As a social worker, what aspects of disability would you teach a group of first-year social work students?
2. What criticisms might you have of the social model of disability?
3. What groups of people initiated the independent living model?
4. In learning about the history of disability, what important considerations do you have to take into account?
5. What made the deinstitutionalization of people with disabilities possible?
6. What major strengths do you foresee you will have in the role of advocate for persons with disabilities?
7. What can be done to increase accessibility for students in the postsecondary classroom?
8. What are the next steps in the disability movement?

Suggested Readings and Resources

The Autism Acceptance Project. *Positively Autistic* [Video]. Retrieved from http://www.taaproject.com

Brown, I. (2011). *The boy in the moon: A father's journey to understand his extraordinary son.* New York, NY: St. Martin's Press.

Canadian Association for Community Living; http://www.cacl.ca

Canadian Association for Social Work Education; http://caswe-acfts.ca/home

Canadian Centre for Disability Studies. (2011). *Disability, development and diversity project*. Retrieved from http://disabilitystudies.ca/ddd-home

Council of Canadians with Disabilities; http://www.ccdonline.ca/en

Elliot, A. (2002). *The collector of Bedford Street* [DVD]. United States: New Day Digital. Retrieved from http://www.newdaydigital.com/The-Collector-of-Bedford-Street.html

Employment and Social Development Canada. (2015). Rethinking disability in the private Sector: Report from the panel on labour market opportunities for persons with disabilities. Retrieved from http://www.esdc.gc.ca/eng/disability/consultations/rethinking_disabilities.shtml

International Association of Schools of Social Work; http://www.iassw-aiets.org

Neudel, E., Gilkey, A., Fay, F. A., Schneider, B., Kusiak, J., Willis, P. A. (2011). *Lives worth living* [Video]. Natick, MA: Storyline Motion Pictures.

Reiff, H. B. (2007). *Self-advocacy skills for students with learning disabilities: Making it happen in college and beyond. A resource for students, parents, and guidance counselors.* Port Chester, NY: Dude Publishing.

TV Ontario. (2015, February 3). The agenda with Steve Paikin: Champions for the disabled. Retrieved from http://www.ccrw.org/2015/02/the-agenda-with-steve-paikin-champions-for-the-disabled

References

Banach, M., Iudice, J., Conway, L., & Couse, L. J. (2010). Family support and empowerment: Post-autism diagnosis support group for parents. *Social Work with Groups, 33*(1), 69–83.

Barker, R. L. (2009). *The social work dictionary* (5th ed.). Washington, DC: NASW Press.

Brown, I., Radford, J. P., & Percy, M. (2007). Historical overview of intellectual and developmental disabilities. In I. Brown & M. Percy, *A comprehensive guide to intellectual & developmental disabilities.* Baltimore, MD: Paul H. Brookes Publishing Co.

Burgstahler, S. E., & Cory, R. C. (Eds.). (2008). *Universal design in higher education: From principles to practice.* Cambridge, MA: Harvard Education Press.

Carter, I., Hanes, R., & MacDonald, J. (2014). Notes from the editors. *Professional Development: The International Journal of Continuing Social Work Education, 17*(2), 3–4.

Carter, I., Park, W., & Cragg, S. (2015). Perceptions of social support among Canadian-born and non-Canadian-born parents of children with developmental disabilities. *Professional Development: The International Journal of Continuing Social Work Education, 18*(1), 56–73.

Carter, I., & Wilson, R. (2011). Reflections on face-to-face and online self-help group participation: Comparing the views of persons with autism with those of parents speaking for their autistic children. *International Journal of Self-Help and Self Care, 5*(4), 353–69.

Covarrubias, I., & Han, M. (2011). Mental health stigma about serious mental illness among MSW students: Social contact and attitude. *National Association of Social Workers, 56*(4), 317–25.

Dunn, P. A., Hanes, R., Hardie, S., Leslie, D., & MacDonald, J. (2008). Best practices in promoting disability inclusion within Canadian schools of social work. *Disability Studies Quarterly, 28*(1), 13–20.

Embry, P. B., Parker, D. R., McGuire, J. M., & Scott, S. S. (2008). Postsecondary disability service providers' perceptions about implementing Universal Design for Instruction (UDI). *Journal of Postsecondary Education and Disability, 18*(1), 34–44.

Employment and Social Development Canada. (2015). Rethinking disability in the private sector: Report from the panel on labour market opportunities for persons with disabilities. Retrieved from http://www.esdc.gc.ca/eng/disability/consultations/rethinking_disabilities.shtml

Encinares, M., & Golea, G. (2005). Client-centered care for individuals with dual diagnoses in the justice system. *Journal of Psychosocial Nursing & Mental Health Services, 43*(9), 29–36.

Goode, J. (2007). Managing disability: Early experiences of university students with disabilities. *Disability and Society, 22*(1), 35–48.

Goodley, D. (2000). Self-advocacy in the lives of people with learning difficulties. In L. Barton (Ed.), *Disability, human rights & society series.* Philadelphia, PA: Open University Press.

Goodley, D. (2011). *Disability studies: An interdisciplinary introduction.* California, CA: Sage Publications Ltd.

Gormley, D., & Quinn, N. (2009). Mental health stigma and discrimination: The experience within social work. *Practice: Social Work in Action, 21*(4), 259–70.

Hanes, R., Carter, I., MacDonald, J., McMurphy, S., & Skinner, S. (2014). Exploring social work and disability in US schools of social work. *Professional Development: The International Journal of Continuing Social Work Education, 17*(2), 5–17.

Hauch, N. (2014). Enhancing independent living within community services for people with physical disabilities in Ontario, Canada. *Professional Development: The International Journal of Continuing Social Work Education, 17*(2), 52–60.

Hebdon, H. M. (2007). Universal design: Making education accessible to all students. *The Exceptional Parent, 37*(5), 70.

Hoefer, R. (2012). *Advocacy and practice for social justice: Incorporating advocacy into the generalist model* (2nd ed.). Chicago, IL: Lyceum Books Inc.

Jansson, B. (2011). Joining a tradition of social reform. In. B. Jansson, *Becoming an effective policy advocate: From policy practice to social justice* (6th ed.). Pacific Grove, CA: Thomson Learning.

Kliewer, C., Biklen, D., & Kasa-Hendrickson, C. (2006). Who may be literate? Disability and resistance to the cultural denial of competence. *American Educational Research Journal, 43*(2), 163–92. doi:10.3102/000283120043002163

Kuluski, K., Williams, A. P., Berta, W., & Laporte, A. (2012). Home care or long-term care: Setting the balance of care in urban and rural northwestern Ontario, Canada. *Health and Social Care in the Community, 20*(4), 438–44.

Laws, J., Parish, S., Scheyett, A., & Egan, C. (2010). Preparation of social workers to support people with developmental disabilities. *Journal of Teaching in Social Work, 30*(3), 317–33. doi:10.1080/08841233.2010.497128

Lewis-Fleming, G. (2007). The military child with special needs transitioning to adulthood. *The Exceptional Parent, 37*(8), 68–76.

Lo, L. (2010). Perceived benefits experienced in support groups for Chinese families of children with disabilities. *Early Child Development and Care, 180*(3), 405–15. doi: 10.1080/03004430802002625

Lopez, V., Clifford, T., Minnes, P., & Ouellette-Kuntz, H. (2008). Parental stress and coping in families of children with and without developmental delays. *Journal on Developmental Disabilities, 14*(2), 99–104. doi:10.1080/03004430802002625

Mackelprang, R. W., & Salsgiver, R. O. (2015). *Disability: A diversity model approach in human service practice.* Chicago, IL: Lyceum Books Inc.

Manor-Binyamini, I. (2010). Mothers of children with developmental disorders in the Bedouin community in Israel: Family functioning, caregiver burden, and coping abilities. *Journal of Autism and Developmental Disorders, 41*(5), 610–7. doi:10.1007/s10803-010-1080-1

Matthews, N. (2009). Teaching the invisible disabled students in the classroom: Disclosure, inclusion and the social model of disability. *Teaching in Higher Education, 14*(3), 229–34.

Meekosha, H., & Dowse, L. (2007). Integrating critical disability studies into social work education and practice: An Australian perspective. *Practice, 19*(3), 169–83.

Milsom, A., & Hartley, M. (2005). Assisting students with learning disabilities transitioning to college: What school counselors should know. *Professional School Counselling, 8*(5), 436–41.

Morris, J. (2001). Impairment and disability: Constructing an ethics of care that promotes human rights. *Hypatia, 16*(4), 1–16.

Neufeldt, A. H. (2003). Disability in Canada: An historical perspective. In H. Enns & A. H. Neufeldt, *In pursuit of equal participation: Canada and disability at home and abroad* (pp. 22–79). Concord, ON: Captus Press.

Oliver, M. (1990). *The politics of disablement.* New York, NY: St. Martin's Press Inc.

Oliver, M., Sapey, B., & Thomas, P. (2012). *Social work with disabled people* (4th ed.). Houndmills, UK: Palgrave MacMillan.

Panitch, M. (2003). Mothers of intention: Women, disability and activism. In D. Stienstra & A. Wight-Felske (Eds.), *Making equality: History of advocacy and persons with disabilities in Canada* (pp. 273–5). Toronto, ON: Captus Press.

Phetrasuwan, S., & Miles, M. S. (2009). Parenting stress in mothers of children with autism spectrum disorders. *Journal for Specialists in Pediatric Nursing, 14*(3), 157–65. doi:10.1111/j.1744-6155.2009.00188.x

Phillips, C. (2003). Steering your own ship: The growth of individual advocacy within the Canadian Association of Independent Living Centres. In D. Stienstra & A. Wright Felske (Eds.), *Making equality: History of advocacy and persons with disabilities in Canada* (pp. 197–219). Toronto, ON: Captus Press Inc.

Prince, M. (2004). Canadian disability policy: Still a hit-and-miss affair. *Canadian Journal of Sociology, 29*(1), 59–82.

Prince, M. (2009). The Canadian disability community: Five arenas of social action and capacity. In M. Prince, *Absent citizens: Disability politics and policy in Canada* (pp. 112–33). Toronto, ON: University of Toronto Press.

Prince, M. (2012). Canadian disability activism and political ideas: In and between neo-liberalism and social liberalism. *Canadian Journal of Disability Studies, 1*(1), 1–34.

Rees, J., & Raithby, M. (2012). Increasingly strange bedfellows? An examination of the inclusion of disability issues in university- and agency-based social work education in a Welsh context. *Social Work Education, 31*(2), 184–201.

Rioux, M. H., & Samson, R. M. (2006). Trends impacting disability: National and international perspectives. In M. A. McColl & L. Jonbloed (Eds.), *Disability and social policy in Canada* (2nd ed., pp. 112–42). Toronto, ON: Captus Press Inc.

Roeher Institute. (2003). *Towards a common approach to thinking about and measuring social inclusion*. Toronto, ON: Author.

Rothman, J. (2003). *Social work practice across disability*. Boston, MA: Allyn & Bacon.

Russo-Gleicher, R. (2008). MSW programs: Gatekeepers to the field of developmental disabilities. *Journal of Social Work Education, 44*(2), 129–56.

Samuels, C. A. (2007). Universal design concept pushed for education. *Education Week, 27*(10), 1–12.

Shakespeare, T. (Ed.). (1998). *The disability reader: Social science perspectives*. London, UK: York House Typographic Ltd.

Shakespeare, T. (2008). Disability, genetics and eugenics. In J. Swain & S. French (Eds.), *Disability on equal terms*. Thousand Oaks, CA: Sage Publications Ltd.

Silverstein, R. (2001). *An overview of the emerging disability policy framework: A guidepost for analyzing public policy*. Baltimore, MD: Paul H. Brookes Publishing.

Stanley, N., Ridley, J., Harris, J., & Manthrope, J. (2011). Disclosing disability in the context of professional regulations: A qualitative UK study. *Disability & Society, 26*(1), 19–32.

Statistics Canada. (2015). Disability in Canada: Initial findings from the Canadian Survey on Disability. Retrieved from http://www.statcan.gc.ca/pub/89-654-x/89-654-x2013002-eng.htm

Stienstra, D. (2012). *About Canada: Disability rights*. Halifax, NS: Fernwood Publishing.

Sue, D. W., & Sue, D. (2013). *Counseling the culturally diverse: Theory and practice* (6th ed.). Hoboken, NJ: John Wiley and Sons.

Taylor, C. (2014). *Improving parental involvement in special education and advocacy*. Vanderbilt Kennedy Center. Retrieved from http://vkc.mc.vanderbilt.edu/notables/2014/12/improving-parental-involvement-in-special-education-and-advocacy/#sthash.vxyUyO8z.dpuf

Thompson-Ebanks, V. (2014). Disability disclosure among college students with psychiatric disabilities in professional majors: Risks and implications for rural communities. *Professional Development: The International Journal of Continuing Social Work Education, 17*(2), 18–28.

Tower, K. D. (2003). Disability through the lens of culture. *Journal of Social Work in Disability & Rehabilitation, 2*(2/3), 5–22.

Trainor, A. (2010). Diverse approaches to parent advocacy during special education home-school interactions: Identification and use of cultural and social capital. *Remedial and Special Education, 31*(1), 34–47.

Tremblay, M. (2003). Lieutenant John Counsell and the development of medical rehabilitation and disability policy. In D. Stienstra & A. Wright-Felske (Eds.), *Making equality: History of advocacy and persons with disabilities in Canada* (pp. 51–71). Toronto, ON: Captus Press Inc.

TV Ontario. (2015, February 3). The agenda with Steve Paikin: Champions for the disabled. Retrieved from http://www.ccrw.org/2015/02/the-agenda-with-steve-paikin-champions-for-the-disabled

Uskun, E., & Gundogar, D. (2010). The levels of stress, depression and anxiety of parents of disabled children in Turkey. *Disability and Rehabilitation: An International, Multidisciplinary Journal, 32*(23), 1917–27. doi: 10.3109/09638281003763804

World Health Organization. (2015). Disability and health: Fact sheet No. 352. Retrieved from http://www.who.int/mediacentre/factsheets/fs352/en/

Zavirsek, D. (2014). Time for recognition: People with disabilities today. *Social Dialogue, 9*(3), 4–5.

Social Work with Diverse Older Adults

15

By Daniel W.L. Lai and Xue Bai

Chapter Objectives

This chapter will help you develop an understanding of:

- The diversity of Canada's aging population
- Theories and perspectives on aging and diversity
- Practice approaches for working with diverse older adults

Introduction

Most "developed" countries, including Canada, are experiencing population aging triggered by low fertility rates and rising life expectancy. In 2014, adults aged 65 and over in Canada numbered 5.6 million, representing 15.7 per cent of the population (Statistics Canada, 2014a), an increase from 4.2 million (13.1 per cent) in 2006 and 2.4 million (9.6 per cent) in 1981 (Turcotte & Schellenberg, 2007; Statistics Canada, 2012a). As baby boomers born in the 1950s and 1960s enter old age over the next 20 years, the older population will grow in both number and proportion. An aging trend is observed within Canada's older population, with those aged 80 or over expected to rise from 1.4 million in 2013 to nearly 5 million by 2063. The proportion of older seniors (aged 80 and over) in the total population will increase to 5.3 per cent in 2026, and then 9.6 per cent in 2045 (Statistics Canada, 2014c).

This chapter will examine diverse experiences and outcomes in Canada's aging population, including differences in well-being and perceptions of aging associated with ethnocultural background, gender, sexual orientation, and age. The chapter will explore theoretical approaches to understanding aging and diversity and practice approaches for diverse older adult populations.

Older Adults in Canada as a Diverse Group

It is limiting to assume that the older adult population shares the same needs and requires the same standardized services. Canada has a diverse older population with substantial differences in terms of age, gender, culture, religion, language, and sexual orientation. An expanded understanding of this field is necessary if social workers are to effectively serve diverse aging populations.

Migration and Older Adults

Over the past century, immigration has greatly altered the profile of Canada's aging population. The 2011 National Household Survey (NHS) reported more than 200 ethnic origins among the Canadian population, and among them 13 ethnic origin groups reported a total of over 1 million people (Statistics Canada, 2013b). Canada has the highest proportion of foreign-born residents of all G8 countries. Foreign-born Canadians numbered 6,775,800 in 2011, representing 21 per cent of the population (Statistics Canada, 2014b). Immigrants will represent 25 to 28 per cent of Canadians by 2031, with this population increasing four times more rapidly than the rest of the population in coming decades (Statistics Canada, 2010).

In recent decades, the primary source countries of immigrants to Canada have shifted from Western European countries to Asian countries, with an increase in immigrants from African and Latin American countries (Chui, Maheux, & Tran, 2007). Between 1981 and 2001, the proportion of immigrants from Western and Northern Europe and the United States declined from 45.5 per cent to 24.6 per cent, and the proportion from Asia increased from 13.9 per cent to 36.5 per cent. In 2010 and 2011, the majority of immigrants to Canada were born in Asian countries, and immigrants from Asian countries contributed roughly 60 per cent of all the immigration population (Chagnon, 2013). In addition, the Philippines, India, China, Iran, Pakistan, Iraq, and South Korea represented seven of the top ten source countries in 2010 (Chagnon, 2013). (The unique challenges of adaptation and acculturation among diverse groups are discussed in Chapter 9 by Debashis Dutta and Ross Klein.)

More specifically, in 2013, 29,539 immigrants from the Philippines came to Canada as permanent residents, which represents 11.41 per cent of all the immigrants in that year. The number of immigrants from the Philippines increased steadily from 12,928 in 2001 to 18,400 in 2006 to 38,617 in 2010. Another major source country is India, where the number of immigrants as permanent residents from this country was 27,901 in 2001 and then 33,847 in 2006 and 34,235 in 2010; in 2013, this number was 33,085, representing 12.78 per cent of all immigrants that year. When it comes to the People's Republic of China, although the number of immigrants from this country has gone down, from 40,365 (16.10 per cent) in 2001 to 33,518 (13.32 per cent) in 2006, 30,391 (10.83 per cent) in 2010, and 34,126 (13.18 per cent) in 2013, it is still the major source country of immigrants to Canada (Government of Canada, 2010, 2014).

The number and proportion of older adults from ethnically and culturally diverse backgrounds have also grown significantly over time. In 2006, approximately 30 per cent of Canada's older adults were immigrants, with 10 per cent arriving at age 50 or older and facing more challenges in adaptation and acculturation because of their age

(Ng, Lai, Rudner, & Orpana, 2012). In 2001, nearly one in four (23 per cent) immigrant seniors belonged to a visible minority group, compared to 0.8 per cent of Canadian-born seniors, increasing from 6.8 per cent of immigrant seniors and 0.4 per cent of Canadian-born seniors in 1981. The proportion of senior immigrants from Asian countries increased from 5.6 per cent to 19.1 per cent. Most visible minority immigrant seniors reside in Alberta (25.5 per cent) and British Columbia (30.7 per cent) (Turcotte & Schellenberg, 2007).

Religious and Linguistic Diversity

Immigration has contributed to religious and linguistic diversity in Canada's aging population. The 2011 NHS identified nine major categories of religious affiliation (see Table 15.1), and 111 different languages were reported being spoken at home (see Table 15.2) by Canadians aged 65 and older (Statistics Canada, 2011b).

Table 15.1 Religious Affiliation of Canadians Aged 65 and Older in 2011

	Number of Canadians 65 and Older (Total)	Number of Immigrants (of Canadians 65 and Older)
Christian	3,755,775	945,570
Jewish	60,835	29,005
Muslim	46,460	45,545
Sikh	46,090	45,100
Buddhist	42,455	38,245
Hindu	38,960	38,510
No religious affiliation	542,995	209,935

Source: Statistics Canada, 2011a.

Table 15.2 Most Common Languages among Canadians Aged 65 to 74 in 2011

Language	Number of Canadians Aged 65 to 74
English	1,650,130
French	622,785
Italian	43,120
Punjabi	29,350
Cantonese	28,020
Chinese (not otherwise specified)	22,760
Portuguese	18,195
Greek	13,770
Selected Aboriginal languages	5,075

Source: Statistics Canada, 2011b.

Ethnocultural Diversity and Aging

Cultural values, norms, and expectations affect perceptions and experiences of aging related to individualism, independence, and autonomy among groups from the "global North," for example, or to collectivism, interdependence, and reciprocity among groups from the "global South" (Lagacé, Charmarkeh, & Grandena, 2012). For instance, these latter groups may emphasize family and community support for older adults and view aging in more positive terms (Lagacé et al., 2012). Studies of Canadian and Portuguese older adults report differences in antecedents of loneliness and coping strategies, with Canadians more likely to identify personal inadequacies, unfulfilling intimate relationships, relocation or separation, and social marginality as causes of loneliness (Rokach & Neto, 2005). Self-reflection and acceptance, distancing and denial, and religion and faith were more common coping strategies among Canadian seniors, while Portuguese older adults engaged more with social or family support networks (Rokach, Orzeck, & Neto, 2004). Further research on increasing ethnocultural diversity of the aging population is imperative, considering the socio-culturally constructed nature of aging and care (Lagacé et al., 2012).

Gender and Aging

In 2014, roughly 45.1 per cent of Canadians aged 65 and older were male and 54.9 per cent were female (Statistics Canada, 2014a). Numerous gender differences affect aging experiences of Canadian women and men, including perceptions of aging, health outcomes and behaviours, and caregiving experiences.

Men and Women's Perceptions of Aging

Older women and men may perceive experiences of aging differently and identify different sources of support in later life. Lagacé and colleagues (2012) found that older immigrant men were more critical than women of the social challenges of aging in Canada, including loss of social status and changes in living arrangements (e.g., seniors' homes). An American study found that older women and men experience different socio-emotional functioning and adaptation to aging, with men demonstrating more inhibited emotion and women coping through strong friendship networks (Consedine, Magai, & Krivoshekova, 2005). Older women may be more likely than men to share feelings with others, seek formal and informal support, and effectively build informal networks (Phillipson, Bernard, Phillips, & Ogg, 2001).

Different psychosocial factors have different impacts on aging and mortality among women and men. For example, among older Canadian women, low levels of social support and social engagement present greater mortality risks, while lower education, perceived control, and physical functioning present greater mortality risks for men (Fry & Debats, 2006). Older women and men draw on a range of social resources to facilitate healthy aging with differing motivations. For example, Narushima, Liu, and Diestelkamp (2013) found that older Canadian women were more likely than men to pursue education programs for social and practical reasons, such as meeting new people, making friends, and keeping physically active.

Gendered Differences in Health

Gender differences exist in health outcomes and behaviours. Some studies report that older women experience better physical health and mortality outcomes than men in certain areas. In a study of four countries, including Canada, Mitnitski and colleagues (2005) report that although older women were frailer than men, they experienced lower mortality. Gonzalez, Suissa, and Emst (2011) found that older Canadian men were at significantly greater risk of rehospitalization and death due to pulmonary disease than women. However, some international studies report that older women experience greater health challenges than men, including poorer general health, higher disability and depressive symptoms (Zunzunegui et al., 2007), and lower cognitive or neuropsychological memory performance (Tippett et al., 2009). Social workers will increasingly find themselves working in disability support roles as population aging increases. A comprehensive discussion on disability and social work can be found in Chapter 14 by Irene Carter.

Older women and men use different strategies to manage health changes in later life. Older women are more likely to use diverse compensatory or self-protective strategies (e.g., positive thinking, disengagement) to alter perceptions or interpretations of situations by restructuring thoughts, emotions, and attributions (Chipperfield, Perry, Bailis, Ruthig, & Chuchmach, 2007). Their use of such strategies predicts fewer hospitalizations and shorter hospital stays (Chipperfield & Perry, 2006). Older women with serious health problems who use positive restructuring beliefs (e.g., "every cloud has a silver lining") report better emotional well-being and life satisfaction (Swift, Bailis, Chipperfield, Ruthig, & Newall, 2008). Older men may benefit more (e.g., reduced hospitalizations) from primary or proactive strategies intended to change external circumstances to meet goals or life demands, such as task modification (e.g., taking more time to do a task, modifying task components) and seeking help (Chipperfield & Perry, 2006).

Gender differences also exist in access to healthcare services and support. For example, Nie, Wang, Tracy, Moineddin, and Upshur (2010) found that older Canadian women were more likely to consult with family physicians, while men were more likely to visit specialists and emergency rooms. Older women may also be less likely than men to have a helper (spouse or nonspouse) at home to provide health and social support and are more likely to rely on help provided by a person outside the home (Douglas, Richardson, Letts, & Wilkins, 2010).

Gender Differences in Caregiving

Women are the main providers of informal caregiving (Dahlberg, Demack, & Bambra, 2007) and provide more hours of care, more intensive personal care, and longer periods of time caregiving than male caregivers (Chiou, Chen, & Wang, 2005; Lin, Fee, & Wu, 2012; Pinquart & Sörensen, 2006). Women's health is more adversely affected by caregiving, with older female caregivers reporting greater caregiving burden than male caregivers, including increased stress, depression, and anxiety (Bedard, Kuzik, Chambers, Molloy, Dubois, & Lever, 2005; Gallicchio, Siddiqi, Langenberg, & Baumgarten, 2002; Navaie-Waliser, Spriggs, & Feldman, 2002; Yee & Schulz, 2000). Gender differences exist in caregiving tasks. In a study of Canadian women and men caring for a terminally ill spouse (Brazil, Thabane, Foster, & Bedard, 2009), female caregivers more often provided support for toileting tasks, and male caregivers more often provided support for mobility tasks. Women reported significantly greater caregiving strain, including physical, personal, familial, and financial effects, and were less likely to receive support from family or friends (Brazil et al., 2009). In a study of older Canadian women and men caring for individuals with Alzheimer's disease (Bedard et al., 2005), female caregivers experienced greater caregiver burden than males, including strain related to caregiving role demands, a sense of role inadequacy, and dealing with more care-recipient problem behaviours (e.g., anger).

Sexual Orientation, Gender Identity, and Aging

Roughly 2.4 per cent of Canadians aged 18 to 59 self-identify as gay, lesbian, or bisexual (Statistics Canada, 2012b). Understanding the unique needs and challenges of seniors who identify as LGBTQ requires attention to their historical and social contexts. LGBTQ older adults have faced a lifetime of cultural, political, and social norms that stigmatized, pathologized, and criminalized LGBTQ identities, thoughts, and behaviours, and a lack of social support associated with marginalization has consequences in later life (Blank, Asencio, Descartes, & Griggs, 2009; Brotman, Ryan, & Cormier, 2003; D'Emilio, 2002). LGBTQ seniors face challenges associated with gender identity, discrimination (including homophobia and heterosexism), family relations, health concerns, and care access, but also experience positive aspects of aging, including self-sufficiency, independence, and effective crisis management (Murray, Numer, Merritt, Gahagan, & Comber, 2012). However, little research attention has been paid to health and aging among LGBTQ seniors in Canada (Murray et al., 2012).

Mental Health Status in LGBTQ Older Adults

Research on LGBTQ older adults in the 1980s and 1990s focused primarily on negative mental health stereotypes, such as experiences of depression and difficulties in coping with aging, while recent studies describe more positive psychosocial functioning among LGBTQ older adults (Fredriksen-Goldsen & Muraco, 2010). Some studies report that LGBTQ older adults are no more depressed than other older adults experiencing good or excellent mental health (Dorfman et al., 1995; D'Augelli, Grossman, Hershberger, & O'Connell, 2001). Older adults openly identifying as gay or lesbian may have higher self-esteem and life satisfaction as well as a lower maladjustment to aging (Fredriksen-Goldsen & Muraco, 2010). However, an American study (Fredriksen-Goldsen, Kim, Barkan, Muraco, & Hoy-Ellis, 2013) found that LGBTQ older adults experience higher risk of poor mental and physical health, disability, smoking, and excessive drinking than heterosexual seniors. A Canadian research review (Murray et al., 2012) reports that LGBTQ seniors experience specific health needs and risks, including certain types of cancer vulnerability.

While some studies report good mental health outcomes for LGBTQ seniors (D'Augelli et al., 2001; Dorfman et al., 1995), others explain that alienation from one's family and exclusion from mainstream society can result in marginalization and isolation. Romantic partnerships among LGBTQ individuals are twice as likely to dissolve compared to heterosexual marriages, potentially because of stressors including societal discrimination (Blank et al., 2009). LGBTQ seniors are more likely to live alone, which is associated with increased health risks (e.g., poorer mental health and nutrition), lower income, and higher risk of institutionalization (Blank et al., 2009). For social workers, who are allies and advocates for LGBTQ communities, it is important to understand how to productively recognize the vulnerability of LGBTQ seniors and ways to promote social action to ameliorate the consequences of such vulnerability. This is further addressed in Chapter 12 by Christine A. Walsh, Carey Mulligan, and Gio Dolcecore.

Access to Healthcare and Social Services for LGBTQ Older Adults

Attitudes among peers and service providers can impact the well-being of LGBTQ older adults. American and European studies of LGBTQ older adults (Stein, Beckerman, & Sherman, 2010; Villar, Serrat, Faba, & Celdran, 2013) describe fears or experiences of rejection or neglect by care providers and other older adults (e.g., care-facility residents) and of going "back into the closet" if placed in care. A study of older Canadian gay men and lesbian women (Brotman et al., 2003) describes the impacts of discrimination on health, service access, and experiences of invisibility. A Canadian review by Murray and colleagues (2012) reports that LGBTQ seniors face challenges with disclosure of sexual orientation to service providers and discrimination, including homophobia and heterosexism, in health and social services.

Adaptation to Aging Processes in LGBTQ Older Adults

Lesbian, gay, and bisexual older adults may be more successful than their heterosexual counterparts at accepting self and status in later life (Fredriksen-Goldsen & Muraco, 2010), as skills garnered to effectively deal with stigmatization and marginalization in early life equip LGBTQ individuals to better deal with stigmatization associated with old age (Berger & Kelly, 2002; Price, 2008). Other factors influencing aging among LGBTQ older adults include gender identity and performance (the way in which gender is socially enacted), sexual behaviours, discrimination, and degree of openness about one's sexual orientation (Blank et al., 2009). Some recent research describes similarities in older adults' well-being regardless of sexual orientation. For instance, declining cognitive functioning in aging may be correlated with gender, but it is not correlated with sexual orientation (Maylor, Reimers, Choi, Collaer, Peters, & Silverman, 2007).

LGBTQ older adults' experiences are intertwined with ethnicity, culture, socioeconomic status, and familial relations (Price, 2008). For example, David and Knight (2008) report that older men identifying as both gay and African American experienced significantly higher levels of ageism than those identifying as gay and Caucasian. Older African-American gay men also experience higher levels of racism and heteronormativity than younger African-American men. Older adults identifying as lesbian are more likely than older gay men to have partners, lower incomes, larger social networks, and to not live alone (David & Knight, 2008). Finally, identity development patterns and experiences, including family relationship construction and function, vary between older lesbian women and gay men (Herdt, Beeler, & Rawls, 1997; Muraco, LeBlanc, & Russell 2008).

Cohort Diversity in the Aging Population

In 2014, roughly 56.3 per cent of Canada's older adults were aged 65 to 74, 30.6 per cent were aged 75 to 84, and 13.1 per cent were aged 85 and older (Statistics Canada, 2014a). **Age cohorts** refer to groups of people who are the same age in the same period of time (Statistics Canada, 2013a). Age cohort differences refer to groups differentiated by age (e.g., 65 to 75 compared to 75 to 85) and are linked with **birth cohort**, which refers to all people born in a given year. Any study investigating differences between age groups in a specific year also examines birth cohort effects since it is impossible to determine whether differences are due to age and development or to birth year (Twenge & Campbell, 2001). Age-related individual development (e.g., behavioural or emotional development) may also vary between birth cohorts. Individuals belonging to specific cohorts can experience aging differently (Fredriksen-Goldsen & Muraco, 2010). For instance, growing up in the 1940s and in the 1960s may produce different age-related developmental changes (Twenge & Campbell, 2001). Historical, social, political, and environmental experiences (e.g., war, natural disasters) have differential developmental effects on groups of different ages.

Age cohort can affect physical and mental health and well-being. For example, O'Hoski and colleagues (2014) found that balance ability (linked to falls) was greater among Canadian seniors from younger age cohorts (50 to 59, 60 to 69) compared to older age cohorts (70 to 79, 80 to 89). Chen, Stewart, Dales, Johansen, Bryan, & Taylor (2005) found that men aged 55 and over had more hospitalizations from pulmonary disease than women, except in the 55 to 59 cohort, where women had more hospitalizations. Most hospitalizations for both genders were between ages 70 to 79. European studies report that older age and birth cohorts experience poorer outcomes in self-esteem, memory problems, instrumental daily living activities, and physical activities (Finkel,

Reynolds, McArdle, & Pedersen, 2007; Heikkinen et al., 2011; McMullin & Cairney, 2004). However, other studies have reported no age cohort differences in aging outcomes. For example, Broeska, Lengyel, and Tate (2013) found that cohort effects did not influence relationships between nutrition and mortality for older Canadian men.

Social support may influence outcomes for different age cohorts. For example, Fiori, Smith, and Antonucci (2007) found age cohort differences in older adults' social networks. Those aged 85 and older were more likely to have smaller networks, more frequent contact with friends than family members, lower contact with friends, and lower activity involvement and emotional support. Younger older adults were more likely to have larger networks, frequent contact with both family and friends, and higher emotional support and activity involvement. European studies report differences in friendships across older age cohorts, with those aged 54 to 64 having more friends and retaining friends longer than those aged 65 to 74 or 75 to 84 (Stevens & Van Tilburg, 2011). American studies describe age cohort differences in adaptation to aging, with those aged 74 to 86 more likely than those aged 65 to 73 to be socially isolated, anxious or depressed, and emotionally inhibited (Consedine et al., 2005). Class inequities may be heightened in later life, with older age groups experiencing the largest income differentials in Canada, and older age groups in lower social classes experiencing lower self-esteem (McMullin & Cairney, 2004).

Case Example 15.1

Susan (age 65) has just retired from her job. She has registered with a seniors' centre in order to keep active in the community. However, she does not feel comfortable taking part in the group activities, which are mainly for oldest-old adults with declining health conditions. Activities include arts and crafts, cards and board games, and community outings. Susan has difficulty fitting in with the group and feels that she cannot build relationships with the other members. She is feeling frustrated with group activities and is not feeling engaged in the community. Susan is wondering if she should continue to attend the seniors' centre activities.

Points to Consider

- If you were a worker at the seniors' centre, what could you do to support Susan?
- What are some other factors that might be impacting Susan's experience?
- How could you support programs for older adults of different ages and health statuses?
- What are some other resources that might help Susan feel engaged in the community?
- What other individuals or organizations could be involved in these support processes?

Theoretical Approaches to Understanding Aging and Diversity

While acknowledging the variations within the aging population, the following theories and perspectives should sensitize social workers to diverse dimensions and experiences of aging, aiding in an understanding of the ways in which these variations intersect and combine in a socially structured process of inequality, leading to disadvantage, discrimination, and oppression.

Life Course Theory and Cumulative Advantage/Disadvantage in Aging

Life course theory views life as a continuing process, with each phase linked to another (Giele & Elder, 1998; Bai & Chow, 2014), with individuals' past experiences influencing their present state, and with the present shaping future possibilities (Dannefer, 2003). Individuals' life events (e.g., education, migration, marriage, widowhood) and trajectories result in changes in status and roles. Life course theory focuses on the interplay of individuals' life events and their historical and socio-cultural contexts, with personal life trajectories embedded in broader social contexts, cultural practices and ideologies, and historical events (Elder, 1995; Dannefer & Setterstein, 2010). These influence individuals' opportunities, life choices, developmental paths, and aging experiences (Stoller & Gibson, 2000). Within population cohorts, aging differs according to gender, ethnicity, religion, social class, family structure, and sexual orientation, and individual capacity to manage life changes varies with differential resource access.

Consistent with a theory underlining the cumulative effects of life events, the **cumulative advantage/disadvantage perspective** (Merton, 1988) interprets diversity of aging experiences as the accumulation of privilege or disadvantage throughout an individual's life. Cumulative advantage refers to "the ways in which initial comparative advantage, trained capacity, structural location, and available resources" combine to widen the gap between "haves" and "have-nots" (Merton, 1988, p. 606). Life course and cumulative advantage/disadvantage perspectives have been used to investigate mechanisms shaping diversity in aging processes (e.g., Bai & Chow, 2014; Dannefer & Setterstein, 2010).

Feminist Theory and Diverse Aging Experiences

Feminist theory prioritizes gender as an organizing principle of power, wealth, and welfare, exploring mechanisms behind older women being undervalued in society, oppression within the family, and comparatively higher rates of poverty. Feminist gerontologists maintain that men and women's socially constructed roles and gendered division of economic and political labour translate into women's vulnerability and subordination, resulting in further inequality in older age (Binstock, 2007; Lewis & Butler, 1972). For example, women are more likely to shoulder unpaid or underpaid caregiving roles, with many leaving or reducing paid employment because of the burden of balancing career and care responsibilities (Allen & Walker, 2009; Kolb, 2014), which affects social and health status and leads to lower income and financial dependency in later life.

Feminist social workers aim to empower women and fight against patriarchy (through advocacy efforts, for example) and raise societal awareness of socially constructed gender inequalities (Mehrotra, 2010; Turner & Maschi, 2014). Efforts by feminist social workers and gerontologists might include advocating for more family-friendly employment policies, comprehensive long-term care services, and adequate financial support for older women. Despite the contribution of feminist theory to understanding diverse aging experiences, older "men" and "women" should not be viewed as homogeneous groups, as significant differences exist within each group (Teater, 2010). Critical thinking about gender affects our learning as students and our practice as social workers. Further discussion on gender-sensitive social work service can be found in Chapter 13 by Sarah Fotheringham.

Intersectionality Theory and Diverse Aging Experiences

Intersectionality theory suggests that different dimensions of disadvantage or oppression (e.g., ageism, racism, sexism, heterosexism) and power relations associated with different identity categories multiply their effects, leading to greater marginalization, exclusion, and oppression (Mattsson, 2014; Sargeant, 2011). Canadian and international research supports this theory's relevance for diverse older populations, reporting that age, gender, sexual orientation, social class, health, and immigrant and visible minority status intersect to generate marginalization and oppression (Cronin & King, 2010; Taylor, 2009) as well as barriers to health and social service access (Kobayashi & Prus, 2011; Sargeant, 2011). Intersectionality analysis can support anti-oppressive practice, enabling social workers to challenge inequality and support client empowerment (Mattsson, 2014). More attention should be paid to intersecting identities and wider social and policy contexts affecting older adults. For further discussion of how intersectionality affects social workers' interventions and client relationships, see Chapter 6 by Miu Chung Yan.

Practice Approaches with Diverse Aging Population

Aging populations face a range of challenges and oppressions that impact older adults' general well-being and access to resources, services, and information (Collins, 2011). Challenges facing diverse older adults include language, housing, transportation, unemployment, and financial difficulties and poverty, as well as deteriorating personal relationships and social isolation (Collins, 2011; Georgiades, 2014; Warburton, Bartlett, & Rao, 2009). Older adults' diverse health and social service needs (e.g., medical services, senior daycare centres, in-home health services) represent an area of concern (Collins, 2011), because older adults face challenges in finding and using appropriate services due to a lack of appropriate services, limited awareness of available resources, service access difficulties, and unfamiliarity with socio-cultural systems (Georgiades, 2014; Warburton et al., 2009). Social workers may adopt a range of practice approaches to effectively and appropriately support diverse older clients.

Anti-oppressive Practice

Anti-oppressive practice aims to empower vulnerable or marginalized individuals and groups by addressing structural inequalities and social hierarchies (Dominelli, 1996); addressing systems of racism, classism, or sexism linked to power imbalances; as well as focusing on broader social, educational, economic, and cultural structures (Clifford, 1995). This can be effective when working with people from diverse immigrant, health, and socio-economic backgrounds (Larson, 2008; Sakamoto, 2007; Strier & Binyamin, 2010). It is appropriate to use anti-oppressive approaches to work with diverse older adults (of different ethnocultural backgrounds or sexual orientation, for example), who may benefit from support and empowerment to enhance social respect and benefits.

For example, in developing anti-oppressive services for LGBTQ older adults, it is vital that social workers allow self-definition of sexual orientation and gender identity, apply new and relevant knowledge in practice, use appropriate language, and provide sensitive and appropriate outreach. It is imperative for social workers to understand the impact of agency, program, and services policies and practices, as well as local, provincial, and federal laws that affect the experiences of LGBTQ older adults (Fredriksen-Goldsen, Hoy-Ellis, Goldsen, Emlet, & Hooyman, 2014; Siverskog, 2014). It is, however, our responsibility to question the potential limitations of anti-oppression in social work practice and professional education. Such limitations and the ways in which we may understand and circumvent them are further discussed in Chapter 3 by Gordon Pon, Sulaimon Giwa, and Narda Razack.

Culturally Sensitive, Appropriate, and Competent Practice

"Culturally sensitive" and "culturally competent" practice are identified as key to providing responsive and effective support to diverse aging populations (Collins, 2011; Georgiades, 2014), aiming to ensure service accessibility and acceptability to diverse communities and enhance practice quality and outcomes (Davis & Donald, 1997; Schim, Doorenbos, & Borse, 2006). Cultural sensitivity is based on knowledge and awareness of cultural influences on well-being and care and involves changes in practitioners' attitudes, values, and awareness of cultural differences and similarities (Hardy & Laszloffy, 1995; Santiago-Rivera, 1995; Schim et al., 2006), such as showing respect, awareness of language and culture, and understanding the importance of spirituality and religion as sources of support (Collins, 2011). Approaches often involve relatively superficial adaptations (e.g., language, practitioner background) of conventional interventions (Wendt & Gone, 2012). Social workers often work with clients that have multiple connections with spiritual or religious communities, requiring that as helping professionals we have an understanding of how spirituality and religion affect our clients as well as ourselves. This topic is further discussed in Chapter 11 by Diana Coholic.

Culturally appropriate practice involves recognizing and responding to relationships between cultural aspects and client outcomes (Johnstone & Kanitsaki, 2009; Shaw, 2005) while considering the "appropriateness" of conventional approaches for diverse groups (Vicary & Bishop, 2005). Services are tailored to the needs of particular populations (Shaw, 2005), including culturally specific services (Anderson, Scrimshaw, Fullilove, Fielding, & Normand, 2003; Henderson, Kendall, & See, 2011; Shaw, 2005) and consideration of service location, procedures, and regulations (Johnstone & Kanitsaki, 2009).

Cultural competence moves beyond knowledge, awareness, and sensitivity, referring to a set of congruent beliefs and values, attitudes, behaviours, and policies (Anderson et al., 2003; Hardy & Laszloffy, 1995; Johnstone & Kanitsaki, 2009; Schim et al., 2006; Wendt & Gone, 2012). This involves integrating and transforming knowledge into specific attitudes, practices, standards, and policies (Davis & Donald, 1997) and requires organizational, institutional, systemic, and policy-level cultural competence (Anderson et al., 2003; Johnstone & Kanitsaki, 2009). Culturally competent services consider and address structural influences on the client, the practitioner, and the institutional power dynamics through empowerment and advocacy (Guarnaccia & Rodriguez, 1996; Wendt & Gone, 2012; Williamson & Harrison, 2010) as well as through partnerships (Collins, 2011). (For further discussion of cultural competence, see Chapter 4 by Marie Lacroix.)

Warburton and colleagues (2009) identify five practice responses for work with older adults from culturally and linguistically diverse backgrounds:

- Recognizing diversity within different cultural groups
- Using strengths-based approaches
- Developing cultural competency
- Cultivating tolerance and anti-discrimination
- Providing information and improved communication and working in partnership

A Canadian example of a culturally relevant approach to practice described by Podnieks and Wilson (2003) is an initiative to increase awareness of elder abuse among faith communities and enhance their capacity to identify and deal with elder abuse through education and empowerment. This approach, involving partnerships with cultural and faith organizations, focuses on Catholic, Jewish, and Muslim faith leaders and involves dissemination of culturally sensitive information, materials, and support in older adults' preferred language. Faith leaders recommended educational materials such as pamphlets, videos, and short sermons written by someone with knowledge of elder abuse, and emphasized the need for training on elder abuse for faith communities (Podnieks & Wilson, 2003).

Case Example: Addressing Intersectionality of Oppression among LGBTQ Older Adults

LGBTQ older adults represent one population facing intersecting forms of discrimination and oppression (e.g., heterosexism, homophobia, transphobia), which are central to their lived experiences (Langley, 2001; Siverskog, 2014). LGBTQ older adults may not be willing to disclose their sexual orientation and gender identity because of fear of oppression. They may be characterized by a degree of "invisibility," since they may hide their identity and social workers will not necessarily know who they are (Langley, 2001). Social workers should develop knowledge about diverse and complex sexuality and gender identities among older adults, beyond heterosexual and binary gender norms (De Montigny, 2011; Siverskog, 2014). In a review of existing literature on aging and sexuality, Fredriksen-Goldsen and colleagues (2014) summarize competencies critical for social workers supporting LGBTQ older adults:

- Critically analyzing one's personal and professional attitudes on sexual orientation and gender
- Understanding social and cultural factors influencing those attitudes
- Understanding social, cultural, structural, and environmental contexts that negatively affect LGBTQ older adults' experiences
- Distinguishing different subgroups of LGBTQ older adults

An anti-heterosexist approach, involving both anti-oppression and empowerment (Langley, 2001; Mattsson, 2014), is one possible approach to social work practice with LGBTQ older adults that involves awareness of heterosexist assumptions influencing individual practice and institutional responses (Langley, 2001; Mattsson, 2014), as well as addressing issues of isolation, fear, shame, and trauma resulting from prior experiences of discrimination (Langley, 2001; Siverskog, 2014).

An example of a program supporting LGBTQ older adults is the Los Angeles LGBT Center's Seniors Services Department (Gratwick, Jihanian, Holloway, Sanchez, & Sullivan, 2014), which involves (1) activities (including enrichment, education, and entertainment activities) providing older adults with opportunities for social interaction and social support networks; (2) case management, facilitating access to services (e.g., affordable housing, mental health, legal and food resources) and support groups for older adults and caregivers; and (3) cultural competency training for service providers, including healthcare professionals, housing organizations, and government agencies, and for social work students. It was reported that public awareness of LGBTQ older adult concerns has increased since providing training to different sectors (Gratwick et al., 2014).

Narrative Approach for Person-Centred Care

A narrative approach emphasizes the importance of clients' lived experience and the importance of narratives (story-based accounts of events) in framing people's understanding of the

Case Example 15.2

Rob (age 70) is a gay man who has recently moved to an assisted living facility. The home has made an effort to ensure that the language used in policies and publications, in meetings with residents, and in communication within the facility is inclusive of sexual minorities. This made Rob feel safe to come out in the facility, and he generally feels accepted by the staff in the home. However, after learning that Rob is gay, a group of residents, who grew up during a period when homosexuality was illegal and considered immoral, isolate him and do not want him to stay in the home. Rob has expressed that he feels upset by this and has come to you for help.

Points to Consider

- As a manager of the facility, what approaches or strategies could you use to handle this issue?
- How could you support Rob while also engaging the other residents?
- How can you effectively engage care-facility staff in these support processes?
- What are some approaches or strategies that could be applied at the institutional level?
- What theories could you apply to guide your intervention approaches?

social world and in shaping identity (Kropf & Tandy, 1998; Roscoe, Carson, & Madoc-Jones, 2011; Wilks, 2005). Narrative approaches involve deconstructing "problem" stories, challenging existing meanings and interpretations, constructing alternative and empowering narratives, and facilitating new meanings and understandings (Caldwell, 2005; Kropf & Tandy, 1998; Poole, Gardner, Flower, & Cooper, 2009; Roscoe et al., 2011). This approach considers social, political, and cultural structures, contexts, and relationships that affect narratives, actions, and identities (Kropf & Tandy, 1998; Roscoe et al., 2011; Wilks, 2005). Social workers and service users share stories and experiences (Roscoe et al., 2011), individually or in groups (Poole et al., 2009), including through creative techniques (e.g., journaling, life maps) (Caldwell, 2005).

Narrative approaches may be useful to support successful aging among diverse older adults (Andrews, 2009; Poole et al., 2009). Positive narratives of aging have strong implications for successful aging (Andrews, 2009) and can be used in life review processes (Caldwell, 2005). Older adults construct life narratives that focus on particular roles (e.g., caring roles) and changes in roles, identities, and stories over time (Kropf & Tandy, 1998; Roscoe et al., 2011; Wilks, 2005). Narrative approaches can support older adults to address anxiety, loss, and devaluation linked to health status, racial or ethnic identity, sexuality, and age (Kropf & Tandy, 1998). Through narrative approaches, social workers are increasingly emphasizing identity construction as a product of social processes. Further discussion on these approaches can be found in Chapter 10 by Catherine Montgomery.

In one Canadian example of a narrative-based intervention, Poole and colleagues (2009) described a narrative therapy group for ethnoculturally diverse older adults coping with mental health and substance misuse challenges. In 90-minute sessions over eight weeks, group work practices were used to build mutual support, and participants identified, created, and shared life stories involving memories, accomplishments, and successes. They were supposed to view themselves as complex individuals with teams of family, friends, and supporters and to develop tools to address challenges. Participants emphasized the importance of group size and diversity, as well as tolerance, acceptance, befriending, empowerment, and lessening guilt linked to the narrative approach (Poole et al., 2009).

Empowerment and Social Work

Empowerment approaches involve individual and collective processes of changing power relations for people (such as diverse older adults) experiencing social, cultural, economic, and political oppression. Empowerment focuses on people's ability to gain control over decisions and actions regarding their own lives, as well as equity and social justice (Askheim, 2003; Breton, 1994; Chapin & Cox, 2002), and works across personal, interpersonal, and political levels of practice through consciousness raising, political awareness, social mobilization, action, and reflection (Askheim, 2003; Breton, 1994; Cattaneo & Chapman, 2010; Chapin & Cox, 2002; Cowger, 1994). This approach addresses power imbalances between service providers and users. Clients are considered experts on their own lives and interests, and social workers act as partners, facilitators, and advocates, helping people to empower themselves by encouraging, assisting, and supporting them to define goals and implement actions though training, mutual support, community building, and social and political action (Askheim, 2003; Cattaneo & Chapman, 2010; Chapin & Cox, 2002; Cowger, 1994; Thompson & Thompson, 2001). Empowerment involves individual increases in social influence, control, self-confidence, self-efficacy, knowledge, and skills, and structural dimensions addressing oppressive social structures and relations (Askheim, 2003; Breton, 1994; Cattaneo & Chapman, 2010; Chapin & Cox, 2002; Thompson & Thompson, 2001).

Diverse older adults may be marginalized or disempowered due to ethnoracial status, poor health, poverty, social isolation, service barriers, and ageism and discrimination. Empowerment approaches focus on resilience and productive aging, challenging stereotypes facing older adults. Older adults are supported to enhance their own life status, control, and self-efficacy by engaging in actions addressing service, income, and housing policies and challenging structural oppression (Chapin & Cox, 2002; Thompson & Thompson, 2001). Manthorpe, Moriarty, Stevens, Hussein, and Sharif (2010) identify practical recommendations for service providers supporting ethnic minority older adults, emphasizing opportunities for involvement in social activities to address social isolation, including voluntary or intergenerational activities, and supporting older adults to play active roles in the management of programs. In another example, Concannon (2009) describes a strategy to promote social inclusion of LGBTQ older adults based on empowering elders to access social services and providing a caring and secure community environment in which diverse older adults can meet.

Enhancing knowledge and skills is critical to empowerment in the aging population. For instance, the Phone Angel Program in New York aimed to empower older Chinese adults and family caregivers (Mui, Glajchen, Chen, & Sun, 2013). Older adult volunteers were trained on caregiving issues such as burden, coping, and problem-solving skills to provide emotional and coping support to isolated caregivers. They provide phone support to caregivers within their ethnocultural community, with monitoring and evaluation carried out by social workers. Most older adults reported positive outcomes, including improved communication skills, mental and emotional well-being, and sense of self, while caregivers reported positive outcomes such as reduced burden and stress (Mui et al., 2013).

Experiential Exercise: Reflect and Act

This exercise aims to enable participants to reflect and take action to increase their awareness and understanding of the experiences of diverse older adults. This includes learning more about the services and supports that are available for diverse older adults in the community, as well as challenges that might face diverse older adults in accessing services to respond to their physical, psychological, social, and material needs.

Case Example 15.3

Jenny (age 72) immigrated to Canada from Shanghai in 2014. She and her husband, who has dementia, live with her adult son. She looks after her husband and cooks for the family as both her son and daughter-in-law have full-time jobs. Jenny's son and daughter-in-law have noticed that she has been feeling very tired, is not sleeping well, and is showing signs of depression. Jenny has expressed feelings of anxiety about food quality and home hygiene and is worried that she is not doing her job right. Her son and daughter-in-law have tried to talk to Jenny, but she has become distant from the family. Her son has come to you for help, as he is concerned about his mother's mental health.

Points to Consider

- As a social worker, what are your concerns about Jenny? What factors might impact her well-being?
- What intervention approaches or strategies could you use for this family?
- Which family members should be involved in these interventions? Why?
- What are some resources that might be used in supporting this family?
- What theories could you apply to guide an intervention for this family?

Step 1: Researching Contacts

- Identify organizations, associations, or other services in your city or community that work with older adults from diverse backgrounds (e.g., different ethno-cultural, socio-economic, or other identity groups).
- Compile a list of organizations, associations, or other services, including contact information, for each one.
- Select one organization that serves a population of older adults about which you have no prior knowledge or understanding.

Step 2: Making Connections

- Contact the selected organization, association, or service to arrange a site visit.
- Make an in-person visit to the organization and meet with staff and with older adults (members or clients) to better understand the client population, the services provided, and the needs the organization is meeting OR
- Identify and take part in volunteer activities offered by the organization to better understand the client population, the services provided, and the needs that the organization is meeting.
- Before visiting the organization and collecting information, explain in detail what the purpose of your visit is and what the information will be used for; obtain informed consent from the organization; and outline steps to protect the privacy and confidentiality of staff and older adults.

Step 3: Making Sense of Experiences and Needs

- Keep notes and write a personal journal to reflect on your thoughts and experiences when interacting with the organization and with the older adults.
- Compile a list describing the different challenges, needs, and strengths of the older adult population that you came to understand through your experience.
- Meet with your classmates or other course participants to share and discuss your experience and your understanding of the experiences of diverse older adults.

Questions to consider during the site visit or volunteering activity and during your reflections and discussions:

- Who is the target population served by the organization? Does the organization target a specific gender group, age group, cultural or religious group, health-status group, or other group?

- In targeting particular populations, how does the organization consider different aspects of identity and oppression?
- What types of services or programs does the organization offer?
- What are the aims or objectives of the organization? What are the aims and objectives of their specific programs?
- How are the organizational programs and practices using approaches based on cultural sensitivity or competency? Empowerment?
- What do the older adults enjoy about the service or program? What is working well?
- What are some of the challenges with the service or program (e.g., accessibility, cost)?
- What are the biggest challenges facing the older adults served by the organization (e.g., health, social, or financial challenges)?
- Did some of the identified challenges surprise you? Why?
- Who are some other older adult groups who might face similar challenges?
- How can these challenges and experiences be understood using a life course perspective? Feminist theory? Intersectionality theory?
- What other services or policy changes might be needed to address these different challenges?

Summary and Conclusion

Differences in ethnocultural background, gender differences, cohort differences, and sexual orientation are just some examples of the diversity found in Canada's aging population. To understand the experiences of diverse aging populations, various theories and perspectives can be applied. *Life course theory* emphasizes the influence of past experiences on older adults' present status and future possibilities, linked to the accumulation of advantages or disadvantages and impacts on aging. *Feminist theory* examines gendered power relations resulting in older women's vulnerability, oppression, and disadvantage (e.g., in division of labour), aiming to empower women and combat patriarchy. *Intersectionality theory* examines interactions between multiple dimensions of identity and disadvantage (e.g., age, gender, sexual orientation) and their effects on life changes and aging experiences.

Drawing on these theoretical perspectives, a range of practice approaches can be adopted by social workers to address the needs of diverse older adults. *Anti-oppressive practice* addresses systems of discrimination and power, including relations between service providers and users. Older adults often experience multiple dimensions of oppression, and addressing the *intersectionality* of discrimination and oppression is crucial through, for example, *anti-heterosexist approaches*. *Culturally sensitive, appropriate, and competent practice* aims to ensure service accessibility, acceptability, and quality for diverse ethnocultural and linguistic communities based on cultural knowledge, attitudes, behaviours, and policies. A *narrative approach* emphasizes the importance of lived experiences and narratives in shaping identities, supporting new and empowering understandings of aging. *Empowerment approaches* aim to change individual and collective power relations for marginalized older adults, supporting control, decision making, and action in their own lives at individual and socio-political levels by enhancing knowledge and skills.

Acknowledgements

The research assistance and information searches provided by Gabrielle Daoust and Lun Li are very much appreciated.

Questions for Review

1. Drawing on the arguments outlined in the chapter, explain why and how social, cultural, structural, and environmental contexts would affect the aging experience of LGBTQ older adults in addition to their personal and life course factors.
2. People holding the multiculturalism perspective claim that harmony and equity exist among different racial and ethnic groups in Canada, and racial and ethnic diversities have been well respected in the provision of services for older adults. To what extent do you agree with them? Why?
3. The primary source countries of immigrants to Canada are said to have shifted from Western European countries to Asian countries in recent years. In what way can the government, organizations, and practitioners better attend to the diverse needs and preferences of older immigrants by using culturally sensitive, appropriate, and competent approaches?
4. The chapter explains how intersectionality theory examines interactions between multiple dimensions of identity and disadvantages and their effects on life changes and aging experience. Can you think of two target groups and apply intersectionality theory to explain how these groups of older people have accumulated disadvantages and been severely oppressed in our society?
5. Considering the gendered differences in various aspects outlined in the chapter, what types of intervention strategies do you think could be used for older male and female adults, respectively, to enhance their well-being in the most effective way?
6. What is the empowerment approach in social work? How can this approach be used to help older female immigrant caregivers who face both caregiving burden and adaptation challenges?

Suggested Readings and Resources

Atira Women's Resource Society. (2011). Building on promising practices across Canada for housing older women experiencing abuse. Retrieved from www.atira.bc.ca/building-promising-practices-across-canada-housing-older-women-experiencing-abuse

Bezalel, R. (1994). *When Shirley met Florence* [Video file]. National Film Board of Canada. Retrieved from www.nfb.ca/film/when_shirley_met_florence

Calgary Catholic Immigration Society. (n.d.). Immigrant seniors services. Retrieved from www.ccis-calgary.ab.ca/index.php?option=com_content&view=article&id=119:immigrant-seniors-services-iss&catid=10:community-development-a-integration-services&Itemid=130

Canadian Women's Health Network. (2012). *Aging, Women and Health.* Retrieved from www.cwhn.ca/en/resources/primers/aging

COSTI Immigrant Services. (n.d.). Seniors service. Retrieved from www.costi.org/programs/seniors.php

Elder Justice Now. (2010). *An age for justice: Confronting elder abuse in America* [Video file]. Retrieved from www.youtube.com/watch?v=-eaJXBj87to

Elgersma, S. (2010, May 26). Immigrant seniors: Their economic security and factors affecting their access to benefits. Parliament of Canada. Retrieved from www.parl.gc.ca/content/lop/researchpublications/07-45-e.htm

Léger, D. (2007). *A Sunday at 105* [Video file]. National Film Board of Canada. Retrieved from http://www.nfb.ca/film/sunday_at_105

Los Angeles LGBT Center. (n.d.). Senior services. See www.lalgbtcenter.org/senior_services

Milan, A., & Vézina, M. (2013, May 13). Senior women. Statistics Canada. Retrieved from http://www.statcan.gc.ca/pub/89-503-x/2010001/article/11441-eng.htm

Multicultural Women and Seniors Services Association; http://www.mwssa.org/about

Ng, E., Lai, D.W.L., Rudner, A.T. (2012). What do we know about immigrant seniors aging in Canada? A demographic, socio-economic and health profile. CERIS—The Ontario Metropolis. Retrieved from http://www.elderabuseontario.com/wp-content/uploads/2014/03/What-do-we-know-about-immigrant-seniors-aging-in-Canada.pdf

Ohama, L. (2001). *Obachan's garden* [Video file]. National Film Board of Canada. Retrieved from http://www.nfb.ca/film/obachans_garden

ProgramsForElderly.com. (n.d.). Urban home—Gay, LGBT retirement community program. Retrieved from http://www.elderabuseontario.com/wp-content/uploads/2014/03/What-do-we-know-about-immigrant-seniors-aging-in-Canada.pdf

Rexdale Women's Centre. (n.d.). Ethno-cultural seniors programs and services. Retrieved from http://www.rexdalewomen.org/programs/programsAndServices-EthnoCultural.html

Ryan, B. (2009). *Healthy aging for gay and lesbian seniors in Canada*. Rainbow Health Ontario. Retrieved from http://www.rainbowhealthontario.ca/resources/healthy-aging-for-gay-and-lesbian-seniors-in-canada

Senior Pride Network. (n.d.). Older LGBTQ resources: Greater Toronto Area. Retrieved from http://www.seniorpridenetwork.com/older-lgbt-resources-gta

Special Senate Committee on Aging. (2007). Active participation in society and economic life. In *First Interim Report: Embracing the Challenge of Aging.* Retrieved from www.parl.gc.ca/Content/SEN/Committee/391/agei/rep/repintfeb07-e.htm#4._Active_Participation_in_Society_and_Economic_Life

The Good Companions. (n.d.). LGBT competency project. Retrieved from www.thegoodcompanions.ca/community-support-services/lgbt-competency-project

Tjepkema, M. (2008). Findings: Health care use among gay, lesbian and bisexual Canadians. Statistics Canada. Retrieved from http://www.statcan.gc.ca/pub/82-003-x/2008001/article/10532/5002598-eng.htm

Webster, A. (2014, May 29). When '70s guys hit their 70s: 3 gay men face aging in "Before You Know It." *New York Times*. Retrieved from www.nytimes.com/2014/05/30/movies/3-gay-men-face-aging-in-before-you-know-it.html?_r=0

References

Allen, K. R., & Walker, A. J. (2009). Theorizing about families and aging from a feminist perspective. In V. L. Bengtson, M. Silverstein, N. M. Putney, & D. Gans (Eds.), *Handbook of theories of aging* (pp. 517–28). New York, NY: Springer.

Anderson, L. M., Scrimshaw, S. C., Fullilove, M. T., Fielding, J. E., & Normand, J. (2003). Culturally competent healthcare systems: A systematic review. *American Journal of Preventive Medicine*, *24*(3), 68–79.

Andrews, M. (2009). The narrative complexity of successful ageing. *International Journal of Sociology and Social Policy*, *29*(1–2), 73–83.

Askheim, O. P. (2003). Empowerment as guidance for professional social work: An act of balancing on a slack rope. *European Journal of Social Work*, *6*(3), 229–40.

Bai, X., & Chow, N. W. (2014). A life-course perspective on elderly residential mobility in Southern China: An adaptation of the amenity retirement migration model. *Journal of Ethnic and Cultural Diversity in Social Work*, *23*(3–4), 309–24.

Bedard, M., Kuzik, R., Chambers, L., Molloy, D. W., Dubois, S., & Lever, J. A. (2005). Understanding burden differences between men and women caregivers: The contribution of care-recipient problem behaviors. *International Psychogeriatric*, *17*(1), 99–118.

Berger, R. M., & Kelly, J. J. (2002). What are older gay men like? An impossible question? *Journal of Gay and Lesbian Social Services*, *13*(4), 55–64.

Binstock, R. H. (2007). Feminism, aging, and the life course perspective. *The Gerontologist*, *47*(5), 705–16.

Blank, T. O., Asencio, M., Descartes, L., & Griggs, J. (2009). Aging, health, and GLBTQ family and community life. *Journal of GLBT Family Studies*, *5*(1/2), 9–34.

Brazil, K., Thabane, L., Foster, G., & Bedard, M. (2009). Gender differences among Canadian spousal caregivers at the end of life. *Health and Social Care in the Community*, *17*(2), 159–66.

Breton, M. (1994). On the meaning of empowerment and empowerment-oriented social work practice. *Social Work with Groups*, *17*(3), 23–37.

Broeska, V. E., Lengyel, C. O., & Tate, R. B. (2013). Nutritional risk and 5-year mortality of older community-dwelling Canadian men: The Manitoba follow-up study. *Journal of Nutrition in Gerontology and Geriatrics*, *32*(4), 317–29.

Brotman, S., Ryan, B., & Cormier, R. (2003). The health and social service needs of gay and lesbian elders and their families in Canada. *The Gerontologist*, *43*(2), 192.

Caldwell, R. L. (2005). At the confluence of memory and meaning: Life review with older adults and families: Using narrative therapy and the expressive arts to re-member and re-author stories of resilience. *The Family Journal: Counseling and Therapy for Couples and Families*, *13*(2), 172–5.

Cattaneo, L. B., & Chapman, A. R. (2010). The process of empowerment: A model for use in research and practice. *American Psychologist*, *65*(7), 646–59.

Chagnon, J. (2013). Migration: International, 2010 and 2011. Statistics Canada. Retrieved from http://www.statcan.gc.ca/pub/91-209-x/2013001/article/11787-eng.htm

Chapin, R., & Cox, E. O. (2002). Changing the paradigm: Strengths-based and empowerment-oriented social work with frail elders. *Journal of Gerontological Social Work, 36*(3–4), 165–179.

Chen, Y., Stewart, P., Dales, R., Johansen, H., Bryan, S., & Taylor, G. (2005). Changing age-pattern of hospitalisation risk of chronic obstructive pulmonary disease in men and women in Canada. *Age and Ageing, 34*(4), 373–7.

Chiou, C. J., Chen, I. P., & Wang, H. H. (2005). The health status of family caregivers in Taiwan: An analysis of gender differences. *International Journal of Geriatric Psychiatry, 20*, 821–6.

Chipperfield, J. G., & Perry, R. P. (2006). Primary and secondary control strategies in later life: Predicting hospital outcomes in men and women. *Health Psychology, 25*, 226–36.

Chipperfield, J. G., Perry, R. P., Bailis, D. S., Ruthig, J. C., & Chuchmach, L. P. (2007). Gender differences in use of primary and secondary-control strategies in older adults with major health problems. *Psychology and Health, 22*(1), 83–105.

Chui, T., Maheux, H., & Tran, K. (2007). Immigration in Canada: A portrait of the foreign-born population, 2006 Census. Statistics Canada. Catalogue No. 97-557-XIE.

Clifford, D. (1995). Methods in oral history and social work. *Oral History, 23*(2), 65–70.

Collins, W. L. (2011). Culturally competent practices: Working with older African Americans in rural communities. *Social Work and Christianity, 38*(2).

Concannon, L. (2009). Developing inclusive health and social care policies for older LGBT citizens. *British Journal of Social Work, 39*(3), 403–17.

Consedine, N. S., Magai, C., & Krivoshekova, Y. S. (2005). Sex and age cohort differences in patterns of socioemotional functioning in older adults and their links to physical resilience. *Ageing International, 30*(3), 209–44.

Cowger, C. D. (1994). Assessing client strengths: Clinical assessment for client empowerment. *Social Work, 39*(3), 262–8.

Cronin, A., & King, A. (2010). Power, inequality and identification: Exploring diversity and intersectionality amongst older LGB adults. *Sociology, 44*(5), 876–92.

Dahlberg, L., Demack, S., & Bambra C. (2007). Age and gender of informal carers: A population-based study in the UK. *Health and Social Care in the Community, 15*(5), 439–45.

Dannefer, D. (2003). Cumulative advantage/disadvantage and the life course: Cross-fertilizing age and social science theory. *The Journals of Gerontology Series B: Psychological Sciences and Social Sciences, 58*(6), S327–37.

Dannefer, D., & Settersten, R. A. (2010). The study of the life course: Implications for social gerontology. In D. Dannefer & C. Phillipson (Eds.), *The SAGE handbook of social gerontology* (pp. 3–20). London, UK: Sage Publications.

D'Augelli, A. R., Grossman, A. H., Hershberger, S. L., & O'Connell, T. S. (2001). Aspects of mental health among older lesbian, gay, and bisexual adults. *Aging and Mental Health, 5*(2), 149–58.

David, S., & Knight, B. G. (2008). Stress and coping among gay men: Age and ethnic differences. *Psychology and Aging, 23*(1), 62.

Davis, P., & Donald, B. (1997). *Multicultural counseling competencies: Assessment, evaluation, education and training, and supervision.* Thousand Oaks, CA: Sage Publications.

D'Emilio, J. (2002). *The world turned: Essays on gay history, politics and culture*. Durham, NC: Duke University Press.

De Montigny, G. (2011). Beyond anti-oppressive practice: Investigating reflexive social relations. *Journal of Progressive Human Services, 22*, 8–30.

Dominelli, L. (1996). Deprofessionalizing social work: Anti-oppressive practice, competencies and postmodernism. *British Journal of Social Work, 26*(2), 153–75.

Dorfman, R., Walters, K., Burke, P., Hardin, L., Karanik, T., Raphael, J., & Silverstein, E. (1995). Old, sad and alone: The myth of the aging homosexual. *Journal of Gerontological Social Work, 24*(1/2), 29–44.

Douglas, A., Richardson, J., Letts, L., & Wilkins, S. (2010). Help at home and perceived health status: Gender differences in a community-dwelling population. *Physical and Occupational Therapy in Geriatrics, 28*(1), 86–100.

Elder, G. H. (1995). Life trajectories in changing societies. In A. Bandura (Ed.), *Self-efficacy in changing societies* (pp. 46–68). Cambridge, UK: Cambridge University Press.

Fiori, K. L., Smith, J., & Antonucci, T. C. (2007). Social network types among older adults: A multidimensional approach. *The Journals of Gerontology Series B: Psychological Sciences and Social Sciences*, *62*(6), P322–30.

Finkel, D., Reynolds, C. A., McArdle, J. J., & Pedersen, N. L. (2007). Cohort differences in trajectories of cognitive aging. *Journal of Gerontology: Psychological Sciences, 62B*(5), P285–94.

Fredriksen-Goldsen, K. I., Hoy-Ellis, C. P., Goldsen, J., Emlet, C. A., & Hooyman, N. R. (2014). Creating a vision for the future: Key competencies and strategies for culturally competent practice with lesbian, gay, bisexual, and transgender (LGBT) older adults in the health and human services. *Journal of Gerontological Social Work*, *57*(2-4), 80–107.

Fredriksen-Goldsen, K. I., Kim, H., Barkan, S. E., Muraco, A., & Hoy-Ellis, C. P. (2013). Health disparities among lesbian, gay, and bisexual older adults: Results from a population-based study. *American Journal of Public Health, 103*, 1802–9.

Fredriksen-Goldsen, K. I., & Muraco, A. (2010). Aging and sexual orientation: A 25-year review of the literature. *Research on Aging*, *32*(3), 372–413.

Fry, P. S., & Debats, D. L. (2006). Sources of life strengths as predictors of late-life mortality and survivorship. *International Journal of Aging and Human Development*, *62*(4), 303–34.

Gallicchio, L., Siddiqi, N., Langenberg, P., & Baumgarten, M. (2002) Gender differences in burden and depression among informal caregivers of demented elders in the community. *International Journal of Geriatric Psychiatry, 17*, 154–63.

Georgiades, S. D. (2014). Greek immigrants in Australia: Implications for culturally sensitive practice. *Journal of Immigrant and Minority Health*. doi:10.1007/s10903-014-0128-2

Giele, J. Z., & Elder, G. H. (1998). *Methods of life course research: Qualitative and quantitative approaches*. London, UK: Sage Publications.

Gonzalez, A. V., Suissa, S., & Emst, P. (2011). Gender differences in survival following hospitalisation for COPD. *Thorax, 66*, 38–42.

Government of Canada. (2010). Immigration overview: Permanent and temporary residents. Retrieved from http://www.cic.gc.ca/englisH/resources/statistics/facts2010/permanent/10.asp

Government of Canada. (2014). Facts and figures 2013: Immigration overview: Permanent residents. Retrieved from http://www.cic.gc.ca/english/resources/statistics/facts2013/permanent/10.asp

Gratwick, S., Jihanian, L. J., Holloway, I. W., Sanchez, M., & Sullivan, K. (2014). Social work practice with LGBT seniors. *Journal of Gerontological Social Work*, *57*(8), 889–907.

Guarnaccia, P. J., & Rodriguez, O. (1996). Concepts of culture and their role in the development of culturally competent mental health services. *Hispanic Journal of Behavioral Sciences*, *18*(4), 419–43.

Hardy, K. V., & Laszloffy, T. A. (1995). The cultural genogram: Key to training culturally competent family therapists. *Journal of Marital and Family Therapy*, *21*(3), 227–37.

Heikkinen, E., Mauppinen, M., Rantanen, T., Leinonen, R., Lyyra, T., Suutama, T., & Heikkinen, R. (2011). Cohort differences in health, functioning and physical activity in the young-old Finnish population. *Aging Clinical and Experimental Research, 23*, 126–34.

Henderson, S., Kendall, E., & See, L. (2011). The effectiveness of culturally appropriate interventions to manage or prevent chronic disease in culturally and linguistically diverse communities: A systematic literature review. *Health and Social Care in the Community*, *19*(3), 225–49.

Herdt, G., Beeler, J., & Rawls, T. W. (1997). Life course diversity among older lesbians and gay men: A study in Chicago. *International Journal of Sexuality and Gender Studies*, *2*(3-4), 231–46.

Johnstone, M. J., & Kanitsaki, O. (2009). Engaging patients as safety partners: Some considerations for ensuring a culturally and linguistically appropriate approach. *Health Policy*, *90*(1), 1–7.

Kobayashi, K., & Prus, S. (2011). Adopting an intersectionality perspective in the study of healthy immigrant effect in mid-to later life. In O. Hankivsky (Ed), *Health inequities in Canada: Intersectional frameworks and practices* (pp. 180–97). Vancouver, BC: UBC Press.

Kolb, P. (2014). Understanding aging and diversity: Theories and concepts. Oxford, UK: Routledge/Taylor & Francis.

Kropf, N. P., & Tandy, C. (1998). Narrative therapy with older clients. *Clinical Gerontologist, 18*(4), 3–16.

Lagacé, M., Charmarkeh, H., & Grandena, F. (2012). Cultural perceptions of aging: The perspective of Somali Canadians in Ottawa. *Journal of Cross-Cultural Gerontology, 27*(4), 409–24.

Langley, J. (2001). Developing anti-oppressive empowering social work practice with older lesbian women and gay men. *British Journal of Social Work, 31*, 917–32.

Larson, G. (2008). Anti-oppressive practice in mental health. *Journal of Progressive Human Services, 19*(1), 39–54.

Lewis, M. I., & Butler, R. N. (1972). Why is women's lib ignoring old women? *International Journal of Aging and Human Development*, 3, 223–31.

Lin, I. F., Fee, H. R., & Wu, H. S. (2012). Negative and positive caregiving experiences: A closer look at the intersection of gender and relationship. *Family Relations, 61*(2), 343–58.

Manthorpe, J., Moriarty, J., Stevens, M., Hussein, S., & Sharif, N. (2010). Black and minority ethnic older people and mental well-being: Possibilities for practice. *Working with Older People, 14*(4), 32–7.

Mattsson, T. (2014). Intersectionality as a useful tool: Anti-oppressive social work and critical reflection. *Affilia: Journal of Women and Social Work, 29*(1), 8–17.

Maylor, E. A., Reimers, S., Choi, J., Collaer, M. L., Peters, M., & Silverman, I. (2007). Gender and sexual orientation differences in cognition across adulthood: Age is kinder to women than to men regardless of sexual orientation. *Archives of Sexual Behavior, 36*(2), 235–49.

McMullin, J. A., & Cairney, J. (2004). Self-esteem and the intersection of age, class, and gender. *Journal of Aging Studies, 18*(1), 75–90.

Mehrotra, G. (2010). Toward a continuum of intersectionality theorizing for feminist social work scholarship. *Affilia, 25*(4), 417–30.

Merton, R. K. (1988). The Matthew effect in science II: Cumulative advantage and the symbolism of intellectual property. *ISIS, 79*, 606–23.

Mitnitski, A., Song, X., Skoog, I., Broe, G., Cox, J. L., Grunfeld, E., & Rockwood, K. (2005). Relative fitness and frailty of elderly men and women in developed countries and their relationship with mortality. *Journal of the American Geriatric Society, 53*, 2184–9.

Mui, A. C., Glajchen, M., Chen, H., & Sun, J. (2013). Developing an older adult volunteer program in a New York Chinese community: An evidence-based approach. *Ageing International, 38*(2), 108–21.

Muraco, A., LeBlanc, A. J., & Russell, S. T. (2008). Conceptualizations of family by older gay men. *Journal of Gay and Lesbian Social Services, 20*(1–2), 69–90.

Murray, E., Numer, M., Merritt, B., Gahagan, J., & Comber, S. (2012). Healthy aging among LGBT seniors in Canada: A review of the literature. *The International Journal of Health, Wellness and Society, 1*(4), 179–92.

Narushima, M., Liu, J., & Diestelkamp, N. (2013). Motivations and perceived benefits of older learners in a public continuing education program: Influence of gender, income, and health. *Educational Gerontology, 39*, 569–84.

Navaie-Waliser, M., Spriggs, A., & Feldman, P. H. (2002) Informal caregiving: Differential experiences by gender. *Medical Care, 40*(12), 1249–59.

Ng, E., Lai, D., Rudner, A., & Orpana, H. (2012). What do we know about immigrant seniors aging in Canada? A demographic, socio-economic and health profile. *CERIS Working Papers*, 88–90.

Nie, J. X., Wang. L., Tracy, S., Moineddin, R., & Upshur, R. E. G. (2010). A population-based cohort study of ambulatory care service utilization among older adults. *Journal of Evaluation in Clinical Practice, 16*, 825–31.

O'Hoski, S., Winship, B., Herridge, L., Agha, T., Brooks, D., Beauchamp, M. K., & Sibley, K. M. (2014). Increasing the clinical utility of the BESTest, Mini-BESTest, and Brief-BESTest: Normative values in Canadian adults who are healthy and aged 50 years or older. *Physical Therapy, 94*(3), 334–42.

Phillipson, C., Bernard, M., Phillips, J., & Ogg, J. (2001). *The family and community life of older people: Social networks and social support in three urban areas.* New York, NY: Routledge.

Pinquart, M., & Sörensen, S. (2006). Gender differences in caregiver stressors, social resources, and health: An updated meta-analysis. *Journal of Gerontology Series B, 61B*, P33–45.

Podnieks, E., & Wilson, S. (2003). Elder abuse awareness in faith communities: Findings from a Canadian pilot study. *Journal of Elder Abuse and Neglect, 15*(3–4), 121–35.

Poole, J., Gardner, P., Flower, M. C., & Cooper, C. (2009). Narrative therapy, older adults, and group work? Practice, research, and recommendations. *Social Work with Groups, 32*(4), 288–302.

Price, E. (2008). Pride or prejudice? Gay men, lesbians and dementia. *British Journal of Social Work, 38*(7), 1337–52.

Rokach, A., & Neto, F. (2005). Age, culture, and the antecedents of loneliness. *Social Behavior and Personality, 33*(5), 477–94.

Rokach, A., Orzeck, T., & Neto, F. (2004). Coping with loneliness in old age: A cross-cultural comparison. *Current Psychology, 23*(2), 124–36.

Roscoe, K. D., Carson, A. M., & Madoc-Jones, L. (2011). Narrative social work: Conversations between theory and practice. *Journal of Social Work Practice: Psychotherapeutic Approaches in Health, Welfare and the Community, 25*(1), 47–61.

Sakamoto, I. (2007). A critical examination of immigrant acculturation: Toward an anti-oppressive social work model with immigrant adults in a pluralistic society. *British Journal of Social Work, 37*, 515–35.

Santiago-Rivera, A. L. (1995). Developing a culturally sensitive treatment modality for bilingual Spanish-speaking clients: Incorporating language and culture in counseling. *Journal of Counseling and Development, 74*(1), 12–7.

Sargeant, M. (Ed.). (2011). *Age discrimination and diversity: Multiple discrimination from an age perspective.* Cambridge, UK: Cambridge University Press.

Schim, S. M., Doorenbos, A. Z., & Borse, N. N. (2006). Enhancing cultural competence among hospice staff. *American Journal of Hospice and Palliative Medicine, 23*(5), 404–11.

Shaw, S. J. (2005). The politics of recognition in culturally appropriate care. *Medical Anthropology Quarterly, 19*(3), 290–309.

Siverskog, A. (2014). They just don't have a clue: Transgender aging and implications for social work. *Journal of Gerontological Social Work, 57*, 386–406.

Statistics Canada. (2010). *Canadian Community Health Survey: Healthy aging (CCHS).* Retrieved from http://www23.statcan.gc.ca/imdb/p2SV.pl?Function=getSurvey&SDDS=5146&lang=en&db=imdb&adm=8&dis=2

Statistics Canada. (2011a). *2011 National Household Survey: Data tables.* Catalogue No. 99-010-X2011032. Retrieved from http://www12.statcan.gc.ca/nhs-enm/2011/dp-pd/dt-td/Rp-eng.cfm?TABID=2&LANG=E&APATH=3&DETAIL=0&DIM=0&FL=A&FREE=0&GC=0&GK=0&GRP=0&PID=105399&PRID=0&PTYPE=105277&S=0&SHOWALL=0&SUB=0&Temporal=2013&THEME=95&VID=0&VNAMEE=&VNAMEF=

Statistics Canada. (2011b). 2011 National Household Survey: Data tables. Catalogue No. 99-010-X2011041. Retrieved from http://www12.statcan.gc.ca/nhs-enm/2011/dp-pd/dt-td/Rp-eng.cfm?TABID=2&LANG=E&APATH=3&DETAIL=0&DIM=0&FL=A&FREE=0&GC=0&GK=0&GRP=0&PID=107557&PRID=0&PTYPE=105277&S=0&SHOWALL=0&SUB=0&Temporal=2013&THEME=95&VID=0&VNAMEE=&VNAMEF=

Statistics Canada. (2012a). The Canadian population in 2011: Age and sex. Retrieved from http://www.statcan.gc.ca/pub/91-209-x/2013001/article/11787-eng.htm

Statistics Canada. (2012b). Same-sex couples and sexual orientation . . . by the numbers. Retrieved from http://www.statcan.gc.ca/dai-quo/smr08/2014/smr08_189_2014-eng.htm#a3

Statistics Canada. (2013a). Chapter 1: Postcensal and intercensal population estimates, Canada, provinces and territories. Retrieved from http://www.statcan.gc.ca/pub/91-528-x/2011001/ch/ch1-eng.htm

Statistics Canada. (2013b). Immigration and ethnocultural diversity in Canada: National Household Survey. Retrieved from http://www12.statcan.gc.ca/nhs-enm/2011/as-sa/99-010-x/99-010-x2011001-eng.pdf

Statistics Canada. (2014a). Annual demographic estimates: Canada, provinces and territories. Catalogue No. 91-215-X. Retrieved from http://www.statcan.gc.ca/pub/91-215-x/91-215-x2014000-eng.pdf

Statistics Canada. (2014b). Canadian demographics at a glance: Section three: Composition of the population. Retrieved from http://www.statcan.gc.ca/pub/91-003-x/2014001/section03-eng.htm

Statistics Canada. (2014c). Population projections: Canada, the provinces and territories, 2013 to 2063. *The Daily*. Retrieved from http://www.statcan.gc.ca/daily-quotidien/140917/dq140917a-eng.htm

Stein, G. L., Beckerman, N. L., & Sherman, P. A. (2010). Lesbian and gay elders and long-term care: Identifying the unique psychosocial perspectives and challenges. *Journal of Gerontological Social Work, 53*, 421–35.

Stevens, N. L., & Van Tilburg, T. G. (2011). Cohort differences in having and retaining friends in personal networks in later life. *Journal of Social and Personal Relationships, 28*(1), 24–43.

Stoller, E. P., & Gibson, R. C. (2000). *Worlds of difference: Inequity in the aging experience*. Thousand Oaks, CA: Pine Forge Press.

Strier, R., & Binyamin, S. (2010). Developing anti-oppressive services for the poor: A theoretical and organisational rationale. *British Journal of Social Work, 40*(6), 1908–26.

Swift, A. A., Bailis, D. S., Chipperfield, J. G., Ruthig, J. C., & Newall, N. E. (2008). Gender differences in the adaptive influence of folk beliefs: A longitudinal study of life satisfaction in aging. *Canadian Journal of Behavioural Science, 40*(2), 104–12.

Taylor, Y. (2009). Complexities and complications: Intersections of class and sexuality. *Journal of Lesbian Studies, 13*(2), 189–203.

Teater, B. (2010). *An introduction to applying social work theories and methods*. Maidenhead, UK: Open University Press.

Thompson, N., & Thompson, S. (2001). Empowering older people: Beyond the care model. *Journal of Social Work, 1*(1), 61–76.

Tippett, W. J., Lee, J., Mraz, R., Eng, P., Zakzanis, K. K., Snyder, P. J., Black, S. E., & Graham, S. J. (2009). Convergent validity and sex differences in healthy elderly adults for performance on 3D virtual reality navigation learning and 2D hidden maze tasks. *CyberPsychology and Behavior, 12*(2), 169–74.

Turcotte, M., & Schellenberg, G. (2007). *A portrait of seniors in Canada, 2006*. Statistics Canada. Catalogue No. 89-519-XIE.

Turner, S. G., & Maschi, T. M. (2014). Feminist and empowerment theory and social work practice. *Journal of Social Work Practice: Psychotherapeutic Approaches in Health, Welfare and the Community, 29*(2), 151–62. doi:10.1080/02650533.2014.941282

Twenge, J. M., & Campbell, W. K. (2001). Age and birth cohort differences in self-esteem: A cross-temporal meta-analysis. *Personality and Social Psychology Review, 5*(4), 321–44.

Vicary, D., & Bishop, B. (2005). Western psychotherapeutic practice: Engaging Aboriginal people in culturally appropriate and respectful ways. *Australian Psychologist, 40*(1), 8–19.

Villar, F., Serrat, R., Faba, J., & Celdran, M. (2013). As long as they keep away from me: Attitudes toward non-heterosexual sexual orientation among residents living in Spanish residential aged care facilities. *The Gerontologist*. doi:10.1093/geront/gnt150

Warburton, J., Bartlett, H., & Rao, V. (2009). Ageing and cultural diversity: Policy and practice issues. *Australian Social Work, 62*(2), 168–85.

Wendt, D. C., & Gone, J. P. (2012). Rethinking cultural competence: Insights from indigenous community treatment settings. *Transcultural Psychiatry, 49*(2), 206–22.

Wilks, T. (2005). Social work and narrative ethics. *British Journal of Social Work, 35*, 1249–64.

Williamson, M., & Harrison, L. (2010). Providing culturally appropriate care: A literature review. *International Journal of Nursing Studies, 47*(6), 761–9.

Yee, J. L., & Schulz, R. (2000). Gender differences in psychiatric morbidity among family caregivers: A review and analysis. *Gerontologist*, *40*(2), 147–64.

Zunzunegui, M. V., Minicuci, N., Blumstein, T., Noale, M., Deeg, D., Jylha, M., & Pedersen, N. L. (2007). Gender differences in depressive symptoms among older adults: A cross-national comparison: The CLESA project. *Social Psychiatry and Psychiatric Epidemiology*, *42*, 198–207.

Social Work and Diversity through an Experiential Lens

16

By Natalie Blake-Noel

Chapter Objectives

This chapter will help you develop an understanding of:

- What it means to work with diverse populations through seven experiential classroom exercises that are intended to elicit critical thinking and individual reflection
- The role and value of self-reflection in practice as future practitioners preparing to work in the field of social work with clients from diverse backgrounds and stories

Introduction

Diversity is an integral part of our society, as evidenced throughout this text. Within the framework of social work and society as a whole, diversity has a strong and ever-present existence. As a social work practitioner, I have witnessed the impact and value of diversity within the delivery of social services in Toronto. Within such a context, diversity is no longer a "buzzword" that is weighted by statistics and a plethora of research, but it pushes through and becomes one of the key cornerstones of regions like Toronto, which is home to an abundance of nationalities, cultures, languages, religions, sexual orientations, and many other rich facets of difference. According to the Ontario government, Toronto is a city where more than 150 languages are spoken every day and 50 per cent of residents were born outside of Canada (Government of Ontario, 2013). Additionally, according to the City of Toronto, the top five visible minority groups in Toronto are South Asian, Chinese, Black, Filipino, and Latin American (City of Toronto, 2014).

The range of clients that I have counselled is a true testament that diversity carries many faces through the varied experiences, life stories, histories, and backgrounds of people. Diversity goes beyond simply what we can see; rather, it is what we experience and choose to learn. What this means is that the beliefs, attitudes, and even worldviews of a member from one cultural, ethnic, or religious group do not necessarily represent those of all members from the same cultural, ethnic, or religious group, and working in a city like Toronto provides a perfect backdrop of this important reality, as illustrated in Case Example 16.1.

Case Example 16.1 describes one of many client experiences that a social worker who deals with diversity may encounter. Essentially, as a practitioner (and also as a person), what one sees on the outside is not the full picture of a client's narrative. Basing a client's identity exclusively on visible or observable indicators is dangerous territory, as the uniqueness of their needs becomes intertwined and often outweighed by sweeping generalizations and judgment rather than respect and appreciation of their diverse needs and strengths. Simply put, if all clients are seen the same way as members of the same group, then ignorance becomes a tool of devaluing difference and instead places emphasis on everyone thinking the same, doing the same, and being the same. And diversity is about just that—difference. It represents "a unique creation of biopsychosocialspiritual elements, different from every other individual not only in terms of genes, but in terms of experiences, influences, perspectives and world view" (Rothman, 2008, p. 7).

Case Example 16.1

Mrs S. was a married mother of two young children who cared for her children during the day while her husband worked. Mrs S., of South Asian descent, enjoyed raising their children and managing the household while her husband was the principal financial supporter for the family.

Mr S., the husband, advised his wife that he would like her to start working so that she could apply her education and skills that she once acquired as a teacher in their native India. He felt that his wife had the ability and capacity to manage and balance both the domestic responsibilities as well as employment responsibilities. This was creating conflict and tension within their marriage because of their polarized views, and therefore resulted in the couple seeking counselling services and supports.

At the onset, the appearance of diversity could likely claim that Mr S. would be endorsing his wife's rearing of the children at home because of the beliefs expressed by some South Asian clients that husbands work while wives raise the children and maintain the household. Traditional gender role expectations, as among the White majority population, remain compelling in most families of Indian heritage. "Women generally shoulder the bulk of domestic responsibilities while men are expected to be the main earners" (Laird, 2008, p. 56). However, the life experience of this specific couple represents their unique needs and challenges as a family unit taking into consideration their cultural values and beliefs. This is a clear illustration that not all South Asian women stay at home to care for their children while the spouse goes to work to financially support the family.

As a social worker, I can unequivocally state that no two clients are ever alike even if they come from the same or even a similar cultural, ethnic, or religious group. Every client presents his or her own story and voice in the therapeutic alliance and as such, especially when providing service in a diverse city like Toronto, it is critical to apply this approach within a practical space. What does this look like as a social worker? In my professional experience, the clients I met on a daily basis came from various backgrounds and walks of life, and I was more successful when I placed myself in the role of a learner and not so much the "expert" that clients often perceive social workers to be. Prior to practising social work, a social worker walks the path of being a student and engaging in academic preparation to one day become a practitioner. While a student, one of the cornerstones of practitioner training is learning social work theories and concepts while also developing professional skills and abilities through the world-of-work experience of field practicums. Once practitioner training is achieved, where does the learning end and the role of practising begin? It simply shouldn't end. Although the formal learning has been successfully achieved upon receipt of an educational diploma or degree, it is critical that a practitioner, whether new or seasoned, continually seek opportunities to learn, especially from the people we serve and support.

This chapter discusses a diversity of issues and complexities within the realm of social work that, although fictional in their creation but reality-based in nature, embody deeply personal and meaningful issues that future practitioners may experience in the therapeutic alliance. The seven exercises in this chapter entail the following experiences:

- Multicultural social work in community and organization settings
- Ethnographic interviewing
- Aboriginal communities
- Immigrant families
- Gay, lesbian, bisexual, transgendered, and queer communities
- Refugees
- Anti-racist/anti-oppressive practice

The Social Worker's Role in the Therapeutic Alliance

Undoubtedly, social workers bring a level of expertise to the therapeutic alliance to facilitate assessments, recommendations, empowerment, and change. However, what happens when the expertise of the social worker plays a primary or dominant role in the therapeutic alliance? Miley, O'Melia, & DuBois (2013) state that "reverence toward social workers as experts fabricates a hierarchy of haves and have-nots. In this view, proficient social work experts have the knowledge, insight, and ideas to bestow on inept clients who lack these qualities . . . Interpreted bluntly, the expert professionals are the champs, and the clients are the chumps!" (p. 134). The expertise of the client is diminished and takes a backseat to the "expertise" of the social worker, which becomes front and centre.

Inasmuch as many clients are seeking some form of expertise, direction, and guidance from social workers, this perception of social workers rescuing or healing clients from their issues becomes magnified and perpetuates the false image of the role and value of social workers. In addition, the social worker's ability to learn from the client is significantly stunted by a sense of power and control over the relationship that essentially tips the scale even further between the perceived "haves" and "have-nots."

However, for the role of social workers to be as effective and authentic to the therapeutic alliance as possible, the value of clients' own experiences and competencies must be one of the foundational pillars in the helping process. Choosing to be a learner in the therapeutic alliance provides not only knowledge and awareness of clients' situations, but equilibrium in the sense of a partnership between both social worker and client. Clients are the experts on their own situations and circumstances—they know their situations

Case Example 16.2

Mr P. was a client from the Middle East who came to me for counselling because he was experiencing depression related to his unemployment. Mr P. was a professional in his home country and was actively seeking work in Toronto in his area of expertise. He was beginning to experience insomnia, limited appetite, a lack of energy, and his optimism for finding work and contributing his skills and abilities to his adopted country was beginning to decline rapidly. Exacerbating his depression, he shared with me that he was unable to financially support his family back home because of his lack of employment, and the inability to support his family was becoming a failed promise. His commitment to support his family back home was rooted in the fact that he was in Canada, and it was believed that upon arrival he would be able to find work and experience an abundance of financial stability and impart monetary support to his family.

During a few sessions with Mr P., we collaboratively worked on his résumé, ensuring that his education and professional experience were effectively marketed to prepare for prospective interviews. His résumé garnished the attention of five firms resulting in a series of interviews, at which point I provided employment coaching and preparation with Mr P., including conducting a few mock interviews.

After his last interview, we had a post-interview counselling session. It was during this session that he advised me that he was not offered a job opportunity by any firm and that his depression was compounded by his sense of rejection and pessimism. During my assessment of Mr P.'s disclosure, it was apparent that Mr P.'s résumé facilitated his success in obtaining interviews, but it appeared that during the interviews he was not experiencing the same level of success. As I continued to assess Mr P.'s situation, I decided to ask Mr P. about a facial feature that he possessed—a unibrow—as I saw a possible correlation between Mr P.'s outward appearance and the interviews he had conducted. Truthfully speaking, I was initially somewhat hesitant to ask Mr P. about his facial feature best beyond that of social workers. "Social workers who practice from an empowerment perspective realize that social workers and clients have complementary roles and recognize the value of clients' experiences and competencies" (Miley, O'Melia, & DuBois, 2013, p. 134). Creating a space to facilitate complementary roles and intentionally recognizing the expertise of clients is the building block to purposefully seeking to learn from clients, essentially placing oneself in the role of learner. Deliberately placing myself in the role of a learner has been one of my key goals as a social worker, and it is a role that I take very seriously. Being a learner has provided me with immense and rewarding opportunities to listen to client stories and narratives and to provide a platform for clients to share their voice when collaboratively developing effective strategies that will help shape their lives. Another key part of my journey as a learner is learning about values, beliefs, ideologies, customs, and traditions from a clientele base that represents a rich tapestry of diversity. Case Example 16.2 provides a key example of this experience as a learner.

because I was not certain how he would receive my question and quest for understanding. However, as a social worker the role of being a learner must involve the ability to ask questions, even questions that may elicit some form of discomfort for the client or the social worker or both within the confines of respect. During our previous sessions, Mr P. was placed in the position of educating me about his educational and career path and his journey to Canada. This discourse and exchange of information became the key building blocks in the helping process; however, the question about Mr P.'s unibrow was one that I believed was steeped in a deeper awareness that reflected a more personal and intimate tone. When asked the question, Mr P. reacted with anticipation and was in fact eager to answer my question, although inwardly I was somewhat fearful of offending him. Mr P. explained to me that, culturally, the unibrow in the Middle East represents a sign of attraction, and women are often attracted to a man with this feature. I was immensely thankful for this opportunity to learn about a cultural aspect within his community that I would not have known had I not asked and placed myself in a position to learn.

With this knowledge, I then shared with Mr P. that, to my knowledge, the perceived standard of attraction and beauty in North America, and more specifically Toronto, does not include men possessing this feature. I shared with him my general observations and characteristics of male appearances and presentations and linked this discussion with his interviews in that the feature of the unibrow may have possibly played a role in him being negatively perceived or misunderstood, resulting in him potentially not being offered a job opportunity. I had no fact to substantiate this, but there was a likelihood of these aspects being connected.

After further discussion and in-depth reflection, Mr P. decided to re-create his appearance and remove this feature. He made this decision with anticipated understanding that if this was a barrier to his employment, he was willing to make changes to market his skills in North America.

As illustrated in Case Example 16.2, being a learner and not the perceived "expert" provides social workers with a platform to gain knowledge and understanding of beliefs, values, practices, traditions, and customs carried by a diverse population. The role of learning also provides the enriched ability to develop partnerships with clients to collaborate on strategies to facilitate the helping process.

The illustrations in Case Examples 16.1 and 16.2 are just a couple of experiences I have encountered first-hand as a practitioner in Toronto. Working with a richly diverse population has involved the capacity to learn about individuals while also valuing and appreciating the importance of other human dimensions, such as religion, culture, ethnicity, gender, and sexual orientation. Is this easier said than done? Absolutely. However, I share these experiences because as a practitioner for over 10 years, it indeed takes time and purposeful intention to see people for who they are while recognizing other dimensions that play a pertinent role in the helping process, especially within the context of a city like Toronto.

Class Exercises: Bridging Theory with Practice

The following section is intended to provide an opportunity and a platform for students to apply theoretical and critical knowledge into a practical experience while discussing, sharing, and exchanging ideas, worldviews, and information within a collective group setting. There is also an emphasis on students engaging in self-reflective and introspective thinking on an individual basis to expose their thoughts about diversity, multiculturalism, and the value of difference.

It is critical to note that each exercise will be most effective if you are honest when sharing your viewpoint and perspective as well as listening to and respecting those of others. The value of respect expressed to clients within a professional context is indicative of the value of respect expressed and demonstrated in these exercises as colleagues in the classroom.

Due to the exceptionally sensitive nature of some of these exercises, the value of respect, active listening, and honesty is underscored and asked to be maintained with integrity.

Exercise #1: Multicultural Social Work in Community and Organizational Settings

You are a social worker at a local community agency in a multicultural community that provides settlement services and supports to individuals, groups, and families who are newcomers to Canada. The organization provides counselling services, employment coaching, referrals, and workshops to the local community based on the strong demographics of refugees and immigrants.

One of your clients advises you that a number of students from the local high school have not been attending school on a regular basis and some have even dropped out. This client, who is a community member and parent of two children who attend the local high school, was informed of this situation by her children who have friends that have been attending school on an irregular basis. It appears that a major reason for some students missing school and even dropping out is due to the apparent pressures of providing financial support and stability to their families. It appears that some of the students are working part-time and full-time jobs in various sectors such as retail, customer service, and general labour to provide some means of income for their family. Many of the students are newcomers to Canada and come from families where their parents are internationally educated professionals; however, the parents are either unemployed or underemployed as a direct result of their educational and professional skills being undervalued or not recognized by the Canadian labour market. Many of these parents cannot afford to have their educational qualifications credentialized or return to school to upgrade their training to meet the Canadian educational standards. Additionally, a lack of "Canadian work experience" has been a common and universal message that some of the parents have been receiving from prospective employers. The emphasis of having work experience in Canada has also created a barrier to employment—at least to sustainable and professionally rewarding employment. This has resulted in some of the unemployment of some parents while others are relegated to working in jobs that are below their educational and professional experience and qualifications.

Shortly after this concerned community member and parent discloses this information to you, your organization receives a phone call from the head of the social work department from the same local high school regarding the issue that has been brought forward to you by the community member. The school social worker discloses that there has been a sharp decrease in student attendance and a steady increase in student withdrawal. This trend has been rooted specifically in the senior grades: Grades 11 and 12 and students who arrived in Canada in the last two years. The social worker has advised you that she and her team of social workers and settlement workers have attempted to contact the parents of some of the students; however, their assessment ascertains that the following may be potential challenges to direct school–parent contact and parental follow-up: linguistic barriers, conflicting work schedules of parents, and lack of knowledge and awareness of the Canadian education system. The school social worker would like to liaise and partner with your organization to explore this issue that has several layers of impact: academic, social, community, and personal.

You approach your team of social workers, equipped with this information, and request a meeting to discuss the multilayered issues that have been presented to you.

Background Information

In your assessment of this situation, it is critical to be aware of some key aspects to facilitate your assessment, understanding, discussion, and strategizing of this case scenario. (For a complementary discussion on social work and immigrant families, see Chapter 9 by Debashis Dhutta and Ross Klein.)

- "A permanent resident is someone who has been given permanent resident status by immigrating to Canada, but is not a Canadian citizen. Permanent residents are citizens of other countries" (Government of Canada, 2015).
- "As many as 65 percent of immigrants can expect to experience a low-income spell within their first 10 years of living in Canada and, of these, roughly one-third will remain in low income for three years or more" (Anisef, Brown, Phythian, Sweet, & Walters, 2010).
- "Canada receives about one-quarter million immigrants and refugees annually from all regions of the world. This is in addition to an already large foreign-born population making up one-fifth of the total population, a fact which speaks to the importance of immigration as one of the pillars of Canadian nation building" (Turegun, 2013).
- Many internationally educated professionals who migrate to Canada experience significant challenges finding work in their chosen profession. "Upon their arrival, they find several roadblocks; lack of Canadian experience, lack of local business and language skills, lack of education and training at a Canadian institution, not to mention discrimination and other hurdles" (Sankey, 2006).
- The topic of "Canadian experience" continues to play a persistent, provocative, and powerful role in multiculturalism in Canada, specifically around the employment and marketability of trained immigrants seeking to use their talents and skills in their new adopted country. The subject matter was under scrutiny by the former Ontario Chief Human Rights Commissioner Barbara Hall. She states that

> those two words—Canadian experience—if you ask someone who has come to this country, I can see it in the crowds of people, their heads start to nod and we have said that prima facie—a rigid requirement for Canadian experience is discriminatory because it shouldn't matter where you got your experience. The question is: are you qualified for the job and what are the skills you need and how do you test for that? (as quoted in Doyle-Marshall, 2014).

- "Educational qualifications from countries of origin are often not transferable in resettlement countries, while jobs held in countries of origin may not be applicable to the skills needed in a more technologically advanced society. Subsequently, the migrant is oftentimes forced to 'begin again' or 'start from scratch.' This search and struggle for gainful employment may result in a decrease in status, poor self-esteem and feelings of hopelessness" (Pedersen, Draguns, Lonner, & Trimble, 2008, p. 314). (For more on organizational level–related diversity issues in social work, see the discussion in Chapter 5 by Douglas Durst.)

Questions for Discussion

1. What other facts would be needed to ensure you and your team have all the necessary information?
2. What would the first steps of partnering with the local high school entail? Explain the step-by-step strategies.
3. As a group of practitioners, please discuss how you would approach this community regarding the issues outlined above.
4. What strategies would you apply that demonstrate effective community work and development?

Exercise #2: Ethnographic Interviewing

"**Ethnographies** are studies that sketch an overall cultural setting, such as that shared by an ethnic group, a village or a neighbourhood. This type of research describes the key norms, rules, symbols, values, traditions and rituals in that setting and show how they fit together" (Rubin & Rubin, 2005, p. 7). Essentially, this type of interviewing is the process by which a social worker can learn about a client's culture and develop an informed understanding of that culture exclusively from the client's perspective without the influence of judgments or assumptions. The profession of social work entails a qualitative element of storytelling by the client with whom we are working. And learning about someone's story involves asking questions, the application of critical listening, and an awareness of the information being received to appreciate the experience of the storyteller. "The worker asks the client to be her/his cultural guide, to explain and explore the dimensions of the client's culture, which impact upon the problem in the eyes of the client" (Rothman, 2008, p. 43).

Social work is considered a study of social sciences, and thus social workers are considered researchers when seeking and obtaining information from clients. "The researcher almost by definition arrives as an outsider: someone who is not part of the social environment in which she or he will do research, has limited knowledge of the people, the normal patterns of everyday conduct, the climate and culture of the place" (Bloommaert & Dong, 2010). As social scientists, we are the outsider stepping into the world of our clients with the objective to obtain data and do so within a context of being a learner and not the "expert." Taking the standpoint of an outsider means trusting the interview process by actively pursuing a client's, or the "insider's," knowledge with the ability to be openly vulnerable by exposing our own limitations of information.

Being an outsider involves asking questions not just for learning, but invites an opportunity to provide fluid conversation with the interviewee. "Interviews are conversations: a particular kind of conversation, but a conversation nonetheless. It is an ordered conversation, one that is structured by questions or topics you may want to see discussed and one in which you will have to make sure that a particular order is being followed" (Bloommaert & Dong, 2010).

Considering that interviews are a form of conversation that encompass critical questions and topics that can lead to practitioner learning and deeper understanding of clients, it is pertinent that we provide clients with this platform to be storytellers of their information. "During this conversation, the ethnographic interviewing process also empowers the client by acknowledging him/her as the expert in this area" (Rothman, 2008, p. 44).

Although ethnographic interviewing is indeed a purposeful and valuable tool for learning and listening, it is just as critical to note that you will not learn absolutely everything about a client's culture. The experience of an individual from one culture will be different from another individual from the same culture. Placing the value of culture before the value of the person is dangerous because it is disempowering and reinforces the notion that people from the same culture are exactly the same. Individuals from the same culture are unique with possible commonalities; however, their difference may likely outweigh their similarities. The bottom line is that the application of ethnographic interviewing is to learn about a client's culture through their perspective, but not to paint every other person from that same culture with the same brush. The value of a person first and culture second is imperative and an ongoing journey of learning. (For more on obtaining qualitative research information from clients, see Chapter 4 by Marie Lacroix.)

Questions for Discussion

With a partner, conduct an ethnographic interview. Critically think about and document a minimum of 10 questions that you would ask your partner regarding his or her culture. Also document the rationale for each question. The interviewee will document his or her thoughts about the questions asked and provide this assessment to the interviewer. This exercise involves each person being the interviewer and the interviewee.

Exercise #3: Social Work with Aboriginal Communities—Part 1

This exercise is somewhat unique in its presentation as it is formatted in two parts because of the deeper complexity of information and reflection around the issues concerning Aboriginal peoples. At times, it can take multiple layers to fully express an individual's story, and this exercise does so in this fashion.

You are a school social worker at a diverse high school with a population of approximately 2,000 students. The high school is situated in an urban city. It is the start of the second semester and you have been newly assigned by the head of the school's counselling department to work with Autumn, a 15-year-old Anishinaabe student who moved to the city with her grandmother last summer from the northern region of the province. Autumn and her grandmother previously lived in a reserve community with a population of 3,200 residents. Autumn is having challenges adjusting to her new school and appears to be socially isolated, as she spends most of her time alone in the library between classes. It appears that she has not made any friends and eats alone in the cafeteria.

Autumn has also been experiencing serious academic challenges. Her teachers have noted that she engages minimally with her classmates in the classroom and will interact only when asked to do so during group work. Autumn rarely engages in class discussions and will attempt to share the answer or her opinion when she is called on by the teacher; however, she maintains a solemn resolve when not participating. Her teachers have remarked that Autumn is respectful when asked to participate and submits her assignments on time. However, Autumn's work is only satisfactory. She is struggling academically in her math, science, and social studies classes, but is doing well in her English and literature classes.

Since the age of 7, Autumn has been raised by her grandmother. Autumn was originally raised by her parents from birth to 5 years of age, but due to marital problems her parents separated, leaving Autumn in the care of her mother. Autumn's parents had been placed in residential schools and met when they both left the school as young adults. Autumn's grandmother had also been placed in a residential school during her childhood and adolescent years. After the marital separation, Autumn's mother felt she could no longer care for her daughter independently and gave Autumn to her mother to be cared for. While growing up with her grandmother, Autumn developed and maintained close friendships with four other girls and boys from the community. At the age of 13, within a span of one year, Autumn lost all four of her friends to apparent suicides. Shortly after the suicide of her last friend, Autumn started to develop disturbing behaviour such as staying up all night in her room and sleeping during the day, resulting in chronic absence in school. As well, she started to engage in self-mutilation by cutting her wrists. It is not clear if Autumn has herself attempted suicide, but the possibility exists.

Autumn's grandmother decided to leave their small northern community to provide Autumn with a fresh start, away from the memories of the past and with the hope that the city can provide her granddaughter with better opportunities for the future.

Autumn has been referred to the school's counselling services by her homeroom teacher, resulting in her being assigned to you as her social worker.

Background Information

In your assessment of this situation, it is critical to be aware of some key aspects to facilitate your assessment, understanding, discussion, and strategizing of this case scenario. (For a complementary, in-depth discussion on Aboriginal social work, see Chapter 7 by Raymond Neckoway and Keith Brownlee.)

- Historically, Aboriginal peoples were the first inhabitants of Canada; however, they currently live on reserves that are often isolated and significantly distant from urban cities across Canada. These reserves are often in hard-to-reach communities and are called home by almost 60 per cent of registered Indians (Angelini, 2012).
- Residential schools were formally initiated in 1910. The primary objective of these schools was to educate Aboriginal children in Christian values by separating them

from the "corrupting influence" of their own language, culture, and their parents (Angelini, 2012).

- The residential school system "separated many children from their families and communities preventing them from speaking their own languages and from learning about their heritage and cultures. In the worst cases, it left legacies of personal pain and distress that continue to reverberate in Aboriginal communities to this day. Tragically, some children were victims of physical and sexual abuse" (as cited in Warry, 2007).
- "In the school system Aboriginal adolescents are identified as having low levels of achievement and retention and high levels of failure, absenteeism and behavioural problems. The causes of this are complex but include feelings of not belonging in the classroom and racism from teachers and peers" (as cited in Briskman, 2007).
- Since 1995, the Royal Commission on Aboriginal Peoples reported that "an Aboriginal adolescent aged 10–19 is 5.1 times more likely to die from suicide than a non-Aboriginal adolescent" (as cited in MacNeil, 2008, p. 13).
- Colonial practices "related to residential schools, reserve communities, loss of traditional lands, and erosion of language and cultural traditions that lead to cultural continuity have created a loss of cohesion and identity in Aboriginal communities which have impacted family health behaviours" (as cited in MacNeil, 2008).
- Self-harming is described as "a wide range of things that people do to themselves in a deliberate and usually hidden way . . . Self-harm can involve: cutting, burning, scalding, banging or scratching one's own body, hair pulling, ingesting toxic substances or objects" (as cited in Fox, 2011, p. 41).

Questions for Discussion: Part 1

1. Given the multilayered cultural dynamics of Autumn's situation, what would be your first steps in activating and initiating the helping process?
2. Thoroughly describe in detail what your first session with Autumn would look like. Include the questions you would ask her and the rationale for asking these questions.
3. What other information would you seek that you believe would be helpful in facilitating your understanding and awareness of the issues impacting Autumn and your role as Autumn's social worker?

Exercise #3: Social Work with Aboriginal Communities—Part 2

The second part of this exercise takes a deeper look at the educational and social dynamics that have transpired based on the family dynamics identified in Part 1 of this exercise.

Background Information

- The stereotypes that members of the Aboriginal communities experience in Canada are persistent and a continuous reminder of biases, misinformation, and lack of knowledge that many people carry when it comes to this group of individuals and other groups as well.
- "There are over 1 million self-identified Aboriginals (including First Nations, Metis and Inuit) in Canada, and over 600 First Nations bands alone with variability in histories, contemporary community characteristics, levels of enculturation, and traditional practices both within and across groups, thus underscoring the need for careful conceptualizations of culture and due attention to Aboriginal diversity" (Walls, Hautala, & Hurley, 2014).
- "It is a failure of Canada's imagination that its original inhabitants continue to suffer the most distorted stereotypes of any non-white group . . . Even more striking, according to a study by Environics Institute, many non-aboriginals recognize their comic book characterization of natives and acknowledge that real discrimination exists" ("Shameful survival of stereotypes," 2011, p. F8).

Questions for Discussion: Part 2

In your group, each student will share either a bias, area of misinformation, or lack of knowledge that you have about Canadians of Aboriginal background and identify and openly discuss where this belief stems from. Each student is then to discuss a practical, realistic, and meaningful way that he or she will genuinely use to shift from this paradigm of thinking that will positively contribute to his or her self-awareness and cultural awareness of Aboriginal peoples as a practitioner-in-training as well as an individual.

Exercise #4: Social Work with Immigrant Families

You are a practitioner at a residential home for seniors and you will be conducting an initial intake as the first step of the admission process. You have been scheduled to meet with a Canadian Pakistani Muslim family regarding the prospective admission of their 70-year-old father, Mr K. At the meeting, six family members attend the meeting with Mr K.: his two sons, the wife of his eldest son, and their three adult children, aged 21–25. Mr K. currently lives with his eldest son and his family. Mr K. emigrated from Pakistan to Canada with his wife and eldest son 50 years ago. At the time, his eldest son was 5 years old. The couple later had another son who was born in Canada. Mr K. and his wife were gainfully employed while raising their young family in the suburbs outside the urban city.

Mr K.'s wife passed away two years ago from cancer, resulting in Mr K. selling the family home and moving in with his eldest son at his son's request. At the time of his wife's death, Mr K.'s two children had already moved out of the house, with the eldest son marrying and moving 20 minutes away from his parents. Mr K.'s youngest son moved out after graduating from university and accepting a job in the United States. He has since returned home to Canada on a temporary leave from work to help the family determine the next steps in their father's care and well-being. Mr K. has recently been diagnosed with osteoporosis and has been experiencing significant challenges with his mobility. He suffers from no other medical conditions.

During the intake meeting, the family members are quite vocal with their position on whether Mr K. should be placed in the residential home. Mr K.'s eldest son is opposed to placing his father in the residential home based on his negative perception of nursing and residential homes as being neglectful and abusive. As well, based on tradition, culture, and religion, he states that it is his responsibility as the eldest son to look after his father for the remainder of his life and to be the primary caregiver, ensuring he is well taken care of and cared for until he passes away. He states that placing his father in a residential home will negatively impact his role, responsibility, and duty as the eldest son. Mr K.'s daughter-in-law and eldest granddaughter support the position of Mr K.'s eldest son, while two of the three adult grandchildren are actively pursuing and initiating for their grandfather to be placed in the home because of the impact it is having on their parents' health. They strongly feel that the residential home will be able to better care for their grandfather, since their parents are juggling home and life responsibilities and it appears to be taking a significant toll on their parents' marriage, although their parents do not admit to this during the meeting.

Mr K.'s youngest son also feels that the residential home will be better suited to care for his father rather than have his brother and his family shouldering the burden, especially given Mr K.'s osteoporosis. Refer to Table 16.1 for each family member's position on Mr K.'s future housing. Prior to his father's diagnosis, the youngest son was comfortable with and fully supported his father being cared for by his brother and his family. However, given the diagnosis, he has begun to explore the possibility and practicality of having his father placed in a residential home instead of being cared for at home where his needs are not likely to be met around-the-clock because of the various work schedules of the family and other life demands and commitments.

From the initial intake meeting, there is a clear presentation of opposing viewpoints and positions in the K. family on where Mr K. should live and who should care for him.

Table 16.1 Mr K.'s Family Members and Their Positions on His Future Housing

In Favour of Residential Home	Against Residential Home
Youngest son	Eldest son
2 grandchildren	Daughter-in-law (eldest son's wife)
	1 grandchild

Background Information

In your assessment of this situation, it is critical to be aware of some key aspects to facilitate your assessment, understanding, discussion, and strategizing of this case scenario. (For further discussion on perspectives on aging and social work practice with diverse older adults, see Chapter 15 by Daniel Lai and Xue Bai.)

- "Islamic teaching emphasizes the duty of adult children towards ageing parents in terms of deference and the provision of material support" (Laird, 2008).
- However, insomuch as the bedrock of religion influences parental obligation and duty, it is not always the case. In fact, "regardless of the strength of their religious convictions, young people of Pakistani and Bangladeshi descent usually expect to provide for aged parents and think of this as a moral obligation. Their parents, in turn, often anticipate assistance from adult children as part of an intergeneration contract of mutual support" (Laird, 2008, p. 85).

Questions for Discussion

In your group, engage in a respectful and healthy discussion about the application of cultural practice in terms of the cultural and religious dynamics revolving in the K. family.

1. What steps would you take to approach the viewpoints and positions of each family member?
2. What specific questions would you ask this family to further explore around their reasons and rationale for supporting or opposing Mr K.'s prospective admission into the residential home?
3. What other factors may be the source of this family situation?

Exercise #5: Social Work and Sexuality with Gay, Lesbian, Bisexual, Transgendered and Queer Communities

Jamie is a 21-year-old woman who has joined the community kitchen program at the homeless shelter where you work as a counsellor and community outreach worker. The community kitchen program is designed for women living in low-income communities who are underhoused or at risk of being homeless to learn about healthy cooking habits and developing healthy eating lifestyles on a fixed income. The secondary objective of the program is for women of all ages within the community who are experiencing personal, social, emotional, or financial challenges to share their stories with one another as a means of providing a network of support and social connectivity. The group of 12 women meets twice a week and makes dinner together with the assistance of a local chef. Once they have finished cooking, they eat their dinner collectively in a large dining area. It is at this time during dinner that the women have an opportunity to talk and discuss issues of their own choosing with the facilitation of two counsellors. The role of the two counsellors is mainly to facilitate a safe and respectful environment ensuring each member has the opportunity to talk, which is on a voluntary basis, and that the information remains confidential within the group.

Jamie recently joined the group, and after her fourth week she asks to speak with you privately after the group has finished dinner and clean up. Once you meet with Jamie, she discloses that she and her parents had a heated argument a few days ago resulting in her parents telling her not to return home. Jamie has since been living on the streets and fears for her health and safety. She did not want to share the information earlier as she was embarrassed to disclose that she is homeless and did not want to be a burden to anyone, including her partner. Jamie refuses to speak to her parents because of the demeaning and destructive insults and threats that they made to her. Jamie revealed to her parents that she is gay and wanted their acceptance and support of her sexual orientation after hiding it from them for eight years. An additional catalyst for Jamie's coming out was to introduce her parents to her girlfriend, whom she has been dating for two years. She felt that she could no longer conceal the truth and wanted the freedom to be honest and to share this major part of her life and identity.

At the age of 13, Jamie knew she was gay and battled with her sexuality throughout high school. With the internal conflict Jamie was experiencing throughout her teenage years, she dated a young man from her high school for two years to try to convince herself that she was not gay and to create an image to her family and friends that she was "happily" involved in a heterosexual relationship. Although her family and friends did not appear to be suspicious of her "relationship," Jamie wanted to ensure her true sexual orientation was concealed because she felt immense pressure from her family to marry and have children after she completed postsecondary studies. As a child of parents who are both educators and from large families, the value of education and family was strongly emphasized in Jamie's home, and Jamie did not want to disrupt the family values. Additionally, with Jamie's mother teaching at her high school, Jamie did not want to embarrass or humiliate her mother or her public image. She felt that her mother's career would be in jeopardy for advancement to principal if she disclosed her sexual orientation and therefore maintained a "heterosexual" relationship in high school to dampen or destroy any speculation or rumours.

After her completion of high school, Jamie broke off her "relationship" and attended university in the city while living at home. She majored in psychology to pursue her long-term goal of becoming a psychologist. It was during her studies at university that Jamie met Dawn, where the two became friends and soon after started a relationship. Jamie kept her relationship a secret to everyone except her cousin Charli, whom she has been close with since childhood. Charli is Jamie's sole confidante and supports Jamie's relationship with Dawn.

During a trip last summer overseas to help build homes for disadvantaged families, Jamie reflected on her life and came to the realization that she could no longer live in secret and yearned for the freedom to share who she is with her family and friends, especially her parents. Upon her return home to start her second year of school, Jamie had several conversations with Dawn and decided to disclose her sexual orientation and her relationship with Dawn to her parents.

Jamie's revelation was not well received, and her parents' reaction and response has negatively impacted her self-esteem and self-worth and even her relationship with Dawn. She has not spoken to Dawn since being kicked out of her home, and she would be unable to stay with Dawn since Dawn lives in residence and shares accommodations with other university students in limited quarters. Charli has offered her home to Jamie, but Jamie does not want to be an additional burden to Charli, who recently got married and is living in a studio apartment with her spouse and her mother-in-law, who is recovering from cancer-related surgery and treatment.

Jamie confides in you that she is extremely anxious about her fractured relationship with her parents, isolation from her girlfriend, and lack of housing accommodations. She doesn't know what to do and is in constant fear of her health and safety.

Background Information

In your assessment of this situation, it is critical to be aware of some key aspects to facilitate your assessment, understanding, discussion, and strategizing of this case scenario. (For further discussion on social work and sexual diversity, see Chapter 12 by Christine A. Walsh, Carey Mulligan, and Gio Dolcecore.)

- "Sexual orientation and gender identity are complex constructs and are difficult to define. Some define sexual orientation as a person's sexual attraction to a gender, others suggest it to be a self-concept and others conceptualize it as comprised of cognitive, behavioural and affective dimensions" (Johnson & Amella, 2013, p. 525).
- "Identity concealment entails youth hiding their true sexual identities by not engaging in activities that will label them as gay or lesbian" (Johnson & Amella, 2013).
- "Homelessness among young people, including both runaways and youths evicted from their homes by parents, is a significant public health crisis. At particular risk for homelessness are lesbian, gay and bisexual (LGB) youths" (Rosario, Schrimshaw, & Hunter, 2011, p. 186).
- "Homeless LGB youth are at far greater risk for psychological symptoms than homeless heterosexual youth. Homeless LGB youth report significantly higher levels of depressive symptoms, anxious symptoms and other internalizing problems relative to homeless heterosexual youth" (Rosario & Schrimshaw, 2012, p. 545).

Questions for Discussion

1. What is your first course of action with Jamie? Why?
2. As it appears that Jamie is experiencing mental health issues, what assessments would you make to confirm this and what are your next steps to support her mental health?
3. What role would you play in terms of Jamie's relationship with her parents and her girlfriend?
4. What role would the women's community kitchen group play in the helping process?

Exercise #6: Social Work, Immigration, and Refugee Work

Nia is a 29-year-old woman whom you have been working with for the past 18 months. You are a social worker at a local government office that provides social assistance, counselling, and career and employment supports. Nia has been on social assistance for the past 10 months, whereby her basic needs—rental accommodations and food—are financially funded by the municipal government. Nia is a refugee and arrived in Canada two years ago. Nia is originally from Mali, a country situated in the western region of Africa. Nia fled her home country because of threats made to her and her young daughter for rejecting the common practice of female genital mutilation. Nia rejected this practice when she was 13 years old and refused to have her daughter undergo this custom. Nia's parents did not agree to the practice and did not have Nia circumcised, especially after having lost their eldest daughter who bled to death as a result of the procedure at the age of 14. Nia was 9 years old at the time her sister died and has not fully recovered from the loss of her sister and friend. As a result of losing their daughter, Nia's parents vowed that Nia would never undergo the traditional and cultural practice of female genital mutilation amidst community and public pressure to honour the common tradition and cultural practice.

As pressure from the community intensified, Nia's parents and two older brothers devised a plan for Nia to leave Mali and to live with her uncle and aunt in Tunisia until things settled down, at which time she could return home without any pressure from the community. Tunisia was also an ideal place for Nia to escape to since female genital mutilation is not commonly practised there. Nia was able to successfully leave Mali and eventually made her way to Tunisia with the help of another uncle who travelled with her as her accompanying adult. Nia lived in Tunisia with her uncle and aunt and attended school and participated in various activities an average teenager would engage in. Nia, however, missed her family and wanted to rejoin her parents and brothers, but didn't know how to find her way back without upsetting her uncle and aunt.

Nia settled in Tunisia and completed high school and eventually earned her nursing degree at a local university. Nia eventually married and had a daughter. Shortly after her daughter's third birthday, Nia learned that her father was terminally ill and decided to return to Mali to be with him before he died. She felt that she would be safe from harm from the community given that so much time had passed and she was now an adult. Nia and her family reunited after being separated for 14 years. The reunion with her family was short lived, though, because Nia was threatened by various members of the community, who asserted that because she dishonoured the custom, her daughter would be forced to undergo the procedure with or without Nia's consent. For fear of her daughter's life, Nia and her husband immediately left Mali and returned to Tunisia, but feared that news would spread in Tunisia of her dishonour. Feeling responsible for the threats, Nia made the hard decision to leave her husband and to seek refuge in Canada with her daughter.

Since her arrival in Canada, Nia has been living with her cousin in a basement apartment. Her cousin, Saleema, who is a full-time librarian and part-time nursing student at the local university, was supporting Nia and her daughter, but because of her school fees Saleema has been unable to continue financially supporting Nia, resulting in Nia seeking financial assistance. Throughout the past 10 months, Nia has been having severe anxiety and problems sleeping and she has been doubting herself about returning to the field of nursing. Although practising nursing, especially with adolescent and young adult females in the area of sexual health, is Nia's lifelong career goal, she is not certain if she has the required abilities or capability. Although she is committed to building a life in Canada with her daughter with the hopes of having her husband join them, Nia fears that she may be denied protection in Canada and forced to return to possible threats and danger in her home country.

Background Information

In your assessment of this situation, it is critical to be aware of some key aspects to facilitate your assessment, understanding, discussion, and strategizing of this case scenario. (For more discussion on social work and refugees, see Chapter 10 by Catherine Montgomery.)

- The World Health Organization defines female genital mutilation (FGM) as "all procedures involving partial or total removal of the external female genitalia or other injury to the female genital organs for non-medical reason" (Conroy, 2009, p. 110).
- FGM "is practiced in at least 34 countries and in diverse cultures affiliated with different religions, including Islam, Christianity and animistic belief systems" (Suardi, Mishkin, & Henderson, 2010, p. 234).
- "Different societies organize and justify female circumcision (FC) differently. In some societies, FC is a pubertal rite of passage into adulthood. In the case of infibulation, carried out before puberty, FC symbolically bestows virginity or to enclose fertility in a girl. In other societies, FC is part of the wedding ritual and initiates the girl into womanhood, marks the start of childbearing and ensures paternity" (Ahlberg, Krantz, Lindmark, & Warsame, 2004, p. 52).

- "FGM is often given as an example of a topic that challenges cross-cultural understanding, but it is also defended as a part of the elaborate rules and cultural systems that are transmitted from generation to generation . . . as a rite of passage" (Corbett, 2008, as cited in Suardi, Mishkin, & Henderson, 2010).
- "If someone intentionally applies force to another person without that person's consent, it is considered an assault (Section 265, [Criminal Code]). Under Canadian law, performing FGM constitutes an assault. It is not an acceptable medical procedure. Additionally, a child cannot give legal consent for FGM. As well, while a child can give consent for medical purposes, no parent, grandparent, or other adult can consent to assault on behalf of the child. Therefore, no one can consent to female genital mutilation for a child" (Mattern, 1998, p. 36).

Questions for Discussion

1. What has been your initial understanding or awareness of female genital mutilation prior to reading this case scenario?
2. Describe in detail the various issues that Nia is possibly dealing with that appear to be impacting her mental health and sense of self-worth and self-esteem.
3. What impact is Nia's refugee status having on her settlement and adjustment to Canada?
4. How does Nia's escape from FGM and her identity as a woman and mother intersect and impact how she views herself and her future goals?

Exercise #7: Anti-Racist/Anti-Oppressive Social Work Practice

You are a social worker at a well-established and well-respected Boys and Girls Club in a diverse part of the city. You provide individual counselling for children and their families, lead recreational and social programs, and outreach to the community. Your organization also partners with five local elementary schools to provide breakfast, tutoring, and reading programs to help facilitate academic, social, and personal success in the children of the community. With strong ties to the academic community and other community partnerships that support student learning and success, your organization has been asked to attend a community session at the local district school board to discuss its viewpoint and argument on the development of an Afrocentric alternative school in the neighbourhood.

For several years, members of the Black community and other community supporters have been requesting that the school board integrate African-centred information and material into the curriculum to support the engagement and success of Black students and to expose all students to the positive contributions of African Canadians. With public and community pressure mounting, the school board has decided to hear from the community and will be hosting a series of hearings to consider the proposal of the community's request for an Afrocentric alternative school. Your organization has been asked to attend the first of many proposal meetings. Your district manager has decided to have a meeting to discuss each social worker's perspective and opinions of a proposed Afrocentric school in the community to ensure there is consensus on the organization's stance on the proposal.

Background Information

In your assessment of this situation, it is critical to be aware of some key aspects to facilitate your assessment, understanding, discussion, and strategizing of this case scenario. (For further discussion on anti-racism and anti-oppression in social work practice, see Chapter 3 by Gordon Pon, Sulaimon Giwa, and Narda Razack.)

- "Research shows that the dropout rate of African-Canadian students exceeds 40% and when the statistics are disaggregated along gender balance, the percentage for Black/African Canadian male students is much higher . . . there is something wrong in the system that is causing this malady of disengagement, underachievement and/or failure. The general assumption is that there are a number of contributing factors including the non-inclusive content of the curriculum, low expectations of teachers and negative school climates" (Brathwaite, 2010).
- "Anti-racist education begins from the premise that racism exists and includes a focus on systemic racism . . . Anti-racist education recognizes intersecting forms of inequality, assumes the role of power in the perpetuation of racism, criticizes racialized inequalities and addresses white supremacy" (Raby, 2004).
- "A focus on Afrocentricity is designed not to exclude other 'centric' knowledge but to contribute to a plurality of perspectives and knowledge about schooling in the Euro-Canadian context. Curriculum in Canadian schools is diversified when programming is culture-specific without marginalizing cultures" (Dei, 1996, p. 177).
- "In September of 2009, Africentric Alternative School in Toronto admitted its first 90 students" (Levine-Rasky, 2014).

Group Discussion

With a partner or in a small group, engage in a respectful and healthy debate whereby each person takes an opposing position on either the advantages or disadvantages of the proposal by the local school board to integrate an Afrocentric alternative school in the community of the Boys and Girls Club. Provide in detail the reasons for your position.

The Role and Value of Self-Reflection in Practice

As a social work practitioner working with individuals from an array of diverse backgrounds, the role and value of self-reflection has been an impetus to my own self-awareness as a person and professional while enhancing my understanding and appreciation of the unique needs of people. Social work training within the education system entails reflecting on one's skills, abilities, belief systems, and the prospective contributions you will make once you start practising.

In my experience and observation, self-reflection is highly endorsed in academia as essential to professional development; however, self-reflection does not end in the classroom or within the pages of a textbook. Self-reflection is an ongoing introspective exercise and experience that plays a salient role in the everyday delivery of social work. "Reflective thinking begins with a state of doubt, hesitation or perplexity and moves through the act of searching to find material that will resolve, clarify or otherwise address the doubt" (Di Gursansky & Le Sueur, 2002, p. 779). As a practitioner, I am continuously trying to better understand my own attitude, approach, behaviours, and responses to the individuals that seek my support and guidance in life situations. It is often assumed that a social worker knows exactly what is going on with a client and holds the answers to remedy the client's life. However, as we discussed earlier, this is far from the truth. The intentionality of being a learner while our clients teach us about themselves and critical areas of their lives is not only fundamental to the therapeutic alliance but also life changing. Self-reflection is about learning and making the deliberate choice to better understand and even expose why I think the way I do and how this impacts and shapes my learning when I am providing individual counselling, group counselling, or working in the community. What am I learning or have learned about myself through an experience with a client that is impacting and shaping my role as a practitioner and also as a person?

Earlier in the chapter, when I discussed the story of Mr P., the professional from the Middle East (Case Example 16.2), I was somewhat challenged to ask him about his personal appearance, fearing that he may react negatively or that my query may appear judgmental or biased in some way. With this experience, I reflected on my initial reservations in asking Mr P. a rather personal question that I felt had possible ties to his professional pursuits, and recognized that my approach was rooted in my attitude of not wanting to create any barriers or distance to the therapeutic alliance between myself and Mr P. Asking such questions may appear as a sign of vulnerability in the eyes of a client, and I realized in my reflection that I did not want to appear vulnerable but rather consistently competent to Mr P. However, as I continued to reflect on this, I became aware that asking such questions, uncomfortable as they may be, is critical to truly knowing our clients' stories, histories, and background. Being vulnerable does not mean you are incompetent, but rather it is a demonstration of knowledge seeking within a mutually supportive environment of exchanging information, ideas, and strategies to facilitate client empowerment.

My reflective thinking was rooted in my own doubt and hesitation, and yet this was the catalyst to my own learning about cultural traditions of the client and to facilitating Mr P.'s own education about the varying cultural aspects of North America and the Middle East. "The centre of reflection seems to be a positive embracing of doubts, anxieties, uncertainties and contradictions which are an integral part of the human condition and attendant upon all forms of intervention. It is the effort to make sense of these and to use them in constructive change (for the self and others) that requires reflection. It is its core function" (Di Gursansky & Le Sueur, 2002, p. 779). This simply means that reflective thinking often starts with vulnerability such as doubts and leads to the desire to want to make sense of this vulnerability to use this knowledge for change of oneself and others.

I often tell my students that when it comes to practising social work, they are a person first and a professional second in order to promote their own reflective thinking of their biases and judgments of others. In the context of a client, I remind students that the client is an individual first and that their culture, religion, sexual orientation, or other aspect of difference comes after. The reality is that we all carry negative attitudes and perspectives toward people that do not look like us or act like us or who are just simply "different" than us. Social workers and social work students are not immune to this mentality and frame of thinking, and this lends itself to the role of self-reflection in this area. It is critical to ask yourself: *How do I not allow my own racism or discrimination of a group of people to impact my work with a client?* This question is personal, provocative, and powerful, as many people claim that they are not racist or prejudiced and they treat everyone the same; however, true reflective thinking will expose the racism and prejudice that we each carry. "There are many factors that impact prejudice and discrimination, including physical difference, established patterns and norms of interaction between various groups, media portrayal of groups, and direct exposure to one another" (Oskamp, 2000, as cited in Wahler, 2012, p. 1060). In other words, difference is all around us and our negative attitudes and behaviours are shaped by these differences. When discussing this in class, I remind my students that upon graduation they will still carry racist and discriminatory beliefs; however, as practitioners-in-training and eventual practitioners, what will the intersection of prejudice and practice look like and how will it impact the therapeutic alliance? These are hard yet necessary questions that require the application of honesty and critical thinking.

A fundamental aspect of answering such questions is exploring consciousness raising. It helps students identify the groups with whom they hold prejudiced beliefs. Consciousness of one's beliefs is the first step in changing values, beliefs, and subsequent behaviours, and reflection is particularly important when examining beliefs about human nature, diversity, and behaviour (Osmo, 2001; Comerford, 2003, as cited in Wahler, 2012) to avoid discriminatory beliefs from affecting social workers' interventions with clients. Essentially, being honest about one's discrimination and critically examining the root of your discrimination and the target of your intolerance are beneficial in professional competence and helping clients beyond one's intolerance.

"Because social workers have the power to impact people's lives, it is of the utmost importance that beliefs, values and opinions that guide actions are explicitly identified and critically examined to reduce the chances of acting out of prejudice or incorrect assumptions" (Osmo and Landau, 2001, as cited in Wahler, 2012, p. 1064). Will this take time? Of course it will, and even for seasoned practitioners it is integral to continuously and deliberately expose discriminatory attitudes and mentality to ensure the therapeutic alliance is not compromised. In my practice, one of my guiding principles is to ensure that a client does not leave my presence the same way he or she came in. This principle is based on my regular engagement in reflective thinking and exposing my own racism and discrimination to ensure that my negative thoughts are consistently examined and do not reach my lips in terms of words spoken to clients. Again this takes time, but is demonstrative of an act of consciousness raising and awareness.

It is critical to be an active participant in reflective thinking to express the values and ethics of social work while engaging in professional competence, accountability, and integrity. And it all starts and ends with honesty.

Summary and Conclusion

The objective and vision of this chapter is to provide a simple and refreshing look at the practical application of diversity within the experiential lens of classroom learning and engagement. With my work as a social worker in Toronto with diverse populations, diversity is beyond a buzzword or a foreign term or concept, but is the actual reality of our society and the work that practitioners in human services engage in on a daily basis regardless of where in the country one works. Essentially, studying diversity can either be the beginning of knowledge for some or the desire or requirement to broaden one's limited understanding or the much-needed and sometimes uncomfortable exercise to challenge one's biases, ignorance, prejudice, or discrimination. It is hoped that through the exercises in this chapter, which have explored a collection of diverse stories and experiences about difference, that on an individual and collective basis readers will have had the opportunity to uncover and expose their own meaning and understanding of diversity while engaging in healthy, constructive, and even uncomfortable conversations and dialogues about approaches and responses that best meet the needs of individuals. Learning about ourselves is just as relevant as learning about and from others, even in the midst of disagreements, misunderstandings, and uncertainties. And learning about diversity is not linear in any way, shape, or form, but is a complex and ongoing process.

And in this process of ongoing and fluid learning, it is up to the learner to reflect on his or her attitudes, approaches, uncertainties, and doubts to facilitate honest, genuine, and uncompromising self-reflection that can only promote and increase professional and personal competence.

Questions for review

1. What does diversity mean to you as a person and a practitioner?
2. What or who influences your understanding of differences? Why?
3. How has your learning been shaped, impacted, or challenged by the class exercises outlined in this chapter?
4. Why is self-reflection important and what is its personal worth to you?
5. What steps are you currently taking or will you take to engage in self-reflective thinking?

Suggested Readings and Resources

Bishop, A. (2002). *Becoming an ally: Breaking the cycle of oppression in people* (2nd ed.). Halifax, NS: Fernwood Publishing.

D'Augelli, A., Grossman, A., Starks, M., & Sinclair, K. (2010). Factors associated with parents' knowledge of gay, lesbian, and bisexual youths' sexual orientation. *Journal of GLBT Family Studies, 6,* 178–98.

Davidson, C., & Hawe, P. (2012). School engagement among Aboriginal students in northern Canada: Perspectives from activity settings theory. *Journal of School Health, 82*(2), 65–74

Gardner, F. (2001). Social work students and self-awareness: How does it happen? *Reflective Practices, 2*(1), 27–40.

Gioia, D. (2014). Reflections on teaching ethnographic fieldwork: Building community participatory practices. *Qualitative Social Work, 13*(1), 144–53.

Johnston, L. (2009). Critical thinking and creativity in a social work diversity course: Challenging students to "think outside the box." *Journal of Human Behaviour in the Social Environment, 19,* 646–56.

Jones, S. (2009). *Critical learning for social work students.* Exeter, UK: Learning Matters

Ontario Human Rights Commission (1996). Female genital mutilation (FGM): Questions and answers (fact sheet). Retrieved from http://www.ohrc.on.ca/en/female-genital-mutilation-fgm-questions-and-answers-fact-sheet

Ontario Human Rights Commission. (2013). Policy on removing the "Canadian experience" barrier. Retrieved from http://www.ohrc.on.ca/en/policy-removing-%E2%80%9Ccanadian-experience%E2%80%9D-barrier

References

Ahlberg, B., Krantz, I., Lindmark, G., & Warsame, M. (2004). It's only a tradition: Making sense of eradication interventions and the persistence of female circumcision within a Swedish context. *Critical Social Policy, 24*(1), 50–78.

Angelini, P. (2012). *Our society: Human diversity in Canada* (4th ed.). Toronto, ON: Nelson Education Ltd.

Anisef, P., Brown, R., Phythian, K., Sweet, R., & Walters, D. (2010). Early school leaving among immigrants in Toronto secondary schools. *Canadian Review of Sociology, 47,*103–28.

Blommaert, J., & Dong, J. (2010). *Ethnographic fieldwork: A beginner's guide.* Bristol, UK: Multilingual Matters.

Braithwaite, O. (2010). The role of the school curriculum to obliterate anti-black racism. *Our Schools, Our Selves, 19*(3), 305–26.

Briskman, L. (2007). *Social work with Indigenous communities*. Sydney, AU: The Federation Press.

City of Toronto. (2014). Toronto facts. Retrieved from http://www1.toronto.ca/wps/portal/contentonly?vgnextoid=dbe867b42d853410VgnVCM10000071d60f89RCRD&vgnextchannel=57a12cc817453410VgnVCM10000071d60f89RCRD

Conroy, M. (2009). Refugees themselves: The asylum case for parents of children at risk of female genital mutilation. *Harvard Human Rights Journal, 109*, 21–131.

Dei, G. (1996). The role of Afrocentricity in the inclusive curriculum in Canadian schools. *Canadian Journal of Education, 21*(2), 170–86.

Di Gursansky, D., & Le Sueur, E. (2010). Authenticity in reflection: Building reflective skills for social work. *Social Work Education, 29*(7), 778–91.

Doyle-Marshall, W. (2014, February 19). Canadian experience—conveniently discriminatory. *Indo Caribbean World*, pp. 1 & 12.

Fox, C. (2011). Working with clients who engage in self-harming behaviour: Experiences of a group of counsellors. *British Journal of Guidance & Counselling, 39*(1), 41–51.

Government of Ontario. (2013). City of Toronto. Retrieved from www.ontarioimmigration.ca/OI/en/living/OI_HOW_LIVE_TORONTO.html

Government of Canada. (2015). Immigration and citizenship. Retrieved from http://www.cic.gc.ca/english/newcomers/about-pr.asp

Johnson, M., & Amella, E. (2013). Isolation of lesbian, gay, bisexual and transgender youth: A dimensional concept analysis. *The Journal of Advanced Nursing, 70*(3), 523–32.

Laird, S. (2008). *Anti-oppressive social work: A guide for developing cultural competence*. London, UK: Sage Publications.

Levine-Rasky, C. (2014). White fear: Analyzing public objection to Toronto's Africentric school. *Race Ethnicity and Education, 17*(2), 202–18.

MacNeil, M. (2008). An epidemiologic study of Aboriginal adolescent risk in Canada: The meaning of suicide. *Journal of Child and Adolescent Psychiatric Nursing, 21*(1), 3–12.

Mattern, C. A. (1998). Canada: Female genital mutilation—workshop manual. *Women's International Network News, 24*(4), 33–7.

Miley, K., O'Melia, M., & DuBois, B. (2013). *Generalist social work practice: An empowering approach*. New York, NY: Pearson Education.

Pedersen, P., Draguns, J. G., Lonnder, W., & Trimble, J. (2008). *Counselling across cultures* (6th ed.). Thousand Oaks, CA: Sage Publications.

Raby, R. (2004). There's no racism at my school, it's just joking around: Ramifications for anti-racist education. *Race Ethnicity and Education, 7*(4), 367–83.

Rosario, M., & Schrimshaw, E. (2012). Homelessness among lesbian, gay and bisexual youth: Implications for subsequent internalizing and externalizing symptoms. *Youth Adolescence, 41*, 544–60.

Rosario, R., Schrimshaw, E., & Hunter, J. (2011). Risk factors for homelessness among lesbian, gay and bisexual youths: A developmental milestone approach. *Children and Youth Services Review, 34*, 186–93.

Rothman, J. (2008). *Cultural competence in process and practice: Building bridges*. New York, NY: Pearson Education.

Rubin, H., & Rubin, I. (2005). *Qualitative interviewing: The art of hearing data* (2nd ed.). Thousand Oaks, CA: Sage Publications.

Sankey, D. (2006, February 4). Job prosperity eludes immigrant professionals. *Calgary Herald*, I1, Front.

Shameful survival of stereotypes. (2011, February 26). *Globe & Mail*, p. F8.

Suardi, E., Mishkin, A., & Henderson, S. (2010). Female genital mutilation in a young refugee: A case report and review. *Journal of Child & Adolescent Trauma, 3*, 234–42.

Turegun, A. (2013). Immigrant settlement work in Canada: Limits and possibilities for professionalization. *Canadian Review of Sociology, 50*(4), 387–411.

Wahler, E. (2012). Identifying and challenging social work students' biases. *Social Work Education, 31*(8), 1058–70.

Walls, M., Hautala, D., & Hurley, J. (2014). Rebuilding our community: Hearing silenced voices on Aboriginal youth suicide. *Transcultural Psychiatry, 51*(1), 47–72.

Warry, W. (2007). *Ending denial: Understanding Aboriginal issues*. Peterborough, ON: Broadview Press.

Conclusion

By Alean Al-Krenawi, John R. Graham, and Nazim Habibov

17

In this volume, the editors consciously sought topics that highlight ways in which we can better understand diversity. A particularly important concept has been the intersection of various parts of our diversities. Each chapter, in its own way, has emphasized how any person's notion of diversity, and the identity that is implicit to this notion, changes over time and place. Multiple facets of diversity—diverse settings, diverse populations, and theories on diversity in social work—have been considered.

One of the most important means for understanding diversity is through self-awareness. When one appreciates one's positionality—such as age, gender, ethnicity, race, sexual orientation, and socio-economic status and how all these things intersect with one another—one is better able to appreciate the different positionalities of others. Self-awareness is paramount (Graham, 2008).

Whatever one's positionality, there can be power relationships. These same notions are interactive; one's degree of power changes over time, place, interaction, and on the basis of the other parties one is interacting with.

Human service agencies, likewise, have their own cultures, which vary over time, place, clients, and personnel involved. Social service organizations change in light of the social, economic, and political circumstances that influence their clients. Any such change invariably has a relationship to identity. Agencies providing services to people of Muslim background, for instance, have adapted their services to respond to issues of post-9/11 Islamophobia (Shier & Graham, 2013). Indeed, a great deal of scholarship has been written on providing culturally appropriate services to Muslim communities in general (Al-Krenawi & Graham, 2008, 2012; Shier & Graham, 2013). Some surprising insights can be taken from an emerging scholarship on diversity. Recent work, for instance, highlights the common experiences of social workers in major urban centres practising with specific cultural populations, and workers in rural, remote areas of the country. There can be problems with dual relationships, incidental encounters, among other facets, common to the rural/remote and to the urban culturally specific practice communities alike (Graham, Shier, & Brownlee, 2012).

Whether it is age, ethnicity, gender, language, nationality, range of ability, sexual orientation, or any other category of diversity there will be interpretations of oneself and of others around oneself. Given the differences—on the level of individual, group, or community—that can be embedded in these identities, there can be positive and negative feelings and responses. In some instances, there can be a backlash to others on the basis of differing identities. This may lead to a situation in which differences and the Other are feared; that is, a "culture of fear" that may occur among people, communities, or broader societies.

Culture of Fear

One way to understand differences is through the term "**multiculturalism**," a term that we define in the glossary. In the past, the term "multiculturalism" was largely associated with negative conceptions in both popular and scholarly circles (Hartman & Gerteis, 2005). A need to somehow "safeguard" culture and identity was perceived by individuals who faced incoming waves of immigration and change. Multiculturalism and diversity were seen as threats to the coherence and unity of society in North America well into the 1970s (and arguably, for some, until today). For instance, American historian Arthur M. Schlesinger, Jr. wrote about drastic consequences if multiculturalism was to be "misused" in education; the title of his paper, "The Disuniting of America," speaks volumes (1991). Cummins and Sayers held a similar view, claiming that cultural diversity was "the enemy from within" (1996, p. 6). Others read multiculturalism as a sort of appeasement policy, a way of "pacifying" the growing number of minorities (D'Andrea, Daniels, & Heck, 1991). This attitude can manifest as a simple annoyance at being faced with difference, to considering such difference a threat to the foundation of a particular community.

A refusal to acknowledge the legitimacy of different groups may result in psychological barriers and fear of the Other (Al-Krenawi, 2014). This "culture of fear" is characterized by the sense that one's values and identity will degenerate upon granting recognition to another. Detrimental practices such as racial profiling, wage discrimination and income gaps, and differential access to education are potential consequences of a "culture of fear," and cultural alienation is not far behind in the progression. Alternatively, custodians of all manner of communal settings can choose to work to manage diversity.

Managing Diversity

With regard to the crucial issue of managing diversity, we offer this wisdom: One does "not always have to endorse the things which we must tolerate in a respectful workplace in order to get the job done" (cited in Rosado, 2006, p. 9). That is, agreement with or support of an idea is not intrinsic to toleration and respect. Importantly as well, workplace diversity is best managed strategically and with a combination of micro-, mezzo-, and macro-planning. Organizations are being encouraged to "move away from merely 'counting heads for the government'" and to think positively and critically in managing diversity. We shall now take a few moments to do just that.

As mentioned above, multiculturalism can be thought of as a kind of mechanism for managing diversity. The management of diversity, then, entails the implementation of the ideas and values of multiculturalism. In doing so, we strive to create a safe space for differences—different cultures, different religions, different sexual orientations, and so on. This demands that a delicate balance be maintained: A too-strong sense of unity can result in an overdevelopment of uniformity, whereas a too-strong sense of diversity can overemphasize differences among individuals (Rosado, 2006). In other words, when striving to manage a diverse setting one is best off treading the middle ground. Doing otherwise incurs the risk of making the environment feel "diverse by force," which can inadvertently accentuate differences rather than allow for a natural highlighting of a range of qualities. This outcome, of course, would be counterproductive. Hence, balance is basic to the success of the project.

Diversity management has been discussed by Ely and Thomas (2001) and Dass and Parker (1999). These researchers suggested a multilevel approach that took into account a number of other contemporary theories for diversity management. At level one we find a resistance to diversity, showing a need for better management of diversity; level two is an approach that approves assimilation or equalization of differences; the third level gives way to a selected legitimacy and access to differences; and finally, the fourth level allows for an active and successful interaction and preservation of diversity.

Al-Krenawi (2014) proposed a two-step model for managing diversity. The first step entails cultivating an understanding of the Other and his or her differences to reach a place of acceptance and respect. The second step is then dedicated to developing an awareness of the advantages of considering the Other as equal to you, since equality is a prerequisite for a healthy society. Step two is predicated on the actualization of step one and an elimination of discrimination (such as prejudice and stereotypes) and skepticism. Al-Krenawi's model aims to help divided communities embrace the multicultural approach in which each group is giving and receiving recognition and respect. We argue that this approach will enhance diversity efforts not only in societies that are divided, but also in localities that are simply comprised of very heterogeneous populations.

Rosado's (2006) model of structural change, total quality diversity, is a third model of diversity management. In this approach diversity is managed in such a way that "the effect of all working together is greater than the sum total of all the parts working independently" (Rosado, 2006, p. 6). The first dimension of this model concerns the individual or "horizontal" level. Similarly to Al-Krenawi's (2014) proposal, this first level aims to help people develop a sense of positive value for difference. Absent this, Rosado contends, a group will fall short of its maximum potential. Nonetheless, according to Rosado the level of individual change is insufficient for achieving success. A second dimension, which centres on institutional change, is crucial to the project. Rosado describes this as the "vertical" dimension of the model, which makes targeted use of group diversity (p. 6). This institutional level change is pivotal because it is at this level that exclusion tends to fester. Furthermore, the change must be more than surface-deep; that is, a team of diverse individuals when brought together must learn how the assets of each individual contribute to the good of the organization as a whole.

Highly holistic in nature, this model of managing diversity takes into account diversity across multiple dimensions of a group.

Significantly, Rosado notes that the management of diversity is not a novel idea. Rather, it has an old, established history. More often than not, however, diversity has been managed for purposes of exclusion. As social workers who are against this, we wish to consider how to manage diversity while making adequate room for the inclusion of all.

Cultures of Inclusion

While the inquiry is still in its nascent phase, **social inclusion** has become a global concern. A recent United Nations (2010) report titled "Analysing and Measuring Social Inclusion in a Global Context" makes this quite clear:

> Creating a society for all is a moral obligation—one that must reflect the commitments to upholding fundamental human rights and principles of equality and equity. There are also strong instrumental reasons for promoting social integration and inclusion. Deep disparities, based on unequal distribution of wealth and/or differences in people's backgrounds, reduce social mobility and ultimately exert a negative impact on growth, productivity and well-being of society as a whole. Promoting social integration and inclusion will create a society that is safer, more stable and more just, which is an essential condition for sustainable economic growth and development.

Thus, we see that from the point of view of international thought leaders that the creation of cultures of inclusion is nothing short of an ethical imperative. Moreover, as the report notes, important practical concerns attest to the necessity of such cultures. We are confident that the theories and techniques presented in this volume will assist the student of social work in making informed and self-reflexive choices about leveraging the diversity that he or she finds everywhere. We conclude with a hope for these, our students, that is well articulated by Rosado: "[To be] persons who are able to . . . identify with humankind throughout the world, at all levels of human need . . . a *transcending* people who know no boundaries, and whose operating life-principle is compassion" (2006, p. 14). We can think of no professional goal more worthy than that.

References

Al-Krenawi, A. (2014, May). *What do we mean by diversity and multiculturalism in the Israeli society?* Paper presented at the conference on Diversity and Multiculturalism. Achva Academic College, Arugo, IL.

Al-Krenawi, A., & Graham, J. R. (2008). *Helping professional practice with Indigenous peoples: The Bedouin-Arab case.* Lanham, MD: University Press of America.

Al-Krenawi, A., & Graham, J. R. (2012). The impact of political violence on psychosocial functioning of individuals and families: The case of Palestinian adolescents. *Child and Adolescent Mental Health, 17*(1), 14–22.

Cummins, J., & Sayers, D. (1996). Multicultural education and technology: Promises and pitfalls. *Multicultural Education, 3*(3), 4–10.

D'Andrea, M., Daniels, J., & Heck, R. (1991). Evaluating the impact of multicultural counseling training. *Journal of Counseling & Development, 70*, 143–50.

Dass, P., & Parker, B. (1999). Strategies for managing human resource diversity: From resistance to learning. *The Academy of Management Executive, 13*(2), 68–80.

Ely, R. J., & Thomas, D. A. (2001). Cultural diversity at work: The effects of diversity perspectives on work group processes and outcomes. *Administrative Science Quarterly, 46*(2), 229–73.

Graham, J. R. (2008). Who am I? An essay on inclusion and spiritual growth through community and mutual appreciation. *Journal of Religion, Spirituality, and Social Work, 27*(1/2), 5–24.

Graham, J. R., Shier, M. L., & Brownlee, K. (2012). Contexts of practice and their impact on social work: A comparative analysis of the context of geography and culture. *Journal of Ethnic & Cultural Diversity in Social Work, 21*(2), 111–28.

Hartman, D., & Gerteis, J. (2005). Dealing with diversity: Mapping multiculturalism in sociological terms. *Sociological Theory, 23*(2), 218–40.

Rosado, C. (2006). What do we mean by managing diversity? *Workforce Diversity, 3*, 1–15.

Schlesinger, Jr., A. M. (1991). The disuniting of America: What we all stand to lose if multicultural education takes the wrong approach. *American Educator: The Professional Journal of the American Federation of Teachers, 15*(3), 21–33.

Shier, M. L., & Graham, J. R. (2013). Identifying social service needs of Muslims living in a post 9/11 era: The role of community-based organizations. *Advances in Social Work, 14*(2), 379–94.

United Nations Department of Economic and Social Affairs. (2010). Analysing and measuring social inclusion in a global context. New York, NY: United Nations Publications.

Glossary

accessibility A term that implies that goods, services, facilities, accommodation, employment, buildings, structures, and premises are able to be reached or obtainable by all members of society. Accessibility legislation refers to the "implementing and enforcing of accessibility standards in order to achieve accessibility for people with disabilities" (Accessibility for Ontarians with Disabilities Act, 2005).

acculturation The process of cultural and psychological change that results after a meeting between cultures. Individuals may show the effects of acculturation through changes in their everyday behaviours and ways of perceiving themselves and the world around them. Groups may show the effects of acculturation through changes in their cultural activities and institutions.

acculturative stress A state of psychological, emotional, physical, or social strain resulting from the process of adapting to a new cultural environment.

advocacy Taking action to defend, represent, or otherwise advance the cause of clients to ensure social justice at the individual, group, and community level (Hoefer, 2012).

age cohort A group of people who are the same age in the same period of time. Age cohort differences are differences that occur between groups of people differentiated by their age bracket (e.g., differences between those aged 65 to 75 and those aged 75 to 85).

agency An individual's capacity to make decisions and act independently of structural constraints.

ally An individual who takes actions to support another's actions in relation to a particular activity (e.g., in response to a social justice issue).

anti-Black racism Refers to the particular type of racism that is specifically targeted toward Black people on one hand, and the resistance to this racism on the other.

anti-colonialism A political struggle that seeks to transform structural and systemic oppressions that are endemic in settler societies. It prioritizes Indigenous sovereignty and Indigenous knowledges while emphasizing Indigenous ways of knowing and being that embrace a holistic understanding of mind, body, and spirit.

anti-oppression An approach used to address oppression that occurs in various forms. The goal of anti-oppression is to address the power imbalances between those who have power and those who do not.

anti-racism approach A theory used to address practices of racism, particularly at the institutional level. The strategies deployed to challenge racism can be targeted at different levels, including the state, institutions, organizations, groups, and individuals.

assimilation A process by which a person or persons acquire the culture, values, and patterns of another group through adopting the social and psychological characteristics of that group.

bias An inclination, feeling, opinion, or particular tendency to be prejudiced in favour of or against a thing, an individual, or a group—often without consideration of the possible merits of alternative points of view.

binary The practice of seeing things as having only two sides wherein there is no opportunity to see things outside of this binary. In social work practice, this is sometimes referred to as an "either/or" approach.

birth cohort A group of people born in the same year. The term is sometimes used more narrowly (e.g., to refer to a group of people born in the same month of the same year) or more broadly (e.g., to refer to a group of people born in the same set of years and who identify as belonging to the same generation).

bisexual A word used to describe a person who enjoys intimate (e.g., sexual, emotional, or spiritual) relationships and encounters with both members of their own gender and members of the opposite gender.

campaign strategies Persuasive, carefully planned tactics used during a campaign, such as for an election or for Missing Aboriginal women, in an effort to change people's opinions through education and promotion.

Canadian Multiculturalism Act Federal legislation passed in 1985 promoting equality and full and equitable participation in society.

capitalism An economic system in which some individuals own the means of production, that is, the capitalist, while others provide their labour for a wage.

Charter of Rights and Freedoms A bill of rights that is entrenched in the Canadian Constitution. It grants political rights to individual Canadian citizens and can challenge the Canadian government's policies and legislations. The Charter became law on 17 April 1982.

cis-gendered A word used to describe an individual whose self-identified gender matches the one that is aligned with her or his biological sex.

civil rights movements A social movement that occurred in the United States between the 1950s and 1960s to end racial segregation and discrimination against Black Americans and to grant them constitutional voting rights.

clan A group of individuals who belong to one of seven clans (e.g., Crane, Loon, Fish, Bear, Martin, Deer, and Bird). Each clan is assigned certain roles (functions) to serve the people. A person born into a clan would assume the duties or functions assigned to that clan.

collaborative strategies Strategies that seek to achieve social change through negotiation and agreed action.

colonialism A process by which representatives from one country acquire full or partial control over another country or a region traditionally controlled by Indigenous peoples. Control is typically achieved through a combination of physical force and coercion. Once control has been secured, colonialist powers establish a presence in the colonized region to exploit local peoples and resources for financial or political gain.

colour-blind approach An approach that views all people as human and believes that differential treatment is not experienced by people because of race.

coming out A process during which an individual reveals his or her sexual or gender identity to others.

community A group of people who are socially connected by geographic space or through a common connection (e.g., a group of people living in a particular village, or a group of social workers interacting across a particular province).

community development The work of capacity building in a community to bring change that improves the community's well-being.

community organizing Working in the community to help develop and organize the group to take action to address a social issue.

conflict/feminist/Marxist conceptual framework These frameworks share a common understanding that power is not equally shared, and real change can only occur when marginalized or oppressed groups have equal power. Those with power will not give it up without conflict.

contest strategies Strategies that apply pressure to change through confrontation and protest and view the issues in terms of unequal power and control.

critical race theory (CRT) A theory advanced by racialized scholars in the United States beginning in the 1980s. These scholars critiqued how legal discourses were not "colour-blind" but instead reproduced systemic and structural racism, with aims to transform the legal system and advance social justice. Today, the central tenets of CRT have been extended beyond its legal origin to consider broader economic, institutional, social, and cultural inequalities. CRT places high value on the lived experiences and narratives of marginalized peoples and communities.

cultural competence "[A] set of congruent behaviours, attitudes, and policies that come together in a system, agency, or amongst professionals and enable that system, agency, or those professionals to work effectively in cross-cultural situations" (Cross, Bazron, Dennis, & Isaacs, 1989). This model helps individuals understand and explore the challenges and advantages of diversity and also helps them develop an ability to interact effectively with people of different cultures and socio-economic backgrounds.

cultural diversity The existence of cultural variety within a particular group or society.

cultural literacy In social work, refers to becoming aware of a client's culture so that one can contextualize and better understand the issues the client conveys and the things he or she discusses. One cannot, of course, gain absolute "literacy" in a culture because not only is culture fluid and always changing, it is also understood differently by people within any cultural group. The model suggests, however, that learning the broad parameters of a culture and then gaining an understanding from the client about how these may or may not be taken up and lived in their life is an important means of understanding and working with clients.

culture The sum of ideas, beliefs, values, knowledge, and way of life of a particular society, group, place, or time; manifested in the art, customs, language, laws, and institutions of the people. Culture captures the lifestyle of a group of people while acknowledging their uniqueness from other groups. Culture guides human behaviour through a complex and dynamic creation of particular meaning, knowledge, artifacts, and symbols.

cumulative advantage/disadvantage perspective The perspective that interprets diversity of aging experiences as the accumulation of privileges or disadvantages throughout an individual's life course, examining the ways in which initial advantages, capacity, structural location, and available resources widen gaps between individuals or groups (Merton, 1988).

decentring Taking a step back from an intervention situation and reflecting on one's personal values and biases and how these affect the intervention process.

disability "[A]ny degree of physical disability, infirmity, malformation or disfigurement that is caused by bodily injury, birth defect, or illness and . . . includes diabetes mellitus, epilepsy, a brain injury, any degree of paralysis, amputation, lack of physical co-ordination, blindness or visual impediment, deafness or hearing impediment, muteness or speech impediment, or physical reliance on a guide dog or other animal or on a wheelchair or other remedial appliance or device" or a "condition of mental impairment or a developmental disability, a learning disability, or . . . a mental disorder" (Accessibility for Ontarians with Disabilities Act, 2005).

disability studies An interdisciplinary convergence of the humanities and social sciences that analyzes the politics of human variation from a variety of viewpoints and disciplines, challenging us to overcome and to address the realities of oppression of people with disabilities.

disadvantage A person or persons who lack or have unequal access to resources such as housing, education, employment, and social services.

diversity A range of characteristics including, but not limited to, age, race, skin colour, ethnic origin, geographic origin, culture, heritage, spoken language, gender, gender and sexual identity, disability/non-disability status, health status, religious and spiritual beliefs, political orientation, educational background, immigration status, and socio-economic status.

dominant cultural group In a given society, the culture of the group of people, typically in the majority, who are able to achieve power and influence over others by shaping and controlling the social, educational, economic, political, and religious institutions of their society. This culture is also sometimes called the majority-group culture.

employment equity The requirement that employers avoid discriminating against employees and potential employees based on such characteristics as gender, race, ethnicity, and disability. Employment equity means more than treating people in the same way; it also requires special measures and the accommodation of differences.

empowerment The belief that one can change one's environment. It involves increasing one's sense of personal strengths and realizing that one can improve one's circumstances.

empowerment perspective In intervention with individuals, groups, families, or communities, the empowerment perspective focuses on strengths and works with those involved on reclaiming their power in a situation over which they feel helpless so that they may become active subjects rather than passive recipients of help.

epistemological Relating to knowledge; the ways one can gain knowledge and make sense of things. One's epistemology is dependent on one's ontology (see *ontological*). If, for instance, one believes that only observable things are real, then one's epistemology will involve direct observation.

equity In social services, the rights of individuals to a fair and equal share of the goods and services in society. Equity programs are designed to engage in proactive practices that increase the likelihood of equal treatment for various disadvantaged groups, such as people with disabilities, Aboriginal peoples, visible minorities, and women.

essentialism The practice of stripping down the complex identity of a group to a set of attributes considered necessary to its identity and function; the discounting of variation among group members.

ethnic group A community of people whose members identify with each other culturally, usually on the basis of a presumed common genealogy or ancestry.

ethnicity Refers to a common heritage that particular groups identify themselves as belonging to—for example, British Isles, Caribbean-Black, Chinese, or Pakistani.

ethnocentricity Being centred or focused on one's own culture and view of the world and believing that that view is inherently superior to that of others.

ethnographies "[S]tudies that sketch an overall cultural setting, such as that shared by an ethnic group, a village, or a neighbourhood. This type of research describes the key norms, rules, symbols, values, traditions, and rituals in that setting, and shows how they fit together" (Rubin & Rubin, 2005, p. 7).

ethnoracial A person who is racialized because of their ethnicity and is also inferiorized in a subordinate way because of their ethnoracial identity.

ethnorelativism The ability not only to accept and respect cultural differences, but also to shift one's perspective to encompass another culture's worldview and thus empathize with individuals from that other culture.

Eurocentrism Around the world, European culture, values, ideas, and beliefs dominate in a way that it is held to be superior to other cultures. Their system of beliefs and thoughts are what produces colonialism and racism and creates the ethnic "other." European culture is also associated with upholding the systems of liberalism and democracy.

experiential phenomenology The study of subjective experience.

feminism An umbrella term used to represent a number of movements and ideologies that are concerned with the political, economic, cultural, and social equality of women.

feminist theory A theory that the socially constructed roles of men and women and the gender-based division of labour in economic and political spheres translate into men's domination and women's vulnerability and subordination.

First Nation The most common definition refers to Aboriginal communities that have a treaty relationship with the federal government of Canada. The second sense of the word refers to individuals whose descendants originate in Turtle Island (North America).

gay A word used to describe a person whose primary sexual orientation is toward members of his or her same gender. The term can be used to describe both men and women, but it is most commonly applied to describe a man who sees himself as being sexually attracted to as well as emotionally or spiritually connected to other men.

gender The psychological experience of being female or male. Gender is typically considered to be a socially constructed state, and it is often differentiated from the biological fact of one's sex.

gender variant Gender nonconformity or fluidity. The term is sometimes used to describe an individual whose self-perception or presentation of her or his gender differs from what members of the surrounding society would consider to be typical.

generalized other A symbolic interactionist concept used to explain how we can understand ourselves by making reference to an "other" that represents the norms, expectations, and regularities that are inscribed onto a role and align the performance of the occupant of the role with the role's meaning held by others (LaRossa & Reitzes, 1993).

hegemonic masculinity The dominant form of masculinity in a society. It is the cultural ideal of a man that subordinates all other types of masculinity and femininity.

hegemony The processes by which the dominant culture or ruling class maintains its dominant position, including the tendency for society to relinquish economic, political, social, and cultural control to the dominant group without question.

heterosexism The belief that being heterosexual (i.e., attracted only to members the opposite sex) is "normal" and that all other forms of sexuality are "abnormal" or "deviant." This belief can occur at individual, group, or institutional levels and can result in discrimination against individuals perceived to be other than heterosexual.

homonationalism The collective energy of political movements that coexist together and strive toward equality for queers and other minority populations.

homonormative The assimilation of heterosexual normalities, or the constructs given to gender and sexual appropriation (Butler, 1999).

homophobia A fear or hatred of gay and lesbian individuals.

identification The social process through which we recognize our membership in a particular social group.

identity "A subjective sense of coherence, consistency, and continuity of self, rooted in both personal and group history" (Henry, Tator, Mattis, & Rees, 1995). Identity may be expressed in various ways, including nationalism, which may be defined as a social and psychological force that provides people with a sense of perceived unity and community based on a shared cultural, linguistic, racial, historical, or geographic experience.

identity exam A technique that invites students and practitioners to explore the principal markers that they consider to be important to identity. Using index cards, the participants first explore the ways in which they define their own identity and, second, explore the ways in which others may perceive their identity. The exercise allows participants to reflect both on stereotypical representations of identity and also on the ways in which perceptions of identity may change in different contexts and according to different points of view.

ideology A complex set of ideas that attempts to explain, justify, legitimate, and perpetuate the circumstances in which a group finds itself. White hegemony over Aboriginal peoples in Canada, for example, has been perpetuated by a racist ideology of White superiority.

independent living A model that regards the person with a disability as a responsible decision maker who is capable of managing his or her own care requirements, indicating a philosophy that people with disabilities should have the same rights and choices as do people without disabilities.

indigenize To increase local participation in or ownership of something.

integration The process of unifying distinctive groups or individuals through full participation in the social, economic, political, educational, and cultural life of a society while retaining one's own unique identity.

intercultural approach An encounter and an exchange between two identities, individuals, or groups where each comes to the encounter with his or her own culture and worldview and give each other meaning. This exchange is redefined each time they meet.

interculturalism The promotion of effective communication and meaningful interaction among members of different cultures.

interlocking Graphically portraying the messy and tangled nature of the interwoven relationships among different disadvantaged social positions of a marginalized group.

intersect Metaphorically, when different disadvantaged social positions are interweaved together to generate a social force that adds to the oppressive condition imposed individually by these social positions.

intersectionality The idea originates from some Black feminists who argue that the oppressive condition challenging women of colour who live in poverty cannot be reduced to either their race, gender, or class. Instead, these three social categories intersect and work together to produce injustice. This idea has been expanded to understand the marginalized condition of people who experience oppression because of their disability, sexual orientation, immigrant status, or other.

intersex A word used to refer to an individual who possesses both male and female genetic or physical sex characteristics. Many intersexed people consider themselves to be part of the trans community (Topp, 2013).

intersubjectivity An interactive process in which active subjects try to exercise their agency to make sense of the context in which they are co-situated and the discourse to which they are co-subjected.

kinship The relations between individuals or family groups. The ties to the relationship can be clan-based, matrilineal, patrilineal, formal, or informal agreements. There are expectations of hospitality and assistance from kin.

lesbian A word used to describe a woman who sees herself as being sexually attracted to as well as emotionally or spiritually connected to other women.

liberal Whites A White person who views him or herself as someone who does not notice the "race" of a person and adopts a colour-blind approach. Overall, liberal Whites see themselves as progressive because they view everybody as equal and do not think racial prejudice exists.

life course theory A way of interpreting life as a continuing process in which past experiences influence an individual's present state and the present shapes future possibilities. Life course theory focuses on the interplay of individuals' life events and the historical and socio-cultural context in which individuals live.

localize To make local; synonym for *indigenize*.

mainstream (agency) The majority, or more accurately the most powerful (even if not a numeric majority), people within society. Such people tend to be of White European heritage, so a "mainstream agency" tends to serve and be built around the needs, ways of being, and norms of such people.

marginalization A form of oppression in which disadvantaged people are isolated from useful participation in the socio-economic system and even potentially leaves them in extreme poverty.

medical model of disability A model of disability that views a person with a disability as having a condition or a deficit that is unwanted. The medical model is criticized as problematic because it judges the person with a disability as being sick on the basis of their ability to function as a normal person does.

mindfulness Activity that encourages awareness to emerge through paying attention on purpose, nonjudgmentally, in the present moment. It is a holistic philosophy and practice that has to do with examining who we are, questioning our view of the world and our place in it, and cultivating an appreciation for the fullness of each of life's moments.

minority group A subordinate group of people who are fewer in number or have less power or control socially, politically, or economically than the dominant group.

multiculturalism (policy) "[A] system of beliefs and behaviours that recognizes and respects the presence of all diverse groups in an organization or society, acknowledges and values their socio-cultural differences, and encourages and enables their continued contribution within an inclusive cultural context which empowers all within the organization or society" (Rosado, 1996, p. 2).

ontological One's beliefs about the nature of existence.

oppression When the group or individual(s) in power control the less powerful through the use of cruel and unfair physical, psychological, social, cultural, or economic force.

Other An individual or a group of people that is perceived to be different from an individual or a group that is in the position to perceive. The basis of this difference may be in any number of perceived attributes, ranging from sex or gender to race or ethnicity to social status to political or religious belief.

patriarchy "A system of thought and social relations that privileges and empowers men, and creates relationships between the genders that disfranchise, disempower, and devalue women's experience" (Payne, 2005, p. 251).

positionality One's social position in relation to others.

positioning From a social psychological perspective, "the discursive process whereby people are located in conversations as observably and subjectively coherent participants in jointly produced storylines" (Davies & Harre, 1999, p. 37).

queer A word used to describe people whose sexual or gender identity does not fit neatly into any of the more strictly defined, socially constructed sexual or gender identities. While sometimes used in a critical or disrespectful way, the term "queer" has been reclaimed as a positive, flexible label by members of the LGBTQ community.

questioning A word used to describe an individual who is questioning her or his sexual identity. This process may involve introspective reflection, interpersonal discussions, and sexual and romantic encounters with others.

race Groupings of people based on perceived or supposed differences and similarities in physical or genetic traits such as skin colour, hair texture, and bone structure. The concept of race is socially constructed; as such, racial categories and their implications for those who are racialized differ from one society to the next.

race relations Interactions between individuals who are perceived as belonging to different socially constructed racial categories. Race relations often involve power differences, with members of more dominant racial groups holding power over members of less dominant racial groups.

racial discrimination Any action or attitude that subordinates or excludes a person or group of people because of their assumed race. Human rights violations and loss of fundamental freedoms often occur with racial discrimination.

racialization The association of certain events, practices, or people with socially constructed race categories. Racialization is often apparent in widely accepted racialized associations that present all members deemed to belong to a particular race in either a negative or a positive way (e.g., associating gang violence with Black people or associating intelligence with Asian people).

racialized Other Refers to the process by which individuals come to be understood as being a member of a racial group, which is different from Whites. This process of becoming raced or racialized often encompasses marginalization, stigmatization, negative stereotyping, and oppression. This process is often referred to as "othering." In becoming the racialized other, such individuals are viewed as constituting the binary opposite of Whites. According to this binary, the racialized "other" is often socially constructed as being inferior to those who are considered the "self" or "White."

racism A form of prejudice that one group exercises over another group at the individual, cultural, and institutional levels. At the individual level, racism involves holding an erroneous belief or attitude that is carried out in the form of an action against another group. At the cultural level, racism is the taken-for-granted prejudicial stereotypes that people are aware of and that are often learned through media, school, and the knowledge that is circulating in the wider of society. At the structural level, racism is the power exercised to exclude one group of people from being able to fully participate within institutional structures. All of these acts of racism, whether they be at the individual, cultural, or structural level, may be intentional or unintentional when enacted by an individual, group, or system.

reacculturation The process that occurs when a person returns to his or her home country after living in another country. The term suggests that the individual must endure a process of learning about and attempting to fit back in to the home country after having acculturated to a foreign country.

religion A faith-based system of worship and belief that typically involves interpersonal relationships, ritualized practices, and shared worldviews.

self-indication process A process in which the individual pieces together and guides his or her action by noting things, assessing them, and giving them a meaning as they may arise in the situation in which he or she is acting. Through this process the individual may accept, reject, or transform his or her self-indication, depending on his or her interpretation of the situation (Blumer, 1969).

sex The state of being biologically male, female, or intersex. It is based on reproductive organs and processes.

social action model Workers who initiate social change to address social issues that are oppressing or marginalizing some members of the community.

social category Products of a social construction process through which people are included or excluded from a certain categorical collective.

social dimensions A categorical collective that is used to classify people, such as gender, race, and ethnicity.

social identity A socially constructed disposition signifying membership in a particular social group.

social inclusion Actions taken by a group or a society to ensure all of its members have equal opportunities to participate in group life, free from discrimination and other unfair barriers.

social intervention A term that refers broadly to various types of intervention practices dealing with social issues in both community and institutional settings. The term encompasses practices of a wide variety of professionals in the social field (social workers, human relations agents, psycho-sociologists, social educators, community workers) and is not necessarily limited to persons with social work degrees. It is frequently used in Quebec and Europe.

social location One's personal demographics in relation to variables such as race, gender, and so on. The variables used in understanding one's social location are those that relate to the ways oppression operates in society. Consequently, understanding one's social location is a means of identifying how one may be impacted by oppression and structural inequality.

social model of disability A model of disability that allows us to view people with disabilities as an oppressed, marginalized, nonethnic minority that is caused by society's failure to provide appropriate services, emphasizing that negative social factors, and not the disability, restrict participation.

social networking Use of computer online communications such as Facebook, Twitter, and LinkedIn to connect with other members of a social group (network).

social planning Involves the collection and analysis of data from the community to find solutions to resolve issues or improve the community's well-being.

social position The rank or placement of an individual or group in a given society and culture.

social support The emotional, informational, or monetary formal or informal assistance one receives from others. Formal supports are professional, such as medical, education, and income supports. Informal supports include family, friends, and volunteer organizations.

social systems framework Arrangements that see the world in terms of interdependent systems that need to keep in balance to function normally. Values and common goals are shared. Also known as a functionalist framework.

spirituality The state of being concerned with the immaterial rather than the material. One's spirituality is understood to include one's search for life purpose and meaning, and connection with self, others, the universe, and a self-defined higher power, either with or without a particular faith orientation.

stigma The result of viewing others without respect as if they are disgraceful. It is the characteristic of another that is deemed negative. It is negative beliefs by a society about members of a group.

strategic exchange A social process through which human actors strategically accept or reject the social power exerted on them in an oppressive social condition to maximize their interest and to minimize their loss.

subordination The act of treating something or someone as less important than something or someone else.

superdiverse society A society in which all people, not just immigrants, are globally connected and mobile, and where time and space are both local and translocal.

systemic racism Racism that is deeply embedded in the structure, functioning, social institutions, and widespread beliefs of a society in such a way that members of one or more racialized groups benefit while members of other racialized groups experience prejudice and discrimination.

totems The specific symbol for a clan (i.e., Crane, Loon, Fish, Bear, Martin, Deer, or Bird). Also known as doo-dems.

transgender A word used to describe a person who perceives her or his gender as different from the one assigned to her or him at birth. An individual may be transgendered without having taken any outward steps (hormonal, surgical, or other) to present as or transition to the felt gender.

transphobia A fear or hatred of transgendered individuals.

two-spirit A term used by First Nations and other Indigenous peoples in North America to refer to members of their cultures whose gender identities have both traditionally male and traditionally female aspects. In non-Indigenous cultures, these individuals are typically thought of as gay, lesbian, bisexual, pansexual, or transgendered.

universal instructional design (UID) An educational process that creates learning environments and teaching strategies that are usable by the greatest diversity of students. The potential needs of all learners are identified and unnecessary barriers to learning are removed, normalizing student diversity and decreasing the need for accommodation.

Whiteness A social construction (rather than a biological category) that connotes a racial hierarchy that is generally invisible to White people, who are often not conscious of its power. Whiteness studies "explore how white people's attitudes and understandings—not about racial others but about *themselves* and *their own status* in the society—factor into the perpetuation and legitimation of racial inequalities. . . . The focus is on identities, ideologies, and norms that are not always understood or even explicitly realized by those who benefit from them" (Hartmann, Gerteis & Croll, 2009, p. 404).

White privilege Unearned benefits of being White, such as not being negatively "racially" profiled by police and security services.

References

Accessibility for Ontarians with Disabilities Act. (2005). S.O. 2005, c. 11.

Blumer, H. (1969). *Symbolic interaction: Perspective and method.* Englewood Cliffs, NJ: Prentice-Hall, Inc.

Butler, J. (1999). *Gender trouble.* New York, NY: Routledge.

Cross, T. L., Bazron, B. J., Dennis, K. W., & Isaacs, M. R. (1989, March). Toward a culturally competent system of care: A monograph on effective services for minority children who are severely emotionally disturbed. Washington, DC: Georgetown University Child Development Center. Retrieved from http://www.mhsoac.ca.gov/meetings/docs/Meetings/2010/June/CLCC_Tab_4_Towards_Culturally_Competent_System.pdf

Davies, B., & Harre, R. (1999). Positioning: The discursive production of selves. In R. Harre & L. van Langenhove (Eds.), *Positioning theory: Moral contexts of intentional action* (pp. 32–52). Oxford, UK: Blackwell Publishers Ltd.

Hartmann, D., Gerteis, J., & Croll, P. R. (2009). An empirical assessment of whiteness theory: Hidden from how many? *Social Problems, 56*(3), 403–24.

Henry, R., Tator, C., Mattis, W., Rees, T. (1995). The colour of democracy: Racism in Canadian society. Toronto, ON: Harcourt Brace and Co.

Hoefer, R. (2012). *Advocacy practice for social justice: Incorporating advocacy into the generalist model.* Chicago, IL: Lyceum Books.

LaRossa, R., & Reitzes, D. C. (1993). Symbolic interactionism and family studies. In P. G. Boss, W. J. Doherty, R. LaRossa, W. R. Schumm, & S. Steinmetz (Eds.), *Sourcebook of family theories and methods: A contextual approach* (pp. 135–63). New York, NY: Plenum Press.

Merton, R. K. (1988). The Matthew effect in science II: Cumulative advantage and the symbolism of intellectual property. *ISIS, 79,* 606–23.

Payne, M. (2005). *Modern social work theory* (3rd ed.). Chicago, IL: Lyceum Books.

Rosado, C. (1996). Toward a definition of multiculturalism. Retrieved November, 21, 2008. http://rosado.net/pdf/Def_of_Multiculturalism.pdf

Rubin, H., & Rubin, I. (2005). *Qualitative interviewing: The art of hearing data* (2nd ed.). Thousand Oaks, CA: Sage Publications.

Topp, S. S. (2013). Against the quiet revolution: The rhetorical construction of intersex individuals as disordered. *Sexualities, 16*(1–2), 180–94.

Index